D1098129

Readings in Monetary Theory

The Series of Republished
Articles on Economics
Volume V

Selection Committee For This Volume

*The participation of the American Economic Association in
the presentation of this series consists in the appointment of
a committee to determine the subjects of the volumes and
of special committees to select the articles for each volume.*

Readings in Monetary Theory

Selected by a Committee of

The American Economic Association

RICHARD D. IRWIN, INC.

HOMEWOOD, ILLINOIS

1951

PREFACE

The considerations which have determined our selection of articles for republication in this volume are numerous. Entirely appropriate articles have been excluded if they have already been published in another volume of this series. An example would be D. H. Robertson's "Survey of Modern Monetary Controversy." We have been keenly aware of the unavoidable problem of alternative cost in the use of limited resources. Consequently, in a few instances we have regretfully omitted articles which were so long that, in the light of limitations on space, their inclusion would have required the omission of several articles of more moderate length. This is particularly true of a number of articles by James W. Angell. For the most part—but we have not made this an invariable rule—we have excluded articles which already have been made easily available in some other volume, such as the various republished articles of John H. Williams.

The boundary lines of no field of knowledge can be drawn with precision, and this is notably true of monetary theory. We have included, without misgivings on this score, a number of articles that deal with commercial banks and with central banking. Studies in aggregative economics stand in the borderland between monetary and price theory, and yet they invariably introduce monetary considerations in very large measure. We have, therefore, included a number of such studies. Equally relevant topics have been largely or wholly excluded, however, because either whole volumes or sections in other volumes of readings have been devoted to them. For this reason we have given only limited space to cycle theory, and we have included no articles on pure interest theory or on foreign exchange and international monetary equilibrium. Since a volume on fiscal policy is projected, we have included only one brief article on this subject.

We have not altogether ignored the matter of coverage of the various aspects of monetary theory, and yet we have leaned somewhat in the direction of making our selections without reference to this consideration. In the light of the various limitations which we deemed it necessary to place upon our choices, it was inevitable that some parts of the field should be only meagerly represented at best.

FRIEDRICH A. LUTZ,
LLOYD W. MINTS,
Co-Chairmen, Selection Committee

September, 1950

CONTENTS

PART III.   MONEY, THE RATE OF INTEREST
AND EMPLOYMENT

PART IV.   MONETARY POLICY

PART I

INTEGRATION OF THE THEORY OF MONEY AND THE THEORY OF PRICE

THE APPLICATION OF THE THEORETICAL APPARATUS OF SUPPLY AND DEMAND TO UNITS OF CURRENCY*[1]

By Edwin Cannan‖

I have used what will perhaps appear a somewhat clumsy phrase in place of the more familiar "Laws of Supply and Demand," or even the "theory of the relation of demand and supply to value," because I think it desirable to suggest that "Supply and Demand" are heads of arrangement rather than the name of a doctrine. When we say that the value of a thing depends on supply and demand, we do not, or at any rate ought not, to mean more than that we think it will be convenient to arrange the causes of changes in value under those two heads.

The stock of some things (such as milk, or even wheat) in hand at any one moment is so small in proportion to the annual produce, that we think of the stream of produce as furnishing the supply, and the ability and willingness of people to consume the thing as furnishing the demand. Of other things, such as land and railways, the annual production is so small compared with the stock, that we think of the stock as furnishing the supply, and the ability and willingness of people to use the thing as furnishing the demand.

Currency belongs to the second class. It is one of those durable instrumental goods of which the stock at any moment is very large in proportion to the annual gross additions to and gross subtractions from the stock.

---

* *Economic Journal,* **31** (1921), 453–61. Reprinted, by the courtesy of the publisher, without change from the original text.

‖ Professor Cannan died in 1935.

[1] Read before Section F of the British Association, Edinburgh, 1921.

We may consequently think of the supply, as we think of the supply of houses, as being the stock rather than the annual produce; and we may think of this supply, as we think of the supply of houses, as being increased by net additions to the stock, and decreased by net subtractions from it.

Following the same line with demand, we must think of the demand for currency as being furnished, not by the number or amount of *transactions,* but by the ability and willingness of persons to *hold* currency, in the same way as we think of the demand for houses as coming not from the persons who buy and re-sell or lease and sub-lease houses, but from the persons who *occupy* houses.   Mere activity in the house market—mere buying and selling of houses—may in a sense be said to involve "increase of demand" for houses, but in the corresponding sense it may be said to involve an equal "increase of supply"; the two things cancel.   The demand which is important for our purposes is the demand for occupation.   In the same way, more transactions for money—more purchases and sales of commodities and services—may in a sense be said to involve increase of demand for money, but in the corresponding sense it may be said to involve an equal increase of supply of money; the two things cancel.   The demand which is important for our purpose is the demand for currency, not to pay away again immediately, but to *hold.*   Just as you are a less important demander of houses if you occupy a £1000 house than if you occupy a £2000 house, so you are a less important demander of currency if you keep on the average £5 in your pocket than if you keep £10.

It may be said that, in addition to the demand of persons and institutions for currency to *hold,* there is also sometimes a demand by banks and governments for currency to *destroy,* as, for example, at present in this country, when the Treasury is buying in Currency Notes and burning them.   But as this demand always, or almost always, comes from institutions which have issued quantities of paper and subsequently repented, it is usually regarded as simply reducing the supply instead of increasing the demand.   In favour of regarding the institution as a demander, it may of course be said that the fact that it acquires the currency to burn rather than to hold is immaterial, since it makes no difference whether the currency acquired is held or burnt, provided it is not reissued. It is, some one may say, all the same whether Currency Notes which have been withdrawn have been burnt or are stored somewhere in the Bank of England. But this is not quite true, since, if the notes were still held, they would appear in the total stock which we have agreed to call the supply, whereas, having actually been destroyed, they no longer appear in the total. Consequently it is more convenient to follow ordinary usage in this matter, and speak of banks and governments which buy up and burn currency as reducing the supply.

To clear up our ideas about the demand for currency, let us think of a few obvious causes of increase and decrease of demand for it.

The most obvious cause of increase of demand for a currency is an increase in the number of persons who use it. At a very early age—often at his or her christening—each new member of the human race begins to hold a small quantity of currency, and the child of six sometimes has more than his father or mother. There are plenty of examples of increase of demand from this source having been sufficient to cause a noticeable increase in the value of a currency which is limited in amount—the Indian rupee after the closing of the Indian mint and the American greenback are often quoted, and the general increase of gold and silver-using populations, though it has not actually raised the value of gold and silver currencies, has at any rate obviously prevented them from falling as fast as they would otherwise have done. The great rise of prices after the Black Death may be given as an example of the converse effect of diminution of population in diminishing the demand for, and consequently the value of a currency.

The introduction of anything which economises currency, i. e. which makes it unnecessary for people to keep so much currency by them on the average, tends to diminish the demand for currency. To take the simplest possible example, suppose a landlord living on his rents paid quarterly, and that neither he nor his farmers have bank accounts. The farmers will have to accumulate a considerable sum in currency towards quarter-day, and this will then be handed over to the landlord, who will only decumulate it gradually as the next quarter wears on. Between them they will always have a large sum of currency, the landlord holding most of it at the beginning of the quarter and the farmers the most of it at the end.   But if a bank is started, and they all open accounts at it, the farmers will no longer accumulate currency to pay rents with, but will accumulate balances at the bank, and when quarter day comes will order the bank (by their cheques) to pay the landlord, who will be content to see their balances transferred to him, and will not want the store of cash which he formerly required. The bank, of course, will provide a new demand for currency, since it will require a full enough till, but enough for it will be very much less than the amount formerly required by the farmers and landlord.

That banks economise currency in this way is obvious, but there is no possible means of discovering or estimating *how much* they econo- mise it.   We may know that we keep an average of £10 a head in currency now, when we have banks, but we cannot possibly form the wildest guess how much we should keep if there were no banks.   Some of us would probably never have been born: the whole situation of the world would be different.   No doubt some other ingenious methods of economising currency would have been devised if some ban had been placed on banking.

A change in the distribution of wealth may cause a change in the demand for currency.   If the rich and banking portion of the people becomes richer, it does not keep appreciably more currency in its pockets, but increases its balance at the bank.   But if the poorer non- banking portion becomes richer, it does accumulate currency, not only in its pockets, but also in money-boxes and mugs on the chimney-piece and other strange places.

Innumerable are the changes of social circumstances which may lead to greater or less economy of currency, and consequently less or greater demand for currency.   The calling up of men for military service, and subsequently the large removal of women from their homes for munition-making and other purposes during the recent war, greatly increased for the time the demand for currency, because the members of families, when separated, found it convenient to keep much more currency by them in the aggregate than when they were living at home and together.

Like the demand for other things, the demand for currency is liable to be varied by the miscalculations of mankind about the future.

If we were all level-headed prophets, fluctuations of prices would be smoothed out.   There would still be slowly rising and falling tides, but waves would disappear.   But in fact we all foresee wrong, and our individual mistakes do not balance each other—we foresee wrong to some extent in unison.   One year we agree in over-estimating the potato crop, and the next year in under-estimating it: when we over-estimate it, our willingness to buy early is less than if we foresaw correctly, and for the time demand is kept below what it would be if prices were kept as stable as possible.   The same thing happens with currency, though it is not nearly so obvious.   If there is a predominating impression that prices in general are going to rise, there will be a predominating tendency to hold commodities for the rise, which will itself raise prices at once.   Every one can see this, but few notice that this tendency to hold goods back, resulting in a rise of prices, is the same thing as a diminution in the demand for currency.   Currency becomes the depreciating article which people in general are less willing to hold. Vice versa, if it is generally expected that prices will fall, most people are more eager to get rid of goods and are more willing to hold currency.

You must not expect to find evidence of increased or decreased willingness to hold currency in actually increased or decreased stocks of currency.   If the total is a fixed amount it cannot vary in that way. The evidence is to be looked for in the fact that more or less goods are actually being given for the unit of currency.   You can have an increased and a decreased demand for houses without finding any alteration in the number or size of houses.

The effect of misguided speculation for the rise or fall of the value of a currency is disguised, so far as internal speculation is concerned, by taking the form, in each individual case, of speculation for the fall or rise of particular commodities.   Very few persons grasp the idea of a rise and fall in the value of their own country's money, and the Money Market is a place where you deal in loans, not in money.   We have not yet risen to the height of having a Currency Market in which you can buy and sell future Board of Trade, Statist and other Index Numbers.   But direct speculation in the currency of other countries is common enough, and is often ill-informed enough to cause great disturbances of values, instead of smoothing them down.   Some time ago, the editor of an Athens newspaper was unable to go to a certain restaurant there because the waiters worried him with questions about the future of Austrian crowns which they were holding.   When the British troops first went to Cologne, they bought German marks because they saw that the mark was "lower than usual."   It is known that many milliards of the depreciated currencies are held by foreigners.   Such holding is, of course, a pure addition to the usual demand for currency, and tends to maintain its value for a time.   Eventually, however, the foreign holders decide to sell, and their decision is much more likely to come at a time when it will make a fall more precipitous than when it will moderate a rise.   This ignorant speculation of foreigners has been the cause of many violent fluctuations of currency values and is a great support of the doctrine that they "depend on confidence."   About that we need not say more than that the price of sugar also is affected at any moment by people's views of what it will be in the future, but we do not say that "the price of sugar depends on confidence."

The supply being taken as fixed, *how much* will a given increase of demand send up the value of currency?   One difficulty in answering the question arises from the fact that we have no easy means of measuring increase of demand, and consequently scarcely know how to exemplify a "given increase of demand."   But one example seems workable.   Suppose that to a country with a particular currency of its own there is added a new province one-tenth as large and with exactly similar characteristics, which has just, by some accident, lost all its own currency, and that the annexing country creates no additional currency, but allows the new province to supply itself as best it can. We may look on this as providing, after some initial disturbance, 10 per cent. of additional demand.   The people in the new province, wanting a medium of exchange, would have to give people in the rest of the country commodities and services to induce them to part with some of their holdings of currency; these sales would send down the prices of commodities and services, and correspondingly elevate the value of currency.   How much in the end, when things had settled down, would depend on what we have learnt from Marshall to call "the elasticity of the demand" for currency.   This has often been supposed to be what he calls "unity," which would mean that an increase of demand would cause an exactly proportional rise in the value of currency and a reciprocal fall of prices.   So that, for example, in the case given above, when the new province was provided with its one-eleventh of the whole currency, prices would be down one-eleventh and the value of the unit of currency up one-tenth.   We can see why if we reflect that when prices fall from eleven to ten, and £10 consequently buys as much as £11 did before, we will find it convenient to carry only £10 about with us instead of the £11 we did before.   So, to induce the old country to part with one-eleventh of its stock, a reduction of prices by one-eleventh will be required and be sufficient.   But we shall do well not to accept this doctrine that the elasticity of the demand for currency is always unity, till we have considered it in relation to supply.   We shall then see reason to doubt it.

Now let us turn to the Supply side of the question, asking ourselves about the effect of alterations in supply of currency.

Given a certain demand, increase of supply, in case of any article, reduces value, and currency is no exception.   The additional supply of currency is usually given by the producer, or issuer, in exchange for commodities and services, and his coming in as a new and additional buyer of such commodities and services raises the price of those things and diminishes the value of what he is offering—that is, currency. Sometimes, indeed, he gives the new currency away in doles and pensions without getting any return (except ingratitude), but this is not essentially different, since then the recipients of his gifts are the new and additional buyers.

Great confusion is often introduced at this point by neglect of the distinction pointed out by Sidgwick between increase of demand and what he calls "extension of demand."   We often say that the demand for a thing has increased when we only mean that people are taking more of it because they can get it cheaper.   It is obvious, however, that it is not this kind of increase of demand that we have in mind when we discuss the effect of increase of demand upon values.   We could not say in the same breath that increase of demand for houses raises the value of houses, and that a fall in the value of houses causes an increase of demand for them.   We can say in the same breath, that increase of demand raises the value of houses, and that the fall of value *extends* the demand for them (or, vice versa, a rise of value *contracts* the demand).   No more in the case of currency than in any other case does the increase of supply defeat itself by causing *increase* of demand. It only *extends* demand, inducing people to hold more currency because the fall of value makes it possible to hold larger amounts with equal sacrifice and necessary to hold larger amounts to secure equal convenience.   People will take the additional currency as they take additional whisky when it is watered and offered to them at a lower rate, but that does not show that, in the absence of increase of demand in the narrower sense, they will take additional whisky or additional currency at the old rate.

The next question is *how much* a given addition to the supply of currency will raise prices and lower the value of the unit of currency? This is really the same question that we have already asked in regard to the effect of a given increase of demand.   The answer is the same— it depends on the elasticity of demand, and there is the same *primâ facie* reason for believing that the elasticity at bottom is unity, so that, always in the absence of any increase or decrease of demand in the narrow sense, an increase in the supply should cause an exactly reciprocal diminution in the value of the currency.   But great doubt is thrown on the doctrine when we reflect that if it were universally true, issuers of legal tender could go on buying goods and services with new issues indefinitely.   The process of doubling the currency in, say, the first month, would indeed gradually bring the purchasing power of the unit down to one-half, but as the issuer at the beginning would be buying very near old prices, and only at the end at the new prices, he would have acquired goods and services worth over three-quarters of the value of the total of the old currency.   By another issue equal to the old currency he would only get half as much, but there is nothing to prevent him issuing twice as much in the second month, four times as much in the third, eight times in the fourth, and so on, and then he will be able to go on acquiring the same amount of commodities per month indefinitely.   Experience seems to show that the unit of a currency falls to zero in value long before the supply of the currency reaches infinity, and believers in the doctrine have been unable to explain why. They have contented themselves with eluding the point by means of propositions, such as "however many kronen the Austrian Government issues, so long as they really circulate, they will always have some value, however small."[2] No doubt; but is it not equally true that so long as they have some value they will continue to circulate? They will stop circulating when they lose all value. The explanation seems to lie in the fact that human intelligence anticipates what is coming. When it is seen that the value of currency is steadily falling, people see that it is more profitable to hold goods than currency, the demand for currency fails to extend in proportion to the enlargement of the supply, and its value consequently falls more rapidly. The issuer very likely redoubles his efforts to keep up with the fall by issuing new currency at a still more rapidly increasing rate, but all to no purpose—he is bound to lose the race, and the reason is that the elasticity of demand is less than unity.

In the converse case, that of reduction in the supply of currency, there is also reason to expect an elasticity less than unity. As general prices fall owing to the reduction, people will endeavour to protect themselves by displaying greater readiness to part with goods and services, and less to part with currency, and anticipation will thus cause the fall of general prices to outrun the diminution of currency. Pushed to the extreme limit, the policy would put a stop to the circulation of the currency, as it would all be hoarded, and exchanges of goods would be made by barter. But things are never pushed so far, because, long before, substitutes for the existing currency are always introduced and check the rise of purchasing power. For example, as soon as a reduction of our present paper currency went so far as to make £1 of it worth more than 113 grains of fine gold, substitutes for it would begin to come into use in the shape of sovereigns and half-sovereigns.

Lovers of paradox might say that a currency may go out of use either because it is too cheap, or because it is too dear, but that is not

---

[2] I quote from Miss Van Dorp's review of Dr. G. M. V. Stuart's Inleiding tot de Leer van de Waardevastheid van het Geld, in *Economic Journal*, June 1921, but I am not sure whether the opinion is that of the author or the reviewer, or both.

the true conclusion of my argument.   The true conclusion is that a continuance of rapid change in either direction will cause a currency to go out of use.   This is perfectly reasonable, stability of value being one of the most important requisites of useful currency, and Gresham's law that bad money drives out good being fortunately quite untrue of the long run.

2

A SUGGESTION FOR SIMPLIFYING
THE THEORY OF MONEY*[1]

By J. R. Hicks‖

After the thunderstorms of recent years, it is with peculiar diffi-
dence and even apprehension that one ventures to open one's mouth
on the subject of money.   In my own case these feelings are particularly intense, because I feel myself to be very much of a novice at
the subject.   My education has been mostly in the non-monetary
parts of economics, and I have only come to be interested in money
because I found that I could not keep it out of my non-monetary
problems.   Yet I am encouraged on reflection to hope that this may
not prove a bad approach to the subject: that some things at least
which are not very evident on direct inspection may become clearer
from a cross-light of this sort.

It is of course very largely by such cross-fertilisation that economics progresses, and at least one department of non-monetary
economics has hardly emerged from a very intimate affair with monetary theory.   I do not, however, propose to resume this particular
liaison.   One understands that most economists have now read
Böhm-Bawerk; yet whatever that union has bred, it has not been
concord.   I should prefer to seek illumination from another point
of view—from a branch of economics which is more elementary,
but, I think, in consequence better developed—the theory of value.

To anyone who comes over from the theory of value to the

* *Economica*, New Series, **2** (1935), 1–19.   Reprinted, by the courtesy of the
publisher and the author, without change from the original text.

‖ Nuffield College, Oxford, England.

[1] A paper read at the Economic Club, November 1934.   The reader is asked
to bear in mind the fact that the paper was written to be read aloud, and to
excuse certain pieces of mischief.

theory of money, there are a number of things which are rather startling.   Chief of these is the preoccupation of monetary theorists with a certain equation, which states that the price of goods multiplied by the quantity of goods equals the amount of money which is spent on them. This equation crops up again and again, and it has all sorts of ingenious little arithmetical tricks performed on it.   Sometimes it comes out as $MV = PT$; and once, in its most stupendous transfiguration, it blossomed into $P = \dfrac{E}{O} + \dfrac{I' - S}{R}$.   Now we, of the theory of value, are not unfamiliar with this equation, and there was a time when we used to attach as much importance to it as monetary theorists seem to do still.   This was in the middle of the last century, when we used to talk about value being "a ratio between demand and supply."   Even now, we accept the equation, and work it, more or less implicitly, into our systems.   But we are rather inclined to take it for granted, since it is rather tautologous, and since we have found that another equation, not alternative to the quantity equation, but complementary with it, is much more significant.   This is the equation which states that the relative value of two commodities depends upon their relative marginal utility.

Now, to an *ingénu,* who comes over to monetary theory, it is extremely trying to be deprived of this sheet-anchor.   It was marginal utility that really made sense of the theory of value; and to come to a branch of economics which does without marginal utility altogether!   No wonder there are such difficulties and such differences! What is wanted is a "marginal revolution"!

That is my suggestion.   But I know that it will meet with apparently crushing objections.   I shall be told that the suggestion has been tried out before.   It was tried by Wicksell, and though it led to interesting results, it did not lead to a marginal utility theory of money.   It was tried by Mises, and led to the conclusion that money is a ghost of gold—because, so it appeared, money as such has no marginal utility.[2]   The suggestion has a history, and its history is not encouraging.

---

[2] A more subtle form of the same difficulty appears in the work of Marshall and his followers.   They were aware that money ought to be subjected to

This would be enough to frighten one off, were it not for two things. Both in the theory of value and in the theory of money there have been developments in the twenty or thirty years since Wicksell and Mises wrote. And these developments have considerably reduced the barriers that blocked their way.

In the theory of value, the work of Pareto, Wicksteed, and their successors, has broadened and deepened our whole conception of marginal utility. We now realize that the marginal utility analysis is nothing else than a general theory of choice, which is applicable whenever the choice is between alternatives that are capable of quantitative expression. Now money is obviously capable of quantitative expression, and therefore the objection that money has no marginal utility must be wrong. People do choose to have money rather than other things, and therefore, in the relevant sense, money must have a marginal utility.

But merely to call that marginal utility X, and then proceed to draw curves, would not be very helpful. Fortunately the developments in monetary theory to which I alluded come to our rescue.

Mr. Keynes' "Treatise," so far as I have been able to discover, contains at least three theories of money. One of them is the Savings and Investment theory, which, as I hinted, seems to me only a quantity theory much glorified. One of them is a Wicksellian natural rate theory. But the third is altogether much more interesting. It emerges when Mr. Keynes begins to talk about the price-level of investment goods; when he shows that this price-level depends upon the

marginal utility analysis; but they were so dominated by the classical conception of money as a "veil" (which is valid enough at a certain level of approximation) that they persisted in regarding the demand for money as a demand for the things which money can buy—"real balances." As a result of this, their invocation of marginal utility remained little more than a pious hope. For they were unable to distinguish, on marginal utility lines, between the desire to save and the desire to hoard; and they necessarily overlooked that indeterminateness in the "real balance" (so important in some applications of monetary theory), which occurs when the prices of consumption goods are expected to change. On the other hand, I must admit that some versions of the Marshallian theory come very close to what I am driving at. Cf. Lavington, *English Capital Market*, chap. 6.

relative preference of the investor—to hold bank-deposits or to hold securities.   Here at last we have something which to a value theorist looks sensible and interesting!   Here at last we have a choice at the margin!   And Mr. Keynes goes on to put substance into our X, by his doctrine that the relative preference depends upon the "bearishness" or "bullishness" of the public, upon their relative desire for liquidity or profit.

My suggestion may, therefore, be re-formulated.   It seems to me that this third theory of Mr. Keynes really contains the most important part of his theoretical contribution; that here, at last, we have something which, on the analogy (the appropriate analogy) of value theory, does begin to offer a chance of making the whole thing easily intelligible; that it is from this point, not from velocity of circulation, natural rate of interest, or Saving and Investment, that we ought to start in constructing the theory of money.   But in saying this, I am being more Keynesian than Keynes; I must endeavor to defend my position in detail.

II

The essence of the method I am proposing is that we should take the position of an individual at a particular point of time, and enquire what determines the precise quantity of money which he will desire to hold.   But even to this simple formulation of the problem it is necessary to append two footnotes.

1. " Point of Time."   We are dealing with an individual decision to hold money *or* something else, and such a decision is always made at a point of time.   It is only by concentrating on decisions made at particular points of time that we can apply the theory of value to the problem at all.   A very large amount of current controversy about money seems to me to be due to the attempt, superficially natural, but, in fact, highly inconvenient, to establish a close relation between the demand for money and *income*.   Now the simple consideration that the decision to hold money is always made at a point of time shows that the connection between income and the demand for money must always be indirect.   And in fact the whole conception of income is so intricate and beset by so many perplexing diffi-

culties, that the establishment of any connection with income ought only to be hoped for at a late stage of investigation.[3]

2. " Money." What sort of money are we considering? For the present, any sort of money. The following analysis will apply equally whether we think of money as notes, or bank deposits, or even metallic coins. It is true that with a metallic currency there is an ordinary commodity demand for the money substance to be considered, but it is relatively unimportant for most of our purposes. Perhaps it will be best if we take as our standard case that of a pure paper currency in a community where there are no banks. What follows has much wider application in reality. Only I would just ask you to keep this standard case in mind, since by using it as a basis for discussion, we may be able to save time a little.

An individual's decision to hold so much money means that he prefers to hold that amount of money, rather than either less or more. Now what are the precise contents of these displaced alternatives? He could reduce his holding of money in three ways:

1. by spending, i. e. buying something, it does not matter what;
2. by lending money to someone else;
3. by paying off debts which he owes to someone else.

He can increase his holding of money in three corresponding ways:

1. by selling something else which he owns;
2. by borrowing from someone else;
3. by demanding repayment of money which is owed by someone else.

This classification is, I think, complete. All ways of changing one's holding of money can be reduced to one of these classes or a combination of two. of them—purchase or sale, the creation of new debts or the extinction of old.

If a person decides to hold money, it is implied that he prefers to do this than to adopt any of these three alternatives. But how is such a preference possible?

---

[3] Cf. Lindahl, *The Concept of Income* (Essays in honour of Gustav Cassel).

A preference for holding money instead of spending it on consumption goods presents no serious difficulty, for it is obviously the ordinary case of a preference for future satisfactions over present. At any moment, an individual will not usually devote the whole of his available resources to satisfying present wants—a part will be set aside to meet the needs of the future.

The critical question arises when we look for an explanation of the preference for holding money rather than capital goods. For capital goods will ordinarily yield a positive rate of return, which money does not. What has to be explained is the decision to hold assets in the form of barren money, rather than of interest- or profit-yielding securities. And obviously just the same question arises over our second and third types of utilisation. So long as rates of interest are positive, the decision to hold money rather than lend it, or use it to pay off old debts, is apparently an unprofitable one.

This, as I see it, is really the central issue in the pure theory of money. Either we have to give an explanation of the fact that people do hold money when rates of interest are positive, or we have to evade the difficulty somehow. It is the great traditional evasions which have led to Velocities of Circulation, Natural Rates of Interest, *et id genus omne*.[4]

Of course, the great evaders would not have denied that there must be some explanation of the fact. But they would have put it down to " frictions," and since there was no adequate place for frictions in the rest of their economic theory, a theory of money based on frictions did not seem to them a promising field for economic analysis.

This is where I disagree. I think we have to look the frictions in the face, and see if they are really so refractory after all. This will, of course, mean that we cannot allow them to go to sleep under so vague a title.

---

[4] I do not wish to deny that these concepts have a use in their appropriate place—that is to say, in particular applications of monetary theory. But it seems to me that they are a nuisance in monetary theory itself, that they offer no help in elucidating the general principles of the working of money.

III

The most obvious sort of friction, and undoubtedly one of the most important, is the cost of transferring assets from one form to another.   This is of exactly the same character as the cost of transfer which acts as a certain impediment to change in all parts of the economic system; it doubtless comprises subjective elements as well as elements directly priced.   Thus a person is deterred from investing money for short periods, partly because of brokerage charges and stamp duties, partly because it is not worth the bother.

The net advantage to be derived from investing a given quantity of money consists of the interest or profit earned less the cost of investment.   It is only if this net advantage is expected to be positive (i. e. if the expected rate of interest ± capital appreciation or depreciation, is greater than the cost of investment) that it will pay to undertake the investment.

Now, since the expected interest increases both with the quantity of money to be invested and with the length of time for which it is expected that the investment will remain untouched, while the costs of investment are independent of the length of time, and (as a whole) will almost certainly increase at a diminishing rate as the quantity of money to be invested increases, it becomes clear that with any given level of costs of investment, it will not pay to invest money for less than a certain period, and in less than certain quantities.   It will be profitable to hold assets for short periods, and in relatively small quantities, in monetary form.

Thus, so far as we can see at present, the amount of money a person will desire to hold depends upon three factors: the dates at which he expects to make payments in the future, the cost of investment, and the expected rate of return on investment.   The further ahead the future payments, the lower the cost of investment, and the higher the expected rate of return on invested capital—the lower will be the demand for money.

However, this statement is not quite accurate.   For although all these factors may react on the demand for money, they may be insufficient to determine it closely.   Since the quantity of available money must generally rise to some minimum before it is profitable to invest it at all, and further investment will then proceed by rather discontinuous jumps for a while, we shall expect to find the demand for money on the part of private individuals, excepting the very well-to-do, fairly insensitive to changes of this sort.   But this does not mean that they are unimportant.   For among those who are likely to be sensitive, we have to reckon, not only the well-to-do, but also all business men who are administering capital which is not solely their own private property.   And this will give us, in total, a good deal of sensitivity.

IV

Our first list of factors influencing the demand for money—the expected rate of interest, the cost of investment, and the expected period of investment—does, therefore, isolate some factors which are really operative; but even so, it is not a complete list.   For we have also to take into account the fact, which is in reality of such enormous importance, that people's expectations are never precise expectations of the kind we have been assuming.   They do not say to themselves "this £100 I shall not want until June 1st" or "this investment will yield 3·7 per cent"; or, if they do, it is only a kind of shorthand. Their expectations are always, in fact, surrounded by a certain penumbra of doubt; and the density of that penumbra is of immense importance for the problem we are considering.

The risk-factor comes into our problem in two ways: first, as affecting the expected period of investment; and second, as affecting the expected net yield of investment.   There are certain differences between its ways of operation on these two lines; but, as we shall see, the resultant effects are broadly similar.

Where risk is present, the *particular* expectation of a riskless situation is replaced by a band of possibilities, each of which is considered more or less probable.   It is convenient to represent these probabilities to oneself, in statistical fashion, by a mean value, and some appropriate measure of dispersion.   (No single measure will be wholly satisfactory, but here this difficulty may be overlooked.)   Roughly speaking, we may assume that a change in mean value with constant dispersion has much the same sort of effect as a change in the particular expectations we have been discussing before.   The peculiar problem of risk therefore reduces to an examination of the consequences of a change in dispersion.   Increased dispersion means increased uncertainty.

If, therefore, our individual, instead of knowing (or thinking he knows) that he will not want his £100 till June 1st, becomes afflicted by increased uncertainty; that is to say, while still thinking that June 1st is the most likely date, he now thinks that it will be very possible that he will want it before, although it is also very possible that he will not want it till after; what will be the effect on his conduct?   Let us suppose that when the date was certain, the investment was marginal—in the sense that the expected yield only just outweighed the cost of investment.   With uncertainty introduced in the way we have described, the investment now offers a chance of larger gain, but it is offset by an equal chance of equivalent loss.   In this situation, I think we are justified in assuming that he will become less willing to undertake the investment.

If this is so, uncertainty of the period for which money is free will ordinarily act as a deterrent to investment.   It should be observed that uncertainty may be increased, either by a change in objective facts on which estimates are based, or in the psychology of the individual, if his temperament changes in such a way as to make him less inclined to bear risks.

To turn now to the other uncertainty—uncertainty of the yield of investment.   Here again we have a penumbra; and here again we seem to be justified in assuming that spreading of the penumbra, increased dispersion of the possibilities of yield, will ordinarily be a deterrent to investment.   Indeed, without assuming this to be the normal case, it would be impossible to explain some of the most obvious of the observed facts of the capital market.   This sort of risk, therefore, will ordinarily be another factor tending to increase the demand for money.

V

So far the effect of risk seems fairly simple; an increase in the risk of investment will act like a fall in the expected rate of net yield;

an increase in the uncertainty of future outpayments will act like a shortening of the time which is expected to elapse before those out-payments; and all will ordinarily tend to increase the demand for money.   But although this is what it comes down to in the end, the detailed working of the risk-factor is not so simple; and since these further complications have an important bearing upon monetary problems, we cannot avoid discussing them here.

It is one of the peculiarities of risk that the total risk incurred when more than one risky investment is undertaken, does not bear any simple relation to the risk involved in each of the particular invest-ments taken separately.   In most cases, the "law of large numbers" comes into play (quite how, cannot be discussed here), so that the risk incurred by undertaking a number of separate risky investments will be less than that which would have been incurred if the same total capital had been invested altogether in one direction.   When the number of separate investments is very large, the total risk may sometimes be reduced very low indeed.

Now in a world where cost of investment was negligible, every-one would be able to take considerable advantage of this sort of risk-reduction.   By dividing up his capital into small portions, and spread-ing his risks, he would be able to insure himself against any large total risk on the whole amount.   But in actuality, the cost of investment, making it definitely unprofitable to invest less than a certain minimum amount in any particular direction, closes the possibility of risk-reduction along these lines to all those who do not possess the command over considerable quantities of capital.   This has two consequences.

On the one hand, since most people do not possess sufficient resources to enable them to take much advantage of the law of large numbers, and since even the large capitalist cannot annihilate his risks altogether in this manner, there will be a tendency to spread capital over a number of investments, not for this purpose, but for another. By investing only a proportion of total assets in risky enterprises, and investing the remainder in ways which are considered more safe, it will be possible for the individual to adjust his whole risk-situation to that which he most prefers, more closely than he could do by investing in any single enterprise.   It will be possible, for example, for him to feel fairly certain that in particular unfavourable eventualities he will not lose more than a certain amount. And, since, both with an eye on future commitments with respect to debt, and future needs for consumption, large losses will lay upon him a proportionately heavier burden than small losses, this sort of adjustment to the sort of chance of loss he is prepared to stand will be very well worth while.

We shall, therefore, expect to find our representative individual distributing his assets among relatively safe and relatively risky investments; and the distribution will be governed, once again, by the objective facts upon which he bases his estimates of risk, and his subjective preference for much or little risk-bearing.

On the other hand, those persons who have command of large quantities of capital, and are able to spread their risks, are not only able to reduce the risk on their own capital fairly low—they are also able to offer very good security for the investment of an extra unit along with the rest. If, therefore, they choose to become borrowers, they are likely to be very safe borrowers. They can, therefore, provide the safe investments which their fellow-citizens need.

In the absence of such safe investments, the ordinary individual would be obliged to keep a very considerable proportion of his assets in monetary form, since money would be the only safe way of holding assets. The appearance of such safe investments will act as a substitute for money in one of its uses, and therefore diminish the demand for money.

This particular function is performed, in a modern community, not only by banks, but also by insurance companies, investment trusts, and, to a certain (perhaps small) extent, even by large concerns of other kinds, through their prior charges. And, of course, to a very large extent indeed, it is performed by government stock of various kinds.

Banks are simply the extreme case of this phenomenon; they are enabled to go further than other concerns in the creation of money substitutes, because the security of their promises to pay is accepted generally enough for it to be possible to make payments in those promises. Bank deposits are, therefore, enabled to substitute money still further, because the cost of investment is reduced by a general belief in the absence of risk.

This is indeed a difference so great as to be properly regarded as a difference in kind; but it is useful to observe that the creation of bank credit is not really different in its economic effects from the fundamentally similar activities of other businesses and other persons. The significant thing is that the person who deposits money with a bank does not notice any change in his liquidity position; he considers the bank deposit to be as liquid as cash.   The bank, on the other hand, finds itself more liquid, if it retains the whole amount of the cash deposited; if it does not wish to be more liquid, but seeks (for example) to restore a conventional ratio, it will have to increase its investments.   But substantially the same sort of thing happens when anyone, whose credit is much above the average, borrows. Here the borrowing is nearly always a voluntary act on the part of the borrower, which would not be undertaken unless he was willing to become less liquid than before; the fact that he has to pay interest on the loan means that he will be made worse off if he does not spend the proceeds.   On the other hand, if the borrower's credit is good, the liquidity of the lender will not be very greatly impaired by his making the loan, so that his demand for money is likely to be at least rather less than it was before the loan was made.   Thus the net effect of the loan is likely to be "inflationary," in the sense that the purchase of capital goods or securities by the borrower is likely to be a more important affair than any sale of capital goods or securities by the lender, made necessary in order for the lender to restore his liquidity position.

Does it follow that all borrowing and lending is inflationary in this sense?   I do not think so; for let us take the case when the borrower's credit is very bad, and the lender is only tempted to lend by the offer of a very high rate of interest.   Then the impairment of the lender's liquidity position will be very considerable; and he may feel it necessary to sell rather less risky securities to an even greater capital sum in order to restore his liquidity position.   Here the net effect would be "deflationary."

The practical conclusion of this seems to be that while *voluntary* borrowing and lending is at least a symptom of monetary expansion, and is thus likely to be accompanied by rising prices, "distress borrowing" is an exception to this rule; and it follows, further, that the sort of stimulation to lending, by persuading people to make loans which they would not have made without persuasion (which was rather a feature of certain phases of the world depression), is a dubious policy—for the lenders, perhaps without realising what they are doing, are very likely to try and restore their liquidity position, and so to offset, and perhaps more than offset, the expansive effects of the loan.

VI

It is now time for us to begin putting together the conclusions we have so far reached.   Our method of analysis, it will have appeared, is simply an extension of the ordinary method of value theory.   In value theory, we take a private individual's income and expenditure account; we ask which of the items in that account are under the individual's own control, and then how he will adjust these items in order to reach a most preferred position.   On the production side, we make a similar analysis of the profit and loss account of the firm. My suggestion is that monetary theory needs to be based again upon a similar analysis, but this time, not of an income account, but of a capital account, a balance sheet.   We have to concentrate on the forces which make assets and liabilities what they are.

So as far as banking theory is concerned, this is really the method which is currently adopted; though the essence of the problem is there somewhat obscured by the fact that banks, in their efforts to reach their "most preferred position" are hampered or assisted by the existence of conventional or legally obligatory reserve ratios.   For theoretical purposes, this fact ought only to be introduced at a rather late stage; if that is done, then my suggestion can be expressed by saying that we ought to regard every individual in the community as being, on a small scale, a bank.   Monetary theory becomes a sort of generalisation of banking theory.

We shall have to draw up a sort of generalised balance sheet, suitable for all individuals and institutions.   It will have to be so generalised that many of the individual items will, in a great many cases, not appear. But that does not matter for our purposes. Such a generalised balance sheet will presumably run much as follows.

Assets	*Liabilities*
Consumption goods	
—perishable	
Consumption goods	
—durable	
Money	
Bank deposits	
Short term debts	Short term debts
Long term debts	Long term debts
Stocks and shares	
Productive equipment (including goods in process)	

We have been concerned up to the present with an analysis (very sketchy, I am afraid) of the equilibrium of this balance sheet. This analysis has at least shown that the relative size of the different items on this balance sheet is governed mainly by anticipation of the yield of investments and of risks.[5] It is these anticipations which play a part here corresponding to the part played by prices in value theory.[6]

Now the fact that our "equilibrium" is here determined by subjective factors like anticipations, instead of objective factors like prices, means that this purely theoretical study of money can never hope to

---

[5] As we have seen, these risks are as much a matter of the period of investment as of the yield. For certain purposes this is very important. Thus, in the case of that kind of investment which consists in the starting of actual processes of production, the yield which is expected if the process can be carried through may be considerable; but the yield if the process has to be interrupted will be large and negative. Uncertainty of the period for which resources are free will therefore have a very powerful effect in interrupting production. Short-run optimism will usually be enough to start a Stock Exchange boom; but to start an industrial boom relatively long-run optimism is necessary.

[6] I am aware that too little is said in this paper about the liabilities side of the above balance sheet. A cursory examination suggests that the same forces which work through the assets side work through the liabilities side in much the same way. But this certainly requires further exploration.

reach results so tangible and precise as those which value theory in its more limited field can hope to attain.   If I am right, the whole problem of applying monetary theory is largely one of deducing changes in anticipations from the changes in objective data which call them forth.   Obviously, this is not an easy task, and, above all, it is not one which can be performed in a mechanical fashion.   It needs judgment and knowledge of business psychology much more than sustained logical reasoning.   The arm-chair economist will be bad at it, but he can at least begin to realise the necessity for it, and learn to co-operate with those who can do it better than he can.

However, I am not fouling my own nest; I do not at all mean to suggest that economic theory comes here to the end of its resources. When once the connection between objective facts and anticipations has been made, theory comes again into its rights; and it will not be able to complain of a lack of opportunities.

Nevertheless, it does seem to me most important that, when considering these further questions, we should be well aware of the gap which lies behind us, and that we should bring out very clearly the assumptions which we are making about the genesis of anticipations. For this does seem to be the only way in which we can overcome the extraordinary theoretical differences of recent years, which are, I think very largely traceable to this source.

VII

Largely, but not entirely; or rather a good proportion of them seem to spring from a closely related source, which is yet not quite identical with the first.   When we seek to apply to a changing world any particular sort of individual equilibrium, we need to know how the individual will respond, not only to changes in the price-stimuli, or anticipation-stimuli, but also to a change in his total wealth.[7]   How

---

[7] The amount of money demanded depends upon three groups of factors: (1) the individual's subjective preferences for holding money or other things; (2) his wealth; (3) his anticipations of future prices and risks.   Changes in the demand for money affect present prices, but present prices affect the demand for money mainly through their effect on wealth and on price-anticipations.

will he distribute an increment (or decrement) of wealth—supposing, as we may suppose, that this wealth is measured in monetary terms?

It may be observed that this second problem has an exact counterpart in value theory. Recent work in that field has shown the importance of considering carefully, not only how the individual reacts to price-changes, but also how he reacts to changes in his available expenditure. Total wealth, in our present problem, plays just the same part as total expenditure in the theory of value.

In the theory of money, what we particularly want to know is how the individual's demand for money will respond to a change in his total wealth—that is to say, in the value of his net assets. Not seeing any *a priori* reason why he should react in one way rather than another, monetary theorists have often been content to make use of the simplest possible assumption—that the demand for money will be increased in the same proportion as total net assets have increased.[8] But this is a very arbitrary assumption; and it may be called in question, partly for analytical reasons, and partly because it seems to make the economic system work much too smoothly to account for observed fact. As one example of this excessive smoothness, I may instance the classical theory of international payments; as another, Mr. Harrod's views on the "Expansion of Bank Credit" which have recently been interesting the readers of *Economica* and of the *Economist*.[9] It would hardly be too much to say that one observed fact alone is sufficient to prove that this assumption cannot be universally true (let us hope and pray that it is sometimes true, nevertheless)—the fact of the trade cycle. For if it were true, the monetary system would always exhibit a quite straightforward kind of stability; a diminished demand for money on the part of some

---

[8] Of course, they say "income." But in this case "income" can only be strictly interpreted as "expected income." And in most of the applications which are made, this works out in the same way as the assumption given above.

[9] The above was written before reading Mr. Harrod's rejoinder to Mr. Robertson. As I understand him, Mr. Harrod is now only maintaining that the expansion of bank credit *may* work smoothly. With that I am in no disagreement.

people would raise the prices of capital goods and securities, and this would raise the demand for money on the part of the owners of those securities. Similarly an increased demand for money would lower prices, and this would lower the demand for money elsewhere. The whole thing would work out like an ordinary demand and supply diagram. But it is fairly safe to say that we do not find this straight-forward stability in practice.

The analytical reason why this sort of analysis is unsatisfactory is the following: The assumption of increased wealth leading to a pro-portionately increased demand for money is only plausible so long as the value of assets has increased, but other things have remained equal. Now, as we have seen, the other things which are relevant to this case are not prices (as in the theory of value) but anticipations, of the yield of investment and so on. And since these anticipations must be based upon objective facts, and an unexpected increase in wealth implies a change in objective facts, of a sort very likely to be relevant to the anticipations, it is fairly safe to assume that very many of the changes in wealth with which we are concerned will be accompanied by a change in anticipations. If this is so, the assumption of propor-tionate change in the demand for money loses most of its plausibility.

For if we assume (this is jumping over my gap, so I must emphasise that it is only an assumption) that an increase in wealth will very often be accompanied by an upward revision of expectations of yield, then the change will set in motion at least one tendency which is certain to diminish the demand for money. Taking this into account *as well as* the direct effect of the increase in wealth, the situation begins to look much less clear. For it must be remembered that our provisional assumption about the direct effect was only guess-work; there is no necessary reason why the direct effect should increase the demand for money proportionately or even increase it at all. So, putting the two together, it looks perfectly possible that the demand for money may either increase or diminish.

We are treading on thin ice; but the unpleasant possibilities which now begin to emerge are sufficiently plausible for their examination to be well worth while. What happens, to take a typical case, if the demand for money is independent of changes in wealth, so that neither an increase in wealth nor a diminution will affect the demand for money?

One can conceive of a sort of equilibrium in such a world, but it would be a hopelessly unstable equilibrium.   For if any single person tried to increase his money holdings, and the supply of money was not increased, prices would all fall to zero.   If any person tried to diminish his money holdings, prices would all become infinite.   In fact, of course, if demand were so rigid, the system could only be kept going by a. continuous and meticulous adaptation of the supply of money to the demand.

Further, in such a world, very curious results would follow from saving.   A sudden increase in saving would leave some people (the owners of securities) with larger money balances than they had expected; other people (the producers of consumption goods) with smaller money balances.   If, in their efforts to restore their money holdings, the owners of securities buy more securities, and the producers of consumption goods buy less consumption goods, a swing of prices, consumption goods prices falling, security prices rising, would set in, and might go on indefinitely.   It could only be stopped, either by the owners of securities buying the services of producers, or by the producers selling securities.   But there is no knowing when this would happen, or where prices would finally settle; for the assumption of a rigid demand for money snaps the connecting link between money and prices.

After this, we shall be fairly inured to shocks.   It will not surprise us to be told that wage-changes will avail nothing to stop either an inflation or a deflation, and we shall be able to extend the proposition for ourselves to interference with conventional or monopolistic prices of any kind, in any direction.   But we shall be in a hurry to get back to business.

VIII

These exercises in the economics of an utterly unstable world give us something too mad to fit even our modern *Spätkapitalismus;* but the time which economists have spent on them will not have been wasted if they have served as a corrective to the too facile optimism engendered by the first assumption we tried. Obviously, what we want is something between the two—but not, I think, a mere splitting of the difference. This would give the assumption that an increase in wealth always raises the demand for money, but less than proportionately; if we had time, it might be profitable to· work out this case in detail. It would allow for the possibility of considerable fluctuations, but they would not be such absurd and hopeless fluctuations as in the case of rigid demand.

However, I think we can do better than that. The assumption which seems to me most plausible, most consistent with the whole trend of our analysis, and at the same time to lead to results which at any rate look realistic, is one which stresses the probable differences in the reactions of different members of the community. We have already seen that a considerable proportion of a community's monetary stock is always likely to be in the hands of people who are obliged by their relative poverty to be fairly insensitive to changes in anticipations. For these people, therefore, most of the incentive to reduce their demand for money when events turn out more favourably will be missing; there seems no reason why we should not suppose that they will generally react "positively" to changes in their wealth— that an increase in wealth will raise their demand for money more or less proportionately, a fall in their wealth will diminish it. But we must also allow for the probability that other people are much more *sensitive*—that an increase in wealth is not particularly likely to increase their demand for money, and may very well diminish it.

If this is so, it would follow that where the sensitive trade together, price-fluctuations may start on very slight provocation; and once they are under way, the rather less sensitive would be enticed in. Stock exchange booms will pass over into industrial booms, if industrial entrepreneurs are also fairly sensitive; and, in exactly the same way, stock exchange depressions will pass into industrial depressions. But the insensitive are always there to act as a flywheel, defeating by their insensitivity both the exaggerated optimism and the exaggerated pessimism of the sensitive class. How this comes about I cannot attempt to explain in detail, though it would be an interesting job, for one might be able to reconcile a good many apparently divergent theories. But it would lead us too deeply into Cycle theory—I will only say that I think the period of fluctuation turns out to depend, in rather complex fashion, upon the distribution of sensitivity and the distribution of production periods between industrial units.

Instead, I may conclude with two general reflections.

If it is the insensitive people who preserve the stability of capitalism, people who are insensitive (you will remember) largely because for them the costs of transferring assets are large relatively to the amount of assets they control, then the development of capitalism, by diminishing these costs, is likely to be a direct cause of increasing fluctuations. It reduces costs in two ways: by technical devices (of which banks are only one example), and by instilling a more "capitalistic" spirit, which looks more closely to profit, and thus reduces subjective costs. In doing these things, capitalism is its own enemy, for it imperils that stability without which it breaks down.

Lastly, it seems to follow that when we are looking for policies which make for economic stability, we must not be led aside by a feeling that monetary troubles are due to "bad" economic policy, in the old sense, that all would go well if we reverted to free trade and *laisser-faire*. In so doing, we are no better than the Thebans who ascribed the plague to blood-guiltiness, or the supporters of Mr. Roosevelt who expect to reach recovery through reform. There is no reason why policies which tend to economic welfare, statistically considered, should also tend to monetary stability. Indeed, the presumption is rather the other way round. A tariff, for example, may be a very good instrument of recovery on occasion, for precisely the reason which free-traders deplore; that it harms a great many people a little for the conspicuous benefit of a few. That may be just the sort of measure we want.

These will be unpalatable conclusions; but I think we must face the possibility that they are true. They offer the economist a pretty hard life, for he, at any rate, will not be able to have a clear conscience either way, over many of the alternatives he is called upon to consider. His ideals will conflict and he will not be able to seek an easy way out by sacrificing either.

3

THE RELATIVE LIQUIDITY OF MONEY
AND OTHER THINGS*

By Edward C. Simmons‖

A brief consideration of the relative liquidity of money and other things may serve to throw light on some troublesome matters. If monetary management is to be relied upon, along with fiscal management, to control the level of activity in a free market economy, the quantity of money must have dimensions. If a dividing line between money and other things cannot be established both in theory and in practice, monetary policy discussions are meaningless. Should money be made more like other things? Should other things be made more like money? Should other things be made less like money? These three questions pose the issue. The position is taken here that the gap between money and other things should be made as wide as possible. The wider the gap the more effective can be monetary management.

We begin with the categorical statement that money is different in its fundamental character from securities and commodities. Money serves as a standard of value and as a medium of exchange. Commonly the list of functions is much more extensive, but the tendency to lengthen the list is to be deplored. Conceptually one needs only the minimum essential functions to establish a dividing line, and these two functions serve to bring out the essence of money. That thing which has parity and the capacity to mediate exchange is money, whether it be a pure token or something having value in another connection.

The phenomenon of liquidity appears in the economy as soon as mediation of exchange appears. Conceptually money can exist as a

* *The American Economic Review,* Supplement, **37** (1947), 308–11. Reprinted, by the courtesy of the publisher and the author, without change from the original text.

‖ Duke University.

pure *numeraire,* but such a money seems unlikely to exist in fact in a free market economy. Every exchange transaction in a money economy involves two operations—selling for money and buying for money—and momentarily at least money is held. It is self-evident that everyone in society cannot hold all his assets in nonmonetary forms. Some of these assets, although they do not serve to mediate exchange, do approach closely to money in possessing near-parity and in possessing general acceptability in that they may be bought and sold readily. Except in special cases, the movement of these things in and out of the possession of the person necessitates the recording of a book gain or loss on the books of account, which are conducted in conformity with the money illusion.

The inevitable result of exchange mediation is to create in the economy a special type of asset which by its nature serves as a store of value and a bearer of options. That is not to say that anything which serves as a store of value is money. Approaching the definition of money by this avenue leads only to the conclusion that everything is more or less money. Unless one proceeds carefully, he may find himself arguing that monetary management is impossible since the supply of money is dimensionless.

The store of value concept of money, although not yielding a satisfactory definition of money, does serve to bring out the liquidity problem. A person holding money and certain other assets, securities and nonspecialized commodities is endowed with a wide range of freedom as to time and kind of outlays. He may spend now or later or never.

Liquidity preference is a complex matter. Why does society seek liquidity? There is some minimum of liquidity that cannot be escaped. The institutional factor of payment patterns obliges some persons to hold money. Frequency and regularity of receipts and disbursements and their coincidence set a theoretical maximum to velocity, but beyond that subjective factors operate. In this paper this residual will be lumped under the one broad heading of uncertainty. The cost and bother of investing small sums for short periods serve to explain some money holding, but beyond this persons hold substantial sums either in money directly or in various assets that serve mainly as store of value against some more or less clearly foreseen contingency. The costs of this action are the opportunity costs of foregone returns. But there is some *quid pro quo,* for an economizing decision lies behind the action of holding low yield or no yield or even negative yield assets. Presumably some imperfectly foreseen future gain will offset the immediate loss.

The nature of the uncertainty elements which lead to piling up of liquid assets cannot be explored. However, the general observation may be made that the liquidity problem must be attacked along the lines of the causes of uncertainty rather than by destroying somehow the parity of money.

One school of thought has proposed that money be made more like other things by applying carrying costs to money. Stamped scrip is one of the practical proposals. In essence this requires that hoarding be distinguishable from normal holding over the interval between receipt and expenditure. But hoarding is a normative concept, for all units of money are held for longer or shorter periods because of the lack of coincidence between receipts and expenditures. The practical result of stamped scrip proposals would be to create units of money with varying discounts, or in other words to destroy the quality of parity. Were this not done with great skill, the outcome might possibly be simply a shift from conventional money to some other thing having greater stability of value. An exchange economy must have a medium of exchange. The liquidity problem cannot be solved by dispensing with a medium of exchange. Attractive as the idea may be at first glance that money should be made like other things, that end is neither desirable nor attainable.

On the other hand, the liquidity problem is not soluble by making other things more like money. That is what we have been busily engaged in doing these past few years. The government debt is our large liquid asset, thanks to our having opened the way to its monetization at the central bank in order to finance the war cheaply. In terms of the small sacrifice of liquidity that has been imposed on government security purchasers, 2 per cent was possibly too high a price to pay to get people to give up money for securities which are only slightly less liquid than money.

We must now face squarely the question of the meaning of liquidity. There are no liquid assets aside from money, unless there is a central bank. In the discussions of liquid assets, it is significant that cash, bank deposits, and government securities are the only things ordinarily considered. Other securities and commodities are not added in when statistical estimates are made. Possibly this is a recognition of the painful truth learned in frequent panics under the national banking system that only a central bank can create liquidity. The shifting of assets among banks, firms, and private persons suffices in normal times, and in periods of boom everything seems to be salable and therefore liquid, but there can be no general movement from assets to money unless the money-creating power of the sovereign is brought into play. At this point, it might be remarked that the gilt-edge quality of government securities rests not only on the power of the sovereign to tax in order to service the debt but also to no small degree to the long established practice of having the central bank stand ready to lend on or purchase government debt instruments. The liquidity of things which may not be absorbed by the central bank is a fair-weather phenomenon. Nonetheless, this fair-weather liquidity is a matter of significance and requires consideration. To the extent that liquidity preference is satisfied in periods of calm by assets that prove to be illiquid in periods of stress, the system is rendered more unstable.

Probably no one would seriously defend the proposition that all things should be made liquid. A monetary policy which would endeavor to make the number of dollars equal to the dollar amount of gross national wealth is patently absurd. Monetary theory has advanced far enough to provide good grounds for holding that even the good bills doctrine is fallacious as a guide to monetary policy. Monetizing all wealth would result only in limitless inflation.

Finally the third question. Should other things be made less like money? This is the really practical question which we now face. We have a large volume of public debt obligations which, under present arrangements, may be converted into bank deposits and currency at the option of the holders. If monetary management is to mean anything at all, the monetary authorities must be in a position to increase and decrease the number of dollars on their own initiative. Really effective monetary management seems to call for open-market operations rather than discount operations, at least where discounting is regarded as a right.   Moreover, open-market operations should probably be conducted in assets which are by nature subject to price fluctuations so that the effect of central bank operations will not be to peg prices and thus create a body of near-money assets.

Unless we are prepared somehow to make the transition to this state of affairs, we shall be unable to utilize the very powerful weapon of monetary management in its proper but not omnipotent role of a stabilizer in meeting coming intense cyclical movements of business activity.   Our public debt policy has closed the way to the employment of this weapon.

The making of other things less like money is not a futile goal. There is little danger that other things will become money in the modern economy.   Interest-bearing obligations are cumbersome at best in the mediation of exchange.   Few commodities other than the precious metals have the required attributes to challenge dollars as now embodied in cash and bank deposits.   Moreover, the tax power is available to discourage the use of such things.   The only real problem is therefore the policy of the central bank; that is, the extent to which other assets will be monetized.

The transition to the ideal world cannot be explored here.   In that happy land, the public debt would exist as perpetual consols. Privately-issued securities would exist only in the form of equities bearing no fixed rate of return or no fixed maturity value.   The central bank would buy and sell such amounts and kinds of assets as necessary to produce appropriate fluctuations in the supply of money. Probably this ideal world is never to be realized, but contemplation of it may assist us to see our way out of the present muddle.

Making other things less like money will not get at the cause of the liquidity problem, which is uncertainty.   A direct attack must be made on that.   However, financial reforms that will reduce liquid assets and reforms that will reduce the uncertainties that make the holding of liquid assets desirable are both hurdles to be cleared on the road to greater economic stability.

PART II

THE DEMAND FOR AND THE SUPPLY
OF MONEY—THE VALUE OF MONEY

4

THE GENESIS OF BANK DEPOSITS*

By W. F. Crick‖

From time to time there crops up with renewed fury a confused and confusing controversy as to the powers of the banks, as the saying is, to "create credit." To a large extent it is a battle of mere words, arising out of over-simplification of monetary theory into bald, unaccompanied statements such as that "every bank loan creates a deposit." A dictum like this, standing alone, has just as much scientific value, and no more, as David's exclamation, in the heat of the moment, that "all men are liars," or the cynical generalisation that no woman knows her own mind. As a verbal embodiment of accounting practice it is perfectly true, but as a contribution to monetary theory it is valueless unless accompanied by its converse, that every repayment of a loan destroys a deposit, and that in consequence the extension of a loan to repay another already outstanding neither adds to nor subtracts from the total of bank deposits. Disregard of this fairly obvious fact is responsible for much misunderstanding and is typical of the basic misconceptions of meaning which give rise to interminable and unconvincing argument. The true centre of any inquiry into the question whether the banks are able, and if so within what limits, if any, to expand or contract deposits is the relations, arithmetic and causal, between bank cash and deposits. Bank cash for this purpose comprises currency held by the banks, together with the balances to their credit at the Bank of England, while bank deposits include all the funds held by the banks to the credit of customers, whether withdrawable on demand or at an agreed period of notice, a distinction, by the way, which in practice has very little force. Any

* *Economica*, 7 (1927), 191–202. Reprinted, by the courtesy of the publisher and the author, without change from the original text.

‖ Midland Bank, London. [Sir Ernest Cassel Travelling Scholar, 1922.]

attempt to arrive at the truth in this investigation must proceed by way of the known practical and statistical facts to provide a solution to the problem of the relationships between bank cash and deposits.

The general stability of cash ratios is too well known to need detailed demonstration. The returns published by the banks are monthly averages of figures taken out on a particular day in each week. Probably the ratio of cash to deposits varies somewhat from day to day; probably too the ratios of which the published figures are averages differ appreciably. We know that the monthly figures vary fractionally, and in the case of some banks at the turn of the half-year, very substantially. Nevertheless, they reveal a degree of steadiness which is obviously much more than accidental. They are, indeed, the result of attempts by each individual bank to adhere to its own particular standard in this matter of the ratio of cash to deposit liabilities. From this relative stability, which applies even more to the banks as a whole than to most of the individual institutions, there are two alternative inferences, one of which must be true, the other false; either changes in the amount of cash available to the banks must bring about multiple changes in the amount of bank deposits; or, if this is not true, then variations in the volume of bank deposits must give rise to proportionate, but smaller, variations in the volume of bank cash. If the first inference be accepted it means that an addition of £x to bank cash results in an addition of £$(x \times a)$ to bank deposits; if the second, a decline of £y in bank deposits gives rise to a fall of £$\dfrac{y}{a}$ in bank cash; the relatively stable ratio between cash and deposits being represented by a. It is easy to say in reply that the question admits "no possible, probable shadow of doubt," but unfortunately that statement provides no convincing solution of the problem, which of these two inferences is correct.

If all the banks be considered together, the question may best be answered by asking and answering a second: What determines the amount of bank cash available to the banks? To assume no change in public habits, and therefore no change of more than transitory duration in the relative amount of currency in active circulation, does not in any way invalidate a discussion of the causes of relatively short-term variations in the volume of bank cash, under conditions of ordinary public confidence in the banks. For the sake of completeness, moreover, it may be noted that if a bank desires to increase its currency holding it can only do so by drawing on its balance at the Bank of England, so that the aggregate of bank cash is unaffected, unless the central bank takes steps, by extending its loans or investments, to make up the aggregate of joint stock bank balances with itself to the level before the addition to currency holdings took place. If, however, gold flows into the Bank of England there is an immediate or almost immediate addition to bank cash. The gold rarely reaches the Bank through a joint stock bank, but even so it is paid in by someone who either keeps his account at a joint stock bank, where by contrast with the Bank of England he may receive interest on his balance, or who shortly passes on the proceeds of the sale, namely a credit at the Bank of England, to someone who does keep such an account. Very soon, therefore, if not at once, an addition to the Bank's stock of gold adds to the available supply of bank cash. But this again assumes that the Bank does not choose to counteract the addition to bank cash by selling bills or securities or reducing its loans.

Consequently the volume of bank cash is determined, over relatively short periods, not by the public, nor by the joint stock banks, not merely by gold movements, but ultimately by the actions of the Bank of England.[1] According as it expands its loans or buys additional securities on the one hand or calls in loans or sells securities on the other, so it counteracts, reinforces or indeed ignores altogether the inflow, outflow or no flow of gold. There is nothing new in this. The Bank had precisely this power before the war, though perhaps it used it less. Since the war it has used it more—on the whole with benefit—though the consequence is that the Bank of England's ratio of reserve to liabilities is much more variable than in the case of the joint stock banks. It is important to note that so long as the budget is balanced by revenue or the proceeds of actual savings, even the

---

[1] For detailed argument leading to this conclusion, see the speech delivered by the Chairman of the Midland Bank Ltd. at the Annual Meeting of Shareholders, January 28th, 1927.

Government has little if any direct control over the supply of bank cash, except for very short periods. It is a function almost exclusively in the hands of the Bank of England.[2] The central institution cannot determine the distribution of the existing amount of cash between the banks, but it can and does determine the total amount outstanding at any particular time.

If, then, the volume of bank cash is determined by the actions of the Bank of England, what in turn determines the direction of these acts? To some extent the Bank's actions are controlled by statute, for it is bound by law to buy or sell gold at fixed prices; to some extent by custom, for it is always ready to discount customers' bills at a rate fixed by itself. But over and above these requirements, either emphasising or neutralising their effects, is the policy of the Bank. And this is determined by reference to a variety of considerations, among them the desire to earn a profit, the ratio of reserve to liabilities, the situation in the money market, the state of the foreign exchanges, and the general conditions of business. There is certainly no definite and direct relation of cause and effect between the deposits of the banks as a whole and the policy behind the actions of the central institution. Consequently the second alternative inference is ruled out, and we are left with the first, namely, that changes in the volume of bank cash result in multiple changes in the volume of deposits.

The acceptability of this conclusion is not merely a matter of reasoning. It can be arithmetically demonstrated and in addition can be reinforced by consideration of actual banking processes. First the arithmetic—and here we shall necessarily be somewhat dull and perhaps a little abstruse. It is the extraordinary side of truth which is stranger than fiction: commonplace truth is anything but exciting, and not always entertaining. For the purpose of the argument we need no such artificial supposition as the existence of a solitary bank. We may, however, make certain simplifications which will be seen in no way to invalidate nor even weaken the argument. We will assume the existence of five banks of equal size in point of deposits, each

---

[2] For statistical, as well as theoretical, argument on this point, see *Midland Bank Monthly Review*, March–April 1926, and for parallel argument applied to the United States see the same journal, May–June 1924, and Benjamin Anderson in the *Chase Economic Bulletin*, November 8th, 1926.

working to the same ratio of cash to deposits. Let us suppose each has £300 millions of deposits and works to a ratio of 10 per cent. Imagine that for some reason or other Bank A receives an addition of £1 million to its cash. It may be, for example, that gold has flowed into the country through a customer of Bank A and that the Bank of England sees no reason for neutralising the increase in its deposits. Bank A's position now is, deposits £301 millions, cash £31 millions, so that its ratio has risen to 10·3. Seeing, however, that its standard ratio is 10, it will be justified in increasing its earning assets at the expense of its cash. What are the possible courses open to it, and what is the result in each case?

Bank A may, in the first place, buy securities. If it buys them from one of its own customers there is no loss of cash, while deposits and investments are raised by an equal amount. But the chances are four to one against the seller of the security being its own customer, so that the purchase probably involves an increase in investments and an equal decrease in cash, deposits being unaffected. Precisely the same holds true if the bank goes into the market and buys bills—the effect will depend upon whether the seller of the bills is a customer of the bank or not. As a third possibility, the bank may increase its overdraft facilities, and in this case there is no effect on its balance sheet until the account is drawn on. When this happens, if the money is paid away to a non-customer there is an increase in loans and advances and an equal decrease in cash, with no change in deposits; if the money is paid to a customer there is an increase in loans and advances and an equal increase in deposits, with no change in cash. If, fourthly, the bank grants new loans, then loans and advances on the one hand and deposits on the other are immediately written up by the same amount, and only when a part or the whole of the loan is paid away to a non-customer is there any reduction in cash, which is accompanied by an equal fall in deposits.

Now two important facts emerge from this analysis. First, even if the policy of the bank renders likely an immediate loss of cash, it is improbable that an amount of cash equal to the full amount or purchase price of all the new earning assets will be removed to other banks. Secondly, if the bank extends new loans (as opposed to allowing new overdrafts) there is likely to be some delay in the loss of cash. It follows that the bank can lend or buy bills or investments to an amount in excess of the new cash received. If it were likely immediately to lose cash to the full extent of its loans or purchases it could only lend or spend £900,000, retaining £100,000 of the newly acquired cash. But as such a result is not likely, the spending or lending of £900,000 only will leave it with more than £100,000 of cash, and therefore a higher ratio than it regards as necessary. The probability is that the bank will lose an amount of its new cash not exceeding four-fifths of the amount of new loans or purchases. Consequently if it lends a full £1 million it will still presumably have £30·2 millions of cash. Its deposits, immediately upon making the new loans or buying the new assets, will be raised by £1 million, but at the same time £800,000 of this initial increase will be lost, with an equal loss in cash. Deposits will therefore be £301·2 and the ratio 10·03, which is still above the prescribed proportion. Consequently Bank A, when it receives an extra £1 million of cash, may with comparative safety increase its earning assets by over £1 million and at the same time effect a small net addition to its own deposits.

For simplicity's sake, however, let us limit A's new loans and purchases to £1 million. We have seen that by lending or spending this amount it loses £800,000 of cash, and this sum, together with £800,000 of new deposits, passes to the other four banks. So far, then, the new cash has added £1,200,000 to the deposits of Bank A and £800,000 to those of the other banks—already a twofold addition to deposits as a whole. Assuming the four banks share equally, each has £300·2 millions of deposits, £30·2 millions of cash, and a ratio of 10·06. Each is therefore faced with the possibility of increasing its earning assets. But the important point is that as all five banks are doing the same thing there will be no net loss of cash to anyone, for what B loses to C, D may lose to B, and so on. It may here be objected that in practice the banker cannot know this.[3] True, he may not at the outset, but it is quite obvious that he will get to know very soon after the first tentative steps have been taken, with no loss of cash, and with the ratio still as a consequence above

---

[3] This seems to be the gist of the objection voiced by the Chairman of Lloyds Bank Ltd. at the Annual Meeting of Shareholders, February 4th, 1927. The argument following in the letterpress, however, is entirely overlooked.

the standard. In the course of a short time each of the four banks will find it possible to spend or lend £1,800,000, for what is the result to each bank? Cash remains stationary at £30·2 millions, earning assets are up £1,800,000, and deposits, since the banks pay by means of cheques on themselves, are up in the aggregate £2 millions, restoring the ratio to 10 per cent. In the meantime A will have found it possible to continue expanding its earning assets without the maximum loss of cash, so that it too will be in the same position as the other four banks.

The final result of the addition of £1 million to the reserves of Bank A is thus achieved by a cumulative process, acting and reacting through all five banks. The cash has been distributed between them and they have, merely by working to a regular ratio, added £10 millions to their aggregate deposits and £9 millions to their earning assets. This they have done by a process of lending or spending in the faith and, indeed, knowledge that they will not suffer a commensurate loss of cash.

Without repeating the argument step by step, it is obvious that the opposite process is equally capable of arithmetic demonstration. If bank cash is curtailed, then so long as regular ratios are adhered to, deposits must fall by a multiple amount, in the case we have taken, by ten times the loss in cash. In both cases, with ratios consistently maintained—as they usually are in fact—changes in the volume of bank cash produce changes of multiple scope in bank deposits. The important point, which is responsible for much of the controversy and most of the misunderstanding, is that while one bank receiving an addition to its cash cannot forthwith undertake a full multiple addition to its own deposits, yet the cumulative effect of the additional cash is to produce a full multiple addition to the deposits of all the banks as a whole.

We may now leave the debating society and the class-room and enter the bank parlour, for the sceptical reader may still have doubts as to the practical facts of the case.

Perhaps the best way of following the sequence of events is by considering the position of a banker faced at the outset of a day's work with the necessity of deciding what policy he must adopt during the day towards the utilisation of his bank's resources and the applications for loans which will probably make their appearance. What are the facts before him? Little more than the precise state of affairs at the close of the previous day's business, with a few general but extremely uncertain indicators of what the immediate future has in store. He knows what amount of loans was outstanding at the close of business the previous evening. He knows what was the extent of the other earning assets, of his customers' deposits, and of the cash held against them. On the other hand, he knows very little of what will happen during the day, which is just what would be of the greatest assistance. He does not know what amount of deposits will be drawn off and therefore the extent of the demands to be presented for cash; he does not know what amount of loans will be repaid nor how far overdrafts will be increased. Consequently, although he can place an accurate figure on the bills falling due on this particular day, he cannot foresee with precision what his position will be at the close of business, apart altogether from new loan and investment transactions. To make the argument clearer, let us assume our banker has made up his mind to grant no fresh loans, to buy or sell no investments, to discount no further bills, and to enter into no new engagements during this particular day. We may now tabulate his knowledge thus, placing an affirmative opposite those items the exact extent of which at the end of the day he can forecast with accuracy, and a negative against those the movements in which during a single day, quite apart from any action of his own, no amount of prescience can foresee:

Capital and Reserve	.. Yes	Premises	..	..	Yes
Deposits ..	.. No	Acceptances, etc.		..	Yes
Acceptances, etc.	.. Yes	Investments	..	..	Yes
		Advances and loans of all			
		kinds ..	..	..	No
		Bills ..	..	..	Yes
		Cash ..	..	..	No
Total ..	.. ?	Total	..	..	?

Obviously we cannot say, with Omar, "He knows about it all; he knows; he knows." The vital figures are those he knows least about, and the proportion of cash to deposits at which he is aiming may be jeopardised by an infinity of unexpected occurrences. How much more impossible, then, to foresee his position when, as he must be, he is called on to make new loans and to shape his assets policy with a view to earning the maximum income consonant with safety! Clearly he must always be at least a day late with his data. For the rest he must rely on judgment—an elusive term, but a very real quality, which distinguishes the banker from the gambler.

Now for a practical case. Our banker, let us say, sets a ratio of 12½ per cent. as his cash objective. At the close of business on Tuesday the ratio of cash to deposits is found to be 14 per cent. He knows how much is falling due the next day on bills, to reinforce still further his cash reserves. He knows the bill market is lively and will want to borrow money. He knows of nothing to suggest heavy withdrawals of cash during the next day. What then will be his policy on Wednesday? Clearly he is losing profit by holding a cash ratio 1½ per cent. higher than he need. His decisions will therefore be affected by the desire to increase earning assets, so that he will be inclined to view loan applications more liberally. But the cash ratio is not the only proportionate figure to be watched. For liquidity's sake he must maintain more or less regular and well-established proportions of the various kinds of assets to the whole. Consequently he will not merely extend loans on all hands. He will probably buy some bills, thus replacing and perhaps more than replacing those falling due. He will lend more at short term, for the liveliness in the bill market gives him good rates of return. All this will be in addition to granting increased accommodation to those customers asking for advances or higher limits of overdraft. Finally, if there is no keen demand for loans, it may be held desirable to increase the bank's holdings of long-term investments. In all these various ways, as already explained, it is open to the banker, by increasing his assets, to effect the addition to his own or another bank's deposits which his relatively high cash holding appears large enough to support.

But suppose our banker's judgment is not of the best, or that it is one of his unlucky days.   For some unknown reason the demands for encashment of deposits are unusually large, while at the same time customers enjoying overdraft facilities draw unexpectedly heavily on their accounts.   The result is a dual depletion of cash. Each pound drawn off in cash effects at most only an equal absolute reduction in deposits, which are already seven or eight times as large as the basis of redeemability.   In the case of an overdraft there is no reduction at all in deposits, though there may be in cash.   But, in addition, the expansion in loans tends to bring about an increase in deposits more than offsetting the decline due to withdrawals of cash. As a result of these movements the ratio falls, let us say, to 11 per cent. What happens on Thursday morning?   The banker obviously cannot lay his hands on quantities of currency outside the bank and add them to his cash reserves.   And although the cheques drawn on his bank and presented at the clearing may be exceeded by his countervailing claims on other banks, he cannot expect much reinforcement from that source.   If he considers the movements of yesterday likely to persist he may sell investments.   He will be most unlikely to sell bills, for that, according to British banking tradition, would be regarded as a sign of weakness.   He will, however, most certainly refrain from instructing his brokers to buy bills in the open market. Further, he may seek to deter borrowers of all kinds by raising his charges for loans, or may harden his heart in dealing with current applications.   He may even call in short-term loans already outstanding.   In one, some, or all of these various ways the banker will seek to reduce his earning assets and concurrently to add to his cash at the expense of other banks or reduce his liabilities on account of deposits.   If his judgment is correct and his plans well laid, in the absence of any extraordinary occurrences like a panic demand for cash, his traditional ratio will be restored.

What now is the moral of the story?   It is just this: that the banker has his ideal of liquidity combined with profit-earning capacity.   His ratios are a golden legend, inscribed in gleaming figures around the facts of yesterday's position.   His knowledge is mainly of the immediate past; he knows with certainty little of the present, still less of the proximate future.   He must rely on his experience and judgment to bring his day's-end figures into conformity with the golden numerals of his ideal. The guiding influence in the exercise of his faculties is provided by his latest known ratios, particularly that of his cash to deposits. But deposits are the adjustable item; cash is a matter very largely of chance or of policy outside his control. Through earning assets the banker contracts or expands his liabilities. Through the banker's balance sheet and the banker's judgment is exerted the ultimate power of cash to determine the scope of deposits. In this indirect but vital way it is cash that controls deposits. But the controlling power of cash is dependent on the skill, the clearsightedness and the discrimination of the practical banker. An incapable, still more an unscrupulous, banker might upset the whole complicated scheme of relationships and throw sand in the monetary machine. Small wonder that irresponsibility and intellectual fatuity seldom if ever find their way into the highest seats of the oligarchy of banking!

We see, then, that cash relies for the effectiveness of the control it exercises over deposits upon the stability of the ratios adopted by the banks as part of their policy, and upon the success attending their efforts to maintain them. Up to the present we have assumed no change in bank policies, but let us suppose that Bank A decides that, having hitherto maintained a cash ratio of 10 per cent., it will be on the safe side in allowing the figure to run down and adopting in its place a level of 8 per cent. Starting from the same data as in the example already set out, the bank may lend or spend £6 millions with safety, knowing that as a result of its action it cannot lose more than £6 millions in cash and will probably lose less. Taking the extreme view, and supposing it loses the whole, its deposits remain at £300 millions, its cash is reduced to £24 millions, and earning assets are increased £6 millions. But bank cash as a whole is absolutely unaffected, so that the other banks each receive £1½ millions, plus £1½ millions of new deposits. Their ratio being raised, they may restore it by lending or spending £13½ millions, without any loss of cash, thus adding £13½ millions to their deposits. Each has now £315 millions of deposits and £31½ millions of cash, with a ratio of 10 per cent. In other words, the change of policy on the part of one bank has added £60 millions to bank deposits as a whole, so that in this case deposits have been controlled, not by a change in the volume of bank cash, but by a change in the ratio maintained by one bank. The example, none the less, reinforces the theory that, subject to bank policy and practical adherence thereto, it is cash that controls deposits.

This is true in particular because as a fact banks rarely change their policies in the matter of cash ratios, and because as a matter of record they adhere quite closely to the figures they adopt. It follows that changes in bank cash are the cause of inflationary and deflationary movements, for there is no guarantee that bank cash, and with it bank deposits, will expand or contract according to the volume of business being currently transacted. Finally, seeing that the volume of bank cash depends on Bank of England policy, the central bank alone, in present conditions, is responsible for any tendency towards inflation or deflation, by which we mean any tendency towards expansion or restriction of the volume of money as related to the volume of business and the current rapidity of circulation. The Treasury, although it has the power of note issue, has nothing whatever to do with the determination of the quantity of bank cash or deposits as long as it neither forces the Bank of England constantly to lend to the Government nor to receive repayment of outstanding loans.[4] The banks, moreover, act as the vehicles of Bank of England policy, by the process of lending or calling in loans and buying or selling bills and investments, without any powers of note issue whatever. The possession or lack of such powers is quite irrelevant to the discussion.

Summing up, then, it is clear—or at least we must hope so—that the banks, so long as they maintain steady ratios of cash to deposits,

---

[4] The Chairman of the Westminster Bank Ltd. appears to hold a precisely opposite view. See article in the *Westminster Bank Review*, November 1926, and Speech to the Annual Meeting of Shareholders, January 27th, 1927, where the rise of £14 millions in the Bank's deposits over the previous year is attributed to increased saving. It would be interesting to know whether the decline of £9 millions registered by the February 1926, figures, as compared with those for the previous month, was due to the reverse process, namely, customers drawing on savings.

are merely passive agents of Bank of England policy, as far as the volume of money in the form of credit is concerned. The proviso being substantially true, so therefore is the principal statement. If the Bank of England were to maintain a steady ratio of reserve to liabilities of the Banking Department, then gold movements would determine the volume of money in the form of bank deposits. The proviso being obviously untrue, except in a minor degree, the major statement is also untrue. The Bank of England is therefore the controller of money supplies. The banks, except for short periods and so long as no permanent change in cash ratios is effected, have very little scope for policy in the matter of expansion or contraction of deposits, though they have in the matter of disposition of resources between loans, investments and other assets. But this is not to say that the banks cannot and do not effect multiple additions to or subtractions from deposits as a whole on the basis of an expansion of or contraction in bank cash. To say that a bank cannot in practice "create" deposits to an indefinite extent is one thing; to say it cannot "create" deposits at all is another. The first assertion is true because a bank cannot make an addition at will to its own cash reserves without reducing its earning assets, while it feels it must conform to a regular ratio. The second is untrue, because we know as a fact that an addition to bank cash is accompanied, or closely followed by, a multiple addition to deposits, which cannot be attributed to any other cause but action by the banks. All of which may seem unnecessarily lengthy as an exposition of accounting and statistical fact, but all of which goes to prove what a flexible instrument is our mother tongue. To some minds the idea of "creating" anything is both objectionable and absurd, but disagreement on matters of terminology should not blind us to the relations, in sequence and amount, between the volume of bank credit outstanding and the quantity of bank cash held against it.

5

THE AMOUNT OF MONEY AND THE BANKING SYSTEM*

By J. E. Meade‖

The object of this note is to illustrate the factors which determine how much the amount of money will be affected in different types of banking system by given changes in that system. I have confined the inquiry to three types of banking system, but the method could easily be extended to cover other types. Finally, I have attempted, by means of statistical material taken from the MacMillan Report, to illustrate the results for the English banking system for the years 1925 to 1930.

I

1. The first banking system which I have considered is of the following type:—No gold coin is in circulation, and the Central Bank alone issues notes. The Central Bank keeps a certain proportion of its note issue and a certain proportion of its deposit liabilities to member banks covered by gold. Member banks keep a certain proportion of their deposit liabilities covered by reserves, *i.e.* by notes or by deposits with the Central Bank; and they also keep a certain proportion of their reserves in the form of deposits with the Central Bank. The amount of money is defined as the total deposit liabilities of the member banks + the amount of notes held by the public. The public keep a certain proportion of their money in the form of notes.

Let G = the amount of gold,

$\quad N$ = the total note issue, of which N_1 is held by member banks and N_2 by the public,

---

* *Economic Journal*, **44** (1934), 77–83. Reprinted, by the courtesy of the publisher and the author, without change from the original text.

‖ University of London.

$B =$ the deposit liability of the Central Bank to the member banks,

$D =$ the deposit liabilities of the member banks,

$M =$ the amount of money,

$l =$ the proportion of its note issue, which the Central Bank covers with gold,

$m =$ the proportion of its deposit liability to member banks, which the Central Bank covers with gold,

$n =$ the proportion of their deposit liability, which member banks cover with reserves,

$p =$ the proportion of their reserves which member banks hold in the form of deposits with the Central Bank,

and $q =$ the proportion of their money, which the public holds in the form of notes.

Then:

$$G = lN + mB,$$
$$N = N_1 + N_2,$$
$$nD = N_1 + B,$$
$$B = p(N_1 + B),$$
$$M = N_2 + D,$$

and $N_2 = qM.$

It follows that

$$M = \frac{G}{n(1 - q)(l - p[l - m]) + lq} \cdot \quad \cdot \quad \cdot \quad \cdot \quad \text{(i)}$$

Let

$$\frac{1}{n(1 - q)(l - p[l - m]) + lq} = t_1.$$

2. If the Central Bank keeps the same proportion of its liabilities, whether they be notes issued or deposit liabilities, covered by gold, l will be equal to m. Let $l = m = l'$.

Then

$$M = \frac{G}{l'(n + q - qn)} \cdot \quad \cdot \quad \cdot \quad \cdot \quad \cdot \quad \text{(ii)}$$

Let

$$\frac{1}{l'(n + q - qn)} = t_2.$$

It is interesting to note that p, the proportion of its reserves, which member banks hold in the form of deposits with the Central Bank, disappears from this equation. This is, of course, exactly what one would expect. If the member banks substitute deposits with the Central Bank for part of their holding of notes, this will have no further effect if the Central Bank keeps the same proportion of gold against notes and against deposit liabilities. It will only have further repercussions if these two proportions are different.

3. Let us suppose that the Central Bank prints an amount of notes equal to its holding of gold $+$ a given fiduciary issue, and maintains a given proportion between the notes so issued but not in circulation and its deposit liabilities to member banks. Let $K =$ the fiduciary issue and $k =$ the proportion between "notes in the banking department" and Central Bank deposit liabilities to member banks.

Then

$$M = \frac{G + K}{n(1 - q)(1 - p[1 - k]) + q} \quad . \quad . \quad . \quad \text{(iii)}$$

Let

$$\frac{1}{n(1 - q)(1 - p[1 - k]) + q} = t_3.$$

In this case it is to be noticed that an alteration in p will affect M. This is naturally so, because now, if the member banks substitute notes for deposits with the Central Bank, this will affect the proportion k between the Central Bank's notes in the banking department and its deposit liabilities.

Up to this point it has been assumed that the member banks keep the same proportion of their deposit liabilities covered by reserves, whether these are "time" or "sight" liabilities. This may not be the case. Let D_1 be the amount of current accounts and D_2 the amount of deposit accounts; let n_1 be the proportion of current accounts covered by reserves and n_2 the proportion of deposit accounts covered by reserves. Let r be the proportion of their deposits which the public keep on current account.

Then

$$D_1 = r(D_1 + D_2)$$

and

$$n = \frac{n_1 D_1 + n_2 D_2}{D_1 + D_2}$$

so that

$$n = n_2 + r(n_1 - n_2).$$

II

In order to determine how sensitive the amount of money is to given changes, it is necessary to differentiate equations (i), (ii) and (iii) in respect to all the possible variables. The results of this process are shown in Table I.

Table I

	1.	2.	3.
dM/dG	t_1	t_2	t_3
dM/dn	$-(1-q)(l-p[l-m])t_1M$	$-(1-q)l't_2M$	$-(1-q)(1-p[1-k])t_3M$
dM/dq	$-\{l-n(l-p[l-m])\}t_1M$	$-(1-n)l't_2M$	$-\{1-n(1-p[1-k])\}t_3M$
dM/dl	$-(n[1-q][1-p]+q)t_1M$	—	—
dM/dm	$-np(1-q)t_1M$	—	—
dM/dl'	—	$-\dfrac{1}{p}M$	—
dM/dk	—	—	$-np(1-q)t_3M$
dM/dp	$+n(1-q)(l-m)t_1M$	0	$+n(1-q)(1-k)t_3M$

All the proportions are $+^{ve}$ and lie between 1 and 0, and l will always in fact be $>m$. It follows that the derivatives are all of the sign shown in the table. In the case of each of the three types of banking system

$$\frac{dM}{dn_1} = r\frac{dM}{dn}, \frac{dM}{dn_2} = (1-r)\frac{dM}{dn}$$

and

$$\frac{dM}{dr} = (n_1 - n_2)\frac{dM}{dn}.$$

III

The third thing which I wish to do is to make some attempt to measure these quantities for England from the years 1925 to 1930.

Table II gives the necessary information for these calculations. R measures "notes in the banking department" of the Bank of England. G, N, R, B, D, N_1 and N_2 are all measured in £ million. G, N, R and B are annual averages of the monthly averages of the columns headed respectively "Gold Coin and Bullion," "Notes in Circulation," "Notes in Banking Department" and "Other Deposits: Bankers" in the MacMillan Report, pp. 302–3. D and N_1 are taken from the columns headed "Total Deposits" and "Cash in Hand" in Table 3 on p. 296 of the MacMillan Report. r is taken from the column headed "Proportion of Current Accounts to Total" on p. 37 of the MacMillan Report.

Table II

	G.	N.	R.	B.	D.	N_1.	$N_2 = N - N_1$	$p = \dfrac{B}{N_1+B}$	$n = \dfrac{N_1+B}{D}$	$q = \dfrac{N_2}{N_2+D}$	$l' = \dfrac{G}{N+B}$	$k = \dfrac{R}{B}$	r.
1925	145	382	26·7	71·3	1603	104	278	0·405	0·109	0·148	0·32	0·374	0·576
1926	149	375	27·6	68·4	1609	103	272	0·4	0·107	0·145	0·336	0·404	0·573
1927	150	373	32·0	66·5	1657	105	268	0·388	0·103	0·139	0·341	0·481	0·562
1928	163	372	46·9	65·7	1709	105	267	0·385	0·1	0·135	0·372	0·714	0·558
1929	147	362	44·5	62·8	1738	104	258	0·377	0·096	0·129	0·346	0·709	0·541
1930	155	358	56·7	64·9	1741	104	254	0·384	0·097	0·127	0·366	0·875	0·529
Av.	151·5	370	—	66·6	1693	—	266·1	0·389	0·102	0·137	0·347	0·592	0·556

It is to be observed that the proportions p, n, q, l' and r are all fairly stable, while the proportion k shows a very large change over these years.   This is largely, no doubt, to be explained by the changes made by the Currency and Bank Notes Act of 1928.   But even between the years 1929 and 1930 there is a large fluctuation in k.   On the other hand, l' is fairly stable.   This suggests that while formally the English banking system is of our third type, in fact it is more similar to the second type examined above.

In order to see how much more or less sensitive our banking system would become to given changes in its structure, it is useful to assume certain values for n_1, n_2, l and m.   Let us suppose, as has often been suggested, that the joint-stock banks hold a smaller proportion of reserves against deposit accounts and a larger proportion against current accounts.   Let us suppose further that the proportion to be kept against deposit accounts is 3 per cent. and that the proportion to be kept against current accounts is chosen in such a way that for the average of the years 1925 to 1930 the same proportion between reserves and total deposits would have been maintained. Then, since $n = n_2 + r(n_1 - n_2)$, we have

$$\cdot 102 = \cdot 03 + \cdot 556(n_1 - \cdot 03),$$
or
$$n_1 = \cdot 16.$$

Similarly, let us suppose that the Bank of England had maintained a proportion of $37\cdot5$ per cent. of its notes backed by gold, and that it had chosen to back such a proportion of its deposit liabilities by gold as would have enabled it to maintain the same note circulation and deposit liabilities to bankers as it did maintain from 1925 to 1930. Then we have

$$lN + mB = l'(N + B)$$
$$\cdot 375 \times 370 + m66\cdot6 = \cdot347(370 + 66\cdot6),$$
or
$$m = \cdot 195.$$

In Table III these proportions are used to calculate values for Table I.

Table III

	$\dfrac{dM}{dG}$[1]	$\dfrac{dM}{dn}$	$\dfrac{dM}{dq}$	$\dfrac{dM}{dl}$	$\dfrac{dM}{dm}$	$\dfrac{dM}{dl}$	$\dfrac{dM}{dk}$	$\dfrac{dM}{dp}$	$\dfrac{dM}{dn_1}$	$\dfrac{dM}{dn_2}$	$\dfrac{dM}{dr}$
1	$12\cdot8$	$-3\cdot37M$	$-4\cdot4M$	$-2\cdot44M$	$-\cdot438M$	—	—	$\cdot203M$	$-1\cdot88M$	$-1\cdot5M$	$-\cdot438M$
2	$12\cdot8$	$-3\cdot84M$	$-3\cdot99M$	—	—	$-2\cdot88M$	—	0	$-2\cdot13M$	$-1\cdot71M$	$-\cdot5M$
3	$4\cdot74$	$-3\cdot44M$	$-4\cdot33M$	—	—	—	$-\cdot163M$	$\cdot171M$	$-1\cdot91M$	$-1\cdot53M$	$-\cdot447M$

[1] The three figures in this column represent t_1, t_2, and t_3 and are calculated by means of the proportion given in Table II from equations (i), (ii) and (iii). t_1 and $t_2 = \dfrac{M}{G}$. They should, therefore, be equal to $\dfrac{N_2 + D}{G}$, which is equal to 12·9, calculated directly from Table I. $t_3 = \dfrac{M}{G + K} = \dfrac{N_2 + D}{G + 260}$, since K is the Fiduciary Issue. $\dfrac{M}{G + K}$ calculated directly from Table I = 4·72. These calculations provide a check on some of the work. I suspect, however, that the correspondence between the two methods of calculating t_3 is largely accidental, since the Fiduciary Issue (*i.e.* the notes in circulation + notes in the banking department — the amount of gold held by the Bank of England) was not fixed at £260 until 1928. I have used the figures for t_1, t_2 and t_3 given in Table III for the purpose of calculating the other figures in Table III.

There are certain comments to be made on this table. All the figures in line 1 and all those in the columns headed $\dfrac{dM}{dn_1}$, $\dfrac{dM}{dn_2}$ and $\dfrac{dM}{dr}$ are in a sense arbitrary and fictitious: they represent the sensitiveness of the amount of money to given changes, in the first place on the assumption that during the years 1925–30 the Bank of England had maintained certain arbitrarily chosen proportions between gold and notes issued and between gold and deposit liabilities, and in the second case on the assumption that the joint-stock banks maintained certain arbitrarily chosen proportions between current accounts and reserves and between deposit accounts and reserves.   Thus in fact, since there is no difference between these proportions and $n_1 = n_2$, $\dfrac{dM}{dr} = 0$. These figures should be taken, therefore, to represent what would have happened if the English banking system had been different in certain ways from what it was in the years 1925–30.

Secondly, all of the figures in Table III are, of course, calculated on the assumption that one factor is altered and that all the other factors are independent and constant.   In many cases it is permissible to assume that the proportions are independent of one another; if the joint-stock banks decide to maintain a larger proportion of reserves to deposits, this is not likely to affect the proportion of notes held by the public to their total holding of money.   But there are two important cases in which independence cannot be assumed.   In the first place, a change in the amount of money may cause a change in prices or money incomes.[1]   If a country is part of an international system, this in turn will probably affect its gold reserves.   Thus a change in any of the proportions would probably affect G if the exchanges were fixed. For this reason the figures in Table III must not be interpreted as measuring the change in the amount of money, which would, in fact, have followed a given change in one of the proportions during the years 1925–30; but rather they are simply measures of the sensitiveness of the English banking system during those years (i.e. measures of what would have occurred if everything else had remained the same). In the second place, if the Central Bank is taking a conscious control of the monetary position—as it quite properly should do—it may not maintain l, m, l' or k constant, but may consciously vary them to offset

---

[1] It is not my purpose in this note to discuss at all whether this must be so, or in what way the change is caused.

changes in the other factors. It is necessary, however, to assume that certain proportions—l and m, or l' or k, for instance—are kept constant by the Central Bank in order to be able to calculate the figures of Table III at all. Thus all the figures in all the columns—except in those headed $\dfrac{dM}{dl}, \dfrac{dM}{dm}, \dfrac{dM}{dl'}$ and $\dfrac{dM}{dk}$—are calculated on the assumption that the Bank of England was maintaining certain proportions constant. As I have said above, l' was much more constant than k during the years 1925–30, while l and m are purely fictitious quantities. Thus line 2 is probably the best measure for the actual position in England during those years.

Thirdly, it is interesting to make certain comments on the figures. First, it is clear that whichever type of banking system England had adopted, the sensitiveness of the system to given changes would not have been very different in most cases. In the case, however, of a change in the amount of gold, with the first or second type of system the change in the amount of money would have been about thirteen times, while with the third type of system it would have been only about five times the change in the amount of gold. Secondly, the introduction of different percentages of reserves against deposit or current accounts would not, *with the arbitrary chosen figures of 3 per cent. against deposit and 16 per cent. against current accounts,* have made the banking system very sensitive to changes in the proportion of deposits held on current or deposit accounts. Thus, if during those years persons had elected to hold 56·6 per cent. instead of 55·6 per cent. of their deposits on current account, the amount of money would have been decreased by about one half of one per cent. Thirdly, it is interesting to observe how sensitive the amount of money is to changes in q, the proportion of their money, which the public hold in the form of notes. Mr. Hawtrey has argued that a boom is stopped and a depression starts largely because q increases as wages rise and a larger proportion of the national dividend goes to those classes who hold a large proportion of their money in the form of currency. Table III shows that if q had increased from 13·7 per cent. to 14·7 per cent., the total amount of money would have decreased by about 4 per cent. However, in order to test the importance of Mr. Hawtrey's theory it is necessary to show not only how sensitive the amount of money is to changes in q, but also that q increases in the later phases of a boom. Table II shows that q was falling steadily in England from 1925 to 1930.   But this period was a peculiar one in England, and to test the theory it would be interesting to calculate $\dfrac{dM}{dq}$ and movements in q for other countries and for other times, in which the phases of the trade cycle were more typical.

6

LIQUIDITY AND A NATIONAL
BALANCE SHEET*

By Roland N. McKean||[1]

This essay is an attempt to analyze the factors determining "liquidity position" and to show the need for a "nation's economic balance sheet" to supplement "the nation's economic budget." Greater precision in thinking about liquid assets and illiquid obligations may enable us to formulate and test improved hypotheses concerning changes in these balance-sheet items and in the level of aggregate demand. Before examining particular types of assets and debts, I shall summarize (1) present views on the relationship between liquidity and spending and (2) the development of the concept of liquidity position.

I. Current Hypotheses About Effects of Changes in Liquidity on Volume of Spending

Practically all schools of thought believe that fluctuations in liquidity influence the level of aggregate expenditure. An increase in the money stock, for example, may induce exchanges of cash for less liquid assets of all varieties—for claims, raising their price and lowering their yield or "the" interest rate; for capital goods, pushing investment to a correspondingly lower position on the marginal efficiency of capital schedule; and for consumers' goods, raising the consumption function and lowering the marginal rate of substitution of consumers' goods for other assets.

* *The Journal of Political Economy,* **57** (1949), 506–22. Reprinted, by the courtesy of The University of Chicago Press and the author, without change from the original text.

|| Vanderbilt University.

[1] I am especially indebted to Professors Milton Friedman and Lloyd W. Mints for helpful criticisms.

Even an old-fashioned Keynesian like Roy Harrod goes along with this when he writes (regarding the postwar inflationary pressure in Britain) : " . . . if in the existing state of affairs there is a tendency for people to save less or to expend old savings, that is due to the low rate of interest and has nothing to do with the large volume of liquid assets, which is merely the mechanism by which that low rate has been brought about."[2] Despite this rather odd way of putting it, he is declaring that new balances will be allocated among different uses so as to equalize the marginal gain obtainable in each direction.[3]

Moreover, Keynesian converts, like A. G. Hart, who emphasize the imperfections of the capital market, would insist that an increase in the stock of liquid assets may increase investment without depressing *observable* interest rates.[4] At least two explanations are possible. One is capital rationing. In a single market for a homogeneous commodity, sellers do not prefer one customer to another, and price tends to move so as to equate quantity demanded and quantity offered. In the loan market, however, sellers (i.e., lenders) classify their customers according to the risk of losing principal and interest payments, and no single interest rate moves so as to equate the quantities offered and demanded. If customers fell into discrete compartments or risk-categories, this would simply mean that several loan markets and interest rates existed. But even within a single broad risk-category, *each* borrower presents a different degree of risk; and a loan to one customer is a different commodity from a loan to another. There can be no smooth supply schedule of loans, no offer of various volumes at a series of interest rates to each category of borrowers. Hence not only must there be many different markets for loans and many interest rates, but, at each resulting rate, some rationing is inevitable. Since there can hardly be as many interest rates as there are degrees of risk, preference among customers must help interest rates allocate funds; for a price to

---

[2] Roy Harrod, *Are These Hardships Necessary?,* London, Rupert Hart-Davis, 1947, 128.

[3] Many would urge, of course, that the marginal gain in certain uses will drop rapidly, so that very little new cash will be devoted to these uses.

[4] A. G. Hart, Assets, liquidity, and investment, *American Economic Review, Papers and Proceedings,* 39 (May 1949), 171–81.

equate quantity demanded and offered in a market for full titles to existing goods is conceivable; but in a market for contracts concerning the future, in an uncertain world, differentiation among customers and rationing at each price seem unavoidable.[5]   A shrinkage in the volume of liquid assets, therefore, may not produce lower supply schedules of loanable funds in all the loan markets (separated according to the degree of risk), so that smaller volumes of loans are negotiated in each market at higher interest rates.   Rather, the shrinkage in liquid assets may produce higher debt-asset ratios, fewer eligible and willing borrowers all along the line, and smaller volumes of loans negotiated at each old interest rate, with the higher-risk borrowers excluded entirely. Conversely, an increased volume of liquid assets may produce lower debt-asset ratios, more eligible borrowers, and a greater volume of loans negotiated at the previously existing pattern of interest rates. Investment may be stimulated without any decline in observable interest rates.[6]

A second explanation can be offered without resort to the concept of "credit rationing," i.e., without encroaching upon the allocative role of interest rates.   Fewer liquid assets may lower *both* demand schedules for, and supply schedules of, loanable funds, since less favorable asset-debt ratios in an uncertain world involve extra risk for both entrepreneurs and lenders.   The result could be a restricted volume of loans without a rise in interest rates.   The supply of loans to high-risk borrowers could dwindle to zero, as they move into even higher-risk categories, where supply and demand schedules never intersect;

----

[5] See *ibid.* for comments on the possibility of having pure competition in the capital market.

[6] Cf. M. W. Reder's Discussion in The theories of J. M. Keynes, *American Economic Review*, 38 (May 1948), 297: "To my way of thinking, it is quite improper to eliminate availability of funds as a determinant of the rate of investment.   However, the model that seems to me correct is neither Keynesian nor neo-classical.

"Such a model would be based squarely upon the fact of capital rationing. Each firm would have its own sources of capital, the supply of which would not be closely related to the rate of interest it must pay. . . . It would be possible to have low open-market rates coupled with a shortage of available funds for borrowers whose securities did not qualify for the open market."

there would be no transactions and no recorded price (as in the market for rubber skillets). On the other hand, supply schedules of loans to low-risk customers (like the government) could increase so that such loans continued to take place at even lower interest rates. Even if interest rates do perform the allocative tasks, a decreased (increased) volume of liquid assets can shift demand and supply schedules for loans so as to discourage (encourage) investment without raising (depressing) observable interest rates.[7] In fact, the complex of observable interest rates may appear to rise (fall) as funds become more (less) "available."

To summarize this introductory section, Keynesians and non-Keynesians alike agree that changes in liquidity positions are likely to influence the level of consumption and investment, though how and how much are still controversial matters.[8]

II. The Development of the Concept of Liquidity Position

Individual businessmen certainly look at more assets than cash and also at the other side of the balance sheet before coming to any conclusions about their liquidity position. A banking firm can hardly base its lending decisions solely upon an examination of cash on hand. Yet, in elaborating the quantity theory of money, economists tended to obscure the other balance-sheet items and to focus attention on the influence of one particular asset—money—which had to be defined arbitrarily. Some—Henry Thornton was one of the earliest, and Henry Simons one of the most persuasive—sought further in the balance sheet for influences on the level of spending and emphasized that liquid assets other than those defined as money were near-moneys or money substitutes.[9] Then, in the 1930's, Irving Fisher developed the

---

[7] These conclusions do not depend upon changing expectations and resulting changes in the demand for loans or in the marginal efficiency of capital.

[8] In order to analyze the effect of balance-sheet items apart from that of income flows, we have to confine the discussion to existing, rather than expected, liquidity positions. A theory of expected liquidity positions or an entire theory of assets would swallow up all theory, inevitably embracing not only expected incomes and outlays but expectations of all sorts.

[9] Henry Thornton, *An Enquiry into the Nature and Effects of the Paper Credit of Great Britain*, London, 1802, 39–43; Henry Simons, Rules versus au-

debt-deflation theory of depressions, stressing private debts and debt burden as partial explanations of fluctuations in aggregate spending.[10] Henry Simons improved the hypothesis, particularly with respect to short-term debts and the liquidation scramble.[11] By and large, however, Fisher and Simons tended to discuss the implications of privately held liquid assets apart from the implications of debts privately owed. They made little attempt to consider the two sides of the balance sheet simultaneously in order to formulate an integrated hypothesis.

Some investigators have attempted to observe the whole balance sheet rather than just certain components. A. G. Hart, in *Debts and Recovery*, was concerned throughout with both assets and liabilities in relationship to each other and to the volume of spending.[12] J. R. Hicks, in 1935, urged that monetary theory ought to be developed by regarding " . . . every individual in the community as being, on a small scale, a bank" and that " . . . the same forces which work through the assets side work through the liabilities side in much the same way. But this certainly requires further exploration."[13]

Homer Jones has tried to investigate the relationship between the balance sheet and the volume of investment spending.[14] He has found that individual savers have a remarkably strong preference for

---

thorities in monetary policy, *Journal of Political Economy,* **44** (February 1936), 5–14, reprinted in *Economic Policy for a Free Society,* Chicago, University of Chicago Press, 1948, 164–72.

Recently, numerous writers have discussed or investigated liquid assets other than money. See, e.g., Hart, Postwar effects to be expected from wartime liquid accumulations, *American Economic Review,* **35** (May 1945), 341–51; U.S. Department of Agriculture, Bureau of Agricultural Economics, Division of Program Surveys, *National Survey of Liquid Asset Holdings, Spending, and Saving: A Survey Conducted for the Board of Governors of the Federal Reserve System,* Washington, 1946; and further analyses reported at intervals in the *Federal Reserve Bulletin.*

[10] *Booms and Depressions,* New York, Adelphi Co., 1932.

[11] *Op. cit.*

[12] Hart, *Debts and Recovery,* New York, Twentieth Century Fund, 1938.

[13] A suggestion for simplifying the theory of money, *Economica,* New series, **2** (February 1935), 12, and 13, n. 2.

[14] Investment prospects, *Journal of Finance,* **2** (April 1947), 15–33.

holding fixed claims (e.g., time deposits, insurance policies, bonds).[15] Furthermore, financial institutions are under legal and moral pressure to hold predominantly fixed claims. Therefore, Jones decided that as the debt-equity ratio rises, there is less "room" for investment because investors refuse to lend and businessmen refuse to borrow when debt-asset ratios are unfavorable. Bankers, accountants, businessmen, farmers, and even individual households keep an eye on debt-asset ratios because they realize that this is an uncertain world. Since the 1945–46 debt-equity ratio was exceptionally low (i.e., the national balance sheet had become heavy with assets compared to private debts), Jones concluded that investment prospects were excellent but that the rise in the debt ratio as investment in fixed claims soared might lead later to a drying-up of investment. We should notice that, as the debt ratio rises, both the demand schedule for and—if it makes sense to speak of them—the supply schedules of loanable funds are lowered without necessarily causing a rise in interest rates, particularly those paid by low-risk borrowers. Perhaps it should be observed also that inflation drives the debt-equity ratio down, encouraging further expansionary investment (at least until prices and incomes rise less rapidly than debt) and that deflation drives the debt-equity ratio up, discouraging investment outlays still further (at least until private debt falls more rapidly than prices and incomes). *During fluctuations,* of course, other influences, notably price and income expectations, may play a dominant role.[16]

III. Analysis of Factors Determining Liquidity Position

First, it is necessary to define several terms. "Liquidity" will be used here to mean merely "moneyness." Usually, an asset's liquidity is described to include the probabilities of getting various fractions of the going price plus the time period necessary to liquidate the asset. Perhaps another element should be added—the time period over which

---

[15] The flow of savings. I, *ibid.,* 3 (October 1948), 6–7.

[16] These attempts to include both assets and liabilities as determinants of liquidity positions and, through them, of outlays appear to be only a beginning. It may be useful, for example, to break down the aggregates and examine the relationship of various types of claims and debts to liquidity positions.

the other characteristics are expected to endure.[17]   Since these components cannot be measured, there is little to be gained by breaking the notion down.   Perhaps it is sufficient to say that the more nearly we regard an asset as substitutable for money, or the more it partakes of the same attractions possessed by money-holdings, the more liquidity the asset has.

"Illiquidity," on the other hand, will be used to mean the opposite of moneyness.   In contrast with the liquidity of claims—the ability to make lower cash balances acceptable—is the "illiquidity" of debts, or the capacity of maturing debts to require the holding of cash balances. That debtors to banks do, in fact, maintain higher balances than they would otherwise keep was demonstrated by the well-known analysis of C. A. Phillips.[18]   After a borrower gets a loan, there is some lag before all the proceeds are checked out.   Indeed, the proceeds may never be completely drawn out, especially since many banks require the maintenance of minimum balances.   As the maturity date approaches, cash is gradually accumulated to retire the debt.   On the average, Phillips estimated that 20 per cent of a bank's created deposits remained with the original bank (though this figure would vary, depending upon a great many factors).   This amounts to saying that, on the average, debtors to banks maintain higher cash balances, to that

---

[17] Many definitions apparently ignore this aspect of liquidity, for instance: "Roughly speaking, the longer the useful or consumable life of the article, the less liquid it is likely to be" (A. A. Berle, Jr., and V. J. Pedersen, *Liquid Claims and National Wealth: An Exploratory Study in the Theory of Liquidity,* New York, Macmillan Co., 1934, 42).   But surely it is not an apt definition of liquidity that makes such a statement valid.   Money, possessing 100 per cent liquidity, is expected to last indefinitely; any asset which depreciates rapidly, whether from use or disuse, does not have much "moneyness."

C. C. Brown excluded from liquidity the ability to exchange for a particular price, which, he said, involved appreciation or depreciation, a separate and confusing quality possessed by assets (*Liquidity and Instability,* New York, Columbia University Press, 1940, 3, 7).   It is true that appreciation or depreciation in real value is a characteristic of both liquid and illiquid assets and is hence something apart from liquidity.   Nevertheless, the tendency not to depreciate or appreciate in nominal value is a trait of moneyness.

[18] *Bank Credit,* New York, Macmillan Co., 1926, chap. 3.

extent, on account of their obligations. This "illiquidity" of debt depends upon lags, the probability of having to pay the face amount without renewal or refinancing, and the time available before repayment. To repeat, the illiquidity of debts is the extent to which they act as a reduction of the moneyness of balance sheets—the extent to which they require the maintenance or acquisition of cash balances.[19]

The liquidity position of a person or spending unit means the "current" position, and "is determined by the *liquidity characteristics* and *money amount* of assets owned, relative to the *maturity schedule* and *money amount* of debts owed."[20]

The liquidity position of the entire economy is the aggregate or combined liquidity positions of private individuals, nonfinancial businesses, financial institutions, and governments. The analysis here, however, will be confined to the liquidity position of individuals and nonfinancial businesses.[21] Only balance-sheet items as they would appear on their books will be considered. Assets and obligations on the books of lending institutions and government units are important to aggregate spending but can best be examined separately.[22] I am concerned with those balance-sheet items which directly affect the consumption and investment outlays of businesses and individuals. Although it is well to remember the similarities between banks and other businesses,[23] separate treatment seems justified by the differences

---

[19] Hart uses the terms "negative liquidity" and "illiquidity" in this same sense in *Money, Debt, and Economic Activity,* New York, Prentice-Hall Book Co., Inc., 1948, 75–76, 133–35.

[20] Brown, *op. cit.,* 151.

[21] Admittedly, the distinction between financial and nonfinancial businesses must be arbitrary, but it is sufficient to include in the former all banks, life insurance companies, savings and loan associations, etc., that accept "deposits" or owe fixed obligations and relend on a large scale.

[22] The federal government's liquidity position (or the size of the public debt) affects legislation and appropriations and may exercise a depressing, or other, psychological influence on private spending. The liquidity position of financial institutions affects their willingness to lend, the illiquidity of private debt to the banks, the ability to borrow from the banks, and hence the liquidity position of nonfinancial businesses and individuals.

[23] As Hicks observed: " . . . the cash reserve a bank keeps against its liabilities is simply a special case of the holding of money against uncertain

—notably that (1) banks' "spending" policy, for the most part, affects the nonfinancial sector's liquidity position rather than directly affecting consumption and investment; (2) banks carry much larger cash reserves (i.e., are probably influenced to a much greater degree by liquidity position) than other businesses; and (3) banks' liquidity positions are directly regulated to a considerable extent by monetary authorities.

In the following sections I shall examine several classes of assets in conjunction with the liabilities, if any, which correspond to them. Claims are matched by different types of debts. Unless one takes into consideration the impact on the debtor's cash-balance requirements, or liquidity position, as well as on the creditor's, a short-term claim against private business will appear to be much the same in its effects as a short-term claim against the government. Yet the net effects are clearly not the same. Three ways in which liquidity position may be affected will form the headings under which these balance-sheet items will be discussed: (A) changing volume of assets and debts, (B) changing liquidity of assets and illiquidity of debts, and (C) changing real value of claims and real burden of debt as the price level fluctuates.

A. Changing Volume of Assets and Debts

CURRENCY, DEMAND DEPOSITS, NEAR-MONEYS, AND EQUITY TITLES NOT MATCHED BY PRIVATE DEBT. It is impossible to say, once and for all, precisely what should be included in such categories as money and near-moneys (i.e., acceptable substitutes, to variable extents, for cash balances).[24] I include currency and demand deposits under money, since they are usually acceptable for either cash-balance or exchange purposes, and I arbitrarily define near-moneys as claims, other than demand deposits, against financial institutions or the federal government. Thus they include time deposits, cash-surrender values of

---

future expenditures, which is practiced to some extent by all businesses, and by many private individuals as well" (*Value and Capital*, Oxford, Clarendon Press, 1946, 241).

[24] For a good statement of the problems involved see M. Bronfenbrenner, Some fundamentals in liquidity theory, *Quarterly Journal of Economics*, **59** (May 1945), 405, 413.

life insurance policies,[25] repurchasable shares in savings and loan associations, travelers' checks, and privately held obligations of the federal government, such as postal savings, short-term bills, and all redeemable and marketable securities.

Currency, demand deposits, near-moneys, and "other fixed claims" (referred to below) have fixed face values, while equity titles are assets having no fixed face amounts.   Fixed claims can, of course, have variable exchange value; they can become worthless or be transformed through foreclosure or agreement into equity titles.   There are a few hybrid types, but most assets fall logically into one of the two classes. So much for the way in which these terms are used here.

Pigou has explained that one effect of an increased amount of money issued by the government is to increase the real value of the total volume of claims and hence to increase the real value of the community's total stock of assets.[26]   This ought to make people feel better off and, since the proportion of real value in the form of liquid claims has increased, in a more liquid position.   An increase (decrease) in the volume of metallic or paper money, *ceteris paribus,* is a clear-cut net addition to (deduction from) the real value of liquid assets, with no offsetting change in the real burden of private debt.[27] Likewise, if the government sells new securities to the central or commercial banks (and spends the proceeds), the volume of demand

---

[25] Despite the similarities between cash-surrender values or "deposits" with insurance companies and other time deposits, many persons feel that the former are seldom regarded as money substitutes.   If it is true that people are extremely reluctant, by and large, to "tap" these liquid reserves, then, in effect, they are not liquid reserves and cannot substitute for cash.   Nevertheless, all these claims can be (and, in an emergency, are) converted into cash; so for purposes of analyzing the theory of liquidity position, I have classed all claims against financial institutions as near-moneys.

[26] The classical stationary state, *Economic Journal,* **53** (December 1943), 342–51, and Economic progress in a stable environment, *Economica,* New Series, **14** (August 1947).

[27] This is true only under the special circumstances existing in the United States.   If currency is issued by commercial banks, the subsequent analysis of demand deposits matched by private debt is applicable.

deposits not matched by any private debt expands,[28] adding to the net liquidity of the community.

Of course, other things do not normally remain the same. Currency in circulation fluctuates according to the form in which people wish to hold their liquid assets. Conversion of currency into deposits, or vice versa, alters the volume of liquid assets other than currency (and also alters the banks' liquidity position, neglected here, unless government action deliberately maintains perfect interconvertibility). In the case of demand deposits not matched by private debt, bank purchase of government bonds from individuals or businesses increases the stock of demand deposits not matched by private liabilities but simultaneously decreases the public's bond holdings. Member-bank purchase of bonds from the government simultaneously reduces the banks' liquidity (and therefore, indirectly, the public's liquidity), though it does not appear on the balance sheet of the nonfinancial public. Analyzing changes in each asset, with other things held the same, serves to point up the distinctions between different balance-sheet items; the obvious abstractions involved emphasize the necessity of observing changes throughout the balance sheets of both the nonfinancial public and the financial institutions.

Another type of liquid asset not matched by private debt is the stock of near-money claims against the federal government, their moneyness depending upon the terms and maturities. Longer-term claims—if support prices are absent or changeable—will have less liquidity than short-terms, though both will be more liquid than corporate bonds with similar maturities. The near-money claims against financial institutions, too, are unmatched by private obligations to the extent that they are offset by government securities, equities, or

---

[28] Debts of state-local governmental units, omitted here because relatively unimportant, are in an intermediate position between federal and private debt. Although local governments possess the taxing power, they do not have the authority to create money or the central government's relationship to the banking system. Moreover, we know that local debts are repudiated and that local governmental balance sheets probably influence their outlays more than in the case of the federal government.

reserves held by financial institutions. An increase (decrease) in the volume of all these near-moneys, *ceteris paribus,* should add to (detract from) the community's liquidity position.

Properties owned outright, also, though not claims to a definite number of dollars, must be an addition to, not a detraction from, liquidity positions. Equity titles vary a great deal in liquidity; common stocks on major stock exchanges, inventories, jewelry, and some types of real estate are among the comparatively liquid properties. Ownership is not matched by an offsetting liability; hence, to the extent that these equity titles have liquidity, they make a net contribution to the community's liquidity position. In the aggregate the real value of these assets probably changes slowly, although the growth of common-stock financing expands the volume of equity titles and improved markets or rapid growth of inventories can shift the composition toward more liquid types.

All the classes of assets discussed in this section make an undiluted contribution to liquidity positions.

DEMAND DEPOSITS, NEAR-MONEYS, AND OTHER FIXED CLAIMS MATCHED BY PRIVATE DEBT. Expansion or contraction of the volume of these claims cannot affect the real value of the community's holdings, because the real value of the new claims is offset by the real burden of the new liabilities. Thus the Pigou line of reasoning is inapplicable. If, moreover, debtors regarded their obligations as detracting from their liquidity positions as much as the owners of claims regarded them as adding to their liquidity positions, then the creation and destruction of the claims could have no net effect on the liquidity position of the community. For two reasons, however, it is unlikely that debtors do feel impelled to increase their cash balances on account of their obligations as much as claim-holders are enabled to reduce their previous cash balances on account of the newly created demand deposits, near-moneys, or other claims: (1) In the case of new private deposits with, matched by new private borrowing from, financial institutions, the debts to the institutions are seldom due on call and are often term loans or long-term bonds, while the claims against the institutions are available on short notice (and, in the case of checking deposits, serve as a circulating medium). The more remote the maturity of the debt to the bank or insurance company and the more immediate the availability of the claim, the greater the excess of the claims' liquidity over the debts' illiquidity. (2) Even if the claims and debts have identical terms and maturities, as in the case of other fixed claims (i.e., against individuals and nonfinancial businesses), the claims are surely regarded as being more liquid than the debts are illiquid. Otherwise, there would be no point in borrowing and lending; expansion of debt would never take place if the borrower believed it necessary to raise his cash balance as much as the creditor lowered his.

In other words, for one or both of the above reasons, claims are more liquid, considered by the holders, than the corresponding debts are illiquid, considered by the debtors.[29] Expansion (contraction) of these claims, *ceteris paribus,* puts the community in a more (less) liquid position, though not to the extent suggested if the matching private debts are overlooked.

Again, it is important to remember that other things do not usually remain the same. Expansion of privately held money or near-money will occur if financial institutions purchase existing corporate bonds, without any change in private liabilities. In this case substitution of highly liquid checking accounts or near-moneys for less liquid long-term bonds adds to the public's (but detracts from the institutions') liquidity position. The effects are similar to, but probably stronger than, the effects of purchasing existing government securities by the banking system. Or institutions may vary their holdings of reserves or cash instead of matching depositors' claims with any kind of earning asset.[30] Debts to institutions can fluctuate without any change in

---

[29] Hart, *Money, Debt, and Economic Activity,* pp. 75–76, 134; Hicks, "A Suggestion for Simplifying the Theory of Money," 10–12; this volume, pp. 13–32.

In the next section I state that, during deflation, claims become less liquid, while debts become more illiquid, but the debts are not likely to develop more illiquidity than the liquidity retained by the claims. That is, before the debtor maintained higher cash balances on account of the liability than the creditor would forego on account of his asset, the two would be likely to retire the loan.

[30] See Jones, The optimum rate of investment, the savings institutions, and the banks, *American Economic Review, Papers and Proceedings,* **38** (May 1948), 321–39, for evidence concerning the extent to which this has occurred.

claims against them (or vice versa). To put it another way, the volume of claims against institutions not matched by (i.e., in excess of) private debts to them will increase if holdings of government securities, equities, or reserves are built up at the expense of private debts to banks.

Another important qualification is that contraction is scarcely ever the result only of lenders' compelling debtors to repay at maturity or "persuading" others to exchange cash for bonds on the open market. Often debtors voluntarily repay their obligations. Their demand for cash is no greater than their desire to get rid of the debts. If the banks are as willing as ever to relend on the same terms, paying off bank loans becomes just a way of "storing" checking accounts. The volume of demand deposits privately held and of debts privately owed does decline; yet under these circumstances the resulting excess reserves must be considered as taking their place. Likewise, if insurance companies, other institutions, or individual lenders remain as anxious as before to lend funds voluntarily repaid, the community's liquidity position is not impaired. This means that the financial institutions' liquidity position, though put to one side in this discussion, is indispensable for interpretation of nonfinancial balance sheets.[31] Ability to borrow, elusive as the notion is, must somehow be recognized as a money substitute and as a part of liquidity positions.

---

[31] In the case of voluntary repayment to commercial banks, the "disappearance" of demand deposits (i.e., the emergence of excess reserves) is simply an alternative to a decline in velocity (though strictly passive behavior by banks would be difficult to demonstrate). Under our banking system today the repayment of loans by private borrowers may be predominantly voluntary. Friedrich Lutz's findings led him to believe that large corporations would accumulate cash during depressions and leave it idle if the banking system did not receive repayments and "destroy" checking accounts: "These comparisons suggest that in a system in which business is not indebted to the banks to any great extent—i.e., in which deposits are created or canceled through the purchase or sale of government securities—business fluctuations may reflect themselves not in an increase or decrease of bank loans and deposits but in a change in the velocity of circulation of deposits and, perhaps, in a change in ownership of deposits between consumers and enterprise" (*Corporate Cash Balances, 1914–43,* New York, National Bureau of Economic Research, 1945, 5).

All the classes of assets discussed in this section make a "diluted" contribution to the community's liquidity position. Demand deposits are naturally more liquid than near-moneys, and the latter are more liquid than other claims (such as trade receivables, privately held mortgages, or corporate bonds); but the argument is similar for all: expansion decreases the cash-balance needs of the holders more than it increases the cash-balance requirements of the debtors, and contraction ordinarily does the opposite.

B. Changing Liquidity of Assets and Illiquidity of Debts

Claims may possess what has been entitled "fair-weather" liquidity,[32] and debts may possess what might be termed "foul-weather" illiquidity. During good times, when there is no mass attempt to call claims, they are extremely liquid and function as good money substitutes; debts, on the other hand, which can be renewed or refinanced easily, are not very illiquid, and little cash reserve is needed to meet obligations. When critical times arrive, however, and general liquidation is attempted, creditors doubt the moneyness of their claims, and debtors encounter increased pressure to pay and greater obstacles to refinancing. Hence claims lose their ability to substitute for cash, and debts acquire the capacity to require the accumulation of cash balances. This foul-weather illiquidity of debts is about what A. G. Hart once entitled the "mythology of maturities."[33] During prosperous times, debts have no effective maturity, because they can easily be refinanced. During bad times the maturity of obligations is very real and, in many cases, accelerated.

To include fluctuating liquidity of claims and illiquidity of debts as determinants of net liquidity positions is to introduce the byproducts of changing liquidity desires. It may appear to erase all distinction between liquidity position and liquidity desire, but, in reality, I believe, it enables us to make the distinction sharper. In a community with absolutely no private debts, fair-weather liquidity

---

[32] Edward C. Simmons, The relative liquidity of money and other things, *American Economic Review, Papers and Proceedings,* **37** (May 1947), 310; this volume, pp. 33–7.

[33] *Debts and Recovery,* 14–15.

and foul-weather illiquidity would not exist, though both the stock of, and the desire for, liquid assets could fluctuate.   In our community, with private debts constituting much of our financial structure, fluctuations can occur in (1) the stock of liquid assets, (2) the desire for liquid assets, and (3) the liquidity of balance-sheet items as a by-product of changing liquidity desire.

CURRENCY, DEMAND DEPOSITS, NEAR-MONEYS, AND EQUITY TITLES NOT MATCHED BY PRIVATE DEBTS.   Currency issues by either the Federal Reserve banks or the Treasury can hardly suffer from fair-weather liquidity any more, and no offsetting private debt exists to suffer from changing illiquidity.   Near-money claims against the federal government, which has the power to substitute cash for its obligations, are not likely to change much in moneyness.[34]   The longer-term securities will have less moneyness than will the short-terms and some degree of fair-weather liquidity, not due to doubts that the government can redeem them but due to changing "shiftability," interest rates, and uncertainty about support policy.

Demand deposits and near-money claims against financial institutions in excess of private debts to them cannot be distinguished, of course, from similar claims which are matched by private debts.   All such claims have in the past been subject to fair-weather liquidity. Demand deposits performed all the functions of money, and claims like time deposits served as cash substitutes satisfactorily most of the time; but, during a crisis when people suspected the soundness of financial institutions and tried to withdraw deposits, the ability of all such claims to act as cash balances declined sharply.   The effect was to undermine liquidity positions where claims and debts remained outstanding—over and above the shrinkage in volume of such claims (including the drain upon bank reserves and the resulting multiple contraction).   Nowadays, it is true, these assets are more homogeneous.   Gold is unobtainable even if people prefer to hold it,

---

[34] As indicated above, state and local securities form a class almost by themselves; for, while these governmental units do not have the power to create money, they do have the power to tax.   In any case, claims against states and local units are sometimes of dubious and fluctuating liquidity.

deposits with banks or savings and loan associations are to a considerable extent insured, and there are some provisions for system liquidity. The sudden demotion of bank deposits to claims of very dubious liquidity is unlikely to be so severe. Nevertheless, deposits may be tied up for a short time, and the liquidity of some near-moneys may deteriorate considerably.

Since the demand deposits and near-money claims discussed in this section are matched by government debt, cash reserves, or equity investments rather than by private debt, the possibility of foul-weather illiquidity of private debt is minimized.[35] Nevertheless, even though no outstanding private debt can be called or sold, holders can sell government debt on the open market, ordinarily raising yields not only on government securities but also on corporate bonds and other private debts and arousing uncertainty about further changes in bond prices. Debtors, potential or existing, may find it more expensive or difficult to remain in debt or to sell new bonds.

Equity titles are subject to great variation in liquidity (but, of course, are not matched by any debts which can fluctuate in illiquidity). During stable or inflationary periods, some equity titles have a fair degree of moneyness. People are at times confident that they can convert them into a certain amount of cash on short notice and may allow them to substitute for cash to some extent. During periods of declining markets and uncertainty, equities possess much less moneyness, and people's cash-balance requirements increase. The quantitative significance of this factor is hard to appraise; it may easily have been underestimated in many discussions of liquidity.

DEMAND DEPOSITS, NEAR-MONEYS, AND OTHER FIXED CLAIMS MATCHED BY PRIVATE DEBT. In the previous section I sketched the fluctuating liquidity of all demand deposits and near-moneys. Other claims (e.g., mortgages and corporate bonds privately held, notes and

---

[35] See Hart, *Money, Debt, and Economic Activity*, 508: " . . . we are in some ways safer in having bank deposits rest on government debt than we would be if they rested on private debt (bank loans). The danger that a business recession may be compounded by bank credit contraction is much reduced: our cash supply is largely deflation-proof."

accounts receivable) are also likely to have fair-weather liquidity. Short-term claims lose moneyness when collectibility seems doubtful; long-term claims lose moneyness when shiftability becomes expensive. The extreme example of loss of liquidity is complete default by the debtor.

All the claims to which this section pertains, however, are matched by private debts. To assert that loss of liquidity by these deposits, cash-surrender values, mortgages, and receivables has a net effect on liquidity positions is to assume that the offsetting obligations do not lose a corresponding amount of illiquidity. This assumption is more than conservative because, during times when the liquidity of claims comes under suspicion, the illiquidity of debt increases. When it appears that collection efforts are imminent or that debts cannot be renewed or refinanced as easily as anticipated, owing debts (whether to institutions, businesses, or individuals) necessitates acquiring higher cash balances than were previously held. Maturities can be taken lightly by debtors when money is easy, yet must be taken seriously when money is tight. Instead of a debt which can without difficulty be refinanced and which therefore requires no offsetting liquidity on the asset side of the balance sheet, the debt becomes practically a subtraction from cash.

Whenever debts are voluntarily repaid, it is the debtor's liquidity desire, not the illiquidity of the obligation, which has changed. But whenever the incentive for repayment lies partly in creditors' demands and the interlocking structure of short-term debt, this pressure can be described as the "increased illiquidity of liabilities." Debtors then have to resort to distress selling of assets, distress saving of funds, and distress calling of other debts owed to them, in the general scramble to restore cash balances. The longer the maturity of the debt (unless it can be accelerated), the less debtors suffer from foul-weather illiquidity, but they cannot escape entirely. If financial institutions and others start selling long-term investments, the debtor corporations may not feel extra pressure, but yields will go up, and new financing by long-term, as well as by short-term, loans is more difficult to obtain. Increased illiquidity of debts implies reduced ability to borrow, whether for refinancing or for other purposes.

Impaired liquidity positions among lenders increase cash-balance requirements for potential, as well as for existing, debtors.

C. Changing Real Value of Claims and Real Burden of Debt as Price Level Fluctuates

Changing real value of claims and real burden of debts due to price-level fluctuations also affects the liquidity of stock. As Pigou has urged, if the price level declines, the real value of fixed claims not matched by private debt increases, assuming that their volume does not shrink proportionately.[36] This means that the real value of the community's total stock of assets rises, with the real value of liquid assets forming a larger proportion than before. Holders of such claims should feel better off and in a more liquid position. (Aggregate demand in real terms should increase, compared to what it would have been in the absence of this effect.)

The argument does not apply to claims matched by private debts because, as the real value of these claims fluctuates, the real burden of private debts changes in an offsetting manner. If the price level falls, for instance, net worth is redistributed in favor of the creditor, but there is no change in the community's real net worth. Presumably, on balance, the community should feel neither better off nor in a different liquidity position, as far as such claims and debts are concerned. But this use of Pigou's argument assumes no money illusion. Debtors and creditors may react differently to price-level changes, especially since those who hold most of the claims are individual savers, while those who owe most of the debts are business firms. Suppose the debtors are more sensitive to changes in real burden than creditors are to changes in real value. Debtors may feel additional pressure or relief from pressure more keenly than creditors feel the increased or decreased real value of their claims. If the price level falls and this sort of money illusion exists, debtors' liquidity positions deteriorate more than creditors' liquidity positions improve, so that

---

[36] The classical stationary state, and Economic progress in a stable environment; see also O. Lange, *Price Flexibility and Employment*, Bloomington, Ind., Principia Press, 1945, 13–19, and Hicks, *Value and Capital*, 334–35.

there is a net reduction in the community's liquidity stock, as far as claims matched by private debts are concerned.[37]

The conclusion is that the liquidity of the community's collection of assets and liabilities is subject to change as price levels fluctuate, not only because some claims are not matched by private debts, but also because the money illusion may cause different groups to attach varying significance to fluctuations in real value and real debt burden.

CURRENCY, DEMAND DEPOSITS, AND NEAR-MONEYS NOT MATCHED BY PRIVATE DEBT.[38]   The conventional Pigou argument should be applicable to all these cases.   Increased real value of these holdings, in the event of a price decline, should reduce the cash-balance needs of the holders and would not be offset by a change in the real burden of any matching private obligations.   The changes in liquidity position due to this effect would be in a stabilizing direction. The money-illusion argument, on the other hand, could not apply to these situations.

----

[37] The existence of "money illusion" here means basing calculations to some extent upon the nominal rather than the real changes in payments, receipts, or balance-sheet items—whether because of irrationality, ignorance, or expectations that some "normal" price level will return.   If the price level falls, creditors may feel neither better off nor more liquid because they believe prices will return to "normal," but debtors may have no option, since repaying interest and principal out of reduced incomes renders them palpably worse off and less liquid (Cf. James Tobin, Money wage rates and employment, in *The New Economics,* ed. Seymour Harris, New York, Alfred A. Knopf, Inc., 1948, 581).

[38] Equity titles do not enter this discussion.   Price fluctuations should produce no change in real value of equities, on the average, and there is no offsetting debt whose real burden might change.   Equity titles are the articles whose fluctuating prices make up a changing price level.   Although uniform, proportionate changes in all prices never occur, there is no presumption that properties in the aggregate acquire or lose real value during fluctuations. (Use of an actual price index as a deflator would show changes; for one thing, even if prices of all properties entered into the index, weights could hardly reflect changes in the composition of equity titles.)   In any case the original argument regarding fixed claims assumed that increased real value of claims without any altered real value of equities increased the proportion of asset values held in comparatively liquid form.

DEMAND DEPOSITS, NEAR-MONEYS, AND OTHER FIXED CLAIMS MATCHED BY PRIVATE DEBT. Changes in the real value of these claims produce no net change in the community's net worth; the Pigou argument does not apply. The money-illusion argument, however, is applicable and may explain a destabilizing or perverse influence on liquidity positions. If changes in real debt burden are felt more keenly by debtors than changes in real value are felt by holders of deposits, bonds, and receivables, the community's position may become more liquid during inflation and less liquid during deflation.

IV. NEED FOR A "NATION'S ECONOMIC BALANCE SHEET"

Problems concerned with liquidity position continually enter into policy discussions. Frequently, in the past, conclusions have been based upon scanty quantitative information. Henry Simons' picture of the "financial good-society," in which the only assets are money and equities, is invaluable as an ideal to keep before us; yet he may have exaggerated the significance of near-moneys.[39] The increased volume of near-money claims not matched by private debt does not seem to have had a marked effect on cash-balance requirements (i.e., on velocity), suggesting that people may look upon government bonds, cash-surrender values, and some kinds of time deposits predominantly as sunk investments rather than as liquid reserves.[40] Foul-weather

---

[39] See Simons, Debt policy and banking policy, *Review of Economic Statistics,* **28** (May 1946), 85–86. Apparently his emphasis on near-moneys was, in large part, the reason he referred to private banks and insurance companies as " . . . the two forms of private business which are least essential to, if not incompatible with, a free-enterprise, free-market system," in his article, The Beveridge program: An unsympathetic interpretation, *Journal of Political Economy,* **53** (September 1945), 217.

[40] Cf. A. G. Hart, Postwar effects to be expected from wartime liquid accumulations, 344.

As life insurance companies and mutual savings banks increased their holdings of government bonds (near-moneys), they showed no consistent tendency to lower the proportion of assets held in the form of cash, though these institutions hoarded and dishoarded cyclically, much as others tried to do (Jones, The optimum rate of investment, the savings institutions, and the banks, 325–29). Warburton urges that savings bonds, on account of their yield, do not function as important near-moneys (Quantity and frequency of

illiquidity on the liability side, also stressed by Simons, may be more significant than the fluctuating volume of checking accounts and near-moneys on the asset side.

Moreover, in the past, conclusions have often been based upon partial analysis of liquidity positions.   We have treated similarly types of claims and debts which were not, in fact, similar and have neglected or underemphasized the changes in certain balance-sheet items.   I believe the discussions of postwar banking policy may be an example of this.   The federal government used part of its surplus to retire bonds held by member banks, restoring their reserves so that they were able to expand loans to private borrowers.   As the surplus drained off demand deposits, the banking system poured them back into circulation.   Since the stock of adjusted demand deposits plus currency in circulation did not decline, the net effect did not appear to alter the economy's liquidity position:

> In short, there is no direct deflationary effect from using a government surplus to repay short-term securities held by banks.   There is only an opportunity for the Federal Reserve to mop up some bank reserves without forcing the banks to call loans or sell securities in the open market.   There is, however, a by-product in the reduction of equities and increase of debt to the banking system.[41]

Dr. Hardy's main point was sufficiently important to overshadow his last sentence.   Deflationary effects of a Treasury surplus on liquidity positions have since been associated almost exclusively with retiring debt held by the Federal Reserve banks or building up Treasury deposits with the Reserve banks.[42]   My analysis suggests that we should not entirely overlook the deflationary influence of increased

---

use of money in the United States, 1919–45, *Journal of Political Economy,* **54** [October 1946], 435–37).

[41] C. O. Hardy, Fiscal operations as instruments of economic stabilization, *American Economic Review, Papers and Proceedings,* **38** (May 1948), 399.

[42] See the repeated references to using the surplus to retire bonds held by the Federal Reserve banks in the article, Bank credit developments, *Federal Reserve Bulletin* (October 1948), 1205–16.   Everyone seems anxious to avoid any suggestion of the errors of the 1945 *Annual Report* which Hardy pointed out.

private indebtedness to the banking system. The original Phillips analysis implies that these debts probably require higher cash balances on the part of borrowers than would be required in the absence of the debts. Retirement of bonds held by member banks out of tax receipts is inflationary compared to paying off debt held by the Federal Reserve banks; yet the transaction as a whole is deflationary. Similar reasoning puts retirement of bonds held by insurance companies, savings and loan associations, or savings banks in a slightly different light. It is true that "this process of shifting out of Government securities results in the creation of bank deposits and bank reserves and is just as inflationary as bank credit expansion,"[43] but again the resulting increase of private debt (when the institutions lend the funds obtained) must increase the cash-balance requirements of the borrowers. A shift from liquid assets offset by public debt to similar assets matched by private debt puts the economy in a less liquid position.[44]

Purchase of government securities by the Federal Reserve banks, though clearly putting the banking system and the public in a more liquid position, makes possible a rise in private debts whose opposite impact on liquidity positions should not be overlooked. In view, too, of the potential illiquidity of private debt, it seems rash to assert confidently that " . . . stability in the Government bond market . . . contributes to the underlying strength of the financial structure of the country."[45] It should at least be acknowledged that the growth of private indebtedness facilitated by supporting government bonds contributes to the underlying weakness of our liquidity position.

To minimize these deficiencies in the future—i.e., to compile rele-

---

[43] *Ibid.,* 1216.

[44] Several other factors, until 1948–49, had been reducing our liquidity: (1) the decline in real value of currency and claims not matched by private debts as prices rose; (2) reduced liquidity of banks as portfolios included fewer governments, as interest rates on short-term governments were permitted to rise, and as reserve requirements were increased (until recently); (3) reduced liquidity of long-term corporate bonds, common stocks, and other equities as yields rose and uncertainty grew; (4) reduced liquidity of inventories; (5) increased illiquidity of short-term debts (implying higher interest charges and decreased "availability" of funds in other ways).

[45] *The Economic Report of the President to the Congress, January 7, 1949,* Washington, U.S. Government Printing Office, 1949, 11.

vant quantitative information systematically, to focus attention on liquidity position as a whole, and to prevent excessive emphasis on an oversimplified income-expenditure analysis—I suggest that a "nation's economic balance sheet"[46] would be an appropriate companion statement to the "nation's economic budget."

In drawing up and interpreting such a financial statement, it might be well to follow business practices as closely as possible.[47] We are trying to isolate balance-sheet relationships which influence business and individual actions. Perhaps we should classify and interpret the aggregates in much the same way that a businessman classifies

---

[46] Interesting developments in this direction include *The Balance Sheet of Agriculture*, Miscellaneous Pub. No. 672 for 1948, by the Bureau of Agricultural Economics, U.S. Department of Agriculture; and the statements of current assets, current liabilities, and working capital of American corporations, quarterly releases by the Securities and Exchange Commission.

Townsend-Skinner's Financial Accounting is an attempt to use part of the economy's balance sheet in diagnosing stock-market fluctuations (see Garfield A. Drew, *New Methods for Profit in the Stock Market,* Boston, Metcalf Press, 1948, 15–16).

[47] F. A. Lutz preferred to use ratios of cash to payments (or cash to sales) to discover whether corporations had in the past possessed "free" cash and wrote that quick or other asset-debt ratios " . . . are definitely of little importance to our special problem. Business management also gives little consideration to such ratios, except as it is necessary to do so to meet requirements of credit grantors" (*op. cit.,* 63).

Ratios of liquid assets to past payments, however, are backward-looking; and ratios of liquid assets to future payments, though subsequently calculable for examining past behavior, are unavailable for appraising current liquidity position. Surely current liabilities constitute a useful estimate of expected payments—that is, of those already scheduled.

Cf. H. W. Arndt, The concept of liquidity in international monetary theory, *Review of Economic Studies,* 15 (1947–48), 26: "It is usual to define the 'liquidity position' of a bank, not in terms of the disposition of its assets only, but in terms of certain *ratios* of assets to liabilities, especially the ratios of cash to deposits and of liquid assets (or, conversely, advances) to deposits. It is clear that this is also the only feasible approach to the concept of 'liquidity position' in the international context. . . . In practice, if the concept is to be of use, it will be necessary, internationally as much as in domestic theory, to devise some rough and ready measure of liquidity position, in the form of some significant ratio."

and interprets his balance-sheet items:[48] (As a working hypothesis, we might assume that individuals and small businesses follow, though less consciously and less religiously, the same principles supposedly followed by corporation comptrollers and executives.) However, for such a combined national balance sheet it would be advisable to have, wherever possible, some additional breakdown according to owners in the case of assets and according to owers in the case of liabilities. Ideally, each group of claims (debts) would be further subdivided into holdings by (obligations of) financial institutions, businesses, farmers, and other individuals.

It is especially important that the claims held, and debts owed, by financial institutions be segregated—probably by having two separate balance sheets, the nation's financial institutions balance sheet and the nation's economic balance sheet, the latter showing only assets and liabilities on the books of nonfinancial businesses and individuals. Ratios computed from the two segregated balance sheets should prove more informative than ratios computed from a combined balance sheet.

In interpreting his balance sheet, the businessman uses various ratios, not just one ratio, to help gauge his liquidity position. He does not, of course, blind himself to other guides—e.g., changes in individ-

---

[48] For example, there could be, on the asset side, currency in circulation (outside the Treasury and Federal Reserve banks); demand deposits; near-money claims (maturing in one year or less from the date of the balance sheet) against the government, against financial institutions, and against nonfinancial businesses and individuals; business inventories; long-term claims (maturing more than one year hence) against the government, against financial institutions, and against nonfinancial businesses and individuals; equity shares listed on major stock exchanges; other equity titles. On the liability side, one could list short-term debts (maturity date one year or less hence) to commercial banks, other financial institutions, businesses, and others; and long-term debts (maturity date more than one year hence) to the same creditors. For an example of the possibilities in this direction see Elwyn T. Bonnell, Public and private debt in 1947, *Survey of Current Business*, **38** (October 1948), 20–23, and the National Bureau's projected preparation of a National Balance Sheet as of the end of selected years (*Agricultural Finance Review*, November, 1947, 93–4).

ual items, price levels, liquidity of receivables, and illiquidity of payables. His allowance for the last two factors, which do not appear on the balance sheet, shows up through his requiring higher asset-debt ratios during deflation than during inflation. During periods of contraction, alert businessmen, bankers, and investors, recognizing impaired liquidity positions due to altered collectibility of claims and renewability of debts (as well as having unfavorable anticipations), probably require higher asset-debt ratios of themselves and of those to whom they extend credit. Again the economist can follow suit. Within the nation's economic balance sheet, several ratios can be observed—not mechanically but in the light of changes in individual items, price levels, and the moneyness of assets and liabilities.

To recapitulate, this analysis has indicated that changes in liquidity may come about through changes (1) in the stock of assets (of varying degrees of liquidity) diluted in some cases by changes in the volume of liabilities (of varying degrees of illiquidity); (2) in the liquidity of various assets which remain outstanding, reinforced in some cases by simultaneous changes in the illiquidity of matching debts; (3) in the real value of claims not matched by private debts and, through the money illusion, in the real value and debt burden of matching claims and debts. I believed it useful to hold other things constant while examining variations in particular balance-sheet items, but I pointed out that other things do not usually remain the same. Changes in one group of assets or debts may be accompanied by offsetting or reinforcing changes in some other group of assets or debts.

Thus the variety of possible influences and the complexity of their interrelationships suggest that no single index (such as the quantity of money, the real value of the stock of money plus government bonds, or the ratio of aggregate liquid assets to aggregate private debt) can tell us as much as we need to know about liquidity position. A study of the national balance sheet as a whole, using several ratios or indexes, along with national income and expenditures, is more likely to throw light on fluctuations. Much discussion has centered around the nation's ecomonic budget, comparable to a corporation's income or sources-and-applications-of-funds statement. A nation's economic balance sheet might be a wholesome supplementary exhibit.

7

SOME FUNDAMENTALS IN THE
THEORY OF VELOCITY*

By Howard S. Ellis||

Direct reversal of cause and effect from the relation maintained by the quantity theory has been rather widely recognized in monetary literature for various particular situations. But a much more categoric assertion of this reversal seems to inhere in the description of economic equilibrium emanating from Keynes and his followers. Marginal efficiency of capital in comparison with interest determines investment, which in turn through the multiplier controls the level of employment or output. Prices are established without direct reference to the effective quantity of money (MV) by the cost functions of individual goods. Volume of output multiplied by prices gives the money requirement for the active circulation; and the residual money becomes the supply available for reserves, with which the liquidity demand function equates to set the rate of interest.

The foregoing representation of the rôle of money in the Keynes analysis will later be shown to be an over-statement of Keynes' real position on the part of Mr. Harrod;[1] but it has the merit of setting in bold relief an important line of causation in that theory. I do not hold that an appeal to empiric evidence would necessarily preclude such causation—indeed it may be found to be quite important. But Mr. Harrod maintains that even the conventional quantity theory leaves the way open for precisely this course of causation, because the

* *The Quarterly Journal of Economics,* **52** (1937–38), 431–72. Reprinted, by the courtesy of the publisher and the author, without change from the original text.

|| The University of California.

[1] R. F. Harrod, "Mr. Keynes and the Conventional Theory," *Econometrica,* vol. 5, no. 1 (January 1937), pp. 74–86.

division of money stock between active circulation and liquidity reserves is left indeterminate. That so astute a theorist as Mr. Harrod can argue in this wise seems to indicate the desirability of a general ordering of the elements in velocity theory. Before submitting its case to the arbitrament of facts, the more conventional theory must be explored for further possibilities of logical formulation.

It is a matter of no controversy to regard the stock of money in the hands of the public as belonging to three main categories: (1) the active circulation, or working balances involved in advancing goods toward consumption; (2) the financial circulation, or balances used for acquiring titles to wealth for speculative or mere holding purposes; and (3) idle balances, hoards, contingency or liquidity reserves, or simply reserves.[2] Since the present inquiry does not pretend to be a "General Theory," it is permissible to restrict the sphere of analysis; and upon this basis the financial circulation, without denial of its pristine importance, has been "impounded in *ceteris paribus.*" Sections I–III examine the basic determinants of the active circulation; their effects upon the number of dollars required *or* upon circular velocity, transactions velocity, and real balances; and finally the interrelations of these three velocity expressions. The analysis of these three sections reveals an almost completely mechanical relation between the rate of turnover of goods and monetary requirement,[3] *or* between the rate of turnover of goods and velocity in its three expressions; but to the surprise of some readers, the description of determinants of *active circulation alone* reveals nothing as to whether causation proceeds from prices to velocity or the reverse. Which line of causation actually prevails in a certain situation depends wholly upon what determines the *division* of money stock into active circulation and hoards. If this *division* rests upon a subjective calculus not in-

---

[2] Not only "money in the hands of the public" but each of its subdivisions raises intricate statistical problems of definition, which are not discussed in this paper.

[3] Throughout these pages, "monetary requirement" refers strictly to the number of *dollars* in working balances and *not* to the *real* size of working balances, which will later be seen to be quite a different matter.

volving given prices but resulting in prices, quantity-theory causation obtains; and if the division depends, not upon a subjective calculus at all, but upon the given product of output times prices, contra-quantity-theory causation obtains.

The first three sections on working balances accordingly maintain neutrality as to causation between prices and velocity; basic determinants work themselves out either in monetary requirement or in velocity. Because of this neutrality, it is hoped that the analysis has positive value *per se* on the mechanics of monetary circulation, aside from the problem of quantity-theory causation. In order finally to cope with this problem, I consider in Section IV the character of hoards or liquidity reserves, giving a definition in terms of previous concepts and examining the hoarding or liquidity-preference calculus. The issue as to causation itself is joined in Section V.

Recurring to the treatment of working balances or the active circulation, we will find in Section I the analysis of an important variable known as "overlapping" and its results on monetary requirement or upon circuit velocity. Another primary variable, the degree of industrial differentiation, is treated in Section II. As a method of progressing by degrees, the results are expressed now, along with the results of overlapping, not only in terms of monetary requirement and circuit velocity, but also in transactions velocity. Section III explains the relation of the Cambridge real-balance doctrine to circuit and transactions velocities in the light of basic velocity determinants—an essential step in approaching the question of hoards and final causation.

I. Working Balances and the "Overlapping" of Payments

Traditionally the factors determining the size of working balances have been described as the *frequency* and *coincidence* of payments or, where longer lists of factors appear, these two embrace their substance.[4] (1) As for frequency, which apparently signifies the *absolute* time length of periods hereafter to be distinguished, we may be content

---

[4] Cf., for example, Irving Fisher, *The Purchasing Power of Money,* 2d ed., (New York, 1922), pp. 352–53.

with the simple relationship that the monetary requirement or the length of time required for an average consumer-producer circuit increases proportionally with extensions of the periods. (2) Nothing is said in the traditional analysis of transactions velocity concerning firm differentiation, apparently under the mistaken notion that this variable affects only circuit velocity. The second variable will be the subject of Section II. (3) At present we are concerned with a third variable, the factor loosely designated as "coincidence." Inasmuch as all money is continuously owned, one person holding a sum until the precise moment when a payment obligation causes its transfer to someone else, coincidence in one sense is always perfect. What then can be meant by coincidence which admits of degrees, and which could therefore be a true monetary variable?

As long as we regard only *one* set of facts, the temporal beginning and end of balance holdings, we come no farther than the observation of this perfect joining. Degrees of coincidence obviously require a contrast between *two* phenomena; it is Professer Angell's distinction to have discovered the essential dichotomy in his "income-expenditure periods" and "payment intervals."[5] The relation between these two magnitudes, called the "degree of overlapping," can be given precise mathematical expression. In conjunction with the absolute lengths of these periods and the number of industrial "stages," degree of overlapping gives a fairly complete analysis of the anatomy of working balances. For this reason Angell's innovation occupies a central place in the present section. The importance of his discovery is, however, jeopardized for his readers by several errors of illustration; and his preoccupation with algebraic relations may account for the lack of a definition and even any very direct description of overlapping itself. I have attempted to supply these essentials, to revise the illustrations to suit what appears to be the author's intention, and to translate them for the benefit of the mechanically minded into graphic devices. To avoid reproducing large sections of Angell's exposition, it is necessary to rely upon the reader's extensive reference to his text for a thoro mastery of the subject; but an ordinarily careful reading of the follow-

---

[5] J. W. Angell, "The Components of the Circular Velocity of Money," *The Quarterly Journal of Economics*, vol. 51 (February 1937), pp. 224–73.

ing somewhat compressed argument, it is hoped, will permit the reader to survive to the subsequent analysis.

The concept of overlapping is approached at the outset more easily by informal description than by rigorous definition.[6]   Business practices, customs, and sometimes laws provide fairly fixed intervals for the payment of most obligations, e.g., daily or weekly wages, monthly rents, salaries, and "house bills," quarterly taxes, annual dues, dividends, et cetera.   For a given private person or business man, these combine in all manner of ways, and, with some margin for personal choice, practically determine for the individual the time-shape of his money holdings under the present category.   The length of time between *like* payments, i.e., from a given "stage" in production to the next succeeding one, of regularly recurring nature, Angell calls the payment interval.   The length of time a balance is held, on the other hand, is the "income-expenditure period."

Degree of overlapping refers to the actual magnitude of monetary requirement or circuit period (which is realized because of the existing relation of income-expenditure periods to payment intervals) in comparison with the maximum and minimum monetary requirements or circuit periods which would be realized by the least and the most "efficient" relations of income-expenditure periods to payment intervals.   This mouth-filling sentence may be explained further in terms of extremes.   When the *longest* payment interval (m), in a sequence of payments relating to the production of a given commodity through *all* the entrepreneur stages (average number $= L$), encompasses all the income-expenditure periods (average length $= i$), it "overlaps" the time-dimension of all working balances $(iL = m)$; the monetary requirement reaches its minimum, circuit velocity its maximum, and overlapping is perfect $(g = 1)$.   At the other extreme, the *average* payment interval (v) encompasses the average time-dimension (i) of working balances of only *one* entrepreneur stage $(v = i, vL = iL)$; the monetary requirement reaches its maximum, circuit velocity its minimum, and overlapping is zero $(g = 0)$.   The general expression for limiting and intermediate values of overlapping can be

---

[6] For the latter, see p. 112 below.

written $g = \dfrac{vL - iL}{vL - m}$.[7] If vL and iL are equal, the numerator of the fraction and hence g are zero; if iL and m are equal the fraction and g are 1.   To understand the real meaning of Angell's measure of over-lapping (g) between these limits, as well as the conceivable minimum and maximum monetary-requirement and circuit-velocity values, we shall need to consider cases.

Angell's first illustration of perfect overlapping[8] is reproduced diagrammatically in Case I:A (p. 96), which represents in a fashion described by the legend the following facts.   Once each day at eight o'clock consumer-laborers pay middlemen for goods consumed since the previous morning; once each day at sixteen o'clock, middlemen pay producers for purchases at wholesale since the previous afternoon; and once each day at twenty-four o'clock, producer-employers pay laborers the daily wage earned since the previous midnight.[9]   Because the time of day when each receives his proceeds comes before the time at which his obligations fall due, each person needs to carry the funds only a fraction of a day.   The total time through which funds are carried in all three stages does not exceed the payment interval.   The

---

[7] This formula is derived from Angell's Equation 3 on p. 239, *op. cit.*, by substituting iL for $1/d$ and solving for g.   In the form given above, the formula has the advantage of brevity and of exhibiting simultaneously both limits of g. For rewriting the formula, for correct values of g in Cases III, IV, and V, for the interpretation of $g = 0$, as well as for invaluable collaboration on the whole subject of overlapping, I am indebted to two members of my seminar, Mr. W. L. Hebbard and Mr. L. F. Mikulich.

[8] *Op. cit.*, p. 233.

[9] Throughout all illustrations on my interpretation any time absorbed in the process of making payment is included in the income-expenditure period of the person who continues to own the money until the moment of legal transfer of ownership.   Angell's assumption of instantaneous transfer not only lends his analysis an avoidable tinge of unreality, but it fails to give the proper subordina-tion in a general theory of velocity to such technical details as the speed of trains, the rapidity of bank-clearings, etc.   The Cambridge cash-balance device accomplishes this subordination, as I do, by looking to the transfer of owner-ship of funds, which is instantaneous.

Value added by manufacture is introduced by Angell later in Case V, but nothing in the nature of perfect overlapping precludes its inclusion here also.

(average) income-expenditure period (i) of ⅓ day, multiplied by the (average) number of stages in the production-consumption circle (i) or 3, equals the (maximum) payment interval (m), one day;[10] that is, $iL = m$ and overlapping is perfect or $g = 1$.

Case I:B, which I have added to Angell's, reveals that individual income-expenditure periods may differ in length without impairing $g = 1$, if their average (i) remains the same so that iL still equals m; and that the number of stages can increase compatibly with perfect overlapping, provided that i is correspondingly shortened to maintain $iL = m$. In Case II, to return to Angell's illustrations, a situation of $g = 1$ can be imagined aside from the simplifying assumptions of Case I, that the *amount* of payments at every transfer of money was everywhere the same, and that all payment *intervals* were the same, "maximum" having no particular significance. In Case II[11] each consumer-laborer pays ⅐ of his weekly wage daily to the middleman, who pays over these receipts without delay to the producer, and the latter pays the accumulated receipts of seven days to the consumer-laborer on week-ends. As Angell explains, the respective income-expenditure periods are now 3.5, 0, and 3.5 days in length;[12] and their average, ⅓ days, multiplied by L, which is 3, equals m or 7 days, the length of the genuine maximum payment interval in the series 1 day, 1 day, 7 days;[13] iL still equals m, and $g = 1$.

Case I:A and B and Case II show perfect overlapping, because with v, L, and m as they are, no change of i could reduce the amount of necessary money or increase circuit velocity. In other words, the number of entrepreneur stages being given, the relation of average and maximum payment intervals to the average income-expenditure

---

[10] In Case I:A, since all income-expenditure periods are alike and payment intervals are also, the terms "average" and "maximum" have no particular significance.

[11] *Ibid.,* pp. 235–36.

[12] After completing Section I, the reader may profitably return to a fuller exposition of Case II which is appended on p. 127 below.

[13] The series 1, 1, 7 will be more readily understood by recognizing that payment intervals must be taken in a purely temporal sense, without reference to the magnitude of cash-balances involved at the respective stages.

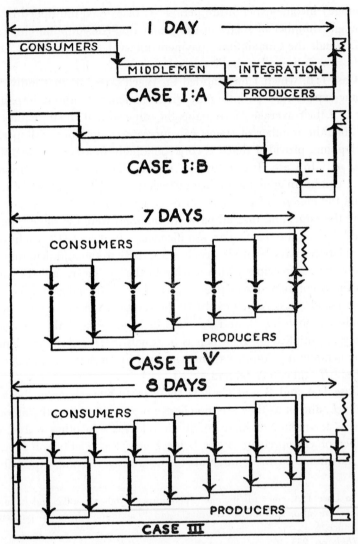

The lapse of time is represented horizontally to the right; an act of payment and its direction, by a heavy vertical arrow; the movement of money from consumers to most remote producers by progress from top to bottom of the chart; size of real balance-holdings, by the vertical, and duration of balance-holding, by the horizontal dimensions of enclosed areas.

[1] The interpretation of Case II requires special reference to p. 127.

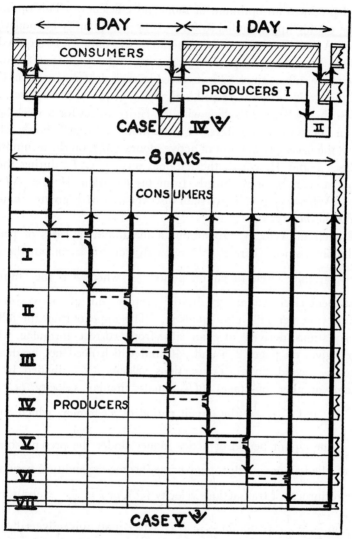

[2] In Case IV the two "strands" of money before integration are distinguished as plain and cross-hatched areas. The one "strand" or sequence of balances after integration is identified by double lines.

[3] In Case V payments are actually traced through for only one sequence of balances: to complete the picture of payments for the whole period, such a sequence would have to be represented as beginning on each day.

period produces an optimum of monetary efficiency. This optimum will be readily apprehended so far as concerns quantity of money: in Case I:A and B, if the daily wage were $7, only $7 is required in balances throughout the productive process, and not less than $7 would conceivably suffice, since $7 is involved in each debt payment; in Case II, if the weekly wage were $49, only $49 is required throughout, and not less than $49 could suffice with the entire wages for a week being paid in one sum each 7 days. Furthermore, as Angell shows, where $g = 1$, the necessary amount of active money (M), on the assumptions of Cases I and II, *equals* the national income (NI) during the m period, as can be seen directly from his equation $M \cdot C = NI$ (p. 225). Whenever $g < 1$, we shall discover that M is greater than NI during the m period.

But circuit velocity also attains a maximum in cases of perfect overlapping, since where $g = 1$ not only does $iL = m$ but the producer-consumer circle or circuit period ($\frac{1}{d}$, where d is the "number of payment circles completed by the average unit of [active] money per unit time period") also equals m. This appears from the following equations derived mechanically from correct formulae which Angell gives on pages 225 and 240 and which need not be demonstrated a second time. Transactions velocity (V) divided by the average number of stages (L) equals circular velocity (C), or $\frac{V}{L} = C$; and $\frac{L}{V} = \frac{1}{C}$, the circuit period of *all* money, which equals also $\frac{1}{d}$, the circuit period of *active* money under the present abstraction of idle balances. But the average income-expenditure period (i) is the reciprocal of transactions velocity (V), or $i = \frac{1}{V}$. Substituting i for $\frac{1}{V}$ in $\frac{L}{V} = \frac{1}{d}$, we obtain $\frac{1}{d} = iL$. This equation is universally valid whatever the overlapping; and since we have seen that perfect overlapping signifies $iL = m$, we can now write: when $g = 1$, then $iL = \frac{1}{d}$.

In Cases I:A and B the articulation of receipts and expenditures is so smooth that the circuit period of money could be reduced only by a reduction of the payment interval itself to something less than 1 day, and in Case II to something less than 1 week: the relationship of i to m is "perfect." Wherever $g < 1$, we shall discover that the value of $\frac{1}{d}$ or iL is greater than m.

Consider next situations in which overlapping, tho less than perfect, is not completely absent. Angell constructs Case III (p. 237) out of Case II by retaining the same assumptions except that middlemen, instead of being able to pay over their receipts immediately to the producers, find that their incoming funds from consumers appear at 5.01 p.m., whereas bills from producers are due at 5.00 p.m. The smooth articulation of previous examples is broken and middlemen must hold balances for nearly 1 day.[14] Since their new balances equal $\frac{1}{7}$ of the weekly wage bill, the monetary requirement is increased to $\frac{8}{7}$ the national income during the longest payment interval (1 week). By the equation $\frac{1}{d} = \frac{M}{NI}$,[15] the circuit period is extended from 7 to 8 days, a mode of expression appropriate to quantity-theory causation in contrast with the expression in terms of monetary requirement. As in Case II, the payment intervals are respectively 1, 1, and 7 days and their average $v = 3$; income-expenditure periods are 3.5, 1, and 3.5 days and their average $i = \frac{8}{3}$; the number of stages $L = 5$; and the maximum payment interval $m = 7$. Supplying these values in the general equation for overlapping on p. 98 above, we obtain $g = \frac{1}{2}$. This figure signifies that as income-expenditure periods and payment intervals actually are, the monetary requirement of $\frac{8}{7}$ the national income during the m interval is halfway between its conceivable minimum at $\frac{7}{7}$, as in Case II, and $\frac{9}{7}$, its conceivable maximum, the nature of which we have yet to portray under the analysis of $g = 0$. Angell himself calls Case III an instance of $g = 0$ and the circuit period 9

---

[14] This is a real case in which "a miss is as good as a mile": if obligations fall due before receipts come in within the payment interval, the lag of receipts may approach the length of the payment interval as a limit without affecting overlapping.

[15] This equation is simply the formula $M \cdot C = NI$ on p. 98 above, with d, circuit velocity of working balances, supplanting C, circuit velocity of all money.

days; but while these values are mutually consistent, an application of the formula or a schematic reproduction such as mine would have revealed why both are wrong.

Another illustration of overlapping less than perfect but not zero is given in Case IV, which assumes considerable significance in the discussion of differentiation in Section II.   It stands in the same relation to Case I:A as Case III does to Case II, and therefore requires no special explanation.   But again Angell carelessly mistakes the character of his illustration and threatens the reader with complete derailment.   Assuming as in Case I a payment interval of one day, he now supposes that

> the producer pays wages precisely at 5.02 p.m. each afternoon; that the consumers or their agents buy finished goods from the retailers precisely at 5.01 p.m. each afternoon; and that the retailers pay the producer precisely at 5.00 p.m. each afternoon.   Then a dollar paid out as wages today . . . cannot be paid out again as wages until the third day. . . . In consequence three times as large a stock of money is needed . . . as in the preceding case.[16]

As a matter of fact, however, with the sequence given by Angell, the last producer needs to hold a money balance only two minutes— 5.00 p.m. to 5.02 p.m., as shown by my diagram of Case IV; and altho the imperfection of overlapping forces the consumers and retailers to hold balances for practically an entire day each, the length of the circuit period $\frac{1}{d}$ is extended to two rather than three days, and the amount of money "necessary" is doubled, not trebled.   Values of $i, v, m,$ and L being ⅔, 1, 1, and 3, the formula for overlapping solves for $g = \frac{1}{2}$ and not 0 as Angell has it; here again his incorrect value of g is consistent with and explained by a mistaken value for the circuit period.   The real degree of overlapping at ½ indicates that income-expenditure periods and payment periods in Case IV are so related as to produce a circuit period of 2 days, i.e., halfway between the conceivable minimum of 1 day, as in Case I, and the conceivable maximum of 3 days.   Before proceeding to this "conceivable maximum" in Case V, I should remark that schemes of pay-

---

[16] *Ibid.,* pp. 234–235.

ments constructed in addition to Angell's cases show various fractional values for g between 1 and 0, not merely $\frac{1}{2}$; and they seem to prove the reliability of the formula.

Finally we come to the situation of "zero overlapping," which Angell supposes to be characteristic of Case V. Having mistaken Cases III and IV for instances of $g = 0$, he actually constructs Case V to take account of value added by manufacture, as revealed in my diagram by the smaller size of balances held by producers farther away from consumers. The only modification of the foregoing analysis required by this added variable is that the number of stages traversed by money in completing the circuit has to be weighted according to the size of balances in the various stages. In this particular case, as Angell correctly says, the weighted or average value of L is 5 and not the unweighted value of 8 got by simply counting stages, including consumers. Our interest attaches to other elements of the scheme. Over the eight-day period national income amounts to $56 or $7 per day. At the close of Day 1 consumers pay $7 to the retailers (Producers I in my diagram) for supplies during the day; at the close of Day 2, Producers I pay from their $7 receipts $1 to consumer-laborers as wages and $6 to the jobbers (Producers II) for purchases during the day. By the close of Day 8, the original $7 expenditures of consumers have returned as wages; and since seven consumer-producer sequences proceed simultaneously, national income amounts to $56 over 8 days. The requisite working balances are $35; and since $d = \dfrac{NI}{M}$, the circuit velocity is 1.6 in 8 days, and the circuit period $\left(\dfrac{1}{d}\right)$ is 5 days.

Taken at its face value, this illustration shows overlapping of zero: the income-expenditure period of one day coincides with the payment interval, and by the general formula $g = \dfrac{vL - iL}{vL - m}$, g becomes 0. Again, taken at its face value, it shows the logical antithesis of Cases I and II where $g = 1$. In place of a circuit period *equal* to the maximum payment interval, the former now extends over *all* the payment intervals added together ($= vL = 5$ days); and the monetary requirement is five times the balance of a single stage, which sufficed in Cases I and II. The absolute length of i and v being as they are, their relation is the most adverse to monetary "efficiency."

Unfortunately, however, Angell's Case V cannot be accepted as strictly legitimate. Unlike Cases III and IV, in which $g = 1$ because the out-payment moment for middlemen precedes in the payment interval the income moment, throwing the sequence of payments out of perfect articulation, Case V actually embodies this perfect articulation, and $g = 1$! Temporal "staggering," such as in Cases III and IV, instead of being carried to a maximum, suddenly gives place to absolute simultaneity. Nothing prevents the $7 expended by consumers at the close of the day from travelling through the entire gamut of seven producers and back into the consumers' hands again instantaneously by mere bookkeeping cancellations.[17] Perhaps Angell did not observe that temporal staggering carried far enough in recurring payment intervals, such as days, simply results again in coincidence! In other words, zero overlapping is a mathematical limit, and as such it cannot be attained in any real illustration, however closely approached. Experimentation with various payment schemes indicates that whereas a value of $g = 0$ requires that $1/d = vL,$ the lowest actual cases which can be constructed give $1/d = v(L-1)$. Had Angell supposed for only one of the seven stages in production that obligations fell due within the payment interval before receipts came in, the perfect coincidence would have disappeared without overlapping being far from zero. This situation would differ in graphic representation so little from Angell's actual example that Case V has been retained to illustrate zero overlapping. But it must be reaffirmed that $g = 0$ represents a limiting and not a realizable case.

That Professor Angell fell into certain errors does not deny the

---

[17] It might well be asked whether bookkeeping cancellation could not entirely dispense with money. The answer is, I believe, negative. Quantitative definiteness is given to the available book-entry credits by the knowledge of the consumers that they cannot "charge" on accounts more than $7 per day, and this defines the money at a positive level. I owe to Prof. Edgar Hoover this suggestion, which seems applicable also to money in a socialist commonwealth.

importance of his discoveries—the isolation of income-expenditure periods and payment intervals, and the quantitative expression of the effects of their relation. "Coincidence" takes on definite meaning; it becomes a true monetary function with measurable results. In concluding this section, let us restate the earlier description of overlapping in the form of a definition. With *given* differentiation (L) in production, and with *given* payment intervals (v, the average, and m, the maximum), overlapping expresses the relation of the amount of money actually employed to the conceivable minimum and maximum amounts of money which would be necessary for the same money work[18] with different income-expenditure periods (i). Or alternatively: with given differentiation in production, and with *given* payment intervals, overlapping expresses the relation of the actual circuit period $\left(\dfrac{1}{d}\right)$ to the conceivable minimum and maximum circuit periods which would be realized with *different* income-expenditure periods.[19] Mathematically it would be equally valid to put the income-expenditure period into the *ceteris paribus* phrase of the two preceding sentences, and let payment intervals come into the position of the variable. But since business practices serve to give the payment intervals a fixity to which the individual balance-holders must adapt themselves, the order in the definitions is justified.

The relation of size of working balances to overlapping is thus an inverse one, balances being at their minimum when $g = 1$ and at their maximum when $g = 0$; but the inverse variation takes place only between the lower and upper limits which are conceivable with *given m, v,* and L values, while the i value changes. Besides overlapping, the other important variables in the anatomy of working balances are the *absolute* lengths of the *m, v,* and i periods, and the number of stages (L). So far as concerns the absolute length of periods, nothing is added to the conventional analysis in the present

---

[18] I.e., to carry on continuous production of given volume without upward or downward revision of prices. This mode of statement is appropriate to contra-quantity-theory causation.

[19] I.e., to carry on continuous production of given volume by an appropriate revision of prices. This statement follows quantity-theory lines of causation.

inquiry. But the degree of overlapping plays so important a rôle in the monetary accompaniments of changed differentiation, that the matter requires separate consideration. An application of the theory to this subject also affords a convenient opportunity for extending the inquiry beyond circuit velocity to the behavior of transactions velocity.

II. Working Balances and Differentiation

Once the duration of payment intervals and their articulation are given for the individual producer or consumer, the time-shape of working balances appears to each holder as a matter of necessity. In Section I we saw that the monetary requirement or the circuit period depends functionally upon (1) the absolute length of income-expenditure periods and payment intervals and (2) upon their interrelation in overlapping, abstracting from (3) changes in the number of productive stages. This third objective determinant of working balances has long been recognized; but how—and indeed in some cases whether—it affects monetary requirements and circuit or transactions velocity have been mooted questions. Schumpeter and Marschak agreed that changes in differentiation (the average L) produce parallel movements in transactions velocity, so that monetary requirements or prices do not change; and Schumpeter added that circuit velocity remains constant.[20] I once brashly characterized this view as "A Spurious Case of Reversed Causation" from quantity-theory lines: if differentiation, for example, decreased, I argued, the "money-work" would be smaller, transactions velocity would be unaffected, and prices would rise.[21] This was also the position taken by Marget.[22] But the real solution of the difficulty, as Angell argues, lies in differing payment arrangements.[23] An application of this reasoning shows that perfect overlapping justifies the Schumpeter-Marschak view, while zero overlapping supports conclusions drawn

---

[20] For a summary of arguments by these writers, cf. my German Monetary Theory, 1905–1933 (reprinted, Cambridge, Mass., 1937), pp. 134–37; 148–53.

[21] Ibid., pp. 197–99.

[22] A. W. Marget, Journal of Political Economy, vol. 40, pp. 488–91.

[23] Angell, op. cit., pp. 257–58, n. 5.

by Marget and myself.   Professor Angell has wisely abandoned an earlier tendency to depreciate the Fisher equation and concept of velocity on the ground that transactions velocity depends upon differentiation.[24]   He now describes in what circumstances *both* circuit and transactions velocities are affected by differentiation.   His argument requires some emendation, but its fundamentals stand.

The diagram of Case I:A shows the merging of two stages under one entrepreneur where overlapping is perfect $(g = 1)$, on the assumption that increased integration does not affect wage and other payment intervals.   The area included within the dotted lines equals the area representing balances for the last stage, now eliminated; nothing happens to alter the money requirement.   Transactions fall from 3 to 2, and transactions velocity falls also from 3 to 2.   Circuit velocity is still 1 per day, or $\frac{1}{d} = 1$ day; and prices remain constant with M as originally given.   Other instances of $g = 1$, such as Case I:B, or Case II with integration or its opposite introduced at any point, give the same results; C is not affected by L, V varies directly and proportionately, and monetary requirements remain constant.

Case V, because it is sufficiently fanciful to incorporate the limiting situation of $g = 0$, never quite attainable actually, illustrates the workings of integration at this extreme.   Let us suppose that a consumers' coöperative venture amalgamates stages 1 and 2 so that the laborers *qua* consumers no longer have to hold separate balances, which amounted to $7 hitherto.   With overlapping initially zero,[25] "it is clear that as L falls, the circular velocity rises in proportion"[26] and V remains the same.   In this instance, the weighted L and the $\frac{1}{d}$ period fall from 5 to 4, circular velocity increases by ¼, V remains

[24] J. W. Angell, "Money, Prices, and Production: Some Fundamental Concepts," *The Quarterly Journal of Economics,* vol. 48, pp. 45–7.

[25] The amount of change in C, tho not the *direction,* will depend upon the stage selected for integration, wherever stages have, as in Case V, unequal weights.   Cf. p. 107 below.

[26] Angell, "Components," *The Quarterly Journal of Economics,* vol. 51, pp. 257–58, n. 5.

the same at 8 for the period of the illustration, while prices rise ¼ with the M as originally given. For V, C, and prices the result is in one sense the converse of integration with $g = 1$.

The algebraic necessity for the foregoing results will be readily seen. Where $g = 1$, $\frac{1}{d}$ or $iL = m$; and since m is unaffected by integration, the circuit period $\frac{1}{d}$ and circuit velocity C cannot be affected. But since $V = C \cdot L$, a fall in L with C constant causes a directly proportional fall in V. Where $g = 0$, $\frac{1}{d}$ or $iL = vL$; as long as v is maintained constant,[27] integration or a fall of L produces a proportional decline in $\frac{1}{d}$ or iL, the circuit period and a reciprocal rise in C. But since $V = C \cdot L$, the rise of C offsets the fall of L, and V remains constant.

So far Angell's analysis is valid and illuminating. Its inaccuracy pertains to integration in cases between $g = 1$ and $g = 0$. Note that *all* real payment and income-expenditure situations must fall short of $g = 0$, and nearly all fall short of $g = 1$, so that we are dealing here with practically all real situations. The shortcomings—easily forgiven because Angell's remarks are compressed into a single footnote—are partly errors of commission, partly of omission. "In the 'average' case," he says, "where g is ½, C and the national income both rise by half the relative amount of the fall in L, while V falls by half this relative amount." But Case IV, if we return to trace the consequence of integration where g is ½, shows quite different results. I have supposed stage 3 to be merged with stage 2, tho the choice here is immaterial. The noteworthy facts appear that, whereas g was ½, it is now 1, as indeed in all cases of two stages it must necessarily be; and furthermore that V *rises* from 3 to 4, while C doubles. With the same M, prices are doubled; or the "necessary money" is halved. Angell gives the correct direction of change for C and for

---

[27] Which is actually impossible but necessary to the maintenance of the imaginable, but unreal, limiting value of $g = 0$.

prices, the wrong direction for the change of V, and the wrong extent of change for all three variables. The cause of these errors is not far to seek—a neglected change in the factor g. For any case with a given value of $g < 1$ but > 0, integration necessarily produces a somewhat higher degree of overlapping, as follows algebraically from the formula $g = \dfrac{vL - iL}{vL - m}$ or from Angell's original version of the same equation.[28] To predict the quantitative change of V, C, and prices or necessary money in a concrete case of integration, we need to know not only the initial overlapping but also the details of the payment and income scheme, so that the effect upon g can be determined.

In two respects, however, even this additional requirement fails to cover all complications. Whether changes in differentiation result in large or small changes in V, C, and prices depends upon monetary requirements in the affected stages relatively to others. This the reader may establish for himself by experimenting for example with Case V. Furthermore, it would remain to be seen whether a change in differentiation might not in practice affect the payment intervals themselves. An assumption of constancy in the i, v, and m items elsewhere would then have to be supplanted by empiric data on the new values.

If the disparate behavior of circuit and transactions velocities in these cases seems peculiar, it may be that one is thinking only of the *subjective* determinants of velocity, since these determinants do necessarily cause circuit and transactions velocities to vary in the same direction in a fixed relation determined by the number of stages. To these subjective moments we shall come in Section V. The validity of the quantity-theory postulates as to causation proceeding from velocity will be seen to depend upon whether the division of money

---

[28] That any change of L, with $g < 1$ but > 0, necessarily changes g does not imply the converse, that a change of g necessarily means a change of L. Changes of g can arise with L constant through variations in i, v or m, as shown earlier.

stock into working balances and hoards follows *subjective* determinants. But because the real-balance approach to velocity, more than the circuit or transactions concepts, is integrated with subjective value theory, it supplies the best apparatus for determining lines of causation. Section III describes the relations between active real balances and circuit and transactions velocities of money in active circulation; Section IV will be concerned with hoards.

III. Real Balances in the Active Circulation

By long established tradition the Cambridge or real-balance analysis runs in terms of income, whereas by a custom nearly as venerable the Fisher analysis refers to transactions. Students approaching these two formulations for the first time are prone to conclude that they deal with distinct phenomena, and no less eminent an economist than Keynes lends his support to the idea that the Cambridge equations naturally "lead up to" one kind of price index, the Fisher equations to another.[29] But there is no inherent reason why the "money-at-rest" viewpoint should be associated with income while the "money-in-motion" view should necessarily be conjoined with transactions; and Robertson has, amongst others, performed a substantial service in demonstrating the substitutability of one set of symbols for the other in dealing with either income or transactions.[30]

The traditional reference in the Cambridge analysis of the real-balance factor k to *real incomes* is beset with three serious causes of misunderstanding, which sometimes impede the attempt to translate this mode of statement into the Fisher terminology. For one thing, a state of fog prevails as to whether k refers to something exclusively pertaining to the consumers' monetary economy, or whether it includes the monetary facts in producers' and consumers' spheres alike. Now there can be no doubt that the latter *is* the true character of the monetary member of the equation, but with equal force the formulation of the theory *seems* to involve the former alternative. Formulae embodying k are widely used as general equations of ex-

[29] J. M. Keynes, *A Treatise on Money*, (New York, 1930), vol. I, p. 238.
[30] D. H. Robertson, *Money*, (New York, 1929), p. 195.

change and not as expressions of the state of affairs in the consumers' sphere alone. Robertson's four formulae setting forth Fisher and Cambridge methods of dealing with incomes and with transactions include the *same* money stock held by the *same* people, simply because the former includes all[31] the money, the latter all the people. Keynes' dissatisfaction with his earlier quantity equation in the *Tract on Monetary Reform* was precisely because its reference to consumption units (k as a ratio to income) "implied that Cash-deposits are used for nothing except expenditure on current consumption, whereas in fact they are held . . . for a vast multiplicity of business and personal purposes."[32]

Despite this Keynes continues to associate the Cambridge type equations with income; and despite Robertson's substitution of one set of symbols for the other, he continues to refer to "income price levels" and "transactions price levels," ignoring the common ground of both equations on the same money, the same balance holders. This sort of misleading phraseology must simply be disregarded: the Cambridge k, altho expressed as a ratio of value held in the form of money to real income, includes all money balances,[33] not merely the balances of people as income receivers. A "pure" consumers' equation would exclude balances held by producers; and it might be very significant when complemented with a "pure" producers' equation to reveal disparate money, velocity, price or turnover factors in the two spheres. But the unspecialized Cambridge equation can no more pretend to this rôle than the general Fisher equation. Both, indeed, are probably superior to such a special consumers' equation, if all factors operative on the cost of living are to be displayed. Circuit velocity, let it be remembered, is the same arithmetic magnitude to producers as to consumers, and it incorporates the balance-holdings of one as much as the other. The same holds true of its counterpart,

---

[31] "All" may be interpreted to include hoards, altho in this Section we are concerned with working balances primarily.

[32] Keynes, *op. cit.*, vol. I, p. 223; cf. also p. 232.

[33] Amongst others, Keynes has set up special equations for consumers alone, *op. cit.*, vol. I, ch. 6 and 10.

the Cambridge k, which should no longer carry the misnomer of "income velocity."[34]

In the second place, it is not always recognized that the traditional k, as a ratio of real balances to income, is the reciprocal of circuit velocity, tho English writers not infrequently advert to the fact.[35] Nothing, of course, prevents the definition of k as a ratio to transactions instead of income, and Cassel has elected this alternative.   In this event k becomes the reciprocal of transactions velocity.[36] The algebraic relations involved may be set forth briefly, but the theoretical consequences of choosing one ratio rather than the other will require careful explanation.

From an earlier connection we recall that $M \cdot C = NI$.   According to a typical Cambridge equation $P = \dfrac{M}{kR}$, where P is the price index, M the money-stock, k the ratio of reserves in the form of money to real income, and R, real income.   Solving both equations for M we obtain $M = \dfrac{NI}{C} = PkR$; but PR and NI, being alternative expressions for the same thing, can be cancelled out, leaving $\dfrac{1}{C} = k$.

---

[34] The circuit period of active money or working balances $(1/d)$ is spoken of even by Angell sometimes as the interval over which the money stock disbursed by consumers returns to their hands.   This proves to be misleading in two respects.   First it suggests that all pieces of money started on their way through production by consumers return to consumers—or more accurately are again disbursed by consumers—by the end of the $1/d$ period.   Reference particularly to Case III or a moment's realistic consideration shows that individual blocks of money can be "sidetracked" on a course returning to consumers long after the termination of the $1/d$ period or perhaps never.   Circuit velocity like transactions velocity is a mere arithmetic average.   Secondly, the concept of the circuit just rejected as too literal or physical suggests some peculiar relevance of circuit velocity (or of k_r) to consumers; the apprehension of the mere average character of these velocity expressions should withdraw the last support from designating them "income" velocities.

[35] Cf. R. G. Hawtrey, *Currency and Credit*, (London, 1930), p. 59; A. C. Pigou, *Industrial Fluctuations*, (London, 1927), p. 152.

[36] Gustav Cassel, *The Theory of Social Economy*, (New York, 1924), pp. 421–33.   In Robertson's equations (loc. cit.), the factor K is the ratio of money held to transactions.

Let us designate this k, which is the ratio of balances to real income, as k_r—the conventional Cambridge velocity factor, and the reciprocal of circular velocity. From an earlier juncture we recall also that $V = C \cdot L$. Substituting $\frac{V}{L}$ for C in the equation $\frac{1}{C} = k_r$, we obtain $\frac{L}{V} = k_r$, or $\frac{1}{V} = \frac{k_r}{L}$. But $\frac{k_r}{L}$ indicates the relation of whatever reserves have been present to a new magnitude, total transactions. Let us designate this new ratio of balances to transactions as k_t. To put the contrasting ratios in juxtaposition: $k_r = \frac{L}{V}$ but $k_t = \frac{1}{V}$.[37]

The ratio to income k_r could equal $\frac{1}{V}$ when, but *only* when, the ratio of real income to transactions remains constant. Pigou rather obscurely implies this in a passage converting his equation of exchange to Fisher's on the assumption of a fixed ratio of "resources" to transactions.[38] Such an assumption is subject to so many and such far-reaching exceptions that they seem to become the rule. Reference to Case I:A, for example, reveals a situation in which integration, by reducing the stages from 3 to 2, reduces Fisher velocity also from 3 to 2. Real balances are not affected in their absolute size; and since income is also unaffected, k as a ratio to income does not change, whence $k_r \neq \frac{1}{V}$. As a ratio to transactions, however, k rises from $\frac{1}{3}$ to $\frac{1}{2}$, since the absolute size of balances cannot be reduced, altho transactions fall by $\frac{1}{3}$. Hence k increases to $\frac{3}{2}$ its former size and $k_t = \frac{1}{V}$. In addition to changed differentiation, changed overlapping shows the same contrast. In Case I, overlapping being perfect both before and after integration, we saw the effect of differentiation alone. But in Case IV we can observe the result of changing

---

[37] At first glance it might seem that the ratio of reserves against income should be *multiplied* instead of *divided* by L, the number of stages in production, to secure the ratio of reserves to transactions. But let $\$10 = NI$, $L = 5$, $k_r = 1$, and $M = \$10$; the Fisher T is then $\$50$, and k_t is $\frac{1}{5}$ or k_r/L. In the current exposition, as before, I abstract from financial transfers.

[38] A. C. Pigou, *Essays in Applied Economics*, (London, 1923), pp. 176–77.

overlapping, from $g = \frac{1}{2}$ with three stages to $g = 1$ with the two stages left after integration.   The transactions V rises from 3 to 4; k as a ratio to income declines from 2 to 1; the absolute size of real balances is halved, but income in real terms remains constant; whence $k_r \neq \frac{1}{V}$. But real transactions are reduced by $\frac{1}{3}$, while absolute balances are halved by the increased overlapping.   As a ratio to transactions, k falls to $\frac{3}{4}$ its former magnitude; whence $k_t = \frac{1}{V}$.[39]   A third circumstance inducing a changed ratio of income to transactions is the appearance of new money-holders, either from an increase of population or a proliferation of firms.   No presumption exists that the additional separate personal or business turnovers which they call into being, or the provisions which they make for contingencies, will increase $k_t T$ by the same percentage as $k_r R$, the obvious reason being that such persons and firms may have no incomes at all or incomes far above average.[40]   But finally the income-transaction ratio varies—the following relation signifies that it always varies markedly—with every change in the national income not accompanied by a proportional change in total turnover of goods and services.   The bearing of this variable upon the classical dispute concerning Keynes' Losses and Hoarding is the subject of later comment.

All of the foregoing inequalities between k and $\frac{1}{V}$ could be eliminated by defining k as k_t, or the ratio to transactions, and this would indeed be desirable for ease in transition from the Cambridge to the Fisher equations.   But since the redefinition would produce inequali-

---

[39] In describing Cases I and IV the assumption is made, as earlier, that the occurrence of integration does not cause any change in the stock of money.

[40] My attention was drawn to this point by E. F. M. Durbin's *The Problem of Credit Policy* (New York, 1935), ch. V, and Appendix, Note 3.   But I ignore Durbin's further idea that the income-transactions ratio varies because the number of industrial stages is associated with the "length of the structure of production."   I reject most of the implications of the latter term, and particularly that any necessary relation prevails between industrial stages and the intensiveness of capitalistic production.   Such changes as actually occur have already been treated under the head of differentiation.

ties in the very same cases for k and $\frac{1}{C}$, the gain would come at a cost to convenience in translating the Cambridge real balance approach into circuit velocity equations such as Angell's. Which of the two alternatives recommends itself will depend largely upon the form of statistical information regarding velocity, but this raises questions beyond the scope of the present inquiry. The purpose here has been to point out an imperative necessity for determining the precise reference of the Cambridge k before proceeding to reason concerning any variable, supposed to affect velocity, in terms of real balances.

A third pitfall in the comprehension of real-balance equations lies in the traditional inclusion under real income of *all* real income whether transferred against money or not, or if the equations refer to real transactions, the inclusion of all transactions, whether monetary or barter. Were the dividing line between barter and money spheres itself in any significant degree a function of the quantity of money or the size of real balances, the inclusion of income or transactions not transferred against money would be requisite. Since this is not the case, the Cambridge practice seems only to complicate the conversion of one set of terms to the other, and to offer, besides, very little hope of statistical fruitfulness. As matters stand, any change in the relative sphere of barter and in differentiation gives an added occasion for the inequality $k_r \neq \frac{1}{V}$, and a case in which even $k_r \neq \frac{1}{C}$ and $k_t \neq \frac{1}{V}$, according to the American practice of limiting both circuit and transactions velocity to monetary income and transactions only. The definition of k_r as a ratio to all income, as an eminent Cambridge economist contends,[41] does indeed make of income something depending solely upon productivity, while the k factor is a pure payments phenomenon. The question, then, is simply whether this gain in theoretical elegance does or does not outweigh the chances of misunderstanding arising out of the inequalities noted and the inadequacy of statistical information about payments in kind.

---

[41] In personal correspondence which I do not feel at liberty to quote.

IV. IDLE BALANCES OR HOARDS

The study of velocity of working balances presented in Sections I–III has revealed certain mechanical connections between the "rapidity of circulation of goods" and money. But nothing in the analysis of these objective connections—the absolute length of income-expenditure periods and payment intervals, their interrelation in "overlapping," and the number of stages—reveals anything as to causation. I have sought to be meticulous by presenting the results of these velocity determinants alternatively in terms of monetary requirements, prices being given, and in terms of prices, money in active circulation being given. It has repeatedly been asserted, tho not yet proven, that direction of causation between money and prices depends upon whether the *division* of money stock between working and idle balances rests upon a value calculus of the money-owner or whether this division is already made for him by objective facts. One particular concept of hoards—paradoxical as it may seem—engulfs both working and idle balances; it therefore obliterates the facts which are crucial for causation. The definition of hoards, far from being a purely terminological question, is vital not only for the whole cause-and-effect nexus in monetary theory but for the general theory of economic equilibrium.

As a result of the publication of the Treatise on Money, the question of what constitutes hoarding was the subject of lively and involved debate between Mr. Keynes and Mr. Robertson in the Economic Journal;[42] and the issue is still being discussed as an open one. The public, it was assumed, suddenly increases its saving quota; by the reduction of demand for consumers' goods, this price-level (P') declines; and consumption entrepreneurs, on the assumption that they resolve to maintain operations at the former level, sell securities to the public for cash in order to meet expenditures. About these facts there was no dispute, but Mr. Robertson maintained that the fall of P' came as a consequence of something to be called hoarding, whereas Mr. Keynes held that this something was not hoarding but Losses.

Mr. Durbin, who has recently reviewed this discussion, supports a concept of hoarding which vindicates Keynes in this particular case

---

[42] In the numbers of September 1921 and September 1933.

and which seems to me to be generally the defensible definition.   But he goes beyond this to argue that Robertson was suddenly introducing a new definition of hoarding into the security-sales case, and that he did not even remain faithful to this definition in the course of his reasoning.   Neither of these contentions holds.   In Banking Policy and the Price Level (1926) hoards are already synonymous with real balances *in general,* and hoarding appears with *every* increase of their ratio to income, or k_r.   On the basis of this definition, Robertson cannot be taxed with inconsistency in finding that security sales increase hoarding: balances are maintained in this wise at their former absolute money magnitude, income of consumption entrepreneurs from sales of goods has fallen off, and the ratio k_r has increased.[43] Durbin, on the other hand, counts the proceeds of the security sales not only in cash reserves, but also, in contrast to Robertson, under "income" as well.[44]   Just what income should imply is not elaborated by real-balance expositions, altho the term certainly suggests net and not gross income, and this interpretation supports Robertson.

But as a ratio to *gross* income or *transactions,* real balances have *not* increased as a consequence of security sales and there is no hoarding.   I do not believe this to be the basis of Keynes' position, nor even of Durbin's main argument supporting him.   But partly because the contrast between k_r and k_t has figured prominently in these pages, and partly because Durbin actually uses gross income (transactions) in his numerical illustrations, it pays to examine this second ratio. Furthermore, in a neglected footnote,[45] Robertson himself says explicitly that "the proportion of the annual volume of transactions which people wish to hold enough money to conduct is unchanged." Securities have merely supplanted the consumers' goods which could not be sold as a consequence of the saving campaign: total transactions, real balances, and k_t, their ratio, have not been altered; there is no hoarding.

From this outcome one might be tempted to dismiss the dispute

[43] D. H. Robertson, "Saving and Hoarding," *Economic Journal,* vol. 43, p. 404; the reduced income is designated as $M_{b'} - X$.

[44] E. F. M. Durbin, *The Problem of Credit Policy* (New York, 1935), p. 253

[45] D. H. Robertson, Mr. Keynes' Theory of Money, *Economic Journal,* vol. 41, p. 403, n. 1.   His supporting argument differs from mine.

over hoarding as "purely terminological," each party being right upon his own definition.   Such a solution implies acquiescence, however, with the general basis of both definitions of hoarding—an increase of the *ratio* of real balances *in general* (without division into categories) to either income or transactions.   That the mere general-ratio definitions do not apprehend the nature of hoarding is the chief point of this section; but a preliminary step is an examination of the contrasts between the two ratios themselves.   Section III laid down the generalization that the two ratios give the same results only when the ratio of income to transactions remains a constant; and the examples of forces distorting this ratio revealed such far-reaching economic variables that the two could never in fact be expected to give results even approximately parallel.   An instance or two may be reviewed for their bearing upon hoarding.   In Case I: A $(g = 1)$, integration did not affect the ratio of balances to income, and so there would be no hoarding or dishoarding on this basis, a reasonable outcome in view of the fact that money-holders have no alternative but to retain the same absolute real balances.   But the ratio of transactions has risen to $3/2$, i.e., an increase of hoarding on the transactions-ratio definition, wholly anomalous in view of the same facts about money-holders.   For the opposite situation $(g = 0)$ portrayed in Case V, converse but equally contradictory results appear.   Integration affects neither transactions velocity nor k_t, and hence there can be neither hoarding nor dishoarding on the transactions-ratio definition; but circuit velocity rises and k_r falls, which signifies dishoarding on the income-ratio definition.   Similar divergences would follow changes of the k_r to k_t relation from other variables described in Section III, amongst them changes of earnings with given turnovers, the general case which includes the Keynes-Robertson situation.

Now the anomalous results of the ratio concepts of hoarding have their origin in the rather obvious fact that hoards are not isolated by putting *all* real balances into one category.   The original connotation of hoards was undoubtedly money withdrawn from circulation, but some sort of false sophistication in monetary theory allowed this common-sense meaning to disappear.   Perhaps the difficulty of isolating hoarded money statistically caused ideas to bow to "facts," or rather to the lack of them. Perhaps the real-balance analysis itself was partly responsible: since *all* money is "at rest," all money is "hoarded"; we cannot separate hoarded from circulating money tho we can express relative intensities of hoarding in the factor k. Neither of these methods of rationalization justifies throwing out the child with the bath. The necessary dichotomy was made conceptually clear in Neisser's methodical inquiry in 1928:[46] working balances are held for the purpose of meeting the regularly recurring inequalities between income and expenditures, idle reserves are held for irregularities in payments and for other purposes. With Angell's inquiry into the "Components" this division assumes mathematical precision: money held longer than one income-expenditure period belongs to the reserves of the particular money owner, the rest *ex definitione* belongs to working balances.[47]

A retrospect to the discussion between Keynes and Robertson will show that the security sales by consumption entrepreneurs resulted in no accretion to idle balances but only a necessary supporting of working balances if operations were to continue as before. Admitting that the ratio of balances to income was increased on the basis of Robertson's interpretation of income, there was no diversion of funds from active circulation to idle balances. The money employed to finance Losses was in active use, not hoarded. When the entrepreneurs in the consumers' goods industries resolved to continue production despite Losses, they launched upon a continued sale of securities merely to meet the day-to-day payments about which there was no choosing. Their "propensity to hoard," as Keynes argued, remained precisely what it was before.[48]

Hoarding upon the definition adopted here affects none of the factors governing the relation of circuit to transactions velocity and the relation of their reciprocals k_r and k_t. If the total money stock

---

[46] Hans Neisser, *Der Tauschwert des Geldes* (Jena, 1928), pp. 18–20; cf. also "Der Kreislauf des Geldes," *Weltwirtschaftliches Archiv*, vol. 33, pp. 365–408.

[47] Angell, *op. cit.*, p. 254.

[48] J. M. Keynes, "Mr. Keynes' Theory of Money: A Rejoinder," *Economic Journal*, vol. 41, pp. 413–19.

in the hands of the public is taken as the basis of computation, an increase of hoarding reduces transactions velocity by the rise of k_t, and it reduces circuit velocity by the rise of k_r, movements of the first pair being L times as great as movements of the second pair. Not every reduction of transactions and circuit velocity nor every rise of k_r and k_t results from hoarding, of course, but according to the definition only such reductions of velocity and increases of real balances as proceed from a transfer of funds from active circulation to reserves. The forces determining this division of the money stock will be investigated in the following section.

V. THE DIVISION OF THE MONEY STOCK AND CAUSATION

Both the "velocity" of money and the amount of "transactions" of goods are hybrids. For, on the one hand, velocity is a weighted average of velocity of working balances and zero velocity of idle balances; and on the other hand, transactions is the product of multiplying quantity of goods by number of turnovers or stages. This has long been recognized. But it is not always recognized (1) that mechanical connections obtaining between T and V (in the Fisher equation) are limited to relations between *turnover* and velocity (or size) of *working balances,* with the absolute exclusion of the other element in T and in V; and (2) that with given mechanical relations of T and V under (1), variations in velocity occur *only* as a result of a changed division of *quantity* of money between working and idle balances.

1. No less a one than von Wieser believed that "Rapidity of circulation of money is not an independently operative cause of changes in the value of money. . . . Money always takes its velocity from goods."[49] This heresy, propagated in recent times by R. H. Lounsbury,[50] involves the notion of "price-neutrality" regarding velocity.

---

[49] Friedrich von Wieser, *Social Economics* (New York, 1927), p. 145.

[50] R. H. Lounsbury, "Velocity Concepts and Prices," *The Quarterly Journal of Economics,* vol. 46, pp. 34–67. After the sufficient answer by C. O. Hardy, in "Velocity Concepts: A Criticism," the author gave a more lucid statement of his *non sequitur* in "Velocity Concepts: A Reply," *The Quarterly Journal of Economics,* vol. 46, p. 570.

Such a conclusion halts at three leagues from the truth. Turnover or number of stages being given, the quantity of goods traded still remains under transactions as a variable causing changes either in prices or in monetary requirements for working balances; and, the basic determinants for working balances being given, the division of money into working and idle balances still remains as a variable causing changes either in prices or in money supply for idle balances. In the third place, even if we restrict our view to the mechanical relation between turnover and velocity or monetary requirements in working balances, changes in turnover are attended by completely offsetting changes in one or other of the latter only when, as explained in Section II, overlapping is perfect. Reduced differentiation necessarily causes a rise in prices or a reduction in monetary requirements when overlapping is less than perfect.

2. Once the scheme of payments in the sense of Sections I–III has been established, money in working balances moves through the productive process with a given *physical rapidity* over which the individual has virtually no control.[51] This rate of physical transfer is uniquely established by the absolute length of income-expenditure periods and payment intervals, by degree of overlapping, and by the number of productive stages. Concerning this rate of physical transfer there need be no mystery: it is the rate at which dollars, *if they circulate at all,* must move; for working balances, rate of physical transfer and velocity in this category coincide. For idle balances, rate of physical transfer and velocity again coincide, but *ex definitione* at zero. In a literal sense, given the determinants of working balances, nothing can happen to the physical transfer rates. If money does not rest in idle balances, it circulates at a predetermined

---

[51] The individual usually has very little control over the time when his receipts come in, this being determined by business usage, which also determines the time of expenditure for the bulk of his outlays. For the latter, however, he can elect to pay at shorter intervals or irregularly within the conventional maximum "charging" period. *If* this choice should enable and induce the receiver of the sums in turn to pay obligations sooner, velocity in general may rise. Conventional "due dates" throughout the system serve at every step, however, to obliterate the effects of individual choices earlier in the productive series.

rate; and whether velocity rises or falls depends upon whether less or more finds its way into idle balances.   Whatever controls this division controls velocity, since it controls the weights assigned to zero rate of idle balances and the "predetermined" rate analyzed in Sections I–III.[52]

According to the quantity theory of money this division is accomplished by a subjective calculus on the part of the money holder. The flow of utilities from holding real wealth in money form against contingencies—it might be against a tempting opportunity to invest —is weighed against the flow of consumption utilities on the one hand and the utility yield of investment on the other.   For this three-fold calculus, the x-axis of utility curves might be taken as dollars, so far as concerns the atomistic individual's own influence on velocity: purchasing power of money would be a parametric function; but since even the individual cannot assume the total supply of money as given by the banking system to be constant, he must think in real terms—to use Marshall's illustration, in wheat.   Marginal utilities of real values devoted to consumption, investment, and reserves are equalized by letting money go into any one of the three where the margin is temporarily too high, by taking it away from a use where the margin is too low.   Money in idle reserves is brought to the desired margin by letting some go into, or by withdrawing some from, working balances sufficiently to raise or lower prices sufficiently to make the money in idle reserves give the requisite real-value provision against contingencies.   Mr. Harrod errs when he states that the quantity theory provides no determinate division of the money stock between working and idle balances.

---

[52] Representations of this fact by symbols differ.   If k, C, and V are taken in connection with *all* the money in the hands of the public, a shift from idle to working balances will show up in changes in the magnitudes of k, C, and V themselves and not in M; but if k, C, and V are taken in connection with working balances only, a shift from idle to working balances increases M, leaving k, C, and V constant.   Both theoretically and practically the former practice seems superior: M can then be regarded as controlled by the monetary authority, while the velocity magnitudes rest partly on payment customs and partly on subjective elements; further, statistical information is more readily and directly available for velocity variations than for division of money into two categories.

Before we proceed to inquire how the real-balance analysis mis-leads Mr. Harrod, as indeed it misleads Professor Angell, we should point out for later reference two correlates of the foregoing "pure" quantity-theory causation.   (1) An increment to M would, *ceteris paribus*, be divided between idle and working balances proportionally to their existing or equilibrium magnitudes; i.e., the Multiplier, as Angell, Knight and Robertson have said, would be circular velocity.[53] (2) The utility of idle balances or "liquidity preference" would de-termine price levels, not interest rates.

This exposition of the real balances version of the quantity theory is purposely "crude and common";[54] for, with the emphasis put upon the *division* of money stock, the quantity theory of real balances undoubtedly makes working balances the dependent and idle balances the independent variable.   This practice, however, is neither necessary nor conventional.   Conventional expositions have not rested upon a dichotomy into working and idle balances; the infrequency and ir-regularity of payments, on the one hand, and contingencies on the other have appeared merely as two *motives* for holding money. Now if motives are thus added together to give *all* the reasons for holding *all* the money, it is an easy step to conclude either that the real-balance theory presents an empty tautology, or that it leaves the division between working and idle balances indeterminate.   Profes-sor Angell writes, "The amount of money people elect to keep by them is the average quantity they actually hold, taking one day with another.   But this is merely tautological: the money stock is what it is."[55]   Mr. Harrod writes, "Now if the quantity required for ac-tive trade were perfectly indeterminate, as it must be by the Quantity

---

[53] J. W. Angell, "The General Dynamics of Money," *Journal of Political Economy*, vol. 45 (June 1937), pp. 337–38; 341–42; F. H. Knight, "Unem-ployment: and Mr. Keynes's Revolution in Economic Theory," *Canadian Jour-nal of Economics and Political Science* (February 1937), p. 110; D. H. Robert-son, "Saving and Hoarding," *Economic Journal*, vol. 43 (September 1933), pp. 409–10.

[54] To employ the flattering phrase by which Mr. Harrod describes his own passages designed for his inept, uninitiated readers.

[55] Angell, "Components," *The Quarterly Journal of Economics*, vol. 51, p. 263.

Theory—for according to that the price level depends on the quantity of money available for active trade, and therefore it is unknown what quantity of money any given amount of active trade will absorb—the residue would be indeterminate also."[56] Angell's error lies in his failing to distinguish money stock and total real balances; the monetary authority determines the former, balance holders the latter, and the price level equates the two magnitudes. Harrod's error lies in his ignoring the fact that the equating comes through a distribution of money between idle and working balances, such that the former by the movement of prices assumes the determinate size given by the real value calculus.

Let us turn next to the chain of causation diametrically opposed to the quantity theory which Harrod represents as Keynes' position. I repeat *verbatim* a summary presented on the first page of this paper: Marginal efficiency of capital in comparison with interest determines investment, which in turn through the multiplier controls the level of employment or output. Prices are established without direct reference to the effective quantity of money (MV) by the cost functions of individual goods. Volume of output multiplied by prices gives the money requirement for the active circulation; and the residual money becomes the supply available for reserves, with which the liquidity function equates to set the rate of interest.

If one were to assert that "the supply of paper money or credit determines the output of goods" one would out-Harrod Harrod to about the same degree as Harrod overstates Keynes' position. This assertion neglects Harrod's limitation of his causal series *to* less than full employment, just as Harrod's version of Keynes neglects the limits put upon his causation by Keynes *within* a condition of less than full employment. Harrod may have been too much impressed by the statements in the General Theory that the quantity theory is valid without qualification for full employment,[57] and by the absence of any explicit statement that the quantity theory has "more or less" validity even short of full employment. This omission and Keynes'

[56] Harrod, "Keynes," *Econometrica*, vol. 5, p. 75.

[57] J. M. Keynes, *The General Theory of Employment, Interest, and Money* (London, 1936), pp. 191, 202, 208–9.

conclusions regarding policy support the view that in his own judgment the degree of validity is "less"; but so far as concerns the formal
structure of the "General Theory," the validity might be "more."

It would be curious indeed if the quantity theory should prove
to be wholly true for full employment and wholly false through the
range of actual employment varying continuously toward that limit.
In this event we should have Mr. Harrod's version of Keynes' theory
or Karl Marx's doctrine of the "socially-necessary circulation value,"
with its automatic hoarding and dishoarding[58] literally true until involuntary unemployment disappeared, and thereafter a rigid quantity
theory with unlimited validity.   Or, as Keynes says:

if there is perfectly elastic supply so long as there is unemployment, and
perfectly inelastic supply so soon as full employment is reached, and if effective
demand changes in the same proportion as the quantity of money, the Quantity
Theory of Money can be enunciated as follows: "So long as there is unemployment, *employment* will change in the same proportion as the quantity of
money; and when there is full employment, prices will change in the same proportion as the quantity of money."[59]

Figure I (p. 124) presents this "quantity theory" in the curve XYZ,
in which prices remain constant through all degrees of employment
to full, and employment and the effective quantity of money (money
times circular velocity) vary together; thereafter prices increase with
quantity of money at a proportion set by circular velocity.

Keynes, however, presents this "quantity theory" merely as a
limiting case.   Real situations involve five "complications," one of
them explaining the appearance of circular velocity in the figures,
and the other four producing a distortion of the price-level function
XYZ to $XY'Z'$ in terms of my Figure I.   (1) With *given* liquidity-
preference, marginal efficiency of capital, and investment-multiplier,
quantity of money determines employment through the interest rate.
Actually, says Keynes, variations in money affect all three of these
basic determinants.   For example, the multiplier might be reduced
if the new income went to wealthier classes, the liquidity-preference

---

[58] Karl Marx, *Capital,* tr. by Moore and Aveling (London, 1887), vol. I, pp.
97-9.

[59] Keynes, *op. cit.,* pp. 295-96; italics his.

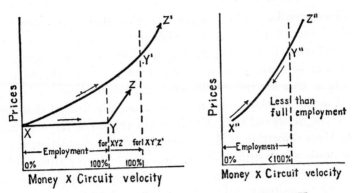

FIGURE I   FIGURE II

1. The slope of YZ and $Y'Z'$ indicates direct and proportional variation of prices with money times circular velocity. Full employment for $XY'Z'$ lies farther to the right than for XYZ because part of the money is "wasted" in raising prices; but the absolute magnitude of employment and output is identical for XYZ and $XY'Z'$.

2. The slope of $X''Y''$ indicates that at first the increase of money goes preponderately into extending employment, but later into raising prices. Whether the downward price-production function in depression exactly corresponds with $X''Y''$ read upward is immaterial for present purposes. $Y''Z''$ indicates pure inflation, as in YZ and $Y'Z'$.

might increase and absorb new money into hoards, or marginal efficiency might rise through favorable expectations proceeding from the monetary policy. (2) If labor is remunerated on the basis of effort and not its efficiency, increasing effective demand encounters diminishing returns. (3) Altho some factors are partly unemployed, others may already have reached an absolute inelastic supply phase. (4) Organized labor may secure upward revisions of the wage unit. (5) User-cost may advance sharply because of expectations of necessity for making earlier replacements.[60]

Now it does not change facts to call them by different names, and yet terms influence ideas. All of the facts modifying an expectation of increasing employment parallel to increased money may be stated in quantity-theory terms, in the sense of its usual employment and not Keynes'. The suppression of this more usual mode of speech through

---

[60] *Ibid.*, pp. 296–303.

most of the General Theory misled Harrod, and it is likely to give greater plausibility to directly contra-quantity theory causation than is actually warranted.

(1) Keynes readily admits that the relation of effective demand to money supply may be embraced under "income-velocity" if (a) income means expected income, and if (b) it means gross income. The second point is eliminated by employing the concept of circuit velocity, which as explained in Section III relates to gross and not to net income. The general doctrine of his book seems to be that the price-level has no determinants separate from costs to a single industry.[61] In this event contra-quantity theory causation obtains, since the monetary requirement for working balances is given, and the remainder goes to determine employment through the interest rate. But if expected income is admitted into the determinants of circular velocity, a factor is admitted which, however much it *affects* costs to single industries, cannot be *deduced from* cost functions in single industries—namely, monetary policy. Personal convictions on this subject give to velocity independent causality. The division of money stock into working and idle balances does not follow from prices, but determines them.

Factors (2), (3), and (5) seem to reduce to the phenomenon of diminishing returns. Under (2) whether labor is remunerated according to efficiency or according to effort determines whether the laborer or the employer bears the brunt of factor (3), diminishing returns; but "income" under the definition of the General Theory includes both wages and profits. Increased replacements, and hence (5), the expectation of them under user-cost, increase *per unit* cost of output only if diminishing returns prevail for the equipment. The factor of diminishing returns in quantity-theory language signifies that T, the volume of transactions, as affected by quantity of goods, does not increase as rapidly as the effective supply of money MV or MC, and so prices rise.

There remains factor (4), the raising of money-wages by the effort of organized labor with the latent assumption that the mone-

---

[61] E.g., *ibid.*, p. 294.

tary authority supplies the additional means for putting into effect the higher rates. This Keynes calls "semi-inflation," because it may be expected to increase employment, being a redistribution of income favorable to the consuming classes. In terms of the quantity theory it is inflation, because quantity of goods has not increased in proportion to the increase of money.

This restatement of the five factors does not itself detract from the Keynes theory. In one passage he himself concludes cautiously that an increase of money will "spend itself partly in increasing the level of employment and partly in raising the level of prices."[62] His conclusions regarding monetary and other policies motivated by the desire to reduce interest naturally rest upon the conviction that the first alternative is the more likely; but the formal structure of his equilibrium analysis permits the latter, and pessimists will incline in this direction. Not merely would the price-function rise more steeply than $XY'Z'$ in Figure I; it would, in consequence of the increased likelihood of misdirected and inefficient production, runaway stock-markets, incautious bank lending and the whole horde of ills attending "semi-inflation," be likely to reach its limit before full employment, and evolve into pure inflation at that limit, or worse, break sharply backward, as in Figure II.

The entire analysis of money and effective demand given by Keynes so far, we learn retrospectively and rather abruptly,[63] has pertained to the short run. For the long run, he believes, "there may be, for example, some fairly stable proportion of the national income more than which people will not readily keep in the shape of idle balances for long periods together," and this notion of a certain secular stability in k_t or circuit velocity would probably find rather general acceptance. The conclusion which Keynes draws is that in *falling* to the level set by available funds for idle balances, interest will extend effective demand. But the *adjustment* to a long term stability in k or circuit velocity does not reveal the quantitative determinants of equilibrium itself. If in the long run people *decide* upon the magnitude

---

[62] *Ibid.*, p. 296.
[63] *Ibid.*, p. 306.

of their idle balances, causation runs from division of money stock to *prices*. Causation can pass from the idle balances to *interest rates* only when people do *not* decide upon that division, i.e., when prices are given, working balances likewise given, and idle balances merely absorb the residual money. Keynes represents people as *deciding* what balances they desire to keep in the long run; he must accept *price levels* as the magnitude finally determined by this decision. The analysis of velocity in the present inquiry therefore supports Robertson in his conclusion that tho "from a short period point of view . . . 'the state of liquidity preference' . . . can be truly represented as exercising a causal influence upon the rate of interest," it has "as its permanent rôle, a share in the determination not of the rate of interest at all but of the price-level."[64]   There is no more momentous issue in contemporary economic theory and policy.

HOWARD S. ELLIS.

UNIVERSITY OF MICHIGAN

A NOTE ON CASE II

My graphic illustration of this arrangement of payments (p. 96) as well as the textual description (p. 95) suppressed a certain complication in order to simplify the argument at an introductory stage. But it is necessary to recognize that, however characteristic of important real situations the scheme of Case II may be, the perfect overlapping which Angell attributes to payments as he describes them here cannot in fact be achieved. Income expenditure periods are given as 3.5, 0, and 3.5 days in length, whereas literally they are 3.5, 0, and 3.0 days for consumers, middlemen, and producers respectively; the average is $2\frac{1}{6}$ days, and $iL = 6\frac{1}{2}$ and not 7 as would be necessary for $g = 1$.

At the end of the seventh day, the consumers' expenditure was, quite as on previous days, transferred instantaneously from consumers to middlemen and from the latter to producers. But unlike previous days, the seventh witnessed an instantaneous transfer of this money back to consumers as laborers. What Angell ignores, in calling this a case of perfect overlapping, is the possibility (as Case V, *q.v.*) of reducing the "necessary money"—in this case by $\frac{1}{7}$—through the simple offsetting of debit and credit to consumer-laborers at the end of the seventh day. Precise analysis of Case II reveals, therefore, that a certain fraction of the total money used to obtain the value of g as equal to 1 actually be-

[64] D. H. Robertson, "A Survey of Modern Monetary Controversy," an address on November 10, 1937, reprinted by the Manchester Statistical Society (Manchester, England, 1937), pp. 17–18.

longs to idle instead of working balances. Any illustration embodying consumer and producer income-expenditure periods of finite length will be embarrassed by a certain amount of balances which are really idle, just as in Angell's case, provided the general scheme of Case II be maintained.

Nevertheless, actual situations may *approach* the complete elimination of idle balances and the attainment of perfect overlapping without departing from the general scheme of receipts and disbursements of Case II. As consumer disbursements are made progressively more frequent, the value of g approaches 1 as a limit. The limiting case, where $g = 1$ and idle balances disappear, may be represented by two triangles with their hypotenuses supplanting the "stairsteps" in my diagram of Case II; infinitesimal amounts are involved in each disbursement, so that a continuous function displaces the former discrete schedule of payments. In this event, the income-expenditure periods become 3.5, 0, and 3.5 days, the circuit period is 7 days, and overlapping is perfect. Angell's Case II and my graphic illustration represent, therefore, an approximation rather than a realization of this state of affairs.

8

MONEY AND INDEX-NUMBERS*[1]

By R. G. Hawtrey||

THE VALUE OF THE UNIT

In monetary theory and in monetary policy alike one of the fundamental ideas is that of the value of money. In monetary theory it is, in a way, *the* fundamental idea. Monetary theory might even be described as nothing more than the theory of how the value of money is determined.

As to the position held by the value of money in monetary policy there is some difference of opinion. But even those who think that monetary policy should not be explicitly guided by any consideration of stabilizing value would recognize that the gold standard itself is to be recommended as a means of keeping the value of money within reasonable limits.

But if we ask what is *meant* by the value of money, we are brought up against certain theoretical difficulties which cannot be certainly or satisfactorily met and which are constantly being felt in the course both of monetary theory and of monetary policy.

Value, in the sense in which it is here used, means value in exchange, and the exchange must be exchange in a *market*. But for the existence of a market, similar exchanges would not be at the same ratio, and the relation indicated by value in exchange would not be determinate at all. A market is limited to a particular time and place.

* *Journal of the Royal Statistical Society,* **93** (1930), 64–85. Reprinted in R. G. Hawtrey, *The Art of Central Banking,* Longmans Green & Co., 1932. Reprinted here, by the courtesy of the publishers and the author, in slightly abridged form.

|| Royal Institute of International Affairs.

[1] Read before the Royal Statistical Society, December 17, 1929, the President, Mr. A. W. Flux, C.B., in the Chair.

At a different place, or at the same place at a different time, the things dealt in may be different, and, in so far as they are similar, their relative values and relative importance may be different.

The monetary unit is no more than a creature of the market. It is the unit in which prices are quoted and bargains are struck. The unit is dependent for its very identity upon the market which employs it.

The market assigns a single, determinate price to each thing dealt in; and thereby it establishes a *value* of the monetary unit in terms of each of the things dealt in. It establishes a multitude of alternative values—values in terms of the several individual things and in terms of all possible collections of them. There is no single value of the unit in terms of things in general, which is theoretically *the* value of the unit.

In what sense and for what purpose, then, does monetary theory require an unequivocal value to be assigned to the unit?

Monetary theory is constantly concerned with tendencies which affect *all* prices equally, or at any rate impartially, at the same time and in the same direction. In order to measure such tendencies, it has to disentangle their effects from the changes in individual prices which are traceable to disturbances of supply and demand, or, more generally, to non-monetary causes.

The Index in the Equation of Exchange

The quantity theory is a device for accomplishing this end. Professor Irving Fisher's Equation of Exchange analyses the total of transactions in a period of time into two factors, the volume of transactions and the price level. The volume of transactions involves the idea of a total of wealth. In order that a number of heterogeneous items of wealth may be aggregated into a sum, they must be expressed in terms of a common unit. They must, in fact, be priced, and they must be priced in the same market. The aggregate so arrived at is a number of monetary units.

With a given price list we can compare any two aggregates of wealth, so long as neither of them contains any items not included in the list. But all such comparisons are relative to the price list and therefore to the market (actual or hypothetical) from which the price list is derived.

The same method which compares two aggregates of wealth with reference to a given price list enables us to compare two price lists with reference to a given aggregate of wealth. Each price list applied to the items of the aggregate gives its own appropriate sum-total of monetary units, the ratio between these totals supplying an index of the difference of price level.

I do not propose to travel once again over the well-worn path of controversy as to the ideal methods of averaging and weighting index-numbers. But I would point out that much of that controversy is in reality irrelevant to the selection of an index-number for Professor Fisher's Equation of Exchange. The equation of exchange itself determines its own type of index-number. Since the equation of exchange proceeds from a comparison of two aggregates of wealth, it must employ the type of index-number which arises from such a comparison, that is to say, the weighted arithmetic mean. The ambiguities inherent in that index, owing to the differences in weighting appropriate to the different periods to be compared, are inherent in the equation of exchange itself.

To this it might be answered that the equation of exchange does not absolutely require the idea of the price level to be derived from the idea of the volume of transactions. We are quite free, if we choose, to arrive at an independent estimate of the price level with whatever methods of weighting and averaging seem best, and then to measure the volume of transactions by dividing the value of transactions by our price index.

I will illustrate the point by a numerical example. Let the commodities dealt in be three in number, equally weighted at the base period, and let their prices be represented at another period by 200, 400 and 800. If the quantities dealt in are the same as at the base period, the total money value of transactions will be 1,400 and the price index will be 466⅔. If we prefer to take the geometric mean, the index will be 400, and we can then arrive at our measure of the volume of transactions by dividing the value of transactions, 1,400, by 400. The result is 3½ instead of 3. That is to say, although the physical quantity of each class of goods dealt in remains absolutely unchanged, the "quantity" for the purposes of the equation of exchange has increased by one-sixth.

If the geometric mean were *the* perfect index-number, this paradoxical result could be defended. It might be argued that the same quantity of goods had become one-sixth more precious as determined by some independent standard, such as marginal utility. But it is not clear that any such independent standard is available, and, even if it is, there is no reason to suppose that the geometric mean has any more connection with it than the arithmetic.

THE INDEX-NUMBER AS A SAMPLE

So long as we are concerned with the price level as something correlative to an aggregate of wealth, we are tied to the arithmetic mean. But there is another standpoint from which we may view the price level, and from which we may assume a wider degree of freedom. Monetary theory is concerned with causes which tend to raise or lower the price level, because they tend to raise or lower all prices to the same proportional extent. If there were no other causes either disturbing prices or interfering with the free action of the general tendency, then any one selection of prices would reveal the tendency as perfectly as any other.

Under the conditions of reality disturbing and interfering causes exist, but every price is nevertheless affected by the underlying monetary movement. A *sample* of prices ought therefore to disclose the magnitude and direction of that movement, provided it is a fair sample. All the index-numbers in practical use are samples, and the technique of index-numbers ought accordingly to be approached from that point of view.

If the non-monetary causes at work were absolutely unknown, we should have no alternative but to take a random sample, and to make it as comprehensive as possible. That is the course of statistical puritanism, which refuses to manipulate the available data, and sternly closes every path by which preconceived ideas can gain access to its operations.

If the non-monetary causes were very many and all small relatively to the monetary, a random sample would still be appropriate. (Any predominating bias among the non-monetary causes would itself be classified as a cause not relatively small.)

Unfortunately these conditions are not fulfilled. A price index-number is liable to be disturbed by non-monetary causes of which the effects are considerable in comparison with those of the monetary causes.

Each of the non-monetary causes affects only one or a few products, but if the products affected are weighted to the extent of 2 or 3 per cent. of the total, and the causes are great enough to double or halve their prices, the result may be to modify greatly or to mask altogether a monetary movement of considerable practical importance. Special caution is required in dealing with certain groups which are usually heavily weighted, particularly (1) cereals, (2) cotton and cotton goods, and (3) coal, iron and steel and engineering products.

ELIMINATION OF NON-MONETARY CAUSES

If we had the means of measuring the effects of the non-monetary causes directly, we could allow for them, and the monetary movement would stand revealed when once the non-monetary movements had been eliminated. But any such measurement is quite impossible. We can say that short crops will raise the prices of cotton or cereals, or that a coal strike will raise the prices of coal, iron and steel, but we cannot say how great the rise of price will be in each case.

We have therefore to fall back on a more rough-and-ready method. We can pick out a limited number of commodities of which we know the prices to have been disproportionately affected by non-monetary causes, and exclude them from the comparison. I do not mean to suggest that a series of index-numbers should be constructed on that principle. It is in the practical application of the series to reveal a monetary movement that expurgation of the kind described becomes necessary. The commodities to be excluded should be chosen not, primarily, because their prices have behaved differently from the predominant trend, but because their prices are known to have been seriously affected by non-monetary causes.

Great inequality of price movements may arise from the action of monetary causes themselves.

Expurgation of the index-number will only yield a satisfactory result if the commodities left in are sufficiently numerous and representative to afford a fair sample. They need not necessarily be commodities of the first importance, provided they are typical in their response to the market.

Non-monetary causes may arise on the side either of demand or of supply. But in general those arising from changes of demand are less likely to require any correction of the index-number. A change in the preferences of the consumer will increase the demand for some products and decrease the demand for others. The rise in some prices will be accompanied by a fall in others. It is true that we cannot assume rise and fall to balance one another exactly. In fact, increasing returns may lower the price of a thing that comes into more extended favour. But that is a change in the conditions of *supply,* and has to be allowed for as such.

And in practice it is rare to be able to identify a considerable price movement as due to a change in demand.

An Index of the Factors of Production

The elimination of non-monetary causes is justified as a *practical* device. We seek to measure a tendency by sampling a number of quantities in each of which the tendency is at work, and we exclude from the sample those quantities in which the effect of the tendency is known to have been distorted or obliterated by disturbing causes.

Nevertheless, the process has its theoretical side. What is it we are eliminating? What kind of correction do we set out to apply to our index-number, and by what standard is the result to be judged more correct after the process than before?

When we class a change of price arising from the conditions of supply as non-monetary, we mean that the change of price is due to a change of *cost*.

This is true of the varying yield of crops and of increasing or diminishing returns, as well as of changes in the processes of manufacture.

A short crop means a smaller volume of production for a given cost of effort and of the factors of production. The rise of price may, it is true, be greater (or less) than in proportion to the consequent increase of cost. But, if so, that means that the effect on price is modified by the conditions of demand. If the crop is half the normal and the price is quadrupled, then a great part of the increase in price represents demand diverted from other products. If the price increases less than in proportion to the shortage, the difference represents demand diverted *to* other products.

It is only in the ideal case, where elasticity of demand is equal to unity, that the demand for other products remains unaffected, and that therefore the method of correcting the index-number by elimination exactly fulfils its purpose. That purpose may be described as the elimination of changes of price that are due to changes of real cost. If cost be defined comprehensively, to include the payments made for all the factors of production and exchange, and therefore to include profit, then cost is equal to price, and every variation in price is due *either* to a variation of real cost, *or* to a variation in the money value of the factors of production and exchange.

If we start with a given change in a price index, we may imagine the change in each separate price to be analysed into the portion (if any) due to a change in real cost, and the residue. We may then suppose the residual portions to be collected into an average or index-number, and this index-number will give us what we are aiming at when we try to eliminate the non-monetary disturbances.

Here is a new aspect of the matter, for the resultant index-number is nothing more nor less than *a price index of the factors of production*.

Such an index could hardly be calculated directly. There is a market in wages, and there can be an index-number of wages. But it would be utterly impossible to construct index-numbers of the other factors of production. The market does not quote a price for each kind of contribution from capital, land, management or organization to the process of production. Interest, depreciation, rent and profit are determined by complex reactions among a number of forces. When the system is in perfect equilibrium, the payments for all these factors conform to definite laws, and theory shows that under those conditions cost may be expressed in terms of cost of effort. The contributions of land and capital to production may be expressed in terms of effort saved. The same is true of cost of management so far as paid for as a separate item. Profit itself is a form of personal remuneration, regulated ultimately, though not very directly, by the labour market. Thus under equilibrium conditions an index of the factors of production would be substantially equivalent to an index of wages. When equilibrium is disturbed, wages may get seriously out of proportion, and what wages gain or lose is lost or gained by profit, which is the residuary item in the total of costs. For the time being an index of wages ceases to be an adequate index of costs.

Consumers' Income and Outlay and Changes of Productivity

The relation of the value of the currency unit to the cost of effort is best seen if we view the productive efforts of the community as a whole.

Producers and dealers employ the workpeople and the material resources of the community to produce a supply of goods and services. All incomes are derived from production, taken in its widest sense to include transport and dealing. Every income is either a payment for services rendered by the recipient (in person or property), or is charged upon other incomes. The unproductive incomes which are not paid for any service rendered can be regarded as a diversion of a part of the productive incomes.

The total of all incomes reckoned in monetary units, or, to give it a convenient name, the consumers' income, is therefore the sum of the payments made for all the services rendered by the factors of production. The consumers' income when spent, that is to say, the consumers' outlay, constitutes the demand for all products. Consumers' income and consumers' outlay must be equal, except in so far as variations occur in the balances of money and bank credit.

Suppose now a change in productivity. The application of effort and the factors of production remaining the same, the physical total of the output is increased or diminished. If the index of the factors of production is to be kept invariable, then the consumers' income and outlay will be unchanged. Demand being unchanged, the price level will fall or rise just in proportion as output is increased or diminished. In fact the elasticity of demand for all products taken together is unity.

It will be observed that here we are employing the idea of an aggregate of wealth, and our method of measuring the price level must be correlative to that idea. For any particular product the changes in output, in cost, and in price will be ascertainable facts. For the aggregate of all products these quantities depend on methods of averaging and weighting.

Next suppose that, productivity being unchanged, the consumers' income changes. There will be a transitional interval during which cash balances and stocks of commodities will be subject to variations, and there will be no longer an equality either of consumers' income and consumers' outlay or of production and consumption. But the interval of disturbance once over, these equalities will be re-established. If production is unchanged, the price level will then have risen or fallen in exact proportion to the consumers' income.

It is a change of this character in the price level that is to be regarded as a change in the value of the monetary unit from the standpoint we are now adopting. More generally we may say that any change in the consumers' income which is not proportional to a change in the amount of the factors of production employed involves a change in the value of the monetary unit. The value of the unit is thus taken to mean its value in terms of the factors of production. Here is a simple formula which eliminates those non-monetary causes that arise on the side of supply. We cannot apply it directly as a test of variations in the value of the unit, because we cannot arrive directly at an index-number of the factors of production. But when we correct an index-number of commodity prices by eliminating price changes due to changes in the conditions of supply, we may regard this as an indirect method of applying the test.

A LABOUR UNIT

Our formula does not altogether avoid the problem of forming an index-number from a weighted average; for while it leaves the aggregate of products on one side, as a factor not entering into the calculation of the value of the unit, it does implicitly involve the idea of the aggregate of factors of production. Even though we do not directly compute this aggregate, the significance of the formula is essentially dependent upon it. A change in the consumers' income involves a change in the value of the monetary unit in so far as it is not accounted for by a change in the factors of production.

In order that they may be aggregated, the factors of production must be expressed in terms of a common unit—in fact they must be priced.

In a certain sense the factors of production are more intimately related together than are commodities. Commodities are only susceptible of comparison in that they all are possible objects of expenditure and are dealt in in the market. The factors of production are likewise objects of expenditure and are dealt in in the market, but *also* they are measurable in terms of effort or man-power.

The material aids to production, land and capital, and the services of organization and management, are valued as means of saving or reinforcing labour. All the factors of production are measurable in terms of productive power, and productive power may be estimated in terms of labour.

That is a broad generalization for which exact truth cannot be claimed. "Labour" is not a perfectly homogeneous thing. An hour's work by an undistinguished able-bodied man may supply a standard of measurement, but as soon as we proceed to compare this with any other kind of hour's work, we find that the comparison has to be made through market value, and market value is determined by the force of demand operating upon various degrees of scarcity, whether natural or artificial. In principle this raises afresh the same problems as an index-number of commodity prices. But we can form the conception of an aggregate of effort or of man-power with suitable corrections for variations of quality among the different kinds of effort. I do not wish to press this idea further than it may legitimately be carried. We cannot ultimately escape from the labour market as the test of the quality of different kinds of effort.

But the hour's work of the undistinguished able-bodied man *does* give us a link between every labour market and every other. And when we are making comparisons of the same community over periods within which the factors of production have undergone no very sweeping change, the condition that the consumers' income varies in proportion to the amount of the factors of production employed has a very definite meaning.

This seems to offer a simple definition of the value of the monetary unit. Its value is its purchasing power in terms of human effort.

Nevertheless, it is not quite so simple as it looks. We cannot assume that the shares of the factors of production in the proceeds of their activity are in their due economic proportions. If a monetary disturbance occurs, and the consumers' income changes relatively to the factors of production employed, the primary effect is likely to be a change in profits, without any proportional change (and perhaps without any change at all) in wages. Therefore we cannot say that the value of the monetary unit is its purchasing power in the labour market.

Unemployment is another complication. If the consumers' income is curtailed by a credit contraction or any other cause, there results not only a reduction of profits but a decline in productive activity. The factors of production will be only partially employed. Clearly for the purposes of our formula it is with the factors of production actually employed that the consumers' income must be compared. The consumers' income is composed of the payments for the services rendered by the factors of production. In so far as no services are rendered there are no payments. In the case of labour the distinction is plain enough. But in the case of land, capital, or management being under-employed, it may not be easy to measure the extent of the services rendered. There is no need here to enlarge upon the difficulties that arise.

THE VALUE OF THE UNIT FOR PURPOSES OF MONETARY POLICY

Having thus arrived at a definition of the value of the monetary unit, I do not want to put it forward as the right theoretical definition to the exclusion of all others. It is quite sufficient to claim for it that the conception I have defined *does* arise in the course of monetary theory, and requires accordingly to be considered.

But when we turn from theory to monetary policy, different criteria have to be applied. As soon as stability of the value of the unit is set up as an aim of monetary policy, the definition of the value of the unit becomes a matter of practical consequence. In order to carry out the policy, we must be clear *what* it is that we want to stabilize; and the definition to be selected must be conditioned by the aim of the policy. The scope and character of the policy may be modified by modifying the definition. We want to select that definition among all those possible which will make the policy of stabilization most beneficial, just as a definition in an Act of Parliament is framed so as to make the application of the Act that which is judged most desirable.

The aims of the policy of stabilization are best described in a negative form, in terms of the evils it seeks to avoid. Critics frequently attack the policy on the ground that no manipulation of money—a mere medium of exchange—can produce additional wealth; that no conjuring trick can produce the substance out of the shadow. That is a misunderstanding. The very same school of thought which makes this criticism is ready enough to expatiate on the dire consequences of the mismanagement of money. Monetary stabilization is not to be regarded as a miraculous *cornucopia* multiplying production without effort, but as a method of avoiding the various disorders, the impoverishment and injustice, which unregulated variations in the value of the unit may cause.

Among these disorders we may concentrate upon three principal groups. First, injustice between debtor and creditor; secondly, disturbance of the relations between values, particularly between wages, prices, and profits; and thirdly, the effect of monetary expansions and contractions upon productive activity.

INJUSTICE BETWEEN DEBTOR AND CREDITOR

The question of injustice between debtor and creditor arises mainly in the case of the rentier, the long-term investor who contracts to receive sums fixed in monetary units in the form of rent or interest and sometimes of the ultimate repayment of capital. In the case of short-term debts there is hardly room for any seriously inequitable change of value to occur, except at a time of extreme monetary instability. Where the instability is kept within moderate limits, its effects upon short-term indebtedness are best dealt with under our other two headings.

Professor Irving Fisher, who has long been one of the most distinguished advocates of monetary stabilization, has always laid special stress on this requirement of justice to the fixed-interest investor. It is easy to show that a seriously unstable unit inflicts injustice. There is no doubt at all that an income fixed in pounds or dollars acquired by an investor in 1896 and retained by him ever since has been enormously depreciated (probably by much more than half) owing to the rise in the price level that has since occurred. There is also no doubt that a similar fixed income acquired in 1920 is being paid in pounds or dollars which represent much more wealth than at the time of the investment.

These are wide movements of prices, about the general tendency and order of magnitude of which there is little dispute. It is when less sensational movements are involved that more precise measurement becomes necessary, and that a choice has to be made between our formula and its rivals.

In what sense must we understand the "value" of the unit, if stabilization of that value is to secure justice to the fixed-interest investor? The question relates, of course, to relatively long periods, and we can disregard the short-period disturbances of the relation between profits and wages.

If real costs remain unchanged, so that a given amount of the factors of production yields the same output, our formula will give the same result as a commodity price index. In order to distinguish between the two, we must suppose a change in real costs or in the productivity of effort.

Take first the effect of diminishing returns. Output is diminished in relation to effort. Suppose that the factors of production employed have increased by 20 per cent., but that the output measured in physical units has increased by only 10 per cent. The question is whether, in order to secure stability, the consumers' income ought to increase by 20 per cent. or by 10 per cent.

Consider the position of the recipient of a fixed income. A fixed income has usually been provided to take the place of an actively earned income. It may be destined for a business man after retirement, or for his widow, or perhaps for someone still active, whose ambitions lie in the direction of art or politics or some other non-remunerative occupation. Whatever the circumstances may be, the calculations made at the time when the money was saved and invested will be based upon a comparison of the income to be expected with other incomes. The man who saves for the sake of his widow will aim at securing her such an income that she can associate without embarrassment with his own social equals. The standard will be set by their incomes, from business or from professions. If their incomes, reckoned in money, change materially, his calculations will, to that extent, prove wrong. If the currency is so regulated that the commodity price level is unchanged, the earned incomes will be reduced in the same proportion as productivity, *i.e.* by one-twelfth. A fixed income will then retain its command over commodities unchanged, but will hold an improved position in comparison with other incomes. The intentions of the man who saved to provide the fixed income would be adequately carried out if the currency were so regulated as to maintain incomes unchanged and to allow a rise of commodity prices by one-eleventh. There is nothing in the idea of a fixed income to require that the possessor should be safeguarded against the effects of a scarcity of natural products from which his neighbours with earned incomes suffer.

Turn next to the case of diminishing costs. The agents of production employed increase by 20 per cent., and output increases by 50 per cent. If the commodity price level is kept fixed, the consumers' income rises by 50 per cent., and the remuneration of a given productive effort rises by one-fourth. The fixed income retains its purchasing power over commodities, but suffers in relativity with the neighbours' earned incomes.

It may be said that the recipient of the fixed income has nothing to complain of, in that he has an undiminished command over goods. But that is no compensation for the loss in relative position. And if we consider what it means in terms of real income, we find that he has to accept the cheap goods made by improved methods or derived from new sources of production as the equivalent of the more highly prized goods previously available. There will not necessarily be any difference of quality. The new cheap machine-made articles may be just as good as those formerly made by hand. But even so they are not really equivalent in the eyes of the consumer.

If the commodity price level is kept fixed, then all those things of which the real cost has not fallen must rise in price. The recipient of a fixed income can only maintain his consumption of these things undiminished if he forgoes the advantage of increasing his consumption of those which have been cheapened.

I do not want to lay any great stress on these arguments founded on justice to the rentier. It is enough for my purpose to show that on the whole the balance of argument is on the side of stabilizing incomes or the remuneration of effort rather than commodity prices.

WAGES, PRICES AND PROFITS

I turn next to the disturbing effects of monetary instability upon the mutual relations of wages, prices and profits. Here one of the governing conditions is that prices are much more easily adjusted than wages. Suppose that any economic change occurs which requires a change in the relation of wages to the price level. The policy of currency stabilization might be interpreted to mean either the stabilization of the wage level or the stabilization of the price level, but it cannot mean both, for they are not consistent with one another. Which is to be preferred?

Suppose that real costs have risen or productivity has declined. To keep the price level constant, the consumers' income and the consumers' outlay must be reduced in proportion to output. The first impact of the reduction will be felt in a shrinkage of profits and a curtailment of production. There will follow an interval, which may be protracted, during which wages have to be brought down to the new equilibrium level.

On the other hand, if the price level is allowed to rise in proportion to the decline in output, that means that consumers' income and consumers' outlay remain unchanged, and the rise of prices comes about naturally and promptly as the result of an unchanged demand meeting with a diminished supply.

The only circumstance that retards the rise of prices is that traders may at first be doubtful whether the rise is justified, and may for a time feed demand from stocks at the old price level. But this cannot continue long, because the traders will be driven to raise prices to protect their stocks from depletion.

Likewise, if productivity is increased or real costs are diminished, a stable price level means increased consumers' income and consumers' outlay. Profits are in the first instance swollen, and an increase in money wages becomes due. The increase in wages lags behind, and may be obtainable only at the cost of friction and possibly of trade disputes.

If it were possible to carry out the stabilization of the monetary unit in terms of human effort with perfect exactitude, the predominant rate of unskilled wages would remain unchanged year after year, decade after decade, generation after generation. The only changes in wages that would ever have to be made would be in the nature of adaptations of the various classes of skilled and semi-skilled rates to the varying demand for the products upon which they are employed, and to the varying scarcity of the qualities and training required.

Undeniably friction would still be possible, but one terribly prolific cause of trade disputes would be avoided if no *general* rise or fall of the wage level were ever needed.

That does not mean that there would be stagnation in wages. But the advance of real wages through industrial progress would always take the form of a fall of prices and not of a rise of money wages.

At this stage it will be relevant to refer to an argument which has been put forward by Professor J. R. Commons of Wisconsin. He has pointed out that an increase in productivity may be accomplished not only by new processes or new discoveries, but by a more effective co-operation on the part of the workmen. He holds that, if improved productivity emanates in this way from the workmen themselves, it should be felt in an increase of money wages rather than a fall of prices. This is, I think, in principle quite right. As a result of their good will or good sense the workmen are in reality offering a greater amount of effort. The factors of production employed are being increased, and the money remuneration should be increased accordingly. If the improvement occurs in one industry only, clearly there ought to be a relative improvement in the remuneration of the workmen to whom it is due. The only reservation which I should make is that in the particular case where the workpeople have artificially raised their wages in the past by an abuse of monopolistic power, it is not equitable (though it may be expedient or inevitable) to reward them for abstaining from this abuse.

TRADE DEPRESSION AND UNEMPLOYMENT

The last of the three troubles caused by monetary instability is the fluctuations in productive activity. That is the most important of the three; it is the unemployment problem.

That deflation or a falling price level causes unemployment is generally accepted. But as to the precise manner and limits of this principle there is room for differences of opinion.

One form in which the principle is sometimes enunciated is that as a fall of wages lags behind a fall of prices, profits are encroached on by costs, and some business, becoming unprofitable, is abandoned. The volume of production is thus diminished and part of the workpeople are thrown out of employment. So stated, the principle is nothing more than an incident of the disparity of wages and prices that we have already considered. The price of labour being too high, the demand for it falls off.

But there is much more in the principle than that. Another formulation of it is that the prospect of falling prices damps down enterprise, because it deters traders from holding stocks of goods. If prices are expected to fall, it pays to postpone purchases and to hasten sales. When the dealers in commodities adopt this course, producers find themselves with fewer orders, and the volume of production shrinks.

This is much nearer to an adequate account of the principle. And it brings out its relation to credit contraction. For credit contraction operates as a deterrent upon holding goods with borrowed money, and therefore produces the same kind of reluctance to buy as the expected fall of prices itself.

But I think the causation of unemployment by monetary contraction is best explained through the consumers' income and outlay. Suppose that anything occurs, whether a credit contraction, a decrease in velocity of circulation or anything else, to cause a reduction in the consumers' income. There will ensue a reduction of the consumers' outlay (not exactly equal, for consumers' balances may be drawn on). Thereby the total effective demand for commodities is curtailed. Dealers find their sales at existing prices falling off, and give smaller orders to the producers for the replenishment of their stocks. The diminished activity of the producers means a further diminution of the consumers' income and outlay. A vicious circle of diminished activity and diminished demand is set up.

This process begins and may even continue for a time without any fall of prices. The fall of prices arises partly from the desire of dealers to sell off stocks in face of the diminished demand, and partly from the desire of producers to keep up output. The reduction of prices in both cases will be tentative, and so long as it is in progress the possibility of a further fall will be present to the minds of both classes of traders as an additional motive for restraining enterprise.

The fall of prices, so far as actually accomplished, is a relief; it makes a given amount of money-demand absorb a greater amount of goods. The difficulty of reducing wages prolongs the depression, because it obstructs the fall of prices.

Given that one of the objects of monetary stabilization is to prevent a restriction of productive activity arising in this way, what form should the stabilization take? So long as productivity is unchanged, it makes no difference whether we stabilize the money value of commodities or the money value of the factors of production. To choose between them, we must suppose productivity to change. Let productivity diminish; for example, let there be a scanty harvest. To keep the price index unchanged, there must be a reduction in the consumers' outlay in proportion to the reduction in the total output of the goods. A credit contraction must be set on foot. If we suppose the elasticity of demand for the products of which there is a shortage to be unity, then, so long as the consumers' outlay is unchanged, the total outlay on each class of products may remain just as it was before. The prices of the scarce products will have risen in direct proportion to their scarcity, and other prices will have remained unchanged. In order to restore the price index to what it was, the outlay on every class of products must be reduced.

Suppose, for example, that a consumer's outlay of £100,000,000 has been applied to 100,000,000 units of goods, and that producers who have hitherto received £20,000,000 for 20,000,000 units find their output reduced to 10,000,000 units, but the price of their product doubled. They still receive £20,000,000 and the other producers can continue to receive £80,000,000 for 80,000,000 units.

But as £100,000,000 is now spent on 90,000,000 units the price level has risen by one-ninth. In order to counteract that rise, the consumers' outlay must be reduced from £100,000,000 to £90,000,000. Every group of producers will find the total proceeds of its sales reduced by 10 per cent. Wages, profits and prices will be thrown out of proportion, and every industry will have to face the adverse effects of flagging demand and falling prices. The producers whose prices have been raised by scarcity will be no exception. Their total receipts are reduced in the same proportion, and they must reduce wages like their neighbours.

The illustration does not depend on elasticity of demand being unity. If the shortage is in a product of which the elasticity is greater than unity, the adverse effect on the producers of that product is greater and on other producers less. If elasticity is less than unity the adverse effect on the former is less and may be more than counteracted, but what they gain their neighbours lose. Whatever the circumstances, the stabilization of the commodity price level in face of scarcity will always tend to cause depression.

On the other hand, any such disturbance is completely avoided if the consumers' income and outlay are stabilized. There is, however, one difficulty that must be mentioned. Suppose that for any reason a decline of productive activity does occur and the available factors of production are under-employed.   Stabilization of the value of the factors of production would imply that the consumers' income and outlay are to remain correspondingly reduced.

This objection relates, however, to the policy of stabilization in general, whether it be the commodity price index or the value of the factors of production that is stabilized.   The answer to it is twofold. First of all, a reduction of activity is nearly always accompanied by relatively greater reduction of the consumers' income and outlay, and the correction of this latter would bring with it a restoration of activity.   And secondly, in the case where this is not so, there is always a natural tendency for production to expand up to capacity, which will work its way unless counteracted by positive measures of credit restriction.

So long as there is no obstacle interposed to the expansion of credit *pari passu* with production, every increment of production brings with it an equal increment of demand.   The same principle reconciles full employment with the growth of population and productive power.

I have shown that in the case where the prices of some products rise owing to scarcity, the stabilization of the consumers' income and outlay works better than the stabilization of the commodity price level.   The contrary case, where there is increased plenty or increased productivity in some industries, requires separate consideration. The prices of the plentiful commodities fall relatively to the others, and, if the price index is to be kept constant, these other prices must be allowed to rise.   If the consumers' income and outlay are kept constant, the full effect of the improved productivity is felt in lower prices, and other prices remain unchanged.

There is no advantage in the latter alternative in regard to productive activity.   The rise of prices in the former would tend to intensify activity, so that the difference, if any, would be in its favour.

But there would be no difference, or at any rate important difference, unless industry as a whole were under-employed.   That is a state of affairs that does not usually occur except as the result of a contraction of the consumers' outlay.   So long as the consumers' outlay remains undiminished, any decline of demand in one direction will always be offset by increased demand in others.

In the particular case where the increased productivity is temporary, where, for example, it is due to an abundant harvest, the general rise of the prices of all other products is distinctly harmful. For when the temporary plenty passes, these other prices must be lowered again at the cost of depression and unemployment.

It is sometimes taken for granted that a fall of prices always causes depression, whatever the cause may be. But this is not so. In so far as the fall is due to diminished real costs or increased productivity in some industries, it has no restraining effect on enterprise. It causes loss to holders of stocks of the commodities affected, for their value falls to the same level as that of the fresh supply. But this loss has no resemblance to the *prospective* loss from a fall of prices which threatens when demand is contracting. A threatened loss in the latter case can be averted or minimized by postponing purchases and hastening sales. But where a reduction of costs has cut down the replacement value of the goods, the sequence of events is quite different. Dealers are forced by competition to reduce the price to the consumer to correspond with the replacement value. The fall of prices being an accomplished fact, there is no motive to postpone purchases.

In the particular case where increased productivity is due to a temporary cause, such as an abundant crop, conditions are somewhat different. There is no definite replacement value to set a standard of price, and dealers may hang back till they believe the price has reached its lowest point. But this is not a case where the dealers' action will affect the activity of the producers.

THE RETAIL INDEX-NUMBER

The foregoing arguments lead up to the conclusion that the most desirable kind of monetary stabilization is stabilization of the consumers' income and outlay—not absolute fixity, but the adjustment of the consumers' income and outlay to the growth of the factors of production, both on account of increasing man-power and on account of accretions of capital.

But still, for practical purposes of monetary policy, we must be guided by the available commodity price index-numbers, and must rely on the elimination of non-monetary disturbances to get the result we seek. We therefore have to choose what index-numbers to use for this purpose.

Some economists (Mr. Keynes among them) have advocated the use of retail index-numbers. At first sight this seems logical, for the consumers' outlay, so far as it is applied to consumption goods, is spent in retail. It is the demand at this final stage that is the test of the state of markets, and it is by their estimate of the retail demand that the producers and wholesale dealers are guided in deciding what prices to ask or to offer at all intermediate stages.

But it is a fatal defect of the retail price index that it only covers a part of the ground. The consumers' outlay is applied not only to consumption goods, but, through the medium of the investment market, to capital goods. In order to be a fair sample, the price index must include capital goods, for example, iron, steel, engineering products and building materials, and this the retail index fails to do.

That being so, it is hardly necessary to consider in detail other defects in a retail index. It is enough to mention the want of sensitiveness, the difficulty of ascertaining the exact meaning of the quotations used in relation to the quality of the goods, and finally the predominance of working-class budgets as the basis of the retail indexes that are actually compiled.

In reality, just because retail demand is transmitted to wholesale markets, and retail prices ultimately govern wholesale prices, the wholesale index is just as representative as the retail index. And it has the advantage of greater sensitiveness and also of greater continuity and definiteness in the specification of the goods priced.

Prices of Stocks and Shares

It has sometimes been held that the price index should not be confined to the commodity markets, but should include the prices of stocks and shares in the investment market.

The consumers' outlay includes outlay on investment. Should not an index-number of things bought with the consumers' outlay include those bought by way of investment?

But *securities* are not really objects of expenditure at all. The true objects of expenditure are the capital goods over which the securities confer rights. The investment market is an intermediary between the outlay of investors on the one side and the production of capital goods on the other.

When an investor buys securities he pays their price to the seller. But the money is not by that transaction spent; it is simply passed on to await investment in the hands of the new owner. It may pass repeatedly from hand to hand and still be in the same condition. But as soon as it is applied to the purchase of a new capital issue, it really is spent on the creation of fixed capital.

The investment market is a body of traders buying and selling securities. Inasmuch as people change their investments from time to time, investors are both buyers and sellers, but in virtue of the growth of savings the purchases of investors exceed their sales. On balance, therefore, the investors' demand is always depleting the supply of securities in the hands of the market. The supply is made good by the new capital issues emanating from the promoters of capital enterprises. In the long run the new capital issues and the savings seeking investment must balance. When, over any interval, they do not balance, the effect is to increase or decrease the amount of securities held by the dealers in the market, and the dealers will thereupon take steps by a suitable movement of prices to bring back their holdings to normal.

The dealers carry part of their holdings of securities by means of bank advances, and any excess or deficiency of the investment money they receive over the money they pay for new issues takes effect in a decrease or increase of the indebtedness of the dealers to the banks.

The functioning of the investment market as an intermediary between investors and promoters is quite unaffected by the price level of the existing securities. Whether the prices be high or low, the purchase and sale of those securities can only transfer the money seeking investment from hand to hand on its journey towards its final destination as capital outlay. The prices determine the amount of *securities* that change hands in this process, but the amount of *money* depends not on the prices, but on the amount of savings seeking investment. The prices of new issues will, it is true, be closely related to the prices of existing securities, but that is because both are affected by the market rate of interest. In the case of the new issues the market rate of interest sets a standard to which the ratio of the expected yield to the capital outlay must conform. In the case of existing securities capital outlay has already been sunk, and price represents the appropriate number of years' purchase of expected yield. Capital outlay in the former case and expected yield in both cases are affected by the commodity price level. But both expected yield and the rate of interest are affected by causes which do not depend directly upon the value of the monetary unit.

The point may be illustrated from recent experience in the United States. Since 1923, when business first revived from the intense depression of 1921, there had been both a substantial fall in the rate of interest and a very large increase in the yield of industrial enterprises. The actual profits of a large and representative selection of concerns more than doubled between 1924 and the spring of 1929. This increase in yield was not attributable to any considerable increase in the consumers' income and outlay, but to improved methods, improved organization and the increased scale of production.

A great part of the sensational rise in the prices of stocks and shares was due to these circumstances. If the expected yield of a share doubles because the price of the product has doubled, and if this rise of price no more than corresponds to a general rise in the commodity price level, then the consequent increase in the price of the share is evidence of a fall in the value of the monetary unit. But if the expected yield doubles in consequence of improved efficiency without any change of prices, the increased price of the share is not being paid for the same thing as before. The *real value* of the shares has increased.

It is essential to include in some form the prices of capital goods in the price index. But if we try to do this by including the prices of stocks and shares, we introduce a quantity of irrelevant matter, which would be even more difficult to disentangle than the non-monetary causes affecting commodity prices. If a price index has to be constructed to verify Professor Irving Fisher's Equation of

Exchange and for no other purpose, there is something to be said for including prices of securities. Professor Fisher includes in the totality of transactions all dealings in securities. But to my mind that is a defect in his formula, and it would be an improvement to exclude all dealings in stocks, shares and pecuniary rights and to restate the Equation of Exchange, as Professor Pigou has proposed, in terms of transactions in goods and services only.

THE WHOLESALE COMMODITY INDEX AND THE EXTERNAL AND INTERNAL PRICE LEVELS

For practical purposes, therefore, we are led to prefer an ordinary wholesale index-number, subject to allowance being made so far as possible for the disturbances due to non-monetary causes. If we wish to measure the change in the value of the monetary unit, we want the most representative index we can get. But if we wish to have prompt warning of the commencement of a change in its value, we shall compose our index rather of the most sensitive commodities than of the most representative. For this reason the American Bureau of Labor index is not altogether satisfactory. It is so comprehensive that it includes a large number of very insensitive prices. The less comprehensive numbers that prevail in Europe are really more useful. In America Professor Fisher's number is noticeably more sensitive than that of the Bureau of Labor.

One more question I must refer to, and that is the relation of internal and external prices. The internal price level is very difficult to sample adequately. The great majority of material products have an international market and contribute to the external price level. The residue is composed mainly of those which are either too bulky in proportion to value or too perishable to stand distant carriage, and for them price quotations are usually very unsatisfactory. The principal part of the internal price level is based upon the prices of *services*—services of construction, repair and cleaning, the preparation and serving of food, retailing, local passenger transport, domestic and personal services. House rent is another important item.

In some countries a prohibitive tariff places the prices of the products which it protects practically in the internal class, but that is so only so long as the tariff remains prohibitive and so long also as the products do not enter into the export market.

In effect, most index-numbers are almost exclusively confined to the external price level. For the purposes of monetary theory this is a serious defect. But it is not necessarily so for the purposes of monetary policy. Plans for price stabilization by one country in isolation from its neighbours are not at the present time within the range of practical politics. The gold standard is an international standard, and price stabilization must mean the stabilization of the world value of gold. For that purpose what we need is an index of world prices.

An index of world prices will be composed of the same commodities that predominate in the European index-numbers we already have. They have the advantages of regular continuous and ascertainable quotations and of sensitiveness. For the elimination of non-monetary causes we must rely on information with regard to world crops, to the opening up or exhaustion of sources of supply, to changes in industrial processes, and to any events, such as Kartel agreements or industrial disputes, which may temporarily affect any important class of industries.

It must be admitted that stabilization of world prices will leave some room for variation in internal price levels. Any country which experiences a disturbance of its balance of payments must suffer from a modification of its internal price level relative to its external. If it maintains the gold standard, the external price level is thereby fixed, and the change is concentrated in the internal. That is a consequence of the gold standard itself, and is not aggravated in any way by the stabilization of gold. Variations in the world value of gold may either increase or diminish the variation of the internal price level on such an occasion, and are not more likely to do one than the other. But on all *other* occasions they are a wanton cause of trouble.

CONCLUSION

We started by saying that monetary theory is concerned with causes which affect all prices. But when it came to detecting those causes by the use of a sample of prices in the shape of an index-number, we found the process to be complicated by the intrusion of non-monetary causes, those confined to particular prices or groups of prices. We are now in a position to state more precisely what is the nature of the monetary causes that we have to detect. They are causes affecting the amount of the consumers' income and outlay otherwise than in proportion to the factors of production. Our sampling should be designed to discover the action of such causes and to separate them from the rest. The reason is that the injuries to the economic system attributed to monetary disorders are traceable to these causes.

Incidentally, this conclusion supplies a definition of inflation and deflation. If these terms mean an *undesirable* excess or deficiency of the means of payment we can say that inflation means an expansion of the consumers' income and outlay, and deflation a contraction, more than in proportion to the factors of production employed.

9

A NOTE ON THE THEORY OF MONEY*

By D. H. Robertson‖

1

In the course of his discussion of the "Cambridge" method of approach to the theory of the value of money (*Treatise on Money*, I, 229–39), Mr. Keynes makes two propositions which may be paraphrased as follows: (1) It is not useful to bring the volume of real income or output R and its price-level P into relation with the total stock of money M by means of a factor K, denoting the proportion of R over which people wish to keep command in monetary form. It is only useful so to bring them into relation with that part of the money stock which is held for the purpose of facilitating the disbursement of *income*; for the remainder of the money stock is held for business and investment purposes not directly connected with the level of output, and is used to purchase things whose price-level may behave very differently from that of output. (2) The price-level proper to equations of the "Cambridge" type is a price-level in which the various items are weighted according to their relative importance in respect of the money balances which they cause to be held, and not (as in equations of the Fisher type, using the concept of velocity of circulation) according to their relative importance in respect of the transactions per unit of time to which they give rise.

I venture to suggest that neither of the propositions is well founded.

2

(1) It is of course true (as is recognised in Marshall's own illustration of the "Cambridge" theory) that many people will have other quantities than their income in mind (for instance, their capital or

---

* *Economica*, **13** (1933), 243–47. Reprinted as Essay VI of *Essays In Monetary Theory*, D. H. Robertson, Staples Press Limited, 1940. Reprinted here, by the courtesy of the publishers and the author, without change from the original text.

‖ Trinity College, Cambridge.

their business turnover) in deciding upon their monetary requirements. But from the fact that their money stock is not exclusively *determined* as a proportion of their income, it does not follow that it cannot usefully be *expressed* as such a proportion; still less that the real value of the whole community's total money stock cannot usefully be expressed (as in the equation $\frac{M}{P} = KR$) in terms of the constituents of real income or output.   For the whole of M is *potentially* expendable against output, and if in any period of time more or less of it were to be so expended than was previously the case, P would alter.   It is of the utmost importance that under certain conditions money which has been imprisoned in what Mr. Keynes calls the "savings deposits" and "business deposits" may seep out, raise the aggregate of incomes and "income deposits," and drive up P.   Such a change is represented in the "Cambridge" approach by a diminution of K: it would not be represented by any change in a symbol which stood for the proportion borne to R by the real value of "income deposits" alone.   Mr. Keynes' charge that "the equation entirely obscures disturbances . . . arising out of a change in the proportion in which deposits are held for the different purposes distinguished above as Savings, Business or Income" seems to me exactly the reverse of the truth.

To give an example: If business becomes more closely integrated[1] than before, a certain amount of money which has been held for the purpose of making payments between firms will become redundant, and will (under normal conditions of trade) presumably be spent or invested in ways which will increase the aggregate of incomes and raise the price-level of output.   There has been no change in the general velocity of circulation of money, or, in other words, in the proportion of annual transactions which people wish to have enough money on hand to conduct; for the volume of transactions has diminished *pari passu* with the volume of business deposits.   But there has

---

[1] In view of the attention attracted by Dr. Hayek's analysis, which tends to a confusion of the two things, it may be as well to state that there is no necessary connection between a change in the degree to which business is integrated, and a change in the degree to which it uses "capitalistic" or "roundabout" methods of production.

been an increase in the velocity of circulation of money *against output,* in other words a decline in the proportion of annual output which people wish to have enough money on hand to purchase. The initiating change has been a change in business practice, not in habits regarding the disbursement of income; but that does not mean that there is no connection between it and the behaviour of the price-level of output. The "Cambridge equation" seems to me well designed to bring out this connection,—and to suggest that a change of this kind calls *prima facie* for compensatory action on the part of the monetary authority.

3

(2) Mr. Keynes' second proposition is concerned not with the *type of transaction-flow* which can properly be brought into relation with the stock of money, but with the *type of index number* which can properly be brought into relation with the stock of money and the flow of money respectively. We can therefore legitimately examine it by means of a simplified case in which the flow of transactions is identical with the flow of real income or output.

Let the annual output be 200 units of wheat and 200 units of cloth. A unit of each commodity is the amount which is sold for £1 in the base period. Let people desire to keep enough money on hand to purchase a year's output of wheat and six months' output of cloth. Then the money stock is £300, of which £200 is "held against" wheat and £100 is "held against" cloth. The Fisher equation $(MV = RP)$ is $300.\frac{4}{3} = 400.1$, and its Marshall counterpart $(M = KRP)$ is $300 = \frac{3}{4}.400.1$. The community's "real balances" KR are the equivalent of nine months' output.

Now, for some extraneous reason, let the price of wheat double, the monetary authority obligingly providing the community[2] with so much extra money as is needed to enable it to increase the money "held against" wheat in proportion, i.e. raising the money stock from

---

[2] This seems to be the procedure visualised by Mr. Keynes. "A rise or fall in the price of certain articles causes a greater fluctuation in the amount of the cash-balances of the community than a similar movement in the price of other articles which give rise to an equal volume of cash-transactions" (*op. cit.,* 77–8).

£300 to £500. The price of cloth remains unaltered. If we weight our index number in the ordinary way, namely according to the relative magnitude of transactions in the two commodities in the base period, we shall weight them both equally, and the new price-level is $\frac{3}{2}$. The Fisher equation becomes $500.\frac{6}{5} = 400.\frac{3}{2}$, and its Marshall counterpart becomes $500 = \frac{5}{6}.400.\frac{3}{2}$.

What has happened? The average velocity of circulation of money has by common consent been reduced, because the new money is being devoted to a use in which money is relatively sluggish. But it is simply stating the same fact in other words to say that the proportion of annual output which people wish to have enough money on hand to purchase is correspondingly increased, or that the community's "real balances" (KR) have become the equivalent of ten months' output instead of nine. Our index number is perfectly designed to reveal this state of affairs.

According to Mr. Keynes we ought, for the purposes of the Marshall equation, to weight wheat twice as heavily as cloth in our index number, because in the base period it occasioned twice as big a holding of money balances. If we do this, the price-level will become $\frac{5}{3}$ instead of $\frac{3}{2}$, the Marshall equation will be $500 = \frac{3}{4}.400.\frac{5}{3}$, and the community's real balances will be unchanged, though its money balances would now buy ten months' output instead of nine. Here, surely, is a great and unhelpful paradox! I cannot resist the conclusion that Mr. Keynes' "cash balances standard" is an unnecessary and confusing complication.

4

Before, however, finally dismissing it as such, we must have regard to one use which Mr. Keynes makes of the distinction which he draws between it and the "cash transactions standard," weighted in the ordinary way. There is, as he points out (*op. cit.*, pp. 237–9) an interval between the date at which a given price is quoted in the market and the date at which the transaction based on this quotation is actually performed. Since people's monetary requirements depend on the transactions to be performed in the quite near future, there is also an interval, but not such a long one, between the date at which a price is quoted and the date at which it affects monetary requirements. For instance, price-quotations made in March may affect monetary requirements in June and monetary transactions in September; while in the last-named month monetary requirements are being influenced by price-quotations made in June, which will influence monetary transactions in December. Hence, if prices are continually rising, the price-level which is relevant to the monetary requirements of September (viz., the price-level quoted in June) will be higher than the price-level relevant to the monetary transactions of September (viz., the price-level quoted in March). This is perfectly true: but it does not mean that we need to use an index number weighted on any other than the ordinary plan. It only means that if the P of our equations is derived from price *quotations,* we must be careful to bring it into relation with other quantities which are relevant to it, and not with other quantities which are not. As regards the Fisher equation, the best way seems to me to be to introduce the concept of "latent money,"—money which does not exist but is affecting the quoted price-level as if it did exist,—the equation referring to a period six months (in the case supposed) later than the date of the price quotation. As regards the Marshall equation, it seems simpler to bring P into relation with the *contemporary* stock of money only, the proportion of annual output (or other flow) over which people wish to keep present command in the form of money being reduced by the fact that they have a confident expectation of being able to get hold of more money by the time they require it. It is of great importance that the result of the intrusion of latent money (as of the increase of any other substitute for real money, such as barter or book-credit) is to destroy the identity which normally exists between a Marshall fraction of the K type and the inverse of the analogous velocity of circulation, causing the former to sink below the latter. But there is no need for, or help in, a specially constructed index number to show that this is so.

A numerical example may help to make the matter plain.[3] For

---

[3] It is assumed (following Mr. Keynes) that the monetary authority is completely complaisant in conforming to and implementing the price-decisions made in the market.

simplicity the volume of transactions is taken as constant at 100 (in fact, of course, in such a period, it is likely to increase somewhat).

	Quoted Price-level (Previously 10)	Money Stock	Value of Transactions	Recorded Velocity of Circulation	Marshall Fraction
March.....	10	100	1,000	10	$\frac{1}{10}$
June.......	15	100	1,000	10	$\frac{1}{15}$
September..	20	150	1,000	$2\frac{2}{3}$	$\frac{3}{40}$
December...	25	200	1,500	$1\frac{5}{2}$	$\frac{2}{25}$
March.....	30	250	2,000	8	$\frac{1}{12}$

Equations relevant to June price-level and money stock (December transactions). $M' =$ latent money.

$$(M + M')V = TP.$$
$$(100 + 100)\,1\tfrac{5}{2} = 100.15.$$
$$M = KTP.$$
$$100 = \tfrac{1}{15}.100.15.$$

10

THE VALUE OF MONEY*

By A. C. Pigou‖

I

The writing of this article has been suggested by Professor Anderson's recent volume on the *Value of Money*. But the article is not directly concerned with the content of that volume. For Professor Anderson's discussion is mainly vigorous controversy, and my view is that controversy on this subject is no longer necessary. The "quantity theory" is often defended and opposed as tho it were a definite set of propositions that must be either true or false. But in fact the formulae employed in the exposition of that theory are merely devices for enabling us to bring together in an orderly way the principal causes by which the value of money is determined. As to what these principal causes are, competent writers of all schools are, I venture to think, really in substantial agreement. The logical machinery of the "quantity theory" has set them by the ears because they have not always realized that it is merely machinery. It is as tho economists who expressed the general theory of value with the help of diagrams should quarrel with those who prefer language or those who prefer algebra. All ways are merely devices for facilitating an orderly arrangement of ideas; and, tho a debate about their comparative convenience and helpfulness is, of course, legitimate, to suppose that this debate implies any fundamental disagreement about the real causes at work would be a grave mistake. Into this mistake, as it seems to me, controversial writers about the "quantity theory" have too frequently fallen; and, therefore, at the outset I insist that,

The Quarterly Journal of Economics, **32** (1917–18), 38–65. Reprinted, by the courtesy of Harvard University Press and the author, without change from the original text.

‖ King's College, Cambridge.

tho the machinery that I shall suggest in the following pages is quite different from that elaborated by Professor Irving Fisher in his admirable *Purchasing Power of Money,* and, as I think, more convenient, I am not in any sense an "opponent" of the "quantity theory" or a hostile critic of Professor Fisher's lucid analysis. He has painted his picture on one plan, and I paint mine on another. But the pictures that we both paint are of the same thing, and the witness of the two, as to what that thing in essentials is, substantially agrees.

II

By money I mean for the purposes of this discussion legal-tender money; and by the value of money I mean the exchange value of a unit of it. The question whether it is proper to use the term value in this sense—a question which Professor Anderson discusses with great elaboration—seems to me to be concerned with linguistic suitability and to have no scientific importance. Economists in general use value to mean "exchange value," and I see no need to invent a new term. But the "exchange value of a unit of money" cannot, of course, be left without further definition. Exchange value in terms of what? The answer, of course is, in terms of commodities. But commodities or, as some prefer to say, "commodities in general," is a vague phrase. In the chapter on "The Measurement of the National Dividend" in my *Wealth and Welfare* the problem of its proper interpretation for various purposes was discussed. For the present purpose it is convenient to adopt a plan similar to that employed by Dr. Marshall in his unpublished paper on the "Pure Theory of Foreign Trade," which has been reproduced in Professor Pantaleoni's *Pure Economics,* and to assume that the value of all commodities other than money in terms of one another is determined independently of the value of money. On this assumption, the value of any combination of commodities in general can be cited in terms of any single commodity. The aggregate of all commodities is represented by so many bushels of wheat; and the value of money by the number of bushels of wheat which a unit of it will purchase. This value is governed, like the value of everything else, by the general conditions of demand and supply. An investigation of the causes upon which the value of money depends means, therefore, just as it would do if we were concerned with lead or tobacco, a detailed analysis of these two groups of forces.   To this analysis, therefore, we may at once proceed.

III

The Demand for Legal Tender Money

In the ordinary course of life, people are continually needing to make payments in discharge of obligations contracted in terms of legal-tender money.   Some of these payments have to be made across the counter, as when commodities are bought for cash; others at some specified date after purchase, as when they are bought on three-months' bills; others at some unspecified date after purchase, as when they are bought vaguely on credit.   Besides the flow of obligations that are thus continually maturing against them, most people have also a flow of claims that are similarly maturing in their favor.   But the obligations and the claims that become due at any moment seldom exactly cancel one another, and the difference has to be met by the transfer of *titles to legal tender*.   Under this name I include actual legal tender (for practical purposes token coins may be reckoned as part of this), bank notes, and bank balances against which checks can be drawn.   If a person is unable to meet his obligations from these sources when they fall due, he will certainly be inconvenienced and will possibly be rendered bankrupt.   Hence everybody is anxious to hold enough of his resources in the form of titles to legal tender both to enable him to effect the ordinary transactions of life without trouble, and to secure him against unexpected demands, due to a sudden need, or to a rise in the price of something that he cannot easily dispense with.   For these two objects, the provision of convenience and the provision of security, people in general (I do not here include bankers, whose special position is discussed later) elect to hold in the form of titles to legal tender the aggregate value of a given quantity of wheat.   In other words, they offer a demand price per unit for titles to legal tender equal to the aggregate quantity of wheat that they have determined upon, divided by the aggregate number of legal tender units for which titles are forthcoming.   There is thus constituted at any given moment a definite demand schedule for titles to legal-tender money. Let R be the total resources, expressed in terms of wheat, that are enjoyed by the community (other than its bankers) whose position is being investigated; k the proportion of these resources that it chooses to keep in the form of titles to legal tender; M the number of units of legal tender, and P the value, or price, per unit of these titles in terms of wheat. Then the demand schedule just described is represented by the equation $P = \dfrac{kR}{M}$. When k and R are taken as constant, this is, of course, the equation of a rectangular hyperbola.

From the demand schedule for titles to legal tender is *derived* a demand schedule for legal tender itself. The derivation is as follows. The titles to legal tender that people hold are kept in two forms, partly in actual money in their pockets and tills, and partly in bank balances. If bankers with whom these balances are deposited retained the whole of them in legal tender in their vaults, the derived demand schedule for legal tender would be exactly the same as the direct demand schedule for titles to legal tender. In fact, however, bankers only keep a money reserve equivalent to a part of the balances that they hold for customers. Hence, whereas that part of their immediately available resources which people choose to keep in cash, constitutes a demand for actual legal tender equal to the corresponding demand for titles to it, that part which they keep in bank notes and bank balances gives rise to a demand different from itself, and smaller. The magnitude of the total derived demand depends, therefore, in part, upon the choice that the general body of the public exercises in this matter. The derived demand schedule for actual legal tender is capable, like the original demand schedule, of being represented by an algebraic formula. Let c be the proportion of his titles to legal tender that the representative man chooses to keep in actual legal tender (including token coins), so that $(1 - c)$ is the proportion that he keeps in bank notes and bank balances; and let h be the proportion of actual legal tender that bankers choose to keep against the notes and balances held by their customers. Then the derived equation of demand for actual legal tender will be:

$$P = \frac{kR}{M} \{c + h(1 - c)\}, \text{ or } M = \frac{kR}{P} \{c + h(1 - c)\}.$$

When c and h, as well as k and R are taken as constants, this equation, like the simpler one from which it is derived, is the equation of a rectangular hyperbola.

It cannot be denied that this formula has a somewhat arid appearance. I propose, therefore, to clothe the dry bones by a brief separate study of each of the variables which it includes. First consider R, representing the community's total real resources of commodities, expressed, for convenience, in terms of so many bushels of wheat. My formula shows that, other things being equal, the larger this variable is, the higher will be the demand schedule for money. It is, therefore, important to observe that R is likely in general to be increased by developments that bring the forces of nature more effectively under man's control; such as an increase in the efficiency of the people individually, or an increase in their collective efficiency either through mechanical inventions or through inventions in business organization. This generalization does not, however, hold good of inventions that facilitate the production of commodities for which the elasticity of demand is less than unity; for an increase in the quantity of these commodities involves a decrease in the aggregate quantity of "wheat value" in existence, and so tends to lessen the quantity of "wheat value" that people need to keep in the form of titles to legal tender. This becomes obvious if we take an extreme case and conceive of a commodity whose quantity is increased with the result of reducing its aggregate wheat value to zero.

Secondly, consider the variable k. When the aggregate wheat value of the community's resources is given, the quantity of wheat value kept in the form of titles to legal tender is determined by the *proportion* of his resources that the average man chooses to keep in that form. This proportion depends upon the convenience obtained and the risk avoided through the possession of such titles, by the loss of real income involved through the diversion to this use of resources that might have been devoted to the production of future commodities, and by the satisfaction that might be obtained by consuming resources immediately and not investing them at all. These three uses, the production of convenience and security, the production of commodities, and direct consumption, are rival to one another. For our present purpose, the use of immediate consumption need not be particularly considered. Its presence mitigates, but never does more than mitigate, the effect of the principal causes with which we have to deal. Practically, the critical question for a business man—and the same class of question has to be asked by everybody—is, as Professor Carver well observes: "will it pay better to have one more dollar in his cash drawer and one less on his shelves, or will it pay better to have one less dollar in his cash drawer and one more on his shelves."[1]

It is easily seen that the satisfaction yielded by successive units of resources devoted to future production diminishes as the number of units so devoted is increased. For nobody denies that the satisfaction a man obtains from the one hundredth unit of any commodity is likely to be less than he obtains from the ninetieth, and nobody supposes that production in general obeys the law of increasing return in a measure adequate to counteract this tendency and to cause the *fruits* of the tenth unit of resources invested in production to yield more satisfaction than those of the ninth. An exactly analogous proposition holds good of the satisfaction yielded by successive units of resources held in the form of titles to legal tender. So far as money is desired as a means for facilitating exchange, this is well shown in the following passage: "Some exchanges could scarcely be made at all without the use of money. In these cases the utility of money is very high, and would equal the utility of the exchanges themselves; that is, the advantage of being able to exchange, over the disadvantage of not being able to make the exchange at all. Some exchanges could only be made with great difficulty without money, in which cases the utility of money would be considerable. Some other exchanges could be made with comparatively little difficulty, in which cases the utility of money would be inconsiderable. And some exchanges could be made as easily without money as with it, in which cases the utility of money will be *nil*."[2] Reasoning of the same general kind clearly holds good

---

[1] *American Economic Association Papers* (1905), 131.

[2] Carver, The concept of an economic quantity, *Quarterly Journal of Economics* (May 1907), 443–44.

in so far as money is desired as a means of providing security.   Thus the curves that represent the desire for resources to be used in production and in money respectively both slope downward; and resources will be devoted to the two uses up to the point at which the last unit of resources devoted to each of them yields the same quantity of satisfaction.   It follows that, other things being equal, the variable k will be larger the less attractive is the production use and the more attractive is the rival money use of resources.

The chief factor upon which the attractiveness of the production use depends is the expected fruitfulness of industrial activity.   If a man understands that, in consequence of mechanical inventions or of an expected rise in the prices of the commodities in whose production he is engaged, a given quantity of resources invested in his business will yield an abnormally large return, he will be more anxious than he otherwise would be to devote resources to production.   In the converse case he will be less willing than he otherwise would be to do this.

The factors which determine the attractiveness of the money use are more complex.   The most obvious is the convenience to be got from a holding of titles to legal tender in the ordinary business of life. This partly depends upon the intervals of time at which people are accustomed to be paid for their services.   If, for example, a man is paid £365 once a year, he is practically certain, on the average, to keep a larger proportion of his resources in titles to legal tender than he would do if he was paid the same amount in daily proportions of £1 each.[3]   It also depends in part upon how far the organization of industry is adapted to allow the discharge of debts without resort, direct or indirect, to titles to legal tender.   The importance of this consideration is well brought out in Sir Theodore Morison's account of the Industrial Organization of an Indian Province.   "A very large number of exchanges," he writes, "were in old days effected by means of barter.   Rents were paid in kind, and debts between the cultivator and the money-lender, tho reckoned in terms of money, were usually settled in grain.   The wages of field laborers and of the village artisans were paid almost entirely in grain, and it was therefore possible for the cultivator in former days to make a large number of transactions in

---

[3] Cf. Fisher, *The Purchasing Power of Money*, 84.

the year without employing money at all. Now that the self-sufficiency of the village is being impaired, the occasions for the use of money are largely increased. The tenant usually pays his rent in money; he also employs money, along with bundles of corn, to pay his laborers; a few articles of foreign manufacture are coming into common use, which are purchased at fairs, and for them money is the only payment accepted."[4] In the modern industrial world, the tendency is, perhaps, on the whole, in the opposite direction. There seems to exist a good deal of cross trade between firms worked by means of book-debts. When a firm buys from one party and sells to another, bills drawn on his debtor are passed forward to his creditor, so that titles to legal tender are required to discharge only one bill instead of two of a given amount. There are also in vogue many elaborate devices, such as the Stock Exchange Clearing House and the Railway Clearing House, for carrying still further this method of economizing the use of bank money, while on the established settling days debts are so far cancelled that only differences have to be directly met. Against these influences has to be set the tendency to specialization of processes to different firms, involving, as it does, an increase in the number of transactions that have to be undertaken prior to the completion of many finished goods. Under the same head falls the increasing volume of speculation and other business indirectly associated with industry that is done on the stock exchanges, and for which, of course, a money basis is needed.

But the attractiveness of the money use does not depend only on the contribution which a holding of titles to legal tender makes to business convenience. It is also affected by another important circumstance. Any holding of titles to legal tender is always capable of being exchanged against some quantity of commodities. Clearly, if it is expected that the quantity of commodities for which, say, a note for one pound can be exchanged will be greater a year hence than it is now, the inducement to hold pound notes now is increased; and, conversely, if it is expected that a pound will buy fewer commodities a year hence, it is diminished. Thus any expectation that general prices are going to fall increases people's desire to hold

[4] Industrial Organization of an Indian Province, 306.

titles to legal tender; and any expectation that they are going to rise has the contrary effect. For this reason the suspicion that a nation will fail to maintain or to restore the full convertibility of a paper currency, immediately lowers the demand for that currency in terms of things, and so raises prices, in terms of that currency.

So far, of the causes that operate by way of the variable k. Consider next the variable c, $i.$ $e.$, the proportion of their titles to legal tender that people choose to keep in actual legal tender in their own pockets and tills. The choice between actual cash and bank notes and bank balances is determined in the main by custom and convenience, and people's habits in this matter are not in all countries fixed. Thus, Professor Irving Fisher writes of recent conditions in America: "Some day in the future, when the use of checks has grown up to its work, it would not be strange if the ratio of checks to money should remain fairly constant. At present, however, we are passing through a long transition period during which the device of using checks instead of money is being extended with prodigious rapidity. This is the dominant feature of the present situation and forms the chief basis of the forecast here attempted. All nations—even those which have used checks for generations—are making a continually larger use of checks relatively to money."[5]

Leaving aside bank notes as being relatively unimportant, we may note the following points. First, the proportion of titles to legal tender held in the form of actual legal tender will be smaller the more people have banking accounts, and, therefore, are *able* to keep their titles to legal tender in the rival form of bank balances. The more people have banking accounts the more widespread and the better organized the banking system will become. The development of branch banks and the cultivation of small accounts in turn causes the numbers of the bank-using public to increase. The chief reason why the proportion of coin to bank money used in India is so much larger than in England is that in the former country the banking system is very imperfectly developed.

Secondly, the proportion of titles kept in actual legal tender will be smaller the more readily checks are accepted in ordinary transac-

---

[5] *American Economic Review* (September 1912), 547–48.

tions—and readiness to accept them becomes more widespread as small tradesmen come to have banking accounts and high-waged employés follow their example. Thirdly, this proportion will be smaller the longer shopkeepers allow their accounts to run before requiring payment; for it is much more convenient to pay large sums by check than coin. The average size of accounts is greater, the larger the proportion of rich people in the community,—the very rich pay scarcely anything in coin. It is also greater the more widespread is the custom of paying for purchases through accounts covering a series of purchases, or through deposits paid in advance rather than over the counter at the moment of purchase. Lastly, the proportion will be smaller, the more convenient and less costly is the machinery by which payments can be made direct from bank balances, without resort to actual legal tender, by the paying public. The fact that checks are subject to a small tax is relevant in this connection. Of course, if there is any question of the solvency of banks, the risk of loss, when titles to legal tender are kept in the form of bank balances, strongly favors the alternative form—an incident that in some panics, like the 1907 panic in the United States, may become of very great significance.

There remains the variable h, that is the proportion of actual legal tender that the banking system chooses to keep against its liabilities to customers. The influences that determine this proportion are similar to those that determine the variable k, i. e., the proportion of their resources that people in general (other than bankers) choose to keep in the form of titles to legal tender. Here, as there, the governing factors are, on the one hand, the convenience obtained and the risk obviated by resources held in the form of a money reserve, and, on the other hand, the advantage that is sacrificed when resources are locked up in this form. It is obvious that the advantage sacrificed is determined by that general productivity of industrial investment that has already been referred to in connection with the variable k. The convenience and security that banking reserves provide are, therefore, all that need to be discussed here. The benefit under these heads that a given quantity of resources will yield depends on the following principal considerations.

The first factor is the internal organization of the banking system for economizing the need for large reserves. Means to this end are the elaborate arrangements of clearing houses, by which cross-debts are balanced against one another, and the further device of a banker's bank associated with the clearing house in such wise that the net balances that remain over after the process of cancellation is complete can be discharged by simple entries in the books of the said bank. Arrangements of this kind not only save the use of coin directly, but also indirectly. By bringing the banks together into some sort of unity, they enable their reserves to be used at need for mutual support. This means that the aggregate reserves, instead of having to guard against the sum of the maximum separate drains that are likely to be made upon the several banks individually, need only guard against the maximum drain that is likely to be made upon the sum of these banks collectively. A much smaller aggregate reserve is necessary for the latter than for the former of these purposes. Hence a one-reserve system can be worked much more economically than a many-reserve system. The English banks as a body, because of the central-ization of a large part of their ultimate reserves in the Bank of England, can safely keep these reserves much smaller relatively to their liabilities than the American banks, at all events before the recent reforms, were able to do.

The second factor is the kind of claims of which banks' liabilities are predominantly made up. If a large part of them are claims by foreign depositors, who are likely to require legal tender for shipment abroad, or by native depositors engaged extensively in foreign trade, actual legal tender—when the legal tender is also an internationally recognized money substance such as gold—is liable to be called for in ways that no elaboration of clearing house or other devices can prevent.

The third factor is the proportion in which bankers' liabilities are in bank notes in the hands of the public or in bank balances. This is important, because in modern states the law tends to insist rigorously upon the retention of large reserves against notes, while (except in the United States) leaving the question of reserves against deposit accounts to the banks' discretion.

Lastly, account must be taken of the temperament of the people in respect of liability to panic and so on, and of the general state of confidence in the banking system. It is obvious that a new bank among an impulsive people will need to keep a larger proportionate reserve than an old and well-tried bank among an unemotional people.

This completes the discussion by which I have aimed at clothing the dry bones of my equation of demand. It remains to explain the relation in which that equation stands to the "equation of exchange" made familiar in the "quantity theory"—an equation, by the way, which would itself be more properly described as an equation of demand. At first sight, it might be thought that the two formulae are in violent conflict. But, in fact, it is easy to show that they are perfectly consistent with one another. In order to do this, it is not necessary to complicate the argument by comparing them in their fully elaborated forms. They are both much simplified when abstraction is made of the operations of banks. When this is done, my formula reduces to $P = \dfrac{kR}{M}$. It is enough to exhibit the relation between this and the corresponding simplified formula of the "quantity theory." In that formula T represents total transactions, M the number of units of titles to legal tender, V the velocity of circulation of these units, and π the price per unit of "commodities" in money. The "equation of exchange" then is $\pi = \dfrac{MV}{T}$. Now since P in my equation is the price of money in terms of things and π in the "quantity theory" equation is the price of things in terms of money, it follows that $P = \dfrac{1}{\pi}$.

Hence $\dfrac{kR}{M} = \dfrac{T}{MV}$ or $kV = \dfrac{T}{R}$.

Evidently in given conditions of production and trade $\dfrac{T}{R}$ may be taken as a constant. It follows that kV also is a constant. So soon as this is perceived, the relation in which the two equations stand to one another is at once apparent. When people decide to keep half as much of their resources as before in the form of titles to legal tender, this *means* that the velocity of circulation is doubled. This has been explained very clearly by Dr. Marshall: "If a person, whether in the course of trade or for his own use, buys for currency goods and services of the value of ten thousand pounds of wheat during a year, and if he retains on the average purchasing power in the form of currency to the value of one hundred pounds, then so far as he is concerned, currency will circulate one hundred times in the year. If he keeps twice as much purchasing power, that is, to the value of two hundred pounds of wheat, then currency will, so far as he is concerned, circulate fifty times in the year, that is, only half as rapidly. Thus generally, *ceteris paribus*, any increase in the ready purchasing power that people choose to keep will diminish proportionately rapidity of circulation, and *vice versa*."

It is thus evident that there is no conflict between my formula and that embodied in the quantity theory. But it does not follow that there is nothing to choose between them. Mine is not, of course, any "truer" than its rival. They are both equally true. The claim that I make on behalf of mine is merely that it is a somewhat more effective engine of analysis. It focusses attention on the proportion of their resources that people choose to keep in the form of titles to legal tender instead of focussing it on "velocity of circulation." This fact gives it, as I think, a real advantage, because it brings us at once into relation with volition—an ultimate cause of demand—instead of with something that seems at first sight accidental and arbitrary. But to argue in the air about the merits of a machine is always a waste of time. I offer this specification of it in order that those interested in monetary theory may test its powers in actual work upon concrete problems.

IV

THE SUPPLY OF LEGAL-TENDER MONEY

The formula set out in the preceding section refers exclusively to demand. But in order to determine the value of anything an equation of supply also is needed. What this is depends upon the substance which a country decides to use as money and the rules under which it is manufactured. The principal alternatives are as follows:

First, the quantity of legal-tender money available at any time may be fixed, as in a country making use exclusively of inconvertible paper notes, by the arbitrary decision of the government. Under an arrangement of this kind, the supply curve of legal tender is obviously a vertical straight line fixed in whatever position the government may choose. Its equation is $M = D$, where D is a constant.

Secondly, some part of the total quantity of legal tender money may be arbitrarily fixed. In practice this is the more usual arrangement. In Germany and France, alongside of the gold currency, many old silver coins circulate as full legal tender. In Germany these amount to some twenty million pounds.[6] In the United States, "gold and silver are legal tender equally with greenbacks, or government notes issued during the Civil War, and the treasury notes issued against the deposits of silver bullion under the Sherman Law of 1890."[7] In Austria inconvertible paper circulates alongside of gold. Under these arrangements the shape of the supply curve is the same as it would be if the arbitrarily regulated part of the supply did not exist; but the whole curve is pushed further to the right. Its equation is $M = \{D + f(P)\}$. It is thus less elastic than it would be in the absence of the arbitrarily fixed part of the circulation.

Thirdly, the whole of the legal tender money in the country may consist of one substance coined freely at the mint, and there may be no difficulties in the way of the import and export of this substance. In that event the quantity of legal tender available in any country in response to a given wheat price per unit is equal to the quantity of the substance in the world *minus* the quantity absorbed in other uses, whether these uses be the currencies of other countries or the arts or anything else whatever. This quantity is determined by the supply curve of the world minus the demand curves for these other uses. The supply of the world may, when the monetary substance is a precious metal, be treated, for periods of moderate length, as practically constant; for the aggregate stock in the world is very large relatively to the total annual output, and, therefore, *a fortiori* relatively to such changes—themselves, from the nature of the industry, probably slow-working—in the annual output as may be induced by changes in (wheat) price. The demand for the currencies of other

---

[6] Pierson, *Principles of Economics*, vol. 1, 425.

[7] Kinley, *Money*, 50.

nations is regulated in the way described in the preceding division of this article. The demand curve for the arts depends for its shape and position, like any ordinary demand curve, upon fashion, taste, the availability of substitutes, such as silver, to fulfil like artistic purposes, and so on. It relates, of course, to the total money substance employed in the arts, and not merely to the new supplies of it absorbed into them during the year. The supply curve of legal tender in the country in which we are interested is derived from the above factors.

Fourthly, the money may consist of two substances freely coined and bound together by some legal tie, as under bimetallism and symmetallism. From the present point of view, the principal difference between moneys of this type and the simpler money discussed above is that, since there is a larger stock of money substance available, a given rise in wheat price is likely to call out a larger additional supply than would otherwise be forthcoming. That is to say, the supply is likely to be more elastic.

Fifthly, the money may consist of one substance coined under a seigniorage. Its supply price is then a compound of the cost of the substance contained in the coin and the seigniorage charge. Therefore, a smaller weight of coined money will be forthcoming at a given wheat price per unit than would be forthcoming if there were no seigniorage. Let the seigniorage be £s per £100, and the equation of supply of the substance of which coins are made, $M = \phi(P)$. Then the corresponding equation of supply of actual coins will be

$$M = \frac{100 - s}{100} \phi(P).^{[8]}$$

Sixthly, the supply may be regulated by an act of state, but the state may be guided by the purpose of maintaining a constant ratio

---

[8] This implies that the wheat value of coined money under seigniorage is higher than it would have been in the absence of seigniorage, but higher by somewhat less than the amount of the seigniorage. This result is not appreciably effected by the policy the state adopts in respect of the gold collected in seigniorage. Whether the state coins it or sells it uncoined, makes no difference at all. Even should the state destroy it, the difference would be imperceptible, since the amount of it is very small relatively to the total supply.

of exchange between its money and that of foreign countries with which it has important trade relations. This is the familiar gold exchange standard. Under it the supply of money in the country under review is a function of the commodity (wheat) price of foreign money, falling as this rises, and rising as it falls. The value of the native money fluctuates in just the same way as it would do, if it consisted of freely minted coins of the substance used in foreign money, but its average level is somewhat lower since less of this substance is required in the currencies of the world as a whole.

Lastly, the supply may be regulated by the state on the plan recommended by Professor Irving Fisher: that is to say, in such a way as to keep its value constant in terms, not of a foreign currency, but of commodities in general at home.

All these various systems of supply are possible and an interesting study might be undertaken into their comparative advantages. That, however, does not fall within my purpose. Nor shall I even attempt to exhibit the diverse ways in which the choice that is made between them affects the special problem of the value of money. Since this article is designed merely to elucidate a method and does not profess to be exhaustive, my discussion will be concentrated upon a single dominant system of money—namely, the simple gold standard, that put third in the preceding classification.

V

DEMAND AND SUPPLY

It is a familiar proposition in pure economic theory that, when the equations of demand and supply for any commodity are given, the value of that commodity is found by their solution: or, in geometrical language, that when the demand curve and the supply curve are given, its value is measured by the ordinate drawn from their point of intersection. This analysis provides a kind of scaffolding by the help of which the causes that bring about changes in value can be investigated. But that investigation is never a simple one, and, when its subject-matter is the value, not of an ordinary consumable commodity, but of money, the difficulties to be overcome are exceptionally great. The most important of these have now to be set out.

First, in the real world we cannot always hope to meet only with causes that act either on demand alone or on supply alone. The same cause may easily act upon both. Certain sorts of inventions, for example, may at once facilitate production generally, thus raising the demand schedule for money, and also facilitate the extraction of gold from the mines, thus lowering the supply schedule. Naturally the result is different from what it would have been if demand alone or supply alone had been affected. From a short period point of view, a 10 per cent increase in the *production* of gold accompanied by an equal increase in the production of commodities generally, means a percentage increase in the *supply* of gold, much less than the corresponding increase in the *supply* of commodities. Consequently, the effect exercised through demand will be predominant. But, from the standpoint of an indefinitely long period, the stock of gold existing at the beginning must be insignificant compared with the quantity produced during this period. The effects upon production and upon supply are, therefore, substantially equal, and the predominance of the demand side disappears.[9] The way in which these complex effects work themselves out is not, however, my present concern. What I am interested to point out is that in the real world we may have to do, not with a one-handed, but with a two-handed cause.

Secondly, even when the cause that is being studied acts on the side of demand only, it is most improbable that it will operate through one only of the various *foci* of causation that are distinguished in my demand formula. It is of great importance that no misunderstanding should arise upon this point. The analysis which that formula embodies enables us to distinguish and to discuss separately the principal elements out of which the demand schedule for money is made up. It provides, in short, at any moment of time a true *anatomy* of demand. But it does *not* imply that in the actual world changes in the elements that are summarized under the different letters of the formulae occur independently. It is perfectly legitimate to draw a

---

[9] Cf. Edgeworth, *Economic Journal,* vol. 5, 436.

picture of the bones of a child's body, to measure how much each bone contributes to the total height, and, if we will, even to calculate what difference would be made to that height if the length of any given bone were doubled and everything else remained the same. But it is not legitimate—on the contrary it is altogether ridiculous —to proceed on the assumption that, as a matter of fact any one bone will double in length while all the others remain unaltered. For we know that in growth there is a certain harmony and that many of the changes that occur in any one part are the result of general causes that affect other parts also. This is true of the economic body no less than of the human body. A general industrial expansion does not involve merely an expansion of resources—a growth in the variable R. It also involves the establishment or extension of banks and banking facilities, and this means that the proportion in which people use bank money relatively to actual legal tender is increased, or, in other words, that the variable c is diminished. Nor is this all. Industrial expansion, since it carries with it larger real income, may easily involve an increase in the proportion of their resources that people choose to keep in the form of titles to legal tender; for a very poor man cannot afford the luxury of money in hand. If this happens, the same cause that has brought about an increase in the variable R, will have affected the variable k in the same sense. Yet, again, k (the proportion of their resources that the public keep in titles to legal tender) and h (the proportion of actual legal tender that bankers keep against their liabilities) are obviously liable to be affected by common causes. A boom in business confidence lessens, whereas a general apprehension of panic increases, both of them. These connections are, of course, set out merely as illustrations, and do not profess to be exhaustive. They may suffice, however, to drive home the point that the different letters of my demand formula do not represent channels each of them reserved, as it were, for the separate action of special private groups of causes. They are rather public channels along all of which a single cause may operate at the same time.

Thirdly: when it has been ascertained that the demand schedule has been modified in a definite manner, the resultant effect upon the value of money is not a single thing. If the quantity demanded at a given price is doubled, the supply schedule relevant to immediate effects will not be the same as that relevant to later effects. The change in demand introduces a *series* of changes in the value of money, extending over a long period and different at each moment of that period. To the question how the value of money will be affected, no intelligent answer can be given without reference to the time that is supposed to have elapsed since the change occurred. This point is easily illustrated. The immediate effect of a fall in the demand for legal tender—we are supposing that the legal tender substance is gold freely coined—is, of course, to reduce its value in greater or less degree. But, so soon as its value has fallen, a reaction is set up by way of foreign trade. Gold having become less valuable relatively to goods in one country—say England—foreigners are stimulated to send goods to England as a means of purchasing gold, and to take out a greater proportion of their debts in the form of gold. In this way the supply of gold is diminished, and the reduction in its value that was brought about at the first shock is partially cancelled after a comparatively short time. But this is not the only reaction. After a somewhat longer time, the fall in the value of gold will lead to an increased use of that metal in the arts of the world as well as in the currencies of foreign countries. This again obviously checks the fall in the value of gold. If the elasticity of the arts demand is given, the extent to which the presence of that demand checks the fall is clearly greater the greater is the normal consumption of the money substance in the arts relatively to its consumption in the currency of the country affected. If the consumption in the arts is given, it is greater the *more elastic* is the arts demand. Nor is even this all. After a still longer interval, the fall in the value of gold may be expected to lead to a restriction of the industry of gold mining, which the fall will have rendered less profitable. It must, indeed, be recognized that this circumstance acts in a way somewhat less direct than is sometimes supposed. Thus Professor Fisher writes: "It is often taken for granted that, as soon as the gold production begins to subside, the price level will begin to subside also. This is a gross error. The price level does not depend directly on the *rate* of gold production, but on the *stock* of gold and other money. The question is not one of an increasing or decreasing annual production of gold. The inflowing stream of gold is of significance only as it affects the contents of the reservoir into which it flows. A lake does not cease rising the instant the freshet filling it reaches its maximum flow. The lake will still continue to rise *so long as the inflow continues greater than the outflow.* This is often long after the inflow has passed its maximum."[10] Nevertheless, of course, in the end the check to gold output checks the fall in its value.

The above three influences all take a certain time to work themselves out. The first is perhaps more rapid than the second, and is certainly more rapid than the third. It would be convenient if we could rigidly separate off periods relevant to each of the three, and say, for instance, that in the first month, the first only would operate, after three months the second, and after four months the third. This, of course, we cannot do. The influences are partly synchronous and partly successive. Their collective effect is that the supply schedule against which the changed demand impinges displays greater and greater elasticity the longer the period over which the effect of that changed demand is being calculated. It follows that that effect is likely to be most considerable at first, and thereafter to be gradually reduced.

Lastly, account must be taken of the fact that the demand schedule and the supply schedule for money are not strictly independent of one another. Hitherto, I have tacitly ignored this fact. To do so is in accordance with the practice of economists in their preliminary exposition of the general laws of demand and supply. It is usual to write the equation of demand $p = \phi(x)$ and the equation of supply $p = \psi(x)$. But of course all economists are aware that, when the element of time is taken into account, a change in the equation of supply may react to alter the equation of demand, and *vice versa*. After a period of liberal supply, people may have become so accustomed to some commodity that the demand schedule is raised to a higher level than it occupied before; and, conversely,

[10] *American Economic Review* (September 1912), 536.

after a period of keen demand, economies of production may have been developed that will set the supply schedule at a lower level than it formerly occupied. This is the familiar doctrine of infant demands and infant industries. It is not susceptible of translation into demand and supply curves, because three variables are involved, but there is no difficulty about expressing it in algebraic formulae. The reason that more prominence is not given to it in economic text-books is that, for a large number of problems, abstraction can be made of it, and greater simplicity thereby attained, without any great loss of accuracy. But all economists know that for some problems it is of great importance. There is reason to think that one aspect of it —reaction of supply changes upon the position of the demand sched-ule—has considerable significance for monetary theory. First, it is not improbable that a large increase in the supply of money might permanently lower the demand schedule by diminishing the pro-portion (c) of their titles to legal tender that people choose to keep in actual cash. That this is likely to happen is suggested by Professor Cannan in the following passage: "Nor do I think that, if the sovereign would only buy what is now half a sovereign's worth of goods, the currency would be doubled; at present my average holding of gold is about £5, and with the rise of prices supposed, it might increase to £6 or £7, certainly not to £10, since I should prefer to go oftener to the bank for cash than I do now rather than to carry double the amount of gold about."[11] If Professor Cannan is right the reaction which he anticipates would, of course, cause a given increase in the supply of money to reduce its value more than it would do if there was no reaction. Secondly in some circumstances a large increase in the supply of money, by making money relatively cheap in terms of things, may give bankers an opportunity to render the basis of credit more "solid" by building up larger proportionate reserves. There is reason to think that this effect followed in some degree upon the large gold production that took place during the fifteen years preceding the war. A development of this kind means, of course, an increase in the variable h and therefore a rise in the de-mand schedule for money. If it takes place, a given increase in the

[11] *Economic Journal* (September 1910), 396.

supply of money will cause the value of money to fall *less* than it would do if this reaction were lacking.

VI

Conclusion

This completes the summary analysis which I proposed to myself in writing this paper. Anyone who has followed it up to this point must, I think, agree, whether or not he is in accordance with the argument set out, that the elements upon which the value of money, and changes in that value, depend are so numerous and complex that *some* technical device for holding them together in order is absolutely essential. To tackle these problems without tools is like going into a modern battle unhelmeted and unarmed. The "quantity theory" furnishes a tool which in the skilled hands of Professor Irving Fisher has accomplished great things. But less experienced craftsmen need, I think, a better—a more completely fool-proof tool. It is this that, in the preceding pages, I have endeavored to provide.

PART III
MONEY, THE RATE OF INTEREST AND
EMPLOYMENT

11

LIQUIDITY PREFERENCE AND THE THEORY OF INTEREST AND MONEY*

By Franco Modigliani‖

Part I

1. *Introduction*

The aim of this paper is to reconsider critically some of the most important old and recent theories of the rate of interest and money and to formulate, eventually, a more general theory that will take into account the vital contributions of each analysis as well as the part played by different basic hypotheses.

The analysis will proceed according to the following plan:

I. We start out by briefly re-examining the Keynesian theory. In so doing our principal aim is to determine what is the part played in the Keynesian system by the "liquidity preference," on the one hand, and by the very special assumptions about the supply of labor, on the other. This will permit us to distinguish those results that are due to a real improvement of analysis from conclusions that depend on the difference of basic assumptions.

II. We then proceed to consider the properties of systems in which one or both Keynesian hypotheses are abandoned. We thus check our previous results and test the logical consistency of the "classical" theory of money and the dichotomy of real and monetary economics.

III. From this analysis will gradually emerge our general theory of the rate of interest and money; and we can proceed to use this theory to test critically some recent "Keynesian" theories and more

---

* *Econometrica*, 12 (1944), 45–88. Reprinted, by the courtesy of the publisher and the author, without significant change from the original text.
‖ University of Illinois.

especially those formulated by J. R. Hicks in *Value and Capital*[1] and by A. P. Lerner in several articles.

IV. Finally, to make clear the conclusions that follow from our theory, we take issue in the controversial question as to whether the rate of interest is determined by "real" or by monetary factors.

In order to simplify the task, our analysis proceeds in general, under "static" assumptions; this does not mean that we neglect time but only that we assume the Hicksian (total) "elasticity of expectation" to be always unity. In Hicks's own words this means that "a change in current prices will change expected prices in the same direction and in the same proportion."[2] As shown by Oscar Lange, this implies that we assume the "expectation functions," connecting expected with present prices, to be homogeneous of the first degree.[3]

Since all the theories we examine or formulate in this paper are concerned with the determinants of equilibrium and not with the explanation of business cycles, this simplification, although it is serious in some respects, does not seem unwarranted.

2. *Three Alternative Macrostatic Systems*

As a first step in the analysis, we must set up a system of equations describing the relation between the variables to be analyzed. In doing this we are at once confronted with a difficult choice between rigor and convenience; the only rigorous procedure is to set up a complete "Walrasian" system and to determine the equilibrium prices and quantities of each good: but this system is cumbersome and not well suited to an essentially literary exposition such as we intend to develop here. The alternative is to work with a reduced system: we must then be satisfied with the rather vague notions of "physical output," "investment," "price level," etc. In what follows we have chosen, in principle, the second alternative, but we shall check our conclusions with a more general system whenever necessary.

---

[1] J. R. Hicks, *Value and Capital* (Oxford, Oxford University Press, 1939), 331 pp.

[2] *Ibid.*, p. 205.

[3] Cf. O. Lange, "Say's Law: a Restatement and Criticism" in *Studies in Mathematical Economics and Econometrics*, edited by Lange, McIntyre, and Yntema (Chicago, The University of Chicago Press, 1942), pp. 67–8.

The equations of our system are:

$$(1) \qquad M = L(r, Y),$$
$$(2) \qquad I = I(r, Y),$$
$$(3) \qquad S = S(r, Y),$$
$$(4) \qquad S = I,$$
$$(5) \qquad Y \equiv PX,$$
$$(6) \qquad X = X(N),$$
$$(7) \qquad W = X'(N)P.$$

The symbols have the following meaning: Y, money income; M, quantity of money in the system (regarded as given); r, rate of interest; S and I, saving and investment respectively, all measured in money; P, price level; N, aggregate employment; W, money wage rate; X, an index of physical output.[4] We may also define C, consumption measured in money, by the following identity:

$$(8) \qquad C \equiv Y - I.$$

Identity (5) can be regarded as defining money income. There are so far 8 unknowns and only 7 equations; we lack the equation relating the wage rate and the supply of labor. This equation takes a substantially different form in the "Keynesian" system as compared with the "classical" systems.

In the classical systems the suppliers of labor (as well as the suppliers of all other commodities) are supposed to behave "rationally." In the same way as the supply of any commodity depends on the relative price of the commodity so the supply of labor is taken to depend not on the money wage rate, but on the real wage rate. Under the classical hypothesis, therefore, the last equation of the system takes the form:

$$(9a) \quad N = F\left(\frac{W}{P}\right); \text{ or, in the inverse form: } W = F^{-1}(N)P.$$

The function F is a continuous function, although not necessarily monotonically increasing.

---

[4] This system is partly taken from earlier writings on the subject. See especially O. Lange, "The Rate of Interest and the Optimum Propensity to Consume," *Economica*, Vol. 5, N. S. (February 1938), pp. 12–32, and J. R. Hicks, "Mr. Keynes and the 'Classics'; A Suggested Interpretation," *Econometrica*, Vol. 5 (April 1937), pp. 147–59.

The Keynesian assumptions concerning the supply-of-labor schedule are quite different.   In the Keynesian system, within certain limits to be specified presently, the supply of labor is assumed to be perfectly elastic at the historically ruling wage rate, say w_0.   The limits mentioned above are given by equation (9a).   For every value of W and P the corresponding value of N from (9a) gives the maximum amount of labor obtainable in the market.   As long as the demand is less than this, the wage rate remains fixed as w_0.   But as soon as all those who wanted to be employed at the ruling real wage rate w_0/P have found employment, wages become flexible upward.   The supply of labor will not increase unless the money wage rate rises relative to the price level.

In order to write the last equation of the "Keynesian" form of our system, we must express this rather complicated hypothesis in functional form.   Taking (9a) as a starting point, we may write:

(9) $$W = \alpha w_0 + \beta F^{-1}(N)P,$$

where α and β are functions of $N, W, P,$ characterized by the following properties:

(10)
$$\alpha = 1, \quad \beta = 0, \quad \text{for} \quad N \leqq N_0,$$
$$\alpha = 0, \quad \beta = 1, \quad \text{for} \quad N > N_0,$$

where N_0 is said to be "full employment."   Equations and inequalities (10) thus state that, unless there is "full employment" ($N = N_0$), the wage rate is not really a variable of the system but a datum, a result of "history" or of "economic policy" or of both.   Equation (9) then reduces to $W = w_0$.   But after "full employment" has been reached at wage rate w_0, the supply of labor ceases to be perfectly elastic: W becomes a variable to be determined by the system and (9) becomes a "genuine" equation.   We should add that, even in the "Keynesian" system, it is admitted that the wage rate will begin to be flexible downward before employment has reached the zero level: but in order not to complicate equation (9) still further we can, without serious harm, leave the hypothesis in its most stringent form.

For generality we may also use equation (9) as it now stands, as the "supply of labor" function of the "classical" theory.   But instead of conditions (10) we have the identities (for all values of N)

(11) $$\alpha \equiv 0, \qquad \beta \equiv 1.$$

Some remarks are also necessary concerning the "demand for money" equation. According to the "quantity theory of money," the demand for money does not depend on the rate of interest but varies directly with money income. Under this hypothesis equation (1) reduces to

(1a) $$M = kY.$$

By properly combining the equations and conditions written above, we obtain three different systems which we will analyze in turn.

I. A "Keynesian" system consisting of equations (1) to (7) and (9) and conditions (10).

II. A "crude classical" system consisting of equations (1a), (2) to (7), and (9), and identities (11).

III. A "generalized classical" system consisting of the equations listed under II but with (1a) replaced by (1).

3. *A Reconsideration of the Keynesian Theory*

In reconsidering the Keynesian system we shall essentially follow the lines suggested by J. R. Hicks in his fundamental paper, "Mr. Keynes and the 'Classics.' "[5] Our main task will be to clarify and develop his arguments, taking into account later theoretical developments.

Close consideration of the Keynesian system of equations [equations (1) to (7) and (9) to (10)] reveals that the first 4 equations contain only 4 unknowns and form a determinate system: the system of monetary equilibrium. We therefore begin by discussing its equations and its solution.

4. *The Transaction Demand for Money*

In a free capitalistic economy, money serves two purposes: (a) it is a medium of exchange, (b) it is a form of holding assets. There are accordingly two sources of demand for money: the transaction demand for money and the demand for money as an asset. This is the fundamental proposition on which the theory of the rate of interest

---

[5] *Econometrica*, Vol. 5 (April 1937), pp. 147–59.

and money rests; it is therefore necessary to analyze closely each source of demand and the factors that determine it.

The transaction demand for money is closely connected with the concept of the income period. We may define the income period as the (typical) time interval elapsing between the dates at which members of the community are paid for services rendered. We shall assume for the moment that this income period is approximately the same for every individual and that it coincides with the expenditure period.[6]

Each individual begins the income period with a certain income arising out of direct services rendered or out of property and with assets (physical and nonphysical) having a certain market value. In his endeavor to reach the highest level of satisfaction he is confronted with two sets of decisions: (a) he must decide what part of his income he will spend on consumption and what part he will save, (b) he must determine how to dispose of his assets.

The first set of decisions presents no special difficulty of analysis. On the basis of his tastes, his income, and market prices he will make a certain plan of expenditure to be carried out in the course of the income period. The amount of money that is necessary for individuals to carry out their expenditure plans is the *transaction demand for money by consumers,* as of the beginning of the period. The average transaction demand, on the other hand, depends on the rate at which expenditure takes place within the period.[7]

The difference between the individual's money income and the amount he decides to spend in the fashion discussed above is the money value of his savings (dissavings) for the income period. It represents the net increment in the value of his assets.

5. *The Demand for Money as an Asset*

Having made his consumption-saving plan, the individual has to make decisions concerning the assets he owns. These assets, let us

---

[6] This means, for instance, that people are required by custom or contract to pay within the income period for what they have consumed in the period (rent, grocery bill, etc.) or else must rely on "consumers' credit."

[7] Thus if expenditure should proceed at an approximately even rate, it would be one-half the initial demand.

note, consist of property carried over from the preceding income period *plus current savings.*

There are essentially three forms in which people can keep their assets: (a) money, (b) securities,[8] and (c) physical assets.

We shall for the moment eliminate the third alternative by distinguishing between entrepreneurial and nonentrepreneurial decisions. We consider as entrepreneurs individuals who hold assets in physical form; decisions concerning the acquisition or disposal of physical assets will accordingly be treated as entrepreneurial decisions and will be analyzed in connection with the schedule of the propensity to invest [equation (3)]. An individual's decision to acquire directly physical assets (say a house) or to reinvest profits in his enterprise can be split into two separate decisions, a decision to lend (to himself) and a decision to increase his entrepreneurial risk by borrowing (from himself).

We are therefore concerned here exclusively with decisions concerning nonphysical assets and with those factors that influence the choice between the first two alternatives. Our problem is to determine whether there is any reason for individuals to wish to hold some or all of their assets in the form of money and thus to demand money over and above the quantity they need for transactions.

In this respect there is little to add to the exhaustive treatment that this subject has received in recent literature.[9]

There are two properties that all assets, whether physical or not, share in different degrees: liquidity and risk. Following a criterion particularly stressed by Jacob Marschak, we shall define liquidity of an asset in terms of the perfection of the market in which it is traded. An

---

[8] Under the name of securities we include both fixed-income-bearing certificates and common stocks or equities. From the strictly economic point of view, common stocks should perhaps be considered as a form of holding physical assets. For institutional reasons, however, equities have very special properties which make them in many respects more similar to bonds than to physical assets.

[9] See, for instance, J. R. Hicks, *Value and Capital,* Chapters XIII and XIV and *passim;* J. M. Keynes, *The General Theory of Employment, Interest and Money* (New York, Harcourt, Brace and Company, 1936), 403 pp.; Mabel Timlin, *Keynesian Economics* (University of Toronto Press, 1942), Chapters V and VI; etc.

asset is liquid if this market is perfect, i.e., an individual's decision to buy or sell does not affect the price finitely; it is illiquid in the opposite case. It is riskless if the price at which it sells is constant or practically so; it is risky if the price fluctuates widely.

Securities clearly share with money the property of being highly liquid assets. Where there is an organized market, securities will not be significantly inferior to money in this respect. They have, however, two clear drawbacks in comparison with cash:

(a) They are not a medium of exchange. Assets generally accrue in the form of money through savings, and a separate transaction is necessary to transform them into securities. This transaction involves both subjective and objective costs.

(b) They are more risky than money since their market price is not constant. Even the "safest" type of securities, on which the risk of default can be neglected, fluctuates in price as the rate of interest moves. There are, it is true, some types of loans for which this last risk can be neglected, namely very-short-term loans. Let us assume, for the sake of precision, that the money market is open only on the first day of the income period; then the shortest type of loans will be those that mature at the end of said period. These types of assets will not be subject to the risk mentioned under (b) since, by assumption, the rate of interest cannot change while they are outstanding.[10]

It is just for this type of assets, however, that the disadvantage mentioned under (a), namely the cost of investment, weighs more heavily; for the yield they promise for the very short duration of the loan can only be small, so that even a moderate cost is sufficient to wipe it out. If, as is likely, the cost of investment does not rise in proportion to the amount invested, then short loans may be an interesting investment for large sums, but not so for small investors. Thus, if this were the only possible form of investment, we should expect that any fall in the rate of interest, not accompanied by a corresponding fall in the cost of investing, would induce a growing number of potential investors to keep their assets in the form of money, rather than securities; that is to

---

[10] Even if this assumption were relaxed, the possible fluctuations in the rate of interest would be negligible and the extent to which they would affect the present value of the securities mentioned above could be disregarded.

say, we should expect a fall in the rate of interest to increase the demand for money as an asset.

In this respect, securities of longer maturity would appear to be superior, since the yield to be gathered by holding them until maturity is larger, while the cost of acquiring them need not be different. But as the importance of the cost element decreases, the importance of the risk element grows. As is well known, a given change in the rate of interest will affect most the present value of those bonds whose maturity is furthest away. If the only reason for owning assets were to earn the income they produce, these price fluctuations would not be so important. For, as long as the owner is in a position to hold the asset until maturity, there would be only a potential loss, a loss of better opportunities. There can be little doubt, however, that for a large part of the community the main reason for holding assets is as a reserve against contingencies. A form of assets whose value is not certain must be, *ceteris paribus,* inferior to one whose value is certain, namely money.

This very fact, besides, gives an additional reason why bonds of longer maturity should be a less safe form of holding assets. For there is much less certainty about faraway income periods than there is about the near future and the possibility that one will have to realize the assets before their maturity, if any, increases accordingly; while, on the other hand, it becomes increasingly difficult to make reliable forecasts about the level of the rate of interest and the future market value of the assets.

Securities, on the other hand, are clearly superior to money in that they yield an income. The ruling rate of interest measures the remuneration to be obtained by accepting the drawbacks and assuming the risks that are characteristic of securities as compared with money. Or, to look at it from another point of view, it measures the cost of holding money instead of securities in terms of forgone income. Thus a fall in the rate of interest has, in any event, the effect of making cash cheaper and hence more attractive as a form of holding assets.

In addition, several other reasons can be mentioned that cause a low rate of interest to discourage the holding of securities. In the first place, the risk element involved in holding securities becomes more pronounced when the rate of interest is low, for a smaller fall in the capital value of the asset is sufficient to wipe out the income already earned by holding the asset.   Thus, for instance, the smaller the rate of interest, the smaller is the *percentage change* in the rate itself necessary to absorb the yield obtained by holding the asset a given length of time.   Again, it has been pointed out by some authors that, as the rate of interest becomes lower, there is some ground to expect that possible movements will be predominantly in the direction of an increase and therefore unfavorable to the holders of securities.

In conclusion then, the lower the rate of interest, the larger will be the number of owners of assets who will prefer to hold these assets in the form of money for the income period; the demand for money to hold (as distinguished from money to spend, previously considered) or demand for money as an asset is a decreasing function of the rate of interest.   Denoting this demand by D_a, we can write

$$D_a = D_a(r)$$

for the schedule of demand for money to hold.

What can we say about the characteristics of this function?   It must clearly be a monotonically decreasing function of the rate of interest; in addition, however, it must have, in the author's opinion, two important properties:

In the first place, there must be some value of r, say r', such that $D_a(r) = 0$ for $r \geq r'$.   For there must be, for every individual, some minimum net yield per income period that will induce him to part entirely with money as an asset.   Hence, if he can find some type of securities such that by holding them for a given number of income periods he expects to obtain a net yield equal to or larger than the minimum, his demand for money to hold will fall to zero.[11]

---

[11] Let i_0 denote the minimum yield (per income period) at which an individual is ready to hold no assets in the form of money during the period. We may also assume, without being unrealistic, that this minimum yield is the same for each income period.   Suppose that the securities which, in his opinion, present the best opportunity are expected by him to produce a net yield (including capital appreciation) i_0', i_1', $\cdots$, i_n' in periods 1, 2, $\cdots$, n. He will be induced to invest provided there is some value of n for which

$$(1 + i_0')(1 + i_1') \cdots (1 + i_n') \geq (1 + i_0)^n.$$

Since this is true for every individual, there must also be some system of interest rates which is sufficient to reduce the aggregate demand to zero.

The second characteristic is more peculiar. Since securities are an "inferior" way of holding assets, it is generally recognized that there must be some minimum rate of interest, say r'', at which nobody will be willing to hold nonphysical assets except in the form of money. When this level is reached, the demand for money to hold becomes "absolute" and the rate of interest cannot fall any lower. Hence, $D_a'(r) = \infty$ for $r \gtreqless r''$.

6. The Demand for Money: Conclusion

We have so far discussed the demand for money as an asset and the transaction demand for money by individuals; to complete the analysis we must consider the transaction demand by firms. In principle, the same considerations apply here as were stated in connection with individuals' transaction demand. Firms, as well as individuals, have an institutional expenditure-receipt pattern and, given this pattern, the average demand depends on the volume of transactions. We must however recognize that, in the case of firms, generalizations are less meaningful since their expenditure and receipt flows are generally less certain and uniform than for individuals.

From M. Timlin's treatment of this subject (*Keynesian Economics*, Chapter III) it would appear that marginal holders should expect any security to yield the same net income, at least during the current period. This however is correct only if the expectations of all dealers about the future short rates of interest agree with the market expectation as shown by the forward rates established in the market. [The forward rate for the nth income period ahead can always be found by comparing the price of riskless securities maturing n periods ahead with those maturing $(n + 1)$ periods ahead.] But if an individual believes this forward rate to be too high he may acquire the security at once even though he may expect that it will yield in the current period less than some other security. For, assuming that he is right, he will be able to realize his capital gain as soon as the market recognizes its error and there is no telling when this will occur. If he should wait until the next income period and hold for the current one the asset that promises to pay a higher yield, he may lose his chance of making the expected capital gain.

Then, too, we must admit that we may have oversimplified the consumers' transaction demand by assuming that individuals have a rigorously defined plan of expenditure at the beginning of the income period. It may very well be that under more realistic conditions they will desire to carry some cash above the amount they plan to spend as a reserve and to avoid ending the period with a zero cash balance. This however does not substantially affect our argument. All we are interested in establishing is that, within an institutional framework, there must be for any given volume (value) of transactions a certain amount of money that is necessary to carry them out. This amount clearly depends on such institutional factors as the length of the income period and the prevailing customs as to the settlement of current purchases by firms and must therefore be substantially independent of the level of the rate of interest. The level of the rate of interest influences decisions concerning the disposition of assets, and *money needed to carry out transactions planned for the coming income period is not an asset.* In particular, there must be some level of the rate of interest that is sufficient to reduce to zero the demand for money to hold, and hence the total demand to its minimum institutional level which depends on the volume of transactions. As the rate of interest rises above this level, the demand for money will be substantially unaffected and will depend exclusively on the level of money income.

On the basis of these considerations we may, in a first approximation, split the total demand for money into two parts: the demand for money to hold, $D_a(r)$, and the demand for money to spend or for transactions, $D_T(Y)$; and write

(12) $$L(r, Y) = D_a(r) + D_T(Y) = M.$$

This is not really necessary for our argument, but is very useful since it will constantly remind us of the two sources of demand for money and it will permit us to analyze more conveniently the part played by each variable.

With this in mind we shall find it useful to consider the functioning of the money market in which decisions concerning the disposition of nonphysical assets are carried out.

7. The Money Market and the Short-run Equilibrium of the Rate of Interest

There are two ways of looking at this market: (a) in terms of flows (savings and net borrowing) and (b) in terms of stocks. It is from this latter point of view that we shall consider it at this moment.

The supply in this market consists of the stock that is not needed for transactions. On the basis of our first approximation (12), this supply, denoted by S_a, will be

$$S_a = M - D_T(Y),$$

and is determined for any value of the money income and the fixed supply of money.

A position of equilibrium in the money market is reached when a system of interest rates is established at which dealers are willing to hold for the income period all the available supply. Or, from a different angle, the system of interest rates is determined by the price (in terms of foregone income) that dealers are willing to pay to hold assets in the form of money for the coming income period.

This can easily be translated into the usual Marshallian supply and demand apparatus, provided we replace the system of interest rates by a single rate r, as shown in Figure 1.

DD is the demand curve for money to hold, sloping downward and to the right (when the price, the rate of interest, rises, the demand falls, as in the case of ordinary commodities). The vertical lines are various supply curves corresponding to different values of Y and the fixed value of M. As the income increases, the supply falls: hence

$$Y_4 > Y_3 > Y_2 > \cdots.$$

Since a fall in supply causes a rise in price, the graph shows clearly that equation (1) gives r as an increasing function of Y.

The characteristics of the D_a function described above are shown in the graph. We noted that, for $r \geqq r'$ the demand falls to zero; hence the graph of DD joins the vertical axis and coincides with it.

On the other hand, when the rate of interest falls to the level r'', the demand for money to hold becomes infinitely elastic. Any increase in the supply of money to hold now fails to affect the rate of interest, for the owners of the extra supply will either desire to hold this in the form of cash; or else they will find some owners of securities, who, being just indifferent as to holding cash or securities, will be willing to sell without any necessity for bidding up the price of securities (lowering the rate of interest). Thus, in Figure 1, when the interest rate r'' is reached, the graph of DD becomes parallel to the D_a axis; the income

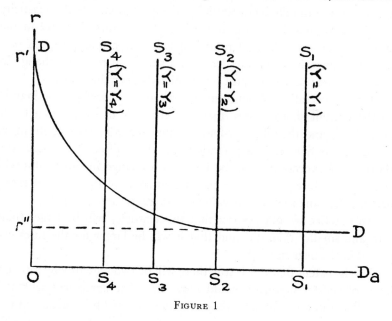

FIGURE 1

corresponding to r'' cannot be more than Y_2; but if income should fall below Y_2 it would not change the interest rate.[12] This situation that plays such an important role in Keynes's *General Theory* will be referred to as the "Keynesian case."

In the diagram we have assumed that there is a single rate of interest r, instead of a whole system of rates for loans of different duration. While it may be assumed that in principle all the rates tend to move in the same direction, we must bear in mind that the extent to

---

[12] From equation (1) we obtain $dr/dY = -L_Y/L_r$ where the subscripts denote partial derivatives. Hence $dr/dY = 0$ if $|L_r| = \infty$.

which a change in the supply of money changes the rates on loans of different maturities depends on the character of interest expectations.

A change in the supply will necessarily affect the short rates (unless the short rate has already reached its minimum). But the extent to which it will affect longer rates depends on the relation between the current spot rate and expected future rates.

To denote the relationship between current and expected rates we may again use the Hicksian elasticity of expectation. If this elasticity is unity, expected short rates move in the same direction and in the same proportion as the spot rate; if it is less than unity, a given percentage change in short rates leads to a smaller percentage change in expected rates; and vice versa for elasticity larger than one.

If the expectations about future short rates are based predominantly on the current shorter rates, then the elasticity of expectation tends toward one and the whole system of rates moves in close conformity. But if dealers have rigid expectations based on different elements, the elasticity of expectation will be low and a change in short rates will affect longer rates only to the extent that some of the discount rates, which determine the present value of the assets, are changed.

In practice we may expect that this elasticity will be larger than zero and smaller than one and that it will be larger for the rates expected in the near future.[13]

To the extent that this is true there will be two reasons why rates on loans of shorter maturity should move in closer agreement with the very short rate: (a) because they are more affected by a change in the current short rate, (b) because the other future short rates (of which they are an average) are more influenced by such a change.

These necessary qualifications do not alter our previous conclusions concerning the determination of equilibrium in the money market. The equilibrium system of interest rates is determined in each period by the condition that the supply of money to hold, which (given M) depends on the transaction demand for money and hence on income, be

---

[13] Denoting by $r_1, r_2, \cdots, r_n$ the short rate of interest anticipated for periods $1, 2, \cdots, n$, we may expect that

$$\frac{\partial r_1}{\partial r_0} > \frac{\partial r_2}{\partial r_0} > \cdots > \frac{\partial r_n}{\partial r_0}.$$

equal to the demand for money to hold. We may therefore proceed to draw the graph of equation (1), $M = L(r, Y)$. This is the LL curve of Figure 3. Any point on this curve shows the equilibrium value of r corresponding to a value of Y and the fixed value of M: it shows therefore positions of possible equilibrium in the money market. We must prove next that only one point on this curve is consistent with the long-run equilibrium of the system.

8. *Saving, Investment, and the IS Function*

The first part of our system yields a second relationship between interest and income. Making use of equations (2) and (3) and the

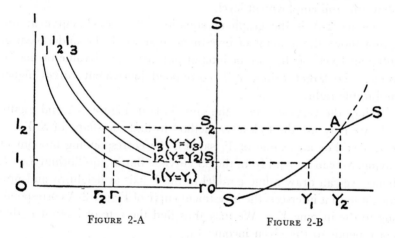

FIGURE 2-A	FIGURE 2-B

equilibrium condition (4) we obtain: $I(r, Y) = S(r, Y)$. In order to gain some idea of the shape of this curve we may again make use of a graphical method illustrated in Figure 2.

Figure 2-B is the graph of equation (3). Since $\partial S / \partial r$ is usually considered small and of unknown sign we have simplified the drawing by eliminating r. This curve describes the relationship between money income and the proportion of it that people choose not to consume. Its position depends on the value of the fixed money wage rate w_0: given the wage rate, to any level of money income there corresponds a certain real income and price level and, therefore, a certain level of money saving. In this diagram Y_2 denotes the highest money income that can be reached with the money wage rate w_0, and A is the full employment relationship between saving and income.

The straight line beginning at A gives the relationship between money income and money saving once full employment has been reached and the second part of condition (10) replaces the first.[14] We have then what is usually called inflation: real income cannot change but money income can rise to any level. As all prices rise simultaneously the amount of real income saved is unchanged while its money value rises in the same proportion as the price level and money income.[15] The dotted curved line, on the other hand, gives a potential relation between S and I if it were possible to raise the real income above the full employment level.

Figure 2-A is the graph of equation (2). Each curve in this graph shows the amount of investment that would be undertaken at different levels of the rate of interest and for a fixed value of the income. To larger values of Y correspond investment curves higher and to the right.

Since the vertical scale is the same in both Figure 2-A and Figure 2-B, we may use the following method to find the shape of $S(Y) = I(r, Y)$: For any value of Y, say Y_1, the corresponding amount of saving, S_1, can be read from the SS curve. But in equilibrium $S = I$, hence we can draw a line parallel to the Y axis at height S_1 and prolong it until it intersects the investment curve of Figure 2-A corresponding to the income Y_1. We may thus find the rate of interest r_1 that corresponds to the given income Y_1.

The character of the relationship between r and Y that emerges from this diagram cannot be established a priori as in the case of the LL curve discussed before. For, as Y increases, S in Figure 2-B increases too, but the corresponding value of r in Figure 2-A may increase

---

[14] This line is the continuation of the radius vector from the origin to A.

[15] This is strictly correct only if inflation does not provoke any permanent redistribution of income; or if the redistribution does not affect the aggregate propensity to save. Since wages rise with prices we can exclude redistributions from working class to nonworking class. But we cannot exclude redistribution from fixed-income receivers (especially owners of securities) to profits. It is difficult to say whether this will change sensibly the aggregate propensity to save; it is probably a good approximation to assume that the effect will be negligible.

or decrease. It all depends on the way the change in income affects the position of the investment curves. If the increase in income tends to raise the desire to save more than the desire to invest, the rate of interest will fall; in the opposite case it will rise.[16] This last possibility is, in our opinion, unlikely to occur, but it may materialize when entrepreneurs are highly optimistic and the existing equipment is already working at capacity.

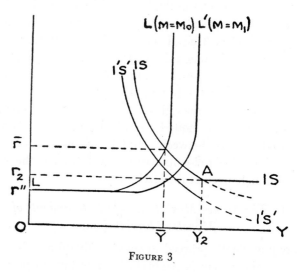

FIGURE 3

The relationship between r and Y emerging from equations (2) and (3) and the equilibrium condition (4) is shown as the IS curve of Figure 3. In the normal case it will slope downward and to the right as in this diagram, but it is conceivable that, at least in a certain range, it may slope upward to the right. In this case $S_Y < I_Y$ and it is usually assumed that the equilibrium of the system will be unstable (and neutral if $S_Y = I_Y$). We shall see, however, that, with inelastic money supply, the negative slope of the IS curve is a sufficient but not necessary condition for stability.

The IS curve must also have another important property. In

---

[16] From $S(r, Y) = I(r, Y)$ we obtain $dr/dY = (S_Y - I_Y)/(I_r - S_r)$, where the subscripts denote partial derivatives. Since $I_r - S_r$ may be expected to be negative, we have $dr/dY \lessgtr 0$ as $S_Y \gtrless I_Y$.

Figure 3, A denotes the equilibrium relationship between full-employment income (Y_2) and rate of interest (r_2). Money income cannot rise above the full-employment level denoted by Y_2 except through inflation, i.e., if wages and prices rise in the same proportion as income. As the stage of inflationary prices and wage increases is reached, the "real" value of investment that it pays to undertake at any interest rate is unchanged since yields and costs change in the same proportion.[17] The money value of profitable investments, on the other hand, rises proportionally to prices and money income. As we have seen above, the same will be true of money savings. It follows that inflationary increases in income raise saving and investment in the same proportion and must therefore leave the equilibrium value of the rate of interest unchanged at the full-employment level r_2. It is for this reason that in Figure 3, to the right of A, the IS curve becomes parallel to the income axis. The dotted curved line beyond A is again the hypothetical relationship between r and Y if it were possible to raise real income above the full-employment level (and if the wage rate should remain unchanged at the level w_0).

9. *The Money Market and the Determinants of Monetary Equilibrium*

We may now finally proceed to consider the process by which the equilibrium of the system is established. For this purpose we must once more revert to the money market which we must, this time, consider in terms of flows rather than in terms of stocks.

---

[17] Following the example of Mr. Keynes we may define the marginal efficiency of an asset as the discount rate that makes the sum of the expected marginal discounted yields equal to the marginal cost of the asset. The expected yields need not all be equal since they depend on the expected net physical yield as well as on expected future prices; and neither is necessarily constant in time. But the expected physical yield does not depend on prices; and, owing to our "static assumption" of unit elasticity of expectation, expected prices change in the same proportion as present prices. Therefore the summation of the yields changes in the same proportion as marginal cost and so does the aggregate value of investments having marginal efficiency equal to or larger than r_2. Under unit elasticity of expectation a given change in all present prices does not modify entrepreneurs' production plans.

In Section 5 we have seen that the rate of interest is established in the money market by the condition that supply of and demand for the stock of money to hold must be equal. This condition is sufficient to determine a position of short-run equilibrium, i.e., a position of equilibrium for the income period. We must now consider under what conditions this level of the rate of interest will also represent a position of long-run equilibrium. As in the textbook analysis of demand and supply, a position of long-run equilibrium is characterized by the fact that neither price nor quantity (demanded and supplied) tend to change any further. In the present case a position of long-run equilibrium will be reached only when the rate of interest does not tend to change from one income period to the other and this in turn is possible only if the stock of money to hold remains constant in time.

Now in each income period people increase their assets by current savings; the money thus saved, since it is not needed for transactions, constitutes an increase in the supply of money to hold. Borrowing, on the other hand, automatically decreases the supply of money to hold by taking cash out of the money market and putting it into active circulation again, through expenditure on investments. If net saving exceeds net borrowing then, on balance, the supply of money to hold will increase above the level of the previous period, say $D_{a \cdot 0}$. But at the old rate of interest (r_0) people will not want to hold the extra supply; they will therefore try to purchase securities and thus will lower the rate of interest. If, on the other hand, at the interest rate r_0 borrowers desire to borrow in the period more than the current amount of money savings, they must induce dealers in the money market to reduce the demand for money as an asset below the previous level $D_{a \cdot 0}$; and this is possible only if the rate of interest rises. There are then three possibilities. (The subscripts 0 and 1 denote quantities in periods zero and one, respectively.)

(1) $S_1 > I_1$: then $D_{a \cdot 1} > D_{a \cdot 0}$ and the rate of interest falls.

(2) $S_1 = I_1$: here $D_{a \cdot 1} = D_{a \cdot 0}$ and the rate of interest is unchanged.

(3) $S_1 < I_1$: then $D_{a \cdot 1} < D_{a \cdot 0}$ and the rate of interest rises.

Recalling our definition of long-run equilibrium, we see at once that only situation (2) satisfies it. In equilibrium then, both demand for and supply of the stock of money to hold and demand for and supply of the flow of saving must be equal.[18]   In addition, however, it is necessary that the flows of saving and of borrowing be themselves constant in time.   This is possible only if two conditions hold: (a) The borrowing that occurs must be equal to the amount of investment that entrepreneurs wish to undertake at the given rate of interest and income level.   The relationship between I_1, r_1, and Y_1 must be described by a point on the corresponding curve of Figure 2-A.   (b) The income (and the rate of interest) must be as large as is required to induce people to go on saving an amount S_1.   The relationship between Y_1, S_1, and r_1 must be described by a point lying on the curve of Figure 2-B.   But if conditions (a) and (b) are satisfied the relationship between Y and r will be described by a point lying on the IS curve of Figure 3.   Thus a position of full equilibrium must be represented by a point lying at the same time on the LL curve (denoting equilibrium between demand for and supply of the stock of money to hold) and on the IS curve (denoting equality and constancy in time of the inflow and outflow of cash in the money market); hence it must be given by the intersection of these two curves.

This is shown in Figure 3 where the equilibrium values of r and Y, thus determined, are denoted by $\bar{r}$ and $\bar{Y}$.   Analytically this corresponds to the simultaneous solution of the two relationships between the income and the rate of interest obtained from equations (1), (2), (3), and (4): $M = L(r, Y)$ and $S(r, Y) = I(r, Y)$.

10. *A Dynamic Model of the Keynesian Theory and the Stability of Equilibrium*

So far our analysis has apparently been "timeless"[19] since it was based on the system of equations of Section 2, in which time does not

---

[18] The classical example of the level of water in a reservoir fits this case perfectly.   The rate of interest, like the level of the water, can be constant only if inflow and outflow are equal.

[19] The word "timeless" has been used here to avoid confusion since the word "static" has already been used to denote the assumption of homogeneity of the first degree of the "expectations functions."

appear explicitly.   A close examination of the last sections, and especially Sections 7 and 9, will reveal, however, that dynamic elements have gradually slipped into our analysis, thanks to the device of "long- and short-run equilibrium," the oldest and simplest device of developing a dynamic theory with a static apparatus.   Actually the criterion that distinguishes short- from long-run equilibrium is essentially a dynamic one: namely, the length of time that is required for certain decisions to be carried out, or, more generally, for certain causes to show their effects.

In our case, the equilibrium of the "money market" is a condition of short-run equilibrium (that determines the rate of interest for each period) because it is the result of decisions that can be carried into effect immediately.   The condition saving = investment, on the other hand, is a condition of long-run equilibrium because the equality of *ex ante* saving and investment cannot be brought about instantaneously.   This is a different way of stating the familiar proposition that the multiplier takes time to work out its full effect.   This well-known fact is in turn explained essentially by the existence of a fundamental time lag: the lag between the time when income is earned and the time when it becomes available for expenditure.   In the economic systems in which we live, people are usually paid for services already rendered. The income earned (or produced) in a period is the value of services rendered which will be paid for at the end of the normal income period; while the income available for expenditure represents payment for services rendered in the previous period.   Decisions as to spending and saving can refer only to the disposable income, and are essentially motivated by it, even though income earned may have some influence.

This explains why the graph of the *IS* curve, unlike the *LL* curve, describes not instantaneous relationships but only possible positions of long-run equilibrium.   When the two curves intersect we have a position of full equilibrium since both short- and long-run conditions are satisfied.

It will therefore be useful at this point to give explicit recognition to the dynamic elements that form the basis of our approach.   This is the purpose of the following system of difference equations which may be considered as the simplest dynamic model of our theory.

(2.1) $M = L(r_t, Y_{d \cdot t}),$
(2.2) $I_t = I(r_t, Y_{d \cdot t}),$
(2.3) $S_t = S(r_t, Y_{d \cdot t}),$
(2.4) $Y_{d \cdot t} = C_t + S_t,$
(2.5) $Y_t = C_t + I_t,$
(2.6) $Y_{d \cdot t} = Y_{t-1}.$

In this system Y denotes income earned and Y_d income disposable. This is a new variable to which corresponds the new equation (2.6). The remaining equations of the system are unchanged.

By repeated substitution the system reduces to the two equations

$$Y_t = Y_{t-1} - S_t + I_t = Y_{t-1} - S(Y_{t-1}, r_t) + I(Y_{t-1}, r_t),$$
$$M = L(r_t, Y_{t-1}).$$

Solving the second equation for r_t and substituting in the first, we obtain a single equation of the form: $Y_t = f(Y_{t-1})$ which determines the time path of the income. By similar procedure we obtain the time sequence of the other variables.

If the system is stable, each variable approaches some definite value which it will maintain in time until there occurs some change in the form of the functional relationship or in some parameter (M or w_0). Equation (2.1) is again the "equation of the money market" that determines the value of r for any period; but we have a position of long-run equilibrium only when $r_t = r_{t-1}$. And this implies $Y_t = Y_{d \cdot t} = Y_{t-1}$ and therefore $S_t = I_t$.

The importance of this system is not limited to the fact that it defines rigorously concepts that were loosely used in our previous analysis. It serves also another important purpose: namely it permits us to determine the conditions of stability for the system.

Following the usual method, we proceed to expand equations (2.1) to (2.3) by Taylor series around the equilibrium values neglecting all terms of degree higher than one. We then obtain:

$$0 = L_r \dot{r}_t + L_Y \dot{Y}_{t-1} + \cdots,$$
$$I_t = I(\bar{r}, \bar{Y}) + I_r \dot{r}_t + I_Y \dot{Y}_{t-1} + \cdots,$$
$$S_t = S(\bar{r}, \bar{Y}) + S_r \dot{r}_t + S_Y \dot{Y}_{t-1}.$$

Subscripts denote partial derivatives taken around the equilibrium values $(\bar{r}, \bar{Y})$ and $r_t = \dot{r}_t - \bar{r}$, $\dot{Y}_t = Y_t - \bar{Y}$. By making use of (4) and (5) and by repeated substitution we obtain the following linear difference equation with constant coefficients:

$$\dot{Y}_t = \dot{Y}_{t-1}\left[1 + \frac{L_Y}{L_r}(S_r - I_r) + I_Y - S_Y\right].$$

The solution of this equation takes the form: $\dot{Y} = \kappa\lambda^t$ or $Y = (Y_0 - \bar{Y})\lambda^t$, since $\dot{Y}_0 = Y_0 - \bar{Y} = \kappa$. Y_0 is determined by the initial conditions and

$$\lambda = 1 + \frac{L_Y}{L_r}(S_r - I_r) + I_Y - S_Y.$$

The stability condition is $|\lambda| < 1$; in the present case this reduces to

$$(2.7) \qquad -\frac{L_Y}{L_r} - \frac{r}{S_r - I_r} < \frac{I_Y - S_Y}{S_r - I_r} < -\frac{L_Y}{L_r}.$$

Since the middle term is the slope of the *IS* curve and the right-hand term is the slope of the *LL* curve, the right-hand condition has a very clear graphical meaning. Stability requires that the slope of the *IS* curve be algebraically smaller than the slope of the *LL* curve. The slope of the *LL* curve cannot be negative ($L_Y > 0$, $L_r \geqq 0$). Also general economic considerations suggest that $S_r - I_r > 0$. Hence this condition is necessarily satisfied if $I_Y - S_Y < 0$, i.e., when the *IS* curve falls from left to right. But this is not necessary. Stability is also possible when the *IS* curve rises in the neighborhood of the equilibrium point as long as it cuts the *LL* curve from its concave toward its convex side.[20]

If the stability conditions are satisfied, the variables approach their equilibrium values, which are the same as those obtained by solving the static system of Section 2. In the opposite case they diverge more and more from these values in a process of cumulative contraction or expansion. In the same way, a change in some of the data will lead to a new stable equilibrium if the new functions satisfy the conditions written above.

---

[20] It is only as $L_r \to \infty$ (demand for money to hold infinitely elastic, *LL* curve parallel to the horizontal axis) that the condition $I_Y - S_Y < 0$ becomes necessary for equilibrium. This holds equally if the supply of money is infinitely elastic for this has the same effect as $L_r = \infty$.

It is interesting to note that, as long as the money supply is inelastic, the system must always have at least one stable solution since eventually the LL curve becomes perpendicular to the horizontal axis and hence its slope must become larger than the slope of the IS curve.

11. *The Determinants of Real Equilibrium*

It is now time to consider the role of the second part of the system in the determination of equilibrium. Equations (5), (6), and (7) *explain* the forces that determine the real variables of the system: physical output, employment, real wage rate.[21]

The most important of these equations is (7), which states the conditions of equilibrium in the production of goods whether for consumption or for investment.[22] Production will be extended up to the point at which the given and fixed money wage rate w_0 is equal to the marginal net product of labor, or, if we prefer, up to the point at which price equals marginal labor cost.[23] This assumes that the only variable factor is labor and the quantity of equipment is fixed; a condition that is approximately satisfied in the case we are considering. Eliminating equation (5) by substitution into (7) we can reduce this part of the system to two equations in the two unknowns X and N, where X' is used for dX/dN:

$$W_0 = X'(N) \frac{Y}{X}, \qquad X = X(N).$$

Since the money income is determined exclusively by the *monetary* part of the system, the price level depends only on the amount of output. If, at any given price level, the fixed wage is less than the marginal product of labor, the forces of competition lead to an expansion of employment and output which forces prices down. This lowers the marginal product of labor until it becomes equal to the wage rate.

---

[21] The price level is also necessary to determine the real wage rate, given the money wage rate W.

[22] The equilibrium price of each type of physical asset is found by capitalizing a series of expected marginal yields at the current rate of interest. The expected yields of the marginal unit need not be equal in each period.

[23] This is a sufficient condition under assumption of perfect competition; the modifications necessary in the case of monopolies cannot be considered here.

If the wage rate exceeded the marginal product of labor, output and employment would contract, which would force prices up. We see clearly from Figure 3 that the amount of employment thus determined will, in general, not be "full employment"; that is, unless the LL curve intersects the IS curve at (Y_2, r_2) or to the right of it.

12. *Underemployment Equilibrium and Liquidity Preference*

This last result deserves closer consideration. It is usually considered as one of the most important achievements of the Keynesian theory that it explains the consistency of economic equilibrium with the presence of involuntary unemployment. It is, however, not sufficiently recognized that, except in a limiting case to be considered later, this result is due entirely to the assumption of "rigid wages"[24] and not to the Keynesian liquidity preference. Systems with rigid wages share the common property that the equilibrium value of the "real" variables is determined essentially by monetary conditions rather than by "real" factors (e.g., quantity and efficiency of existing equipment, relative preference for earning and leisure, etc.). The monetary conditions are sufficient to determine money income and, under fixed wages and given technical conditions, to each money income there corresponds a definite equilibrium level of employment. This equilibrium level does not tend to coincide with full employment except by mere chance, since there is no economic mechanism that insures this coincidence. There may be unemployment in the sense that more people would be willing to work at the current real wage rate than are actually employed; but in a free capitalistic economy production is guided by prices and not by desires and since the money wage rate is rigid, this desire fails to be translated into an economic stimulus.

In order to show more clearly that wage rigidities and not liquidity preference explain underemployment equilibrium we may consider the results to be obtained by giving up the liquidity-preference theory and assuming instead the crudest quantity-of-money theory while keeping the assumption of rigid wages. This can be done by merely replacing equation (1) of our system by the equation

[24] The expression "rigid wages" refers to the infinite elasticity of the supply curve of labor when the level of employment is below "full."

(1a) $$M = kY.$$

Since M and k are constant this equation is sufficient to determine money income. Equations (5), (6), and (7) determine directly physical output and employment as we saw in Section 10. Once more there is no reason to expect that the level of employment thus determined will be "full employment"; and yet the system will be in equilibrium since there will be no tendency for income, employment, and output to change.

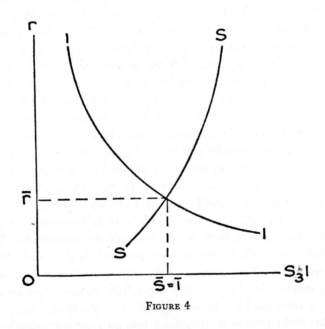

FIGURE 4

It is very interesting to see what part is played under these conditions by equations (2) and (3), the savings and investment equations that have been so much stressed by all the Keynesians. Since the income is determined by equation (1a), equation (2) reduces to an "orthodox" supply-of-saving schedule, giving saving as a function of the rate of interest. For the same reason, equation (3) reduces to a demand-for-saving schedule. Both schedules can be represented in a Marshallian supply and demand diagram as is done in Figure 4. The intersection of these curves, i.e., the equilibrium condition, demand $=$ supply, determines the level of the rate of interest.

Finally let us notice that, in this system also, the rate of interest depends on the quantity of money, or more exactly on the ratio M/W. A change in M (W constant) raises real income and shifts both the SS and II curves to the right.   The net result will be a fall in the rate of interest, if the increase in income raises the desire to save more than the desire to invest (normal case); a rise, in the opposite case.

In spite of these significant similarities between the present system and the Keynesian system, in which we recognize the existence of liquidity demand for money, there remains one very important difference; this difference is to be found in the role played by the rate of interest in the determination of equilibrium.   In both cases the level of employment depends on the quantity of "active" money.   But in the Keynesian system this depends on the rate of interest and consequently also on the propensities to save and invest.   In the present case the quantity of active money is fixed and independent of the rate of interest.   Hence the propensities to save and invest are not a part of the mechanism determining employment; they merely determine the amount of resources devoted to the improvement of the means of production.

We now proceed to consider the determinants of equilibrium in a system in which we do away not only with the liquidity-preference theory but also with the assumption of rigid wages.

13. *The Logical Consistency of the Quality Theory of Money and the Dichotomy of Monetary and Real Economics*

In order to discuss the quantity theory of money we substitute equation (1a) for (1) and replace conditions (10) by the identities (11).

It was shown in Section 8 that a given change in prices will change income, investment, and saving in the same proportion.   Consequently, after Y in equations (2) and (3) is replaced by the expression given in (5), the saving and investment equations may be written in the form

$$(3.2) \qquad \frac{I}{W} = I\left(r, \frac{P}{W}X\right),$$

$$(3.3) \qquad \frac{S}{W} = S\left(r, \frac{P}{W}X\right).$$

Next we divide both members of equations (4) and (5) by W obtaining

$$(3.4) \qquad \frac{S}{W} = \frac{I}{W},$$

$$(3.5) \qquad \frac{Y}{W} \equiv \frac{P}{W}X,$$

$$(3.6) \qquad X = X(N),$$

$$(3.7) \qquad \frac{W}{P} = X'(N),$$

$$(3.9) \qquad N = F\left(\frac{W}{r}\right).$$

$$\left[(3.8) \qquad \frac{Y}{W} \equiv \frac{I}{W} + \frac{C}{W}\right].$$

Equations (3.2) to (3.7) and (3.9) form a system of 7 equations in the 7 unknowns I/W, S/W, P/W, Y/W, r, X, N. These unknowns are therefore determined. Next we can write equation (1a) in the form $M = kPX = Wk(P/W)X$. But since P/W and X have already been determined, this equation determines the money wage rate and hence the price level, money income, etc. This is essentially the "classical" procedure, and we can only repeat the classical conclusions to the effect that the real part of the system, namely, employment, *interest rate,* output, or real income, do not depend on the quantity of money. The quantity of money has no other function than to determine the price level.

This result does not, of course, depend on any special feature of our system. It will always follow, provided all the supply and demand functions of commodities[25] and labor are homogeneous of the zero degree; and since we are proceeding under "static" assumptions, all

---

[25] "Commodities" are, in this context, all goods except money.

the supply and demand functions must be homogeneous of zero degree, if people behave rationally.[26]

This conclusion, which is very old indeed, has some interest since it has been recently challenged by Oscar Lange. Of all the recent attacks against the traditional dichotomy of monetary and real economics, Lange's criticism is by far the most serious because it maintains that "the traditional procedure of the theory of money involves a [logical] contradiction."[27] We propose to show, however, that, while Lange's criticism of Say's law cannot be questioned, it does not invalidate the logical consistency of the procedure of the quantity theory of money.

According to Lange, Say's law implies that the amount of cash people desire to hold is always identically equal to the quantity in existence: denoting by D_n and S_n the demand and supply of money respectively, we can write this as $S_n \equiv D_n$. Lange then states that "a proportional change of all prices does not induce a substitution between different commodities"[28] and concludes that "the demand and supply functions of commodities are, *when Say's law holds*, homogeneous of zero degree."[29] But the homogeneity of the supply and demand functions for commodities does not depend on Say's law: it depends on the assumption of rationality and the homogeneity of the expectation functions. Since a proportional change in all prices does not change the price ratios it also does not change the marginal rate of substitution, and therefore does not induce a substitution between different commodities.

Let us now consider a system in which there are n goods ($n - 1$ commodities and money). As is well known, there are only $n - 1$ prices to be determined, the price of money being unity, and $n - 1$

---

[26] For a proof of this statement see O. Lange, "Say's Law: A Restatement and Criticism," *op. cit.*, pp. 67 and 68. Professor Lange shows that the homogeneity of first degree of all expectation functions is a sufficient condition for all demand and supply equations for "commodities" to be homogeneous of zero degree.

[27] *Ibid.*, p. 65.

[28] *Ibid.*, p. 63.

[29] *Ibid.*, p. 63. Italics ours.

independent supply and demand equations, for one follows from the rest. Since the supply and demand functions for commodities are homogeneous of zero degree, the quantities demanded of the $n-1$ commodities are functions of the $n-2$ price ratios $p_i/p_{n-1}(i=1, 2, \cdots, n-2)$, where p_{n-1} is chosen arbitrarily.[30]   At the same time the demand and supply function to be eliminated is also arbitrary; we may, if we choose, eliminate one of the $n-1$ referring to commodities; we are then left with $n-2$ equations for commodities to determine the $n-2$ price ratios. Hence the price ratios are determined. To determine the actual prices we use the demand and supply equation for money as was done above. In Lange's system this is written:

$$k \sum_{i=1}^{n} p_i S_i = M, \qquad \text{or also} \qquad k p_{n-1} \sum_{i=1}^{n} \frac{p_i}{p_{n-1}} S_i = M,$$

where S_i denotes the equilibrium quantity supplied and demanded of the ith commodity. Since k is a constant this equation determines p_{n-1} and consequently all other prices.

As long as Say's law is not assumed, this procedure is perfectly legitimate; and we cannot escape the classical conclusion that money is "neutral," just a "veil." If, however, Say's law holds, the demand and supply of money are identically equal. The nth equation is therefore not a genuine equation. Thus we have only $n-2$ independent equations to determine $n-1$ prices: the system is not determinate. In Lange's own formulation, the nth equation degenerates into the identity

$$k p_{n-1} \sum_{i=1}^{n} \frac{p_i}{p_{n-1}} S_i \equiv M,$$

which is satisfied by any value of p_{n-1} whatever; the price level is thus indeterminate.[31]

Hence one of Lange's conclusions, namely that "Say's law pre-

---

[30] In our own system p_{n-1} was arbitrarily chosen as the wage rate.

[31] Then k changes in inverse proportion to p_{n-1} instead of being a constant.

cludes any monetary theory,"[32] is perfectly justified.   But Lange goes on to draw a conclusion which does not follow, namely that "the traditional procedure of the theory of money involves a contradiction. Either Say's law is assumed and money prices are indeterminate, or money prices are made determinate—but then *Say's law and hence the neutrality of money* must be abandoned."[33]   But the traditional theory of money is not based on Say's law.   The necessary condition for money to be neutral is that the $n - 1$ "real" demand and supply equations be homogeneous of order zero and this homogeneity does not "disappear when Say's law is abandoned."[34]   Under "static" assumptions money is neutral even without assuming Say's law, if only people are assumed to behave "rationally"; this is all that the classical theory assumes and needs to assume.[35]

The most serious charge against the classical dichotomy can thus be dismissed, as long as we maintain our "static" assumptions.

14. *Liquidity Preference and the Determinants of the Rate of Interest under the Assumption of Flexible Wages*[36]

With this in mind we may now proceed to analyze our third system consisting of equations (1) to (7), (9), and identities (11).   In this system we recognize that there are two sources of demand for money, the transaction demand and the liquidity demand.   But, as in the case just analyzed, we make no restrictive assumptions as to the supply-of-labor equation.   The suppliers of labor as well as the suppliers of all other commodities are supposed to behave "rationally." It follows that the only difference between the present case and the

---

[32] O. Lange, *op. cit.*, p. 66.

[33] *Ibid.*, p. 65.   Italics ours.

[34] *Ibid.*, p. 66.

[35] Lange's result seems due to a failure to distinguish between necessary and sufficient conditions.   Say's law is a sufficient condition for the neutrality of money but not a necessary one.   Lange asks me to inform the reader that he agrees with my conclusion.   This conclusion, however, does not invalidate his result that under Say's law the money prices are indeterminate.

[36] The expression "flexible wages" is used here and in the following pages for brevity in place of the more exact expression "homogeneity of zero degree of the supply-of-labor function."

case just considered is in equation (1). As in the previous case, the last 7 equations form a determinate system which is sufficient to determine the 7 unknowns it contains, namely *the "real" variables of the system and the rate of interest.*

By use of equation (5) or (3.5) equation (1) takes the form

$$(3.1) \qquad M = L\left(r,\ W\frac{P}{W}X\right).$$

Since r and P/W are already determined, this equation determines the 8th unknown of the system, the wage rate: and therefore also the price level, money, income, etc.[37]

We thus reach the conclusion that under "static" assumptions and "flexible" wages, *the rate of interest and the level of employment do not depend on the quantity of money.*

Two questions arise at once: (a) what determines the rate of interest and (b) what part do the rate of interest and liquidity demand for money play in the determination of equilibrium.

Strictly speaking, the rate of interest is determined by all the equations of a Walrasian system *except the supply-of-and-demand-for-money equation.* But it is clear that in the first approximation of partial-equilibrium analysis, the determination of the rate of interest must be associated with equations (3.2) and (3.3), the saving and investment schedules. To explain the level of the rate of interest we could use once more Figure 4, changing the variables measured on the horizontal axis from S or I into S/W or I/W. We must add at once, however, that these two schedules should in no way be confused with the schedules of supply of and demand for savings (or supply of and demand for securities) used in the textbook explanation of the determination of the rate of interest.

Equation (3.3) only tells us what part of their income people wish to devote to increasing their assets rather than to consumption, at different levels of the rate of interest.

In a similar fashion equation (3.2) shows that by devoting output worth I/W to the improvement of the means of production, it is possible to increase real income by an amount $(I/W)(1+r)$ per unit of

---

[37] Except in the Keynesian case considered later (Section 16).

time.   The value of r depends on the given technical conditions, on the quantity I/W and $(P/W)X$ according to the relation expressed by equation (3.2).   This shows clearly the fundamental factors that determine the rate of interest.   The given technical conditions, expressed by the production function [equation (3.6)], together with *tastes* of people for earning and leisure, expressed by the supply-of-labor function [equation (3.9)], give the level of real income that can be reached.[38] The saving schedule, equation (3.3), tells us what part of this income the community desires to save.   The technical conditions (inventions, quantity of capital already in existence, etc.) expressed by the marginal-efficiency-of-investment function (3.2), determine the marginal efficiency of the amount of investment that the giving up of consumption permits undertaking: this is the equilibrium rate of interest.

Let us now examine what part is played by liquidity preference in the present system.   On the basis of the given rate of interest determined in the fashion discussed above, people decide what quantity of money they want to hold as an asset.   Hence, provided the liquidity demand is finite, the rate of interest, together with the supply of money, determines the quantity of active money and therefore the price level. Thus under "flexible" wages, *the desire to hold assets in liquid form does not determine the rate of interest, but determines the price level.* It follows that any factor that influences the demand for money as an asset, either directly or through the rate of interest, will have a repercussion on the price level, unless it is counteracted by an appropriate change in the quantity of money.   This will in particular be the case with changes in the propensities to save and to invest.

15. *Liquidity Preference under Rigid and Flexible Wages—an Example*

In order to see clearly the different implications of the liquidity-preference theory under different hypotheses as to the supply of labor we may briefly consider the effects of a shift in the investment schedule [equation (2) or (3.2)].

Suppose that the system is in equilibrium at money income Y_0: the

---

[38] Under flexible wages there is, of course, always full employment under the conditions mentioned in Section 16.

flow of investments is I_0, and its marginal efficiency, r_0, is the equilibrium rate of interest.   Now let us assume that for some reason the rate of investment that seems profitable at any level of the rate of interest falls.   In particular the marginal efficiency of the rate of investment I_0 falls to the level $r_1 < r_0$.   In order for the system to reach a new position of equilibrium, it is necessary that the rate of interest fall to this level.   Except under special circumstances, to be considered later, as the rate of interest falls, the demand for money as an asset rises, and a certain amount of current money savings remains in the *money market* to satisfy the increased demand.   If the supply of money is not properly increased, this, in turn, implies a fall in money income.

Under the conditions of our last model (flexible wages) the fall is brought about by an all-around reduction in wages and prices.   The price level reaches its new equilibrium position when the supply has been increased sufficiently to satisfy the liquidity demand for money associated with the interest rate r_1.[39]   The net effect of the shift is then to depress the interest rate, the money income, and money wages without affecting the real variables of the system, employment, output, real wage rate.[40]

But if money wages are rigid downward, the reduction in money income, made necessary by the fall in the rate of interest, becomes a reduction in real income and employment as well.   The effect of the shift in the investment schedule is now to start a typical process of contraction so frequently described in Keynesian literature.   As producers of investment goods make losses, they have no other choice than to dismiss workers, even though their physical productivity is unchanged.   This, in turn, reduces the demand for consumption goods and causes unemployment to spread to this sector.   Real income falls along with money income (the price level is likely to fall to a smaller extent).   The fall in money income increases the supply of money to

---

[39] The rate of interest must necessarily fall to the level r_1, for the real income and therefore the amount of real savings will be unchanged, and the marginal efficiency of this amount of real savings is r_1, by hypothesis.

[40] The real wage rate clearly cannot fall.   If the real wage rate had fallen, entrepreneurs would try to expand employment while the supply of labor would, if anything, contract.   If it had risen, the opposite situation would occur, and neither of these situations is compatible with equilibrium.

hold; the fall in real income decreases saving and raises its marginal efficiency above the level r_1.[41]   This double set of reactions leads finally to a new equilibrium, with a smaller money and real income, less employment, higher real wages (since the price level falls) and a rate of interest somewhere below r_0 and above the new "full employment interest" r_1.[42]   In terms of our graphic apparatus, a decreased marginal efficiency of capital (or increased propensity to save), shifts the IS curve to the left, as shown by the curve $I'S'$, and lowers interest rate and income, money as well as real income.

16. *Two Limiting Cases:* (A) THE KEYNESIAN CASE

There is one case in which the Keynesian theory of liquidity preference is sufficient by itself to explain the existence of underemployment equilibrium without starting out with the assumption of rigid wages. We have seen (Section 5) that, since securities are inferior to money as a form of holding assets, there must be some positive level of the rate of interest (previously denoted by r'') at which the demand for money becomes infinitely elastic or practically so.   We have the Keynesian case when the "full-employment equilibrium rate of interest" is less than r''.   Whenever this situation materializes, the very mechanism that tends to bring about full-employment equilibrium in a system with "flexible" wages breaks down, since there is no possible level of the money wage rate and price level that can establish full-employment equilibrium.

From the analytical point of view the situation is characterized by the fact that we must add to our system a new equation, namely $r = r''$.   The system is therefore overdetermined since we have 9 equations to determine only 8 unknowns.

Equations (3.2) and (3.3) are sufficient to determine the value of the real income (since r is already determined).   But this value will in general not be consistent with the value of the real income determined by the last four equations.   More workers would be willing to

---

[41] Except if the IS curve is not monotonic decreasing, in which case the process of contraction will be more pronounced.

[42] If there was no full employment in the initial situation, then r_1 is simply the rate of interest that would maintain the old level of employment.   This conclusion is also subject to the qualification mentioned in footnote 41.

work at the ruling real wage rate than are employed, but efforts at reducing real wages and increasing employment are bound to fail. For any fall in wages and prices increases the supply of money to hold but cannot lower the rate of interest below the level r'' since the demand for money as an asset is infinitely elastic. As Keynes would say, labor as a whole will not be able to fix its own real wage rate.

It appears clearly that, in this case, equilibrium is determined by those very factors that are stressed in the typical Keynesian analysis. In particular, real income and employment is determined by the position and shape of the saving and investment function, and changes in the propensity to invest or to save change real income without affecting the interest rate.

The price level on the other hand is in neutral equilibrium (at least for a certain range of values). It will tend to fall indefinitely as long as workers attempt to lower money wages in an effort to increase employment; and it can only find a resting place if and when money wages become rigid.

In this case the Keynesian analysis clearly departs from the classical lines and it leads to conclusions that could scarcely have been reached by following the traditional line of approach.

Whether the situation we have characterized as the "Keynesian case" is typical of some or all modern economic systems is a factual question which we cannot attempt to answer here. It is beyond doubt however that its interest is not purely theoretical.[43]

---

[43] In the *General Theory* Keynes explicitly recognizes that the situation described as the "Keynesian case" does not seem, so far, normally to prevail in any economic system. This situation, on the other hand, certainly plays an important part in some phases of the business cycle, when a great feeling of uncertainty and the anticipation of price reductions increase the attractiveness of liquidity and, at the same time, decreases the propensity to invest. Besides, it may also soon become a normal feature of some economies if there should come to prevail a real scarcity of investment outlets that are profitable at rates of interest higher than the institutional minimum. Modifying a well-known statement of Hicks we can say that the Keynesian case is either the Economics of Depression or the Economics of Abundance. (Hicks's original statement: "The General Theory of Employment is the Economics of Depression" is found in "Mr. Keynes and the 'Classics,'" *op. cit.*, p. 155.)

(B) THE CLASSICAL CASE

We have the classical case when the equilibrium rate of interest is sufficiently high to make the demand for money to hold zero or negligible. Graphically, the *IS* curve of Figure 3 intersects the *LL* curve in the range in which *LL* is perpendicular to the income axis. Under these conditions changes in the rate of interest (except possibly if they are of considerable size) tend to leave the demand for money unchanged or practically so; $L_r = 0$ or negligible and $M = L(Y)$. The properties of a system satisfying this condition have already been sufficiently analyzed in Sections 11 and 12.[44]

17. *Preliminary Conclusions*

This brings to an end the first part of our analysis which aimed principally at distinguishing, as far as possible, to what extent the results of the Keynesian analysis are due to a more refined theoretical approach (liquidity preference) and to what extent to the assumption of rigid wages. We may summarize the results of our inquiry in the following propositions:

I. The liquidity-preference theory is not necessary to explain underemployment equilibrium; it is sufficient only in a limiting case: the "Keynesian case." In the general case it is neither necessary nor sufficient; it can explain this phenomenon only with the additional assumption of rigid wages.

II. The liquidity-preference theory is neither necessary nor sufficient to explain the dependence of the rate of interest on the quantity of money. This dependence is explained only by the assumption of rigid wages.

---

[44] To what extent the "classical case" is met in practice is again a factual question. In our opinion a moderately high rate of interest is sufficient to make it unattractive to hold assets in the form of cash and therefore to induce members of the community to limit their holdings to the amount necessary for transactions (which is determined by the institutional set-up). It is perhaps not unreasonable to expect that under normal conditions a "pure" rate of interest (i.e., net of default risk) in the neighborhood of 5 per cent might be sufficient to reduce the demand for money to hold to negligible proportions.

III. The result of the liquidity-preference theory is that the quantity of active money depends not only on the total quantity of money but also on the rate of interest and therefore also on the form and position of the propensities to save and to invest. Hence in a system with flexible wages the rate of interest and the propensities to save and to invest are part of the mechanism that determines the price level. And in a system with rigid wages they are part of the mechanism that determines the level of employment and real income.

We proceed now to make use of our results for two purposes: (a) To examine critically some of the theories that have their logical foundation in the Keynesian analysis. (b) To state some general conclusions about the determinants of the rate of interest.

PART II

18. *General Remarks about the Assumption of Wage Rigidity in the Keynesian Theories*

In the *General Theory* Keynes does of course recognize the fundamental importance of the relation between money wages and the quantity of money as is shown by his device of the wage units. This very fact, on the other hand, has had the effect of obscuring the part played by wage rigidities in the determination of economic equilibrium. This can be clearly seen in a large body of literature based on the Keynesian analysis, and will be illustrated with a few examples.

(A) Let us first consider the role of investment.

The statement that unemployment is caused by lack of investment, or that a fall in the propensity to invest or an increase in the propensity to save will decrease employment, has become today almost a commonplace.

As we have seen, however, lack of investment is sufficient to explain underemployment equilibrium only in the "Keynesian case," a situation that is the exception and not the rule.

It is true that a reduced level of employment and a reduced level of investment go together, but this is not, in general, the result of causal relationship. It is true instead that the low level of investment and employment are both the effect of the same cause, namely a basic maladjustment between the quantity of money and the wage rate.   It is the fact that money wages are too high relative to the quantity of money that explains why it is unprofitable to expand employment to the "full employment" level.   Now to each level of employment and income corresponds a certain distribution of the employment between the production of consumption and investment goods determined by the saving pattern of the community.   Hence, when the over-all level of employment is low there will be a reduced level of investment as well as a reduced level of consumption.   And the level of investment is low because employment is low and not the other way around.

What is required to improve the situation is an increase in the quantity of money (and not necessarily in the propensity to invest); then employment will increase in every field of production including investment.   Again, it is true that, in general, a fall in the propensity to invest (the propensity to save being constant) tends to decrease employment (and that an increase in the same propensity has the opposite effect), but this occurs only because it decreases (or increases) the quantity of money available for transactions relative to the money wage rate and therefore makes it profitable to contract (or expand) employment.   Exactly the same result could be obtained by deflating (or inflating) the quantity of money directly. That a change in the marginal efficiency of investment has no direct influence on aggregate employment can be clearly seen in the "classical case" when the demand for money to hold is zero or negligible. In this case the change mentioned above does not affect employment, but only the rate of interest and therefore, at most, the distribution of the unchanged amount of employment between consumption and investment.

In conclusion, then, the statement that unemployment is caused by lack of investment assumes implicitly that every possible economic system works under the special conditions of the "Keynesian case"; and this is clearly unwarranted.   In general the reduced level of investment is not a cause, but just a symptom of unemployment, which in turn is due to essentially monetary disturbances.

This formulation is not only more correct but carries also important implications about the concrete form of economic policies necessary to relieve unemployment.

(B) Another typical result of understressing the assumption of rigid wages is to be found in connection with the concepts of a "natural rate of interest" and of "cumulative inflation" and "deflation" of Wicksellian analysis.[45]

This "natural rate" is the equilibrium (and therefore full-employment) interest rate of a system with flexible wages and not of a Keynesian system with rigid wages. Under "flexible" wages, as we know, the equilibrium rate of interest does not depend on the quantity of money. But, because of the time required for a new position of equilibrium to be reached when some of the conditions change, it will depend on the rate of change of M. Thus the money authority will be able to keep r below (or above) its equilibrium value by increasing (or decreasing) the quantity of money without limit; we thus get a process of cumulative inflation or deflation. Under Keynesian assumptions this ceases to be true; but only because wages are assumed rigid and in this condition, as we have seen, it is in general possible to change the rate of interest with a finite change in the quantity of money.[46]

(C) As a last example, we may quote Lange's "optimum propensity to consume."[47] This concept, outside of its theoretical in-

---

[45] See J. Marschak, "Wicksell's Two Interest Rates," *Social Research,* Vol. 8, (November 1941), pp. 469–78.

[46] The case is more complicated if the relation between Y and r described by the IS curve is not monotonic decreasing in the relevant range. It might then appear that an attempt of the money authority at reducing the interest rate will result in a fall in income and employment. This is the result reached by Marschak. Actually as the money authority expands the quantity of money by open-market policy it finds that the rate of interest eventually rises along with income and employment instead of falling. If the money authority insists on keeping the interest rate at the planned level it will have to go on expanding the quantity of money. This will either push the system to some new equilibrium if the planned rate is equal to or larger than the full-employment rate, or it will cause inflation if the planned rate is below this level. But in no event will an initial attempt at lowering r by open-market policy lead to a contraction of income.

[47] Oscar Lange, "The Rate of Interest and the Optimum Propensity to Consume," *Economica,* Vol. 5, N. S. (February 1938), pp. 12–32.

terest, is only of practical importance if for some reason, money wages and money supply are absolutely inelastic. In general all that is required to increase employment is to expand the quantity of money (or at worst reduce wages) without any necessity for interfering with the propensity to consume.[48]

19. *Lerner's Theory of the Rate of Interest*

We proceed now to consider the typically "Keynesian" theory of the rate of interest and money due to A. P. Lerner. We choose Lerner's theory, because its extremism and its clear-cut formulation permit of a useful criticism.

The substance of Lerner's argument, as far as we can make out, is this: The "classical theory" that saving and investment determine the rate of interest must be rejected: saving and investment, being identically equal, cannot determine interest. This is instead determined by the quantity of money according to a demand-for-money function, say $M = f(r)$.[49]

The first argument is clearly unimportant since it is based on definitions. If one accepts the Keynesian definitions then, of course, actual (or *ex post*) saving and investment are identical; and clearly the *ex post* identity, saving $\equiv$ investment, cannot determine either the rate of interest or income. This however does not prove that the propensities to save and to invest are irrelevant to the determination of interest.

We know on the contrary, that, under assumption of flexible wages, neither of Lerner's arguments holds. In this case the rate

---

[48] If the demand for money is infinitely elastic the propensity to consume plays an important role in the determination of employment. In this case the optimum level of consumption C' would clearly be $C' = Y' - I(r'', Y')$, where Y' is full-employment income and r'' the critical level of the rate of interest for which $L_r = \infty$.

[49] See especially, "Alternative Formulations of the Theory of Interest," *Economic Journal,* Vol. 48, (June 1938), pp. 211–30; and "Interest Theory—Supply and Demand for Loans or Supply and Demand for Cash?" This latter paper has been recently made available to me by Mr. Lerner in manuscript form; it is to be published in the *Review of Economic Statistics.* The present criticism is also the result of a long personal discussion and correspondence.

of interest is independent of the quantity of money and, except in limiting cases, is determined only by the propensities to save and to invest [equations (3.2) and (3.3)].

Let us stress, in order to avoid misunderstandings, that we perfectly agree with Lerner and with all the Keynesians that saving and lending are the result of two independent decisions; our equation (3.3) is a saving schedule and not a schedule of supply of loanable funds. However we cannot agree with Lerner that to treat saving as a "demand-for-securities schedule" is, without qualifications, a serious blunder, or that the classical analysis as to the effect of shifts in the desire to invest or to save is right by pure chance. We must remember that saving and lending coincide when the demand for money to hold is zero or constant. The quantity theory of money starts out with the assumption that the demand for money to hold is identically zero: $D_a'(r) \equiv 0$ or $M = L(Y)$. Now this assumption is unsatisfactory for a general theory, but may be fully justified under certain conditions.

We know that, when the equilibrium rate of interest is sufficiently high, the demand for money to hold does become zero, even if it is not assumed to be identically zero. And, under historically realized conditions, the equilibrium rate of interest may be sufficiently high to make the demand for money to hold so negligible and so scarcely affected by observed changes in the interest rate that this demand can, safely, be neglected. Interest becomes a factor of secondary importance and can be dropped along with many others which certainly do influence the demand for money but are not sufficiently relevant to warrant separate consideration. Under these conditions, the assumption $M = L(Y)$ will give a satisfactory approximation to economic reality.[50] Under changed historical conditions this assumption is no longer justified and it becomes necessary to take into account new factors to avoid oversimplifications.[51]

---

[50] The fact that hoarding and unemployment have always developed in certain phases of the business cycle is not an objection to that. For these are features for a theory of business cycles to explain. Here we are only comparing static theories.

[51] Thus for example, the outcome of a certain physical experiment may be influenced, to a slight extent, by changes in humidity. Then, if the experi-

When we recognize that the demand for money to hold need not be zero (and as long as it is finite), saving and lending coincide only when the demand for money to hold is constant, that is to say, in equilibrium. The equality of money savings and lending becomes an equilibrium condition which, under flexible wages, *determines the price level, not the rate of interest.* And this in turn may explain the traditional lack of attention to the demand for money to hold in connection with the theory of interest.

Thus Lerner's theory cannot explain the rate of interest in a system with "flexible" wages. Let us then see whether it holds within the limits of his (tacit) assumption of rigid wages. We will agree at once that under this assumption the rate of interest depends on the quantity of money, but this is true only in a very special sense. If we look at our "Keynesian" model we find that we have 7 equations in 7 unknowns and two arbitrary quantities or "parameters," M and W_0. The solution of the system gives each of the 7 variables as functions of these arbitrary parameters: $\bar{r} = r(M, W)$, $\bar{Y} = Y(M, W)$, $\bar{N} = N(M, W)$, etc. On the basis of previous considerations these can be written:

$$(5.1) \qquad \bar{r} = r\left(\frac{M}{W}\right), \qquad\qquad (5.2) \qquad \bar{Y} = Y\left(\frac{M}{W}\right), \text{ etc.}$$

If this is the sense in which Lerner states that r is a function of M, his statement is formally correct. But in the first place it is not very helpful for understanding the determinants of the rate of interest. In a system with rigid wages practically every economic variable depends on the quantity of money (and the money wage). The rate of interest depends on M as much as the price of shoes or employment in ice-cream manufacturing. In the second place it has nothing to do with Keynes's liquidity preference: r depends on M even if we neglect the liquidity demand for money (see Section 11). Hence if Lerner's equation, $M = f(r)$, corresponds to our equation (5.1), then it is not a demand-for-money schedule, but an empirical rela-

---

ment is carried out in a place in which the observed variations in humidity are not sufficient to affect the outcome sensibly, it is perfectly justifiable to neglect it. If the same experiment were conducted somewhere else, where humidity is known to be highly unstable, precautions should be taken in interpreting the results.

tionship obtained by previous solution of a system of equations of which the demand for money itself is one. And his approach certainly throws no light on the determinants of the rate of interest.

The only alternative is to consider Lerner's equation as a true demand for money corresponding to our equation (1): $M = L(r, Y)$. But why has the second variable been omitted? The answer is clear; by concentrating attention on the liquidity preference and the demand for money to hold, sight has been lost of the demand for money to spend. Thus we go from one extreme to the other; instead of neglecting the influence of the rate of interest as in the "quantity theory," we neglect the part played by income in determining the demand for money. The results of this unjustified omission are serious in many respects. The most serious is that it leads to the conclusion (reached by Lerner) that saving and investment play no part in the determination of the rate of interest.[52] Figure 3 shows on the contrary that equations (2) and (3) play as vital a role as the demand-for-money equation. It is clear also that changes in the propensity to save or to invest or in the wage rate, lead directly to changes in the interest rate.

To defend his point Lerner is forced to say that changes in these propensities affect the rate of interest *because* they change the demand for money, i.e., because they shift the graph of $M = f(r)$.[53] But this is true and by definition only if Lerner identifies $M = f(r)$ with our equation (5.1). Since this equation is obtained by pre-

---

[52] In "Alternative Formulations of the Theory of Interest," Lerner writes: "For the first, easy step [from the classical to the modern theory of interest] is the insinuation of Liquidity Preference as a junior partner in the old established one-man firm in the business of interest-determination, and the second . . . step is to put Saving-Investment, the senior partner, to sleep, as a preliminary to kicking him out" (*op. cit.*, p. 221).

[53] That this is Lerner's point of view may be seen for instance in the following passage from a letter written to me in June, 1943. Discussing the effects of an increase in the propensity to invest in the "classical case" (demand for money to hold equal zero) he writes: "Even in that case there must be a fall in income which decreases the need for cash which lowers the rate of interest so that the investors have a signal that they should increase investment, but an infinitesimal decrease in employment is sufficient to bring about any necessary fall in the rate of interest. . . . "

viously solving the whole system, it contains the relevant parameters of the functions which determine the rate of interest. A change in any of these parameters changes or shifts the function $r = r(M/W)$ accordingly. But, as we have already seen, equation (5.1) cannot possibly help us in understanding the determinants of the rate of interest.[54]

Another consequence of Lerner's formulation is that it leads to the conclusion that the interest rate can always be lowered by increasing the quantity of money, at least to the point where the demand becomes infinitely elastic; while the truth is that no finite change in the quantity of money can hold the interest rate below the full-employment level.[55]

Let us finally note that Lerner's theory is not fully satisfactory even in the "Keynesian case." It is true that in this case saving and investment do not determine the rate of interest, but it is equally clear that the rate of interest does not depend on the quantity of money.

In conclusion, to say that the rate of interest is determined by the schedule $M = f(r)$ is useless and confusing if this schedule is arrived at by previous solution of the entire system; it is an unwarranted simplification, full of serious consequences, if this function is treated as an ordinary demand function. And the statement that the propensity to save and invest plays no part in determining the rate of interest is true only in a limiting case: the Keynesian case.

20. Hicks's Theory—the Rate of Interest and the Cost of Investing in Securities

In *Value and Capital* Hicks has developed what is probably the most daring attempt at reducing the rate of interest to a purely monetary phenomenon.

---

[54] To give another example, we can solve the system to obtain, say, the equilibrium output of shoes (Q) as a function of the quantity of money: $Q = f(M, W)$ or $M = F(Q, W)$. But to say that a change in tastes changes the output *because* it shifts this function is formally correct but perfectly useless as a tool of analysis.

[55] Proper qualifications must be made for the case in which the IS curve is not monotonic decreasing.

In Hicks's own words the rate of interest is explained by the "imperfect moneyness" of securities. "The imperfect moneyness of those bills which are not money is due to their lack of general acceptability: it is this lack of general acceptability which causes the trouble of investing in them"[56] and it is this trouble, namely "the trouble of making transactions [i.e., of purchasing securities] which explains the short rate of interest."[57]   And these same factors also explain the long rate since the long rate is some average of the short rates plus a premium to cover the risk of (unanticipated) movements in the future short rates.[58]

Thus the rate of interest is explained by the fact that securities are not a medium of exchange and is determined essentially by the cost of making loan transactions.   This is certainly an unusual theory of interest and an astonishing one, to say the least; it appears irreconcilable with the theory we have developed throughout this paper.

Hicks's theory finds its origin in an attempt to answer a question posed by the Keynesian analysis.   The reason that induces people to hold assets in the form of cash rather than securities is that the value of even the safest type of securities is not certain: it is subject to changes due to movements in the rate of interest.   Now, as we have seen, this risk decreases as the duration of the loan transaction becomes shorter: and it disappears entirely on loans that last only one "Hicksian week" (or one income period in our model) since by hypothesis the rate of interest cannot change.   There must then be some other reason to stop people from holding all of their assets in the form of securities and thus reducing their demand for "money to hold" to zero; this reason can only be the cost of investing in this riskless type of loans.   This is Hicks's starting point: and so far there seems to be no difference from our own approach as developed in Section 5.   But from these correct premises Hicks draws the wrong conclusion: namely *that it is the cost of investing that explains the*

---

[56] *Value and Capital*, p. 166.

[57] *Ibid.*, p. 165.

[58] *Ibid.*, Chapter XI.

rate of interest. To say that the cost of investing is necessary to explain *why* the demand for money to hold is not always zero and to say that it *explains* the rate of interest are quite different statements. There is a logical gap between the two. Thus, for example, from the correct premise that the cost of automobiles in New York cannot fall to zero because they have to be transported from Detroit, there does not logically follow the conclusion that the cost of cars in New York is explained or determined by the cost of transporting them.

There is a different way of explaining the rate of interest, which is not less satisfactory for the fact of being obvious: namely that for certain categories of people (entrepreneurs as well as spendthrifts) it is worth while to pay a premium to obtain spot cash against a promise to pay cash in the future. This is the course we have followed: and it is clearly all that is necessary to explain the existence of the rate of interest. The cost of investing continues to play an important part in our theory: (a) it explains why the demand for money to hold is not identically zero; (b) it explains why the rate of interest can never fall below a certain level in a free capitalistic economy; and hence it explains the peculiarities of the Keynesian case. But it is clear that it is not necessary to explain the rate of interest.

Our next task is to show that the cost of investing is also not sufficient to explain the nature of interest. To this end we must disprove Hicks's statement that if people were to be "paid in the form of bills . . . there would be no cost of investment and therefore . . . no reason for the bills to fall to a discount,"[59] i.e., no rate of interest. It is easy to show that, even if "bills" were to be used as medium of exchange, there would be no reason for the rate of interest to fall to zero.

Let us consider first the case of a "stationary state." It is well known that the stationary state is characterized by the fact that the rate of change of the quantity of capital is zero; the marginal efficiency of the existing quantity of capital is equal to the rate of in-

---

[59] *Ibid.*, p. 165.

terest, say r_0, that makes net saving equal to zero.[60]   Now it is theoretically conceivable that, in this state, securities might replace money
as a medium of exchange;[61] their purchasing power would be objec-
tively determined by their discounted value since, by hypothesis, the
future rate of interest is known and constant.   Their aggregate
value would also be constant but, since individual savings need not
be zero, there would be a net flow from dissavers to savers.   Under
these conditions it is clear that securities would continue to yield the
rate of interest r_0, even though they would be performing the function of a medium of exchange.   Thus, as far as the stationary state
goes, Hicks's conclusion does not follow: the interest rate would be
zero only in the special case $r_0 = 0$.

Next let us consider an expanding economy, in which the net
level of saving and investment is not zero, and let us assume again
that it is technically possible for securities to be accepted as a medium
of exchange.[62]

In this economy, if there is to be no inflation, it is necessary
that the rate of money investment be not larger than the rate of
(*ex ante*) saving.   Now there are two possibilities:

(a) There exists some mechanism by which the net increase in
outstanding securities cannot exceed net savings.   Then the competition of borrowers to obtain loans will automatically determine
the level of the rate of interest.

(b) There is no limitation as to the issuance of new securities
per unit of time.   Then, of course, the rate of interest would be
zero, since there would be no necessity for borrowers to compete.
But the result would clearly be a situation of unending and progressive inflation.   In the first case the stability of the quantity of active
money and therefore of the price level is assured by the fact that
savers would increase their "hoards" of securities-money, at a rate
equal to the net increase in the value of outstanding securities.   But

---

[60] For a more detailed description of the conditions that give rise to a stationary state see, for instance, M. Timlin, *Keynesian Economics,* Chapter IV.

[61] See, for instance, *ibid.*, p. 53.

[62] This would require that all people agree at all times on the present value
of every security.

in the second case there is nothing to stop the price level from rising indefinitely, except if it so happens that the "full employment" rate of interest is zero or negative.[63]

We may therefore safely conclude that the rate of interest is not explained by the fact that securities are not money.   Once we recognize this, the complicated and confusing Hicksian theory about the imperfect moneyness of securities becomes unnecessary and should, in our opinion, be abandoned.

To say that different assets share in different degrees the quality of "moneyness" either has no meaning or it is based on a confusion between liquidity and the properties of a medium of exchange.   It is true that different assets have different degrees of liquidity, since the liquidity depends on the perfection of the market in which a good is traded.   And it is also true that money is probably, under normal conditions, the most liquid of all assets.   But the property of money is that it is accepted (freely or by force of law) as a medium of exchange: and liquidity does not make money out of something that is not money.   Whatever one's definition of liquidity, to say that a government bond, a speculative share, a house, are money in different degrees, can at best generate unnecessary confusion.   It is true that money and securities are close substitutes, but this connection is to be found elsewhere than in degrees of moneyness; it depends on the fact that both money and securities are alternative forms of holding assets in nonphysical form.   Securities are thus close substitutes for money, but not for money as a medium of exchange, only for money as an asset.

Having shown that the cost of investment neither explains nor determines the rate of interest, we will agree with Hicks that "the level of that [short] rate of interest measures the trouble involved in investing funds . . . to the marginal lender."[64]   One cannot disagree

---

[63] We are well aware of the fact that the excess of money investment over (*ex ante*) saving does not lead to inflation, unless there is full employment to begin with, or until full employment is reached.   It remains true however that, except in the case mentioned in the text, a zero rate of interest must eventually lead to inflation.

[64] *Op. cit.*, p. 165.

with this statement any more than with the statement that the price of butter measures the marginal utility of butter to each member of the community.[65]   Both statements are either tautologies or definitions of rational behavior.   They are tautologies if they mean that all those who found it convenient to perform a certain transaction have done so.   They are definitions of rational economic behavior if they state the conditions under which economic agents will maximize their satisfaction.[66]   But it is clear that whether these statements are tautologies or definitions they are not sufficient to explain either the price of butter or the level of the rate of interest.

To conclude then we agree with Hicks that the rate of interest is at least equal to the cost of investing to the marginal lender, but this statement is not very helpful for understanding the rate of interest.   But the Hicksian theory that the rate of interest is determined or simply explained by the imperfect moneyness of securities must be discarded as faulty.

21. *Saving and Investment or Supply of and Demand for Cash?—Conclusions*

It will now be useful, in concluding this paper, to restate in brief form the general theory of interest and money that emerges from our analysis.

We believe that the best way of achieving this aim is to show how, by means of our theory, we can answer the controversial question that has caused so much discussion in recent economic literature.

Is the rate of interest determined by the demand for and supply of cash?   Or is it determined by those "real factors," psychological and technological, that can be subsumed under the concepts of propensity to save and marginal efficiency of investment?

We consider it to be a distinct advantage of our theory that we

---

[65] More exactly: the ratio of the price of butter to that of any other commodity measures the ratio of their respective marginal utilities.

[66] If anything, Hicks's statement is less illuminating, since there is, at least theoretically, the possibility that the rate of interest may exceed the cost of lending idle funds to the marginal lender: it is this very possibility that gives rise to the "classical case."

can answer both questions affirmatively. We do not have to choose between these two alternatives any more than between the following two: Is the price of fish determined by the daily demand and the daily supply; or is it determined by the average yearly demand and the cost of fishing?

Since we have maintained throughout this paper that, in general, saving and lending are independent decisions, we must clearly agree that the "daily" rate of interest is determined by the demand for and supply of money to hold (or, for that matter, by demand for and supply of loanable funds).[67] It is this very principle that has formed the base of our analysis of the money market (Section 7). But we cannot stop at this recognition and think that this is sufficient for a general theory of the rate of interest.

To come back to our example, it is certainly true that the daily price of fish is entirely explained by the daily catch of fish. But if we want to understand why the daily price fluctuates around a certain level and not around a level ten times as high, we must look for something more fundamental than the good or bad luck of the fishermen on a particular day. We shall then discover that the number of fishermen and the amount of equipment used does not change daily but is determined by the condition that the average returns, through good and bad days, must be sufficiently high to make the occupation of fishing (and investment in fishing equipment) as attractive as alternative ones.

What is obviously true for the price of fish must also hold for the price of loans. The statement that the "daily" rate is determined by the "daily" demand for and supply of money (or, more exactly, of money to hold) does not greatly advance us in the understanding of the true determinants of the rate of interest. This theory by itself is insufficient to explain, for instance, why in countries well-equipped and of great saving capacity, like England or the United States, the system of rates of interest fluctuates around low levels (2 or 3 per

---

[67] In this respect we have nothing to add to the arguments developed by Hicks in Chapter XII of *Value and Capital*. There are enough equations to determine all the prices on each Monday and it makes no difference which equation is eliminated.

cent for the pure long rate and much less for short rates); while it fluctuates around much higher levels (5 or 6 per cent or more for the long rate) in countries poor in savings or rich but scarcely developed. Is that because in the last-mentioned countries the supply of cash is insufficient? Clearly not. The explanation for this difference can only run in terms of those more fundamental factors, technological and psychological, that are included in the propensity to save and the marginal efficiency of investment.

As we have shown in our model the equality of demand and supply of loanable funds is the equilibrium condition for the week (or for our income period) and determines the equilibrium rate of interest (or system of rates) for the week. It corresponds to the short-run equilibrium condition of the Marshallian demand and supply analysis: price equals marginal cost. But the stock of money to hold (the supply) tends itself to change and thus push the "daily" rate toward the level at which the flow of money saving equals the flow of money investment. The condition, (*ex ante*) saving = (*ex ante*) investment, corresponds to the long-run Marshallian condition (under perfect competition): price = average cost including rent.

The first condition is satisfied even in the short period since it is the result of decisions that can be carried out instantaneously (see Section 5). The second is a long-run condition and therefore may actually never be satisfied: but it is necessary to explain the level toward which the weekly rate tends (even though this level may never be reached since the long-run equilibrium rate of interest itself changes).

Thus, to complete our theory, we must be able to explain what determines the level of long-run equilibrium. At this point we find that our answer is not unique since it depends on the assumptions concerning the form of the supply-of-labor schedule.

I. As long as wages are flexible, the long-run equilibrium rate of interest is determined exclusively by real factors, that is to say, essentially by the propensity to save and the marginal efficiency of investment. The condition, money saving = money investment, determines the price level and not the rate of interest.

II. If wages are rigid it is still true that the long-run equilibrium rate of interest is determined by the propensities to save and to invest but the situation is now more complicated; for these propensities depend also on money income and therefore on the quantity of active money which in turn depends itself on the level of the rate of interest. Thus, unless wages are perfectly flexible or the supply of money is always so adjusted as to assure the maintenance of full employment, the long-run equilibrium rate of interest depends also on the quantity of money and it is determined, together with money income, by equations (1), (2), and (3) of our model.   We want however to stress again that the dependence of the rate of interest on the quantity of money does not depend on liquidity preference.   In a system with rigid wages not only interest but also almost every economic variable depends on the quantity of money.

III. Finally our theory of the rate of interest becomes even less uniform when we take into account the "Keynesian case."   In this case clearly the long-run equilibrium rate of interest is the rate which makes the demand for money to hold infinitely elastic.   The economic theorist here is forced to recognize that under certain conditions the rate of interest is determined exclusively by institutional factors.

12

ECONOMIC PROGRESS IN A STABLE ENVIRONMENT*

By A. C. Pigou‖

I

In actual life the process of economic change is dominated by technical developments resulting from scientific discoveries and is closely associated with changes in the size of the population of working age. In what follows I shall rule both these things out of account. I shall assume, moreover, that the stock of money circulating outside the banks is fixed and that the Government does not attempt to control investment with a view to regulating employment. Finally, I shall assume that the State nowhere intervenes by fixing maximum prices below, or minimum prices above, those which would rule in a free market. This implies that at the ruling prices there are no unsatisfied demands or unwanted supplies; in other words that markets are everywhere cleared, or, if we will, that all parts of the economic system are always in market equilibrium—to be sharply distinguished from what I shall call in a moment thorough-going equilibrium.

The theme I propose is this. Let us imagine ourselves situated in an initial year in which some investment is taking place, and let us ask what thereafter, subject to the conditions set out in the last paragraph, will happen. The enquiry is most conveniently conducted in two divisions; first on the assumption that people make net savings —I use this term as equivalent to net investment—solely on account of the material returns which they expect them presently to yield, so that, if these expected returns were nil, there would be no net saving; and, secondly, on the more realistic assumption that saving

* *Economica,* New Series, **14** (1947), 180–88. Reprinted, by the courtesy of the publisher and the author, without change from the original text.

‖ King's College, Cambridge.

is partly motivated by a desire to hold capital wealth as such as a source of prestige, individual security and so on. On the first assumption the analysis is straightforward, but on the second some awkward puzzles may—not must—present themselves.

II

In Frank Ramsey's well known article, "A mathematical theory of saving,"[1] the first of these two assumptions is implicitly adopted. On this basis Ramsey observes that, for the economic system in any closed community to be in thorough-going equilibrium, the rate of return obtainable from the marginal unit of capital must be equal to the representative man's rate of time preference. So long as there is any difference between these two things, that will constitute a continuing stimulus towards net investment or towards net disinvestment; so that the state of the economic system is continually changing. When there is net investment or disinvestment there cannot be thorough-going equilibrium; when there is thorough-going equilibrium there cannot be net investment or net disinvestment. Here we are supposing that in our initial year some net investment is taking place, so that we have to do with a forward, not a backward, movement. What are the characteristics of this movement?

There is one preliminary complication to be cleared out of the way. We may properly, for the present purpose, disregard cyclical fluctuations in the proportion of available work-people actually employed, but we must not exclude the possibility of a trend of change in this proportion. The monetary authorities being assumed to hold the stock of money circulating outside the banks constant, if the income velocity of money varies, its variations cannot be offset by compensating variations in this stock. As we shall see in a moment, the gradual expansion in the stock of capital will entail a gradual fall in the rate of interest in terms of consumption goods. This may be expected to entail a gradual fall in the income velocity of money and, therefore, in money income, or effective demand. Other things being equal, this should set up a downward pressure on money wage rates, which, so far as it is resisted, will promote unemployment.

---

[1] *Economic Journal* (December 1928).

The pressure will diminish as the rate at which the rate of interest is falling decreases. Hence the proportion of productive resources out of employment might be expected to become smaller and the proportion actually employed larger as the years pass. This movement can, however, hardly be other than slow and weak; and in any case, so far as it is realised, should reinforce rather than counteract the broad tendencies I am about to describe. We need not, therefore, trouble ourselves about it. What then are these broad tendencies?

First, under the pressure of the excess of the rate of interest in terms of consumption goods over the representative man's rate of time preference, new investment will be continuously taking place, the stock of capital in existence will continuously grow, and, therefore, in the conditions we are supposing, the stock of capital actually at work will continuously grow.

Secondly, with the stock of capital at work increasing and the stock of labour (as we are supposing) constant, the rate of return to investment, and so the rate of interest in terms of consumption goods—a slightly ambiguous concept—will, in the absence of technical change, become continuously smaller.

Thirdly, there will be a reaction on the size of real income. Since we are supposing the population of working age to be constant, the aggregate stock of resources, capital *plus* labour, available for work must be continuously increasing. Granted that the percentage of employment is not decreasing, real output or income is bound continuously to expand unless the effective length of the working day is being contemporaneously cut down fast enough to offset this tendency.

By the effective length of the working day, whether for labour or for capital, is meant the proportion of the twenty-four hours in which work of standard efficiency is being done; so that a twelve hours' actual day is not 50 per cent. longer than, but of the same length as, an eight hours' day if work in the shorter day is 50 per cent. more efficient. It should be noted that for capital the effective length of the working day is not necessarily the same as it is for labour; since it is possible to operate the same equipment with one, two or three shifts of labour per day; and, the shorter the working day for labour is, the more inducement employers have to introduce multiple

shifts.   So far as they succeed in doing this, reductions in the effective
length of the working day for labour will be associated with expansions
for capital.   That, however, is a secondary matter and we may ignore
it.   What may be expected to happen to the effective length of the
working day for labour?

The more capital there is the greater is the capacity of the community to produce real income; and people may be expected to
take out some part of their more favourable conjuncture in extra
leisure.   This is not, indeed, *necessary*.   The effort-cost of producing
a given quantity of consumers' goods having diminished, people
might decide, in consequence, to increase the amount of their effort.
In fact, however, the progressive growth of capital, which has taken
place in modern times, has been accompanied by a downward trend
in the hours of labour.   Moreover, it is well known that wealthier
countries on the whole enjoy shorter working hours than poorer
countries.   These considerations suggest, though, of course, they
do not prove, that enlargements in the stock of capital are likely, as
a rule, to entail contractions in the effective length of the working day
for labour.

Now the size of a community's real income or output depends,
in given conditions of technique and so on, on the size of the stocks
of capital and labour in existence, the proportions of these stocks
actually engaged in work and the effective length of the working day.
We have seen that, as the years pass, the stock of capital will be
increasing while, we are supposing, the stock of labour and the proportions of both stocks actually at work, will at worst be constant.
These conditions in combination make for an increase in real income.
True, a third factor, the accompanying decrease in the effective length
of the working day, will cause real income to increase less fast than
it would do otherwise.   But, except in a practically impossible limiting case, it cannot cancel the *whole* of the increase that would have
occurred apart from it.   Hence real income must continuously grow.

Thus as the years pass, with the population of working age constant
and no alteration in technique, three major developments must take
place; a continuing increase in the stock of capital both in existence
and actually at work; a continuing fall in the rate of interest in

terms of consumption goods; and a continuing increase in real income. There remains the question what will happen to the volume of annual investment. Since the economic system is moving towards a goal at which, if it is ultimately attained, this will be nothing, it must at *some* stage enter upon a decreasing phase. It need not, indeed, enter upon that phase immediately or even soon after our initial year is left behind. For, while the fall in the rate of interest, taken by itself, tends to make the rate of investment fall, the associated increase in real income, taken by itself, tends to make it grow. Still, eventually, whether before, in or after our initial year, it is bound to start downwards on a final movement towards nothing.

The general nature of the process—if we like to be pompous, the 'dynamic process'—that I have been describing is plain enough. What of the goal towards which it is moving? We cannot suppose that the representative man's rate of time preference is ever negative, no matter how large an income he has. Hence there can be no question of the rate of interest in terms of consumption goods falling to zero, in consequence of the expansion in the stock of capital, *before* it has come to equality with this rate of time preference. It does not strictly follow from this that there must be some stock of capital in respect of which the rate of interest and the rate of time preference would have equal positive values. For conceivably the two rates, one or both of them always falling, might approach each other asymptotically without actually coinciding in respect of any finite stock of capital. We may, however, I think, disregard this possibility—it is a mathematical toy—and conceive that there *is* a goal with a finite stock of capital, a nil rate of investment and a positive rate of interest, in terms of consumption goods, such that, *if* the economic system hit it, in the absence of technical or population change it would stay there in the thorough-going equilibrium of a stationary state. Indeed there *may* (not, of course, must) be several alternative goals—positions of thorough-going equilibrium—at which the economic system would come to rest if it once got there. But this is a trivial point; because, since we suppose ourselves to start with a state of things in which some investment is taking place, the first point of intersection between the rate of interest curve and the rate of time preference curve (in respect of stationary states) at which the system arrives must be a stable one, and, even though other points of stable equilibrium also exist, there are no means, in the conditions we are supposing, by which the economic system can get to them.   Thus for practical purposes there is only one goal in which we need interest ourselves.

The question still remains whether the economic system need ever hit that goal; whether it might not, after coming close to it, overshoot the mark and thereafter, with alternating investment and disinvestment, oscillate about it for ever.   We need not, I think, trouble ourselves unduly about this suggestion.   For, as the goal is approached, the force impelling to movement, in this case the gap between the rate of interest and the rate of time preference, becomes progressively weaker and advances are made by smaller and smaller steps—a quite different state of affairs from that illustrated by the celebrated pig cycle.   As the first hero struggles panting up the final slope of Mount Everest, it is exceedingly unlikely that he will overshoot his mark and thereafter step backwards and forwards across it for ever.   He will sit down; and, for so long as he dare, stay sat down.   This, too, then is a toy.   On the assumption we have so far been making the economic system will eventually reach and stay at what we may call, if we like, the Ramseyan thorough-going equilibrium—the classical stationary state.

III

So far we have built our analysis on the first of the two assumptions distinguished above, namely that people save merely for the sake of the material return that they expect presently to receive—for the sake, that is to say, of the rate of interest in terms of consumption goods—so that, if this rate were nil, there would be no net saving. We now turn to the other and more realistic assumption.   People are led to save in part by a desire actually to hold wealth for the amenity, so to speak, derived from holding it; the representative man with an income not too small would almost certainly save something—be ready to supply some resources for investment—even if the rate of interest were nil.   This greatly complicates our problem.

For now a thorough-going equilibrium requires, not that the rate of interest in terms of consumption goods shall be equal to the rate of time preference, but that it shall be less than the rate of time preference by some quantity that represents the rate of amenity return from marginal saving. The. rate at which *borrowings and lendings* take place is, indeed, the rate of interest alone without any amenity allowance. The reason is that, when a man borrows resources from another man, no addition is made to his net capital assets, because what he receives is exactly offset by the capital debt created against it. In like manner, when a man lends to another man, no deduction is made from his net capital assets. Therefore what he borrows carries no increment of amenity, and no such element enters into what he pays for loans. But the rate of interest plus the amenity allowance is what the representative man, who in the last resort is both demander and supplier, balances in his mind against the burden he suffers in withdrawing from consumption and supplying (to himself) for investment the marginal apple so supplied. This fact opens up a possibility excluded on our previous assumption, namely that the rate of interest in terms of consumption goods may fall to nothing *before* the stock of capital has become large enough for this rate of interest plus this amenity value to have come to equality with the rate of time preference. This possibility need not, of course, be realised. It may quite well happen that the rate of interest plus our amenity value comes to equality with the rate of time preference while the rate of interest is still positive. In that case everything happens just as it would do in the conditions described in the last section. But it is no longer *necessary* for thorough-going equilibrium to be attained with a stock of capital in respect of which the rate of interest in terms of consumption goods is still positive. If thorough-going equilibrium is *not* attained while that is still so, while the earlier stages of the movement forward from our initial year are as we found them to be on our first assumption, presently a critical point is reached, and we are confronted with a new kind of situation.

The essential fact is this. Since money can be held without appreciable cost it is impossible for the money rate of interest to be less than nothing. Further, since in a thorough-going equilibrium there can be no expectation of a change in relative values, all commodity rates of interest must be the same as the money rate. It follows that no sort of rate of interest can be less than nothing. Hence, in the conditions we are supposing, it may be impossible for the economic system to attain its goal—an equilibrium in which the rate of interest in terms of consumption goods plus the amenity value of marginal saving is equal to, that is to say, is as small as, the rate of time preference. What then will happen?

This is where Lord Keynes comes on the scene. His argument is broadly this. People still want to save. This follows from the fact that the rate of interest plus the amenity value of marginal saving is greater than the rate of time preference. But they will not save by making new real investment at negative interest because it is open to them to hold money at nil interest. Consequently, the representative man will progressively draw money out of the circulation into savings deposits, so that, in the absence of new creations of money, money income must progressively fall or—another way of saying the same thing—money income must fall through the income velocity of money being reduced. Now in these circumstances, if the rate of money wages is held rigid in spite of growing unemployment, unemployment must grow; the proportion of available resources at work contracting roughly in proportion to the contraction in money income. But this process will not go on for ever. The representative man's rate of time preference is sure to be substantially larger for small real incomes than for large, because with a smaller real income he is under stronger pressure to focus attention on the present moment. The contraction of employment entailing, as it does, a corresponding contraction of real income, carries with it, therefore, an increase in this rate. Presently the rate rises so far that it reaches equality with the rate of interest plus the money measure of the amenity value of marginal savings proper to the stock of capital that has been attained. At this point the economic system comes into equilibrium. People no longer desire to save anything, and, therefore, money income no longer contracts. The stock of capital is the same as it was when the rate of interest became nothing; but employment, and therewith real income, is smaller—maybe much smaller. The situation thus reached, provided that money wage rates are still maintained, is one of stable equilibrium—the low level equilibrium that I have sometimes called Lord Keynes's Day of Judgment. Whether real income then is lower, not merely than it was at the critical moment when the rate of time preference became nothing, but than it was in our initial year, depends, of course, on how far distant from that critical moment our initial year was.

This solution is clearly valid provided that the money wage rate is in fact rigidly maintained in the face of heavy and growing unemployment. It is, however, very hard to believe that, in given conditions of technique and so on, the proportion of available resources at work will be determined permanently, as this solution requires, by such superficial things as the money and price situation. In the Keynesian equilibrium wage earners, having infinite time at their disposal, are surely bound to see through the money façade to the realities behind. There must, it would seem, be *some* proportion of employment, not necessarily, of course, "full" employment, to the attainment of which they would set themselves irrespective of the monetary situation. If this is in fact so, the position proper to Lord Keynes's Day of Judgment will not be attained or even approached. Money wage rates will continually fall to prevent employment from falling; but the income velocity of money and money income will also continuously fall. Thus money wage rates, money income and money prices will all move downwards for ever, while employment and real income remain fairly stable and fairly good. With money wage rates free to vary to any extent, this and not the Keynesian Day of Judgment appears *prima facie* to be the goal of the economic process.

But this appearance is deceptive. As the money rate of wages falls the money price of consumption goods falls also. This entails that the value in terms of consumption goods of the stock of money, and, along with this, that of other sorts of non-instrumental property, such as Old Masters, which are specially attractive as receptacles for, or embodiments of, savings, expands. This means that the total stock of property, as valued in consumption goods, which is held by the public becomes progressively larger and larger. It must be remembered, indeed, that not all the stock of money held by the public constitutes a net asset to them. Part of it is offset by debts from them to the banks in respect of advances and discounts. In 1938, the last full pre-war year, these amounted to 1,200 millions as against 2,160 millions of deposits; while the note circulation was 485 millions. Thus of the public's aggregate money holdings, notes and deposits together, only some 1,400 millions out of a total of 2,600 millions constituted a net element in their holding of property. Hence the addition made to this holding of property as valued in consumption goods when prices fall is smaller than it might perhaps be thought to be at first sight. None the less, it is likely to be substantial. Now the amenity value in terms of satisfaction derived from holding an additional unit of property evidently becomes smaller the more units of property (as measured in consumption goods) that there are; while, with a given real income, the value of a unit of satisfaction in terms of consumption goods is, of course, given. Hence, with employment the same as it was when the rate of interest first became nothing, the marginal amenity yield of savings expressed in consumption goods must become smaller and smaller as money income contracts, until finally, it plus the rate of interest coincides with the rate of time preference and a genuine equilibrium is established. Henceforward the stock of capital, employment and real income remain for ever what they were at the critical moment when the rate of interest first became nothing. That rate itself continues for ever at nothing; the rate of time preference continues for ever at that level above nothing at which it stood then; and the marginal amenity yield of (nil) new savings is for ever equal to the excess of the rate of time preference above nothing. Real income, being the same as it was at the critical moment, is obviously larger than it was in our initial year.

To sum up then. If, as the years pass and capital accumulates, the rate of interest in terms of consumption goods plus the marginal amenity yield of savings becomes equal to the representative man's rate of time preference before the rate of interest falls to nothing, thorough-going equilibrium will be then and there established and there are no complications. But, if, before this equality can be achieved, the rate of interest has fallen to nothing, the upshot is uncertain. If money wage rates are rigidly maintained, at this point the economic engine will be put into reverse until a new low level equilibrium is established with a lower, perhaps a much lower, level of employment and real income. If, on the other hand, money wage rates move downward freely, equilibrium will ultimately be established with the stock of capital, employment, real income, the rate of interest and the rate of time preference standing as they stood when the rate of interest first reached nil level, but with the marginal amenity yield of nil new savings so far contracted that this plus the rate of interest is no longer greater than, but is equal to, the rate of time preference.

IV

The foregoing analysis holds good, of course, only on the basis of the assumptions set out at the beginning of this article. It is extremely improbable that these assumptions will ever be satisfied in practice. For, even if we allow the population of working age to be stable and the faculty of invention to disappear, it is ridiculous to suppose that the public authorities would stand passive in the case of catastrophic disturbances. If a situation arose in which money income was being driven inexorably downwards in the way contemplated in the last section, no government would allow money wage rates to rush downwards very far; legal minimum rates would inevitably be established. This would very likely be done soon enough to prevent the type of final equilibrium described on pp. 250–251 from emerging. But, equally, no government could allow the movement towards the Keynesian equilibrium, with its massive unemployment, to proceed very far. It would be bound to intervene by itself undertaking on behalf of the community investment at negative rates of interest or by adopting some other means to arrest the downrush of money income. Thus the puzzles we have been considering in the last section are academic exercises, of some slight use perhaps for clarifying thought, but with very little chance of ever being posed on the chequer board of actual life.

13

PRICE FLEXIBILITY AND FULL EMPLOYMENT*

By Don Patinkin‖

At the core of the Keynesian polemics of the past ten years and more is the relationship between price flexibility and full employment. The fundamental argument of Keynes is directed against the belief that price flexibility can be depended upon to generate full employment automatically. The defenders of the classical tradition, on the other hand, still insist upon this automaticity as a basic tenet.

During the years of continuous debate on this question, the issues at stake have been made more precise. At the same time, further material on the question of flexibility has become available. This paper is essentially an attempt to incorporate this new material, and, taking advantage of the perspective offered by time, to analyze the present state of the debate.

In Part I, the problem of price flexibility and full employment is presented from a completely static viewpoint. Part II then goes on

* *The American Economic Review*, 38 (1948), 543–64. Reprinted, by the courtesy of the publisher and the author. (Advantage has been taken of this reprinting to correct and modify several parts of the article. The major changes are the following: the addition of the latter part of the last paragraph of § 5, as a result of discussions with Milton Friedman; the addition of paragraphs three and four of § 6, as a result of comments by Donald Gordon, Franco Modigliani, and Norman Ture; the correction of the last paragraph of § 6 and Table 1 of § 11 in accordance with Herbert Stein's comment on the original article in the *American Economic Review*, XXXIX (1949), 725–26; and the addition of the last three paragraphs of § 14, in the attempt to clarify some points left ambiguous in the original article. All significant additions are enclosed in brackets.)

‖ Hebrew University, Jerusalem. In the process of writing this paper the author acknowledges having benefited from stimulating discussions with Milton Friedman, University of Chicago, and Alexander M. Henderson, University of Manchester.

to discuss the far more important dynamic aspects of the problem. Finally, in Part III, the implications of the discussion for the Keynesian-classical polemic are analyzed. It is shown that over the years these two camps have really come closer and closer together. It is argued that the basic issue separating them is the rapidity with which the economic system responds to price variations.

I. STATIC ANALYSIS

1. The traditional interpretation of Keynesian economics is that it demonstrates the absence of an automatic mechanism assuring the

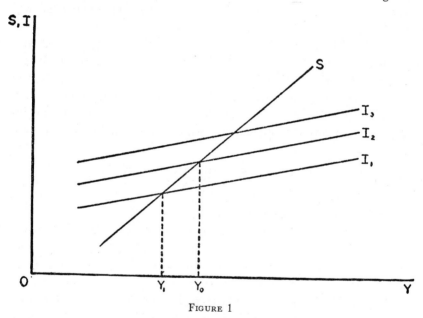

FIGURE 1

equality of desired savings and investment at full employment. The graphical meaning of this interpretation is presented in a simplified form in Figure 1. Here desired real savings (S) and investment (I) are each assumed to depend only on the level of real income (Y). I_1, I_2, and I_3 represent three possible positions of the investment schedule. Y_0 is the full employment level of real income. If the investment desires of individuals are represented by the curve I_1, desired savings at full employment are greater than desired investment at full employment. This means that unemployment will result: the level of income will drop to Y_1, at which income desired savings and investment are equal. Conversely, if I_3 is the investment curve, a situation of overemployment or inflation will occur: people desire to invest more at full employment than the amount of savings will permit. Only if the investment schedule happened to be I_2 would full employment, desired investment and savings be equal. But since investment decisions are independent of savings decisions, there is no reason to expect the investment schedule to coincide with I_2. Hence there is no automatic assurance that full employment will result.

2. The classical answer to this attack is that desired savings and investment depend on the rate of interest, as well as the level of real income; and that, granted flexibility, variations in the interest rate serve as an automatic mechanism insuring full employment.

The argument can be interpreted as follows: the savings and investment functions (representing what people desire to do) are written as

$$S = \Omega(r, Y)$$
$$I = \Psi(r, Y)$$

where r represents the rate of interest.

Consider now Figure 2. On this graph there can be drawn a whole family of curves relating savings and investment to the rate of interest—one pair for each level of real income. In Figure 2, these pairs of curves are drawn for the full employment income, Y_0, and for the less than full employment income, Y_1. On the assumption that for a given rate of interest people will save and invest more at a higher level of income, the investment curve corresponding to $Y = Y_0$ is drawn above that corresponding to $Y = Y_1$; similarly for the two savings curves. The curves also reflect the assumption that, for a given level of real income, people desire to save more and invest less at higher rates of interest.

Consider now the pair of curves corresponding to the full employment income Y_0. If in Figure 2 the interest rate were r_1, then it would be true that individuals would desire to save more at full employment than they would desire to invest. But, assuming no rigidities in the interest rate, this would present no difficulties. For if the interest rate were to fall freely, savings would be discouraged, and investment stimulated until finally desired full employment savings and investment would be equated at the level $S_0 = I_0$. Similarly, if at full employment desired investment is greater than desired savings, a rise in the interest rate will prevent inflation. In this way

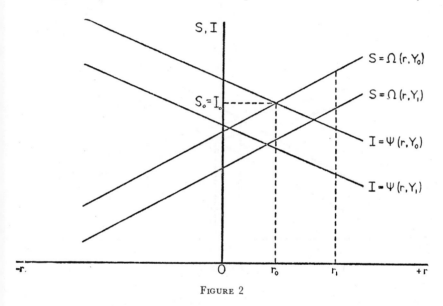

FIGURE 2

variations in the rate of interest serve automatically to prevent any discrepancy between desired full employment investment and savings, and thus to assure full employment.

This argument can also be presented in terms of Figure 1: assume for simplicity that desired investment depends on the rate of interest as well as the level of real income, while desired savings depends only on the latter. Then downward variations in the interest rate can be counted on to raise the investment curve from, say, I_1 to I_2. That is, at any level of income people can be encouraged to invest more by a reduction in the rate of interest. Similarly, upward movements of the interest rate will shift the investment curve from, say, I_3 to I_2. Thus desired full employment savings and investment will always be equated.

3. The Keynesian answer to this classical argument is that it greatly exaggerates the importance of the interest rate. Empirical evidence has accumulated in support of the hypothesis that variations in the rate of interest have little effect on the amount of desired in-

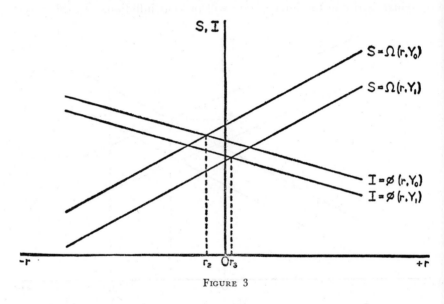

FIGURE 3

vestment. (That savings are insensitive to the interest rate is accepted even by the classical school.) This insensitivity has been interpreted as a reflection of the presence of widespread uncertainty.[1] The possible effect of this insensitivity on the ability of the system automatically to generate full employment is analyzed in Figure 3. For simplicity the savings functions corresponding to different levels of income are reproduced from Figure 2. But the investment functions

[1] Cf. Oscar Lange, *Price Flexibility and Employment* (Bloomington, Indiana, Principia Press, 1945), p. 85 and the literature cited there. For an excellent theoretical discussion of this insensitivity, cf. G. L. S. Shackle, "Interest Rates and the Pace of Investment," *Economic Journal,* Vol. LVI (1946), pp. 1–17.

are now represented as being much less interest-sensitive than those in Figure 2. If the situation in the real world were such as represented in Figure 3, it is clear that interest rate variations could never bring about full employment. For in an economy in which there are negligible costs of storing money, the interest rate can never be negative.[2] But from Figure 3 we see that the only way the interest rate can equate desired full employment savings and investment is by assuming the negative value r_2. Hence it is impossible for the full employment national income Y_0 to exist: for no matter what (positive) rate of interest may prevail, the amount people want to save at full employment exceeds what they want to invest. Instead there will exist some less than full employment income (say) Y_1 for which desired savings and investment can be brought into equality at a positive rate of interest, (say) r_3 (cf. Figure 3).

Thus once again the automaticity of the system is thrown into question. Whether the system will generate full employment depends on whether the full employment savings and investment functions intersect at a positive rate of interest. But there is no automatic mechanism to assure that the savings and investment functions will have the proper slopes and positions to bring about such an intersection.[3]

4. Sometimes attempts are made to defend the classical position by arguing that the investment function is really higher (or the savings function lower) than represented by the Keynesians—so that desired full employment savings and investment can be equated at a positive rate of interest (cf. Figure 3). But this is beside the point. [The fundamental disagreement between Keynesian and classical economics lies in the former's denial of the automaticity of full employment posited by the latter.] Hence a successful restatement

---

[2] Note that in a dynamic world of rising prices, the effective rate of interest may become negative. But even here the *anticipated* **effective** rate cannot be negative. For in that event there would again be an infinite demand for money.

[3] [I have discussed this whole question of the contrast between the classical and Keynesian positions in greater detail elsewhere. *Cf.* "Involuntary Unemployment and the Keynesian Supply Function," *Economic Journal* LIX (1949), 376–78.]

of the classical position must demonstrate the existence of some automatic mechanism which will always bring about full employment.
Thus to argue that *if* the investment or saving function is at a certain level, full employment will be brought about is irrelevant; what
must be shown is that there exist forces which will *automatically*
bring the investment or saving functions to the required level.   In
other words, the issue at stake is not the *possible,* but the *automatic,*
generation of full employment.

5. [To the Keynesian negative interest rate argument replies
have been made by both Haberler and Pigou.[4]   Just as the crude
Keynesian argument of § 1 was answered by introducing a new variable—the rate of interest—into the savings function, so the more
refined argument of § 3 is countered by the introduction of yet another variable—the real value of cash balances held by the individuals
in the economy.   Thus, denoting the amount of money in the economy M_1 (assumed to remain constant) and the absolute price level
by p, Pigou's saving schedule is written as

$$S = \Gamma\left(r, \, Y, \, \frac{M_1}{p}\right).]$$

His argument is as follows: if people would refuse to save anything at negative and zero rates of interest, then the desired savings
schedule would intersect the desired investment schedule at a positive
rate of interest regardless of the level of income (*cf.* Figure 3).   The
willingness to save even without receiving interest, or even at a cost,
must imply that savings are not made solely for the sake of future
income (*i.e.,* interest) but also for "the desire for possession as such,
conformity to tradition or custom and so on."[5]   But the extent to

---

[4] [G. Haberler, *Prosperity and Depression* (League of Nations, Geneva,
1941), 3rd ed., pp. 242, 389, 403, 491–503.]

A. C. Pigou, "The Classical Stationary State," *Economic Journal*, LIII
(1943), 343–51; "Economic Progress in a Stable Environment," *Economica*,
n. s. XIV (1947), 180–90.   Although these articles deal only with a stationary
state, their basic argument can readily be extended to the case in which net
investment is taking place.

[In the subsequent text, I shall follow the exposition of Pigou; but the argument holds also with respect to Haberler.]

[5] *Ibid.*, p. 346.

which an individual wishes to save out of current income for reasons other than the desire of future income is inversely related to the
real value of his cash balances.[6]   If this is sufficiently large, all his
secondary desires for saving will be fully satisfied.   At this point the
only reason he will continue to save out of current income is the primary one of anticipated future interest payments.   In other words,
if the real value of cash balances is sufficiently large, the savings func-

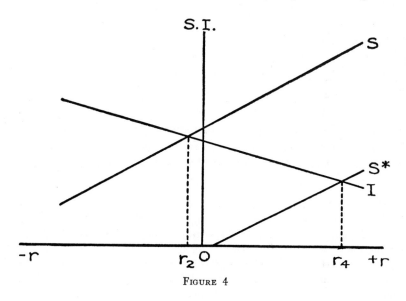

FIGURE 4

tion becomes zero at a positive rate of interest, regardless of the income level.

A graphical interpretation of this argument is presented in Figure 4.   Here S and I are the full-employment savings and investment
curves of Figure 3 (*i.e.*, those corresponding to $Y = Y_0$), and r_2 is
again the negative rate of interest at which they are equal.   Pigou
then argues that by increasing the real value of cash balances, the
full employment savings curve shifts to the right until it is in such
a position that no savings are desired except at positive rates of in-

---

[6] And all his other assets too.   But the introduction of these other assets
does not change Pigou's argument; while concentration on money assets brings
out its (the argument's) basic aspect.   *Cf.* below, § 6.

terest.   This is represented by the savings curve S*, which becomes zero for a positive rate of interest.   (In fact, S* shows dissaving taking place for sufficiently low rates of interest.)   The full employment savings curve S* clearly intersects the full employment investment curve I at the positive rate of interest r_4.   Thus by changing the real value of cash balances, desired full employment savings and investment can always be equated at a positive rate of interest.

How can we be sure that real cash balances will automatically change in the required direction and magnitude?   Here Pigou brings in his assumptions of flexible wage and price levels, and a constant stock of money in circulation.   If full employment saving exceeds investment, national income begins to fall, and unemployment results. If workers react to this by decreasing their money wages, then the price level will also begin to fall.   As the latter continues to fall, the real value of the constant stock of money increases correspondingly. Thus, as the price level falls, the full employment saving function continuously shifts to the right until it intersects the full employment investment function at a positive rate of interest.[7]

---

[7] The exact price level is determined when to our preceding four equations is added the liquidity preference equation, $M_0 = (r, Y, p)$, where M_0 represents the given amount of money in the system.   (As will be shown in the next section, the "stock of money" relevant for the liquidity equation is completely different from the "stock of money" relevant for the Pigou analysis of the savings function; hence the use of two different symbols—M_0 and M_1.)   We then have the complete system of five equations in five variables:

$$I = \Phi(r, Y)$$
$$S = \Gamma\left(r, Y, \frac{M_1}{p}\right)$$
$$I = S$$
$$Y = Y_0$$
$$M_0 = \Lambda(r, Y, p).$$

Under the Pigovian assumptions this system is consistent; its equations are satisfied for a positive rate of interest.

[The workings of a more general system of equations under the Pigovian assumption are described in detail in Parts IV and V of the reference cited in footnote 3 above.   In this more detailed treatment, the full employment level, Y_0, is not arbitrarily defined—as is done in the present paper—but emerges instead from the economic behavior functions themselves.]

This is the automatic mechanism on which Haberler and Pigou rely to assure full employment. It is essential to note that it will operate regardless of the interest-elasticities of the savings and investment functions—provided they are not both identically zero. [It should also be emphasized, as Haberler does, that although this argument has been presented above as an answer to Keynes, it is of much older origin. In particular, it is implicit in classical theorizing on the quantity theory of money. The crucial step in this analysis, it will be recalled, comes at the point where it is argued that as a result of increasing the amount of money in the economy, individuals' cash balances are larger than desired at the existing price level, so that they will attempt to reduce these real balances by increasing their money expenditures. The main contribution of Haberler and Pigou is to show how this set of forces must, and can, be introduced into the Keynesian analytical apparatus.]

6. The inner mechanism and distinctive characteristic of the Pigou analysis can be laid bare by considering it from a larger perspective. It is obvious that a price reduction has a stimulating effect on creditors. But, restricting ourselves to the private sector of a closed economy, to every stimulated creditor there corresponds a discouraged debtor. Hence from this viewpoint the net effect of a price reduction is likely to be in the neighborhood of zero. The neatness of the Pigou approach lies in its utilizing the fact that although the private sector considered in isolation is, on balance, neither debtor nor creditor, when considered in its relationship to the government, it *must be* a net "creditor." This is due to the fact that the private sector always holds money, which is a (non-interest bearing) "debt" of government. If we assume that government activity is not affected by the movements of the absolute price level,[8] then the net effect of a price decline must always be stimulatory.[9] The

---

[8] Pigou makes this assumption when he writes the investment function (which presumably also includes government expenditure) as independent of the absolute price level. *Cf.* footnote 7 above.

[9] It must be emphasized that I am abstracting here from all dynamic considerations of the effect on anticipations, etc. These will be discussed in Part II of the paper.

community gains at the "expense" of a gracious government, ready, willing, and able to bear the "loss" of the increased value of its "debt" to the public.

More precisely, not every price decline need have this stimulating effect. For we must consider the effect of the price decline on the other assets held by the individual. If the decline reduces the real value of these other assets (*e.g.*, houses and other forms of consumer capital; stock shares; etc.) to an extent more than offsetting the increased value of real cash balances,[10] then the net effect will be discouraging. But the important point is that no matter what our initial position, *there exists* a price level sufficiently low so that the total real value of assets corresponding to it is greater than the original real value. Consider the extreme case in which the value of the other assets becomes arbitrarily small.[11] Clearly even here the real value of the fixed stock of money can be made as large as desired by reducing the price level sufficiently. Thus, to be rigorous, the statement in the preceding paragraph should read: "There always exists a price decline such that its effect is stimulatory." From this and the analysis of the preceding section, we can derive another statement which succinctly summarizes the results of the Pigou analysis: "In the static classical model, regardless of the position of the investment schedule, there always exists a sufficiently low price level such that full employment is generated." In any event, it is clearly sufficient to concentrate (as Pigou has done) on cash balances alone.[12]

[This analysis is subject to at least two reservations, neither one of which has been considered by Haberler or Pigou. First of all, we have tacitly been assuming that the depressing effect of a price decline on

---

[10] A necessary (but not sufficient) condition for this to occur is that the price level of assets falls in a greater proportion than the general price level.

[11] I am indebted to M. Friedman for this example.

[12] *Cf.* above, footnote 6. Another possible reason for Pigou's emphasis on cash balances to the exclusion of other assets is that the relative illiquidity of the latter makes them less likely to be used as a means of satisfying the "irrational" motives of saving. Hence the inverse relationship between other assets and savings out of current income might not be so straightforward as that between real cash balances and savings.

a debtor is roughly offset by its stimulating effect on a creditor; hence the private sector, being on balance a creditor with respect to the government, can ultimately be stimulated by a price decline. But allowance must be made for the possibility of a differential reaction of debtors and creditors. That is, if debtors are discouraged by a price decline much more than creditors are encouraged, it may be possible that there exists no price decline which would have an encouraging effect on expenditures. In brief, the Keynesian aggregative analysis followed by Pigou overlooks the possibility of microeconomic "distribution effects."

Secondly, we have so far considered only the effects of a change in real balances on household behavior; that is, on the consumption (or, its counterpart, the savings) function. It seems only natural to extend the analysis to include the influence of real cash balances on firms, and, hence, on the investment function as well. However, this extension cannot be made automatically, inasmuch as the respective motivations of firms and households are not necessarily the same. Nevertheless, it does seem reasonable to assume that investment decisions of firms are favorably influenced by a higher level of real balances. Once we take account of firms, the differential reactions mentioned in the preceding paragraph become increasingly significant. If firms are, on balance, debtors with respect to households and government, then a persistent price decline will cause a wave of bankruptcies. This will have a seriously depressing effect upon the economy which may not be offset by the improved status of creditors. Furthermore, in most cases of bankruptcy the creditors also lose. For these reasons it is not at all certain that a price decline will result in a positive net effect on the total expenditures (consumption plus investment) function. On this point much further investigation—of a theoretical as well as an empirical nature—is required.]

From the preceding analysis we can also see just exactly what constitutes the "cash balance" whose increase in real value provides the stimulatory effect of the Pigou analysis. This balance clearly consists of the net obligation of the government to the private sector of the economy. That is, it consists primarily of the total interest- and non-interest-bearing government debt held outside the treasury and central bank, [plus the net amount owed by the central bank to member banks]. Thus, by excluding demand deposits and including government interest-bearing debt and member bank reserves, it differs completely from what is usually regarded as the stock of money.

These same conclusions can be reached through a somewhat different approach. Begin with the ordinary concept of the stock of money as consisting of hand-to-hand currency and demand deposits. Consider now what changes must be made in order to arrive at the figure relevant for the Pigou analysis. Clearly, government interest-bearing debt must be added, since a price decline increases its value. Now consider money in the form of demand deposits. To the extent that it is backed by bank loans and discounts, the gains of deposit holders are offset by the losses of bank debtors.[13] Thus the net effect of a price decline on demand deposits is reduced to its effect on the excess of deposits over loans, or (approximately) on the reserves of the banks held in the form of hand-to-hand currency [and deposits in the central bank]. Finally, hand-to-hand currency held by individuals outside the banking system is added in, and we arrive at exactly the same figure as in the preceding paragraph.

For convenience denote the stock of money relevant for the Pigou analysis by M_1. Note that this is completely different from M_0 of footnote 7: for M_0 is defined in the usual manner as hand-to-hand currency plus demand deposits. This distinction is of fundamental importance. [One of its immediate implications is that central bank open market operations which do not change the market price of government bonds affect the economic system only through the liquidity preference equation.] Since such operations merely substitute one type of government debt (currency) for another (bonds), they have no effect on M_1 and hence no direct effect on the amount of savings. [Even when open market purchases do cause an increase in the price of government bonds, the changes in M_0 and M_1 will not, in general, be equal. The increase in M_0 equals the total amount of money expended for the purchase of the bonds; the increase in M_1 equals the increase in the value of bonds (both of those bought and those not

[13] Cf. M. Kalecki, "Professor Pigou on 'The Classical Stationary State'—A Comment," Economic Journal, LIV (1944), 131–32.

bought by the central bank) caused by the open-market operations.[14] Corresponding statements can be made for open-market sales.]

7. How does the Pigou formulation compare with the original classical theory?[15] Although both Pigou and the "classics" stress the importance of "price flexibility," they mean by this term completely different things. The "classics" are talking about flexibility of relative prices; Pigou is talking about flexibility of absolute prices. The classical school holds that the existence of long-run unemployment is *prima facie* evidence of rigid wages. The only way to eliminate unemployment is, then, by reducing *real* wages. (Since workers can presumably accomplish this end by reducing their *money* wage, this position has implicit in it the assumption of a constant price level—[or at least one falling relatively less than wages].) Pigou now recognizes that changing the relative price of labor is not enough, and that the absolute price level itself must vary. In fact, a strict interpretation of Pigou's position would indicate that unemployment can be eliminated even if real wages remain the same or even rise (namely, if the proportionate fall in prices is greater than or equal to that of wages); for in any case the effect of increased real value of cash balances is still present.[16]

---

[14] [It might be argued that through its effect on the interest rate, open-market purchases affect the value of assets other than government securities; hence, this change in value should also be included in the change in M_1. This is a point which deserves further investigation. The main question is whether there exists an offset to this improvement in the position of bondholders of private corporations.]

[15] Pigou, of course, introduces the absolute price level into the analysis of the real sector of the economy, whereas classical economics insists that this sector must be considered on the basis of relative prices alone. [As I have shown elsewhere, on this point classical economics is definitely wrong. For, in a money economy, the demand for any good must, in general, depend on the absolute price level, as well as on relative prices. This is a direct result of utility maximization. *Cf.* "Money in General Equilibrium Theory: Critique and Reformulation," *Econometrica,* XVIII (1950), and references cited there.]

[16] The role of real wages in Pigou's system is very ambiguous. At one point (p. 348, bottom) he assumes that reduced money wages will also decrease real wages. At another (p. 349, lines 20–38) no such assumption seems to be involved. "As money wage-rates fall . . . prices fall and go on falling." *Ibid.*

The Pigou analysis also differs from those interpretations of the classical position which, following Keynes, present the·effect of a wage decrease as acting through the liquidity preference equation. to increase the real value of M_0 and thereby reduce the rate of interest; this in turn stimulates both consumption and investment expenditures— thus generating a higher level of national income. To this effect, Pigou now adds the direct stimulus to consumption expenditures provided by the price decline and the accompanying increase in real balances. Consequently, even if the savings and investment functions are completely insensitive to changes in the rate of interest (so that the effect through the liquidity equation is completely inoperative), a wage decrease will still be stimulatory through its effect on real balances and hence on savings.

8. Before concluding this part of the paper, one more point must be clarified. The explicit assumption of the Pigou analysis is that savings are. directly related to the price level, and therefore inversely related to the size of real cash balances. This assumption by itself is, on *a priori* grounds, quite reasonable; [indeed, in a money economy it is a direct implication of utility maximization (above, note 15)]. But it must be emphasized that even if we disregard the reservations mentioned in the preceding sections, this assumption is insufficient to bring about the conclusion desired by Pigou. For this purpose he *implicitly* makes an additional, and possibly less reasonable, assumption. Specifically, in addition to postulating explicitly the direction of the relationship between savings and the price level, he also implies something about its *intensity*.

The force of this distinction is illustrated by Figure 5. Here S and I are the full employment savings and investment curves of Figure 3 (*i.e.*, those corresponding to $Y = Y_0$) for a fixed price level, p_0. The other savings curves, S_1, S_2, S_3, S_4, represent the full employment savings schedules corresponding to the different price levels p_1, p_2, p_3, p_4, respectively. In accordance with the Pigou assumption, as the price level falls, the savings function shifts over to the right. (That is p_1, p_2, p_3, p_4, are listed in descending order.) But it may well be that as the real value of their cash balances continues to increase, people are less and less affected by this increase. That is, for each successive increase in real balances (for each successive price level decline) the savings function moves less and less to the right, until eventually it might respond only infinitesimally, no matter how much prices fall. In graphical terms, as the price decline continues, the savings function might reach S_3 as a limiting position. That is, no matter how much the price level might fall, the savings function would never move to the right of S_3.[17] In such an event the declining price level would fail to bring about full employment. The validity of the Pigou argument thus depends on the additional assumption that the intensity of the inverse relationship between savings and real cash balances is such that it will be possible to shift over the savings function to a position where it will intercept the investment function at a positive rate of interest: say, S_4 (*cf.* Figure 5).

What is at issue here is the reaction of individuals with already large real balances to further increases in these balances. Consider an individual with a cash balance of a fixed number of dollars. As the price falls, the increased real value of these dollars must be allocated between the alternatives of an addition to either consumption and/or real balances.[18] How the individual will actually allocate the increase clearly depends on the relative marginal utilities of these two alternatives. If we are willing to assume that the marginal utility of cash balances approaches zero with sufficient rapidity relative to that

---

[17] Mathematically this may be stated as follows. Write the savings function as

$$S = \Gamma (r, p, Y).$$

(*Cf.* footnote 7, above.) Pigou's explicit assumption is

$$\Gamma_p(r, p, Y) > 0$$

where Γ_p is the partial derivative of S with respect to p. Let $Y = Y_0$ represent the full employment income. Then the argument here is that the savings function, Γ, may still be of a form such that

$$\lim_{p \to 0} \Gamma(r, p, Y_0) = \Gamma^*(r, Y_0)$$

for any fixed r—where Γ^* is any curve which intersects the investment curve at a negative rate of interest. (In the argument of the text, Γ^* is taken to be S_2 in Figure 5.) Pigou tacitly assumes that the savings function approaches no such limit; or that if it does, the limiting function intersects the investment function at a positive rate of interest.

[18] I am abstracting here from the possible third alternative, investment.

of consumption, then we can ignore the possibility of the savings curve reaching a limiting position such as in Figure 5.   That is, we would be maintaining the position that by increasing the individual's balances sufficiently, he will have no further incentive to add to these balances; hence he will spend any additional real funds on consumption, so

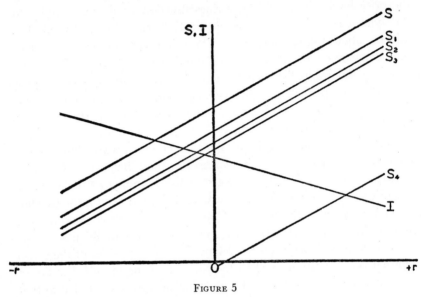

FIGURE 5

that we can make him consume any amount desired.   If, on the other hand, we admit the possibility that, for sufficiently large consumption, the decrease in the marginal utility of cash balances is accompanied by a much faster decrease in the marginal utility of consumption, then the individual will continuously use most of the additional real funds (made available by the price decline) to add to his balances.   In this event, the situation of Figure 5 may well occur.

9. I do not believe we have sufficient evidence—either of an

---

[19] Empirical studies on the effect of real balances on savings have been made by L. R. Klein, "The Use of Econometric Models as a Guide to Economic Policy," *Econometrica*, Vol. XV (1947), pp. 122–25.   Klein's procedure was incorrect in that he used a series for M_0, instead of M_1 in fitting his equations (*cf.* last paragraph of § 6 above).

a priori or empirical[19] nature—to help us answer the question raised in the preceding paragraph. The empirical evidence available is consistent with the hypothesis that the effect of real balances on savings is very weak. But even granted the truth of this hypothesis, it casts no light on the question raised here. What we want to know is what happens to the effect of real balances on savings as these real balances increase in size. Even if the effect were arbitrarily small, but remained constant regardless of the size of real balances, there could be no convergence of savings functions like that pictured in Figure 5. In the face of this lack of evidence, we have to be satisfied with the conclusion that, subject to the [reservations of §§ 6 and 8, Haberler and Pigou have] demonstrated the automaticity of full employment within the framework of the classical static model[20]—the main mechanism by which this is brought about being the effect of a price decline on cash balances.

The statement of this conclusion immediately raises the interesting question of how this set of forces, [emphasized by Haberler and Pigou,] could have been overlooked by Keynesian economists, in general, and Keynes himself, in particular. Questions of this type can rarely be answered satisfactorily—and perhaps should not even be asked. Nevertheless, I think it is both possible and instructive to trace through the exact chain of errors in Keynes's reasoning which caused him to overlook these factors.

I submit the hypothesis that Keynes recognized the influence of assets on saving (consumption), but unfortunately thought of this influence only in terms of physical capital assets. This was his fundamental error.[21] From it immediately followed that in his main discussion of the (short-run) consumption function, where he assumed a *constant* stock of capital, the possible influence of assets was not (and

---

[20] It must be re-emphasized that this conclusion holds only for static analysis. The modifications that must be introduced once dynamic factors enter are discussed in Part II.

[21] Note that there are really two distinct errors involved here. The first is the obvious one of the exclusion of monetary assets. The second is that what is relevant for the influence on saving is not the *physical* asset, but its *real* value in terms of some general price level.

could not) even be considered.[22]   But as soon as Keynes discussed a period sufficiently long for noticeable capital growth, the influence of assets on savings was immediately recognized.[23]   Even here, Keynes could not come to the same conclusion as Pigou.   For Keynes restricted himself to physical assets, and thus rightfully pointed out that it would be "an unlikely coincidence" that just the correct amount of assets should exist—*i.e.,* that amount which would push over the savings function to such a position where full employment could be generated.   Compare this with the determinate process by which just exactly the "correct amount" of real cash balances is brought into existence in the Pigou analysis.   (See above, § 5, paragraph 4.)

This exclusion of physical assets from the short-run consumption function was subconsciously extended to all kinds of assets.   Here was the last link in the chain of errors.   For later when Keynes began to examine the effects of increased real cash balances (brought about either by price declines or increases in the amount of money), he did not even consider their possible influence on consumption.   Instead, he concentrated exclusively on their tendency, through the liquidity function, to lower interest rates.[24]   (*Cf.* above, § 7, last paragraph.)

Looking back on the nature of these errors, we cannot but be struck by the irony that they should have emanated from the man who did most to demonstrate the fundamental inseparability of the real and monetary sectors of our economy.

---

[22] J. M. Keynes, *The General Theory of Employment, Interest, and Money* (New York, Harcourt, Brace, and Co., 1936), Chap. 8.   See especially pp. 91–5, where Keynes considers the possible influence of other factors besides income on consumption, and does not even mention assets.

[23] *Ibid.,* p. 218, second paragraph.

[24] *Ibid.,* pp. 231–34, 266.   The following passage is especially interesting: "It is, therefore, on the effect of a falling wage- and price-level on the *demand for money* that those who believe in the self-adjusting quality of the economic system must rest the weight of their argument; though I am not aware that they have done so.   If the quantity of money is itself a function of the wage- and price-level, there is, indeed, nothing to hope for in this direction.   But if the quantity of money is virtually fixed, it is evident that its quantity in terms of wage-units can be indefinitely increased by a sufficient reduction in money wages. . . . "   (*Ibid.,* p. 266.   Italics not in original.)

II. Dynamic Analysis: The Question of Policy

10. [The Haberler-Pigou analysis discussed in Part I makes two contributions. First, in its emphasis on the effects of a price on savings *via* its effects on real balances, it introduces into the Keynesian analytical apparatus a set of forces hitherto overlooked by the latter. (For convenience this will be referred to as the Pigou effect—though, as mentioned at the end of § 5 above, it is of much older origin.) Secondly, it proceeds to draw the implications of this set] of forces for static analysis, and summarizes its results in the following theorem (*cf.* §§ 5 and 6): *There always exists a sufficiently low price level such that, if expected to continue indefinitely,*[25] *it will generate full employment.*[26] (For convenience this will be referred to as the Pigou Theorem.) The purpose of this part of the paper is to accomplish a third objective: *viz.*, to draw the implications of the Pigou effect for dynamic analysis and policy formulation. It must be emphasized that the Pigou Theorem tells us nothing about the dynamic and policy aspects which interest us in this third objective. (This point is discussed in greater detail in § 12.)

Specifically, consider a full employment situation which is suddenly terminated by a downswing in economic activity. The question I now wish to examine is the usefulness of a policy which consists of maintaining the stock of money constant, allowing the wage and price levels to fall, and waiting for the resulting increase in real balances to restore full employment.

At the outset it must be made clear that the above policy recommendation is *not* to be attributed to Pigou. His interest is purely an intellectual one, in a purely static analysis. As he himself writes: " . . . The puzzles we have been considering . . . are academic exercises, of some slight use perhaps for clarifying thought, but with very little chance of ever being posed on the chequer board of actual life."[27]

---

[25] This qualifying phrase incorporates in it the restriction of the Pigou argument to static analysis.

[26] I am overlooking here the reservations discussed in §§ 6 and 8 above.

[27] "Economic Progress in a Stable Environment," *Economica,* n. s. XIV (1947), 188.

In reality, Pigou's disavowal of a deflationary policy (contained in the paragraph from which the above quotation is taken) is not nearly as thoroughgoing as might appear on the first reading. The rejection of a price decline as a practical means of combatting unemployment may be due to: (a) the conviction that dynamic considerations invalidate its use as an immediate policy, regardless of its merits in static analysis; (b) the conviction that industrial and labor groups, sometimes with the assistance of government, prevent the price flexibility necessary for the success of a deflationary policy. A careful reading of Pigou's disclaimer indicates that he had only the second of these alternatives in mind; *i.e.*, that he felt that the policy would not work because it would not be permitted to work. What I hope to establish in this part of the essay is the first alternative: namely, that even granted full flexibility of prices, it is still highly possible that a deflationary policy will not work, due to the dynamic factors involved.

Nevertheless, nothing in this part of the paper is intended (or even relevant) as a criticism of Pigou, since the latter has clearly abstained from the problem of policy formulation. If sometimes the terms "Pigou effect" and "Pigou Theorem" are used in the following discussion, they should be understood solely as shorthand notations for the concepts previously explained.

11. The analysis of this section is based on the following two assumptions: (a) One of the prerequisites of a successful anti-depression policy is that it should be able to achieve its objective rapidly (say, within a year). (b) Prices cannot fall instantaneously; hence, the larger the price level fall necessary to bring about full employment *via* the Pigou effect, the longer the time necessary for the carrying out of the policy. (If no price fall can bring about full employment, then we can say that an infinite amount of time is necessary for the carrying out of the policy.)

There are at least two factors which act toward lengthening the period necessary to carry out a policy based on the Pigou effect. The first is the possibility that the effect of an increase in cash balances on consumption is so small, that very large increases (very great price declines) will be necessary. [Certainly there is a burden of proof on the supporters of a policy of absolute price flexibility to show that this is not so;] that the economic system is sufficiently responsive to make the policy practical.   So far no one has presented the required evidence.

The second factor is a result of the price decline itself.   In dynamic analysis we must give full attention to the role played by price expectations and anticipations in general.   It is quite possible that the original price decline will lead to the expectation of further declines.   Then purchasing decisions will be postponed, aggregate demand will fall off, and the amount of unemployment increased still more.   In terms of Figures 1 and 3, the savings function will rise (consumption will be decreased) and the investment function fall, further aggravating the problem of achieving full employment.   This was the point on which Keynes was so insistent.[28]   Furthermore, the uncertainty about the future generated by the price decline will increase the liquidity preference of individuals.   Thus if we consider an individual possessing a fixed number of dollars, and confronted with a price decline which increases the real value of these dollars, his uncertainty will make him more inclined to employ these additional real funds to increase his real balances, than to increase his expenditures.[29]   In other words, the uncertainty created by the price decline might cause people to accumulate indefinitely large real cash balances, and to increase their expenditures very little if at all.   [Finally, the bankruptcies caused by the inability of creditors to carry the increased real burden of their debt (above, § 6) will strengthen the pessimistic outlook for the future. The simultaneous interaction of these three forces] will further exacerbate these difficulties.   For as the period of price decline drags itself out, anticipations for the future will progressively worsen, and uncertainties further increase.   The end result of letting the Pigou effect work itself out may be a disastrous deflationary spiral, continuing for several years without ever reaching any equilibrium position. Certainly our past experiences should have sensitized us to this danger.

Because of these considerations I feel that it is impractical to depend upon the Pigou effect as a means of policy: the required price

---

[28] See his discussion of changes in money wages, *op. cit.*, pp. 260–69, especially p. 263.   *Cf.* also J. R. Hicks, *Value and Capital* (Oxford, Oxford University Press, 1939), and O. Lange, *op. cit.*

[29] *Cf.* above, § 8, last paragraph.

decline might be either too large (factor one), or it might be the initial step of an indefinite deflationary spiral (factor two).

On this issue, it may be interesting to investigate the experience of the United States in the 1930's. In Table I, net balances are computed for the period 1929–32 according to the definition in § 6. As can be seen, although there was a 19 per cent *increase* in real balances from 1930 to 1931, real national income during this period *decreased* by 13 per cent. Even in the following year, when a further increase of 19 per cent in real balances took place, real income proceeded to fall by an additional 18 per cent. For the 1929–1932 period as a whole there was an increase in real balances of 46 per cent, and a decrease in real income of 40 per cent.

It will, of course, be objected that these data reflect the presence of "special factors," and do not indicate the real value of the Pigou effect. But the pertinent question which immediately arises is: To what extent were these "special factors" necessary, concomitant results of the price decline itself! If the general feeling of uncertainty and adverse anticipations that marked the period is cited as one of these "special factors," the direct relationship between this and the decline in price level itself certainly cannot be overlooked. Other proposed "special factors" must be subjected to the same type of examination. The data of the preceding table are not offered as conclusive evidence. But they are certainly consistent with the previously stated hypothesis of the impracticability of using the Pigou effect as a means of policy; and they certainly throw the burden of proof on those who argue for its practicality.

12. The argument of the preceding section requires further explanation on at least one point. In the discussion of the "second factor" there was mentioned the possibility of an indefinitely continuing spiral of deflation and unemployment. But what is the relation between this possibility and the Pigou Theorem (*cf.* § 10) established in Part I? The answer to this question may be expressed as follows:

On the downswing of the business cycle it might be interesting to know that there exists a sufficiently low price level which, if it were expected to continue existing indefinitely, would bring about full em-

[*Table I*]

Year	Money in Circulation Outside Treasury and Federal Reserve System	Market Value of Government Interest-bearing Debt Held Outside Government Agencies and the Federal Reserve System	Member Bank Deposits in the Federal Reserve System	Nonmember Bank Deposits in the Federal Reserve System	Other Federal Reserve Accounts	Reserve Bank Credit Outstanding Excluding that Based on Reserve Bank Holdings of U.S. Government Securities	Treasury Deposits in Member and Nonmember Banks	Postal Savings	Net Balances (M_1) $(1) + (2)$ $+ (3) + (4)$ $+ (5) - (6)$ $- (7) + (8)$	Cost of Living Index (p)	Net Real Balances $\frac{M_1}{p}$ $(9) - (10)$	Real National Income
	(1)	(2)	(3)	(4)	(5)	(6)	(7)	(8)	(9)	(10)	(11)	(12)
1929	4.5	14.5	2.4	0.0	0.4	1.3	0.4	0.2	20.2	1.22	16.6	89.9
1930	4.2	13.9	2.4	0.0	0.4	0.5	0.3	0.2	20.4	1.19	17.1	76.3
1931	4.7	15.1	2.3	0.1	0.4	0.6	0.4	0.6	22.1	1.09	20.3	66.3
1932	5.3	16.0	2.1	0.1	0.4	0.6	0.4	0.9	23.7	.98	24.2	54.2

All money figures are in billions of dollars.

Data for series (1), (3), (4), (5), (6) were obtained from *Banking and Monetary Statistics*, p. 368. On pp. 360–67 of this book their interrelationships are discussed. For (7) see *ibid*, pp. 34–5. For (8) see *Statistical Abstract of the United States*, 1947, p. 419.

Being unable to find an official series for (2), I used the following procedure: Total outstanding government debt at face value was classified according to maturities (0–5 years, 5–10, and over 10) on the basis of *Banking and Monetary Statistics*, p. 511. These classifications were multiplied by price indexes for government bonds with maturities of more than 3 and less than 4 years, more than 6 and less than 9, and more than 10, respectively (Standard and Poor, *Statistics: Security Price Index Record*, 1948 edition, pp. 139–44). The sum of these products was used as an estimate of the market value of the total government debt. The ratio of this to the face value of the total debt was computed, and this ratio applied to the face value of government debt held outside the Treasury and Federal Reserve System (*Banking and Monetary Statistics*, p. 512) to yield an estimate of the required series.

Series (10): Bureau of Labor Statistics, cost of living index, *Survey of Current Business*, Supplement, 1942, p. 16.

Series (12): National income in billions of 1944 dollars. J. Dewhurst and Associates, *America's Needs and Resources* (New York, The Twentieth Century Fund, 1947), p. 697.]

ployment.   Interesting, but, for policy purposes, irrelevant.   For due
to perverse price expectations and the dynamics of deflationary spirals,
it is impossible to reach (or, once having reached, to remain at) such
a position.

    The implication of these remarks can be clarified by consideration
of the cobweb theorem for the divergent case.   Assume that a certain
market can be explained in terms of the cobweb theorem.   It is desired

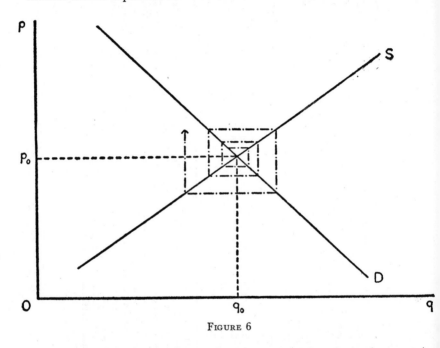

FIGURE 6

to know whether (assuming unchanged demand and supply curves)
the designated market will ever reach a stationary position; that is,
whether it will settle down to a unique price that will continue indefinitely to clear the market.   This question is clearly divided into two
parts: (a) does there exist such a price, and (b) if it does exist, will the
market be able to attain it.   In the case of the cobweb presented in
Figure 6 it is clear that such a price does exist.   For if the price p_0
had always existed and were expected to exist indefinitely, it would
continuously clear the market.   But Figure 6 represents the case of a
divergent cobweb; hence the market will never be able to reach the

price p_0. In brief, even though p_0 exists, it is irrelevant to the workings of the market. The analogy to the argument of the preceding paragraph is obvious.[30]

III. Conclusions

13. The conclusions of this paper can be summarized as follows: in a static world with a constant stock of money,[31] price flexibility as-

---

[30] The distinction of this section can be expressed in rigorous mathematical form using the dynamic system which has become familiar through the work of Samuelson and Lange (P. A. Samuelson, "The Stability of Equilibrium: Comparative Statics and Dynamics," *Econometrica,* Vol. IX [1941], pp. 97–120; Lange, *op. cit.,* pp. 91 ff.). Consider a single market and let D, S, and p represent the demand, supply and price of the particular good, respectively. Let t represent time. Then we can write this system as

(a) $D = f(p)$ demand function

(b) $S = g(p)$ supply function

(c) $\dfrac{dp}{dt} = h(D\text{-}S)$ market adjusting function

The last equation has the property that

(d) $\text{sign } \dfrac{dp}{dt} = \text{sign } (D\text{-}S)$

i.e., price rises with excess demand and falls with excess supply. Consider now the static system identical with (a) — (c), except that it replaces (c) by

(e) $D = S$

As long as (e) is not satisfied, we see from (d) that the system will not be in stationary equilibrium, but will continue to fluctuate. Thus the existence of a solution to the static system (a), (b), (e) (*i.e.,* the consistency of (a), (b), (e)) is a *necessary* condition for the existence of a stationary solution for the dynamic system (a), (b), (c). But this is not a sufficient condition. For the static system (a), (b), (e) may have a consistent solution which, if the dynamic system is not convergent, will never be reached.

Thus Pigou has completed only half the task. Setting aside the difficulties of § 8, we can accept his proof of the *consistency* of the *static* classical system. But that still leaves completely unanswered the question of whether the classical *dynamic* system will converge to this consistent solution. In this and the preceding section I have tried to show why such convergence may not occur in the real world. (I have discussed these issues in greater detail elsewhere. *Cf.* footnote 3, above.)

[31] Throughout Part III, unless otherwise indicated, "stock of money" is to be understood in the M_1 sense of the last paragraph of § 6.

sures full employment.   (I abstract here again from the difficulties raised in §§ 6 and 8.)   But in the real dynamic world in which we live, price flexibility with a constant stock of money might generate full employment only after a long period; or might even lead to a deflationary spiral of continuous unemployment.   On either of these grounds, a full employment policy based on a constant stock of money and price flexibility does not seem to be very promising.

All that this means is that our full employment policy cannot be the fairly simple one of maintaining a constant stock of money and waiting for the economic system to generate full employment automatically through price declines.   Other policies will be required. One possible alternative policy can be inferred from the Haberler-Pigou analysis itself: there are two ways to increase real balances. One is to keep the money stock constant and permit prices to fall.   An equally effective way is to maintain the price level constant, and increase the stock of money by creating a government deficit.[32]   This method of increasing real balances has the added advantage of avoiding one of the difficulties encountered previously (§ 11), for a policy of stabilizing the price level by increasing money stocks avoids some of the dangers of uncertainty and adverse anticipation accompanying general price declines.   Nevertheless, there still remains the other difficulty—that individuals may not be very sensitive to increases in real balances.   If this turned out to be true, we would have to seek still other policies.

14. [On the basis of the analysis presented in this paper it is possible to re-examine the question which has been a favorite one of economists these past years: namely,] What is the distinctive characteristic of Keynesian analysis?   It certainly cannot be the claim to have demonstrated the possibility of the coexistence of underemployment equilibrium and flexible prices.   This, in its day, served well as

---

[32] Considered from this perspective, the Pigou analysis presents in a rigorous fashion part of the theoretical framework implicit in the fiscal-monetary policy of the Simons-Mints position.   Cf. the recently published collection of essays of Henry C. Simons, *Economic Policy for a Free Society* (Chicago, University of Chicago Press, 1948); and Lloyd W. Mints, "Monetary Policy," *Revue of Economic Statistics,* Vol. XXVIII (1946), pp. 60–9.

a rallying cry.   But now it should be definitely recognized that this is an indefensible position.   For flexibility means that the money wage falls with excess supply, and rises with excess demand; and equilibrium means that the system can continue on through time without change. Hence, *by definition,* a system with price flexibility cannot be in equilibrium if there is any unemployment;[33] [but, like any other proposition that must be true by definition, this one, too, is uninteresting, unimportant, and uninformative about the real problems of economic policy].

Nor should Keynesian economics be interpreted as asserting that just as an underemployment equilibrium is impossible, so, too, in a static system may a full-employment equilibrium be impossible.   That is, the static system may be at neither an underemployment equilibrium, nor a full-employment equilibrium.   In other words, the static system may be inconsistent.   (This is the negative interest rate argument of § 3.)   For Pigou's and Haberler's discussion of the effect of a declining price level on real balances shows how this inconsistency is removed.   It is, of course, still possible to maintain this interpretation of Keynes on the basis of the reservations of §§ 6 and 8.   But I think this is neither necessary nor advisable.   For the real significance of the

---

[33] This can be expressed mathematically in the following way: let N^S and N^D be the amounts of labor supplied and demanded, respectively; w, the money wage rate; and t, time.   Then a flexible dynamic system will, by definition, contain an equation of the general type

$$\frac{dw}{dt} = f(N^D - N^S)$$

where

$$\text{sign } \frac{dw}{dt} = \text{sign } (N^D - N^S).$$

If by equilibrium is meant a situation such that

$$\frac{dw}{dt} = 0$$

then clearly this system cannot be in equilibrium unless

$$N^D - N^S = 0$$

i.e., unless there is full employment.

Keynesian contribution can be realized only within the framework of *dynamic* economics.   Whether or not an underemployment equilibrium exists; whether or not full employment equilibrium always will be generated in a static system—all this is irrelevant.   The fundamental issue raised by Keynesian economics is the *stability of the dynamic system:* its ability to return automatically to a full-employment equilibrium within a reasonable time (say, a year) if it is subjected to the customary shocks and disturbances of a peacetime economy.   In other words, what Keynesian economics claims is that the economic system may be in a position of underemployment *dis*equilibrium (in the sense that wages, prices, and the amount of unemployment are continuously changing over time) for long, or even indefinite, periods of time.

But this is not sufficient to characterize the Keynesians.   Everyone agrees that there exist dynamic systems which will not automatically generate full employment.   What distinguishes one economic school from the other is the system (or systems) to which this lack of automaticity is attributed.   If the Keynesian message is applied to an economic system with no monetary policy (if such a thing is possible to define), then it is purely trivial.   For few would claim automaticity of full employment for such a system.   Keynesian theory acquires meaning only when applied to systems with more intelligent monetary policies.   Here an element of arbitrariness is introduced; for what is termed "Keynesian" depends entirely on the choice of the monetary policy to be used as a criterion.

On the basis of Keynes' writings, I believe it is clear that he was primarily interested in attacking the policy of assuring full employment by manipulation of the interest rate through open market operations.[34]   But to Keynes, this policy was equivalent to one of wage flexibility;[35] for (he erroneously thought) the only effect of a wage decline was to increase the real value of the stock of money (in the M_0,

---

[34] *Cf.* Keynes, *op. cit.,* pp. 231–34; 266–67.

[35] "There is, therefore, no ground for the belief that a flexible wage policy is capable of maintaining a state of continuous full employment;—any more than for the belief that an open market monetary policy is capable, unaided, of achieving this result.   The economic system cannot be made self-adjusting along these lines."   (*Ibid.,* p. 267.)

not M_1, sense; *cf.* above, last paragraph of § 6) and thereby decrease the rate of interest—just as in open market operations. As we have pointed out above (end of §§ 6 and 7), these policies are really not equivalent. For open market operations may change only M_0, whereas a wage and price decline change the real value of M_1 as well. Hence, open market operations may act only through the liquidity preference equation, whereas a policy of price flexibility acts also through the savings function (*cf.* above, footnote 7 and end of §§ 6 and 7).

Let us now assume that even if Keynes had recognized the distinction between open market and wage flexibility policies (*i.e.*, if he had recognized the Pigou effect) he still would have continued to reject the latter as a means of assuring full employment. This is not an unreasonable assumption; for most of the objections cited above (§ 11) against the use of a policy based on the Pigou effect, are the very same ones that Keynes uses in arguing against open market operations.[36]

Granted this assumption, I believe it is useful to identify the Keynesian position against one which maintains that full employment can be automatically achieved *via* the Pigou effect by maintaining a constant stock of money, and providing for wage and price flexibility. It is now possible to delineate three distinct theoretical formulations of the Keynesian position—differing in varying degrees from the classical one: (a) Most opposed to the classical position is the Keynesian one which states that even if there were no problem of uncertainty and adverse anticipations (that is, even if there were a static system), and even if we were to allow an infinite amount of time for adjustment, a policy of price flexibility would still not assure the generation of full employment. (This is the negative interest rate argument of §§ 3 and 8; [or the argument based on differential creditor-debtor responses of § 6].)

(b) Then there is the position which states that, in a static world, price flexibility would always assure full employment. But in a dynamic world of uncertainty and adverse anticipations, even if we were to allow an infinite adjustment period, there is no certainty that full employment will be generated. That is, we may remain indefinitely in

---

[36] *Cf.* the passages cited in footnote 34, above.

a position of underemployment disequilibrium. (c) Finally, there is the Keynesian position, closest to the "classics," which states that even with uncertainty full employment would eventually be generated by a policy of price flexibility; but the length of time that might be necessary for the adjustment makes the policy impractical.

Although these positions are quite distinct theoretically, their policy implications are very similar. (In what way would the policies of a man advocating position (a) differ from those of a man advocating (c) and stating that the adjustment would take ten years?) The policies would in general be directed at influencing the consumption and investment functions themselves, in addition to manipulating the amount of money. Thus the policies may advocate tax reductions to stimulate consumption and investment (the Simons-Mints school); or may insist on direct government investment to supplement private investment (Hansen, *et al.*). In this way we could cross-classify Keynesian positions according to their advocated policies, as well as their theoretical foundations.

[Finally, it should be noted that none of the preceding three formulations of the Keynesian position is dependent upon the assumption of wage rigidities. This assumption is frequently, and erroneously, attributed to Keynesian economics as a result of two related misconceptions as to its nature. First of all, as we have seen, the attempt to interpret Keynes' analysis of unemployment within a static equilibrium framework makes it mandatory, by definition, to assume the existence of wage rigidities. The dynamic approach followed in this paper obviates this necessity.

A second implication of restricting ourselves to static equilibrium analysis is that *involuntary* unemployment can, *by definition,* exist only if there are wage rigidities. For if there were no wage rigidities, the wage level could assume any value; and for each such value there would be a corresponding, and presumably different, amount of labor supplied. Thus at the intersection point of the demand and supply curves—the only point of interest in static equilibrium analysis—workers are providing all the labor they wish to at the equilibrium wage. There can be no question of involuntary unemployment. Only if there are wage rigidities—a minimum wage

w_0, below which the workers refuse to go—can the situation be different. For then the supply curve of labor is parallel to the quantity axis at the height w_0 until a certain point (say) N_1, is reached; only afterwards does the curve begin to rise. If the demand curve is now assumed to intersect the supply curve in its horizontal portion at, say, the quantity N_0, then we can say that *involuntary* unemployment to the extent $N_1 - N_0$ exists; for at the equilibrium wage rate, w_0, workers desire to provide a maximum of N_1 units of labor, and are instead providing only N_0.

However, once we throw off the restrictions of static equilibrium analysis, we also free ourselves of the necessity of assuming wage rigidity as a necessary precondition of involuntary unemployment. For, during any given period of time, the dynamic workings of the system may well keep the workers at a point *off their supply curve*. In this departure from the supply curve lies the *involuntariness* of the unemployment. The important point here is that this situation can exist regardless of the shape of the supply curve; that is, even if wages are not rigid. One's view on the length of time such a situation can continue clearly depends on one's choice of the three alternative Keynesian positions delineated above. All this has been dealt with at length elsewhere,[37] and there is no need for any further repetition here.[38]]

---

[37] Cf. reference cited in footnote 3 above.

[38] It might be added that in the light of Chapter 19 of the *General Theory* —the chapter which provides the climax to Keynes' argument, and which explicitly examines the effects of wage flexibility—it is difficult to understand how wage rigidities can be considered a basic assumption of the Keynesian theory of unemployment. From this chapter it is quite clear that wage rigidities are *not* an *assumption* of Keynes' analysis, but rather a policy conclusion that follows from his investigation of the probable effects of *wage flexibility*.

Further explicit evidence that Keynes, in his theory of unemployment, was concerned with a regime of flexible prices is provided by the following passage from the *General Theory* (p. 191): "in the extreme case where money wages are assumed to fall without limit in face of involuntary unemployment . . . there will, it is true, be only two possible long period positions—full employment and the level of employment corresponding to the rate of interest at which liquidity preference becomes absolute (in the event of this being less than full employment)."

14

THE MISPLACED EMPHASIS IN CONTEMPORARY BUSINESS-FLUCTUATION THEORY*

By Clark Warburton‖

Many contemporary economists, particularly those who have been influenced by the writings of Lord Keynes, have placed great emphasis upon maladjusted savings-investment relationships as a basic causal factor in business fluctuations, both cyclical and secular. Other economists who have reviewed the evidence set forth concerning the importance of these relationships have concluded that maladjustment in those relationships was not a significant causal element in the great depression of the 1930's.[1]

The present writer is in agreement with the conclusion that the cause of the great depression must be sought elsewhere than in savings-investment relationships. The purpose of this article is to point out that the emphasis of contemporary economists on these relationships has been misplaced, because a far more potent factor of economic instability in recent years, namely, erratic variation in the quantity of money, has been ignored.

The quantity of money is not left out of the Keynesian system of relations. In fact, one of the four major factors determining the level of employment and income, in Keynes's analytical system, is

---

* The Journal of Business of the University of Chicago, 19 (1946), 199–220. Reprinted, by the courtesy of the University of Chicago Press and the author. All significant additions are included in brackets.

‖ Principal economist, Division of Research and Statistics, Federal Deposit Insurance Corporation. The views expressed are personal views only.

[1] Martin V. Jones, "Secular and Cyclical Saving Propensities," *Journal of Business*, XVII (1944), 1–15, and "Secular Trends and Idle Resources," *ibid.*, p. 68; and George Terborgh, *The Bogey of Economic Maturity* (Chicago: Machinery and Allied Products Institute, 1945).

the quantity of money.[2]   Nevertheless, four vital aspects of the quantity of money and its variability have been ignored by Keynes and by American economists imbued or tinged with Keynesian economics: (1) the statistical data bearing on the amplitude and timing of variation in the quantity of money relative to the amplitude and timing of variation in the three psychological factors stressed by Keynes; (2) the direct influence of changes in the quantity of money on prices and business fluctuations; (3) the relation of variability in the quantity of money and its resulting business fluctuations to the Keynesian psychological factors and to the rate of interest; and (4) the nature of the forces which control the quantity of money in the United States and have therefore produced monetary instability.

AMPLITUDE AND TIMING OF VARIATION IN THE QUANTITY OF MONEY AND IN THE KEYNESIAN PSYCHOLOGICAL FACTORS

Economists in the United States have made various statistical applications of portions of the Keynesian analysis and of the related concepts that have been developed by followers and critics of Keynes; but no one has attempted to compare the amplitude and timing of variation in the four chief factors in Keynes's system: the quantity of money, liquidity-preference, propensity to consume, and prospective yield on new capital.[3]   Such a comparison might be expected

---

[2] The other three are the psychological factors: propensity to consume, liquidity-preference, and the marginal efficiency of capital or prospective yield on new capital (John Maynard Keynes, *General Theory of Employment, Interest, and Money* [New York, Harcourt, Brace & Co., 1936], pp. 246–47). Keynes also mentions the wage-unit, as determined by the bargains reached between employers and employed, as a separate variable; but, since he measures the quantity of money in terms of wage-units, the two concepts together represent the quantity of money measured in customary units (see also Sherwood M. Fine, *Public Spending and Postwar Economic Policy* [New York, Columbia University Press, 1944], p. 31; and Mabel F. Timlin, *Keynesian Economics* [Toronto, University of Toronto Press, 1942], pp. 7–10).

[3] The term "prospective yield on new capital" is used here in preference to either of Keynes's terms, "investment demand-schedule" and "marginal efficiency of capital," and to Irving Fisher's "rate of return over cost," all of which Keynes defines as identical (*op. cit.*, pp. 136 and 140), or to Lerner's "marginal efficiency of investment."   None of these terms is self-explanatory, but "pros-

to throw considerable light on the causal sequences involved in business fluctuations, particularly in the case of the transformation of the prosperity of the 1920's into the great depression of the 1930's. The data for the United States are especially important, since the great depression originated in this country and spread over the world through its effects upon international trade.[4]

As various writers have pointed out, empirical data do not provide direct measurement of Keynes's psychological factors. Empirical data relate to the results of these factors, together with other forces operating in the economy. However, it is possible to select data which are related to the psychological factors in the sense that significant variability in those factors should be reflected in the data. Data of this type which are utilized here are as follows: (1) ratio of cash balances held by individuals and business to their expenditures for the final products of the economy as a series influenced by liquidity-preference; (2) ratio of consumer expenditure to disposable income of individuals as a series influenced by propensity to consume; and (3) corporate security issues for productive use as a series influenced by the prospective yield on new capital. Annual data for these series, for the period 1919–45, and for the quantity of money per capita are given in Table 1 and are plotted on a semilogarithmic scale in Figure 1.

Table 1 also gives two measures of variability of these data: (1) deviations from the average for the entire period, excluding the war years, or from a trend line based on the period 1923–28 and (2) percentage change from the previous year, adjusted for trend. For these measures of variability the average for the years prior to 1941 is used in the case of the ratio of consumer expenditure to disposable

---

pective yield on new capital" is more suggestive than the other terms of Keynes's explanation of his concept: "the marginal efficiency of capital is here defined in terms of the *expectation* of yield and of the *current* supply price of the capital-asset. It depends on the rate of return expected to be obtainable on money if it were invested in a *newly* produced asset" (*ibid.,* p. 136).

[4] Hal B. Lary and Associates, *The United States in the World Economy* (Washington, U.S. Department of Commerce, 1943), pp. 169–83; and Ragnar Nurkse, *International Currency Experience: Lessons of the Inter-war Period* (Princeton, League of Nations, 1944), pp. 107–9.

Table 1

DATA FOR THE UNITED STATES, 1919–45, REFLECTING THE MAJOR KEYNESIAN FACTORS "DETERMINING THE LEVEL OF EMPLOYMENT AND INCOME"

YEAR	DATA INFLUENCED BY—				PERCENTAGE DEVIATIONS FROM—				PERCENTAGE CHANGE FROM PREVIOUS YEAR			
					Trend Based on 1923–28		Average (Excluding 1941–45)					
	Quantity of Money: Average Cash Balances of Business and Individuals per Capita*	Liquidity-Preference: Ratio of Cash Balances to Payments for Final Products†	Propensity To Consume: Ratio of Consumer Expenditure to Disposable Income‡	Prospective Yield on New Capital: Corporate Securities for Productive Use§ (In Millions of Dollars)	Quantity of Money per Capita*	Ratio of Cash Balances to Payments for Final Products†	Ratio of Consumer Expenditure to Disposable Income‡	New Corporate Securities for Productive Use§	Quantity of Money‖	Ratio of Cash Balances to Payments for Final Products‖	Ratio of Consumer Expenditure to Disposable Income	New Corporate Securities for Productive Use
1919	$324	0.458	0.861	¶	−1	−7	−5	¶				
1920	360	.470	.909	¶	+7	−6	......	¶	+8	+2	+6	¶
1921	335	.533	.961	$864	−3	+5	+6	−13	−10	+12	+6	¶
1922	340	.541	.902	1,335	−5	+6	−1	+35	−1	......	−6	+55
1923	367	.518	.871	1,624			−4	+64	+5	−5	−3	+22
1924	371	.523	.875	1,941	−2		−4	+96	−2	......	−6	+20
1925	395	.529	.886	1,824	+2		−2	+84	+4		+1	−6
1926	405	.519	.902	1,801	+1	−3	−1	+82	−3		+2	−1
1927	413	.539	.893	1,781	+1		−2	+80	−1	+3	−1	−1
1928	422	.548	.894	1,495			−2	+51			−1	−16
1929	415	.523	.889**	1,787	−4	−6	−2	+81	−5	−6	−1	+20
1930	402	.573	.918	1,929	−10	+2	+1	+96	−6	+8	+3	+9
1931	389	.678	.909	796	−15	+20		−20	−6	+17	−1	−59
1932	342	.770	.943	203	−28	+34	+4	−79	−15	+12	+4	−74
1933	314	.725	.953	106	−35	+25	+5	−89	−11	−7	+1	−48
1934	329	.669	.935	63	−34	+14	+3	−94	+2	−9	−2	−41
1935	357	.658	.927	94	−31	+11	+2	−90	+6	−3	−1	+49
1936	386	.622	.906	379	−27	+4		−62	+5	−7	−2	+303
1937	403	.601	.903	635	−26	−1	−1	−36	+2	+4	......	+68
1938	399	.648	.930	428	−29	+6	+2	−57	−4	+7	+3	−33
1939	421	.641	.911	191	−27	+3		−81	+3	−2	−2	−55
1940	458	.648	.898	489	−23	+3	−1	−51	+6	......	−1	+156
1941	508	.620	.846	741	−17	−2	−7	−25	+8	−5	−6	+52
1942	567	.644	.754	292	−10		−17	−70	+9	+3	−11	−61
1943	701	.670	.729	133	+9	+3	−20	−87	+21	+3	−3	−54
1944	821	.718	.858	303	+24	+9	−6	−69	+14	+6	+18	+128
1945	966	0.801	0.901	610	+42	+21	−1	−39	+15	+11	+5	+101

* From population at mid-year, including members of the armed forces abroad, as estimated by the Bureau of the Census, and average total money held by business and individuals as estimated in "Quantity and Frequency of Use of Money in the United States, 1919–1945," *Journal of Political Economy*, Vol. LIV, No. 5 (October 1946). Trend based on 1923–28 is 2.86 per cent increase per year.

† Ratio of cash balances of business and individuals to payments for final products, as estimated in "Quantity and Frequency of Use of Money in the United States, 1919–1945." Trend based on 1923–28 is 1.13 per cent increase per year.

‡ For 1919–43, from "Monetary Expansion and the Inflationary Gap," *American Economic Review*, XXXIV (1944), 307 and 309; 1944 and 1945, from data in *Survey of Current Business*, XXVI, No. 2 [February 1946], 8. Average ratio for 1919–40 is 0.908.

§ Corporate security issues for productive uses, as estimated by *Moody's Investors Service*, from *Survey of Current Business*. Average for 1921–40 is $989 million.

‖ Adjusted for trend.

¶ Not available.

** Figure given is comparable with those for succeeding years; figure comparable with those for preceding years is 0.883.

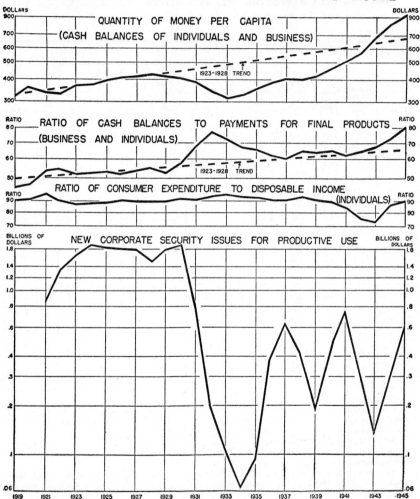

FIGURE 1.—Because of difference in scale, changes in the ratio of cash balances to payments for final products and in the ratio of consumer expenditure to disposable income are exaggerated in comparison with changes in the quantity of money per capita.

income and in the case of corporate security issues for productive use; while the trend is used in the case of the ratio of cash balances to payments for final products and for the quantity of money per capita. The period 1923–28 is chosen as base for the trends because it is the only period as long as five years, in the quarter of a century covered by the data, with a fairly stable price level and a relatively high level of production. The slopes of the trends are approximately the same as for trends fitted to data for the entire period.

These data suggest the conclusions and hypotheses listed below concerning the amplitude and timing of variation in the Keynesian psychological propensities relative to those in the quantity of money and concerning the comparative independence and importance of these variables. The conclusions regarding liquidity-preference are as follows:

1. For the interwar period (1919–41) variations in liquidity-preference tended to be inverse to variations in the quantity of money. This, of course, is in accord with common-sense reasoning. It simply means that, when business and individuals find their cash balances shrinking, they attempt to conserve them; when they find those balances growing at an unusually rapid rate, they use them more freely.[5]

---

[5] Rist has emphasized this effect in the past and its recognition by early writers on economics: "The idea that velocity of circulation slows down when the amount of money increases, and vice versa, is not only unsupported, but directly contradicted by experience. History shows that the velocity of circulation increases when the quantity of money increases *rapidly,* and diminishes when the volume of goods offered for sale increases more rapidly than the stock of money." "Far from the one compensating the other, the quantity of money factor is reinforced by the rapidity of circulation factor. This truth, forgotten like so many others in the nineteenth century, was realized in the eighteenth by Cantillon and Verri" (Charles Rist, *History of Monetary and Credit Theory from John Law to the Present Day* [New York, Macmillan Co., 1940], pp. 116 and 118).

[The term "liquidity-preference," as used here, refers to holdings of money relative to the rate of expenditure for goods and services, rather than to holdings of money relative to holdings of income-earning investments to which Keynes applied the term in his definition (*op. cit.,* p. 166). Use of the term in the former sense is implied by Keynes' discussion of the liquidity function and

2. At the beginning of the great depression, intensification of liquidity-preference lagged behind monetary deficiency; and at the depth of the depression its relaxation moved ahead of, or concomitant with, monetary expansion. In fact, in 1929, when the quantity of money per capita fell 4 per cent below its trend, liquidity-preference also fell. Apparently, in that year people made contracts on the assumption that the normal degree of growth in their cash balances would occur but, in meeting those contracts, had to part with cash which they would normally have kept. But the shrinkage in money was followed by enhanced liquidity-preference the next year. Relaxation of liquidity-preference in 1933, though the average amount of money held was substantially less than in the preceding year, was apparently due to the belief, after the banking holiday, that monetary contraction had been halted.[6]

3. The foregoing lead to the following hypotheses: (a) that liquidity-preference is primarily a function of deviation in the quantity of money from a normal rate of expansion and should therefore be regarded as a dependent, rather than an independent, variable in the set of equations used in the Keynesian type of analysis; and (b) that changes in liquidity-preference should be regarded as an accentuating, rather than an originating, factor in business depression.

4. During World War II the decline in liquidity-preference normally following an abnormal degree of monetary expansion did not appear by the end of 1945. Whether this is to be regarded primarily as the usual lag or to be considered as significantly influenced

---

the income-velocity of money (pp. 199–209). Also, a change in liquidity-preference in the latter sense can alter effective demand only through an effect on liquidity-preference in the former sense. For a discussion of the relationship between these two concepts of liquidity-preference and their relation to business fluctuations, see my article, "Monetary Velocity and Monetary Policy," *Review of Economics and Statistics,* XXX (November 1948), pp. 304–14.]

[6] These conclusions are strengthened by data for periods shorter than a year. The stoppage of normal growth in the quantity of money occurred early in 1928, about two years prior to a significant rise above normal in the ratio of cash balances to expenditures for final products. In 1933, monetary contraction was stopped in March, and the change from a rising to a falling ratio of cash balances to expenditures for final products came at about the same time.

by wartime price controls, rationing, and restrictions on business capital expansion is not discussed here.[7]

The conclusions and hypotheses regarding propensity to consume are as follows:

1. For most of the interwar period, the amplitude of variation in the propensity to consume appears to have been small relative to the amplitude of variation in the quantity of money.

2. The character of the variation in the propensity to consume is an increase in consumption relative to income in times of depression and a decrease of consumption relative to income in times of boom.

3. The foregoing lead to these hypotheses: (a) that variation in the propensity to consume could be omitted from the set of equations used in the Keynesian type of analysis without seriously affecting the conclusions with respect to business depression and boom drawn from such analysis and (b) that changes in propensity to consume should be regarded as a slight mitigating factor in business depression rather than as an accentuating or originating factor.

4. During World War II the propensity to consume, as measured by the ratio of consumer expenditure to disposable income, was abnormally low. The conditions producing this abnormality are related to war financing rather than to typical business fluctuations or to the occasional degradation of a business recession into a deep depression.[8]

The conclusions and hypothesis suggested by the data for corporate security issues for productive use are as follows:

1. The amplitude of fluctuations in the prospective yield on new capital is greater than that in the other three major variables in the Keynesian analysis. This is in accord with common-sense reasoning

---

[7] The first two years of rapid monetary expansion—1942 and 1943—was a period with an extremely high rate of growth in production. It is therefore the monetary expansion in 1944 and 1945, rather than in the preceding years, which would be expected, on the basis of past experience, to be followed by a declining liquidity-preference or a rising circular velocity of money.

[8] See my "Monetary Expansion and the Inflationary Gap," *American Economic Review*, XXXIV (1944), 304 and 308–11, and "Volume of Savings, Quantity of Money, and Business Instability," *Journal of Political Economy*, LV (June 1947), 222–33.

and traditional theory, since profits are presumed to bear the brunt of the effects of economic change.

2. At the beginning of the great depression, the prospective yield on new capital lagged not only behind monetary contraction (per capita) but also behind the downturn in security prices and in rate of production. For the more moderate cyclical fluctuations during the period covered by the data, changes in the prospective yield on new capital appear to have been approximately concomitant with such fluctuations, with some tendency toward a lag.

3. The foregoing lead to the hypothesis that the expectations of business regarding the prospective yield on new capital are dominated by the experience of the recent past and therefore should be regarded as an accentuating, rather than an originating, factor in business fluctuations.[9]

The dominant conclusion suggested by the foregoing data is the primacy of variability in the quantity of money, relative to the expanding amount needed to accompany growth in population and increase in productivity, as the originating factor in business fluctuations, particularly with respect to violent fluctuations, such as the great depression of the 1930's. Perhaps the most remarkable feature of contemporary business-fluctuation theory is the unanimity with which economists have ignored the timing and amplitude of changes in the quantity of money in the United States relative to changes in population, output, consumer spending, prices, and employment.[10]

---

[9] This conclusion has also been stated by Stanley Lebergott (see his "Forecasting the National Product," *American Economics Review,* XXXV [1945], 63–4).

[10] Keynes, in the *General Theory,* has a number of references to business conditions in the United States. He notes (pp. 322–23) that employment was very satisfactory in 1928–29 and that there is no evidence of overinvestment in the true sense, but he has no reference to the data regarding the quantity of money.

Alvin H. Hansen's chapter on "Monetary Policy in the Depression" in his *Fiscal Policy and Business Cycles* ([New York, W. W. Norton & Co., 1941], pp. 66–82) does not refer to the changes in the quantity of money or circulating medium which occurred in the 1930's. In a later chapter he states: "The

Footnote 10—(*Continued*)

modern banking system, with its freedom to create demand deposits on a fractional reserve basis, essentially issues 'paper money' through the loan-deposit operation. And this 'multiplication of currency' has given us an *ever-expanding* money supply corresponding more or less to the increasing volume of trade" (p. 91; italics supplied).

Frank H. Knight states that the assumption that the total quantity of money is constant seems to be a close enough approximation to the facts to function as a hypothesis for a general explanation of the cycle ("The Business Cycle, Interest, and Money," *Review of Economic Statistics,* XXXIII [1941], 59). He includes the lending or deposit-creating power of the banking system in the total quantity of money but makes no mention of the relation of this deposit-creating power to the reserves held by commercial banks or of the degree or timing of fluctuations in those reserves.

Leonard P. Ayres in *Turning Points in Business Cycles* (New York, Macmillan Co., 1939) gives no data regarding the total circulating medium or quantity of money and has no discussion of the factual data regarding the timing of changes in that quantity relative to the factors enumerated above. Neither does [Elmer C. Bratt in *Business Cycles and Forecasting* (Chicago, Business Publications, 1937); or] John Maurice Clark in *Strategic Factors in Business Cycles* (New York, National Bureau of Economic Research, 1935); [or James Arthur Estey in *Business Cycles* (New York, Prentice-Hall, 1941); or] Joseph A. Schumpeter in his two-volume treatise, *Business Cycles* (New York, McGraw-Hill Book Co., 1939); or Jan Tinbergen in *Statistical Testing of Business Cycles* (Geneva, League of Nations, 1938). Neither do any of the twenty-one articles—written by John M. Clark, Howard S. Ellis, Mordecai Ezekiel, Alvin H. Hansen, Ralph G. Hawtrey, Friedrich A. von Hayek, Nikolai D. Kondratieff, Oscar Lange, Abba P. Lerner, Friedrich A. Lutz, Fritz Machlup, Wesley C. Mitchell, Hans Neisser, Bertil Ohlin, Dennis H. Robertson, Paul A. Samuelson, Joseph A. Schumpeter, Jan Tinbergen, and John H. Williams—selected by a committee of the American Economic Association (Gottfried Haberler, chairman) for republication in *Readings in Business Cycle Theory* (Philadelphia, The Blakiston Co., 1944).

Even those economists who give considerable attention to changes in the quantity of the circulating medium or money as a causal element in the course of the business cycle appear to have overlooked the available factual data regarding the amplitude and timing of changes in the quantity of money in the United States relative to these aspects of variability in other data, particularly for the period of transition from the prosperity of the 1920's to the great depression of the 1930's. This is the case with James W. Angell, *The Behavior of Money* (New York, McGraw-Hill Book Co., 1936) and *Investment and Business Cycles* (New York, McGraw-Hill Book Co., 1941); Gottfried von Haberler, *Prosperity and Depression* (Geneva, League of Nations, 1937); and Seymour

Footnote 10—(*Continued*)

E. Harris, *Economics of Social Security* (New York, McGraw-Hill Book Co., 1941).

Angell, for example, gives annual estimates as of June 30 of "circulating money" (currency outside banks plus deposits subject to check, with certain adjustments for comparability of data) for the period 1890–1934, showing the largest figure as of June 30, 1929 (*Behavior of Money,* p. 175). A few pages later he gives, for the period 1919–34, monthly figures separately for the two components—currency outside banks and circulating deposits—but not for their total. When these two series are combined, the high figure for "circulating money" is December, 1927 (except for an isolated peak in November, 1929). A graph of the figures shows an upward trend of 5 per cent per year during the years 1922–27, a leveling-off for the years 1928 and 1929, and sharp decline during the years 1930–32. Angell's conclusion (p. 60) that both outside currency and deposits "tend to move with or after, but apparently never *before,* the several broad indices of production, trade and the like" seems contrary to his data. Reviewers of Angell's book (Frederick A. Bradford, *Quarterly Journal of Economics,* LI [1937], 364–73; Lauchlin Currie, *American Economic Review,* XXVI [1936], 789–91; Howard S. Ellis, *Journal of Political Economy,* XLIV [1936], 693–96; Charles O. Hardy, *Journal of the American Statistical Association,* XXXII [1937], 225–27; and Hans Neisser, *Annals,* CXC [1937], 260–61) also failed to note the facts indicated by Angell's monthly data. The monthly estimates are ignored by Angell in *Investment and Business Cycles,* though the facts indicated by them would have considerable bearing on the arguments in that book.

Harris (*op. cit.,* p. 326) recognizes the instability of the quantity of money, but the latter part of his statement—"in 1929–1932 the decline was excessive, thus aggravating the *depression that accounted for the initial reduction in the supply of money*" (italics supplied)—is inconsistent with the fact that monetary contraction began a year before the peak of business activity in the summer of 1929.

Lauchlin Currie, who emphasized "the importance of the supply of money as a factor affecting business conditions" in the first chapter of *The Supply and Control of Money in the United States* (Cambridge, Harvard University Press, 1934) and whose estimates of the supply of money as of June 30 for the period 1921–33 showed significant increases each year from mid-1922 to mid-1928, a negligible increase from mid-1928 to mid-1929, and "drastic contraction from 1929 to 1932," failed in that book to draw the obvious conclusion that monetary deficiency led the transition from prosperity to depression, though he does emphasize the inadequacy of monetary policy from 1929 to 1932. Even this degree of recognition of the facts regarding the timing of changes in the quantity of money appears to have been completely forgotten in his testimony before the Temporary National Economic Committee, on May 12, 1939. In that testi-

Footnote 10—(*Continued*)

mony Currie emphasized the relation of "income-producing expenditures that offset savings" to the national income, with no mention of the relation of the quantity of money to the amount of expenditures which constitute either the national income or those classified as "income-producing expenditures."

The followers and critics of Keynesian theory, who in recent years have almost monopolized the material regarding business fluctuations published in the leading economic journals, have uniformly ignored the factual data regarding the quantity of money. I have checked the *American Economic Review, Quarterly Journal of Economics, Journal of Political Economy, Review of Economic Statistics,* and *Econometrica* for the nine years since publication of Keynes's *General Theory.* I have not found a single article which reveals acquaintance with the factual data regarding the quantity of money in the United States, though the importance of monetary stability and reasonable growth is recognized in several of them. The articles published during these years dealing chiefly, or significantly, with business fluctuations, the conditions of full production, and related topics are too numerous to list here, but they include articles written by the following authors, in addition to articles by persons mentioned elsewhere in this footnote: Moses Abramovitz, Edward Adams, Clay J. Anderson, Montgomery D. Anderson, R. R. Bangs, Richard C. Bernhard, E. M. Bernstein, Richard M. Bissell, Jr., Morris A. Copeland, Johan Eivarsen, Walter Egle, William Fellner, J. Marcus Fleming, J. K. Galbraith, George Garvy, Donald W. Gilbert, Trygve Haavelmo, Everett E. Hagen, Albert G. Hart, R. F. Harrod, H. Gordon Hayes, J. M. Hicks, Joshua C. Hubbard, Nicholas Kaldorf, Tjalling Koopmans, E. M. Lachmann, Stanley Lebergott, Wassily W. Leontief, S. Morris Livingston, David W. Lusher, J. Marshak, Max Millikan, Franco Modigliani, Oskar Morgenstern, Jacob L. Mosak, Gunnar Myrdal, E. G. Nourse, J. H. G. Pierson, J. J. Pollak, Carl Pribram, Edward Adams Richardson, Wilhelm Ropke, Charles Frederick Roos, Walter S. Salant, Sumner H. Schlichter, E. S. Shaw, Henry C. Simons, Harold M. Somers, Arthur Smithies, Hans Staehle, Wolfgang F. Stolper, Alan R. Sweezy, John M. Thompson, Willard L. Thorp, Gerhard Tintner, Henry Hilgard Villard, Ruthledge Vining, C. R. Whittlesey, A. B. Wolfe, and Theodore O. Yntema.

Evidently most professional economists have joined the ranks of the businessmen described by Joseph French Johnson in his discussion of the psychological effects of a change in the price level: "Men do not and probably never will thoroughly understand the relation between money and goods. To them money is a thing of fixed and changeless value; goods are what they make and sell, and changes in prices are always attributed to changes in the demand for or supply of goods. As a result, when a rising demand for money is not met by an increased supply, and the prices of commodities here and there begin to weaken, business men are unable to explain the phenomenon and are puzzled and distressed" (*Money and Currency* [Boston, Ginn & Co., 1905], pp. 165–66).

RELATION OF VARIABILITY IN QUANTITY OF MONEY TO PRICES AND BUSINESS FLUCTUATIONS

In the Keynesian system of relations, liquidity-preference, propensity to consume, and the prospective yield on new capital are relatively independent of the quantity of money.[11] Change in each is given a place among the causal elements responsible for business fluctuations at least equal in importance to change in the quantity of money. This treatment is in striking contrast to the theory of prices and business fluctuations developed prior to World War I. In the economic theory of the early twentieth century, significant variability in all three of these factors was assumed to result, directly or indirectly, from two general forces: first, economic progress and modification of customs and habits and, second, changes in the quantity of money relative to the rate of economic progress and modification of customs or habits.[12] The first of these general forces was assumed

---

[11] Keynes recognizes that some interaction exists among the various variables, but he aims to discover those variables whose changes *mainly* determine in practice the national income (or dividend) and the quantity of employment (*op. cit.* p. 247).

[12] The designation "early twentieth-century" theory is used in this article because I have found more complete statements of the relation of monetary and price theory to business fluctuations in books published in the decade prior to World War I than in those published prior or subsequent to that decade. However, the theory of prices and business fluctuations presented by prominent writers in that decade is sufficiently consistent with and intimately related to the main tenets of the "classical" theory of value and to monetary and price theory contemporary with "classical" theory that it would be proper to speak of "traditional" or "orthodox" economic theory rather than of "early twentieth-century" theory. That is, in speaking of "early twentieth-century" theory I am talking about concepts developed through more than two centuries of controversy, rather than a new theory developed between 1900 and 1914. I am, however, referring to aspects of traditional economic theory which were emphasized and elaborated in writings of the early part of the twentieth century, notably Joseph French Johnson, *op. cit.;* Irving Fisher, *Elementary Principles of Economics* (New York, Macmillan Co., 1912); Herbert J. Davenport, *The Economics of Enterprise* (New York, Macmillan Co., 1913); and Wesley Clair Mitchell, *Business Cycles* (Berkeley, Calif., University of California Press, 1913).

to produce secular trends rather than short-term fluctuations, so that the problem of business fluctuations was regarded primarily as a problem of variability in the quantity of money. However, the effect upon business of changes in the quantity of money is exerted via the medium of price changes, and the pre-Keynesian theory of business fluctuations is therefore intimately related to the theory of prices.

Early twentieth-century price theory had two main subdivisions: first, the limiting case of full and complete competition, worked out on the assumption of virtually instantaneous adjustment to the forces of demand and supply, and, second, the application of this theory to the real world on the assumption that competition is the dominant, but not the exclusive, aspect of the price-setting mechanism. In practice the effects of a change in demand or in supply, either of a specific commodity or of money (circulating medium), are felt, first, in some particular part of the economy and spread from that part to the rest of the economy through the medium of price differentials created at each stage of adjustment. Each succeeding competitive adjustment narrows the preceding differentials and creates others, with the final result after a considerable lapse of time—provided that, in the meantime, no new original change occurs in demand or supply —closely approximating the limiting case.

The first subdivision of early twentieth-century price theory has been retained by contemporary economists under the concept of long-run equilibrium price theory; the second part has been ignored by Keynes and other contemporary economists, who have searched for the chief cause of business fluctuations in savings-investment relationships.[13] Early twentieth-century economists assumed, as a par-

---

[13] This part of early twentieth-century, or traditional, price theory and the closely associated theory of business fluctuations are not mentioned by Keynes in his chapter, "The Postulates of the Classical Economics," in the *General Theory* (pp. 4–22), nor in his essay, "The Theory of the Rate of Interest," in *The Lessons of Monetary Experience* (New York, Farrar & Rinehart, Inc., 1937), pp. 145–52. As has been pointed out in an article by Wolfgang F. Stolper ("Monetary, Equilibrium, and Business-Cycle Theory," *Review of Economic Statistics*, XXV [1943], 88), Keynes stated in 1933, in his essay in *Festschrift für Arthur Spiethoff* (Munich, 1933), pp. 124–25, his belief that

ticular application of their general price theory, that a decrease or an increase in the quantity of money—other than the amount of expansion required by growth in population, increased productivity per capita, and changing habits in the use of money—reduces or raises, respectively, the level of commodity prices.   However, this process takes an appreciable length of time, since there is nothing in an increased or decreased supply of money to cause an instantaneous change in all prices.   The first change occurs at the point where the additional money is introduced into or taken out of the economy and is expressed in an increased or decreased demand for the goods and services desired by the persons directly affected by the change in the quantity of money; *or,* if the change in the quantity of money is merely relative to growth in population and economic progress, that is, if the money supply is constant while the need or demand for money is increased because of growing population and productive capacity, business enterprises may be faced with a general ina-

---

application of the conclusions of "traditional economics" to the real world was impossible without the aid of a developed theory of "monetary economics," and he implied that up to that time no such theory had been developed.

Keynes's *General Theory* is, in fact, an attempt to develop a substitute for the early twentieth-century theory of the process by which the "limiting case" of price equilibrium is reached in the actual world, on the assumption that this phase of theory had never been treated by the "classical" economists or their successors.   Keynes's substitute, as some of his reviewers have pointed out (especially J. R. Hicks, "Mr. Keynes and the 'Classics,' a Suggested Interpretation," *Econometrica*, V [1937], 147–59; and Wassily W. Leontief, "The Fundamental Assumption of Mr. Keynes' Monetary Theory of Unemployment," *Quarterly Journal of Economics*, LI [1936], 192–97), does not differ greatly from the already well-developed theory which he assumes to be nonexistent—except for terminology and the vital point of emphasis upon savings-investment relationships rather than upon variability in the quantity of money relative to population growth and economic progress.

Keynes and his American followers appear to be largely unacquainted with books published prior to World War I in which the relation of monetary and price theory to business fluctuations is more clearly described than by the "classical" economists, whose views are the target of the *General Theory* (p. 3 n.).   Keynes also passes over passages in Mill, Marshall, and other "classical" economists pertaining to interrelations among the quantity of money, rate of interest, and business fluctuations.

bility to sell all their output at prevailing prices. In view of the fact that production takes time and that production costs are influenced by contracts, custom, and the resistance of employees to reduced wages, the process of adjustment to the new price level required by the changed quantity of money (relative to productive capacity) produces price differentials, which increase or reduce the profitability of business.[14]

Changes in the profitability of business, especially in the profits of manufacturers, are, per se, changes in prospective yield from the use of new capital assets (marginal efficiency of capital or investment demand-schedule, as defined by Keynes). Under early twentieth-century theory, therefore, changes in the quantity of money, particularly if they are rapid and large, produce business fluctuations or intensify fluctuations originating in other factors, such as innovations or changes in the character of demand, both because of the direct effect upon the demand for the output of business and because of the indirect effect via price differentials, changing profit margins, and business prospects.

In brief, monetary deficiency, either in the form of contraction or of a rate of expansion less than that required by economic progress, is the major cause of business depression and declining employment. Monetary expansion at a more rapid rate than economic progress, on the other hand, is the major cause of business recovery

---

[14] Specific references to this aspect of price theory prior to World War I are hardly necessary, since it was so universally accepted. However, mention may be made of statements by Alfred Marshall and by the American economists mentioned in n. 13. Marshall's statements were made in his *Economics of Industry* (London, Macmillan & Co., Ltd., 1879) and in a paper read in 1885, both of which were quoted by him in testimony before the Royal Commission on the Depression of Trade and Industry in 1886 (*Official Papers by Alfred Marshall* [London, Macmillan & Co., Ltd., 1926], pp. 7–9). Marshall particularly stressed the effect upon the profits of manufacturers of changes in prices resulting from change in the quantity of money.

For statements of American economists regarding this direct connection between change in the supply of money and business profits, see Johnson, *op. cit.*, pp. 104–5, 113–16, 121–31, and 161–71; Fisher, *op. cit.*, pp. 184–91; Davenport, *op. cit.*, pp. 280–92; and Mitchell, *op. cit.*, pp. 512–62.

and increasing employment, with the limiting case when labor and productive facilities are fully employed. Beyond that point further monetary expansion still affects prices and profits and creates injustice among various economic classes. Early twentieth-century theory is therefore in agreement with the hypotheses formulated above on the basis of statistical data for the period since World War I.

Relation of Changes in the Quantity of Money to the Keynesian Psychological Factors and to the Rate of Interest

Under the price theory of the early twentieth-century, as is noted above, change in the prospective yield on new capital (investment demand-schedule or marginal efficiency of capital, in Keynes's terminology) is primarily the result of a sufficiently severe variation in the quantity of money to constitute monetary deficiency or excessive monetary expansion. This is also the case with liquidity-preference, which was discussed by pre-Keynesian theorists as the demand for money to hold or to hoard or as the rapidity of circulation of money or by some other phrase expressing rate of use of money.[15]

---

[15] In using the terms "liquidity-preference," "demand for money," "rapidity of circulation," and "rate of use of money" as synonyms, I am not assuming that they are identical unless carefully defined to make them identical. However, the first two concepts are essentially the reciprocal of the latter two; "liquidity-preference" and "demand for money" referring to the amount of money held by individuals (or individuals and business enterprises) relative to their income or to their expenditures for consumption (or for consumption and acquisition of capital assets); and "rapidity of circulation" and "rate of use of money" referring to such expenditures or to all expenditures from income (or from income and proceeds of sale of assets) relative to the amount of money held. For more precise definitions of the concepts to which Keynes applies the term "liquidity-preference" see Max Millikan, "The Liquidity-Preference Theory of Interest," *American Economic Review*, XXVIII (1938), 247–60. For my use of the term "rate of use of money" see "Monetary Theory, Full Production, and the Great Depression," *Econometrica*, XIII (1945), 114–28, and "The Volume of Money and the Price Level between the World Wars," *Journal of Political Economy*, LIII (1945), 150–63. The rate of use of money, thus defined, differs from "rapidity of circulation" or "efficiency of money," as used by nineteenth-century theorists (e.g., John Stuart

The Keynesian approach places less emphasis than early twentieth-century theory on the relation of changes in the quantity of money to liquidity-preference or rate of use of money and results, in part, in different conclusions regarding the direction of movement of the two variables relative to each other.   This difference in emphasis and conclusions has two important aspects: the first relating to a short-run situation and its relation to business fluctuations; the other to a more permanent effect on prices, output, and employment.   With respect to the first, the Keynesian analysis regards liquidity-preference and the quantity of money, as far as a direct relationship is concerned, as independent variables, with any relationship connecting them operating through the rate of interest.

In contrast, early twentieth-century theory, as has been noted above, emphasized the price differentials resulting from monetary expansion or contraction and assumed that the wide profit margins in the former case stimulate businessmen to use their receipts with more than usual promptness and that the narrow or disappearing profit margins in the latter case make businessmen cautious and hesitant in their commitments.   An increase in the quantity of money, therefore, tends to be accompanied by a more rapid rate of use of money, and a decrease in the quantity by a less rapid rate of use.[16] Changes in rate of use of money, therefore, accentuate business fluc-

---

Mill, *Principles of Political Economy, 1848*, Book III, chap. viii, sec. 3, pp. 494–95 in the Ashley edition (London, Longmans, Green and Co., 1920)), but is closely related thereto and may be assumed to be influenced by the same basic forces.

[16] Cf. the following: "The reader will have noticed that all writers who regard the demand for money as the factor determining changes in the velocity of circulation reach the same conclusion. The demand for money increases when prices are falling (that is to say the velocity of circulation decreases) and conversely. Thus variations in demand accompany and reinforce upward or downward movements in the price level, *but cannot be considered as the initial factor determining such movements*. This must be sought elsewhere: either, when it is a case of prolonged fall in prices in a rapid increase in the production and sale of goods, or when prices are rising, in an increase in the currency, or, for cyclical variations, in an increase in credit" (Rist, *op. cit.*, pp. 352–53).

tuations resulting from changes in the quantity of money. This is particularly true with respect to the prolongation of a depression induced by monetary contraction.[17]

The character of the association between a change in the quantity of money and a change in the rate of use of money is thus, according to early twentieth-century theory, the direct opposite of the conclusion reached from the Keynesian analysis. Under pre-Keynesian theory an increase in the quantity of money tends to be associated with an increase in the rate of use of money, while under the Keynesian analysis an increase in the quantity of money tends to be associated (indirectly) with greater liquidity-preference or a decrease in the rate of use of money, with the corresponding associations in the case of a decrease in the quantity of money.

In the case of a change in rate of use of money other than that associated with a change in the quantity of money, as, for example, an outburst of "hoarding" or a change in habits of use of money, early twentieth-century theory and the Keynesian theory of liquidity-preference lead to similar results, but by different lines of reasoning. Such a decrease in the rate of use of money, according to early twentieth-century theory, has an immediate shrinking effect on demand —therefore upon production and income—and tends to produce a business recession. However, such a situation is assumed to be temporary, since the forces of competition will adjust prices and costs to the new demand-and-supply situation; the final effect, after an appropriate lapse of time, is that the "hoarders" have deprived themselves of goods and services to which they were entitled by the prevailing income-distribution processes and have permitted those goods and services to go to other persons, in return for a pledge from society that they (the "hoarders") may obtain goods and services of an equivalent money value at some time in the future. Under the Keynesian system the latter effect is not assumed, and, by implication, output and employment are assumed to remain permanently at a lower level. The real conflict of opinion at this point is with respect to the permanence of price and cost rigidities and the strength

---

[17] Davenport, *op. cit.*, pp. 300–4.

of the competitive influence.   Otherwise, the difference between the older theory and that of contemporary economists imbued with Keynesian concepts is the slight emphasis by the former, and the heavy emphasis by the latter, on autonomous changes (that is, changes not induced by changes in the quantity of money) in liquidity-preference.

Under early twentieth-century theory little attention was given to changes in the psychological factor designated by Keynes as the propensity to consume.   Discussions of this concept were in terms of the tendency to save, and it was assumed that this tendency is so much a product of custom and habit that short-run variations are un-important.   However, the actual volume of savings, according to early twentieth-century theory, is a result of business fluctuations and of changes in the rate of interest.   We turn, therefore, to the difference between the two theories of the rate of interest prior to commenting on the early twentieth-century view of the savings-investment relationship which has figured so prominently in con-temporary business-fluctuation theory.

In Keynes's principal statement of his system of variables the rate of interest is treated as a variable, dependent partly on the state of liquidity-preference and partly on the quantity of money.[18]   How-ever, in other passages, Keynes appears to treat the quantity of money as dependent upon liquidity-preference and the rate of interest, with the rate of interest dependent upon liquidity-preference and the prospective yield on new capital.[19]   The latter is regarded by Lange as the true Keynesian position and by some contemporary economists as the one most in accord with reality.[20]   Keynes and Lange both recognize that under traditional theory the rate of interest is assumed to be affected by changes in the quantity of money; but Hans Neisser, in a recent article, speaks of the "classical" view, under which the level of the interest rate is con-

---

[18] *General Theory*, p. 246.

[19] *Ibid.*, pp. 199–200.

[20] Oscar Lange, "The Rate of Interest and the Optimum Propensity To Consume," *Economica*, V n. s. (1938), 12–32; reprinted in *Readings in Business Cycle Theory*, pp. 169–92.

sidered to be independent of the quantity of money.[21]   Evidently there is confusion among contemporary economists, both as to the character of the interest-rate theory developed in the nineteenth century and as to the real situation regarding the dominant direction of causal influence connecting the rate of interest and the quantity of money.

The interest theory developed in the nineteenth century and accepted in early twentieth-century theory, like price theory, had two main subdivisions: first, a theory of a natural rate determined by the demand for and supply of loans under the condition of monetary stability, with the demand influenced primarily by prospective profits and the supply by savings offered for loan, and, second, a theory regarding departures from the natural rate induced by changes in the quantity of money.[22]

Keynes recognizes this dual character of the orthodox theory of

---

[21] "The New Economics of Spending: A Theoretical Analysis," *Econometrica*, XII (1944), 247.

[22] Mill's principal statement of this interest-rate theory is as follows: "The rate of interest will be such as to equalize the demand for loans with the supply of them."

"The rate of interest bears no necessary relation to the quantity or value of the money in circulation.   The permanent amount of the circulating medium, whether great or small affects only prices; not the rate of interest. . . .

"But though the greater or less quantity of money makes in itself no difference in the rate of interest, a change from a less quantity to a greater, or from a greater to a less, may and does make a difference in it" (Mill, *op. cit.*, Book III, chap. xxiii, secs. 1 and 4, pp. 637 and 645–46).

Marshall made a similar statement in 1887 to the Royal Commission on the Values of Gold and Silver, *Official Papers by Alfred Marshall*, pp. 51–2.

The term "natural" rate of interest was used in various ways by nineteenth-century economists (see Rist, *op. cit.*, pp. 298 and 317).   In my discussion here it is used in a Wicksellian sense [(*Lectures on Political Economy* [London, George Routledge & Sons, 1935], II, p. 193) or as a synonym for Marshall's "equilibrium level" (*Principles of Economics,* eighth edition [London, Macmillan and Co., 1920] p. 534)—which may be regarded as essentially identical concepts (see Arthur Marget's comment on Wicksell's usage (*Theory of Prices,* II [New York, Prentice-Hall, 1942]), p. 202)—rather than with the meaning given to it by Mill (*op. cit.* 638), which may be described as the median natural or equilibrium rate over a period of time.]

the rate of interest but concludes that the two subdivisions of the orthodox theory are not related to each other and that the true character of the relationship between the rate of interest and the quantity of money was not observed by the classical economists. He puts aside the theories developed by his predecessors with the statement:

> . . . no reason has been given why a change in the quantity of money should affect either the investment demand-schedule or the readiness to save out of a given income. Thus the classical school have had quite a different theory of the rate of interest in . . . the theory of value from what they have had in . . . the theory of money. They have seemed undisturbed by the conflict and have made no attempt, so far as I know, to build a bridge between the two theories.[23]

This passage is an especially striking illustration of Keynes's preoccupation with certain theories of those nineteenth-century writers whom he designates as "classical" and his neglect of other contributions to orthodox theory as developed prior to World War I. The price theory of the nineteenth and early part of the twentieth century did provide a strong and substantial bridge between the two phases of the theory of the rate of interest—the natural rate unaffected by the quantity of money and the actual rate markedly affected by changes in the quantity of money but tending to swing toward the natural rate.

The main girders of the nineteenth-century bridge between the two parts of its theory of interest are the beliefs, mentioned above, that a decrease or an increase in the quantity of money (other than the amount of expansion required by growth in population, technical progress expressed in increased productivity per capita, and changing habits of use of money) reduces or raises, respectively, the level of commodity prices; that this process takes an appreciable length of time; and that the price differentials which occur in the process are such as to reduce or increase, respectively, the profits of business, particularly of manufacturers and merchants. A change in the profits of business, especially in the profits of manufacturers, means, per se, a change in the prospective yield from the use of new capital

---

[23] *General Theory*, pp. 182–83.

assets (investment demand-schedule or marginal efficiency of capital, as defined by Keynes). This change in the investment demand-schedule, under pre-Keynesian theory, decreases or increases the demand for loans subsequent to a decrease or an increase in the quantity of money and thereby pulls (down or up, respectively) the market rate of interest to the natural rate, after having been pulled away from the natural rate (up or down, respectively) by the decrease or the increase in the supply of money offered for loan as a direct and immediate result of the decrease or the increase in the quantity of money.[24]

The early twentieth-century theory of the relation of the aggregate volume of savings to the takings of investment funds by business enterprises—a problem which has been of much concern to contemporary economists—was closely related to the theory of the relation of prices and of the rate of interest to the quantity of money. Under this view, as Neisser points out with respect to the classical view, opportunities for investment are believed to be virtually unlimited.[25]

---

[24] Rist states (*op. cit.*, pp. 127–30) that eighteenth-century writers accurately describe this situation but that Marshall and other nineteenth-century economists failed to do so. However, the proposition is strongly implicit in much of nineteenth-century theory, particularly in Marshall's testimony referred to above (n. 23); and I find it difficult to understand Keynes's claim that classical economists had no bridge between the two aspects of the theory of interest.

For a more detailed discussion of the relation between the rate of interest and changes in the quantity of money and of the "upside-down" application of this relationship to practical monetary policy see my "Business Stability and Regulation of the Cost of Money," *American Journal of Economics and Sociology*, IV (1945), 175–84, and "Volume of Savings, Quantity of Money, and Business Instability," *loc. cit.*

[25] Neisser distinguishes three possible positions which may be taken regarding the savings, investment, and rate-of-interest complex which he designates, respectively, as the "new economics of spending," the Keynesian position, and the classical view. He describes the classical view as follows: " . . . opportunities of investment are virtually unlimited and will be utilized provided the interest rate declines sufficiently; the level of the propensity is, therefore, deemed immaterial. The level of the interest rate is considered independent of the quantity of money" (*op. cit.*, p. 247).

However, the necessary condition for the utilization of these opportunities which Neisser describes as the classical view, namely, a sufficient decline in the rate of interest, is only one of two necessary conditions. The other condition which must be fulfilled if businessmen are to take advantage of the investment opportunities surrounding them is a stable or steadily increasing quantity of money. Price differentials associated with monetary contraction tend to be such that profit margins are low, and investment opportunities which under normal circumstances would be quickly seized with a sufficiently low rate of interest may not be attractive even with a zero rate.

Contemporary economists who are convinced that a maladjustment exists between the savings of individuals normally resulting from their incomes and their propensity to consume, on the one hand, and business takings of investment funds, on the other hand, and that this maladjustment is so serious that the government must take some special action to create adequate "offsets" to savings appear to be unacquainted with the early twentieth-century theory of the process by which the savings of indivduals and business takings of investment funds are adjusted to each other. Under this theory variation in the rate of interest acts as an adjusting medium; but this action is satisfactory only when the rate of interest is not pulled away from the natural rate by variations in the quantity of money other than those needed to maintain a stable price level.[26]

The two conditions necessary for satisfactory mutual adjustment of the savings of individuals and business takings of investment funds are interrelated because of the relation of the rate of interest to the quantity of money. However, the importance of monetary expansion at a reasonable rate is due more to the direct effect of monetary deficiency or instability than to the indirect effect through the rate of interest. It is only when the prospective investment yield on capital is not made abnormal by price differentials associated with rising or falling prices—that is, only under conditions of a stable price level—that the savings-adjustment mechanism, via fluctuations in the

---

[26] Johnson, *op. cit.*, pp. 150–55.

rate of interest, operates with reasonable smoothness.[27]   If there is monetary contraction and falling prices and, consequently, a poor outlook for profits because of the relative rigidity of costs, the demand for capital funds will fall below the usual rate of savings; and if there is excessive monetary expansion and rising prices and, therefore, high profits because of the relative rigidity of costs, the demand for capital funds will rise above the usual rate of savings.   But under monetary contraction, business losses occur, which are, per se, negative savings; and the reduced employment and production resulting from business recession reduce the incomes of other persons and force them to draw on their savings or go into debt; it is this process of dissavings which brings the amount of savings down toward or equal to the amount taken by business.[28]   Under conditions of monetary expansion, on the other hand, the increased profits of businessmen, who habitually save more than other classes in the population, particularly when they have marked increases in income, tend to increase the aggregate amount of savings, since the resulting price rise tends to contract the consumption of wage-earners rather than their savings, which are slight in any case.

The economic theory of the early twentieth century thus leads directly to final conclusions regarding savings-investment relations

---

[27] One possible exception to price-level stability without disturbance to the savings-adjustment mechanism is a gradual fall in prices in accord with increased productivity. Whether the quantity of money should expand with technological progress in order to maintain a stable price level or whether such progress should be expressed in a falling price level was an unsettled point in early twentieth-century theory (see, e.g., the article by Allan G. B. Fisher, "Volume of Production and Volume of Money," *American Economic Review,* XXV [1935], 197–211). The argument in favor of monetary expansion to accompany the trend in productivity is that this provides more incentives to business to make full use of improved techniques of production; the argument against such expansion is that the benefits of technological progress are more quickly and fairly distributed among the entire population by a falling price level in line with productivity.

[28] Nineteenth- and early twentieth-century theory was not concerned with the question of whether savings and business takings of investment funds were ever precisely equal to each other, and did not develop sufficiently technical and precise definitions to handle this problem.

which are similar to those reached by the more roundabout reasoning of Keynes and neo-Keynesians, but with much more emphasis upon the independence and importance of variation in the quantity of money as a causal influence in the adjustment process.

FORCES CONTROLLING THE QUANTITY OF MONEY

To understand the forces governing the quantity of money, as in the case of those governing the quantity of coal that is mined, it is necessary to look both to the demand and to the supply and to scrutinize and appraise with care the conditions of both, in order to select or see those which, as a matter of practice, are the limiting and therefore the dominant factors in the total supply. Contemporary economists have concentrated their attention on certain aspects of the demand for money—particularly those associated with the concept of liquidity-preference—and in doing so have lost sight of the nature of the money-creating industry and the conditions under which it operates in the United States.

The conditions influencing the supply of money in the United States are examined by the author in articles published elsewhere.[29] Accordingly, these conditions are sketched here with extreme brevity and without mention of modifying minor factors which do not interfere with the dominant factors. The money supply of the United States consists of bank deposits and currency, of which by far the greater part is composed of bank deposits. Bank deposits expand and contract with the acquisition or relinquishment of assets by commercial banks. Commercial banks, in view of the fact that their own obligations are an acceptable means of payment, have an inherent tendency to acquire additional assets and therefore to expand their total assets to the limit permitted them by law and the conditions under which they operate. The market rate of interest is not an

---

[29] "Monetary Policy in the United States in World War II," *American Journal of Economics and Sociology,* IV (April 1945), 375–83; ["Monetary Control under the Federal Reserve Act," *Political Science Quarterly,* LXI (December 1946), pp. 505–34; and "Bank Reserves and Business Fluctuations," *Journal of the American Statistical Association,* XLIII (December 1948), pp. 547–58].

important factor in the volume of assets acquired by commercial banks, since it is always profitable for them to acquire additional assets as long as the rate of interest is judged to be sufficient to exceed ever so slightly the managerial and risk elements in the market rate of interest.[30]   Examination of the facts indicates that banks do, in practice, expand their assets close to the limit permitted by law and the conditions under which they operate and that this has been the case not only in former times but also in recent years.

The chief limitation upon the expansion of bank assets and deposits is the amount of reserves available to them and the percentage reserve requirements imposed upon them.   Since 1917, when reserves were concentrated in the Federal Reserve banks, the reserves available to commercial banks have depended directly upon the volume of assets held by the Federal Reserve banks, inasmuch as the aggregate amount of reserves of member-banks is necessarily equal to the difference between the amount of assets held by the Reserve banks and the sum of the capital accounts of those banks and their liabilities in the form of circulating notes and foreign and government deposits. However, at certain periods during the past quarter of a century, notably in 1934–36 and 1939–41, conditions other than reserves became limiting factors on the extent or rate of expansion of bank assets and deposits.   These conditions were the customary or required capital ratios and the greatly reduced volume of bank capital, the normal lags in the distribution of excess reserves behind their creation and in the expansion of bank assets behind the receipt of excess reserves, and the accentuation of these lags by uncertainties regarding future monetary and other governmental policies.

The volume of assets of the Federal Reserve banks, except under the special condition of large gold imports at a time when those banks

---

[30] The market rate of interest includes not only risk and managerial elements but also "pure interest," representing compensation for the use of the money loaned.   Investors other than banks require such compensation, since they must relinquish assets which might be used for other purposes.   Banks as a group, do not require such compensation, since they do not have to relinquish other assets except when they have exhausted (to the practical limit) their excess reserves.

do not have a sufficient volume of other assets for compensating sale, is controlled directly by the decisions of Federal Reserve authorities with respect to open-market operations, applications for rediscounts, and the terms of purchase of United States government obligations from member-banks.

The influence of Federal Reserve action, together with monetary policies such as the Treasury price of gold, has been so overwhelmingly dominant that it is a realistic and truthful statement to say that the supply of money in the United States is the result of the *de facto* monetary policy of the United States government. The conclusion cannot be avoided that federal government agencies, particularly the Federal Reserve authorities, have been responsible for the drastic and erratic variability of the quantity of money in the United States since the close of World War I.

Conclusion: Monetary Policy and Business Fluctuations

Many contemporary economists, particularly those whose thinking has been dominated by the Keynesian analysis and who have taken the position described by Neisser as the "new economics of spending," have arrived at conclusions regarding the cause of business fluctuations which depart greatly from those emphasized by economists writing prior to World War I. In reaching these novel conclusions, contemporary economists have ignored available factual data regarding variation in the quantity of money; they have neglected an important phase of the relation of changes in the quantity of money to prices and business profits and prospects which had been recognized by eighteenth-, nineteenth-, and early twentieth-century economists; and they have failed to acquaint themselves with the nature and mode of operation of the money-creating industry.

These defects in the approach to the theory of business fluctuations have led contemporary economists to inaccurate conclusions regarding the character of monetary policy and its results since World War I and to conclusions regarding monetary and other governmental policies necessary for prosperity and stability which differ greatly from those reached by generations of astute thinkers during the preceding centuries. The conclusions of contemporary economists relative to monetary policy which must be challenged include: (1) a general identification of monetary policy with interest-rate manipulation; (2) a more definite identification of central bank rediscount rate with monetary policy; (3) the nature of monetary policy during the crucial period of the transition from the prosperity of the 1920's to the great depression of the 1930's; and (4) the belief that monetary policy produced a low rate of interest in the early 1930's.

The general identification of monetary policy with interest-rate control or manipulation pervades contemporary literature on business fluctuations. It is implicit throughout Keynes's *General Theory* and appears with great frequency in the books and articles referred to above (n. 11). One example only will be specifically mentioned here, taken from a book published subsequent to the flood of articles on the Keynesian analysis which appeared during the first few years after the *General Theory*. Mabel Timlin, in a discussion of the effects of a change in the quantity of money, concludes that central-bank action to increase the quantity of money, through open-market operations, may generate or accentuate a business expansion and that, if a central bank should endeavor to bring about a deflation by reducing the quantity of money, the effects would tend to be reversed. This correct and important conclusion is followed, a few pages later, by a discussion of the implications of Keynesian economics, in which monetary management is described solely in terms of manipulation of the rate of interest (through changes in the quantity of money) with complete forgetfulness of the other effects of a change in the quantity of money and implying that the aim and essence of monetary policy is interest-rate control.[31]

Keynes himself was obviously baffled by the logical consequences of his identification of interest-rate manipulation with monetary policy, as applied to the situation in the United States in 1929. He noted that the prospective yield on new capital was falling rapidly, that continuation of the high level of business required a very low long-term rate of interest, that use of a high rate of interest to over-

---

[31] Timlin, *op. cit.*, pp. 158–59 and 182–83.

come speculative excitement would check all reasonable new investment, and that an increase in the rate of interest "belongs to the species of remedy which cures the disease by killing the patient." He concluded that "the most enlightened monetary control might find itself in difficulties, faced with a boom of the 1929 type in America, and armed with no other weapons than those possessed at that time by the Federal Reserve System; and none of the alternatives within its power might make much difference to the result."[32] Yet he had no suggestion for a monetary policy suitable for use under the 1929 conditions in the United States or for the powers necessary for achievement of a suitable monetary policy.

General identification of monetary policy with interest-rate manipulation has been accompanied by a more specific assumption that the central bank rediscount rate may be used as a representation of monetary policy at a particular period of time. It is true, of course, that the rate of rediscount may be one of the tools of monetary policy, but a reduction in the rediscount rate may be an unused tool because of other conditions attached to rediscounting. In the United States, monetary policy is expressed not in any one announced condition under which commercial banks may acquire reserves at the Federal Reserve banks but in the whole set of conditions which determine (a) the actual amount of reserves and the required reserve ratio and (b) the amount of such reserves and the required ratio which the banks can confidently expect in the future.

The general identification of monetary policy with interest-rate manipulation and the more specific assumption that monetary policy is expressed in the rediscount rate have obscured, in the eyes of followers of Keynesian economics, the real character of monetary policy in the United States during the crucial period of transition from the prosperity of the 1920's to the great depression. When attention is focused on changes in the actual quantity of reserves of member-banks and on the operations of the Federal Reserve banks which controlled the quantity of those reserves, the conclusion is inescapable: (a) that in the late 1920's the *de facto* monetary policy was that of

---

[32] *General Theory*, pp. 323 and 327.

prohibiting growth and (*b*) that during the early 1930's, with an ineffective interlude or two, the *de facto* monetary policy was that of contraction.   Monetary deficiency throughout the period from 1928 to 1933—absence of normal growth followed by contraction—was produced by failure of the Federal Reserve banks to acquire enough assets to maintain a reasonable growth in the amount of bank reserves.[33]

Some economists in recent years have called attention to the necessity of distinguishing between various types of interest rates.   In the United States such a distinction is especially necessary between (*a*) Federal Reserve rediscount rates and short-term open market rates in the financial centers and (*b*) prevailing bank-customer rates and yields on corporate bonds.   The former have only a slight bearing on the rate of interest paid by business enterprises for new capital and therefore have little relevance to the interest-rate concept which is involved in the Keynesian analysis.   The latter are more reliable indicators of the rate of interest which must be paid for new capital. Many Keynesian economists, as a result of their identification of the central bank rediscount rate with monetary policy, appear to assume that the early 1930's was a period when the rate of interest was comparatively low, whereas, in fact, the rate of interest in that period appears abnormally high.   The most reasonable interpretation of the factual data, in the light of the theory of interest, is that the rate of interest—in the sense used in Keynesian analysis—was pushed up in the late 1920's by monetary deficiency and was maintained by the same means at an abnormally high rate until after the banking holiday in 1933.

Throughout the latter part of 1928, all of 1929, and the first half of 1930 the rate of interest charged on commercial loans by Federal Reserve member banks in leading cities was higher than in the first few months of 1928.   During the period from the middle of 1930 to the

---

[33] The data taken into consideration in reaching this conclusion include not only the total reserves of Federal Reserve member banks but also the distribution of member-bank reserves among reserve city, central reserve city, and country banks and the magnitude of operations of banks not members of the Federal Reserve System.

banking holiday in 1933 the average rate on such loans was slightly lower (4.5 per cent compared with 4.7 per cent) than during the first quarter of 1928 but was substantially higher than "normal," as indicated by a trend projected from the six-year period ending early in 1928, during which expanding bank reserves permitted the quantity of money to grow at a reasonable rate. Corporate bond yields tended downward during the early and middle 1920's, but this decline was halted in the middle of 1928. During the ensuing four years corporate bond yields (with some irregularity) were rising and throughout the entire period 1929–33 they were substantially above the projection from the six-year period ending early in 1928.[34]

In drawing the conclusion that interest rates were maintained at an abnormally high rate from the middle of 1928 to the banking holiday, I am necessarily expressing a personal opinion regarding the normal level of the rate of interest at that time. This opinion, of course, cannot be definitely proved or disproved, since there is no way of determining the normal interest rate in the absence of monetary expansion at a reasonable rate. My opinion is based on the following considerations: (1) that the long-term tendency for a fall in the rate of interest, regarded by economists of the eighteenth, nineteenth, and early twentieth centuries as a normal accompaniment of economic progress, was interrupted in the 1920's by the extraordinary demand for loans associated with the construction necessary for adaptation of the economy to the use of motor vehicles; (2) that toward the close of the 1920's the construction boom associated with the adaptation of the economy to motor vehicles passed its climax; (3) that, in the absence of some other special factor, the rate of interest would have tended to drop to a level comparable with and probably below that prevailing during the early years of the twentieth century; (4) that this fall in the rate of interest back to its long-term trend would have been, in the absence of monetary deficiency, approximately as rapid as the fall during the middle 1920's; and (5) that projection of the downward trend during the period 1922–27 therefore gives a reason-

---

[34] Board of Governors of the Federal Reserve System, *Banking and Monetary Statistics* (Washington, D.C., Board of Governors of the Federal Reserve System, 1943), pp. 463, 464, and 468–70.

able estimate of the normal rate of interest for several years subsequent to those years. Not until 1935 did the rate of interest fall close to this estimated normal. This is indicated in Figure 2, which gives for each year of the period 1919–45 a composite interest rate derived from the average interest rate charged by banks on commercial loans and average corporate bond yields.[35]

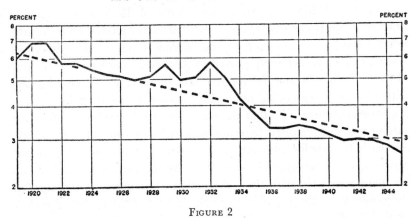

ESTIMATED AVERAGE ANNUAL INTEREST RATES
1919 - 1945

AVERAGE OF CORPORATE BOND YIELDS (MOODY'S) AND BANK
RATES ON COMMERCIAL LOANS IN PRINCIPAL CITIES ——
TREND BASED ON 1922 – 1927 — — —

FIGURE 2

Since 1935 this composite commercial-loan–bond-yield rate of interest has drifted downward in approximate accord with the projection of the 1922–27 trend, but about one-fourth of 1 per cent below that projection, and in recent years has reached a figure slightly under 3 per cent. Whether the projection of the 1922–27 trend has or has

[35] The composite rate used in Fig. 2 is the mid-point between (a) the annual weighted average rate charged by banks on customers' loans or on commercial loans, as reported by the Board of Governors of the Federal Reserve System, and (b) the annual average yield on corporate bonds, all groups, as reported by Moody's *Investors Service*. The figures for the two series are given in *Banking and Monetary Statistics*, and the *Federal Reserve Bulletin*.

not reached the level of a long-term projection from the nineteenth and early twentieth centuries is a question on which it is difficult to reach even a personal judgment, because of the lack of comparability of the available data over such a long period. However, I can see no factual basis for a supposition that average interest rates in recent years have been abnormally low, relative to the level which they might have been expected to reach with normal economic progress and the adjustment of the economy to motor vehicles.

The novel conclusions—as compared with orthodox theory—reached by contemporary economists with respect to the nature of the connection between savings-investment relationships and business fluctuations and regarding the character of governmental policies necessary for "full" production and employment are, it now seems clear, the result of erroneous assumptions and conclusions regarding the character and effect of monetary policy during the period of transition from the prosperity of the 1920's to the great depression and during the subsequent years. Devotees of the Keynesian concepts have substituted the concept of inadequate investment or insufficient "outlets" for savings for the concept of monetary deficiency and the concept of governmental fiscal (debt) policy for monetary policy in its proper sense of policy with respect to the quantity of money. These substitutions have been made by contemporary economists in order to fill an artificial vacuum created by their failure to look at available data and to acquaint themselves with the ideas of their predecessors and the motivating elements in the operations of the money-creating industry. Contemporary business-fluctuation theory in the United States cannot progress further without elimination of its misplaced emphasis on savings-investment relationships and a re-examination of the significance of changes in the money supply.

This criticism of the conclusions of contemporary economists is not a criticism of the Keynes-Lange set of relations, except on the score of emphasis and direction of causation in the real world. The major conclusions [respecting monetary theory] which are properly drawn from [these relations] are identical with the conclusions of orthodox theory: (1) that monetary policy should be concerned, not with the rate of interest per se, but with the maintenance of a suitable quantity of money, to the end that monetary contraction or a lesser degree of monetary deficiency will not precipitate or accentuate a business depression and that excessive monetary expansion will not carry a business boom beyond reasonably full employment into the realm of an upward spiral in the prices of the products of the economy[36] and (2) that government fiscal policy should not, through the meeting of government expenses by the direct issue of money or the sale of an excessive quantity of government obligations to the banking system, interfere with monetary policy.

---

[36] For mathematical treatments of the Keynes-Lange system of relationships, developed in a way which bears on this interpretation of Keynesian economics, see Franco Modigliani, "Liquidity Preference and the Theory of Interest and Money," *Econometrica,* XII (1944), 45–88; and Arthur Smithies, "The Quantity of Money and the Rate of Interest," *Review of Economic Statistics,* XXV (1943), 69–76.

15

THE RATE OF INTEREST, THE BANK RATE, AND THE STABILIZATION OF PRICES*[1]

By Gustav Cassel‖

Economic theory is in its essence a theory of price. Its main function is to explain the whole process by which prices are fixed at their actual heights. It is, therefore, natural that the theory should from the very outset be based on the conception of price. It is not necessary, as the old economists used to do, first to develop a special "theory of value,"—usually very difficult to grasp for the student,—and wait until a relatively late stage to introduce the conception of price. In my *Theory of Social Economy* I take the much more direct and simple way of at once introducing an abstract unit in which all values are reckoned. The investigation is then from the very start an investigation of prices; we have nothing to do with "values," and we need not trouble our students with those numberless definitions of value that generally lie as stumbling-blocks in the way of a youth eager to penetrate to the actual and central problems of economic life.

When we postulate an abstract unit in which all prices are reckoned, we are able to study all problems concerning relative prices; that is, we can master the whole domain usually comprised under the heading of general economic theory. There remains, however, one essential question to be solved. The question is, how the unit itself is determined, or, in other words, how the absolute height of prices is fixed. This question forms the object of the theory of money, and its solution is in fact the only essential task of this theory.

The rate of interest is a matter of relative price, namely, the price

* *The Quarterly Journal of Economics,* **42** (1927–28), 511–29. Reprinted, by the courtesy of the publisher, without change from the original text.
‖ Professor Cassel died in 1945.
[1] The substance of an address delivered at American Universities in 1928.

for the right of disposal of a certain amount of capital for a certain time. This definition is formed directly on the model of the business man's habit of looking upon these matters. We pay so many dollars for the right to dispose of one hundred dollars for one year. The sum paid for this right is precisely the rate of interest. On this point science can for once be in complete accordance with practical economics. The theory of interest attains far greater simplicity when the rate of interest is thus from the very outset defined as a price of a certain service. No part of economic theory has suffered more than the theory of interest from the idea that it should be obligatory first to explain the whole economic system in an imagined moneyless society before daring to approach our actual economic life, so essentially based upon the conception of money. Such horrible formulas as "the general overvaluation of present goods in relation to future ones," which were invented by advocates of a separate theory of value for explaining the phenomenon of interest, were as deficient in scientific stringency as they were unnecessarily difficult for the student to grasp.

The theory of interest as a part of the general theory of prices is capable of being developed in a very elementary form. The function of the rate of interest is, like that of all other prices, to force demand and supply to meet one another. The demand for disposal of capital is always so strong that it would be absolutely impossible to satisfy it if nothing had to be paid for the service in question. Disposal of capital is always supplied in a certain scarcity, and the rate of interest has to compress demand so far that it can be satisfied. This is the fundamental explanation of interest.

If the rate of interest were lower than it actually is, forces would be called forth compelling the rate of interest to rise again to the actual height required for the maintenance of equilibrium. A lowering of the rate of interest would particularly affect the prices of such goods as require much disposal of capital for their production. For instance, house-rents would be particularly strongly affected, because they represent to a great extent payment for disposal of capital. Thus, the demand for housing would be strongly increased, and could not be satisfied without increasing claims being put upon disposal of capital. As, however, the supply of this service is limited, such claims would immediately force the rate of interest to rise again. This is the principle of scarcity.

But we have also to take account of a subsidiary principle, namely, the principle of substitution. If the rate of interest were substantially lower, we could use much more machinery and much more real capital of all descriptions to satisfy the same needs that we now satisfy. We should thereby save much labor and perhaps also other factors of production. Thus a substitution of disposal of capital for these other factors would take place. But this would mean a very much increased demand for disposal of capital, forcing the rate of interest to rise again to its equilibrium level. Further, a lower rate of interest would induce people to make all buildings and constructions and a lot of other things much more durable, naturally at an increased cost for the moment, but with a reduction in the annual cost of the use of these durable goods. This again would be a substitution of disposal of capital for other factors of production, and the effect would be an increased demand for disposal of capital, pressing up the rate of interest. The necessity of paying interest always stands in the way of a technical development which in itself would be very profitable and very advantageous, but which must be restricted within certain limits in order that the claims on disposal of capital should not outgrow the possibility of meeting them.

The rate of interest, on the other hand, has also a certain importance for the supply of capital. Capital is supplied by saving. Some people consume more than they earn, and this over-consumption must be subtracted from the savings of the community before we get to the net savings that form the source from which the whole process of production has to meet its need for disposal of capital. These net savings probably do not vary very much with the usual fluctuations in the rate of interest. Still, the rate of interest is an essential factor for keeping up the supply of net savings at its actual height. At a very low rate of interest—say, one or two per cent—people would not care to accumulate capital to anything like the extent that they actually do now. Human life is too short to make it profitable for anybody to part with a capital of $100,000 in order to receive a ridiculous rent of $1,000 a year in exchange. It is imaginable that we could do that if we could reckon with living for some hundreds of years.   But as our remaining term of life usually does not exceed twenty-five or thirty-three years, we pretend to have something like a twenty-fifth or thirty-third part of our capital as annual interest, if we should abstain from consuming the capital itself.   But that is as much as to say that we insist upon having a rate of interest of 4 or, at least, 3 per cent.

We are now ready to proceed to the second part of the great price-fixing problem, namely, the question how the absolute height of prices is determined.   The rate of interest that comes to be fixed in connection with all other prices by our system of equations is, as we know, reckoned in so many per cent and does not contain the dimension of money.   This rate of interest is, therefore, unlike other prices, absolutely determined by the system of equations, that is, by the conditions of equilibrium of the economic system.   The rate is thus independent of the choice of the monetary unit, and it remains the same at whatever height this unit is fixed.   This rate may therefore rightly be called the equilibrium rate of interest.

Let us begin with a very elementary observation.   If the supply of means of payment valid in our monetary standard were quite unlimited, any price could be paid and prices would continue to rise indefinitely.   An indispensable condition of stability is, therefore, that the supply of means of payment should be limited and thus that a certain scarcity in this supply should exist.   The absolute height of prices and the purchasing power of the unit of money will indeed exclusively depend upon this scarcity, in so far as any height of prices and any purchasing power of the unit may be established, provided the supply of means of payment is suitably adjusted.   This simple observation is the kernel of the *Scarcity Theory of Money,* as I have developed it since the beginning of this century, and as it is particularly expounded in my *Theory of Social Economy.*

Every monetary system is primarily characterized by the way in which it realizes the scarcity of the supply of means of payment.   The simplest case is that where we have a paper currency administered by a central bank.   This case also reflects most faithfully the theoretical conditions from which we have started here.   In developing our general theory of relative prices we have postulated the existence of a monetary standard; that is, we have postulated a unit in which all prices are reckoned, but we have left aside the question of how this unit is fixed.   Now this is precisely the case of the paper standard.   It is based on an absolutely abstract unit, and a fixation of this unit is arrived at only by the central bank's regulation of the supply of means of payment valid in the unit.   In a paper standard these means of payment primarily consist of the notes of the central bank.   The purchasing power of the monetary unit is therefore determined by the scarcity that the central bank chooses to give to its note circulation. Now, the central bank has, of course, several means whereby it is able to restrict its issue of notes.   The ultimate and essential means is, however, always the price that the bank charges for its advances, that is, *the bank rate*.   If the bank rate is kept too low, other means of restriction will not help: people will find it advantageous to borrow at the bank, and thus the supply of means of payment will swell independently of any restrictions.   For the theoretical treatment of the subject we may therefore concentrate our attention upon the bank rate, and assume it to be the only means by which the bank regulates its note issue.

The question then is: how high shall the bank rate be?   By what principles shall the central bank be guided in fixing its rate?   The answer is easy enough as soon as we have perceived that there exists a definite equilibrium rate of interest.   If the bank rate is lower than this equilibrium rate, people will go to the bank for covering their needs for capital, and the bank will have to issue notes in order to meet such needs.   This leads to an unnecessarily large issue of notes, and fresh purchasing power is created without any more goods having been produced, and this increase of nominal purchasing power is bound to force up prices.   Thus the result is simply an inflation of the currency.

On the other hand, if the bank rate is kept higher than the equilibrium rate of interest, people will find it profitable to pay their debts to the bank, and thus notes will begin to flow back to the bank and the supply of means of payment will be restricted.   The consequence is a reduction of nominal purchasing power and a general fall in prices. What takes place in this case is a process of deflation.

The conclusion from this is clear. Stability of prices is possible only when the bank rate is kept equal to the equilibrium rate of interest. When this is done, the bank does not in any way interfere with the capital market, which is therefore left to find its natural equilibrium. We have here arrived at the exact solution of the central problem of money, and we shall see that this solution immediately clears up the whole series of difficult questions connected with this central problem. There can be no other solution, and other formulas that have been represented as being solutions of the problem of monetary stabilization are theoretically defective.

However, it has to be observed here that our solution does not give the bank any immediate practical guidance for its banking policy. The bank cannot know at a certain moment what is the equilibrium rate of interest of the capital market. The only practical way of ascertaining what is the correct bank rate is, therefore, by observing the results. If, at a certain bank rate, prices are seen to rise continually, the bank may be sure that the rate is too low. Vice versa, when prices fall, the bank may conclude that the rate is too high. The bank has to adjust its rate so that no general tendency either to a rise or to a fall in prices arises. The practical rule is, therefore, that the bank rate should be so adjusted as to keep the general level of prices as constant as possible.

The general level of prices is, however, a statistical construction, and altho we are well aware what is meant by this average, we must admit that it has no absolute theoretical meaning. The practical rule at which we arrive has therefore not quite the same exactness as our theoretical solution of the problem. But the rule is the only one that can be used as a practical guide for the central bank. We must be satisfied with knowing that the exact solution is included in the practical rule. When the bank rate is equal to the equilibrium rate of interest, and no disturbing factors derange the equilibrium, all prices remain constant, and therefore also the general level of prices.

A bank rate that is thus regulated comes as near to the equilibrium rate of interest as it is practically possible to ascertain. With such a bank rate, therefore, the whole economic life is approximately regulated as if the bank rate were at every moment kept exactly equal to the theoretical equilibrium rate of interest.   By applying this practical rule, therefore, we secure the highest possible stability both for the general process of price-fixing and for the whole economic life.   In fact, we eliminate as far as possible all the disturbances arising out of deviations of the actual rate of interest from the equilibrium rate. We have seen in the first part of this paper how strong and far-reaching the influence of the rate of interest is, and how it includes every important side of our economic life.   We must conclude from this that any deviation of the actual rate of interest from the true equilibrium rate may be the cause of very serious and very widespread disturbances. We have, however, no means of completely discovering these evil effects or of measuring them quantitatively.   But they are all the more dangerous for that very reason, and we have every cause to do our utmost to prevent such deviations of the actual rate of interest from the equilibrium rate.   This, however, can be done only if the central bank adheres strictly to the rule of maintaining the general level of prices at an invariable height.

Many other devices for the regulation of the supply of means of payment by the central bank have been suggested.   Some people contend that the general level of prices ought not to be kept constant, but ought rather to be continually *raised at a moderate rate.*   They promise us several advantages from such a monetary policy, particularly a more vivid spirit of progress.   But then they entirely forget that the bank rate that would have to be applied for this purpose would be lower than the equilibrium rate of interest.   A policy, however, that involves a continual deviation of the bank rate, and therefore also of all rates of interest actually applied in the community, from the equilibrium rate of interest, is a very hazardous policy indeed, involving continual disturbances at all points of the economic life, disturbances which nobody can survey and which we have no means of controlling.   A society conscious of what it was doing would certainly never accept a recommendation of such a very dubious character.

The same must, of course, be said of all other schemes for regulating a paper standard.   A continuous fall of the general level of prices, as recommended by some people as a program of justice, is from our

point of view equally to be condemned.   Again, the idea that cyclical
fluctuations of the general level of prices are valuable as a stimulus to
enterprise and a tonic for economic health is in itself very vague and
dangerous, but is seen to be still more so if we consider all the evil
economic effects of the continual falsification of the rate of interest
that must be involved in a monetary administration on such lines.

How, then, are we to judge the gold standard from this point of
view?   The gold standard is, as I usually represent it, nothing else than
a paper standard in which the purchasing power of the monetary unit
is so regulated as practically to coincide with that of gold.   The aim
of a gold-standard administration is not to keep the general level of
prices constant, but to keep the price of one single commodity, namely,
gold, as invariable as possible.   If the purchasing power of gold as
against other commodities should happen to remain constant, the gold
standard is obviously identical with a paper standard regulated according to the principles just laid down.   But if the value of gold varies,
the gold standard involves a regulation of the purchasing power of
the monetary unit in accordance with the variations of that of gold.
This is indeed a very artificial and complicated system.   It is clear
that, in order to bring about such variations, it is necessary to keep the
bank rate higher or lower than the equilibrium rate of interest, according to the requirements of the situation of the moment.   Under such
circumstances the gold standard involves continual deviations in opposite directions of the actual rate of interest from the equilibrium rate.
The disturbing effects of such a policy are obviously quite impossible
to survey, and the fact that the world has been persuaded to accept
them without resistance can be explained only by the ignorance that
has prevailed as to the real effects of the gold-standard system as a
disturbing factor in the process by which the true rate of interest is
fixed.

Must we then conclude that the gold standard has to be rejected
altogether as entirely incompatible with the needs of a rationally regulated social economy?   Well, if the value of gold relatively to other
goods should continue to fluctuate as it has done hitherto, the answer
must undoubtedly be yes.   The only condition on which modern
society can accept the gold standard is that some means be found

whereby it is possible to regulate the value of gold so as to keep gold at a constant purchasing power as against other commodities.   For the future, the prospect is that, without such a deliberate regulation of the value of gold, an increasing scarcity of gold will make itself felt, with the result that the general level of prices in every gold standard will be subject to a continual and unlimited fall.   It should be possible to prevent this by economizing in the monetary use of gold.   Ever since the war I have advocated such a policy of economy in the use of gold.   The International Economic Conference in Genoa in 1922 endorsed this policy, which has also later found important expression in the refusal of certain countries to let gold coins enter again into circulation.   No doubt it ought to be possible by such means to stabilize the value of gold at its present height, at least for the next few decades. If this is done, the gold standard may be adhered to as a satisfactory solution of the world's monetary problem as it now presents itself, as determined by the events of history.   But if the gold-economizing policy does not succeed, or if it at a future time is found no longer possible to carry through, the unavoidable consequence must be that the gold standard will have to be abolished, and that the world's economy will have to be based on paper standards regulated with the single purpose of keeping the general level of prices constant.

It is a very natural idea that the bank rate must stand in some proportion to the rate of interest of the capital market.   Indeed, central banks have long been aware of their duty to watch the movements of the capital market and to adjust their bank rate accordingly.   For a hundred years the Bank of England has accumulated experience in bank administration along these lines.   Scientific men have also tried to work out the connection between the bank rate and the rate of the capital market.   Endeavors have thus been made to put the bank rate in some relation to the profits of real capital.   This is, however, a very vague conception and it seems impossible to find an exact definition for it.   It must also be observed that profits may be increased, and are very often strongly increased, on the ground that plant is more fully employed.   There seems to be no reason why such an increase in profits should affect the bank rate, at least directly.   The rate of profits derived from real capital also depends very greatly upon how much money has been spent on this capital, that is, what the cost was when it was constructed. This, however, being a thing of the past, is irrelevant for present economic action and should have no influence on the bank rate. The profits are also naturally very different in different enterprises. Attempts have therefore been made to refer the bank rate to the average return of all capital already invested. This is positively wrong. Interest can never be regulated according to such an average, but has rather to be referred to the marginal return, the "return of the last investment." But the return of the last investment made at the present time must always be, or tend to be, equal to the bank rate. People will go on investing as long as there is any profit over and above what they have to pay to the bank. Thus the bank authorities can obtain no guidance from such a rule.

If we consider these different attempts for a moment, it stands out quite clearly that there can be no other solution of the problem than that here presented. The bank rate must in theory be referred to the equilibrium rate of interest as defined by the conditions for an equilibrium of the whole process of price-fixing. The practical guide for the central bank must be sought in the stability of the general level of prices. The bank rate that results in such a stability being attained represents as truly as possible "the real rate of interest of the capital market" and may be taken as a practical definition of that rate. It is impossible to advance further, and no more exact definition of the rate of the capital market can be given if it is required that this definition should allow us to ascertain the actual height of the rate.

It is necessary now to pay some attention to the special conditions of a progressive society. From our present point of view this society deserves particular attention because it has a continually growing need for means of payment. These means must be supplied by the bank, and will be supplied if the bank rate is adjusted to the theoretical equilibrium rate of interest. In this case all need for capital for buying goods or services is covered by the actual savings of the society without having recourse to the bank. But the need for more means of payment that is characteristic of the progressive society is met by the bank advancing money for the purpose at the bank rate.

It is well now to clear up a complication which, for the sake of simplicity, I have hitherto set aside.   Our whole reasoning has been based upon the tacit assumption that there is only one rate of interest on the capital market.   We know that this is not the case.   There are, firstly, the differences arising out of different risks; but we may disregard these and take account only of the differences in the rate of interest which result from the fact that the rate is paid for disposal of capital under different conditions.   The most conspicuous difference is that between short-term and long-term loans.   It is customary to speak of a "money market" as distinct from the "capital market."   There is, of course, no sharp line of demarcation between these two markets, which indeed are related to one another by innumerable connections.   As, however, different rates are usually quoted for loans under different conditions, it may be asked to what rate of interest the bank rate should be adjusted.   The answer is clear enough.   The bank rate ought to coincide with the particular rate of interest that must be paid for such loans as are usually supplied by the bank.   Then other rates will adjust themselves to this rate and the result will be seen in the stability of the general level of prices, which is a proof of the correctness of the bank rate.

In business circles, and even in political discussions, the question is very often raised, how the rate of interest affects the prices of commodities.   The practical business man is perhaps most often inclined to believe that an increase in the rate of interest is bound to increase the cost of all products and therefore to enhance prices, and he finds it very confusing when he hears a scientific economist or a representative of a central bank proclaim that the rate is increased in order to force prices down.   It is obviously the duty of economic science to remove this confusion, and we are now in a position to do so.   Going back to the general theory of prices, we have first observed that the rate of interest is a price for a service and that this price enters into the cost of production just as the price of any other service required in the process of production.   Thus, no doubt, a rise in the rate of interest is followed by a corresponding rise in the prices of the goods for the production of which disposal of capital has been required.   We must, however, always remember that the general theory of prices is exclusively concerned with relative prices and does not tell us anything about the absolute height of prices. The latter question is exclusively an object of the theory of money. If by a suitable bank policy the general level of prices is kept invariable, every rise in some prices must necessarily be counterbalanced by a fall in others. If the equilibrium rate of interest increases, only those goods will rise in price for the production of which a particularly large amount of disposal of capital has been required, whereas other prices must sink so low that the average level of all prices remains unaltered.

A quite different question is that of the influence of the bank rate. As long as the bank rate coincides with the equilibrium rate of interest, it has no particular influence on prices. But if the bank rate is raised above the equilibrium rate of interest, the demand for loans is affected. As I have already explained, people begin to reduce their debts to the bank. The community is provided with means of payment in a more restricted manner, and the nominal purchasing power of the market is reduced, with the result that prices in general must fall. In this way the raising of the bank rate above the equilibrium rate of interest of the capital market brings about a fall of the general level of prices. Conversely, a reduction of the bank rate below the equilibrium rate of interest is, as we have seen, bound to raise the general level of prices. These effects are quite separate from the effects of fluctuations in the equilibrium rate of interest; and it is absolutely impossible to come to any clear understanding of the matter until people learn to distinguish between the bank rate and the equilibrium rate of interest of the capital market.

Thus far we have confined ourselves to a discussion of static conditions, the term taken in the wider sense already indicated. It is necessary, however, to say some few words about interest in a social economy under dynamic conditions. What I particularly have in view is the rôle of interest as a regulator of trade cycles.

In order to meet its *present* desire for more complete equipment with real capital, society is always in need of saving. These savings are supplied by the individual saver, who saves in order to accumulate funds for *future* needs. Thus, the objects in view in both cases are entirely different, and there is no direct connection between the desire to supply the present society more fully with real capital and the desire of individuals to save for coming years.   Still, the possibility of satisfying the former desire is strictly limited by the second.   If, as a result of certain causes, say, of a technical nature, the first desire increases and becomes more intense, these causes have no direct influence on the second desire.   The increased demand for disposal of capital is not immediately followed by an increase of savings.   An equilibrium can then be brought about only by a rise in the rate of interest restricting the demand for disposal of capital.   It is possible, however, that this rise in the rate of interest will also have a certain influence on saving and bring about a moderate increase in the amount of capital placed at the disposal of production.   In this case the result is a certain increase in the total amount of real capital produced, the productive forces of the society being drawn from the service of consumption to the production of real capital, and perhaps also more intensely used. We then have what is generally called a rising tide in the cyclical movement of trade.   A reaction comes when the production of real capital can no longer bear the burden of the high rate of interest.   A general set-back in the rate of production of real capital takes place and a period of depression follows.   The consequence is a heavy fall in the rate of interest.   The new low rate acts as a stimulus for a renewed activity in the construction of real capital and a new rising tide is engendered.

In both phases of the cyclical movement the rate of interest works as a regulator tending to keep the movement within narrower limits. This is obviously a very important function of the rate of interest.

If the central bank, during a rising tide, keeps its bank rate too low and does not raise it in accordance with the rise in the natural rate of the capital market, the consequence must be, as in the case we have already discussed, that the market borrows unduly much from the bank and becomes too abundantly supplied with means of payment.   The immediate result is that purchasing power is put at disposal for an increased construction of real capital, and the rising tide acquires an artificially increased strength.   This effect is, however, much increased in consequence of the rise in prices that must follow upon the excessive supply of means of payment.   What actually takes place is an inflation of the currency, depriving large groups of income-earners of a part of their real income and placing these means at disposal for further construction of real capital. We have here to do with a compulsory saving representing perhaps the most important source for supplying the means required for the rising tide. The fact that a central bank fails to raise its bank rate in accordance with the actual situation of the capital market very much increases the strength of the cyclical movement of trade, with all its pernicious effects on social economy. This is an evil which ought to be prevented in a rationally organized society, and it can be prevented provided the bank regulates its rate in accordance with the natural rate of the capital market. But here again it is impossible for the central bank to know exactly what this "natural rate" is, and in this case too the bank has only to regulate its rate so that the general level of prices is kept as constant as possible. Supposing the bank succeeds hereby in entirely eliminating the rise and fall of the general level of prices, which always accompanied the trade cycles as we knew them before the war, the whole cyclical movement of trade must become very much attenuated. For it will then be deprived of the great stimulus derived from the continual falsification of the capital market that is a consequence of an alternately too abundant and too scanty supply of means of payment.

This observation throws a clear light on the futility of the mathematical wave-theory of life. It has become a fashion among economists, or rather among statisticians without a thoro economic training, to look upon everything that happens in economic life as subordinate to statistical curves and subject to being predicted by a mathematical analysis of these curves. Against this determinism we now have to put up the incontestable fact that a rational regulation of the bank rate lies in our hands, and may be accomplished if we only perceive its importance and decide to go in for such a policy. It cannot be doubted that with a bank rate regulated on these lines the conditions for the development of trade cycles would be radically altered, and that indeed our familiar trade cycles would be a thing of the past. In this case it is plain enough that our future is not determined by mathematical curves but by our own intelligence and will. But if this is so, the whole so-called science of business-forecasting inevitably becomes very much discredited. What the economist can do is to examine present facts and proposed lines of action, and to show how they are likely to influence the development of economic life. But he can never make a prediction of our future independent of our own actions. And we should never lose sight of the fact that the future is influenced by coming events about which we know nothing, and the prediction of which in any case does not belong to economic science.

PART IV

MONETARY POLICY

16

RULE VERSUS AUTHORITIES IN
MONETARY POLICY*

By Henry C. Simons‖

The monetary problem stands out today as the great intellectual challenge to the liberal faith. For generations we have been developing financial practices, financial institutions, and financial structures which are incompatible with the orderly functioning of a system based on economic freedom and political liberty. Even more disturbing, perhaps, than the institutional trend is the trend of thinking and discussion among special students of money—the fact that economists have become accustomed to deal with monetary problems in a manner which impliedly belies their professed liberalism.

The liberal creed demands the organization of our economic life largely through individual participation in a game *with definite rules*. It calls upon the state to provide a stable framework of rules within which enterprise and competition may effectively control and direct the production and distribution of goods. The essential conception is that of a genuine division of labor between competitive (market) and political controls—a division of labor within which competition has a major, or at least proximately primary, place.

A liberal system adapted to modern conditions would be, of course, exceedingly complex, by comparison with an authoritarian collectivism. It would involve a large measure of political control: outright collectivism in some areas; deliberate enforcement of competition in others; prevention of extreme inequality, largely via taxation, in the distribution of property, income, and power. Moreover, such a sys-

---

* *The Journal of Political Economy*, **44** (1936), 1–30. Reprinted, by the courtesy of The University of Chicago Press, without change in the original text.

‖ Professor Simons died in 1946.

tem is attainable, through economic reconstruction, only by years of careful planning and wise legislation; and, once realized, however perfectly, it would require continuous modification, with at least minor changes in the rules, to meet new developments and new conditions.

There is thus little point in contrasting a liberal system and a planned economy—except for the coincidence that the latter phrase has been appropriated by reformers who have little sympathy with, and less understanding of, the liberal position.

There is imminent danger, however, that actual governmental policies will undermine irreparably the kind of economic and political life which most of us prefer to the possible alternatives. This danger manifests itself mainly in three ways: (1) in the displacement of price competition by political (governmental or monopoly) control in many areas where such competition, if established, preserved, and properly canalized, is peculiarly competent for promoting the general welfare; (2) in the neglect of the unquestioned positive responsibilities of governments under the free-enterprise system; and (3) in measures and policies which involve delegation of legislative powers and the setting-up of *authorities instead of rules.*[1]

It is this danger of substituting authorities for rules which especially deserves attention among students of money. There are, of course, many special responsibilities which may wisely be delegated to administrative authorities with substantial discretionary power; health authorities, for example, cannot well be limited narrowly in their activities by legislative prescriptions. The expedient must be invoked sparingly, however, if democratic institutions are to be preserved; and it is utterly inappropriate in the money field. An enterprise system cannot function effectively in the face of extreme uncertainty as to the action of monetary authorities or, for that matter, as to monetary legislation. We must avoid a situation where every business venture becomes largely a speculation on the future of monetary policy. In the past, governments have grossly neglected their positive responsibility of controlling the currency; private initiative has been allowed

---

[1] These views have been presented more fully by the writer in a tract entitled *A Positive Program for Laissez Faire: Some Proposals for a Liberal Economic Policy,* Public Policy Pamphlet No. 15, Chicago, University of Chicago Press, 1934.

too much freedom in determining the character of our financial structure and in directing changes in the quantity of money and money-substitutes. On this point there is now little disagreement. In our search for solutions of this problem, however, we seem largely to have lost sight of the essential point, namely, that definite, stable, legislative rules of the game as to money are of paramount importance to the survival of a system based on freedom of enterprise.

Indeed, it may be said that economists, as students of money and banking, have accepted and propagated the first serious heresy among liberals. Managed currency (along with protectionism) is the prototype of all current "planning" schemes—in the sense of all the illiberal connotations of planning. To be sure, many economists still protest vigorously against proposals for currency management; but they and their teachers before them joined zealously in the movement for central banking—and it is precisely here that the heresy is clearly manifested.

This unwitting defection among custodians of the liberal faith is explicable, and may be apologized for, in terms of an unfortunate habit of distinguishing too sharply between currency and banking problems, and in terms of a disposition to look upon banking arrangements as merely a detail or subsidiary system within the supposedly automatic mechanism of the gold standard. Only of late is it clearly realized that the money problem has been swallowed up in the credit problem, or that gold has long been reduced largely to the status of a decorative symbol within a welter of national policies as to central banking, government finance, and foreign trade.

Economist-liberals are now on the defensive. On most fronts, however, their position is, or can be made, very strong intellectually. Conspicuous weakness is to be found only with respect to the problems of money and banking. There is little agreement, and not much relevant discussion, as to how the monetary rules of the game might effectively be altered to prevent or greatly to mitigate the affliction of extreme industrial fluctuations. We cannot effectively answer radical critics of the present system, or expose the stupid schemes of plausible reformers, by saying that the problems which they find in other areas are really just problems of money (although this observation is usually correct and pointed), when we have no good solutions to propose, with some unanimity, in the money field.

Our problem is that of defining an adequate monetary system based on simple rules and of finding the way toward such a system. We cannot seek merely to return to some arrangement of the past. The monetary problem was never solved in the past. There is no adequate system of rules to be found in earlier arrangements—except in the sense that the specific form of the rules was formerly, in a more flexible economy, a matter of less importance. Moreover, we have become so habituated to the fact and to the idea of "management," especially with respect to banking, that we shall find it hard either to reject the palliatives which management offers or even to face squarely our intellectual task.

It is significant that the most stimulating contribution to recent discussion, namely, the conception of a neutral money, comes from a group of economists who have held most firmly to the essential tenets of old-fashioned liberalism. In this conception we have, perhaps, a clue as to how the practical problem may ultimately be solved— although it must be conceded that the conception rather defies precise definition or easy translation into concrete proposals.

An effort at such translation was made recently by a group, including the present writer, in connection with some tentative proposals for banking reform.[2] These proposals contemplated (*a*) putting demand-deposit banking on a 100 per cent reserve basis and, more tentatively, (*b*) eventual fixing of the total quantity of circulating media (currency plus demand deposits).[3]

The fixing of the quantity of circulating media is attractive as a principle of monetary policy for several reasons: (1) it avoids reliance on discretionary (dictatorial, arbitrary) action by an independent monetary authority and defines a statutory rule which might be enacted by the competent legislature without substantial delegation of its powers; (2) it provides automatically for downward adjustment of

---

[2] See mimeographed memorandum on "Banking and Currency Reform" (with Supplement and Appendix), prepared and circulated by several Chicago economists in November 1933. See also the pamphlet mentioned above, n. 1.

[3] The two features of the scheme are clearly separable, each calling for appraisal on its merits. The banking proposals might be adopted along with many different monetary arrangements, including the international gold standard.

commodity prices as output expands through improvement in technical efficiency; (3) it represents a rule which, from the viewpoint of a contractual, enterprise economy, is ideally definite and simple; (4) it is clear enough and reasonable enough to provide the basis for a new "religion of money," around which might be regimented strong sentiments against tinkering with the currency. It requires little or no judgment in its administration; it defines a policy in terms of means, not merely in terms of ends; it is compatible with the rule of balancing governmental revenues and expenditures; and it gives to "inflation" a simple meaning which would be conducive to long-term stability in, and observance of, this section of the rules of the economic game.

With all its merits, however, this rule cannot now be recommended as a basis for monetary reform. The obvious weakness of fixed quantity, as a sole rule of monetary policy, lies in the danger of sharp changes on the velocity side, for no monetary system can function effectively or survive politically in the face of extreme alternations of hoarding and dishoarding. It is easy to argue that something would be gained in any event if perverse changes were prevented merely as to quantity, but the argument is unconvincing. The fixing of the quantity of circulating media might merely serve to increase the perverse variability in the amounts of "near-moneys" and in the degree of their general acceptability, just as the restrictions on the issue of bank notes presumably served to hasten the development of deposit (checking-account) banking.

This possibility is clearest in the case of savings accounts (time deposits), where one faces a real difficulty of preventing, and even of defining, effective circulation.[4] The questions which may be raised

---

[4] All reform proposals which depend on or imply a categorical distinction between circulating media (say, demand deposits) and non-circulating near-moneys (time deposits, savings accounts, treasury bills, commercial paper of large corporations) are exposed to serious criticism on that account. Moreover, those who argue that the 100 per cent reserve system need not be a seriously disturbing innovation, because of the opportunities for expansion of savings-deposit banking, are in effect proposing that we undertake radical institutional changes for utterly trivial gains. Indeed, they are really arguing for drastic reform on the grounds that its intended effects would never be realized.

in this case alone are, indeed, sufficiently involved to dictate one's passing immediately, in discussion, to a broader and less practical approach.

The problem of synchronous industrial (employment) fluctuations is a problem (a) of rigidities in crucial areas of the price structure—of adjustments made through output and employment instead of through prices and wage-rate—and (b) of perverse flexibility in the total turnover (quantity and velocity) of effective money. Assuming now a limited flexibility in prices and wages, let us try to see what would be the nature of better or ideal conditions on the financial side. What arrangements as to the financial structure would be conducive to lesser or minimum amplitude of industrial fluctuations?[5]

An approximately ideal condition is fairly obvious—and un-attainable. The danger of pervasive, synchronous, cumulative mal-adjustments would be minimized if there were no fixed money con-tracts at all—if all property were held in a residual-equity or common-stock form. With such a financial structure, no one would be in a position either to create effective money-substitutes (whether for circu-lation or for hoarding) or to force enterprises into wholesale efforts at liquidation.[6] Hoarding and dishoarding (changes in velocity) would,

---

[5] If one finds this question unclear, and the following discussion confusing, for lack of definite assumptions regarding currency, one may assume, for the moment, any monetary system which does not provide for the deliberate off-setting of velocity changes by wholesale changes of quantity. The intention, however, is to focus attention on monetary factors outside the central field of currency and to inquire as to the conditions in the field of private finance which would be most (and least) conducive to stability under any particular set of rules as to the currency.

[6] It might be argued that the emphasis here is misplaced, and that what may be called "voluntary liquidation" is quantitatively more important than liquidation forced by creditors. Undoubtedly, there have been enormous accumulations of cash and near-moneys, and wholesale reductions of debts which might easily have been renewed or refunded, by firms which could anticipate no threat of bankruptcy in the significant future. Whatever the facts, however, the observation is hardly in point, as the following comments may indicate:

1. We are concerned in this paper with monetary factors—with the finan-cial structure as a source of aggravation in booms and depressions. Voluntary

to be sure, still occur; but the dangers of cumulative maladjustment would be minimized.[7]

Not far short of the ideal is a financial system in which all borrowing and lending takes the form of contracts in perpetuity—contracts on which repayment of principal can never be demanded. Given a large volume of financing on such contracts, the mere burden of the fixed annuity charges might occasionally lead to extensive effort among enterprisers to become more liquid. The protection against demands for payment of principal, however, leaves the total of fixed claims relatively small. Moreover, these perpetuities, being subject to sub-

---

liquidation (as evidenced by voluntary reduction of debts and by the augmenting of reserves of cash and near-moneys) must be regarded, on the other hand, as induced essentially by relative-price maladjustments, i.e., as attributable to monopoly and other sources of price rigidity. The distinction between monetary and non-monetary factors seems indispensable analytically; and, from the viewpoint of practical policy, it is certainly useful to separate the factors which have to do with currency, banking, fiscal practice, and business finance from those which have to do with industrial monopoly, the labor market, and public regulation of utility charges. To suggest that monetary factors be conceived and defined very broadly, as relating to other phases of private finance as well as to banking, is not to question the importance of non-monetary factors.

2. Given monopoly and limited flexibility of prices, the efforts of even a small percentage of firms to meet unrenewable and unrefundable obligations of early maturity, or to guard against prospective difficulties, may create or greatly aggravate the maladjustments which dictate liquidation (suspension of investment, hoarding) by firms whose debts represent no threat whatever to continued solvency. It may be appropriate to ask how much voluntary liquidation has been "caused" by involuntary liquidation elsewhere, whatever the difficulties of answering the question quantitatively.

[7] Even with such a simple financial structure, decentralization of security markets would be further conducive to stability. The concentration of security trading in a few large centers greatly facilitates hysterical mob movements of bullishness and bearishness; and it is dangerous, indeed, to have such sensitive and conspicuous barometers of speculative temper in a system where they easily create the conditions which they predict. The maintenance of ready markets (liquidity) for investment assets is possible only with great risks and costs; we have probably gone much too far in facilitating gambling in property rights and in fostering the dangerous illusion of general liquidity of investments.

stantial change of selling prices, would be relatively unattractive as money-substitutes in hoards.

Only a little farther away from the best system is one where all borrowing and lending contracts are entered into for long periods— say, for at least fifty years. Here there would be the added danger that such maturities as did occur during a depression would be availed of to augment money hoards,[8] but the percentage of total obligations falling due in any critical period would probably be small.

---

[8] To some critics it may seem a mistake to emphasize the possibilities of depression-aggravation from bond maturities without mentioning the possible aggravation of booms through new issues. Here, however, an appearance of elegant symmetry would conceal a real distortion. Obligations of distant maturity (as already implied) are subject to substantial changes of selling-prices, even apart from changing prospects of their discharge. At the time of issue, bonds are little nearer to money, and hardly more acceptable as media for use in hoards, than are other property rights generally. They come close to the money category, or become significant as money-substitutes, only as they approach maturity—i.e., only as they become short-term debts. (These distinctions obviously relate merely to differences of degree along a continuous scale, as is inevitable with reference to any realistic and useful conception of money and money functions.) At all events, the possible inflationary effect of bond flotation is simply not of the same order of magnitude as the possible deflationary effect of their retirement. The issue of long-term bonds during a boom is unlikely, in itself, to alter much the velocity of circulating media; but the discharge of such obligations in a depression may induce the former holders to increase their cash reserves by something like the amount of the funds so received, i.e., to hoard on a scale which otherwise would have been difficult or impossible. Bond issues might be concentrated heavily in periods of speculative optimism, and they might be absorbed largely by inflationary dishoarding; but the form of issue (whether of bonds or stocks or partnership equities) could hardly be regarded as an important independent factor. Under the existing financial organization, of course, bond flotations of large magnitude are likely to be coincident with general credit expansion and dishoarding; and thus, whatever the qualitative control of banking and whatever the actual content of bank portfolios, the increase of deposit currency will serve to absorb such issues. Moreover, a merely empirical study of industrial fluctuations (especially of the so-called "long cycles") may easily lead to unfortunate inferences as to causation or (evading a slippery conception) to gross underestimate of the importance of banking and of the results attainable by reform in that area.

Coming on down the scale, the economy becomes exposed to catastrophic disturbances as soon as short-term borrowing develops on a large scale. No real stability of production and employment is possible when short-term lenders are continuously in a position to demand conversion of their investments, amounting in the aggregate to a large multiple of the total available circulating media, into such media. Such an economy is workable only on the basis of a utopian flexibility of prices and wage-rates. Short-term obligations provide abundant money-substitutes during booms, thus releasing money from cash reserves; and they precipitate hopeless efforts at liquidation during depressions. The shorter the period of money contracts, the more unstable the economy will be; at worst, all money contracts would be in the form of call loans.

Thus we move rapidly out of sight of ideal or even tolerable conditions if there develop special institutional arrangements for financing a large volume of investment commitments (which are, or, to permit steady and efficient functioning of the economy, would have to be, essentially permanent and continuing) through intermediaries (banks) which obtain funds for lending by issuing demand and near-demand claims to the original lenders (depositors). If the state gives special status to banking corporations, if their obligations become the established medium of payment, and, what is perhaps more important, if these obligations come to be considered as good as (or, for convenience, better than) currency for use as reserves, then the banking system acquires in effect the prerogative of currency issue and places the government under the practical necessity of giving these private obligations virtually the status of public debts. Demand-deposit banking represents a gigantic development of call-loan financing; moreover, the practical difference between demand deposits and time deposits (savings accounts) is slight indeed.

The fact that such a system will be exposed repeatedly to complete insolvency is perhaps not a matter of primary concern, for government intervention to protect at least the great majority of banks may be taken for granted. What matters is the character of the financial structure which banking creates—and the fact that, in the very nature of the system, banks will flood the economy with money-substitutes during booms and precipitate futile efforts at general liquidation afterward.

Two special circumstances serve to make such a financial system still more sensitive to disturbances: (1) the maintenance by banks of relatively small cushions of owner equities; and (2) the practice of making short-term loans which represent secondary, unsecured claims. Thus, a relatively small decline of security values properly raises question as to the solvency of banks and induces widespread effort to improve the quality of bank assets. Moreover, bankers as holders of unsecured claims naturally respond to signs of unfavorable business conditions with sharp contraction of loans. Certainly, it is an unhappy arrangement whereby those who can demand prompt repayment (can discontinue lending) are, because of the preferred position of other creditors in bankruptcy, compelled to attempt immediate liquidation in the face of the slightest uncertainty.

The notion has somehow become prevalent that banks ought to invest only or largely in short-term commercial paper; indeed, one finds here the rationale of a great enterprise in banking reform. Anyone who is not something of an economist can see that banks, acquiring funds subject to call, should lend only upon promise of early repayment; but the notion, while plausible, is entirely spurious. Indeed, the adherence to this cardinal rule of conservative lending serves (would serve), not to mitigate the affliction of banking, but to compound it; for banks thus increase the volume of short-term debts, not merely in acquiring funds, but in lending them as well. It must be accounted one of the most unfortunate effects of modern banking that it has facilitated and encouraged the growth of short-term financing in business generally.[9]

---

[9] If banks were to confine their investments to long-term obligations, several benefits would accrue. Business would be less exposed to paralyzing withdrawals of working capital; and the banks would largely lose the power, dangerous to themselves as well as to the community, of precipitating chaotic liquidation. Bankers, freed from the illusion of liquidity, would have to face more squarely the necessity of meeting demands for cash by transferring (selling) their investments; thus, their own judgment, if not the demands of de-

The penultimate step away from the ideal financial system carries us to one under which all matured (demand) and maturing obligations are legally convertible into some particular commodity like gold, whose total available supply is only a trivial fraction of the amounts which creditors are in a position to demand. And finally, the worst financial structure is realized when many nations, with similar financial practices and institutions and similar credit pyramids (and narrowly nationalist commercial policies), adopt the same commodity as the monetary standard. When one thinks of the total potential creditor-demands for gold for hoarding, in and after 1929, it seems almost beyond diabolical ingenuity to conceive a financial system better designed for our economic destruction. The anomaly of such a system is perhaps abundantly evident in the strong moral restraints and inhibitions which dissuade many people from exercising their legal rights under it.

Given the vagaries of commercial, fiscal, banking, and currency policies in the various countries, and given the character of national financial structures and price rigidities, it is to the writer a

---

positors, would probably lead them to maintain more nearly appropriate cushions of stockholder equities. There might be significant gains, moreover, in better allocation of investment funds, for investment in long-term securities would probably mean more fundamental and more thorough analysis of the debtor enterprises. Certainly there are disadvantages in a system under which large volumes of funds are allocated primarily with respect to the borrower's immediate outlook and the opportunities for liquidation ahead of other creditors.

Of course, there would also be some disadvantages for the banks. Thorough analysis of prospective investments would be expensive. Moreover, short-term paper has one attractive feature, namely, that one can seldom be expected to tell what it is worth. Thus owners, depositors, and examiners are frequently spared for considerable periods the awareness that banks are insolvent— usually, indeed, until that distressing condition has passed. With portfolios of securities on the other hand, the magnitude of stockholder equities would be seriously exposed to the bitter test of prices on the security exchanges.

It seems, at all events, that desirable changes in the content of bank portfolios might be defined roughly in terms of transfer from earlier to later kinds of assets in the following list: (1) short-term commercial paper; (2) long-term private obligations; (3) federal securities; (4) legal-tender currency.

source of continued amazement that so many people of insight should hold unwaveringly to the gold standard as the best foundation of national policies.[10]   The worship of gold, among obviously sophisticated people, seems explicable only in terms of our lack of success in formulating specifications for a satisfactory, independent national currency—and certainly not in terms of the need of stable exchange-rates for orderly international commerce.   Indeed, it indicates how little progress liberals have made in showing, by way of answer to revolutionists, what kind of money-rules might be adopted to make capitalism a more workable system.

On the other hand, the desire to hold to something, in the face of perplexity, invites understanding sympathy—for certainly we have made little progress in defining attractive alternative systems.   Some students propose pure dictatorship, under powerful monetary authorities; others, the stabilization of various price-indexes; not to mention the many irresponsible proposals for indefinite inflation, based on the notion that our ills are traceable to deficiency of consumer-purchasing-power.   Of all these schemes, those which contemplate stabilization of price-indexes are least illiberal; but they, too, are unsatisfying.   They define programs in terms of ends, with little discussion of appropriate means; they call for an authority with

---

[10] This is not the place to argue the matter in any detail.   See the writer's memorandum to the Commission of Inquiry into National Policy in International Economic Relations (Hutchins Commission), published in their report, *International Economic Relations,* Minneapolis, University of Minnesota Press, 1934, 344–49.

It may be noted that the gold-standard arrangement simply does not define a monetary system based on rules in any sense consistent with our usage in this paper.   It defines a policy merely in terms of its end or objective, and not in terms of means—not in terms of rules of operation.   To be sure, such rules might be established.   To illustrate, Congress might establish a monetary authority with large powers and with a definite mandate (1) to buy and sell gold freely at a fixed price and (2) to maintain a fixed, constant proportion between the amount of its gold holdings and the total amount of money (including demand deposits) in circulation.   It is doubtful whether much enthusiastic or intelligent support could be recruited for such a scheme—or for any other which would establish real rules for the operation of the gold-standard system.

a considerable range for discretionary action, and would require much intelligence and judgment in their administration; and they would leave us exposed to continuous legislative (if not administrative) tinkering, since no particular price-index has much greater inherent reasonableness than many others, and since most of them would serve badly the end of profit stability.[11]

In a free-enterprise system we obviously need highly definite and stable rules of the game, especially as to money. The monetary rules must be compatible with the reasonably smooth working of

---

[11] The choice of a particular price-index, as the basis of a definitive rule of policy, presents serious difficulties. If monetary uncertainties are to be minimized and the monetary authority limited to a strictly administrative function, the commodities whose prices are included in the index must be (1) commodities which can (with a minimum of difficulty) be sharply defined in terms of physical specifications, (2) commodities which (as so defined) are and probably will continue to be actively traded in highly organized and highly competitive markets. The index must be highly sensitive; otherwise, the administrative authority would be compelled to postpone its actions unduly after significant disturbances or (Heaven forbid!) obliged to use discretion in anticipating changes. All prices subject to deliberate regulation, whether by producers or governmental agencies, obviously should be excluded—and all prices which are likely to fall into this class in the significant future!

If a reasonably inclusive, representative index could be designed in accordance with these specifications, it would still be very unsatisfactory. Such an index, governed predominantly by the prices of standardized, basic commodities, would give us an excessively "inflationary" rule, for the production of these commodities is likely to be affected most markedly by the progress of technical efficiency; with such an index we should depart far indeed from the ideal of a neutral money. Moreover, an index of this kind would be peculiarly sensitive to changes and disturbances originating abroad; thus, it might often dictate monetary measures which would be undesirable and merely disturbing domestically. It would seem best to employ an index made up primarily of prices of "domestic," rather than of internationally traded, goods; but it would probably not be possible to construct an index of this kind which would be at all satisfactory in terms of the other considerations which we have noted.

The writer's notion as to how these conflicting considerations should be weighed, for a judicious, practical decision, may be inferred roughly from the order in which they are mentioned above.

the system.[12] Once established, however, they should work me-chanically, with the chips falling where they may. To put our present problem as a paradox—we need to design and establish with the greatest intelligence a monetary system good enough so that, hereafter, we may hold to it unrationally—on faith—as a religion, if you please. The utter inadequacy of the old gold standard, either as a definite system of rules or as the basis of a monetary religion, seems beyond intelligent dispute. But if that

---

[12] The literature of money, however, seems on the whole greatly to over-stress this consideration and to minimize the prospects of automatic adjust-ment through anticipations, under a definite and stable monetary constitution. This may be the result of the widespread practice of discussing the question of what monetary policy should be, in terms of an implied assumption that knowledge of that policy is to be the exclusive possession of an inscrutable monetary authority. The outcome, at all events, is a critical appraisal of possible rules of policy which relates mainly to difficulties of the transition period rather than to the operation of these rules as established bases of anticipations.

This criticism is conspicuously applicable to the usual discussion of "jus-tice" as between debtors and creditors. It is clear that, given a minimum of uncertainty as to money, differences in the monetary rules would tend to be compensated by differences in interest yields. The same point is relevant, moreover, if less obvious and decisive, with respect to "forced saving" and induced maladjustments generally. If the monetary constitution called for a rising, instead of a stable or a declining, price-level, economic behavior would be modified considerably in every sphere—in the labor market, among em-ployers and labor leaders as well; in the determination of the "administered" prices, by both public and private agencies; and, of course, in the money markets.

Generally speaking, it is very difficult to judge the merits of any precise rule of monetary policy on the basis of experience in an economy where no such rule has obtained and where economic behavior has been profoundly in-fluenced by the extreme monetary uncertainty. (The common criticism of price-level stabilization, on the basis of our experience during—and after—the twenties, is thus without much force.) The primary objective of reform should be that of minimizing this kind of uncertainty for the future. From the point of view of ultimate operation, it seems likely that many different rules would serve about equally well. Thus, it is appropriate to focus atten-tion on the difficulties of transition—explicitly.

system lacks peculiarly the virtues which now seem important, they are also patently lacking in most of the systems proposed as substitutes.

Thus, traditional liberalism, if not hopelessly or more fundamentally decadent for other reasons, is at least seriously embarrassed by the difficulty of answering urgent monetary questions in a manner consistent with its central tenets. It is the purpose of this paper, not to present any simple answer or solution, but merely to define the problem more closely and perhaps to provide some basis for ultimate consensus on definite proposals.

The problem of booms and depressions is one which must be attacked from both sides, (*a*) by policies designed to give us a more flexible price structure and (*b*) by measures which will minimize the aggravations attributable to the character of the monetary system and financial structure. The former attack, however, must always be regarded as primary. With adequate price flexibility, we could get along under almost any financial system; with extreme rigidities (reflecting widespread partial monopoly), the most drastic monetary and financial reform, even an ideal financial structure, could not protect us from serious disturbances of production and employment.

For the present, we obviously must rely on a large measure of discretionary money management—on a policy of offsetting and counteracting, by fiscal and banking measures, the effects of monopoly and custom upon prices and wage-rates. Such a policy, however, must be guided by a more fundamental strategy and by the need for early abandonment of temporizing expedients;[13] other-

---

[13] The alternative position would hold that sheer temporizing is less dangerous than definite commitment to any precise, inflexible monetary rule. Given stabilization of a price-index, organized groups might establish the "administered" prices and wage-rates at a level which would prohibit tolerable functioning of the economy as a whole. To guard against this contingency, the monetary authority might be set up as a kind of agency of monopoly control, with an implied policy of countering every general increase of monopoly prices and wages with deliberate inflation of the whole price-level.

Such therapy would alleviate the patient's distress by eliminating possibility of his recovery. We cannot long preserve existing political and economic institutions by countering the infection of monopoly with the opiates of monetary

wise, political control must degenerate into endless concessions to organized minorities, with gradual undermining of the "constitutional structure" under which free-enterprise economy and representative government can function.[14]

The possibilities of genuine economic reconstruction, and the requirements of sound liberal strategy, may be defined in terms of three objectives: (1) restoration of a maximum of competitiveness in industry (including the labor markets); (2) transition to a less preposterous structure of private money contracts; (3) ultimate establishment of a simple, mechanical rule of monetary policy. As regards this third objective, the writer feels that his earlier persuasion as to the merits of the rule of a fixed quantity of money was fundamentally correct, although the scheme is obviously too simple as a prescription under anything like present conditions. Its limitations, however, have to do mainly with the unfortunate character of our financial structure—with the abundance of what we may call "near-moneys"—with the difficulty of defining money in such manner as to give practical significance to the conception of quantity.

---

dictators. The uncertainties of business as to, notably, wage-rates and freight-rates may be as serious as those relating to money; but it would seem sheer folly deliberately to create monetary uncertainties in the hope of salutary counteraction or offsetting effects. Especially alarming, along these lines, is the possibility of a long-continued struggle between the monetary authority, raising the price-level to diminish unemployment, and labor organizations seeking, with able assistance from the Department of Labor, to advance wage-rates ahead of price-level changes—and even, avowedly, to assist the monetary authority by increasing purchasing power! At all events, under such a monetary scheme, the controlled parts of the price structure would probably be manipulated in such manner as to require an indefinite, revolution-creating inflation; indeed, this seems to define the real threat of Fascism in this country and the likely route toward it. If monopoly proves fatal to capitalism, inflation will be the announced cause of death.

[14] As evidence of the grave moral dangers of present policies, one only need mention two superlative contributions of our legislature and executive to the degradation of representative government: the silver legislation and the Guffey-Snyder Bill.

Under what financial conditions would the simple rule of fixed quantity become reasonably satisfactory? In principle, the answer is easy: under the ideal financial structure described above. If this seems to be a counsel of despair, one may add that perfection is not necessary practically. On the other hand, it requires some temerity to specify how far the ideal conditions might safely be sacrificed.

To propose abolition of all borrowing, or even of all borrowing at short term, is merely to dream. It would seem feasible, however, to undertake gradual and systematic reordering of financial practices, to the end of limiting quite narrowly the amount and the possible quantity fluctuations of the generally acceptable near-moneys. This would mean, above all, the abolition of banking, i.e., of all special institutional arrangements for large-scale financing at short term. Demand-deposit banking would be confined (in effect, at least) to the warehousing and transferring of actual currency. Savings banks would be transformed into strictly mutual institutions or investment trusts. Narrow limitation of the formal borrowing powers of other corporations would obviously be necessary, to prevent their effectively taking over the prerogatives of which banking corporations as such had been deprived. Further limitations might also be necessary with respect to financing via the open account (book credit) and instalment sales, although other prohibitions might provide adequate protection indirectly against these evils. If such reforms seem fantastic, it may be pointed out that, in practice, they would require merely drastic limitation upon the powers of corporations (which is eminently desirable on other, and equally important, grounds as well).[15]

Banking is a pervasive phenomenon, not something to be dealt with merely by legislation directed at what we call banks. The experience with the control of note issue is likely to be repeated in the future; many expedients for controlling similar practices may

---

[15] These other grounds, of course, have to do mainly with the monopoly problem. For the writer's views, see the pamphlet mentioned in n. 1.

prove ineffective and disappointing because of the reappearance of prohibited practices in new and unprohibited forms. It seems impossible to predict what forms the evasion might take or to see how particular prohibitions might be designed in order that they might be more than nominally effective. But we perhaps approach insight when we conceive the problem broadly as that of achieving a financial structure in which the volume of short-term borrowing would be minimized, and in which only the government would be able to create (and destroy) either effective circulating media or obligations generally acceptable as hoards-media. More narrowly (with reference to depressions), the problem is one of moving toward a system in which creditors would be unable quickly to demand, and to require enterprises generally to undertake, rapid and impossible liquidation.

Whatever the best-detailed solutions as to financial practices and their control, it seems that some arrangements compatible with rigid fixing of the quantity of effective money may be feasible as a long-term objective of reform. Given such arrangements, the danger of alternate hoarding and dishoarding tendencies, to be sure, would still remain; but it would remain as a problem to be dealt with exclusively via efforts to obtain greater flexibility (competitiveness) in the economy. The problem of industrial fluctuations cannot be solved, and should not be attacked, exclusively by monetary devices. The best monetary system, so to speak, would tolerate occasional disturbances without alleviation, accepting them as a reasonable cost of maintaining the best structure of relative prices and as a means for preventing a continued accumulation of basic maladjustments which could only issue politically in disruption of the system itself.[16]

---

[16] That the fixed-quantity policy would go too far in this direction, however, is a contention to conjure with. Speculative movements with respect to money will always be somewhat cumulative and self-aggravating, even given the most drastic reforms in the field of private finance. Thus, conceding the merits of long-run fixity in the quantity of money, one may argue that provision should be made for temporary changes to offset changes in velocity. But this view, however commendable in principle, has not been, and probably cannot be, translated into significant practical proposals. The difficulties of drafting

In the present critical situation we should not balk at bold schemes for restoring the free-enterprise system to a securely workable basis. The requisite measures, radical in the money field and more radical elsewhere, will become possible politically only with the revival or development of a real religion of freedom, of a strong middle-class movement, and of values (and revulsions) of a rather intense sort. These necessary conditions, however, might soon appear, through popular disillusionment with respect to recently popular economic nostrums and policies, as the perhaps natural alternation in a cycle of opinion and prejudice.

If this favorable climate of opinion does appear, it will behoove liberals to make the most of the opportunity (otherwise probably their last) and, avoiding plausible compromises, to focus their efforts on basic reforms. In particular, this may be interpreted to mean (a) that no concessions can be made as regards the restoration of highly competitive conditions and (b) that few concessions can be made in the effort to remodel our permissible financial prac-

---

satisfactory rules based on elaborate statistical measures of velocity seem decisive. On the other hand, if one wants a system based on rule, it would be folly to enact legislation calling for secular constancy in the quantity of money but leaving the administrative authority free to make "temporary" changes at its own discretion.

These considerations emphasize one great advantage of a price-index rule, namely, that it defines, within a definite long-term rule, appropriate measures for dealing with velocity changes. However, it is possible that, with a more flexible price structure and a narrowly limited amount of short-term financing, the anchor of a fixed quantity of circulating media might suffice to induce prompt reversal of hoarding and dishoarding movements. And moderate cyclical fluctuations might wisely be accepted as the price paid for the conspicuous superiority of the fixed-quantity rule in terms of other considerations. Substantial sacrifice might well be made to obtain greater simplicity and definiteness; to avoid the inherent limitations of index numbers, especially as elements in permanent legislation; to escape the continuing disturbance of positive monetary action; and to dispense with powerful administrative authorities. On the other hand, the price-index rule is eminently preferable for the immediate future—and certainly will remain the more expedient solution unless and until a highly competitive economy is realized and the structure of private money contracts drastically modified.

tices to the end of making feasible and easily workable a definite, mechanical set of rules of the economic game as to money.[17]

For the moment, of course, we must be reconciled to pure management in the money field. We must rely on government action —on political efforts to bring down the prices which remain far out of line; on such injections of fiscal stimulants as may be necessary to prevent recurrence of wholesale liquidation; and, above all, on the prompt and drastic measures for debt retirement which may soon become imperatively necessary to prevent a disastrous inflationary boom. It should be feasible, however, increasingly to concentrate the monetary powers of governmental agencies in fewer hands and, later on, to bring the appropriate agencies more closely within the control of law, through the adoption of rules, expressed perhaps in terms of price indexes. Such measures, at all events, seem essential in a program for avoiding revolutionary changes in economic and political institutions.[18] For the most sanguine view,

---

[17] The so-called 100 per cent scheme of banking reform can easily be defended only as the proper first step toward reconstruction of our whole financial organization. Standing by itself, as an isolated measure, it would promise little but evasion—small effects at the price of serious disturbance—and would deserve classification as merely another crank scheme.

[18] Indeed, the time seems fully ripe for a declaration by Congress and the Administration against further increase in the American price-level. This does not imply that early and rapid recovery is now assured or that the federal budget should promptly be balanced; but it does mean that the gravest dangers are involved in relying upon further reduction in the commodity-value of the dollar for correction of the relative-price maladjustments which still impede recovery. A sound program must now undertake to bring about reduction of those controlled prices and wage-rates which remain high relative to other prices. The problem of relative-price maladjustments must be worked out along the line of the present general level, if reasonable precautions are to be taken against a chaotic boom, wholesale dishoarding, and uncontrollable inflation.

There may now be little agreement on the merits of price-index stabilization as a permanent rule of monetary (fiscal) policy; but there would probably be a surprising unanimity among reputable economists on the proposition that fiscal and banking policy henceforth should not permit any further rise of prices generally. At all events, announcement by the Administration (with supporting Congressional resolutions) of its intention to use all its powers to

however, they define only a proximate objective in monetary reform —a way of escape from present chaos and a step toward a more satisfactory ultimate solution.

The shortcomings of price-index stabilization, as the fundamental basis of a monetary system, are numerous and serious from either an analytical or an empirical viewpoint. It is easy to maintain that such a rule falls far short of the ideal in monetary arrangements—far too easy, indeed, when those who criticize are not obliged or inclined to define the better rules by comparison with which the one in question is so defective. The advocates of a stable price-level (with all the irritating excesses of their advocacy) are proposing a solution which is genuinely consistent with traditional liberal principles—and, precisely on that account, are faring rather badly in the debate which the proposal has provoked among professional economists and journalists. The most vigorous and pungent criticism comes from specialists who themselves have no intelligible solutions to offer and who generally have been spared the suspicion that a solution in terms of definite rules is of any importance.[19]

---

prevent a further rise in the level of prices is the first important step which can be taken to reduce uncertainty as to monetary conditions in the near future. With such an important beginning, we might move on afterward to more and more definitive rules, as political and economic developments permit.

To appreciate the danger of our present position, a moment's reflection should suffice: simply contemplate the political fate of any leader who, in the midst of the credit inflation now imminent, would try to stand in the way or to impose real checks. As a mob, we have probably learned much less than nothing since 1929; the long depression has only put us in the mood to draw and quarter anyone who would deny us the release of an exciting prosperity. And, incidentally, those political leaders who talk most about balanced budgets and sound currency would, by virtue of the magnificent simplicity of these nostrums, probably do least to check wholesale dishoarding and expansion of private credit. But a reasonable rule of policy, erected now, might save us where nothing else would.

[19] In the writer's opinion, the same issue is, or rather ought to be, fundamental in the current controversy as to qualitative versus quantitative control of credit. Qualitative control not only implies avoidance of all definite, meaningful rules; but, while espoused by persons peculiarly hostile to government

If price-level stabilization is a poor system, it is, still from a liberal viewpoint, infinitely better than no system at all. And it seems now highly questionable whether any better system is feasible or possible at all within the significant future. Given the present financial structure, and given the present multitude of uncoordinated monetary measures and monetary authorities, is there any other rule of policy around which some order and system might be achieved? How else may the present chaos of private financial practices, central-bank action, fiscal measures, and tariff changes be pulled together into something which resembles a monetary sys-

---

interference with private business, it also implies a much broader range of political interference and a less specialized conception of appropriate governmental function. Indeed, qualitative control of credit essentially amounts to political control over the *direction* of private investment. Control over the quantity of media, on the other hand, is consistent with the narrowest conception of the proper rôle of political control—with the narrowest definition of control of the currency. Those who argue for greater and more direct control of quantity by political agencies would argue quite as vigorously that the *allocation* of investment funds should be directed only by the freest competition —that this allocation should be entirely freed from the influence of Congress, the Treasury, any monetary authority, or any organization of bankers in the form of bankers' banks.

The so-called 100 per cent scheme was suggested, at least by its Chicago proponents, largely, if not primarily, with the notion that reform along such lines would serve to minimize the danger of increasing political control over the direction of investment, i.e., the danger, both of socialization of banking in its present form and of "financial planning" administered by organizations of private banks. From this viewpoint one may deplore the mass of legislation which has given special status to banking corporations and the development of many kinds of supervision and regulation (qualitative control) which has served to differentiate the obligations of banks from other private obligations and to facilitate their use as money. If a rigid separation could be achieved between the business of warehousing and transferring funds and that of mobilizing funds for lending and investment, the state might properly limit its regulation of the latter type of business to the provision of ordinary safeguards against fraud and the maintenance of competitive conditions in the investment markets.

The 100 per cent banking scheme has been characterized as socialistic; and advocates of quantitative control have been charged with the intention of turning the banking business over to politicians. While both observations are

tem? How else can we possibly escape from a situation where monetary policy is merely the composite of the uncertain daily actions of an indefinite number of agencies, governmental and private? Some ordering of this chaos is imperative. It may be achieved, either by setting up a superior, independent authority or by bringing the totality of monetary measures under the discipline of some rule; and only the advocates of price-index stabilization have offered a feasible way out along the latter lines.

This solution, if unsatisfying, is likewise not simple administratively. Question is often raised as to whether stabilization of a price-level is possible. The problem is better formulated, however, when we ask by what agency it might best be undertaken and what methods would be appropriate in its execution.

The task is certainly not one to be intrusted to banking authorities, with their limited powers and restricted techniques, as should be abundantly evident from recent experience. Ultimate control over the value of money lies in fiscal practices—in the spending, taxing, and borrowing operations of the central government. Thus, in an adequate scheme for price-level stabilization, the Treasury would be the primary administrative agency; and all the fiscal powers of Congress would be placed behind (and their exercise religiously limited by) the monetary rule. The powers of the government to inject purchasing power through expenditure and to withdraw it through taxation—i.e., the powers of expanding and contracting issues of actual currency and other obligations more or less serviceable as money—are surely adequate to price-level control. At present, monetary powers are dispersed indefinitely, among governmental

---

intellectually beneath notice, they might be countered, for purposes of vulgar debate, with the remark that most defenders of qualitative control are impliedly espousing syndicalist ideas and, for their own purposes, a corporative state. At all events, the task for serious students, here as elsewhere, is that of defining carefully the proper spheres for competitive and political controls and of discovering how each may best be implemented in its own sphere. If the 100 per cent scheme has any merit, it is largely that of directing attention to this problem in connection with the reform of a financial system which has acquired a functional complexity that renders useful analysis as difficult as it is important.

agencies and private institutions, not to mention Congress itself. Since the powers of the legislature are ultimate and decisive, a program looking toward co-ordination and concentration of responsibility must focus on fiscal policy as its mode of implementation.

The scheme clearly requires the delegation of large administrative powers. The Treasury might be given freedom within wide limits to alter the form of the public debt—to shift from long-term to short-term borrowing or vice versa, to issue and retire demand obligations in a legal-tender form. It might be granted some control over the timing of expenditures. It might be given limited power to alter tax rates by decree and to make refunds of taxes previously collected. How wide and numerous these powers should be, need not concern us here. Any legislation granting such authority, however, must also impose the duty and responsibility of exercising that authority in accordance with a sharply defined policy.[20]

---

[20] Congress would really be the administrative agency in any event. It could always revoke the powers of the monetary authority or nullify that agency's efforts to execute the price-index rule. Observance of the rule would require appropriate budgetary practice and thus would depend basically upon revenue and appropriation measures. The administrative function of the monetary authority might therefore be conceived mainly in terms of temporary devices for checking or ironing out small aberrations of the index. Its main responsibility, properly, would be that of giving advice and making recommendations to the executive and to the legislature with respect to the budget.

It may be interesting, if gratuitous, to note some features of fiscal practice under a properly executed price-index policy. The old perversity of fiscal changes would, of course, disappear. We should have to get accustomed— assuming continued increase in "physical production"—to the novel phenomenon of chronic budget deficits accompanied by declining interest charges of, at least, not accompanied by corresponding growth of the interest-bearing debt. (That this experience might induce widespread financial insanity is perhaps an argument in favor of a quantity-rule.) The Treasury would systematically borrow when interest rates were high and reduce its interest-bearing debt when rates were lowest; in other words, it would consistently make open-market purchases of its obligations when their prices were highest and sell them when their prices were abnormally low.

Under either a price-index or a quantity rule, by the way, there would

Given the suitable mandate, the grant of administrative powers should err, if at all, on the side of generosity. The more adequately implemented the rule of monetary policy, the easier will be its actual execution. The greater the powers available for its execution, the smaller will be the probable demands for their exercise. If it is clear that the administrative authority is adequately equipped to make the rule effective, then the rule will be, to some extent, self-enforcing, in so far as the actions of enterprisers and speculators come to be predicated upon its enforcement.

Not only must the price-level rule be implemented through fiscal measures; it must also serve as a control upon all governmental measures which have significant monetary effects. In other words, it must be accepted by the community, and obeyed by legislatures, as the guiding principle of government finance—as the basic criterion of sound fiscal policy.[21] While the rule cannot wisely be written

---

presumably be no justification for a complex structure of federal debt. Treasury obligations might properly be confined to two simple forms, lawful money and consols or perpetuities (which would facilitate deletion of the usual textbook observations about benefits to future generations and probable service-life of public improvements).

[21] It may be interesting to note that the whole argument of this paper might properly be developed with primary emphasis upon problems of government finance. With the growth of deposit currency and central banking, not only has monetary policy been left without substantial foundation in legislative rule and without adequate implementation but fiscal policy also has lost its appropriate orientation. Nominally, of course, it has been ordered in terms of the requirements of the gold standard—and it may be conceded that the prestige of gold has occasionally enforced some discipline in government finance. But the rule of maintaining convertibility or redemption has the obvious limitation of any legislative policy which is defined merely in terms of its end. There was no assurance that budgetary arrangements (or the behavior of the banking authorities) would actually be consistent with continued adherence to the rule—and even little prospect that blame for its violation would fall upon those really responsible. Whatever the other limitations of the gold-standard system (see n. 10), its administration, at all events, was left largely to the banking authorities, with only vague recognition that reckless accumulation of federal indebtedness might give rise to difficulties.

One consequence is the conspicuous absence, in both popular and academic discussion, of anything that might seriously be called principles of sound

into our fundamental law, it must provide the same sort of limitation
and mandate as would a constitutional provision. As things stand
now, there is almost nothing which a dominant party may not do
or leave undone financially, without rebuke. (There is still some
moral pressure, to be sure, against outright issue of paper money;
but this only invites evasion through the use of short maturities
and through resort to the inelegant expedient of paying the banks
to create money for the Treasury.) A federal administration can
now spend far beyond its revenues, and grossly debase the currency,
without even placing itself on the defensive before public opinion.
On the other hand, the "principles" to which reactionaries would
have us return are perhaps worse than none at all. That the old
moral prohibitions have lost their force is here not altogether an

---

fiscal practice. (For eloquent testimony on this point, see the textbooks on
public finance.) There are no accepted criteria for criticism; there is no real
basis for intelligent public opinion and, thus, little opportunity for effective
democratic control. Moreover, within the uncertain limits set by the requirements of the gold standard, there are indefinitely large opportunities for doing
things backward in the field of government finance (as well as in banking)—
and political pressures assure that these opportunities will be fairly well
exhausted.

Just as the financial system is conducive to utterly perverse changes in the
quantity of credit, so likewise does it lead almost inevitably to extreme perversity in fiscal changes. During periods of expanding profits and credit
inflation, tax rates are reduced, expenditures increased, and long-term obligations retired (instead of being refunded and increased to permit the impound-
ing of currency). In the face of declining production and employment, taxes
are increased (especially the critical excises), expenditures are usually curtailed, and money is obtained by borrowing (instead of being created by the
Treasury or released from previously accumulated balances). Moreover,
little real comfort can be found in recent recognition of this perversity, for it
promises only temporary, one-sided correction in the case of expenditures
and, thus, perhaps greater ultimate confusion.

It may seem a counsel of sheer cynicism or of utter despair to suggest that
all our established fiscal practices should be entirely reversed—and, as regards
the possibilities of reform within our present financial organization, it is so
intended. Sound fiscal policies are impossible (cannot even be defined) without precise and firmly established rules of monetary policy; but the early adoption of, or rapid movement toward, such rules is entirely feasible.

occasion for regret. But we cannot get along without some such rules—without some moral sanctions and mandates which politicians must obey in matters of finance. And there is probably nothing more promising than the idea of a stable price-level as a symbol articulating deep-rooted sentiments and as a source of discipline in fiscal practice.[22]

A serious practical shortcoming of stable money programs lies in the fact that they are sponsored most vigorously by persons who want the price-level raised sharply before it is stabilized. Thus the scheme is likely to be realized, if at all, on the basis of dangerously large concessions to the demands of debtors, in terms of stabilization at a level involving serious maladjustments and internal strains, and under conditions which would present great difficulties in administration and execution. If the undertaking is to get under way auspiciously, it is imperative that the level chosen should be low enough to require only the minimum of action and display of power by the monetary authority during the trying first years. (The possibility that the level would be fixed too low is of theoretical, rather than practical, interest.) Drastic administrative measures to overcome the inertia of an upward movement would jeopardize the political security of the rule and would also involve unfortunate disturbances in lines of business exposed to the direct impact of such measures. The advocates of stable money will do well not to offer the community one last big spree after the pledge is taken, and not to promise a perpetuity of blissful inebriation.

The issues which such proposals raise with respect to gold are issues which may largely be neglected for some years to come. In the United States we might stabilize on the basis of a price-index, while maintaining indefinitely the present gold price. Indeed, un-

---

[22] To assure popular approval, strong moral support, and thus political stability, it would be desirable, under a price-index rule, to employ an index whose changes would correspond roughly to changes in living-costs for families of modal income. Some weight certainly should be given to this consideration; but, adding it to those mentioned in n. 11, one sees that the best attainable index must fall far short of what is desirable on this, or on any other, particular criterion.

less the orgy of devaluation which we invited in 1933 does finally occur, we shall, with world-recovery, find it easy both to maintain the present price of gold and to reduce continuously the enormous barrier to trade which our tariff legislation has erected. The possibilities of such a program are indicated in the report of the Commission of Inquiry into National Policy in International Economic Relations:[23]

It may be argued that, while there is unlikely to be any occasion for justifiable increase in the dollar price of gold, it might soon be expedient to lower the price: (*a*) to prevent a wastefully large accumulation of gold by the United States; (*b*) to promote distribution of our surplus stock among countries which have real need for additional reserves; (*c*) to check an over-rapid recovery or a potentially dangerous boom at home; or even (*d*) as one means of putting pressure on the reserves of a too rapidly expanding banking system. To any of these ends, however, a more attractive means is at hand, namely, reduction of our tariff duties, even beyond those already recommended. This strategy would afford us a better protection against an unhealthy boom and against over-large investment in gold; it would affect other nations in the same manner economically as would a lowering of our gold price; and it would probably be even more effective toward improving the spirit of international commercial relations.

Not least of the merits of this procedure is the prospect it offers for raising the internal prices of export products (notably, cotton and wheat) relative to other prices. Indeed, it might in the end prove to be an adequate justification of our recent gold policy, that it created this opportunity for gradually and systematically repairing the injury of our past tariff policy to agriculture. Our drastic devaluation, whatever its short-term effects, is likely to lead, slowly and over a long period, to a rise of our price level which could serve no good purpose and might work serious injury. However, if we undertake by tariff reductions systematically to correct favorable balances of payments, and even to send abroad part of our present stock of gold, we could avoid the upward pressure on many industrial prices, while allowing our export staples to enjoy the full effect of the devaluation.

The scheme here proposed is perhaps more elegant in principle than it could ever be in actual application. But it may be worth noting that, just as devaluation offered to post-war France a means of returning to gold without internal deflation, so devaluation offers to the United States a means for scaling down its barriers to trade *without internal deflation*. This opportunity, moreover, presents itself, fortunately from the viewpoint of domestic politics, at a time when

[23] *International Economic Relations,* 96–8.

there is widespread demand for just the assistance to agriculture that it so clearly offers. Furthermore, an expression by our government of the intention to prevent, by this procedure, any enduring injury to foreign countries from our devaluation, would do much to smooth the way for future international understandings as to both monetary and commercial policy.

In this connection two observations are especially in point. (1) It is likely, in view of the condition of our balance of payments prior to devaluation, and in view of the prospect that many of the foreign measures for resisting gold drains will disappear with world recovery, that our present price of gold will prove distinctly excessive, unless measures are taken to offset the long-term effects of its sharp increase. (2) There are many strong considerations, not heretofore invoked in these pages, against resorting to reduction of our gold price in the future. Many of those who bitterly condemn our devaluation program will readily agree that little is now to be gained by trying merely to retrace our steps. If the rise in the price of gold may be held to have worked injury and injustice, it is still unlikely that reduction of that price at a much later date would accomplish much toward repairing the inequities. Those who lost (or gained) by the increase would be largely a different group from those who gained (or lost) from the reduction. Thus, all in all, a number of strong considerations appear to support the proposal for utilizing systematically the potentially large opportunities for tariff reduction which our recent devaluation promises to yield in the future. On this view, tariff reduction might be regarded as an agency of monetary stabilization for the near future and, quite consistently, as a means for helping agriculture at the same time.

The whole argument here may be regarded as supporting the position that our bargaining efforts should be directed especially toward concessions with regard to exchange controls, quota limitations, and similar barriers to our exports. These barriers, largely the product of the acute emergency, may be regarded in part as compensatory to our emergency gold policy. The prospect of their removal will depend partly on our willingness to make the concessions necessary to preservation of reasonable balance. The only major or equivalent concessions which we could offer are (1) reduction of our gold price and/or (2) lowering of our tariff barrier. There are reasons for our preferring the second of these, and no apparent reasons why it should not be equally attractive to other nations.

Price-level stabilization thus seems, on the whole, extremely attractive as the basis of a liberal-conservative policy in the field of money and government finance for the next decade. Whether the price-index rule would be as satisfactory under conditions which could be realized only over a longer period as the rule of a fixed quantity of money, may merit discussion in academic circles and may provide a promising point of departure for analysis and exposition; but the question is not of practical significance now. Given the inevitable limitations of any particular index, however, the former rule might ultimately acquire or manifest serious shortcomings. It is thus appropriate to observe that all the changes in our financial structure which seem necessary to make feasible the adoption of the fixed-quantity rule are changes which would also facilitate the operation of the price-index rule. The existence of a large volume of privately created money-substitutes, with alternate expansion and contraction, might tax seriously the powers of a monetary authority seeking to prevent price-level changes. Thus, if the stability of an index is to be maintained with the least resistance and the minimum of disturbing administrative measures, it is essential that the power to issue money and near-money should increasingly be concentrated in the hands of the central government.

As regards policies for the significant future, it therefore matters little whether price-level stabilization is conceived as a definitive reform or as a transition expedient in a long-term program pointed toward ultimate stabilization of the quantity of money. On either view, the same radical (if not drastic) changes in the field of private finance are clearly appropriate. Most of them, moreover, are necessary, on other grounds as well, for the preservation of economic freedom and political democracy.

CONCLUSIONS

The following observations may now be submitted, to define the author's general position and to guard against misinterpretation:

1. A democratic, free-enterprise system implies, and requires for its effective functioning and survival, a stable framework of definite rules, laid down in legislation and subject to change only gradually and with careful regard for the vested interests of participants in the economic game. It is peculiarly essential economically that there should be a minimum of uncertainty for enterprisers and investors as to monetary conditions in the future—and, politically, that the plausible expedient of setting up "authorities" instead of rules, with respect to matters of such fundamental importance, be

avoided, or accepted only as a very temporary arrangement. The most important objective of a sound liberal policy, apart from the establishment of highly competitive conditions in industry and the narrow limitation of political control over relative prices, should be that of securing a monetary system governed by definite rule.

2. To assure adequate moral pressure of public opinion against legislative (and administrative) tinkering, the monetary rules must be definite, simple (at least in principle), and expressive of strong, abiding, pervasive, and reasonable popular sentiments. They should be designed to permit the fullest and most stable employment, to facilitate adjustment to such basic changes (especially in technology) as are likely to occur, and, secondarily, to minimize inequities as between debtors and creditors; but the problems here, while of first importance, should be conceived and dealt with mainly as problems of a transition period. Once well established and generally accepted as the basis of anticipations, any one of many different rules (or sets of rules) would probably serve about as well as another.

3. The responsibility for carrying out the monetary rules should be lodged in a federal authority, endowed with large administrative powers but closely controlled in their exercise by a sharply defined policy. The powers of the monetary authority should have to do primarily or exclusively with fiscal arrangements—with the issue and retirement of paper money (open-market operations in government securities) and perhaps with the relation between government revenues and expenditures; in other words, the monetary rules should be implemented entirely by, and in turn should largely determine, fiscal policy.

4. Political control in this sphere should be confined exclusively to regulation of the quantity of money and near-money, the *direction* of investment (the allocation of investment funds) being left to the control of competition and kept as far as possible outside the influence of political agencies (or central banks).

5. A liberal program of monetary reform should seek to effect an increasingly sharp differentiation between money and private obligations and, especially, to minimize the opportunities for the creation of effective money-substitutes (whether for use as circu-

lating media or in hoards) by private corporations. The abolition of private deposit-banking is clearly the appropriate first step in this direction, and would bring us in sight of the goal; but such a measure, to be really effective, must be accompanied, or followed closely, by drastic limitation on the formal borrowing-powers of all private corporations, and especially upon borrowing at short term.

6. A monetary rule of maintaining the constancy of some price-index, preferably an index of prices of competitively produced commodities, appears to afford the only promising escape from present monetary chaos and uncertainties. A rule calling for outright fixing of the total quantity of money, however, definitely merits consideration as a perhaps preferable solution in the more distant future. At least, it may provide a point of departure for fruitful academic discussion.

17

A MONETARY AND FISCAL FRAMEWORK
FOR ECONOMIC STABILITY*

By Milton Friedman‖[1]

During the late 19th and early 20th centuries, the problems of the day were of a kind that led economists to concentrate on the allocation of resources and, to a lesser extent, economic growth, and to pay little attention to short-run fluctuations of a cyclical character. Since the Great Depression of the 1930's, this emphasis has been reversed. Economists now tend to concentrate on cyclical movements, to act and talk as if any improvement, however slight, in control of the cycle justified any sacrifice, however large, in the long-run efficiency, or prospects for growth, of the economic system. Proposals for the control of the cycle thus tend to be developed almost as if there were no other objectives and as if it made no difference within what general framework cyclical fluctuations take place. A consequence of this attitude is that inadequate attention is given to the possibility of satisfying both sets of objectives simultaneously.

In constructing the monetary and fiscal framework proposed in this paper, I deliberately gave primary consideration to long-run objectives. That is, I tried to design a framework that would be

---

* *The American Economic Review*, **38** (1948), 245–264. Reprinted, by the courtesy of the publisher and the author, without change from the original text.

‖ The University of Chicago.

[1] [An earlier version of this paper was presented before the Econometric Society on September 17, 1947, at a meeting held in conjunction with the International Statistical Conferences in Washington, D.C. I am deeply indebted for helpful criticisms and constructive suggestions to Arthur F. Burns, Aaron Director, Albert G. Hart, H. Gregg Lewis, Lloyd W. Mints, Don Patinkin, and George J. Stigler.]

appropriate for a world in which cyclical movements, other than those introduced by "bad" monetary and fiscal arrangements, were of no consequence. I then examined the resulting proposal to see how it would behave in respect of cyclical fluctuations. It behaves surprisingly well; not only might it be expected not to contribute to cyclical fluctuations, it tends to offset them and therefore seems to offer considerable promise of providing a tolerable degree of short-run economic stability.

This paper is devoted to presenting the part of the analysis dealing with the implications of the proposal for cyclical stability. Nonetheless, in view of the motivation of the proposal it seems well to begin by indicating the long-run objectives adopted as a guide, even though a reasonably full discussion of these long-run objectives would not be appropriate here.

The basic long-run objectives, shared I am sure by most economists, are political freedom, economic efficiency, and substantial equality of economic power. These objectives are not, of course, entirely consistent and some compromise among them may be required. Moreover, objectives stated on this level of generality can hardly guide proximate policy choices. We must take the next step and specify the general institutional arrangements we regard best suited for the attainment of these objectives. I believe—and at this stage agreement will be far less widespread—that all three objectives can best be realized by relying, as far as possible, on a market mechanism within a "competitive order" to organize the utilization of economic resources. Among the specific propositions that follow from this general position, three are particularly relevant: (1) Government must provide a monetary framework for a competitive order since the competitive order cannot provide one for itself. (2) This monetary framework should operate under the "rule of law" rather than the discretionary authority of administrators. (3) While a truly free market in a "competitive order" would yield far less inequality than currently exists, I should hope that the community would desire to reduce inequality even further. Moreover, measures to supplement the market would need to be taken in the interim. For both purposes, general fiscal measures (as contrasted with specific intervention) are the most desirable non-free-market means of decreasing inequality.

The extremely simple proposal which these long-run objectives lead me to advance contains no new elements. Indeed, in view of the number of proposals that have been made for altering one or another part of the present monetary or fiscal framework, it is hard to believe that anything completely new remains to be added. The combination of elements that emerges is somewhat less hackneyed; yet no claim of originality can be made even for this. As is perhaps not surprising from what has already been said, the proposal is something like the greatest common denominator of many different proposals. This is perhaps the chief justification for presenting it and urging that it receive full professional discussion. Perhaps it, or some variant, can approach a minimum program for which economists of the less extreme shades of opinion can make common cause.

This paper deals only with the broad outlines of the monetary and fiscal framework and neglects, or deals superficially with, many difficult, important, and closely related problems. In particular, it neglects almost entirely the transition from the present framework to that outlined here; the implications of the adoption of the recommended framework for international monetary arrangements; and the special requirements of war finance. These associated problems are numerous and serious and are likely to justify compromise at some points. It seems well, however, to set forth the ultimate ideal as clearly as possible before beginning to compromise.

I. The Proposal

The particular proposal outlined below involves four main elements: the first relates to the monetary system; the second, to government expenditures on goods and services; the third, to government transfer payments; and the fourth, to the tax structure. Throughout, it pertains entirely to the federal government and all references to "government" should be so interpreted.[2]

---

[2] The reason for restricting the discussion to the federal government is simply that it alone has ultimate monetary powers, not any desire to minimize

1. A reform of the monetary and banking system to eliminate both the private creation or destruction of money and discretionary control of the quantity of money by central bank authority. The private creation of money can perhaps best be eliminated by adopting the 100 per cent reserve proposal, thereby separating the depositary from the lending function of the banking system.[3] The adoption of 100 per cent reserves would also reduce the discretionary powers of the reserve system by eliminating rediscounting and existing powers over reserve requirements. To complete the elimination of the major weapons of discretionary authority, the existing powers to engage in open market operations and the existing direct controls over stock market and consumer credit should be abolished.

These modifications would leave as the chief monetary functions of the banking system the provision of depository facilities, the facilitation of check clearance, and the like; and as the chief function of the monetary authorities, the creation of money to meet government deficits or the retirement of money when the government has a surplus.[4]

2. A policy of determining the volume of government expendi-

---

the role of smaller governmental units. Indeed, for the achievement of the long-run objectives stated above it is highly desirable that the maximum amount of government activity be in the hands of the smaller governmental units to achieve as much decentralization of political power as possible.

[3] This proposal was advanced by Henry C. Simons. See his *A Positive Program for Laissez-Faire: Some Proposals for a Liberal Economic Policy*, Public Policy Pamphlet No. 15, University of Chicago Press, 1934; Rules *vs.* authorities in monetary policy, *Journal of Political Economy*, **44** (February 1936), 1–30. Both of these are reprinted in Henry C. Simons, *Economic Policy for a Free Society*, Chicago, University of Chicago Press, 1948.

[4] The adoption of 100 per cent reserves is essential if the proposed framework is to be entirely automatic. It should be noted, however, that the same results could, in principle, be achieved in a fractional reserve system through discretionary authority. In order to accomplish this, the monetary authorities would have to adopt the rule that the quantity of money should be increased only when the government has a deficit, and then by the amount of the deficit, and should be decreased only when the government has a surplus, and then by the amount of the surplus.

tures on goods and services—defined to exclude transfer expenditures of all kinds—entirely on the basis of the community's desire, need, and willingness to pay for public services. Changes in the level of expenditure should be made solely in response to alterations in the relative value attached by the community to public services and private consumption. No attempt should be made to vary expenditures, either directly or inversely, in response to cyclical fluctuations in business activity. Since the community's basic objectives would presumably change only slowly—except in time of war or immediate threat of war—this policy would, with the same exception, lead to a relatively stable volume of expenditures on goods and services.[5]

3. A predetermined program of transfer expenditures, consisting of a statement of the conditions and terms under which relief and assistance and other transfer payments will be granted.[6] Such a program is exemplified by the present system of social security under which rules exist for the payment of old-age and unemployment insurance. The program should be changed only in response to alterations in the kind and level of transfer payments the community feels it should and can afford to make. The program should not be changed in response to cyclical fluctuations in business activity. Absolute outlays, however, will vary automatically over the cycle. They will tend to be high when unemployment is high and low when unemployment is low.[7]

4. A progressive tax system which places primary reliance on

[5] The volume of expenditures might remain stable either in money or real terms. The principle of determining the volume of expenditures by the community's objectives would lead to a stable real volume of expenditures on current goods and services. On the other hand, the usual legislative procedure in budget making is to grant fixed sums of money, which would lead to stability of money expenditures and provides a slight automatic contra-cyclical flexibility. If the volume of real expenditures were stabilized, money expenditures would vary directly with prices.

[6] These transfer payments might perhaps more appropriately be regarded as negative revenue.

[7] It may be hoped that the present complex structure of transfer payments will be integrated into a single scheme co-ordinated with the income tax and designed to provide a universal floor to personal incomes. But this is a separate issue.

the personal income tax.   Every effort should be made to collect
as much of the tax bill as possible at source and to minimize the
delay between the accrual of the tax liability and the actual collection of the tax.   Rates, exemptions, etc., should be set in light of
the expected yield at a level of income corresponding to reasonably
full employment at a predetermined price level.   The budget principle might be either that the hypothetical yield should balance government expenditure, including transfer payments (at the same
hypothetical level of income) or that it should lead to a deficit sufficient to provide some specified secular increase in the quantity of
money.[8]   The tax structure should not be varied in response to
cyclical fluctuations in business activity, though actual receipts will,
of course, vary automatically.[9]   Changes in the tax structure should

---

[8] These specifications about the hypothetical level of income to be used and
the budget principle to be followed are more definite and dogmatic than is
justified.   In principle, the economic system could ultimately adjust to any tax
structure and expenditure policy, no matter what level of income or what
budget principle they were initially based on, provided that the tax structure
and expenditure policy remained stable.   That is, there corresponds some
secular position appropriate to each possible tax structure and expenditure
policy.   The best level of income and the best budget principle to choose
depend therefore on short-run adjustment considerations: what choice would
require the least difficult adjustment?   Moreover, the level of income and budget
principle must be chosen jointly: the same final result can obviously be obtained
by combining a high hypothetical income with a surplus budget principle or a
low hypothetical income with a deficit budget principle or by any number
of intermediate combinations.   My own conjecture is that the particular level
of income and budget principles suggested above are unlikely to lead to results
that would require radical short-run adjustments to attain the corresponding
secular position.   Unfortunately, our knowledge about the relevant economic
interrelationships is too meager to permit more than reasonably informed conjecture.   See Section IV below, especially footnote 22.

[9] The principle of setting taxes so as to balance the budget at a high level of
employment was suggested by Beardsley Ruml and H. Chr. Sonne, *Fiscal and
Monetary Policy,* National Planning Pamphlet no. 35 (July 1944).

Since the present paper was written, the Committee for Economic Development has issued a policy statement in which it makes essentially the same tax
and expenditure recommendations—that is, it calls for adoption of a stable tax
structure capable of balancing the budget at a high level of employment, a

reflect changes in the level of public services or transfer payments the community chooses to have. A decision to undertake additional public expenditures should be accompanied by a revenue measure increasing taxes. Calculations of both the cost of additional public services or transfer payments and the yield of additional taxes should be made at the hypothetical level of income suggested above rather than at the actual level of income. The government would thus keep two budgets: the stable budget, in which all figures refer to the hypothetical income, and the actual budget. The principle of balancing outlays and receipts at a hypothetical income level would be substituted for the principle of balancing actual outlays and receipts.

II. Operation of the Proposal

The essence of this fourfold proposal is that it uses automatic adaptations in the government contribution to the current income stream to offset, at least in part, changes in other segments of aggregate demand and to change appropriately the supply of money. It eliminates discretionary action in response to cyclical movements as well as some extraneous or perverse reactions of our present monetary and fiscal structure.[10] Discretionary action is limited to the determination of the hypothetical level of income underlying the stable

---

stable expenditure policy, and primary reliance on automatic adjustments of absolute revenue and expenditures to provide cyclical stability. They call this policy the "stabilizing budget policy." The chief difference between the present proposal and the C.E.D. proposal is that the C.E.D. is silent on the monetary framework and almost silent on public debt policy, whereas the present proposal covers both. Presumably the C.E.D. plans to cover monetary and debt policy in separate statements still to be issued. See *Taxes and the Budget: A Program for Prosperity in a Free Economy,* a statement on national policy by the Research and Policy Committee of the Committee for Economic Development (November 1947).

[10] For example, the tendency under the existing system of fractional reserve banking for the total volume of money to change when there is a change in the proportion of its total stock of money the community wishes to hold in the form of deposits; the tendency to reduce tax rates and increase government expenditures in booms and to do the reverse in depressions; and the tendency for the government to borrow from individuals at the same time as the Federal Reserve System is buying government bonds on the open market.

budget; that is, essentially to the determination of a reasonably attainable objective. Some decision of this kind is unavoidable in drawing up the government's budget; the proposal involves a particular decision and makes it explicit. The determination of the income goal admittedly cannot be made entirely objective or mechanical. At the same time, this determination would need to be made only at rather long intervals—perhaps every five or ten years—and involves a minimum of forecasting. Further, as will be indicated later, errors in the income goal tend to be automatically neutralized and do not require a redetermination of the goal.

Under the proposal, government expenditures would be financed entirely by either tax revenues or the creation of money, that is, the issue of non-interest-bearing securities. Government would not issue interest-bearing securities to the public; the Federal Reserve System would not operate in the open market. This restriction of the sources of government funds seems reasonable for peacetime. The chief valid ground for paying interest to the public on government debt is to offset the inflationary pressure of abnormally high government expenditures when, for one reason or another, it is not feasible or desirable to levy sufficient taxes to do so. This was the justification for wartime issuance of interest-bearing securities, though, perversely, the rate of interest on these securities was pegged at a low level. It seems inapplicable in peacetime, especially if, as suggested, the volume of government expenditures on goods and services is kept relatively stable. Another reason sometimes given for issuing interest-bearing securities is that in a period of unemployment it is less deflationary to issue securities than to levy taxes. This is true. But it is still less deflationary to issue money.[11]

---

[11] See Henry C. Simons, On debt policy, *Journal of Political Economy*, **52** (December 1944), 356–61.

This paragraph deliberately avoids the question of the payment of interest to banks on special issues of government bonds, as has been proposed in some versions of the 100 per cent reserve proposal. The fundamental issue involved in judging such proposals is whether government should subsidize the use of deposit money and a system of check clearance and if so, what form the subsidy should take.

The large volume of government bonds now outstanding raises one of the

Deficits or surpluses in the government budget would be reflected dollar for dollar in changes in the quantity of money; and, conversely, the quantity of money would change only as a consequence of deficits or surpluses.   A deficit means an increase in the quantity of money; a surplus, a decrease.[12]

Deficits or surpluses themselves become automatic consequences of changes in the level of business activity.   When national money income is high, tax receipts will be large and transfer payments small; so a surplus will tend to be created, and the higher the level of income, the larger the surplus.   This extraction of funds from the current income stream makes aggregate demand lower than it otherwise would be and reduces the volume of money, thereby tending to offset the factors making for a further increase in income.   When national money income is low, tax receipts will be small and transfer payments large, so a deficit will tend to be created, and the lower the level of income, the larger the deficit.   This addition of funds to the current income stream makes aggregate demand higher than it otherwise would be and increases the quantity of money, thereby tending to offset the factors making for a further decline in income.

---

most serious problems in accomplishing the transition from the present framework.   This problem would be eased somewhat by the monetization of bonds that would occur in the process of going over to 100 per cent reserves.   But there would still remain a substantial volume.   Two alternatives suggest themselves: (1) freeze the volume of debt at some figure, preferably by converting it into perpetuities ("consols"); (2) use the monetization of the debt as a means of providing a secular increase in the quantity of money.   Under the second plan, which, on a first view, seems more attractive, the principle of balancing the stable budget would be adopted and the government would commit itself to retiring, through the issuance of new money, a predetermined amount of the public debt annually.   The amount to be retired would be determined so as to achieve whatever secular increase in the quantity of money seemed desirable.   This problem, however, requires much additional study.

[12] These statements refer, of course, to the ultimate operation of the proposal. Under the second of the alternatives suggested in the preceding footnote, the change in the quantity of money during the transitional period would equal the excess of government expenditures over receipts plus the predetermined amount of money issued to retire debt.

The size of the effects automatically produced by changes in national income obviously depends on the range of activities government undertakes, since this will in turn determine the general order of magnitude of the government budget. Nonetheless, an essential element of the proposal is that the activities to be undertaken by government be determined entirely on other grounds. In part, this element is an immediate consequence of the motivation of the proposal. The motivation aside, however, it seems a desirable element of any proposal to promote stability. First, there is and can be no simple, reasonably objective, rule to determine the optimum share of activity that should be assigned to government—short of complete socialization—even if stability were the only objective. Changes in circumstances are likely to produce rapid and erratic variations in the share that seems desirable. But changes in the share assigned government are themselves likely to be destabilizing, both directly and through their adverse effects on anticipations. The attempt to adapt the magnitude of government operations to the requirements of stability may therefore easily introduce more instability than it corrects. Second, the share of activity assigned government is likely to have far more important consequences for other objectives—particularly political freedom and economic efficiency—than for stability.[13] Third, means other than changes in the share of activity assigned government are readily available for changing the size of the reaction to changes in income, if experience under the proposal should prove this desirable. And some of these means need not have anything like the same consequences for other objectives.

Under the proposal, the aggregate quantity of money is automatically determined by the requirements of domestic stability. It follows that changes in the quantity of money cannot also be used— as they are in a fully operative gold standard—to achieve equilibrium

---

[13] An example of the relevance of these two points is provided by the tendency during the 'thirties to recommend an increase in the progressiveness of the tax structure as a means of increasing the propensity to consume and hence, it was argued, employment. Applied to the postwar period, the same argument would call for a shift to regressive taxes, yet I wonder if many economists would wish to recommend regressive taxes on these grounds.

in international trade. The two criteria will by no means always require the same changes in the quantity of money; when they conflict, one or the other must dominate. The decision, implicit in the framework recommended, to select domestic stability means that some other technique must be used to bring about adjustments to changes in the conditions of international trade. The international arrangement that seems the logical counterpart of the proposed framework is flexible exchange rates, freely determined in foreign exchange markets, preferably entirely by private dealings.[14]

III. EFFECT OF PROPOSAL UNDER PRESENT INSTITUTIONAL CONDITIONS

The fluctuations in the government contribution to the income stream under the proposed monetary and fiscal framework are clearly in the "right" direction. Nonetheless, it is not at all clear that they would, without additional institutional modifications, necessarily lead either to reasonably full employment or to a reasonable degree of stability. Rigidities in prices are likely to make this proposal, and indeed most if not all other proposals for attaining cyclical stability, inconsistent with reasonably full employment; and, when combined with lags in other types of response, to render extremely uncertain their effectiveness in stabilizing economic activity.

A. Price Rigidities

Under existing circumstances, when many prices are moderately rigid, at least against declines, the monetary and fiscal framework described above cannot be expected to lead to reasonably full employment of resources, even though lags in other kinds of response are minor. The most that can be expected under such circumstances is a reasonably stable or moderately rising level of money income.

---

[14] Though here presented as a byproduct of the proposed domestic framework, flexible exchange rates can be defended directly. Indeed, it would be equally appropriate to present the proposed domestic framework as a means of implementing flexible exchange rates. The heart of the matter is that domestic and international monetary and trade arrangements are part of one whole.

As an extreme example, suppose that the economy is in a relatively stable position at reasonably full employment and with a roughly balanced actual government budget and that the great bulk of wage rates are rigid against downward pressure.   Now, let there be a substantial rise in the wage rates of a particular group of workers as a consequence either of trade union action or of a sharp but temporary increase in the demand for that type of labor or decrease in its supply, and let this higher wage rate be rigid against downward pressure. Employment of resources as full as previously would imply a higher aggregate money income since, under the assumed conditions of rigidity, other resources would receive the same amount as previously whereas the workers whose wage rates rose would receive a larger aggregate amount if fully employed.   But if this higher money income, which also of course would imply a higher price structure, were attained, the government would tend to have a surplus since receipts would rise by more than expenditures.   There is nothing that has occurred that would, in the absence of other independent changes, offset the deflationary effect of the surplus.   The assumed full employment position would not therefore be an equilibrium position.   If attained by accident, the resultant budgetary surplus would reduce effective demand and, since prices are assumed rigid, the outcome could only be unemployment.   The equilibrium level of income will be somewhat higher than before, primarily because transfer payments to the unemployed will be larger, so that some of the unemployment will be offset.   But there is no mechanism for offsetting the rest.   The only escape from this situation is to permit inflation.

As is widely recognized, the difficulty just described is present also in most other monetary and fiscal proposals; they, too, can produce full employment under such circumstances only by inflation.   This dilemma often tends, however, to be concealed in their formulation, and, in practice, it seems fairly likely that inflation would result.   The brute fact is that a rational economic program for a free enterprise system (and perhaps even for a collectivist system) must have flexibility of prices (including wages) as one of its cornerstones.   This need is made clear by a proposal like the present.   Moreover, the adoption of such a proposal would provide some assurance against cumulative deflation and thereby tend to make flexibility of prices a good deal easier to achieve since government support for monopolistic practices of special occupational and industrial groups derives in large measure from the obvious waste of general deflation and the need for protection against it.

B. Lags in Response

Our economy is characterized not only by price rigidities but also by significant lags in other types of response. These lags make impossible any definitive statement about the actual degree of stability likely to result from the operation of the monetary and fiscal framework described above. One could reasonably expect smaller fluctuations than currently exist; though our ignorance about lags and about the fundamental causes of business fluctuations prevents complete confidence even in this outcome. The lag between the creation of a government deficit and its effects on the behavior of consumers and producers could conceivably be so long and variable that the stimulating effects of the deficit were often operative only after other factors had already brought about a recovery rather than when the initial decline was in progress. Despite intuitive feelings to the contrary, I do not believe we know enough to rule out completely this possibility. If it were realized, the proposed framework could intensify rather than mitigate cyclical fluctuations; that is, long and variable lags could convert the fluctuations in the government contribution to the income stream into the equivalent of an additional random disturbance.[15]

About all one can say about this possibility is that the completely automatic proposal outlined above seems likely to do less harm under the circumstances envisaged than alternative proposals which provide for discretionary action in addition to automatic reactions. There is a strong presumption that these discretionary actions will in general be subject to longer lags than the automatic reactions and hence will be destabilizing even more frequently.

The basis for this presumption can best be seen by subdividing into three parts the total lag involved in any action to offset a disturbance:

---

[15] See Milton Friedman, Lerner on the economics of control, *Journal of Political Economy*, **55**, 5 (October 1947), 414, especially footnote 12.

(1) the lag between the need for action and the recognition of this need; (2) the lag between recognition of the need for action and the taking of action; and (3) the lag between the action and its effects.

The first lag, which is nonexistent for automatic reactions of the kind here proposed, could be negative for discretionary proposals if it were possible to forecast accurately the economic changes that would occur in the absence of government action. In view of the record of forecasters, it hardly needs to be argued that it would be better to shun forecasting and rely instead on as prompt an evaluation of the current situation as possible. The lag between the need for action and the recognition of that need then becomes positive. Its exact magnitude depends on the particular discretionary proposal, though the past record of contemporary interpreters of business conditions indicates that it is not likely to be negligible.[16]

The second lag is present even for automatic reactions because all taxes will not or cannot be collected at source simultaneously with the associated payments, and transfer payments will not or cannot be made immediately without some kind of a waiting period or processing period. It is clear, however, that this lag can be reduced to a negligible time by appropriate construction and administration of the system of taxes and transfer payments. For discretionary action, the length of the lag between the recognition of the need for action and the taking of action depends very much on the kind of action taken. Action can be taken very promptly to change the form or amount of the community's holdings of assets by open market purchases or sales of securities or by changes in rediscount rates or reserve requirements. A considerably longer time is required to change the net contribution of the government to the income stream by changing the tax structure. Even though advance prescription for alternative possibilities eliminates any delay in deciding what changes to make in tax rates, exemptions, kinds of taxes levied, or the like, administrative considerations will enforce a substantial delay before the change becomes effective. Taxpayers, businesses or individuals acting as intermediaries in collecting the taxes, and tax administrators must all be informed of the change and

---

[16] *Ibid.*, 414, especially footnote 11.

be given an opportunity to make the appropriate adjustments in their procedures; new forms must be printed or at least circulated; and so on.

The longest delay of all is likely to be involved in changing the net contribution of government to the income stream by changing government expenditure policy, particularly for goods and services.   No matter how much advance planning may have been done, the rate of expenditure cannot be stepped up or curtailed overnight unless the number of names on the payroll is to be the only basis in terms of which the expenditure is to be controlled or judged.   Time is involved in getting projects under way with any degree of efficiency; and considerable waste in ceasing work on projects abruptly.

The third lag, that between the action and its effects, is present and significant both for automatic reactions and discretionary actions, and little if anything can be done about it by either legal or administrative reform of the fiscal and monetary structure.[17]   We have no trustworthy empirical evidence on the length of this lag for various kinds of action, and much further study of this problem is clearly called for. Some clues about the direction such study should take are furnished by *a priori* considerations which suggest, as a first approximation, that the order of the various policies with respect to the length of this lag is the reverse of their order with respect to the length of the lag between the recognition of the need for action and the taking of action. Changes in government expenditures on goods and services lead to almost immediate changes in the employment of the resources used to produce those goods and services.   They have secondary effects through the changes thereby induced in the expenditures of the individuals owning the resources so employed.

The lag in these induced changes might be expected to be less than the lag in the adjustment of expenditures to changed taxes or to a changed amount or form of asset holdings.   Changes in taxes make the disposable incomes of individuals larger or smaller than they would otherwise be.   Individuals might be expected to react to a change in

---

[17] Reforms of other types, for example, reforms increasing the flexibility of prices, might affect this lag.

disposable income as a result of a tax change only slightly less rapidly than to a change in disposable income as a result of a change in aggregate income.

These indications are, however, none too trustworthy. There are likely to be important indirect effects that depend on such things as the kinds of goods and services directly affected by changed government expenditures, the incidence of the changes in disposable income that result from changed expenditures or taxes, and the means employed to finance government deficits. For example, if deficits are financed through increases in the quantity of money and surpluses are used to reduce the quantity of money, part of the effect of changes in government expenditures or taxes will be produced by changes in interest rates and the kind and volume of assets held by the community. The entire effect of open-market operations, changes in rediscount rates and reserve requirements, and the like will be produced in this way, and it seems likely that these effects would take the longest to make themselves felt.

The automatic reactions embodied in the proposal here advanced operate in part like tax changes—in so far as tax receipts vary—and in part like expenditure changes—in so far as transfer payments vary; and like both of these, some part of their effect is through changes in the quantity of money. One might expect, therefore, that the lag between action and its effects would be roughly the same for automatic reactions as for discretionary tax changes, a good deal shorter for automatic reactions than for discretionary monetary changes, and somewhat longer for automatic reactions than for discretionary changes in government expenditures on goods and services.

This analysis, much of which is admittedly highly conjectural, suggests that the total lag is definitely longer for discretionary monetary or tax changes than for automatic reactions, since each of the three parts into which the total lag has been subdivided is longer. There is doubt about the relative length of the total lag only for discretionary expenditure changes. Even for these, however, it seems doubtful that the shorter lag between action and its effects can more than offset the longer lag between the need for action and the taking of action.

Given less extreme conditions than those required to convert the present proposal into a destabilizing influence, the reduction achieved in the severity of fluctuations would depend on the extent and rapidity of price adjustments, the nature of the responses of individuals to these price changes and to the changes in their incomes and asset holdings resulting from the induced surpluses or deficits, and the lags in such responses.   If these were such as to make the system operate reasonably well, the improvement would tend to be cumulative, since the experience of damped fluctuations would lead to patterns of expectations on the part of both businessmen and consumers that would make it rational for them to take action that would damp fluctuations still more.   This favorable result would occur, however, only if the proposed system operated reasonably well without such aid; hence, in my view, this proposal, and all others as well, should be judged primarily on their direct effects, not on their indirect effects in stimulating a psychological climate favorable to stability.   It must be granted, however, that the present proposal is less likely to stimulate such a favorable psychological climate than a proposal which has a simpler and more easily understood goal, for example, a proposal which sets a stable price level as its announced goal.   *If the business world were sufficiently confident of the ability of the government to achieve the goal,* it would have a strong incentive to behave in such a way as greatly to simplify the government's task.

IV. Implications of the Proposal if Prices Are Flexible and Lags in Response Minor

The ideal possibilities of the monetary and fiscal framework proposed in this paper, and the stabilizing economic forces on which these possibilities depend, can be seen best if we put aside the difficulties that have been detaining us and examine the implications of the proposal in an economy in which prices of both products and factors of production are flexible[18] and lags in other types of response are minor.

---

[18] The concept of flexible prices, though one we use continually and can hardly avoid using, is extremely difficult to define precisely. Fortunately, a precise definition is not required for the argument that follows. All that is necessary for the argument is that there be a "substantial" range of prices that are not "rigid" because of long-term contracts or organized noncontractual

In such an economy, the monetary and fiscal system described above would tend toward an equilibrium characterized by reasonably full employment.

To describe the forces at work, let us suppose that the economy is initially in a position of reasonably full employment with a balanced actual budget and is subjected to a disturbance producing a decline in aggregate money demand that would be permanent if no other changes occurred.[19]   The initial effect of the decline in aggregate demand will be a decline in sales and the piling up of inventories in at least some parts of the economy, followed shortly by unemployment and price declines caused by the attempt to reduce inventories to the desired level.   The lengthening of the list of unemployed will increase government transfer payments; the loss of income by the unemployed will reduce government tax receipts.   The deficit created in this way is a net contribution by the government to the income stream which directly offsets some of the decline in aggregate demand, thereby preventing unemployment from becoming as large as it otherwise would and serving as a shock absorber while more fundamental correctives come into play.

These more fundamental correctives, aside from changes in relative prices and interest rates, are (1) a decline in the general level of prices which affects (a) the real value of the community's assets and (b) the government contribution to the income stream, and (2) an increase in the stock of money.

The decline in the general level of prices that follows the initial decline in aggregate demand will clearly raise the real value of the community's stock of money and government bonds since the nominal value of these assets will not decrease.   The real value of the remainder

agreements to maintain price and that these prices should react reasonably quickly to changes in long-run conditions of demand or supply. It is not necessary that there be "perfect" flexibility of prices, however that might be defined, or that contracts involving prices be subject to change at will, or that every change in long-run conditions of demand or supply be reflected instantaneously in market price.

[19] The same analysis would apply to disturbances producing only a temporary decline. The reason for assuming a permanent decline is to trace through the entire process of adjustment to a new equilibrium position.

of the community's assets may be expected to remain roughly the same, so the real value of the total stock of assets will rise.[20]   The rise in the real value of assets will lessen the need for additional saving and hence increase the fraction of any given level of real income that the community will wish to consume.   This force, in principle, would alone be sufficient to assure full employment even if the government maintained a rigidly balanced actual budget and kept the quantity of money constant, since there would presumably always be some price level at which the community could be made to feel rich enough to spend on consumption whatever fraction or multiple of its current income is required to yield an aggregate demand sufficient to permit full employment.

This effect of a lower price level in increasing the fraction of current private (disposable) income devoted to consumption is reinforced by its effect on the government's contribution to the income stream.   So long as the price level, and with it money income, is below its initial level, the government will continue to run a deficit.   This will be true even if employment is restored to its initial level, so that transfer payments and loss in tax receipts on account of unemployment are eliminated.   The tax structure is progressive, and exemptions, rates, etc., are expressed in absolute dollar amounts.   Receipts will therefore fall more than in proportion to the fall in the price level; expenditures, at

---

[20] If the real value of other assets of the community should fall, this would simply mean that the price level would have to fall farther in order to raise the real value of the community's total stock of assets.   Note that under the proposed framework, all money in the community is either a direct government obligation (nondeposit currency) or is backed one hundred per cent by a direct government obligation (deposits in the central bank).   If this analysis were to be applied to a fractional reserve system, the assets whose aggregate real value could be guaranteed to rise with no directly offsetting fall in the real value of private assets would be the total amount of government obligations (currency and bonds) held outside the treasury and central bank.   On this and what follows, see A. C. Pigou, The classical stationary state, *Economic Journal,* **53** (December 1943), 342–51, and Economic progress in a stable environment, *Economica,* New Series, **14** (August 1947), 180–90.   Also Don Patinkin, Price flexibility and full employment, to be published in the September 1948 number of this *Review.*

most, proportionately.[21]   Because of the emergence of such a deficit,
the price decline required to restore employment will be smaller than if
the government were to maintain a rigidly balanced actual budget, and
this will be true even aside from the influence of the deficit on the stock
of money.   The reason is that the price level will have to fall only to
the point at which the amount the community desires to add to its
hoards equals the government deficit, rather than to the point at which
the community desires to add nothing to its hoards.[22]

The decline in the price level may restore the initial level of employ-

---

[21] The effect of the lower price level on expenditures depends somewhat on
the precise expenditure and transfer policy adopted.   If, as is called for by the
principle of determining the expenditure program by the community's objectives, the real volume of government expenditures on goods and services is kept
cyclically stable and if the program of transfer payments is also stated in real
terms, expenditures will decline proportionately.   If government expenditures
on goods and services are kept cyclically stable in dollar terms, or the program of transfer expenditures is stated in dollar terms, expenditures will decline
less than proportionately.

[22] If the real volume of government expenditures on goods and services is
kept cyclically stable and the transfer program is also stated in real terms, the
aggregate expenditures of government under fixed expenditure and transfer
programs would tend to be the same fraction of the full-employment income
of society no matter what the price level.   This fraction would be the maximum net contribution the government could make to the income stream no
matter how low prices, and with them money income and government receipts,
fell.   Consequently, this force alone would be limited in magnitude and
might not, even in principle, be able to offset every disturbance.   If either
program is in absolute terms, there would be no limit to the fraction that the
government contribution could constitute of the total income stream.

An alternative way to describe this effect is in terms of the relation between the expected expenditures and receipts of consumers, business, and
government.   It is a condition of equilibrium that the sum of the desired
expenditures of these groups equal the sum of their receipts.   If the government maintains a rigidly balanced budget, equilibrium requires that consumers
and business together plan to spend what they receive (*i.e.,* not seek to add to
their money hoards).   If the government runs a deficit, consumers and business together need not plan to spend all they receive; equilibrium requires that
their planned expenditures fall short of their receipts by the amount of the
deficit (*i.e.,* that they seek to add to their hoards per period the amount of the
deficit).

ment through the combined effects of the increased average propensity to consume and the government deficit. But so long as a deficit exists, the position attained is not an equilibrium position. The deficit is financed by the issue of money. The resultant increase in the aggregate stock of money must further raise the real value of the community's stock of assets and hence the average propensity to consume. This is the same effect as that discussed above except that it is brought about by an increase in the absolute stock of money rather than by a decline in prices. Like the corresponding effect produced by a decline in prices, the magnitude of this effect is, in principle, unlimited. The rise in the stock of money and hence in the average propensity to consume will tend to raise prices and reduce the deficit. If we suppose no change to occur other than the one introduced to start the analysis going, the final adjustment would be attained when prices had risen sufficiently to yield a roughly balanced actual budget.

A disturbance increasing aggregate money demand would bring into play the same forces operating in the reverse direction: the increase in employment would reduce transfer payments and raise tax receipts, thus creating a surplus to offset part of the increase in aggregate demand; the rise in prices would decrease the real value of the community's stock of money and hence the fraction of current income spent on consumption; the rise in prices would also mean that even after "overemployment" was eliminated, the government would run a surplus that would tend to offset further the initial increase in aggregate demand;[23] and, finally, the surplus would reduce the stock of money.

As this analysis indicates, the proposed fiscal and monetary framework provides defense in depth against changes in aggregate demand. The first line of defense is the adjustment of transfer payments and tax receipts to changes in employment.[24] This eases the shock while

---

[23] The limit to the possible effect of the surplus on the current income stream would be set by the character of the tax structure, since there would probably be some maximum percentage of the aggregate income that could be taken by taxes no matter how high the price level and the aggregate income.

[24] It should be noted that this is the only effect taken into account by Musgrave and Miller in their calculations of the possible magnitude of the

the defense is taken over by changes in prices. These raise or lower the real value of the community's assets and thereby raise or lower the fraction of income consumed. They also produce a government deficit or surplus in addition to the initial deficit or surplus resulting from the effect of changes in employment on transfer payments and tax receipts. The final line of defense is the cumulative effect of the deficits or surpluses on the stock of money. These changes in the stock of money tend to restore prices to their initial level. In some measure, of course, these defenses all operate simultaneously; yet their main effects are likely to occur in the temporal order suggested in the preceding discussion.

Even given flexible prices, the existence of the equilibrating mechanism described does not of course mean that the economy will in fact achieve relative stability. This depends in addition on the number and magnitude of the disturbances to which the economy is subject, the speed with which the equilibrating forces operate, and the importance of such disequilibrating forces as adverse price expectations. If the lags of response are minor, and initial perverse reactions unimportant, adjustments would be completed rapidly and there would be no opportunity for disequilibria to cumulate, so that relative stability would be attained. Even in this most favorable case, however, the equilibrating mechanism does not prevent disturbances from arising and does not counteract their effects instantaneously—as, indeed, no system can in the absence of ability to predict everything in advance with perfect accuracy. What the equilibrating mechanism does accomplish is, first, to keep governmental monetary and fiscal operations from themselves contributing disturbances and, second, to provide an

effect of automatic variations in government receipts and expenditures. (R. A. Musgrave and M. H. Miller, Built-in flexibility, *American Economic Review* (March 1948), 122–28.) They conclude that "the analysis here provided lends no justification to the view now growing in popularity that 'built-in flexibility' can do the job alone and that deliberate countercyclical fiscal policy can be dispensed with." While this is a valid conclusion, it does not justify rejecting the view that "built-in flexibility" can do the job alone, since the "analysis here provided" takes no account of what have been termed above the "more fundamental correctives."

automatic mechanism for adapting the system to the disturbances that occur.

Given flexible prices, there would be a tendency for automatic neutralization of any errors in the hypothetical income level assumed or in the calculations of the volume of expenditures and revenues at the hypothetical income level. Further, it would ultimately be of no great importance exactly what decision was reached about the relation to establish between expenditures and revenue at the hypothetical income level (*i.e.*, whether exactly to balance, to strive for a deficit sufficient to provide a predetermined secular increase in the quantity of money, etc.). Suppose, for example, that errors in the assumed income level, the calculated volume of expenditures and receipts, and the relation established between expenditures and receipts combined to produce a deficit larger than was consistent with stable prices. The resulting inflationary pressure would be analogous to that produced by an external disturbance and the same forces would come into play to counteract it. The result would be that prices would rise and the level of income tend to stabilize at a higher level than the hypothetical level initially assumed.

Similarly, the monetary and fiscal framework described above provides for adjustment not only to cyclical changes but also to secular changes. I do not put much credence in the doctrine of secular stagnation or economic maturity that is now so widely held. But let us assume for the sake of argument that this doctrine is correct, that there has been such a sharp secular decline in the demand for capital that, at the minimum rate of interest technically feasible, the volume of investment at a full-employment level of income would be very much less than the volume of savings that would be forthcoming at this level of income and at the current price level.[25] The result would simply be

---

[25] Because of the effect discussed above of price changes on the real value of assets, and in this way on the average propensity to consume, it seems to me that such a state of affairs would not lead to secular unemployment even if the quantity of money were kept constant, provided that prices are flexible (which is the reason for including the qualification "at the current price level" in the sentence to which this footnote is attached). But I am for the moment accepting the point of view of those who deny the existence or importance of this

that the equilibrium position would involve a recurrent deficit sufficient to provide the hoards being demanded by savers. Of course, this would not really be a long-run equilibrium position, since the gradual increase in the quantity of money would increase the aggregate real value of the community's stock of money and thereby of assets, and this would tend to increase the fraction of any given level of real income consumed. As a result, there would tend to be a gradual rise in prices and the level of money income and a gradual reduction in the deficit.[26]

V. CONCLUSION

In conclusion, I should like to emphasize the modest aim of the proposal. It does not claim to provide full employment in the absence of successful measures to make prices of final goods and of factors of production flexible. It does not claim to eliminate entirely cyclical fluctuations in output and employment. Its claim to serious consideration is that it provides a stable framework of fiscal and monetary action, that it largely eliminates the uncertainty and undesirable political implications of discretionary action by governmental authorities, that it provides for adaptation of the governmental sector to changes

---

equilibrating force. Moreover, if the quantity of money were constant, the adjustment would be made entirely through a secular decline in prices, admittedly a difficult adjustment. Once again changes in the government contribution to the income stream and through this in the quantity of money can reduce the extent of the required price change.

[26] This and the preceding paragraph, in particular, and this entire section, in general, suggest a problem that deserves investigation and to which I have no satisfactory answer, namely, the characteristics of the system of equations implicit in the proposal and of their equilibrium solution. It is obvious that under strictly stationary conditions, including a stationary population, the equilibrium solution would involve constancy of prices, income per head, etc., and a balanced actual budget. The interesting question is whether there is any simple description of the equilibrium solution under specified dynamic situations. For example, are there circumstances, and if so what are they, under which the equilibrium solution will tend to involve constant money income per head with declining prices, or constant prices with rising money income per head, etc.? It is obvious that no such simple description will suffice in general, but there may well be broad classes of circumstances under which one or another will.

occurring in other sectors of the economy of a kind designed to offset the effects of these changes, and that the proposed fiscal and monetary framework is consistent with the long-run considerations stated at the outset of this paper.   It is not perhaps a proposal that one would consider at all optimum if our knowledge of the fundamental causes of cyclical fluctuations were considerably greater than I, for one, think it to be; it is a proposal that involves minimum reliance on uncertain and untested knowledge.

The proposal has of course its dangers.   Explicit control of the quantity of money by government and explicit creation of money to meet actual government deficits may establish a climate favorable to irresponsible government action and to inflation.   The principle of a balanced stable budget may not be strong enough to offset these tendencies.   This danger may well be greater for this proposal than for some others, yet in some measure it is common to most proposals to mitigate cyclical fluctuations.   It can probably be avoided only by moving in a completely different direction, namely, toward an entirely metallic currency, elimination of any governmental control of the quantity of money, and the re-enthronement of the principle of a balanced actual budget.

The proposal may not succeed in reducing cyclical fluctuations to tolerable proportions.   The forces making for cyclical fluctuations may be so stubborn and strong that the kind of automatic adaptations contained in the proposal are insufficient to offset them to a tolerable degree.   I do not see how it is possible to know now whether this is the case.   But even if it should prove to be, the changes suggested are almost certain to be in the right direction and, in addition, to provide a more satisfactory framework on which to build further action.

A proposal like the present one, which is concerned not with short-run policy but with structural reform, should not be urged on the public unless and until it has withstood the test of professional criticism. It is in this spirit that the present paper is published.

18

FEDERAL RESERVE POLICY AND THE FEDERAL DEBT[*][1]

By Lester V. Chandler||

It is common knowledge that monetary management in this country has for several years been strongly influenced, if not dominated, by considerations related to management of the federal debt.   With this debt amounting to more than $250 billion and comprising about 60 per cent of all outstanding debt in the country, the foremost objective of our monetary policy has come to be "the maintenance of an orderly market in government securities" and the prevention, or at least a limitation, of the rise of yields on these securities, especially on the long-term issues.   Though the rise of this new objective has been the subject of widespread discussion, the writer believes that its full implications are not generally appreciated.   The purpose of this article, therefore, is to trace the rise of this policy objective and to raise some questions concerning its consequences.

The Evolution of the Policy before Pearl Harbor

Prior to 1937 Federal Reserve purchases and sales of government securities were primarily for the purpose of influencing the volume of member bank reserves and of member bank borrowings at the Reserve Banks.   These were, of course, designed to affect interest rates, includ-

---

[*] *The American Economic Review,* **39** (1949), 405–29.   Reprinted, by the courtesy of the publisher and the author, without change from the original text.

|| Princeton University.

[1] [This material will become part of a broader study of the process of inflation in the United States since 1939, a study which the writer could not have undertaken without generous financial assistance from the Merrill Foundation for Advancement of Financial Knowledge, Inc.]

ing yields on governments, but the effects were expected to result mainly from changes in the ability and willingness of banks to lend and purchase securities.   But in 1937, apparently for the first time as a major policy objective, the Federal Reserve bought long-term governments for the purpose of limiting their price decline.   After reaching high levels in late 1936, the prices of long-term governments and high-grade corporate bonds began to fall early in 1937.   This decline did not extend to Treasury bills and notes.   The Reserve System thereupon initiated what it called its "flexible portfolio policy," purchasing more than $200 million of the longer-term bonds and reducing its holdings of the shorter-term notes and bills by about $150 millions.   The decline of government bond prices was stopped and reversed.[2]   By such operations the System influenced directly—not merely through its effects on bank reserves—the yields on both long- and short-term government securities and indirectly the yields on others.

The avowed purpose of this policy was (1) to exert an influence toward orderly conditions in the money market, and (2) to facilitate the orderly adjustment of member banks to the increased reserve requirements effective May 1, 1937.[3]   In justifying its policy the Board said,

In recent years the bond market has become a much more important segment of the open money market, and banks, particularly money-market banks, to an increasing extent use their bond portfolios as a means of adjusting their cash position to meet demands made upon them.   At times when the demands increase they tend to reduce their bond portfolios and at times when surplus funds are large they are likely to expand them.   Since prices of long-term bonds are subject to wider fluctuations than those of short-term obligations, the increased importance of bonds as a medium of investment for idle bank funds makes the maintenance of stable conditions in the bond market an important concern of banking administration.[4]

The System continued its flexible portfolio policy from early 1937 until after Pearl Harbor, though no extensive operations were neces-

---

[2] Board of Governors, *Annual Report*, 1937, 5–7.
[3] *Ibid.*, 6.
[4] *Ibid.*, 7.

sary in 1938 and early 1939.[5]   Its next major operation in governments occurred in September, 1939, when the outbreak of war in
Europe led to a sharp decline of bond prices.   To stop this decline the
System did two things: (1) It announced that all the Reserve Banks
stood ready to lend on government securities at par value to non-
member as well as member banks, the discount rate to be the one applicable to such loans to member banks.   The rate at New York and
Boston was 1 per cent, and five other Reserve Banks instituted a preferential 1 per cent rate on loans secured by governments.   (2) It purchased nearly $500 million of bonds in the open market.   The Board
justified these stabilizing purchases on two principal grounds: (1) To
"exert a steadying influence on the capital market, which is an essential
part of the country's economic machinery, and disorganization in
which would be a serious obstacle to the progress of economic recovery," and (2) to safeguard the large United States government portfolio of the member banks from "unnecessarily wide and violent
fluctuations in price."[6]

At only one other time between late 1939 and Pearl Harbor did the
Federal Reserve find it necessary to purchase governments to cushion
a decline of their prices.   This was in the spring of 1940, following the
invasion of Norway and Denmark and later the Low Countries, when
bond prices began to decline and the Reserve System added somewhat
to its holdings.[7]   During the rest of 1940 the System decreased its
holdings of long-term governments by about $300 million, thereby re-
tarding the rise of bond prices that occurred as outside demand re-
covered strongly, partly because of large additions to bank reserves
resulting from voluminous gold inflows.   The Reserve Banks maintained their holdings of governments practically stable during 1941

---

[5] For evidence that the Federal Open Market Committee continued to be
concerned with maintaining an orderly market in governments, see Board of
Governors, *Annual Report,* 1938, 77–9.   In the early part of 1939 the System
allowed its holdings of Treasury bills to decline markedly because they could
be replaced only on a virtually no-yield basis.   By the end of the year it held
no bills.

[6] Board of Governors, *Annual Report,* 1939, 5.

[7] Board of Governors, *Annual Report,* 1940, 3–4.

until the price break following Pearl Harbor, at which time they bought $60 million of bonds and $10 million of bills.

In summary, by the time the United States entered World War II the "maintenance of an orderly market for government securities" had already become an important consideration in Federal Reserve policy. The Reserve System was buying and selling governments to protect member banks against "unnecessarily wide and violent fluctuations" in the prices of the government securities that they held; to exert an indirect influence on other interest rates in the market; and to remove obstacles to economic recovery. It had not yet, however, reached the point of "pegging" government prices at stated levels and standing ready to buy all these securities offered to it at the pegged prices. In other words, it was maintaining an "orderly market for governments" in the sense of preventing "disorderly" changes in their prices and yields, but it was not yet maintaining a rigid yield pattern.

FEDERAL RESERVE POLICY DURING THE WAR

Upon our entrance into the war, the maintenance of an "orderly market for government securities" at low interest rates became not merely an important objective, but the clearly dominant objective, of Federal Reserve Policy. The Board of Governors assured the public on December 8, 1941 that the Federal Reserve could and would see that the Treasury was supplied with all the money that it needed for war finance.

The existing supply of funds and of bank reserves is fully adequate to meet all present and prospective needs of the Government and of private activity. The Federal Reserve System has powers to add to these resources to whatever extent may be required in the future.

The System is prepared to use its powers to assure that an ample supply of funds is available at all times for financing the war effort and to exert its influence toward maintaining conditions in the United States Government security market that are satisfactory from the standpoint of the Government's requirements.[8]

This promise was amply fulfilled. The war effort may at times have been impeded by other shortages, but it never suffered from a lack of

---

[8] Board of Governors, *Annual Report,* 1941, 1.

money.   Thanks to a highly liberal Federal Reserve policy, the Treasury could get from the Reserve Banks or from commercial banks any funds that it needed beyond those secured by taxation and by borrowing from non-bank sources.   Of the $230 billion increase of the federal debt from June, 1940 to December, 1945, nearly $75 billion was taken by commercial banks and $22 billion by the Reserve Banks.

Moreover, a generous Federal Reserve policy enabled the Treasury to borrow these tremendous sums of money at low and slightly declining rates of interest.   At the time of our entrance into the war the excess reserves of member banks amounted to nearly $7 billion, and during the preceding five years they had only rarely been less than $2 billion.   Under these conditions and with a shrunken demand for investable funds, the whole structure of interest rates had fallen to low levels, and rates on safe short-term paper were low indeed.   This situation was continued throughout the war period.   In March, 1942 the Federal Open Market Committee agreed with the Treasury that the general market for governments "should be maintained on about the then existing curve of rates (but that this did not mean special support for issues which might be out of line or that any issue must be held at par or at any other fixed price)."[9]   The pattern of pegged rates above which market yields were not permitted to rise until well after the end of the war was ⅜ of 1 per cent on 90-day Treasury bills, ⅞ of 1 per cent on 12-month certificates of indebtedness, and higher rates on longer-term issues ranging up to 2½ per cent on the longest-term taxable bonds.

The Federal Reserve helped maintain this pattern of low yields on governments in two principal ways.[10]   First, but less important, was the maintenance of low discount rates.   The Reserve Banks stood ready to make advances at a discount rate of 1 per cent to both mem-

---

[9] Board of Governors, *Annual Report*, 1942, 104.   See also pp. 12 and 106.

[10] We need not deal at length with the lowering of reserve requirements of central reserve city banks from 26 to 20 per cent in 1942, the exemption of War Loan Deposit Accounts from member bank reserve requirements and FDIC assessments beginning in 1943, and the 1942 legislation authorizing the Federal Reserve to purchase securities directly from the Treasury but limiting such holdings at any one time to $5 billion.

ber and non-member banks up to the full par value of any government security offered as collateral, and they established a preferential rate of ½ of 1 per cent on advances to member banks secured by governments maturing or callable within a year.   Since the member banks owned an ample volume of the shorter-maturity issues, only the ½ of 1 per cent rate was significant in most cases.   This willingness of the Federal Reserve to lend at low interest rates was reassuring to some banks, but few of them found it necessary or desirable to take advantage of the opportunity.   Banks needing funds could secure them more cheaply by selling low-yield Treasury bills to the Reserve Banks.   Federal Reserve discount rates had already become largely meaningless.

The much more important method of preventing yields on government securities from rising above the pattern agreed upon with the Treasury was Federal Reserve open-market operations.   The System relinquished its initiative and its accuracy of control over the volume of governments that it held in order to prevent yields from rising above the established pattern.   The loss of initiative by the Federal Reserve was most obvious in the case of Treasury bills.   On April 30, 1942, the Federal Open Market Committee ordered the Reserve Banks to buy all Treasury bills offered to them at ⅜ of 1 per cent yield.   And in October of that year it ordered the Reserve Banks to grant repurchase options to sellers of bills, permitting them to repurchase at ⅜ of 1 per cent yield the bills that they had sold to the Reserve Banks.   In this way the yield on Treasury bills was held constant until mid-1947. Moreover, Treasury bills were made as safe and liquid as money itself so the banks had no reason to hold large excess reserves.   In a similar way, the Federal Reserve stood ready to buy all 12-month certificates of indebtedness offered to it at its ⅞ of 1 per cent posted buying rate. Though no rates on longer-term issues were formally posted and publicized, the Federal Reserve nevertheless purchased these issues in whatever quantities were necessary to prevent their yields from rising above the established pattern, and it sometimes sold them as their yields fell below the pattern levels.   Thus the Federal Reserve lost almost completely its initiative in open-market operations; its holdings of governments were determined by the Treasury as issuer of the securities and by other institutions and persons as buyers and sellers of them.

It had to monetize all the outstanding governments that others were not willing to buy and hold at the established pattern of rates.[11]

As mentioned earlier, the pattern of yields on governments agreed upon by the Federal Reserve and the Treasury reflected, in general, the pattern prevailing in the market in the early part of 1942. The principal exception related to 90-day Treasury bills, whose yield averaged less than 0.30 per cent in April, 1942 and which were pegged at the higher level of 0.375 per cent at the end of that month. It developed later that the short-term Treasury bills with their ⅜ of 1 per cent rate and even the 12-month certificates with their ⅞ of 1 per cent rate were less attractive to investors than the longer-term securities with yields up to 2½ per cent. This trend became clear only after the end of 1942. During the first year of our participation in the war, Reserve Bank holdings of governments rose about $3.7 billion, the increase being about equally distributed between the shorter-term bills and certificates on the one hand and the longer-term notes and bonds on the other. But during the remainder of the war and for some time thereafter, offerings to the Federal Reserve were composed almost entirely of bills and certificates. In fact, while its holdings of bills and certificates rose from $1.9 billion at the end of 1942 to $22.4 billion at the end of 1946, the Federal Reserve was able, owing to the strong outside demand for them, to reduce its holdings of the longer-term notes and bonds from $4.1 billion to $1.4 billion. And even so, the longer-term issues rose to a premium, the longest maturities reaching a peak premium of about 7 per cent and their yield declining to about 2.1 per cent in early 1946.

---

[11] The London *Economist* (August 4, 1945), 161–62, has argued that the loss of initiative by central banks originated not during the war but during the Great Depression when central banks initiated easy-money policies. They could assure the continuance of cheap money only by standing ready to supply all the money that the public elected to hold at low interest rates. This is in a sense true, but the cheap-money policy of the depression period was initiated to encourage general business recovery and could presumably be reversed if spendings approached a dangerously high level. We shall see later that an easy-money policy aimed primarily at holding down interest costs to the Treasury and protecting bondholders against loss in terms of money may lack this element of reversibility.

Though other factors contributed, the principal reason for this shift of investors' preferences toward the longer-term issues was undoubtedly the announced policy of the Treasury of not raising the interest rates to be carried by successive new issues and the Federal Reserve policy of preventing the prices of governments from falling below the pegged levels.   In such a situation the conventional distinction between short and long maturities lost much of its meaning.   So long as the Federal Reserve continued to support the prices of the longer-term issues, every one of them was perfectly liquid at the pegged price, as much so as the shortest-maturity Treasury bill.   An investor could rationally prefer a shorter-term government with a low yield over a longer-term government with a higher yield only to the extent (1) that the longer-term issue was selling at a premium over the Federal Reserve support price and there was a risk that its price would decline, or (2) that the Federal Reserve would lower its support prices.   In view of the fact that both official pronouncements and the problems of debt management strongly indicated that yields on the longer-term governments would be prevented from rising significantly not only during the war but also for an indefinite period thereafter, it is small wonder that the Federal Reserve as residual buyer came to hold a large proportion of the shorter-term low-yield issues, thereby adding to bank reserves, while other investors bid down the yields on the longer-term issues.

THE FEDERAL RESERVE AND GOVERNMENT SECURITY PRICES SINCE THE END OF THE WAR

Remembering the history of its policy before World War II, and especially before 1937, one might have expected the Federal Reserve to abandon its easy-money policy and to quit supporting the prices of government securities on a low-yield basis as the Treasury ceased to be a net borrower and began to reduce its debt in 1946 and as inflation gained momentum.   But no significant change of policy occurred until mid-1947.[12]   Until this time the Federal Reserve con-

---

[12] It is true that the Federal Reserve in the spring of 1946 eliminated the right of non-member banks to borrow on government securities at the 1 per cent rate; that about the same time it eliminated the preferential rate of ½ of 1 per cent on advances secured by governments maturing within a year; and

tinued virtually without change the wartime pattern of its support prices, though its officials repeatedly warned Congress that without additional powers they could not simultaneously continue to support government security prices and combat inflation effectively. The first departure from the pattern of yields maintained during the war came in July, 1947 when the Federal Open Market Committee eliminated the ⅜ of 1 per cent posted rate on Treasury bills and announced that the yield on bills would thereafter be expected to find its proper position in the market relative to the rate on certificates, which continued to be pegged at ⅞ of 1 per cent. The Committee emphasized, however, that the System would continue to purchase and hold bills to the extent necessary to maintain an orderly market.[13] The second departure from the wartime pattern came in August, 1947 when the Federal Open Market Committee discontinued its ⅞ of 1 per cent buying rate on certificates and embarked on a policy of preventing yields from rising above the Treasury issuing rate on new certificates. The Treasury thereafter gradually raised the rate on newly issued certificates to 1⅛ per cent. This permitted the yield on Treasury bills to move up to about 1 per cent. These levels prevailed until the late summer of 1948.

The third departure from the wartime pattern occurred in December, 1947 when the Federal Reserve lowered somewhat its support prices of longer-term governments. As already noted, the prices of these longer-term securities were considerably above par in 1946 and early 1947. In April, 1947 the average premium on taxable bonds with 15 or more years to maturity was about 4.6 per cent and the yield had declined to 2.19 per cent. Believing that these yields were too low, the Treasury sold between April and the end of October about $1.8 billion of bonds out of its own investment accounts, and in October offered for sale a new issue of nonmarketable 2½ per cent bonds.[14] These sales, coupled with the rise of short-term rates, large

that in the summer of 1946 it raised acceptance buying rates from ½ of 1 per cent to 1 per cent. But for reasons that will be indicated later these actions were relatively ineffective.

[13] Board of Governors, *Annual Report,* 1947, 93.

[14] Federal Reserve Bank of Boston, *Monthly Review* (January 1948), 7.

flotations of corporate securities, and a general rise of the private de‧ mand for loan funds, caused the prices of long-term governments to fall and yields on the longest-term issues to rise to 2.37 per cent in November.   The decline was apparently considered too rapid, for the Federal Reserve stepped in and increased its holdings of bonds by about $2 billion during November and up to December 24.   Then, the day before Christmas, the Federal Open Market Committee low‧ ered its support prices for the longer-term issues.   No government security was allowed to fall below par, however, and the Federal Re‧ serve purchased vigorously to support the new pattern of prices.[15]

The fourth departure from the older yield pattern came in August, 1948 when the Secretary of the Treasury announced that on October 1 the rate on new certificates would be raised from 1⅛ to 1¼ per cent.

Several aspects of these Federal Reserve and Treasury actions in 1947 and 1948 should be noted.   (1) The structure of yields on gov‧ ernments was permitted to rise somewhat, the yields on short-term issues rising more than those on longer-terms.   Between June, 1947 and October, 1948 the yield on bills rose from 0.375 to about 1.1 per cent, the yield on certificates from 0.875 to 1.25 per cent, and the yield on the longest-term bonds from 2.2 to 2.48 per cent.   Yields on other comparable types of debt moved in a roughly parallel manner. (2) These actions indicate a shift of stabilizing operations away from short-term rates and toward long-term rates.   From early 1942 until

---

[15] The Federal Open Market Committee's decision to take such action was arrived at in its meeting on December 9, 1947.   Action was to be deferred until after the Treasury's January refunding operations had been completed unless market selling increased substantially.   "It was understood that . . . the executive committee would continue the existing prices at which Govern‧ ment securities were being supported until after the Treasury January refund‧ ing had been completed, at which time prices of bonds should be permitted to decline rapidly, if the market did not support itself, to a level not more than 100½ and not less than par on the longest restricted 2½ per cent issue and to not less than par on 1⅛ per cent one-year certificates.   It was also understood that if, before the completion of the January refunding, market selling should increase substantially, the executive committee would be authorized to permit prices to decline to the level stated above as rapidly as was consistent with the maintenance of orderly market conditions."   Board of Governors, *Annual Re‧ port,* 1947, 97.

July, 1947, the Federal Reserve pegged the bill rate at the low level of 0.375 per cent with the result that the yields on long-term governments tended to be depressed below their 1942 levels. But the 1947–1948 actions show a tendency toward concentrating attention on preventing the longest-term rate from rising above 2½ per cent while allowing shorter-term rates to rise relative to it. (3) These actions indicate some willingness of the Federal Reserve and the Treasury to reintroduce a degree of upward flexibility in interest rates. But the implications of these actions for the future must not be exaggerated. In the first place, they do not indicate that the Federal Reserve has abandoned its objective of "maintaining an orderly market for government securities" at low-yield levels. Both by its pronouncements and by its continued security purchases in the face of inflation, the Federal Reserve has indicated that the maintenance of government security prices is still a dominant policy objective. And in the second place, the fact that the Federal Reserve has allowed some rise of interest rates does not necessarily mean that it will permit further significant increases. This point will be amplified in later paragraphs.

FEDERAL RESERVE SUPPORT OF GOVERNMENT SECURITY PRICES IN THE FUTURE

Will the Federal Reserve in the foreseeable future abandon the support of government security prices and the maintenance of low yields as the dominant objective of its open-market operations in order to be free to combat inflation vigorously? All the available evidence indicates that this is highly unlikely with respect to the long-term governments, though future policy with regard to short-term issues is more uncertain. Several officials, including the chairman of the Board of Governors, the former chairman, and the president of the Federal Reserve Bank of New York, have stated emphatically their determination to prevent the long-term rate from rising above 2½ per cent.

Typical of their statements is that of Marriner Eccles, former chairman, in December, 1947:

The one thing you cannot do is to have confidence shaken in that 2½ per-cent rate. If you let that go below par, there is always a question, where does it go? Because people remember, a great many of them, what happened after the last war when they let those securities go below par.[16]

Though the Federal Reserve and the Treasury appear determined to prevent yields on the longest-term governments from rising above 2½ per cent in the "foreseeable future," they appear less reluctant to allow the yields on short-term issues to rise above the levels prevailing in mid-1948, so long as the rise is not great enough to upset the market for long-term governments. Eccles stated in April, 1948,

I want to make another matter clear: We have never made the statement that we should support all Government securities at par. What we have said is that we should maintain the 2½ percent rate on the long-term bonds. That should be the basic long-term rate.

The short rate should be permitted to fluctuate to the extent that it can be useful.[17]

President Sproul of the Federal Reserve Bank of New York agreed with this principle.[18]   In August, 1948 Eccles again argued the rate

[16] *Hearings Before the Joint Committee on the Economic Report* (December 10, 1947), 620. See also Eccles' statement in *Hearings Before the Joint Committee on the Economic Report* (April 13, 1948), 16. Chairman McCabe takes a similar position: " . . . I have a very strong conviction that it is vitally necessary to support the 2½ per cent bonds. . . . I would not say it is our policy forever. I say for the foreseeable future." *Hearings Before the House Banking and Currency Committee* (August 2, 1948), 101. For a concurring statement by President Sproul of the Federal Reserve Bank of New York, see *Hearings Before the Joint Committee on the Economic Report* (May 12, 1948), 101–2. Secretary of the Treasury Snyder stated, "I think we are definitely committed to a support of the 2½ percent rate." See *Hearings Before the House Banking and Currency Committee on S. J. Res. 157* (August 4, 1948), 250.

Several specialists in the money market have pointed out to the writer that practically all the public statements of Federal Reserve officials have been to the effect that the long-term rate will not be allowed to rise above 2½ per cent, not that the bonds will be supported at or above par. These observers believe that the distinction may be significant, for the Federal Reserve might contend that a bond price fractionally below par would still produce a yield of only "approximately 2½ per cent."

[17] *Hearings Before the Joint Committee on the Economic Report* (April 13, 1948), 16.

[18] *Hearings Before the Joint Committee on the Economic Report* (May 12, 1948), 93.

on certificates should be raised above 1⅛ per cent, and seemed—
though his statement was not clear on this point—to favor a gradual
withdrawal of Federal Reserve support from short-term governments while firmly supporting the long-term issues.[19] It seems very
doubtful, however, that yields on Treasury bills and certificates can
be raised very much above the levels attained by the autumn of
1948 without forcing the Federal Reserve to buy large quantities of
long-term government bonds to prevent their yield from rising above
2½ per cent. This is in line with Eccles' appraisal of the situation
in April, 1948:

> . . . Short-term rates probably cannot be raised much more without unsettling
> the 2½ percent rate for long-term Treasury bonds.
>
> When I say "cannot be raised much more," I am thinking in terms of an
> eighth of 1 per cent to a maximum, say, of one-quarter. If you made the certifi-
> cate rate 1¼ that would be raising it an eighth. If you raised it a full quarter,
> ultimately that would be 1⅜. There may be, under certain conditions, a pos-
> sibility of going as far as 1½ in a short-term rate, but I certainly can't foresee
> that now.
>
> Clearly you can't let the short-rate go up to a point where pressure on the
> long-term rate result, so you have to support the long-term market.[20]

Secretary Snyder had stated earlier that, "We feel there are very
narrow limits in which you can consider increased interest rates."[21]
Sproul, relying heavily on the argument that even the longest-term
bonds are in effect demand obligations so long as their price is supported by the Federal Reserve, believes that there is somewhat more
room to raise the short-term rates without upsetting the 2½ per cent

---

[19] *Hearings Before the House Banking and Currency Committee on S. J. Res.
157* (August 3, 1948), 181–82.

[20] *Hearings Before the Joint Committee on the Economic Report* (April 13,
1948), 18. Eccles later stated, " . . . so long as you hold the 2½ per cent
rate . . . the range within which the short-term rate can rise would be within
its present 1⅛ and I would say possibly 1½ per cent." *Hearings Before the
House Banking and Currency Committee on S. J. Res. 157* (August 3, 1948),
182–83.

[21] *Hearings Before the House Banking and Currency Committee* (November
25, 1947), 50.

rate on the long-term obligations.[22]   But he would probably agree with Eccles that so long as the 2½ per cent long-term rate is prevented from rising, short-term credit cannot be made expensive; it can only be made a little less cheap.

In summary, it appears that both Federal Reserve and Treasury officials have decided that for "the foreseeable future" they will not allow the yield on the longest-term governments to rise above 2½ per cent and that yields on the shorter-term issues will not be allowed to rise to a point where they will endanger the stability of the long-term rate.

Federal Reserve and Treasury officials have offered many reasons for continuing to stabilize the yields on government securities at low levels despite the upward sweep of inflation.   Among those most frequently advanced are the following: (1) Increased rates on the federal debt would add to the already large interest burden.[23] They point out that with interest charges already amounting to about $5 billion a year and averaging 2 per cent of the outstanding debt, every increase of one-half of a percentage point in the average rate would add about $1.25 billion to federal interest costs.   It is important to note here that the Treasury could follow either of two general lines of action if it were decided to terminate the policy of maintaining low interest rates.   The first would be to refund at higher interest rates only the maturing debt, allowing the rest of the outstanding debt to decline in price.   This would postpone the full increase of interest charges, but it would impose capital depreciation on banks, insurance companies, and other holders.   The other line of action would be to refund the entire debt at whatever rates of interest were required to prevent government securities from falling below par in the face of tightened credit conditions.   Though

---

[22] *Hearings Before the Joint Committee on the Economic Report* (May 12, 1948), 93.

[23] Board of Governors, *Annual Report*, 1945, 5–6. *Hearings Before the House Banking and Currency Committee* (November 25, 1947), 50. *Hearings Before the Joint Committee on the Economic Report* (November 28, 1947), 246–47.

this would protect holders against capital depreciation, it would immediately increase significantly the interest costs of the Treasury. Neither Federal Reserve nor Treasury officials seem willing to follow either course of action except to the limited extent of raising somewhat the shorter-term rates of interest. (2) Fluctuating prices and yields on governments would greatly complicate the Treasury's refunding operations—a serious matter with $49 billion of the debt falling due within a year and nearly $100 billion within five years.[24] (3) An increase of the yield on governments, which without an increase of coupon rates would mean a decline of their prices, would impose capital losses on financial institutions and other holders and might lead to panicky selling and loss of confidence in financial institutions.[25] Officials recall the drastic decline of bond prices in 1920 when the federal debt was only $26 billion and point to the greater possibilities of panic now that the debt is ten times as large and represents about 60 per cent of all debt in the country. Eccles has stated that with the public debt as large as it is today a free market is out of the question if that is taken to mean an unmanaged, unsupported market. The real question cannot be whether yields shall be free or pegged; it must relate to the levels at which pegging will occur. "There is no natural level. . . . "[26] (4) A decline in the prices of marketable government securities might lead to wholesale redemptions of the nonmarketable savings bonds, which are in effect demand obligations. (5) A moderate rise of the yields on government securities would not be effective as an anti-inflation measure.[27] Federal Reserve officials have argued that a rise of rates so small that it would not greatly increase interest costs to the Treas-

---

[24] See Eccles' statement in *Hearings Before the House Banking and Currency Committee on S. J. Res. 157* (August 3, 1948), 183.

[25] Board of Governors, *Annual Report,* 1945, 7. *Federal Reserve Bulletin* (January 1948), 11. *Hearings Before the Joint Committee on the Economic Report* (November 25, 1947), 140. *Hearings Before the Joint Committee on the Economic Report* (December 10, 1947), 620. *Hearings Before the Joint Committee on the Economic Report* (May 12, 1948), 101–2.

[26] *Federal Reserve Bulletin* (November 1946), 1231–32.

[27] *Federal Reserve Bulletin* (January 1948), 15–16. *Hearings Before the Joint Committee on the Economic Report* (November 25, 1947), 139.

ury or cause serious capital losses to holders of bonds would not be a strongly restraining factor. (6) Low interest rates and generally easy credit eased the process of reconversion and will help to maintain high levels of employment and production.[28] As late as May, 1948 Sproul contended that allowing long-term governments to decline more than fractionally below par would interfere with private flotations of loans and might have deleterious effects on production and employment.[29]

EFFECTS ON THE FUNCTIONING OF THE ECONOMY

If, as seems likely but not certain, the Federal Reserve continues to stabilize the yields on government securities at low levels, refusing to let the longest-term rates rise above 2½ per cent and limiting the rise of short-term rates to levels consistent with the longest-term rate, what effects will this have on the operation of the economy? The most obvious effect, of course, is to hold down interest charges on the federal debt, thereby limiting the amount of taxes that must be collected for this purpose, and to protect holders of government securities from capital losses in terms of money, though not in terms of purchasing power. These results are far from insignificant. But much more important, I believe, are the effects on monetary policy, the behavior of the money supply, and the cost and availability of funds for private investment and consumption purposes.

With the adoption of this policy, the functioning of the Federal Reserve has been radically altered. This is most apparent in the case of open-market operations. Traditionally, this was the one instrument over which the Federal Reserve had complete and accurate control; the System could buy or sell precisely that amount of securities which it considered appropriate in light of existing and prospective economic conditions. But under its present policy of stabilizing government prices according to a selected pattern it has lost almost completely its initiative and its accuracy of control over its holdings of governments. It must as residual buyer purchase all the govern-

---

[28] Secretary of the Treasury, *Annual Report*, 1946, 3.

[29] *Hearings Before the Joint Committee on the Economic Report* (May 12, 1948), 101–2. See also his testimony on pp. 94–95.

ments that others are unwilling to hold at the selected pattern of support prices. It must (1) purchase them not only from commercial banks but also from all other types of holders, and (2) purchase them regardless of the purposes for which the sellers will use the money. These two points are so important that they will be developed further.

In the past it has ordinarily been expected that the Federal Reserve would affect the supply of money and loanable funds primarily through the commercial banking system. It was a system of "bankers' banks"; it lent primarily to commercial banks, and even its open-market operations were undertaken primarily to affect the volume of commercial bank reserves and lending power. But with this new policy of supporting the prices of governments regardless of the type of institution or person selling them, access to Federal Reserve credit is no longer limited to commercial banks, but also extends to savings banks, insurance companies, many other types of financial institutions, nonfinancial corporations, and individuals. This might not have been an important change prior to 1933 when the federal debt was small, but as Table 1 suggests, it is of the greatest importance when the federal debt held outside the government and the Federal Reserve amounts to nearly $200 billion and that held by nonbank investors amounts to more than $130 billion. So long as the Federal Reserve follows its present policy all these institutions and persons are in a position to secure at their option very large amounts of additional money by selling their governments to the Reserve Banks at the support prices. And the decision as to the amount of new money to be issued in this way lies with the holders of securities, not with the Federal Reserve. The cost of this money is, of course, the yield sacrificed on the securities sold; it is an "opportunity cost." Thus, when the Federal Reserve changes the yield pattern on governments, it is in effect changing the cost of money to sellers of the securities.

Moreover, in pursuing its present policy the Federal Reserve cannot refuse to buy and monetize governments even if it disapproves of the purpose for which the new money will be used. Holders may exchange their securities for money to be used for (1) consumption, (2) purchase or construction of capital goods, (3) repayment of debt, (4) purchase of other securities, new or old, or (5) increase of idle balances. The Federal Reserve is powerless to prevent monetization of the government debt at the selected pat-

Table 1

HOLDINGS OF UNITED STATES GOVERNMENT SECURITIES, DIRECT AND FULLY GUARANTEED[a]

(*In billions of dollars*)

Type of Holder	Holdings as of March 31, 1948	Holdings as of June 30, 1948	Increase from June 30, 1940 to March 31, 1948	Holdings on March 31, 1948 as a Percentage of Holdings on June 30, 1940
Commercial banks	$65.4	$16.1	$49.3	406
Mutual savings banks	12.1	3.1	9.0	390
Insurance companies	23.8	6.5	17.3	366
Other corporations and associations	21.8	2.5	19.3	872
State and local governments	7.5	0.4	7.1	1875
Individuals	66.8	10.3	56.5	649
Total held outside the Federal Reserve and U. S. Government agencies and trust funds	197.4	38.9	158.5	507

[a] *Federal Reserve Bulletin* (June 1948), 700. This table includes not only marketable government issues that are directly supported, but also nonmarketable issues—principally savings bonds—which are not directly supported by the Federal Reserve. Even these, however, are indirectly supported, for the Treasury must redeem them on demand and—to the extent that its surplus and sales of nonmarketable issues are inadequate—refund them with marketable issues which are supported by the Federal Reserve.

tern of interest rates even if the new money is used directly to inflate spendings for consumption or capital goods or is used to supply liberal low-cost loans for these purposes.

In short, we are now on what may be called a "low-yield government security standard," for the Federal Reserve stands ready to monetize all the debt that others are unwilling to hold at the selected pattern of yields. And the commercial banks can, of course, expand their credit by a multiple of any new reserves furnished to them by this process, just as they can in response to increases of the monetary gold stock.

This new policy has made Federal Reserve discount rates practically ineffective as they are raised above the level of the lowest yields on government securities held by member banks. For example, in mid-1946 the Reserve Banks discontinued the ½ of 1 per cent preferential discount rate, so that their 1 per cent discount rate was the lowest one remaining. This had practically no effect on the credit situation, for commercial banks were holding more than $1 billion of Treasury bills on which the yield was only 0.375 per cent, and about $14 billion of other governments maturing within a year on which the highest yield was 0.875 per cent. The discount rate increases to 1¼ per cent in January, 1948 and to 1½ per cent in August, 1948 were largely ineffective for similar reasons. In the autumn of that year banks held well over $20 billion of governments maturing within a year and carrying a maximum yield of 1¼ per cent. Thus, discount rates below the yields on governments may tend to ease credit, but rates above the yields on governments which banks can sell freely to the Federal Reserve are likely to be largely meaningless. Even the "psychological effects" of rate advances above the yields on governments are likely to be insignificant when banks are largely out of debt to the Reserve Banks and know that they can remain so by selling governments at their own option.

Similarly, increases of Federal Reserve buying rates on acceptances are largely ineffective above the yield level on Treasury bills. Banks needing funds will sell Treasury bills rather than acceptances to secure needed funds, and they will shift from bills to acceptances whenever yields on acceptances rise significantly above the Treasury bill rate. The acceptance rate will continue to be of little importance, however, so long as the volume of outstanding acceptances remains at a low level.

The Reserve System can still use "moral suasion," but this instrument, too, is seriously weakened by the fact that member banks are practically out of debt to the Reserve Banks and know that they can remain so while they have so many governments that they can sell to the Federal Reserve.

Even the efficacy of increasing member bank reserve requirements is seriously reduced by the Federal Reserve policy of buying governments freely at the sellers' option. By mid-1948 the Board of Governors had already raised member bank reserve requirements to almost the limit of their statutory authority; there remained only the power to raise requirements against demand deposits in central reserve cities from 24 to 26 per cent. In August, however, Congress gave the Board power to raise reserve requirements by an additional 4 percentage points against demand deposits and 1½ percentage points against time and savings deposits. By using these powers to the full, the Federal Reserve could add about $3.5 billion to the volume of reserves required against existing deposits with member banks. But it is far from certain that such a policy would either force a reduction of bank credit or curtail a rise, for member banks can easily replenish their reserves by selling some of their governments—of which they hold more than $55 billion—to the Reserve Banks. An increase of reserve requirements can retard the expansion of bank credit for private purposes only to the extent that banks are reluctant to reduce their holdings of governments in order to acquire other assets. This point will be discussed more fully in a later section.

The Federal Reserve support program also alters the relationship of the Treasury to monetary controls. In the first place, the Treasury determines the coupon rates to be borne by its issues, so that while the Federal Reserve is committed to supporting governments at or near par the Treasury also determines within narrow limits the pattern of market yields. At times the Treasury has followed the advice of Federal Reserve officials, but at other times it has refused to do so and has insisted on maintaining lower interest rates than the Federal Reserve desired. Rumor has it that the Federal Reserve tried unsuccessfully during the war period to get the Treasury to raise yields on its shortest-term issues, and Eccles has testified that just after the war and again in early 1948 the Treasury refused to follow Federal Reserve recommendations that short-term rates be increased.[30]   In the second place, the Treasury's taxation-spending policies affect the behavior of the money supply even while the Federal Reserve maintains a fixed yield pattern on governments.   A fiscal policy that raises the propensity to save out of a given level of national income or that reduces the expected profitability of new investment tends to reduce the demand for bank credit and the creation of new money, while a fiscal policy that induces less national savings or that inhibits investment spendings less tends to increase the volume of new money created by the banking system.   In the third place, the willingness of the Federal Reserve to buy governments at the sellers' option reduces greatly the anti-inflationary effect of Treasury redemptions of securities held by the Federal Reserve and commercial banks.   When banks lose reserves as a result of Treasury retirement of Federal Reserve holdings, they can easily repair their reserve position by selling securities out of their own portfolios to the Reserve Banks.   For example, it is estimated that during the first half of 1948 the Treasury retired $4 billion of securities held by the Federal Reserve.   This tended, in the first instance, to reduce bank reserves, but during the same period the Federal Reserve was forced to restore $2.8 billion to bank reserves by purchasing governments in the market.[31]   Treasury retirements of debt held by the Federal Reserve can tighten credit only to the extent that banks are reluctant to sell governments in order to repair their reserve position and acquire other assets.

We come now to a crucial question: To what extent, if any, can

---

[30] *Hearings Before the House Banking and Currency Committee on S. J. Res. 157* (August 3, 1948), 187–88.

[31] This does not pretend to be a complete discussion of the effects of fiscal policy. Its purpose is merely to point out that with everyone free to sell securities to the Federal Reserve, the use to which the Treasury applies its surplus revenues is less important than it would be if banks and others did not have access to the Reserve Banks at their own option. A full discussion of the subject would have to discuss separately (1) the effects on private consumption, saving and investment resulting from collecting taxes in excess of government spendings, and (2) the effects of using the surplus (a) to build up Treasury balances in its own vaults, at the Federal Reserve, or at commercial banks, (b) to retire Federal Reserve-held debt, (c) to retire commercial bank held debt, and (d) to retire debt held by others.

credit for private investment and consumption purposes become more costly and less freely available so long as the Federal Reserve continues its readiness to monetize the government debt at low interest rates and the entire community retains its freedom to shift funds at will among the various branches of the long- and short-term money market? Would even a further rise of the demand for loan funds and/or a further decline of the propensity to save tighten credit for private purposes? My judgment is (1) that the cost of private credit can rise in a roughly parallel manner to the increases in yields on governments produced by changes in Federal Reserve support levels, but (2) so long as "prosperity" continues, the cost of private credit cannot rise much *relative to* the yield on governments, and the availability of credit for private purposes cannot be lessened very much.

These conclusions are based on two general considerations: (1) The Federal Reserve maintains its yield pattern on governments at any given time by standing ready to issue money (and reserves to banks) in exchange for any government securities that others are not willing to hold at the pattern of yields. (2) All holders—institutional and individual—retain their freedom to shift their funds at will between government securities and all other types of assets in such a way as to equalize the marginal attractiveness of all types of assets. The differences that have prevailed between yields on various governments and other securities presumably measure the marginal estimate of differences in risk and liquidity. Several factors could permit yields on private securities to rise relative to those on governments: (1) A rise of the estimated risk and illiquidity of private securities relative to governments. This is not likely to be important while the inflation continues. (2) Inertia. Having already made up their portfolios, some investors may be slow to sell governments in order to purchase private securities whose yields have risen. (3) Specialization of financial institutions and individual investors. Since some investors specialize in holding certain types of securities, their funds do not flow freely into other branches of the money market. (4) Policies of "balanced portfolios" and diversification of types and maturities held. Strongly imbued with these ideas, many investors may hestitate to upset what they consider to be a balanced portfolio in order to shift to other securities. Commercial banks, with their present low ratio of capital accounts to total assets, may in some cases be reluctant to load themselves heavily with risky obligations. All these factors contribute to the immobility of funds among the various branches of the money market and might permit some tightening of credit for private purposes while yields on governments are held constant. The Federal Reserve was apparently relying largely on these "frictions" when it expressed hope that by increasing member bank reserve requirements it could tighten private credit somewhat without a significant rise in the yields on governments. But it is easy to overestimate the immobility of credit.

Several developments since the prewar period may have increased the mobility of funds from government securities into other branches of the money market. Among these are: (1) The large volume of government securities held by institutional and other investors. As mentioned earlier, investors in this country hold nearly $200 billion of federal securities, an amount considerably in excess of all other outstanding debt obligations and equal to many times the annual net increase of private debt. Even if the flow of current savings were very small and the demand for funds very high, investors as a group would have to sell only a small percentage of their governments to be able to absorb all new private issues during any year. The importance of this point is magnified by the fact that every net sale of governments to the Federal Reserve, whether by banks or others, adds an equivalent amount to member bank reserves and permits a multiple expansion of commercial bank loans and investments. (2) The widespread ownership of government securities. If most of the outstanding governments were owned by only a few types of financial institutions specializing in a few types of private credit, the mobility of funds out of governments and into the other branches of the money market might be quite restricted. But this is not the situation, as Table 1 shows. The mobility of credit would seem to be enhanced by the fact that virtually all types of institutional and individual investors who ordinarily lend in the various branches of the money market hold these large volumes of governments that they can sell to secure funds for lending. (3)

The fact that investors' holdings of governments are so much larger, as a proportion of total assets as well as in absolute amounts, than they were in the prewar period. For example, government securities as a percentage of their total assets increased between 1939 and 1948 from 30 per cent to 62 per cent in mutual savings banks, from 40 per cent to 70 per cent in commercial banks, and from 27 per cent to nearly 50 per cent in life insurance companies. This tremendous growth in their government holdings—which in many cases occurred largely because of the scarcity of other debt obligations —should make for an increased willingness to shift out of governments and into other type of securities, for investors are likely to feel that they are now overly safe, overly liquid, and too dependent on government obligations.

We conclude, therefore, that though the immobility of credit among the various branches of the money market will probably permit some rise in the cost and some decrease in the availability of credit for private purposes even while yields on governments are pegged at a given level, credit is nevertheless a highly mobile commodity. Though its direct objective is to control yields on government securities, the Federal Reserve is effectively controlling, though less precisely, yields on outstanding and new issues of private debt obligations. It was, I believe, the late Lord Keynes who once bemoaned the fact that central banks, operating largely through discount rates and open-market operations designed to regulate the volume of commercial bank reserves, were unable to control with any accuracy long-term interest rates. He could not make such a complaint in the United States today, but he might not be happy to know that the Federal Reserve is using this newly developed power to hold interest rates at low levels and to assure the easy availability of investible funds despite the onrush of inflation.

It is beyond the scope of this article to assess quantitatively the contribution that our low-interest, easy-money policy has made to the height and duration of inflation. Such an attempt would require, among other things, an estimate of the interest elasticity of private saving, private investment, and hoarding. A few relevant observations will, however, be made.

In the first place, the continued assurance of a liberal supply of loanable funds and money at low rates of interest which are kept stable or allowed to rise only within a very narrow range cannot fail to be an unstabilizing factor in an economy in which expectations concerning the marginal efficiency of capital fluctuate widely relative to the propensity to save. Such a policy is, of course, appropriate to a period when the marginal efficiency of capital is so low relative to the propensity to save that investment and saving are equalized at a level of national income so low as to produce widespread unemployment. But it is not appropriate to a period in which the marginal efficiency of capital is so high relative to the propensity to save that saving and investment can be equalized only at progressively higher inflationary levels of national income. To assure a liberal supply of credit at low interest rates in such a period is to say, in effect, that the inflation shall not be hindered by any increase in the cost or decrease in the availability of investible funds; despite any rise in the propensity to consume, despite any increase in public and private demands for funds for investment spendings, despite any increase in the demand for money for transactions purposes as price levels rise, the Federal Reserve stands ready to assure an ample supply of low-cost money by issuing new money itself and by providing commercial banks with additional reserves to support new monetary issues by them. The rate of investment spendings need not be limited to the amounts the community is willing to save out of a given level of national money income, for the Federal Reserve must under its present policy create, or provide reserves to permit the creation of, enough new money to meet the surplus demand.

Such a policy seems beautifully designed to sustain continued inflation in an economy in which all the major groups—workers, farmers, and business enterprises—attempt to maintain their real purchasing power at levels exceeding the available supply of goods and services by demanding increases of their money incomes to offset, or more than offset, each rise of prices. Economists have generally condemned as unstabilizing in its effects the Federal Reserve policy, enunciated in the early nineteen-twenties, of "accommodating industry, agriculture, and commerce" at relatively stable rates of interest.   But the present Federal Reserve policy of stabilizing yields on government securities at low levels produces comparable results. With demand uncontrolled, the Federal Reserve can stabilize interest rates at low levels only at the cost of losing control over the money supply.

In the second place, I believe that the inflationary contribution of the present Federal Reserve policy is underestimated by those who concentrate their attention on interest rates rather than on the supply and availability of investible funds.   Some appear to contend that low interest rates do not make much of a contribution to inflation, for they do not increase very much either the propensity to consume or the inducement to invest.   I believe that this analysis is not correct.   It seems to assume that the market for investible funds is perfectly competitive, with the supply of investible funds being rationed solely through increases and decreases of interest rates which are highly sensitive.   It would be more realistic to recognize that many interest rates are relatively sluggish and that much of the rationing of credit is effected by non-price methods, such as the lender talking the borrower into taking a smaller or larger amount of credit than he asked for, the lender regretfully informing the borrower, "Sorry, but I'm loaned up," tightening or relaxing standards of creditworthiness, refusal to underwrite a new security issue because "the present market is too tight," and so on.   A tight money policy by the Federal Reserve can have a much more restrictive effect on private investment and on consumer borrowing than would be expected from a somewhat sluggish upward movement of the interest rate structure as the supply of investible funds is restricted.   Conversely, the present easy money policy of the Federal Reserve probably enhances inflation more by assuring a highly ample supply and availability of loan funds than by maintaining interest rates at low depression levels.

Conclusions

Without attempting a full analysis of our war finance program, I should like to conclude with a few comments on the Federal Reserve's support program since the end of the war.   In the first place, it is impossible to evaluate Federal Reserve policy without considering as well the attitudes and policies of the Treasury and Congress. Federal Reserve officials probably share the general fear of initiating policies that might prove to be too restrictive and that might precipitate the economy into deflation, but they seem to have less of a bias toward liberal credit than do the Treasury and Congress. The Treasury has displayed an understandable but probably not justifiable determination to hold down interest costs on the federal debt, and Congress has both feared that "prosperity" would be brought to an end and refused to use its taxation-spending powers to halt the inflation. So long as fiscal policy plays such an important role in our economy and is so closely related to the functioning of the monetary system, it is probably to be expected that Federal Reserve authorities will try to cooperate with fiscal authorities and will be influenced by the attitudes of the executive and legislative departments. Most economists favor a coordination of fiscal and monetary policies, but they should recognize that recent experience emphasizes the difficulties of securing such coordination on a satisfactory basis. If Federal Reserve and fiscal authorities disagree, should the Federal Reserve insist on taking actions that would embarrass the fiscal authorities? Should the Treasury have veto or directive power over the Federal Reserve, or should the Federal Reserve have control over certain Treasury actions, such as determining interest rates on the federal debt? Should we establish an agency to coordinate fiscal and monetary policies? How can fiscal authorities be induced to pay more attention to the broad economic effects of their policies? To at least some extent, the unsatisfactory nature of our fiscal-monetary policy since the end of the war must be laid to the unsatisfactory division of authority between the Federal Reserve and those responsible for fiscal policy.

In the second place, it is important to distinguish between a policy of maintaining a rigid pattern of yields on government securities and a policy of merely maintaining an orderly market for governments. As pointed out earlier, a policy of maintaining a rigid yield pattern or of holding the fluctuations of yields within narrow limits is likely to be incompatible with the maintenance of economic stability, for the central bank can achieve stability of interest rates only by surrendering its control over the money supply. On the other hand, the maintenance of an orderly market in governments need not conflict with the objective of promoting economic stability if this is interpreted to mean that the Federal Reserve should buy and sell securities in such a way as to promote orderly adjustments of security prices and yields. For example, under such a policy the Federal Reserve might sell securities, or at least curtail its purchases, in order to establish higher yields but still prevent "disorderly" movements. Such a policy would be difficult to administer, however, and the Federal Reserve would have to choose between accuracy of its control over yield levels and accuracy of its control over the money supply.

In the third place, it is not at all clear just why Federal Reserve and Treasury officials have continued since the end of the war to peg yields on governments at low levels. Some of the frequently offered justifications were given in an earlier section, but they may be rationalizations rather than motivating reasons. These seem to boil down to three principal arguments: (1) Higher interest rates would increase costs to the Treasury, (2) Higher yields without higher coupon rates would impose capital depreciation on institutional and individual holders of the government debt, and (3) Higher yield levels or the uncertainty attending the upward movement of yields, would increase the difficulty of private financing and might initiate a business recession. These arguments are of varying weight and may indicate differing policy decisions.

The argument that yields should be pegged at low levels to keep down the cost of government is unconvincing, even if all outstanding governments were immediately refunded at higher interest rates so that the full burden of increased interest costs would be felt at once. (a) It does not follow that minimizing interest costs tends to keep down the total cost of government. With interest costs making up only about one-eighth of the total costs of the federal government, total governmental costs may actually be increased if the low-interest policy enhances inflation significantly. (b) If it is felt that higher interest rates would be an "unjust" enrichment of the rentier class, the problem should be attacked through taxation rather than general credit policy. (c) Even if low interest rates do decrease total governmental costs, the avoidance of increased taxes for this purpose is less important than the promotion of economic stability. Interest costs are transfer rather than exhaustive payments, and the shifts of income involved in paying them out of higher tax collections are presumably less arbitrary than the shifts of wealth and income induced by inflation.

Also unconvincing is the argument that yields on governments should be pegged at low levels to protect holders of government securities against capital losses. (a) It is not clear that buyers of marketable government securities may properly ask for protection against a depreciation of their securities in terms of money. (b) The policy of preventing securities from depreciating in terms of money has not protected bondholders against loss of purchasing power. Many holders of the federal debt would probably be injured less by a decline in the monetary value of their bonds than by the loss of purchasing power induced by the continuance of easy-money. In general, it seems unwise to employ general credit policy to protect bondholders against capital losses in terms of money if this enhances inflation and reduces the purchasing power of all groups with relatively fixed money incomes. (c) It is not necessary to peg yields at low levels to protect holders of governments against capital losses in terms of money; the alternative is to refund the outstanding governments by issuing new securities with coupon rates high enough to enable the securities to sell at par value in the face of the tightened credit conditions imposed by the Federal Reserve in the pursuance of its function of general economic stabilization. I am not convinced that the government is under any moral obligation to protect the holders of its obligations against capital losses in terms of money, but if this is to be our national policy it should be accomplished through appropriate adjustments of coupon rates rather than by having the Federal Reserve relinquish its control over the money supply in order to maintain a pattern of interest rates established by the Treasury at some time in the past. Such a policy would require that coupon rates on federal obligations be changed from time to time, perhaps frequently, and would probably be criticized by the Treasury, Congress and perhaps some investors who are accustomed to dealing in the conventional types of government securities.   But policy should recognize that stability of bond prices, stability of coupon rates, and the maintenance of effective control over the money supply will at times be incompatible with each other in our economy.   In my opinion it is of first importance that the Federal Reserve regain its freedom to control the money supply in the interest of economic stabilization, so that either the stability of government bond prices or the stability of coupon rates on those bonds should be sacrificed.

The third argument for continuing an extremely easy money policy since the end of the war—that higher yields would increase the difficulty of private financing and might initiate a business recession —is also unconvincing.   It does have the merit of dealing with the objective, economic stabilization, that should be the primary concern of a central bank, but I do not believe that this objective would have indicated the assurance of an unlimited supply of low-cost money during the postwar period, and I suspect that Federal Reserve officials would not have thought so either if they had not been swayed by considerations related to holding down interest costs to the Treasury and protecting holders of government securities against capital depreciation.   The Federal Reserve frequently tightened credit to halt overexpansions before the Great Depression, and it must have recognized that the slowing down of inflation during the postwar period required some restriction of private investment spendings so long as the propensity to consume remained high and government spendings for domestic and foreign purposes continued to be large. It is true, of course, that general credit restrictions are difficult to administer with precision and that they may not merely halt inflation but also precipitate a decline, but it does not follow that during a period of a high propensity to consume, large government spendings, and a very high marginal efficiency of capital it is necessary to assure an unlimited supply of low-cost funds in order to avoid a cumulative decline of economic activity.

The growth of the federal debt to $250 billion so that it equals one and a half times all other outstanding debt obligations does represent a marked change in our financial structure and gives rise to difficult problems of debt management. Yields on governments will probably continue for some time to dominate yields on private obligations. This, however, is no valid argument for maintaining an unvarying interest rate structure. A monetary policy aimed at securing economic stability requires control of the volume of investible funds, and with a widely varying demand this will sometimes mean variable interest rates. If, as a matter of national policy, we decide to continue protecting holders of governments against capital losses in terms of money, we should do so by varying the amount of interest paid to them, not by having the Reserve Banks passively monetize all the federal debt offered to them at a virtually invariable structure of interest rates.

19

FISCAL OPERATIONS AS INSTRUMENTS OF ECONOMIC STABILIZATION*

By Charles O. Hardy‖

This paper deals chiefly with the quantitative aspects of fiscal control; that is, with the use of Treasury operations to stabilize the total amount of income, as measured in money terms. Qualitative controls, designed to influence the pattern of expenditures, aim primarily at objectives other than stabilization. For example, excises which discourage a particular type of consumption or subsidies which encourage a particular type of production may be used to promote health or morals, to develop a backward region, or to give something to one group of people at the expense of another group. The effects of such selective controls on the total volume of productive activity are incidental.

I shall discuss only federal finance. State and local governments cannot operate effectively on the level of total money income, for two reasons. The first of these is patent; namely, that money income is so fluid that any expansion or contraction of expenditures engineered by local finance is diffused quickly over the whole economy. So far as the local government is concerned the effects are dissipated, just as are those of the operations of single business units. The same consideration applies to operations of the government or the central banking system of a small country. Only a very large country (or an international organization of smaller countries) can hope to stabilize its economy through either fiscal or monetary policy.

* *The American Economic Review,* Supplement, **38** (1948), 395–403. Reprinted, by the courtesy of the publisher, without significant change from the original text.

‖ Mr. Hardy died in 1948.

The second reason why local government finance is impotent as a tool of stabilization is that a local government, having no power to issue money and no control over the central banking system, must finance its expenditures by tax revenues or by borrowing the current savings of the community. Like a private corporation, it can increase its own expenditures only by reducing the spending capacity of some one else. The effect of its operations on the volume of bank credit, if any, is beyond the control of the local government, and subject to that of the central monetary authority.

I. Three Types of Fiscal Control

Surplus or Deficit. The type of fiscal control which has been most discussed in recent years is control through the net balance of expenditures and revenues—the cash surplus or deficit—which is supposed to exercise a direct influence over the volume of private purchasing power.

Tax Management. By tax management I mean changing the form and incidence of taxation, with a view to influencing the volume of private expenditure. Enthusiasts for this idea believe, or hope, that it will some day be possible to check inflation by shifting the tax structure so as to throw the burden more heavily on those incomes which would otherwise be spent most quickly. For times of depression, they suggest another structure be provided, the incidence of which would be on incomes that are feeders of idle balances. Taxation combined with equivalent expenditure would channel these funds into the income stream with the same immediate results as the spending of newly-created money. Ideal tax management, from the standpoint of stabilization, would follow these two patterns alternately, and thus exercise a constant stabilizing influence.

So far as I can see, however, there is no way to identify such income for tax purposes. The factual basis of this whole scheme of tax management is highly speculative; I know of no attempts to carry it through in practice. The generally accepted relationship between the size of individual incomes and the rate of turnover of cash has no statistical, and very little theoretical, justification. All taxes are deflationary, except perhaps those business taxes which are so high as to encourage wasteful spending and discourage resistance to wage demands and increases in the prices demanded by those who supply goods and services to industry.

An excess profits tax of 90 or 95 per cent is probably inflationary because of its stimulus to uneconomic spending, whereas the same tax with rates of 50 per cent or 25 per cent would be deflationary. Hence, I am not one of those who are distressed that the excess profits tax of World War II was taken off at the wrong time, although a sharp reduction of the rate would have been more timely than outright repeal. Its maintenance at wartime rates would probably have increased the inflationary pressures of the last two years.

My tentative conclusion, which is not based on adequate study, is that tax management is a promising field for further study from the standpoint of encouraging progress, but is not likely to contribute much to the solution of the short-run stabilization problem. In the long run, the most promising possibility is probably "incentive taxation," designed to subsidize investment, stimulating expenditure in the short run and increasing real income in the long run. So far this is the happy hunting ground of the amateur rather than the professional economist. It is of little interest in the current situation when investment needs no prodding.

DEBT MANAGEMENT. The third type of fiscal program, debt management, includes the choice between the issuance of types of security which will be bought by banks and those which are preferred by individuals and savings institutions. It includes also the use of non-marketable securities like the savings bonds and non-redeemable securities like the terminal leave bonds to sterilize purchasing power. During the war we tried to hold down the volume of spending by limitations on bank ownership of certain types of bonds and by drives to push bonds into the ownership of individuals. But since this purpose conflicted with the Treasury's interest in selling the bonds with a minimum of work and risk of failure, loopholes were left open. There was a large amount of surreptitious bank buying through loans to directors and officers, the bonds being transferred later to bank ownership as they became eligible.

The logical extremes of types of debt management control are, in deficit finance, the choice between the issuance of interest-bearing securities and of paper money; in surplus finance the choice between hoarding cash and depositing surplus funds in reserve-free accounts of commercial banks.   In planning for a deficit it may be argued that the only purpose of interest on the public debt is to reduce its liquidity and discourage expenditures on the part of the holders; hence when deficit finance is used to stimulate private spending, the deficit should be financed by the issuance of greenbacks.   It seems likely that a larger stimulus to spending would result from the same sized deficit financed by paper money than by issuing interest-bearing securities.   If this is correct, there is little excuse for paying interest when the purpose is to stimulate expansion; if it is incorrect there is no need to pay interest at any time.   Conversely, in surplus financing the maximum restrictive effect would be attained by keeping the surplus locked up in cash, or—what amounts to the same thing—by paying off debt at the Federal Reserve Banks without any offsetting Reserve System acquisition of new assets.   This brings me to my first main point, the dependence of fiscal policy on the cooperation of the banking authorities.

II. Relations between Fiscal Policy and Central Banking Policy

Surplus or Deficit Financing.   It is obvious that deficit spending does not increase total spending unless the deficit is financed in such a way that it does not correspondingly decrease private spending. In *practice,* in a flexible currency-credit system, the use of a fiscal deficit to increase total expenditures (leaving out the case of paper money) involves selling securities to banks and providing them with the reserves necessary to support an expansion of credit; that is, to carry the securities without liquidating other securities or loans.   Or, securities may be sold to non-banking organizations which have sold or will sell their old holdings to the banks.   Here again an expansion of bank credit will ordinarily be necessary to facilitate the operation. Thus the effect of deficit financing and of expansionist debt management depends on support from the central bank.

Likewise the quantitative significance of a Treasury surplus depends upon the concurrent policy of the Reserve System.   I have pointed out above that to collect an excess of taxes over expenditures and lock it up, or to retire securities held by the Federal Reserve Banks, would be highly deflationary. This seems to be accepted by everybody. But there is no such common knowledge of the rest of the story. There is widespread acceptance of an erroneous doctrine that the anti-inflationary effect of a surplus is due to, or is accentuated by, the use of the surplus to retire securities held by the commercial banks. This idea is implicit in the *Annual Report* of the Board of Governors for 1945, and it runs through Governor Eccles' recent testimony before Congressional committees.[1] Yet it is clear that if the money drawn out of private deposits as taxes comes back to the banks in redemption of securities, excess reserves are created. At the end of the operation, the banks have the same amount of reserves they had before, while deposits, and consequently reserve requirements, have been decreased by the payment of tax checks. The banks can make new loans to the full amount of the excess of taxes over government expenditures. The contrary impression is apparently due to a facile assumption that reversing a pump will put the water back in the well. During the war, everybody became aware that inflation of the money supply resulted from the sale of securities to the banks. Why then does not deflation result from the reverse procedure—a cash surplus used to retire these securities?

What is overlooked is the vital role of central bank policy in the whole process. The financing program of the deficit years was inflationary, but not because the bonds were sold to the banks. Selling

---

[1] See *The Economic Report of the President* (January 1948), 30; *Annual Report* of the Board of Governors of the Federal Reserve System (1945), 3, 14; anti-inflation program as recommended in the President's Message of November 17, 1947; *Hearings* before the Joint Committee on the Economic Report, 80th Cong., 1st sess., testimony of Marriner S. Eccles, pp. 137, 164.

There are many other passages in Federal Reserve publications which state correctly the relation between budget surplus, debt retirement, and bank contraction. See *Federal Reserve Bulletin* (May 1946), 461, 464, 466; October 1946, 1098–99; May 1947, p. 775; November 1947, p. 1342.

In the passages cited from the *Annual Report of 1945,* the apparent error may be due to the inexplicit use of the term "bank holdings," where Federal Reserve holdings are meant.

securities to banks is not of itself any more inflationary than selling them to anybody else. The crucial fact of war finance was that the banks were enabled by Federal Reserve support to buy bonds without a corresponding reduction of their existing investments and loans. This was not true of any other class of buyers. The new deposits created in lending to the government were added to the existing stock of money; the new expenditures were superimposed on the existing flow of expenditures. The expansion of money flow could parallel the expansion of production so long as the expansion of the war effort consisted primarily of the absorption of idle resources and secondarily of the conversion to war purposes of resources that had been producing heavy capital goods whose product would have been remote in time anyway. Price inflation followed when this was no longer possible.

But the repayment of bank-held securities does not automatically contract the scale of banking activities in the way that the acquisition of those securities expanded the scale of banking activities. The reserves that were created to make possible the expansion are still held by the banks. Unless the Federal Reserve System mops up the reserves that are set free by the cancellation of deposits through taxation, the loss of bond investments by the banks makes possible an expansion of loans to business, or the purchase of bonds formerly owned by business, either of which restores to active use the funds that were taken away in taxes. It is as though the taxpayers borrowed from the banks new money to pay their taxes in the first place.

In short, there is no direct deflationary effect from using a government surplus to repay short-term securities held by banks. There is only an opportunity for the Federal Reserve to mop up some bank reserves without forcing the banks to call loans or sell securities in the open market. There is, however, a by-product in the reduction of equities and increase of debt to the banking system.

DEBT MANAGEMENT AND CENTRAL BANK POLICY. Debt management is also closely tied into central banking policy. The main point of debt management from the standpoint of prosperity and depression is to make it an indirect way of expanding and contracting the amount of purchasing power in the hands of the public. If long-term bonds are refunded into low-yield short-term certificates, and the latter are sold to the banks, the former holders of the bonds get bank deposits and are put in a position to make new investments. The possibility of doing this depends on the presence of excess reserves in the banking system; and the creation and destruction of excess reserves is the keystone of central banking. In essence, debt management is thus a more roundabout way of doing what we used to call open market operations.

TAX MANAGEMENT AND CENTRAL BANK POLICY. I said above that the most effective way of budgeting for expansion through a deficit would be to finance the entire deficit by expanding the money supply. There would be something to be said for a "no tax" policy if deflationary forces were so strong that the operation would not overdo the desired correction and give us a roaring inflation. But there is a prejudice against increasing the national debt, and there is sentiment in favor of taxing the rich in order to melt them down. Hence, instead of concluding merely that we should have lower taxes, or none, in time of deflation, the theorist plans to adapt the *kinds* of taxes levied to the alternating requirements of prosperity and depression eras. If the tendency is toward depression, use taxes which will fall chiefly on large incomes; if it is toward inflation, lay aside the whole theory since it suggests the use of regressive taxes. During the depression it was very fortunate for the flowering of the fiscal theory of stabilization that the kinds of taxes which had the greatest equalitarian appeal, were precisely the ones that seemed to fit in with a stabilization program. This remained true so long as the problem was one of stabilizing against deflation.

Some attention should perhaps be given to the contention, rather common among political leaders, that all taxes paid by business are inflationary because they enter into the cost of production. Of course, what some of our political leaders mean when they say that a tax is inflationary is that the combined effect of levying the tax and spending the proceeds is inflationary. This may or may not be true, according to the incidence of the tax. It is to be noted, however, that when there is slack in the banking system, taxes may be financed by bank expansion just as well as any other business expenditure. When this occurs the tax viewed by itself is quantitatively neutral, but the tax and corresponding expenditure taken together are inflationary.

III. Relative Efficiency of Fiscal Controls and Credit Controls

During the twenties economists developed an almost superstitious reverence for the supposed power of central banks to stabilize business through rediscount rates and open market operations. During the 30's there was a reaction against this view; some went to the other extreme and denied that central banking powers are strong enough to be of any value. Fiscal controls commanded the same sort of unquestioning allegiance that central bank controls had enjoyed in the twenties.

On this question I have only four things to say, none of which requires long discussion:

(1) Of the two sets of apparatus the central banking scheme seems to me more powerful than the fiscal one, though neither method alone is as effective as both used together, especially for expansion. Fiscal policy for expansion will not work without active central banking support; though for a contraction it will work if the central bank merely keeps total bank reserves stable. Central banking policy will have some effect in either direction if fiscal policy is merely neutral. It will bring about contraction very effectively, but for expansion purposes it is not much more than permissive. You can only slacken a string; it is of no use to push hard on it. If they should work against one another, no general statement can be made as to the result.

(2) There is very little historical material with which to check theoretical findings as to the efficacy of either method. The case of the United States during the thirties is generally supposed to support the view that central banking powers are inadequate and fiscal powers adequate, but no conclusions can safely be drawn from the experience of a period in which both methods are being used for the same purpose at the same time. The relative mildness of the depression of the thirties in England, where there was substantially no deficit financing, points to the opposite conclusion.

(3) Because the theory of fiscal management was developed in the thirties under the influence of the depression, it has been worked out chiefly as a technique of preventing or checking deflation. On the

other hand, the theory of central banking policy was developed at a time when most of the interest in stabilization related to the prevention of inflation.

(4) Although the theory of control of the flow of income through fiscal management was developed as a sort of by-product of the development of Keynesian economics, it is really no more Keynesian in its assumptions than is the theory of management through central banking operations. The Keynesian system intensified the demand for an effective instrument of control over the level of activity, because it treated as permanent integral characteristics of the economy certain maladjustments which in non-Keynesian economics are treated as aberrations from normal human conduct. The Keynes of 1924 and of 1930 was a devotee of the doctrine of control through rediscount rates and open market operations. The Keynes of 1936 was an advocate of fiscal controls because, along with many non-Keynesians, he had decided that central banking controls used alone were too weak—a conclusion foreshadowed by two or three sentences in the *Treatise on Money*.[2]

IV. OPEN-MARKET OPERATIONS OF THE TRUST FUNDS

The newest form of fiscal control is the use of the securities in the government trust funds, chiefly the social security reserve funds, in open-market operations. This was suggested in 1946 by Roland Robinson.[3] An interesting account of its use has recently been published.[4] This relates to sales of long-term securities held by the trust funds, to prevent declines in long-term interest rates, the securities being replaced in the trust funds by special issues and the money used by the Treasury to retire bank-held debt.

It is clear that there has been close cooperation between the Federal Reserve System and the Treasury in these operations. Nevertheless, it is risky to have two kinds of open market operations controlled by different agencies. The only permanent guarantee that they will not be used at cross-purposes would be the permanent subordination of

---

[2] Vol. II, 1930, p. 170.

[3] *Postwar Economic Studies of the Federal Reserve System*, No. 3, 78.

[4] *Federal Reserve Bulletin* (November 1947), 1349.

one agency to the other. This brings me to my final point, which relates to the location of responsibility for the monetary and credit policy of the national government.

V. INDEPENDENCE OF MONETARY AUTHORITY

Our monetary system is organized on the theory that the monetary authority should be an independent agency operating in the public interest to provide the amount of money necessary to meet the needs of industry and commerce.

The stabilization functions of the Federal Reserve System were being performed in a crude way by the Treasury before the Reserve System was established. Treasury balances were shifted back and forth between sub-Treasury hoards and commercial bank balances as the fluctuating needs of the banks were indicated by seasonal ease or strain and by occasional panics. The Federal Reserve Act originally provided that the Secretary of the Treasury and the Comptroller of the Currency should be members of the Federal Reserve Board, a relationship which was terminated in 1935. Since then, as before then, however, the Treasury has at times practically dictated the credit policies of the Reserve System—as has been true also in other countries. The control was greatest in 1917–19 and in 1941–46, but it would probably have been just as effective in the later years of the depression of the thirties if the objectives of the two agencies had not coincided.

In my judgment the reasons which led to entrusting the stabilization policy to a body independent of the Treasury were cogent when the System was established, and are still just as cogent. Treasuries always favor cheap money; especially, of course, when they are borrowing more than they are paying off. The functions of stabilizing the economy and minimizing the interest burden on the Treasury are separate and distinct. They did not conflict in the middle thirties because the banking policy was to provide cheap money for business cycle reasons, while the Treasury was running a deficit, necessitating Treasury borrowing in the open market. But Federal Reserve banking policy and Treasury policy conflict whenever the central bank has the problem of controlling or terminating too rapid an expansion of credit.

The current boom has revived the conflict and stimulated ingenious plans to circumvent the difficulty without a conflict of authorities.   The issue of location of authority is being postponed, and the economic issue is being fogged, by Reserve System's acceptance of the claim that the fiscal interests of the Treasury and the economic interest of the country in the monetary system really coincide.   There has been widespread acceptance of the doctrine that high interest rates are of no value in checking a boom—although the same authorities seem to say that cheap money is essential to the maintenance of full employment.   The real point is not the effect of the higher rates, but the by-product effect on rates of the things that would have to be done to check inflation; or stating it the other way round, the effect on inflation of the things that have to be done to keep interest rates from rising.   Now that this issue is forced to the front by the sweep of inflation, we are being told that stability of the bond market is itself essential to the prevention of further inflation.   It is feared that a rise in long-term rates on government bonds would precipitate a wholesale cashing of savings bonds and dumping of marketable bonds.   This tendency to inverse elasticity—holders selling on declines and buying on advances—does appear occasionally in speculative markets in periods of rapid price change, but has never been so chronic as to discredit the general practice of price-cutting on the part of sellers who want to move their goods quickly.   Keynes thought that inverse elasticity was of considerable importance with respect to *wages,* but he always treated a rise of *interest rates* as a stimulant to buying of bonds, and vice versa.

The scheme recently recommended by the Reserve System, involving isolation of most of the short-term government debt from the rest of the money market, offers a partial solution, though it is not clear that it would protect the long-term money market from the competition of corporate securities and commercial loans.   I believe that such a special reserve of short-term securities would be worth adding to the monetary structure, especially if the Treasury would agree, in return for this much protection of its short-term market, to withdraw its objections to stabilization of the total volume of money by Federal Reserve open market operations.

We are relying on very slender evidence in making a sacred white ox of the parity of government bonds. We shall never know whether a 99⅞ quotation for long-term bonds would wreck the country until we try it, but we know that no calamitous results followed the decline of government bonds below 85 in the early 20's. The risks attached to a lowering of the peg under the bond market must be weighed against the risks of continuing to blow up the bank credit structure in the process of supporting that market. The basic fact of inflation is that the supply of money is outrunning the demand for it. While our tax policy is anti-inflationary, Reserve System policy has not been such as to make the tax policy effective. And the present debt management policy is basically inflationary; so long as we must keep the bond market rigidly pegged we cannot grapple seriously with the control of inflation at its source.

20

THE "CHICAGO PLAN" OF BANKING REFORM*

By Albert G. Hart‖

I

A Proposal for Making Monetary Management Effective in the United States

i

1. A proposal for the radical reform of the American banking system by requiring reserves of 100 per cent. against all deposits subject to cheque has been made during the last two years from several quarters. General attention was first called to it by a memorandum circulated in mimeographed form by a group of economists at the University of Chicago.[1] Simultaneously, and quite independently, the same notions were developed by Dr. Laughlin Currie, of Harvard University.[2] Another independent inventor of very similar ideas was Mr. Bostrom, now of the University of Texas, whose proposals are sketched below. From conversations with various American economists I am convinced that the same notion occurred to economists at several other centres of economics at the same time, although their findings have not happened to be published. A book on the

---

* *The Review of Economic Studies*, **2** (1935), 104–16. Reprinted, by the courtesy of the publisher and the author, without change from the original text.

‖ Columbia University.

[1] Another account of the proposal from the point of view of the Chicago group is to be found in the pamphlet, *A Positive Program for Laissez Faire*, Chicago, University of Chicago Press, 1934, by Mr. Henry Simons, where the scheme is placed in its setting as part of a larger programme of the economic reform along liberal lines.

[2] *Cf.* his *Supply and Control of Money in the United States*, Cambridge, Mass., 1934.

proposal, founded in part on the Chicago memorandum already alluded to, is at present being prepared by Professor Irving Fisher.[3]

It is interesting to note that the plan has some support in the political world as well as among economists. In June, 1934, Bills were introduced in both houses of Congress (by Senator Cutting and Representative Patman respectively) requiring the maintenance of 100 per cent. reserve against chequing deposits.

2. The proposal has been advocated on three main grounds. One, which was prominent at the beginning but has since receded, is the obvious consideration that if chequing deposits were backed by reserves of 100 per cent. their holders and the public in general would be relieved of the risk of destruction of deposits by bank failures. All immediate interest in this aspect of the plan is removed by the advent of the Federal Deposit Insurance Corporation. A second contention is that the adoption of the scheme would make it possible to retire and cancel a large part of the national debt. This claim will be examined in the course of this note, and reasons will be shown for believing that it is illusory. The third ground for advocacy of the scheme is that it would create a situation favourable for truly effective monetary control. This, in the writer's opinion, is the real substance of the argument in favour of the scheme. Accordingly the discussion of this note will turn upon the questions this raises; though the necessity of considering the problems of transition to the system proposed will afford an opportunity of dealing with the claim that it could be used to reduce the national debt.

3. The second section of this note will be devoted to a brief analysis of the implications of the various forms of the proposal. In the third

---

[3] Professor Hayek points out that Professor Ludwig von Mises took a rather similar position several years ago, *Geldwertstabilisierung und Konjunkturpolitik,* Jena, 1926, 81*ff.*, advocating the extension of the principle of Peel's Act to all note-issuing banks and to commercial banks where cheques are in use. As will presently be seen, however, the "Chicago Plan" diverges from the principle of Peel's Act in that it looks toward a managed rather than an automatic currency. Another aspect of Peel's Act (the fixed "uncovered" issue) would be administratively so very cumbrous in a system of thousands of banks, such as exists in the United States, that it does not appear in any of the variants of the present proposal known to me.

section the weaknesses of the American banking system which the scheme is aimed to remove will be pointed out; and the aptness both of this scheme and of various others for the abolition of these weaknesses will be discussed. The fourth section contains an examination of the problems which would arise in the course of transition to the proposed system; while the fifth section outlines the considerations upon which the writer feels the scheme can properly be supported as a practical recommendation.

ii

1. In the core of the "Chicago Plan" is the proposal that all banks carrying deposits subject to cheque should be required by law to hold against those deposits reserves of 100 per cent. in the form of vault cash or deposits at a Federal Reserve Bank.[4] This would not require any change in the present relation between depositor and banker (except for the possibility of heavier service charges, which will be discussed in the fourth section, below), nor in the present system of cheque clearance. But the reserve requirements of the bankers against chequing deposits would be raised from the present sum of about $2,000 million to a sum presumably of $20,000 million or so.[5] Accordingly it would be necessary both to multiply the amount of reserve funds in existence and to get the additional funds into the hands of the banks.

2. The standard form of the "100 per cent. scheme" proposes the printing of the necessary reserve cash and its dissemination to the banks which need it by purchasing banking assets with the newly-printed paper in the name of the central monetary authority.[6] A second proposal (which, as we shall presently see, differs but little in principle from the first) is that the necessary reserve funds be created by printing

---

[4] From this central provision the plan is often called the "100 per cent. system."

[5] Proponents of the "100 per cent. system" generally favour also the abolition of the present three per cent. required reserve against savings deposits, which would release a few hundred millions of reserves. This, like other implications of the scheme for savings deposits, cannot be gone into here.

[6] This was the proposal of the original Chicago memorandum, and is followed by Mr. Simons, Dr. Currie, and Professor Fisher.

paper money and put in the hands of the banks which need reserves by simple gift. Even so, of course, the printing of this paper would be non-inflationary, since it would be immobilised by the increased reserve requirements.[7]

A third proposal, which diverges somewhat more from the standard scheme, is for the transfer of all chequing deposits from the banks to a government body (say the Post Office), banks being forbidden to carry deposits subject to cheque in future. This would involve uprooting some of the habits of the depositor; but for the banker the change would be comparatively slight, as it is proposed that each banker should issue debentures (to be held by the Post Office) in the amount of the chequing deposits transferred. These debentures would simply replace the banker's former demand deposits among his liabilities.[8]

3. All these proposals are aimed at preventing the creation or destruction of circulating medium (cash or deposits subject to cheque) except through the conscious action of the central monetary authority. A banker who made a loan, e.g., could not simply write new chequing deposits on the books, but must be able to make the funds available by transferring previously existing deposits.[9] Similarly, the repayment of loans would not result in a reduction in the amount of chequing deposits on the books, but in the accumulation of circulating medium by the lenders. Only the central monetary authority would continue to enjoy the present power of commercial banks to "create credit" by buying fresh assets. What we may call (adapting a remark of Senator

---

[7] This proposal, which originates with Professor Frank Knight, has not—so far as I know—been advanced in any published writing.

[8] This proposal is made in an unpublished manuscript of Mr. Bostrom, and is also hinted at by Dr. Currie, op. cit. While differing superficially from the other two variants, it has in common with them the removal of the volume of circulating medium from private control.

[9] This would make universal the present practice of the American mutual savings banks, which (since deposits in these banks cannot themselves be used in payment) make advances in the form of cheques on commercial banks. The balances on which these cheques are drawn are accumulated by the deposit of cheques and cash brought in by savers to the savings bank.

Gore about the Federal Home Loan Banks) the "free and unlimited coinage of debt" would be abolished.

4. It cannot be pretended, however, that this would do away with all monetary influences not originating with the central authority. Bankers could still call more loans than they made (though if they did they would accumulate excess reserves not—as now—to about one tenth of the loans called, but to the full amount). Economy of money payments (e.g., by using private debts of third parties as means of payment) could still be attained; and even without economy of payments changes in the amount of payments financed with a given volume of money (i.e., changes in "velocities") could readily occur. Some important elements in the monetary situation would thus be beyond the reach of management; but the quantity of cash plus chequing deposits would certainly be completely controllable.

iii

1. Virtually all schemes of monetary policy rely on the quantity of cash and chequing deposits as their principal instrument. It is proposed now to keep the quantity constant, now to let it increase with population, now to vary it so as to keep some price index stable; but almost invariably quantity of circulating medium occupies a central place. This is due not to any delusion among economists that variations in this quantity are the only important factor in the monetary situation, but to a well-grounded conviction that the other factors are decidedly less manageable than this.

It has already been intimated that the only valid ground for advocating the "100 per cent. system" is that it would bring this quantity under control, and thus enable monetary management through the quantity to be made effective. To make clear why such a device should be recommended, however, it is necessary to study the factors which at the present time limit the power of the central authorities to control the quantity of circulating medium. These, besides handicaps self-imposed by the monetary authorities,[10] are of two types: There

---

[10] The policy, e.g., of the Federal Reserve toward the acceptance market (as several writers on Federal Reserve policy have pointed out) has often weakened other aspects of the system's policy.

exists a set of "automatic" forces which cause changes in the form or location of the circulating medium to affect its quantity.   In addition there are elements in the structure and usages of the banking system which give the member banks a considerable degree of power to thwart the policy of the central bank.   For both of these defects in present arrangements, it is claimed, the "100 per cent. system" would provide a remedy.

2. The chief of the "automatic" forces is the curious (though historically natural) arrangement under which conversion of chequing deposits into cash or *vice versa* influences the total quantity of both in existence.[11]   This has shown itself most glaringly in the present depression, in consequence of the enormous increase in the volume of cash held by the public.[12]   As the banks found their depositors turning deposits into cash, the fractional reserves held against the deposits withdrawn provided but a small part of what was needed.   Earning assets therefore had to be turned into reserve funds in order to maintain the statutory reserve proportions.   But the member banks if left to themselves could increase their free reserves only by a small proportion (on the order of ten per cent.) of the assets liquidated.   If, however, the central bank aided them by buying part of the assets and thus creating new member bank reserves, its own reserve requirements were so constituted as enormously to reduce its "free gold" and thus eventually exert deflationary pressure.   Even the Glass-Steagal Act of 1932, which greatly reduced the gold requirements of the Federal Reserve Banks by permitting them to post bonds as note collateral, did not entirely remove this perverse elasticity.[13]

---

[11] On this and the other automatic effects *cf.* the masterly account of Dr. Currie, *op. cit.* The present sketch is largely along the lines he there lays down.

[12] For the benefit of future historians of monetary doctrines, I hazard the opinion that the chief reason for the sudden popularity of the "100 per cent. system" lies in American experience with the hoarding movement of 1932–33.

[13] The pressure on the member banks arises directly from the fractional reserve system; while the inability of the central bank to relieve it altogether arises from the divergent requirements for reserves against notes (40 per cent. in gold—or now in "gold certificates") and against deposits in member banks (35 per cent. of the member bank reserves, which in turn are 0 per cent.

3. Similarly, a redistribution of chequing deposits among banks may affect their total quantity. A flow either of customers' deposits or of bankers' deposits to metropolitan banks, e.g., tends to increase reserve requirements, since legal reserve ratios are higher for banks in important centres. Thus such a flow may exert a deflationary force. In the opposite case the effect is reversed.[14] Both change in location and change in form of the circulating medium being beyond the reach of monetary regulation, these reactions must be viewed as serious handicaps for the central monetary authorities.

4. Over and above these more or less automatic forces, there are other difficulties in carrying out monetary policy through influencing the member banks. When open-market operations are used to cut down member bank reserves with a view to contraction, the member banks may—and on occasion do—offset the change by exercising their right to rediscount. It is only the tradition of avoiding continuous indebtedness to the Reserve Banks which enables them to influence member bank reserves at all without raising rediscount rates to fantastic heights. Expansion, on the other hand, requires not only the basis of an increased amount of reserve funds but the acquisition by member banks of additional earning assets. If—as has happened recently—the banks are unable to find a sufficient volume of satisfactory short-term assets and hesitate to acquire further long-term assets for fear of capital losses, it may be impossible under the present organisation of the banking system to bring about expansion at all.[15]

---

against government deposits, 3 per cent. against "time deposits," and 13 per cent., 10 per cent., or 7 per cent.—according to the location of the bank—against "demand deposits"). If member bank deposits turn into cash, therefore, the requirements for reserves at the central bank rise from 4.55 per cent. to 40 per cent. in the most favourable case.

[14] This, incidentally, offers a foothold in monetary theory for the otherwise unacceptable argument that prosperity could be restored by "restoring farm purchasing power," since this would draw funds to country banks.

[15] This inability of the member banks to expand their assets appears to be a phenomenon only of the catastrophic phase of the present depression. Prior to 1932 a substantial excess of reserves over legal requirements was unknown. Accordingly it is possible to argue that this difficulty of management will be removed by the eventual resumption of "normal" banking.

5. The adoption of a "100 per cent. system" would eliminate both these possibilities of counter-management by bankers and the automatic perverse movements previously described.[16] With reserves of 100 per cent. an outflow of deposits (whether over the counter or through the clearinghouse) could be faced with complete equanimity, as the shrinkage of deposits would release just enough reserve funds to meet the drain. It may be noted, however, that this guarantee against unplanned variations in the circulating medium would be bought at the price of a certain rigidity. This would be a comparatively unimportant thing if the goal was a currency system under which the volume of circulating medium was to vary not at all or only slightly.[17] But if (e.g.) substantial variations in velocity of circulation are anticipated, and it is proposed to offset them by varying the quantity, the question arises how the funds are to be put in circulation. Ideally, we might propose manipulation by tax remission or increase of government expenditures (financed by printing paper) when expansion was desired and tax increases or diminution of expenditure in the contrary case. Failing this (which would demand a very high degree of flexibility of the administration), it would be necessary to work through open-market operations. In the absence of the possibility of expansion through bank loans, it might very well prove that these operations produced substantial fluctuations on security markets.[18] But unless it was desirable to produce large and sudden changes in the volume of circulating medium this would scarcely be of great importance.

6. The "100 per cent. system," as has just been argued, would be an effective remedy for the weaknesses of the banking system which now unfit it either for automatic functioning or for use as an instrument of monetary management. But other remedies are, of course, possible; and it is proposed in the next few paragraphs to comment on some of those which have been proposed.

---

[16] In so far as bankers held reserves against savings deposits, the variability of these reserves might, however, have very much the effects above described.

[17] It may be noted that the original Chicago memorandum implied constancy of the circulating medium; and for this purpose the "100 per cent. system" would be ideal.

[18] For this suggestion I am indebted to Professor Gregory.

7. One proposal for reform is the development of branch banking, which some of its numerous supporters seem to feel would remedy all the present defects of American banking. While there is good reason to believe such a development would be more helpful than harmful, it may be doubted both that it is likely to be at all rapid and that its ultimate effects will be so beneficial as is often supposed.

The political objections (especially on the part of the West) to branch banking development are well known. What is not so generally realised is that the organisation of the American banking system is such that even in the absence of political opposition the concentration of banking would not be likely to go forward very fast. In the first place the tradition and personnel requisite for a giant branch banking business must be built up gradually; and outside of California there is no large American bank which has it. The "branch offices" in operation elsewhere in the country are almost all located in the same city as their head offices, and are to all intents and purposes merely counters of the head offices which for greater accessibility are placed a few doors down the street. Their autonomy in making advances is very limited. This in itself would take some time to overcome. In addition, however, the system of correspondent relations among American banks sets up obstacles to concentration. Large urban banks devote themselves largely to the business of acting as "correspondent" for country banks, which involves the holding and investment of idle balances, clearance of cheques and drafts, and often aid in time of trouble. These relations to a considerable extent replace the branch banking organisation of other countries. What is important in the present connection, however, is the fact that to launch upon a campaign of branch development would involve for any large bank the loss of this very profitable business. When it is remembered also that the small banks are in themselves a very powerful political force, it may be conceded that the growth of branch banking (to a degree of concentration, say, comparable to that of England) is likely to be a matter of decades.

In any event it is to be doubted that branch banking in itself would clear the ground for successful monetary management, if the present reserve system were maintained. Both the automatic and the banker-controlled sources of weakness would remain; and in fact the power of member banks to act independently would tend to grow with the size of the banks. The greater amenability to management of the British and Scandinavian banking systems (as compared to the American) is to be attributed rather to temperamental differences and to basic differences of economic structure between the countries than to the superficial organisation of the banking system into a very small number of banks.

8. Putting branch banking aside, however, it would be possible to propose a system of modifications of the fractional-reserve system of banking which would approximate the degree of control offered by the "100 per cent. system." A programme of this sort may be sketched briefly as follows:

(a) The "automatic" effects of transfer of funds among different types of deposits on the volume of deposits could be eliminated by equalising reserve requirements (in terms of reserve deposits at the Federal Reserve plus vault cash) on all chequing balances of individuals and governmental bodies regardless of location, and abolishing reserve requirements on all savings deposits and on bankers' deposits. This would tend to establish a direct relation between the total amount of reserves and the total amount of chequing deposits which constitute effective money.

(b) The "automatic" effects of transfer of funds from cash to deposits or *vice versa* on the amount of chequing deposits could be eliminated by offsetting the flow of funds into or out of member banks through open-market operations. This calls for a reduction of central bank reserve requirements against notes to a figure approximating that against chequing deposits in the hands of the public, i.e., on the order of three or four per cent.[19]

(c) The power of member banks to alter the amount of reserves in opposition to the will of the central bank could be taken away by

---

[19] See above, p. 442, note 13. From this point of view the Federal Reserve Bank Note (the gold requirement against which is only five per cent.) is very nearly an ideal instrument; and it may be considered very unfortunate that these notes are now being withdrawn again after their great expansion at the time of the banking crisis.

the complete abolition of the rediscount privilege.[20]   The proposal of
the Reserve Board that it should have power to alter reserve requirements is also desirable from this point of view.

(d) The disappearance of circulating medium through bank failures is made practically impossible by the present system of deposit
insurance, and could be made completely so by extending the insurance
to cover all chequing deposits.

9. Some such system of reform could be made to cover all the
principal technical weaknesses against which the "100 per cent. system" is aimed, with one exception.   This is the possibility that member banks, when endowed with excess reserves to induce them to
expand the circulating medium, may refuse to do so.   This is a matter
of the first importance at the present time; but it is extremely difficult
to judge whether it is ever again likely to be so.   The question of the
relative merits of such a scheme and the "100 per cent. system" for
the United States, in any case, cannot well be decided without considering the problems of transition, to which it is now proposed to turn.

iv

1. In considering the advisability of such a scheme as the "100 per
cent. system" economists are under obligation to consider not only
how it would function if established but whether it could ever be put
in operation, and if so on what terms.   In principle the same question
arises about the alternative rearrangement of the fractional reserve
system; but in this case it is much less serious.

The only one of the four changes of the fractional reserve system
suggested which might have serious transitional effects is the stand-
ardisation of reserve requirements.   This would certainly entail some
redistribution of reserve funds, and according to the ratio chosen might

---

[20] This need not involve the giving up of the arrangements by which the
Federal Reserve can intervene to ease pressure on member banks.   If open
market operations left some individual bank in difficulties it could be relieved
by the use of the established practice of a sale of securities to the Reserve
Bank subject to a repurchase agreement.   But a *right* of member banks to
obtain accommodation on definite conditions, such as exists at present, is a
heavy handicap on Federal Reserve efforts to force bank contraction.

leave the banks either with excess reserves or with a deficiency. Open-market operations along present lines would, however, be adequate to adjust the level of reserve balances. If reserve requirements against "savings deposits" were dropped, this would create a temptation to encourage their use as means of payment, and steps would have to be taken to prevent this. (This problem is similar to one which would arise in transition to a "100 per cent. system," as we shall see.)

With the "100 per cent. system," however, possibilities of inconveniences in transition are legion. The discussion of this note will be confined to four of these possibilities, which strike the writer as of prime importance: (a) The transition would probably in itself induce fluctuations in the demand for money. Could these be so handled as to avoid dangerous fluctuations in prices and the volume of employment? (b) Would it be possible, in view of the great importance of the banks on the capital market, to effect such a transition without radical disturbances in this quarter? (c) Is there not danger, in the process of making chequing deposits more manageable, of driving business to other and less manageable methods of payment? (d) Might not the transition leave the institutions succeeding to the non-monetary functions of the banks dangerously weak?

Each of these problems takes on somewhat different forms according to the method of transition proposed; and here again there is no limit to the number of possible alternatives. It is proposed to consider only the three already mentioned, however: (A) Chequing deposits to be left with the banks and reserves to be provided by open-market purchases of banking assets (standard plan); (B) chequing deposits to be left with the banks and reserves to be provided by gift (Professor Knight's plan); (C) chequing deposits to be transferred to the Post Office, the banks to issue debentures to the Post Office in settlement of the obligations so arising (Mr. Bostrom's plan). In each case it will be assumed that the transition, once initiated, is to be carried through quickly (say within a year).

2. The first transitional problem arises from the fact that under any of the forms of the "100 per cent. system" the separation between cash assets (pocket money and balances subject to cheque) and other

assets held by the public would be much more sharply drawn than at present.[21]   Even in the United States, where the line is probably more distinct than elsewhere, cash holdings shade off gradually into investments.   If, therefore, the public were called upon to estimate their demand for money it is extremely likely that they would hit it wrong, and that even at a constant level of prices and incomes they would presently find their balances either redundant or deficient.[22]   In these circumstances, if the efforts of individuals to readjust their cash holdings were not to lead to radical monetary changes, it might be necessary for the central authority presently to find means to alter the total amount of cash plus chequing deposits substantially.[23]   This problem would arise in much the same form under each of the three schemes, except that under the second the lack of a large portfolio of saleable securities might prove embarrassing.

3. The second problem springs from the great importance of bankers on the American capital market.[24]   It follows from this that if they were impelled to bring about sweeping alterations in the character of their portfolios the capital market might be very seriously upset.

---

[21] This would apply with special force if (as Mr. Simons and some other proponents of the plan urge) savings deposits and other forms of short-term debt were refunded into long-term obligations; for this would broaden the gap between money and other assets very substantially.   Some of the reasons for the proposal to abolish savings deposits as well as "uncovered" chequing deposits will appear in connection with the three other transitional problems; though limitations of space make it impossible to develop all the issues connected with savings deposits in this paper.

[22] The writer is inclined to guess that cash requirements would be over-estimated at the outset, and that the excess might amount to as much as $4,000 or $5,000 million.

[23] Even if the goal were an "automatic" currency with a constant volume, it might be extremely dangerous not to have some body with discretionary power to offset such changes in the demand for money, at least for the first few years.

[24] The assets of American "commercial" banks aggregate somewhat more than the present national debt of the United States, or somewhat less than that of England.   In addition to this the mutual savings banks have assets amounting to about one-third those of the commercial banks.

Since the first (or "standard") form of the "100 per cent. system" envisages the transfer of a large part of banking assets to the central authority, it raises this issue in an especially acute form.

Under the standard plan of transition the greater part of the $18,000 million or so of additional reserves which would be needed would be provided through the purchase of banking assets by the central authority. The preference would presumably be for government securities, railway and public utility bonds, etc.; though it would probably be expedient also to rediscount a considerable amount of bank loans.[25] The tendency of these operations would be to leave bankers with the custody of savings deposits (or possibly with debenture liabilities created by refunding savings deposits into long-term debts). But the open-market operations would strip them of precisely the types of assets which American tradition holds appropriate to savings banks (with the sole exception of their mortgages), and leave them with just the sort of asset (unsecured loans and loans with stock-market collateral) which American savings-bank practice frowns upon.[26] It may scarcely be doubted that conscientious bankers in such circumstances would embark upon a campaign of rearranging their portfolios so as to attain a conventional distribution of assets, and that this would be profoundly disturbing to the capital market, especially since bankers are overwhelmingly the largest holders of the classes of loans they would be trying to liquidate. Incidentally this would tend still further to increase the handicaps which the organisation of the capital market imposes upon small enterprises, which the writer would consider a very unfortunate turn of events.

This objection would not apply, however, to the other two variants.

---

[25] Federal Reserve figures indicate that to obtain the necessary amount of reserves many banks would have to sell practically all of their "investments," and a considerable number would be obliged to rediscount substantial proportions of their loan portfolios as well.

[26] The American money market lacks almost entirely the type of financial house found in England which obtains funds by accepting savings deposits and holds a portfolio of bills. American savings banks invest almost altogether in well-secured urban mortgages and in the better classes of domestic bonds; and it is felt that a banker should have such assets in his portfolio to match his savings deposits even though commercial banking is his primary business.

The second (the gift of reserve funds) would amount to leaving bankers' assets undisturbed while relieving them of their liability for demand deposits. There is nothing in this to make their distribution of assets unsatisfactory. The same conclusion follows from the examination of the third scheme; for if liabilities to demand depositors were replaced by debenture liabilities to government the latter would not be felt to be so pressing as to require readjustment. Both schemes, by relaxing the pressure for "liquidity," would tend to reduce the premiums on certain types of assets and to induce a gradual redistribution.[27]

4. The third problem is of fundamental importance; for if the setting up of a "100 per cent. system" would tend to reduce the economic importance of the quantity of cash and chequing balances this would strike at the very root of monetary management. A repetition of the fiasco of bank-note regulation—which drove monetary transactions into the less manageable form of chequing on bank balances— would be disastrous. It must be recognised, moreover, that some forms at least of the proposals made tend to encourage the substitution of savings deposits and other forms of debt for cash and chequing deposits as means of payment.

As has already been pointed out, inflow or outflow of chequing deposits would not under a "100 per cent. system" affect the banker's earning assets. This would remove most of the present inducements to the banker to submit himself to the heavy expenses of carrying chequing accounts. Two inferences may be drawn: that bankers would be willing to carry chequing accounts only subject to heavy service charges, and that they would be strongly tempted to devise means for making "savings deposits" in fact serve as means of payment. Bank customers, to avoid service charges, would be inclined to co-operate in the development of such practices, which would tend to bring the "elasticity of credit" in again at the back door.[28] Furthermore, cus-

---

[27] The tendency would presumably be to reduce the charges on mortgages and unsecured advances relative to those on loans to government and to the call money market.

[28] This is one reason for the feeling of some advocates of the "100 per cent. system" that its success would require the abolition of the savings deposit.

The condition for the effective use of savings deposit as a substitute for

tomers would be offered strong inducements to adopt means of doing business which economise cash transactions, especially by using the private debts of third parties (not bankers) as means of payment.

To some extent repressive measures (such as prohibition of payment of savings deposits except on presentation of the passbook and restrictions on the negotiability of private instruments of debt) might serve to keep down such practices. But undoubtedly the most effective measure would be to ensure that the use of cheques remained, as at present, cheaper and more convenient than alternative modes of settlement. Under the third proposal (administration of chequing accounts by government) this could be done directly. Under the other two schemes, however, it would require a subsidy to bankers who carried chequing accounts, on such a basis as to prevent the growth of service charges to a point which would discourage the use of cheques. The effects of such a subsidy on bank earnings will be discussed in connection with the problem of the successor institutions in the next paragraph.

5. The fourth of the transitional problems is the character of the financial institutions which would succeed the present banks. As has already been indicated, every present bank would be succeeded by a chequing agency and some sort of savings institution, which might or might not be under combined management. Three questions arise here: the composition of assets and liabilities (already treated in part under the first head of this section), the problem of reserves, and the question of earnings. The first two will here be discussed together.

"chequing deposits" should here be stated. It is that cheques drawn against savings deposits should be reconverted into savings deposits after use. If a banker permitted a cheque to be drawn against a savings balance and the cheque was deposited in a chequing account, the banker would be obliged to find reserves to the amount of the cheque, just as if he had made a loan. But redeposit in a savings account would promptly release the reserves again. Even so, if the savings account was in a different institution from the first, the banker who permitted the drawing of the cheque would lose reserves, which would be a serious hindrance to the growth of such a method of payment.

It is disquieting to reflect that such transactions would be very simple between depositors in the same bank, and that savings institutions might devise arrangements for interavailability of deposits.

If savings deposits remained in their present form, but most of the present reserves were absorbed in the 100 per cent. reserve against chequing deposits, the reserve proportions of the successor institutions would be so thin as to make them very vulnerable to runs. Since, furthermore, as has been argued above, radical changes in bank portfolios would be likely under the standard form of transition, the unsettlement of the transitional situation in itself would be likely to induce runs under this plan. But to encourage savings bankers to carry large reserves, or to insure savings deposits, would be to revive many of the aspects of banking which the "100 per cent. plan" is aimed to abolish. Advocates of the "100 per cent. plan" are thus under obligation either to urge the refunding of savings deposits into long-term obligations[29] or to propose that the savings institutions maintain very low reserve proportions. As the latter arrangement would be likely to be fragile, the probability that a refunding might become necessary would in any case remain in the background.

The earnings question also affects the probable strength of the successor institutions, and incidentally links it intimately with the other transitional problems. If the standard form of transition were followed, the earning assets of the successor institutions would be on the order of half those of the present commercial banks, and gross earnings would be reduced roughly in this proportion except as the successor institutions could raise revenue by imposing heavy service charges on chequing depositors. In the present state of bank earnings this would mean not only the destruction of the net earnings of most banks, but the serious impairment of their ability to pay a return to savings depositors or even cover current losses. The standard proposal amounts to taxing bankers in the amount of the earnings on the assets they must part with to get the necessary reserves. Part of the tax could be shifted by service charges, part could perhaps be absorbed by eliminating numerous minor services offered free to depositors; but part would fall with confiscatory force on the equity of bank stockholders and even on savings depositors.

---

[29] Mr. Simons goes the length of suggesting that these obligations be converted into shares, giving the successor institutions the form of investment trusts with unusually stable portfolios.

This would be avoided, of course, if a subsidy were given the bankers to meet the expense of offering chequing facilities. Considerations of equity to bank stock-holders and savings depositors thus join with considerations of the ill-effects of heavy service charges on the modes of payment the public would use in commending such a subsidy. In view of the present state of bank earnings and of the very limited opportunities for economy on expenses, it would probably be considered appropriate to make this subsidy substantially equivalent to the earnings on the assets the banks were obliged to sell.[30]

On the second plan of transition, the subsidy which would be necessary to induce bankers to offer chequing facilities would be added to their present gross earnings, as their assets would be undisturbed. This would be as thoroughly inequitable as the appropriation of gross earnings under the first plan (without the subsidy). The appropriate remedy would be a tax on bankers proportioned to the holdings of demand deposits at the moment of transition, as each banker would continue to hold the corresponding assets regardless of the later flux and reflux of chequing deposits. The yield of the tax and the amount of subsidy should roughly balance.

On the third plan the bankers would be left with substantially unimpaired earnings, while the transfer of deposits to the Post Office would relieve them of heavy expenses. Accordingly it would be equitable to require them to pay interest on the debentures held by the Post Office at such a rate as would offset this saving.

6. From this sketch it may be concluded that workable methods of transition to a "100 per cent. system" could be found. The "standard" scheme, however, would have definitely objectionable transitional effects through its influence upon bank portfolios, and has

---

[30] This is the consideration which, as Professor Jacob Viner has suggested to the writer, destroys the claim that the "100 per cent. system" could be used to wipe out the national debt. It would be possible, by converting the assets bought into government securities, to achieve a nominal cancellation of much of the principal of the debt. But the interest charge, which is the economic substance of the debt, would be replaced by the subsidy on chequing accounts. To prove the contrary would require a demonstration that bankers could absorb a tax which removed half their gross earnings.

the further disadvantage that it lends itself to the fallacious claim that the "100 per cent. system" would eliminate the national debt.   Under any of the proposed schemes difficult problems of equity toward bank proprietors and savings depositors would be certain to arise.   None of them, finally, would avoid the necessity of adjusting the volume of circulating medium to fluctuations of demand, at least at the outset.

V

1. The argument just concluded indicates that even allowing for transitional difficulties the "100 per cent. system," properly handled, could bring about the results claimed for it in the improvement of the effectiveness of American monetary management.   But in this it is no more than on a par with other programmes which could be devised, such as that sketched in the third section of this paper.   Advocates of the scheme, accordingly, are bound to defend it not as the sole means to effective monetary control, but as the best of several economically workable alternatives.

2. To take this position, however, is to go somewhat outside the field of "pure economics"; for the considerations which may be urged in favour of the "100 per cent. system" are essentially political.   Space does not admit of a full discussion of this side of the matter; but the three chief arguments of this sort may here be touched upon: (*a*) As compared with alternative proposals, the "100 per cent. system" has the advantage of going with the grain of public prejudice.   A proposal to take steps so that the depositor's money should literally "be in the bank" is one the man in the street can understand and sympathise with.   (*b*) Banking reform along more conventional lines tends to involve the government more and more deeply in the lending business; and the danger that bank accommodation might become intimately linked with political patronage is serious.   It would scarcely be going too far to say that such a development on a large scale would wreck the American political system.   (*c*) An institutional separation of lending operations from the administration and creation of chequing deposits would have the healthy effect of making it clear that regulation of the quality of bank assets did not constitute a monetary policy. Our monetary system has definitely ceased to be automatic; but if the

central authorities content themselves with having a "banking policy"
monetary policy tends to become merely a by-product.

3. It is on such grounds rather than on purely "economic" considerations that reasoned advocacy of the "100 per cent. system" is
possible.   Whether or not one finds them adequate to justify whole-
hearted support of the practical proposals, the discussion of the scheme
is to be welcomed.   We can scarcely hope for any great improvement
of the American monetary system until it comes to be realised that
chequing deposits are money, that their creation and destruction are
matters of public concern, and that to avoid major monetary disturbances these deposits must be watched and regulated.   Whatever
may come of the scheme itself, the debate upon it can scarcely fail to
bring about a healthy consciousness of these facts.

CLASSIFIED BIBLIOGRAPHY OF ARTICLES ON MONETARY THEORY

Any attempt to define the field of monetary theory today and to delimit it from other branches of economics faces a difficult problem. Monetary theory is no longer confined to explaining the value of money. In recent years it has been extended to include almost all aggregative economics. A bibliography on monetary theory inevitably overlaps the areas marked out by other specialties, particularly international monetary relationships, determination of the level of income and employment, business cycles, fiscal policy, and distribution theory (with respect to the determination of the rate of interest). An exhaustive bibliography of monetary theory, broadly defined, would require an entire volume. Fortunately the Blakiston Series of Republished Articles on Economics contains bibliographies on some of the above specialties, and where that is the case the following list of articles has been materially shortened by exclusion of most of the items that appear in these other bibliographies. These other bibliographies should, therefore, be used to supplement the following one if further references are desired.

In the following bibliography the selection of articles on international monetary relationships is confined to those articles appearing later than those listed in the bibliography in *Readings in the Theory of International Trade;* for earlier articles in that area that bibliography should be consulted. Similarly there has been no attempt to include below the relevant articles included in the bibliographies of *Readings in Business Cycle Theory* and *Readings in the Theory of Income Distribution.* Space limitations have made necessary the elimination of several categories of articles which might justifiably be included, since they are closely related to categories which do appear below. For instance, articles on the consumption function are excluded (as dealing chiefly with the problem of ascertaining the shape and position of the function), although articles on the multiplier, the liquidity pref-

457

erence function, and the entire General Theory are included.   Articles on banking have been excluded, as most of them do not contribute much to monetary theory or policy.   Likewise excluded are articles dealing with the availability of funds for financing business and articles on the security markets.   In view of the prospect of a separate volume of Readings on public finance, articles on war finance are excluded below.   Also excluded is the whole controversy over capital theory, despite its close relationship to interest theory.   A rather tortuous line has been drawn through the articles on wage and price flexibility in an attempt to include articles dealing with changes in the real value of cash balances but attempting to exclude most of the controversy over the movement of real and money wage rates. Articles on the theory of income determination are included, but the discussion of secular stagnation is omitted.   Articles on monetary policy in general and those on the monetary problems of this country are included, but the many recent articles on the domestic monetary problems of foreign countries are excluded.   Discussions of taxation alone are excluded, but discussions of fiscal policy are included if related to monetary policy and its price and employment objectives. Book reviews, except for a few of article length, are excluded.

The articles are classified into a relatively small number of groups A more finely divided classification would merely multiply the prob lems of classifying individual articles, many of which cut across even the present classes.   The present classification is thought to provide fairly useful divisions, however.   Within each class, articles are listed alphabetically by author, except for attempts to keep replies and rejoinders with the articles which gave rise to them.

In compiling this bibliography, a list of articles for the period 1938–1944, compiled by Professor Mints, served as a beginning. Earlier articles have been excluded for the most part.   The final bibliography covers the major journals through June 1950 and others through June 1949.   This method of constructing a bibliography inevitably leaves some gaps and involves different judgments.   Space limitations argued against attempting to fill more than a few of the gaps, so no judgment is implied on articles which might well appear in the bibliography and which do not. The articles in French and German were selected by Professor Lutz, and the articles in Italian by Paolo Sylos Labini.

No attempt has been made to include articles in banking journals, except for *Lloyds Bank Review,* nor in Federal Reserve publications, except for the *Postwar Economic Studies.* Nor has any attempt been made to include all articles reprinted in such well-known collections as Robertson's *Essays in Monetary Theory.* Anyone using this bibliography will do well to look at such volumes as well as at other Blakiston volumes in the Series of Republished Articles on Economics. For a bibliography of articles before 1938, see especially Saulnier, *Contemporary Monetary Theory* (New York, Columbia University Press, 1938).

I wish to express my indebtedness to Professor Lutz and to Sylos Labini for preparation of the foreign bibliography, and above all to Professor Mints, not merely for his direct contribution to the bibliography but for his constant advice throughout my task.

Harlan M. Smith

Outline of the Bibliography

I. MONETARY THEORY

I-A. *The Value of Money*

Includes articles on the quantity theory of money or employing a quantity theory approach. Discussions of credit expansion are included here. Articles dealing solely with the construction of index numbers or the behavior of indexes over selected time periods are excluded from the bibliography. Discussions of Keynes' *Treatise* are included here rather than in I-B.

AFTALION, A., Les experiences monetaires recentes et la theorie quantitative, *Revue d'Economie Politique*, XXXIX (1925) 657–85, 813–41, 1009–31, 1236–64.

AMOROSO, L., Prezzi e moneta, *Giornale degli Economisti*, VII, new series (1949) 1–10.

ANDERSON, O., Ist die Quantitätstheorie statistisch nachweisbar? *Zeitschrift für Nationalökonomie*, II (1930–31) 523–78.

BACHI, R., Panorami monetari, *Moneta e Credito* (1948) 114–25.

BELL, J. W., Recent literature on money and banking, *Harvard Business Review*, XVII (Winter 1939) 222–36.

BERNACER, G., Die grundgleichung des geldwertes, *Weltwirtschaftliches Archiv*, LV (1942) 465–510.

———, Der preis des geldes, *Schmoller's Jahrbuch für Gesetzgebung, Verwaltung und Volkswirtschaft*, LXVII (1943) 137–76.

BILIMOVIČ, A., Kritische und positive bemerkungen zur geldtheorie, *Zeitschrift für Nationalökonomie*, II (1930–31) 352–75, 695–732.

LE BRANCHU, J. Y., La théorie quantitative de la monnaie au XVI° siècle, *Revue d'Economie Politique*, XLVIII (1934) 1241–56.

BREGLIA, A., Moneta ed economia vincolata, *Giornale degli Economisti*, LIII (1938) 173–84.

BUCK, H., Means of payment and prices in Canada 1900–46, *Canadian Journal of Economics and Political Science*, XIII (1947) 197–207.

CAPODAGLIO, G., Un problema di fondo e di flusso: il costo della moneta metallica equello della moneta bancaria, *Rivista Italiana di Scienze Economiche*, VIII (1936) 419–32.

CHESSA, F., I succedanei della moneta, *Rivista Bancaria*, XVIII (1937) 817–32.

CLARK, C., Public finance and changes in the value of money, *Economic Journal*, LV (1945) 371–89.

COPELAND, M. A., Tracing money flows through the United States economy, *American Economic Review*, XXXVII (1947, supplement) 31–49.

*CRICK, W. F., The genesis of bank deposits, *Economica*, VII (1927) 191–202.

CROSS, I. B., A note on lawful money, *Journal of Political Economy*, XLVI (1938) 409–13.

———, A note on the use of the word "currency," *Journal of Political Economy*, LII (1944) 362–63.

CRUM, W. L., and VANDERBLUE, H. B., The relations of a commercial bank to the business cycle, *Harvard Business Review*, III (1924–25) 297–311.

* Reprinted in the present volume.

DEL VECCHIO, G., Ricerche sopra la teoria generale della moneta, *Annali di Economia dell'Universita Bocconi*, VIII (1932) 71–614.

——, Le nuove teorie economiche della moneta, *Rivista Bancaria*, XIII (1932) 737–43.

——, Les nouvelles théories économiques de la monnaie, *Revue d'Economie Politique*, XLVII (1933) 1265–74.

DUESENBERRY, J., The mechanics of inflation, *Review of Economic Statistics*, XXXII (1950) 144–49.

ECKER, L. L., Money and banking, *Harvard Business Review*, IX (1930–31) 505–14.

EDER, G. V., Effect of gold price changes upon prices for other commodities, *Journal of the Royal Statistical Society*, CI (1938) 173–87.

*ELLIS, H. S., Some fundamentals in the theory of velocity, *Quarterly Journal of Economics*, LII (1937–38) 431–72.

FISHER, I., Our unstable dollar and the so-called business cycle, *Journal of the American Statistical Association*, XX (1925) 179–202.

FRASER, L. M., The equation of exchange: a suggestion, *Economica*, VI, new series (1939) 67–77.

GLENDAY, R., Business forecasting: a quantitative investigation of the influence of money on trade development, *Journal of the Royal Statistical Society*, XCV (1932) 1–55.

HAWTREY, R. G., and others, Discussion on Mr. Glenday's paper, *ibid.*, 56–75.

GOODWIN, R. M., The supply of bank money in England and Wales, 1920–38, *Oxford Economic Papers*, V (1941) 1–29.

GORDON, R. A., Period and velocity as statistical concepts, *Quarterly Journal of Economics*, LV (1940–41) 306–13.

——, The treatment of government spending in income-velocity estimates, *American Economic Review*, XL (1950) 152–59.

GRAGNANI, C., Sofismi sulla moneta, *Rivista di Politica Economica*, XXV (1935) 1044–67.

GRIZIOTTI, B., Le funzioni economiche finanziarie e politiche della moneta, *Rivista Internazionale di Scienze Sociali*, XLII (1934) 781–93.

GÜNTHER, A., Eine gesellschaftliche theorie des geldes, *Zeitschrift für Nationalökonomie*, X (1941) 101–12.

GUTMAN, F., Gut und geld, *Jahrbücher für Nationalökonomie und Statistik*, CXXXIV (1931) 546–63.

*HAWTREY, R. G., Money and index numbers, *Journal of the Royal Statistical Society*, XCIII (1930) 64–85; reprinted in *The Art of Central Banking*, 303–31, London, Longmans Green, 1932.

*——, Consumers' income and outlay, *The Manchester School*, II (1931) 45–64.

HICKS, E., Alexander Del Mar, critic of metalism, *Southern Economic Journal*, VI (1939–40) 314–32.

HOLTZ, D., Geldwert und staatskredit, *Finanzarchiv*, NF 8 (1940–41) 274–316.

HOLZMANN, F. D., Income determination in open inflation, *Review of Economic Statistics*, XXXII (1950) 150–58.

* Reprinted in the present volume.

HUBBARD, J. B., Some recent literature on money and banking, *Harvard Business Review,* XIV (1935–36) 113–28.

HUNTINGTON, E. V., On the mathematical hypotheses underlying Carl Snyder's trade-credit-ratio theorem, *Econometrica,* VI (1938) 177–79.

KEMMERER, E. W., The prospect of rising prices from the monetary angle, *Annals of the American Academy of Political and Social Science,* CLXXXIII (1936) 255–62.

LINTNER, J., The theory of money and prices, *The New Economics,* 503–37, New York, Knopf, 1947.

LORIA, A., Keynes sulla moneta, *Riforma Sociale,* XXXVIII (1931) 113–20.

MARGET, A. W., The "rate of sale" and the "velocity of circulation of goods": A comment, *Economica,* VI, new series (1939) 450–55.

MATSUOKA, K., On the quantity theory of gold, *Kyoto University Economic Review,* IX (1934), No. 1., 76–94.

*MEADE, J. E., The amount of money and the banking system, *Economic Journal,* XLIV (1934) 77–83.

MICHELL, H., The impact of sudden accession of treasure upon prices and real wages, *Canadian Journal of Economics and Political Science,* XII (1946) 1–17.

MOELLER, H., Wandlung der geldtheorie, *Finanzarchiv,* NF 6 (1938) 1–13.

MORGAN, J. N., Can we measure the marginal utility of money?, *Econometrica,* XIII (1945) 129–52.

MUHS, K., Der parallelismus von preis und produktionsbewegung, *Jahrbücher für Nationalökonomie und Statistik,* CXLIII (1936) 665–77.

————, Die aufgaben des geldes, *Schmoller's Jahrbuch für Gesetzgebung, Verwaltung und Volkswirtschaft,* LXIV (1940) 129–66.

MURAD, A., The nature of money, *Southern Economic Journal,* IX (1942–43) 217–33.

NAKATANI, M., Deposit currency and its velocity of circulation in Japan, *Kyoto University Economic Review,* XIV (1939), No. 4, 33–50.

NOGARO, B., Die Abhängigkeit des preisniveaus von der geldmenge, *Weltwirtschaftliches Archiv,* XLVIII (1938) 207–35.

————, La théorie de l'inflation à la lumière des expériences monétaires contemporaines, *Revue d'Economie Politique,* LVII (1947) 34–64.

NÖLL VON DER NAHMER, R., Geld-kaufkraft- "kapital" und ihre gegenseitigen beziehungen, *Finanzarchiv,* NF 9 (1941–43) 79–94.

NUSSBAUM, A., The meaning of inflation, *Political Science Quarterly,* LVIII (1943) 86–93.

OLIVER, H. M., A note on velocity, *Review of Economic Statistics,* XXXI (1949) 153–54.

PATINKIN, D., Relative prices, Say's law, and the demand for money, *Econometrica,* XVI (1948) 135–54.

————, The indeterminacy of absolute prices in classical economic theory, *Econometrica,* XVII (1949) 1–27.

* Reprinted in the present volume.

HICKMAN, W. B., The determinacy of absolute prices in classical economic theory, *Econometrica*, XVIII (1950) 9–20.

LEONTIEF, W. W., The consistency of the classical theory of money and prices, *ibid.*, 21–4.

PHIPPS, C. G., A note on Patinkin's "Relative prices," *ibid.*, 25–6.

PEARSON, F. A., Gold and prices, *Academy of Political Science, Proceeding*, XVI (1934–36) 37–45.

PETER, H., Wandlungen des geldes, *Schmoller's Jahrbuch für Gesetzgebung, Verwaltung und Volkswirtschaft*, LXIV (1940) 61–78.

*PIGOU, A. C., The value of money, *Quarterly Journal of Economics*, XXXII (1917–18) 38–65.

POINDEXTER, J. C., Some misconceptions of banking and interest theory, *Southern Economic Journal*, XIII (1946–47) 132–45.

RICCI, U., Considerazioni sulla utilità della moneta, *Giornale degli Economisti*, LII (1937) 712–33.

———, Einige strittige fragen üebr die kurve des geldnutzens, *Weltwirtschaftliches Archiv*, LVII (1943) 113–40.

RIST, C., Théories relatives à l'action de l'or et du taux d'escompte sur ie niveau general des prix, *Revue d'Economie Politique*, XLIX (1935) 1495–1534.

———, Doctrines relatives a l'action de l'or sur les prix (1850–1936), *Revue d'Economie Politique*, L (1936) 1473–1526.

ROBERTSON, D. H., New light on an old story, *Economica*, XV, new series (1948) 294–300.

———, A note on the theory of money, *Economica*, XIII (1933) 243–47. Reprinted in *Essays in Monetary Theory*, 92–7. London: King, 1940.

SHIBATA, K., An examination of Professor Cassel's quantity theory of money, *Kyoto University Economic Review*, VII (1932) No. 1, 52–84.

SHIRRAS, G. F., and CRAIG, J. H., Sir Isaac Newton and the currency, *Economic Journal*, LV (1945) 217–41.

SOKOLOFF, A. A., Die geldvermehrung und die preisscheren, *Archiv für Sozialwissenschaft und Sozialpolitik*, LXIV (1930) 433–52.

TAKATA, Y., Money, the economic veil, *Kyoto University Economic Review*, XV (1940) No. 4, 25–43.

VILLARD, H. H., Monetary theory, *A Survey of Contemporary Economics*, 314–51. Philadelphia, Blakiston, 1948.

VINING, R., A process analysis of bank credit expansion, *Quarterly Journal of Economics*, LIV (1939–40) 599–623.

WARBURTON, C., Monetary theory, full production, and the great depression, *Econometrica*, XIII (1945) 114–28.

———, The volume of money and the price level between the world wars, *Journal of Political Economy*, LIII (1945) 150–63.

———, Quantity and frequency of use of money in the United States, 1919–45, *Journal of Political Economy*, LIV (1946) 436–50.

* Reprinted in the present volume.

WARBURTON, C., Bank reserves and business fluctuations, *Journal of the American Statistical Association*, XLIII (1948) 547–58.

———, Monetary policy and business forecasting, *Journal of Business of the University of Chicago*, XXII (1949) 71–82.

———, The secular trend in monetary velocity, *Quarterly Journal of Economics*, LXIII (1949) 68–91.

WARREN, G. F., and PEARSON, F. A., Relationship of gold to prices, *Journal of the American Statistical Association*, XXVIII Proceedings (March 1933, supplement) 118–26.

KEMMERER, E. W., Discussion: Gold and prices, *ibid.*, 126–32.

———, The gold situation, *Academy of Political Science Proceedings*, XVI (1934–36) 88–96.

WATKINS, L. L., The expansion power of the English banking system, *Quarterly Journal of Economics*, LIII (1938–39) 1–37.

WEINBERGER, O., Über verfahrensweisen zur bestimmung des geldlichen grenznutzens, *Zeitschrift für die Gesamten Staats-wissenschaften*, XCIII (1932) 385–441.

WIJNHOLDS, H. W. J., Geldmenge, umlaufsgeschwindigkeit und preisniveau, *Weltwirtschaftliches Archiv*, L (1939) 583–611.

WOLFF, R., Liaison entre prix et monnaie, *Revue d'Economie Politique*, XLVIII (1934) 1691–1764.

I-B. Monetary Equilibrium

Includes Wicksellian and the later Swedish analysis, ex-ante and ex-post concepts, the Robertsonian period analysis, and the savings-investment controversy.

ANDERSON, M., A formula for total savings, *Quarterly Journal of Economics*, LVIII (1943–44) 106–19.

AOYAMA, H., A critical note on D. H. Robertson's theory of savings and investment, *Kyoto University Economic Review*, XVI (1941) No. 1, 49–73.

BENINI, R., Il posto del risparmio in un programma di economia induttiva, *Giornale degli Economisti*, I, new series (1939) 331–35.

DANIELS, G. W., The circulation of money in relation to production and employment, *The Manchester School*, IV (1933) 15–29.

———, Spending and investing, *The Manchester School*, V (1934) 102–17.

EGLE, W., Zur frage des "neutralen" geldes, *Zeitschrift für Nationalökonomie*, IX (1939) 12–30.

ELLIS, H. S., Monetary policy and investment, *American Economic Review*, XXX (1940 supplement) 27–38.

FAIN, G., Epargne réelle et épargne monétaire, *Revue d'Economie Politique*, LIX (1949) 335–51.

FORSTMANN, A., Zur monetären gleichgewichtsproblematik, *Schmoller's Jahrbuch für Gesetzgebung, Verwaltung und Volkswirtschaft*, LXVII (1943) 577–625.

FRUMENTO, A., Considerazioni critiche sulla polemica intorno al risparmio, *Giornale degli Economisti*, IL (1934) 819–31.

GRAZIANI, A., Sofismi sul risparmio, *Rivista Bancaria*, XIII (1932) 977–83.

HANSEN, A. H., A note on savings and investment, *Review of Economic Statistics,* XXX (1948) 30–3.

LERNER, A. P., Saving and investment: definitions, assumptions, objectives, *Quarterly Journal of Economics,* LIII (1938–39) 611–19; Reprinted in *The New Economics,* 626–33, New York, Knopf, 1947.

———, Saving equals investment, *Quarterly Journal of Economics,* LII (1937–38) 297–309; Reprinted in *The New Economics,* 619–25, New York, Knopf, 1947.

MAHR, A., Neutrales geld und wirtschaftssystem, *Zeitschrift für Nationalökonomie,* XI (1944) 1–11.

PREISER, E., Sparen und investieren, *Jahrbücher für Nationalökonomie und Statistik,* CLIX (1944) 257–309.

REYNAUD, P., Essais sur la monnaie neutre: I-Monnaie neutre et économie réelle, *Revue d'Economie Politique,* LI (1937) 1192–1216; II-Monnaie neutre et échanges internationaux, *Revue d'Economie Politique,* LI (1937) 1367–93.

SCHNEIDER, E., Ersparnis und investition in der gescholssenen volkswirtschaft, *Schmoller's Jahrbuch für Gesetzgebung, Verwaltung und Volkswirtschaft,* LXVII (1943) 35–64.

SHACKLE, G. L. S., Myrdal's analysis of monetary equilibrium, *Oxford Economic Papers,* VII (March 1945) 47–66.

STRIGL, R., Der Wicksellsche Prozess, *Weltwirtschaftliches Archiv,* LV (1942) 443–64.

WALKER, E. R., Savings and investment in monetary theory, *Economic Record,* IX (1933) 185–201.

WARBURTON, C., Volume of savings, quantity of money, and business instability, *Journal of Political Economy,* LV (1947) 222–33.

WILSON, J. S. G., Investment in a monetary economy, *Economica,* XVI, new series (1949) 321–35.

I-C. Liquidity, Hoarding, the Demand for Money, Interest

Includes articles on the determination of the rate of interest which are not confined to nonmonetary explanations. For articles on the effectiveness of interest rate manipulations by monetary authorities under various conditions see III-A, III-B, and III-C. The liquidity-preference function is treated in articles listed below and in I-D.

ADARKER, B. P., and GHOSH, D., Mr. Keynes' theory of interest, *Indian Journal of Economics,* XXI (1941) 285–300.

ALEXANDER, S. S., Mr. Keynes and Mr. Marx, *Review of Economic Studies,* VII (1939–40) 123–35.

BEHRMAN, J. N., The short-term interest rate and the velocity of circulation, *Econometrica,* XVI (1948) 185–90, 370.

BRONFENBRENNER, M., Some fundamentals in liquidity theory, *Quarterly Journal of Economics,* LIX (1944–45) 405–26.

BROWN, A. J., The liquidity-preference schedules of the London clearing banks, *Oxford Economic Papers,* No. 1 (1938) 49–82.

BROWN, A. J., Interest, prices, and the demand schedule for idle money, *Oxford Economic Papers,* No. 2, (1939) 46–69.

BURGESS, W. R., Factors affecting changes in short term interest rates, *Journal of the American Statistical Association,* XXII (1927) 195–201.

*CANNAN, E., The application of the theoretical apparatus of supply and demand to units of currency, *Economic Journal,* XXXI (1921) 453–61.

DANIEL, J. L., Interest rates: Long-term vs. short-term, *Econometrica,* VIII (1940) 272–78.

DATTA, B., Interest and the complex of preferences, *Indian Journal of Economics,* XIX (1939) 491–99.

DAVENPORT, H. J., Interest theory and theories, *American Economic Review,* XVII (1927) 636–56.

DAVIES, G. R., Factors determining the interest rate, *Quarterly Journal of Economics,* XXXIV (1919–20) 445–61.

D'SOUZA, V. L., Theory of interest reconsidered, *Indian Journal of Economics,* XIX (1939) 473–81.

DUNCAN, A. J., "Free money" of large manufacturing corporations and the rate of interest, *Econometrica,* XIV (1946) 251–53.

KISSELGOFF, A., A reply, *ibid.,* 254.

ELLSWORTH, P. T., Mr. Keynes on the rate of interest and the marginal efficiency of capital, *Journal of Political Economy,* XLIV (1936) 767–90.

FAN-HUNG, Keynes and Marx on the theory of capital accumulation, money, and interest, *Review of Economic Studies,* VII (1939–40) 28–41.

FELLNER, W., Monetary policies and hoarding in periods of stagnation, *Journal of Political Economy,* LI (1943) 191–205.

———, Monetary policy and the elasticity of liquidity functions, *Review of Economic Statistics,* XXX (1948) 42–4.

———, and SOMERS, H. M., Alternative monetary approaches to interest theory, *Review of Economic Statistics,* XXIII (1941) 43–8.

———, and ———, Note on "stocks" and "flows" in monetary interest theory, *Review of Economic Statistics,* XXXI (1949) 145–46.

FETTER, F. A., Interest theory and price movements, *American Economic Review,* XVII (1927 supplement) 62–105.

FISHER, I.; MITCHELL, W. C.; PALYI, M.; MITCHELL, W. F.; KNIGHT, F. H.; and KARSTEN, K. G., Interest theory and price movements: Discussion, *ibid.,* 106–22.

FLEMING, J. M., The determination of the rate of interest, *Economica,* V, new series (1938) 333–41.

FLORIN, R., Théorie des encaisses et théorie de l'interêt, *Revue d'Economie Politique,* LVI (1946) 178–89.

GOODWIN, R. M., Keynesian and other interest theories, *Review of Economic Statistics,* XXV (1943) 6–12.

GRUSON, C., La préférence pour la liquidité, *Economique Appliquée,* I (1948) 301–56.

HAHN, A., Anachronism of the liquidity preference concept, *Kyklos,* I (1947) 203–20.

* Reprinted in the first volume.

HART, A. G., Assets, liquidity, and investment, *American Economic Review,* XXXIX (1949 supplement) 171–81.

MARSCHAK, J., Role of liquidity under complete and incomplete information, *ibid.,* 182–95.

FRIEDMAN, M.; GOODWIN, R.; MODIGLIANI, F.; and TOBIN, J., Liquidity and uncertainty: Discussion, *ibid.,* 196–210.

HAWTREY, R. G., Interest and bank rate, *The Manchester School,* X (1939) 144–52.

HICKS, J. R., A reply, *ibid.,* 152–55.

HAWTREY, R. G., A rejoinder, *ibid.,* 155–56.

HAYES, H. G., Hoarding and the competitive equilibrium, *American Economic Review,* XXVIII (1938) 89–91.

*HICKS, J. R., A suggestion for simplifying the theory of money, *Economica,* II, new series (1935) 1–19.

KEYNES, J. M., The theory of the rate of interest, *The Lessons of Monetary Experience; Essays in Honor of Irving Fisher,* New York; Farrar and Rinehart, 1937, 145–52.   Reprinted in *Readings in the Theory of Income Distribution,* Philadelphia, The Blakiston Company, 1946, 418–24.

KISSELGOFF, A., Liquidity preference of large manufacturing corporations (1921–1939), *Econometrica,* XIII (1945) 334–44.

KRAGH, B., Two liquidity functions and the rate of interest: A simple dynamic model, *Review of Economic Studies,* XVII (1949–50) 98–106.

KRISHNASWAMY, A., Marshall's theory of money and income, *Indian Journal of Economics,* XXII (1941) 121–43.

LANDAUER, C., Staat und zins, *Archiv für Sozialwissenschaft und Sozialpolitik,* LXI (1929), Heft 3, 449–64.

LERNER, A. P., Alternative formulations of the theory of interest, *Economic Journal,* XLVIII (1938) 211–30.   Reprinted in *The New Economics,* New York, Knopf, 1947, 634–54.

———, Interest theory—supply and demand for loans or supply and demand for cash, *Review of Economic Statistics,* XXVI (1944) 88–91.   Reprinted in *The New Economics,* New York, Knopf, 1947, 655–61.

FELLNER, W. J., and SOMERS, H. M., Comment on Dr. Lerner's note, *Review of Economic Statistics,* XXVI (1944) 92.

LESER, C. E. V., The consumer's demand for money, *Econometrica,* XI (1943) 123–40.   See Errata, *ibid.,* 268.

LOKANATHAN, P. S., Interest and investment, *Indian Journal of Economics,* XIX (1939) 483–90.

LUKAS, E., "Geldüberhang" und "Geldüberfluss," *Finanzarchiv,* NF 10 (1943–45) 1–17.

LUSHER, D. W., The structure of interest rates and the Keynesian theory of interest, *Journal of Political Economy,* L (1942) 272–79.

LUTZ, F. A., The structure of interest rates, *Quarterly Journal of Economics,* LV (1940–41) 36–63.   Reprinted in *Readings in the Theory of Income Distribution,* Philadelphia, The Blakiston Company, 1946, 499–529.

* Reprinted in the present volume.

MARX, D., JR., The structure of interest rates: Comment, *Quarterly Journal of Economics,* LVI (1941–42) 152–56.

LUTZ, F. A., La monnaie et le taux d' interêt, *Economique Appliquée,* I (1948) 229–42.

*MCKEAN, R. N., Liquidity and a national balance sheet, *Journal of Political Economy,* LVII (1949) 506–22.

MAKOWER, H., and MARSCHAK, J., Assets, prices and monetary theory, *Economica,* V, new series (1938) 261–88.

MARCUS, E., The interest-rate structure, *Review of Economic Statistics,* XXX (1948) 223–26.

MARGET, A., Zur Dogmengeschichte des Begriffes einer "Umlaufsgeschwindigkeit der Güter" und seines verhältnisses zur umlaufsgeschwindigkeit des geldes, *Zeitschrift für Nationalökonomie,* IV (1932–33) 188–219.

MARSCHAK, J., Volksvermögen und kassenbedarf, *Archiv für Sozialwissenschaft und Sozialpolitik,* LXVIII (1933) 385–419.

———, Vom grössensystem der geldwirtschaft, *Archiv für Sozialwissenschaft und Sozialpolitik,* LXIX (1933) 492–503.

MEHTA, J. K., Coordination of the theories of interest, *Economic Journal,* XLVIII (1938) 251–63.

MELVILLE, L. G., The theory of interest, *Economic Record,* XIV (1938) 1–13, 161–75.

REDDAWAY, W. B., and DOWNING, R. I., Zero rates of interest, *Economic Record,* XV (1939) 94–7.

MELVILLE, L. B., A further comment, *ibid.,* 97–8.

MILLIKAN, M. F., The liquidity-preference theory of interest, *American Economic Review,* XXVIII (1938) 247–60.

———; ELLSWORTH, P. T.; MORTON, W. A.; and MARGET, A. W., Summaries of papers on general interest theory, *American Economic Review,* XXVIII (1938 supplement) 69–72.

*MODIGLIANI, F., Liquidity preference and the theory of interest and money, *Econometrica,* XII (1944) 45–88.

MORGAN, E. V., The future of interest rates, *Economic Journal,* LIV (1944) 340–51.

MORGAN, T., Interest, time preference and the yield of capital, *American Economic Review,* XXXV (1945) 81–98.

MORTON, W. A., Liquidity and solvency, *American Economic Review,* XXIX (1939) 272–85.

NEISSER, H., Volksvermögen und Kassenbedarf, *Archiv für Sozialwissenschaft und Sozialpolitik,* LXIX (1933) 484–91.

NIXON, S. E.; BRYDEN, J. T.; and HACKETT, W. T. G., Interest rates in Canada, *Canadian Journal of Economics and Political Science,* III (1937) 421–48.

OHLIN, B., Alternative theories of the rate of interest, *Economic Journal,* XLVII (1937) 423–27.

OU, P. S., Ex-ante saving and liquidity preferences, *Review of Economic Studies,* XI (1943–44) 52–6.

* Reprinted in the present volume.

PHILIP, K., A statistical measurement of the liquidity preference of private banks, *Review of Economic Statistics*, XVI (1949–50) 71–7.

REDER, M., Interest and employment, *Journal of Political Economy*, LIV (1946) 243–57.

RICCI, U., Die kurven des geldnutzens und die theorie des sparens, *Zeitschrift für Nationalökonomie*, III (1931–32) 307–32.

ROBERTSON, D. H., Mr. Keynes and "finance": A note, *Economic Journal*, XLVIII (1938) 314–18.

KEYNES, J. M., Comment, *ibid.*, 318–22.

ROBERTSON, D. H., Mr. Keynes and "finance," *ibid.*, 555–56.

———, Mr. Keynes and the rate of interest, *Essays in Monetary Theory* (1940), London: King, 1940, 1–38. Reprinted in *Readings in the Theory of Income Distribution*, Philadelphia, The Blakiston Company, 1946, 425–60.

ROBINSON, J., The concept of hoarding, *Economic Journal*, XLVIII (1938) 231–36.

ROBINSON, R. I., Money supply and liquid asset formation, *American Economic Review*, XXXVI (1946) 127–33.

ROOS, C. F., and VON SZELISKI, V., The determination of interest rates, *Journal of Political Economy*, L (1942) 501–35.

SALANT, W. S., The demand for money and the concept of income velocity, *Journal of Political Economy*, XLIX (1941) 395–421.

SCHNEIDER, E., Zur liquiditätstheorie des zinses, *Weltwirtschaftliches Archiv*, LXII (1949) 123–30.

DE SCITOVSKY, T., A study of interest and capital, *Econometrica*, VII, new series (1940) 293–317.

SHACKLE, G. L. S., The nature of interest rates, *Oxford Economic Papers*, I, new series (1949) 100–20.

SHAW, E. S., False issues in the interest-theory controversy, *Journal of Political Economy*, XLVI (1938) 838–56.

*SIMMONS, E. C., The relative liquidity of money and other things, *American Economic Review*, XXXVII (1947 supplement) 308–11.

SMITHIES, A., The quantity of money and the rate of interest, *Review of Economic Statistics*, XXV (1943) 69–76.

SOMERS, H. M., Monetary policy and the theory of interest, *Quarterly Journal of Economics*, LV (1940–41) 488–507. Reprinted in *Readings in the Theory of Income Distribution*, Philadelphia, The Blakiston Company, 1946, 477–98.

SOMERVILLE, H., Interest and usury in a new light, *Economic Journal*, XLI (1931) 646–49.

CANNAN, E.; ADARKAR, P.; SANDWELL, B. K.; and KEYNES, J. M., Saving and usury: A symposium, *Economic Journal*, XLII (1932) 123–37.

DENNIS, L., and SOMERVILLE, H., Usury and the canonists: continued, *ibid.*, 312–23.

SPENGLER, J. J., Economic opinion and the future of the interest rate, *Southern Economic Journal*, III (1936) 7–28.

STAFFORD, J., The future of the rate of interest, *The Manchester School*, VIII (1937) 125–46.

* Reprinted in the present volume.

SWAN, T. W., Some notes on the interest controversy, *Economic Record,* XVII (1941) 153–65.

THIRLBY, G. F., The rate of interest, *South African Journal of Economics,* VII (1939) 1–17.

————, Demand and supply of money, *Economic Journal,* LVIII (1948) 331–55.

TINBERGEN, J., Some problems in the explanation of interest rates, *Quarterly Journal of Economics,* LVI (1946–47) 397–438.

TOBIN, J., Liquidity preference and monetary policy, *Review of Economic Statistics,* XXIX (1947) 124–31.

TOWNSHEND, H., Liquidity-premium and the theory of value, *Economic Journal,* XLVII (1937) 157–69.

VALK, W. L., Die dynamische bedeutung des böhmschen verlustprinzips und die volkswirtschaftliche liquiditätsfrage, *Weltwritschaftliches Archiv,* LVI (1937) Heft 2, 466–75.

WALDE, G., Die umlaufageschwindigkeit des geldes als begriff der geldwerttheorie, *Finanzarchiv,* NF 6 (1937–38) 712–31.

WALLICH, H. C., The current significance of liquidity preference, *Quarterly Journal of Economics,* LX (1945–46) 490–512.

WARBURTON, C., Monetary velocity and monetary policy, *Review of Economic Statistics,* XXX (1948) 304–14.

TOBIN, J., A rejoinder, *ibid.,* 314–17.

WESTERFIELD, R. B. (chairman), Abstracts of discussions on the future of interest rates, *American Economic Review,* XXXII (1942 supplement) 217–26.

I-D. *The Keynesian General Theory*

Includes review articles and commentaries on *The General Theory of Employment, Interest and Money.* Articles dealing primarily with liquidity preference are found in I-C, those on price and wage rigidity in I-E, and those on the multiplier in I-G.

AMONN, A., Keynes' "Allgemeine Theorie der Beschäftigung," *Jahrbücher für Nationalökonomie und Statistik,* CXLVII (1938) 1–27, 129–57.

ANGELL, J. W., Keynes and economic analysis today, *Review of Economic Statistics,* XXX (1948) 259–64.

BACCHI ANDREOLI, S., La teoria keynesiana in Italia, *Bancaria* (1949) 941–52, 1029–49.

BAUER, P. T., Die allgemeine theorie von Keynes und ihre kritiker, *Zeitschrift für Nationalökonomie,* IX (1939) 99–106.

————, Remarques sur la theorie generale de Lord Keynes, *Revue d'Economie Politique,* LVI (1946) 121–34.

BETTELHEIM, C., Revenue national, épargne et investissements chez Marx et Keynes, *Revue d'Economie Politique,* LVIII (1948) 169–97.

CHAMLEY, P., La théorie générale de l'emploi, de l'interêt et de la monnaie, *Economique Appliquée,* I (1948) 357–99.

DARRELL, J., The economic consequences of Mr. Keynes, *Science and Society,* I (1936–37) 194–211.

DEHN, E., Zur geld- und konjunkturtheorie von Professor Keynes, *Zeitschrift für Nationalökonomie*, IX (1939) 273–82.

——, Zur allgemeinen theorie von Professor Keynes, *Zeitschrift für Nationalökonomie*, IX (1939) 385–413.

DERVAUX, P., Réflexions sur l'interêt, l'épargne et l'investissement, á propos de la théorie générale de J. M. Keynes, *Revue d'Economie Politique*, LV (1945) 149–77.

EHRHARDT, A., Les raisonnements fondamentaux de la "Théorie Générale" de Keynes, *Revue d'Economie Politique*, LIX (1949) 183–206, 369–84.

EINAUDI, L., Della moneta "serbatoio di valori" e di altri problemi monetari, *Rivista di Storia Economica*, IV (1939) 133–66.

ELLIS, H. S., The state of the new economics, *American Economic Review*, XXXIX (1949) 465–77.

FITCH, L. C., Comments on Keynesian economics, *Political Science Quarterly*, LXII (1947) 418–27.

FORSTMANN, A., Arbeit oder beschäftigung?: Kritische betrachtungen zu J. M. Keynes' "Allgemeine Theorie der Beschäftigung," *Finanzarchiv*, NF 5, (1937–38) 375–488.

FORT, D. M., A theory of general short-run equilibrium, *Econometrica*, XIII (1945) 293–310.

GRAZIANI, A., Vecchie e nuove teorie sull' interesse, *Rivista di Politica Economica*, XXVII (1937) 945–54.

GRUCHY, A. G., J. M. Keynes' concept of economic science, *Southern Economic Journal*, XV (1948–49) 249–66.

HABERLER, G., The place of *The General Theory of Employment, Interest, and Money* in the history of economic thought, *Review of Economic Statistics*, XXVIII (1946) 187–94.

——, La place de la théorie générale de l'emploi, de l'interêt et de la monnaie dans l'histoire de la pensée economique, *Economique Appliquée*, I (1948) 211–28.

HAHN, L. A., Wage flexibility upwards, *Social Research*, XIV (1947) 148–67.

HANSEN, A. H., Keynes and the General Theory, *Review of Economic Statistics*, XXVIII (1946) 182–87.

HARROD, R. F., John Maynard Keynes, *Review of Economic Statistics*, XXVIII (1946) 178–82.

HENDERSON, H. D., Mr. Keynes' attack on economists, *The Spectator*, (February 14, 1936) 263.

HICKS, J. R., La théorie de Keynes apres neuf ans, *Revue d'Economie Politique*, LV (1945) 1–12.

HOOVER, C. B., Keynes and the economic system, *Journal of Political Economy*, LVI (1948) 392–402.

KAHN, E., Keynes' influence on theory and public policy, *South African Journal of Economics*, XVI (1948) 70–4.

KLEIN, L. R., Theories of effective demand and employment, *Journal of Political Economy*, LV (1947) 108–31.

LYDALL, H. F., Unemployment in an unplanned economy, *Economic Journal*, LVI (1946) 366–82.

Mosse, P., La notion d'expérience marginale, la théorie générale de J. M. Keynes et le problème de l'interêt, *Revue d'Economie Politique,* LVIII (1948) 88–132.

von Mühlenfels, A., Allgemeine theorie der beschäftigung des zinses und des geldes, *Schmoller's Jahrbuch für Gesetzgebung, Verwaltung und Volkswirtschaft,* LXII (1938) 221–29.

Neisser, H., Keynes as an economist, *Social Research,* XIII (1946) 225–35.

Pagni, C., Keynes contro i classici: Una nuova teoria della occupazione, dell'interesse e della moneta, *Giornale degli Economisti,* LII (1937) 197–201.

Papi, G. U., Recenti vedute teoriche inglesi sulla disoccupazione, *Giornale degli Economisti,* I, new series (1939) 1–25.

Peter, H., Keynes' neue allgemeine theorie, *Finanzarchiv,* NF 5 (1937–38) 51–84.

Robinson, E. A. G., John Maynard Keynes, 1883–1946, *Economic Journal,* LVII (1947) 1–68.

Roos, C. F., The demand for investment goods, *American Economic Review,* XXXVIII (1948 supplement) 311–20.

Jones, H., The optimum rate of investment, the savings institutions, and the banks, *ibid.,* 321–39.

Dunlop, J. T., The demand and supply function for labor, *ibid.,* 340–50.

Copeland, M. A., and Gordon, R. A., Keynesian economics, savings, investment, and wage rates: Discussion, *ibid.,* 351–56.

Rueff, J., The fallacies of Lord Keynes' general theory, *Quarterly Journal of Economics,* LXI (1946–47) 343–67.

Tobin, J., The fallacies of Lord Keynes' general theory: Comment, *Quarterly Journal of Economics,* LXII (1947–48) 763–70.

Rueff, J., Reply, *ibid.,* 771–82.

———, Les erreurs de la théorie générale de Lord Keynes, *Revue d'Economie Politique,* LVII (1947) 5–33.

Samuelson, P. A., Lord Keynes and the general theory, *Econometrica,* XIV (1946) 187–200.

Schüller, R., Keynes' theorie der nachfrage nach arbeit, *Zeitschrift für Nationalökonomie,* VII (1936) 475–82.

Schumpeter, J. A., John Maynard Keynes 1883–1946, *American Economic Review,* XXXVI (1946) 495–518.

———, Keynes and statistics, *Review of Economic Statistics,* XXVIII (1946) 194–96.

Scott, I. O., Professor Leontief on Lord Keynes, *Quarterly Journal of Economics,* LXIII (1949) 554–67.

Leontief, W., Comment, *ibid.,* 567–69.

Haberler, G., Further comment, *ibid.,* 569–71.

Sen, S. R., Sir James Stewart's general theory of employment, interest and money, *Economica,* XIV, new series (1947) 19–36.

Simons, H. C., Keynes's comments on money: A review of Keynes's *The General Theory of Employment, Interest and Money, The Christian Century,* LIII (July 22, 1936) 1016–17.

Stafford, J., Mr. Keynes on employment and output, *The Manchester School,* VII (1936) 55–60.

SWEEZY, P. M., John Maynard Keynes, *Science and Society,* X (1946) 398–405.

SYLOS LABINI, P., The Keynesians (A letter from America to a friend), *Banca Nazionale del Lavoro Quarterly Review* (1949) 238–42.

TAKATA, Y., Unemployment and wages: A critical review of Mr. Keynes' theory of unemployment, *Kyoto University Economic Review,* XII (1937) No. 2, 1–18.

TARSHIS, L., An exposition of Keynesian economics, *American Economic Review,* XXXVIII (1948 supplement) 261–72.

WILLIAMS, J. H., An appraisal of Keynesian economics, *ibid.,* 273–90.

CHANDLER, L. V.; WARBURTON, C.; and REDER, M. W., A consideration of the economic and monetary theories of J. M. Keynes: Discussion, *ibid.,* 291–98.

TRACHTENBERG, I., Soviet comments on Keynesian theories of full employment, *Science and Society,* X (1946) 405–09.

TRANCART, G., La révolution Keynesienne, *Revue d'Economie Politique,* LIX (1949) 88–94.

VICKREY, W., Limitations of Keynesian economics, *Social Research,* XV (1948) 403–16.

WILSON, E. B., John Law and John Keynes, *Quarterly Journal of Economics,* LXII (1947–48) 381–95.

WRIGHT, D. McC., The future of Keynesian economics, *American Economic Review,* XXXV (1945) 284–307.

I-E. Price and Wage Flexibility

Includes articles on the effects of price and wage rigidity and on the results to be expected from general wage cuts in depression. Articles dealing primarily with the measurement of real and money wage movements are in general excluded from the bibliography.

BACKMAN, J., Price inflexibility and changes in production, *American Economic Review,* XXIX (1939) 480–86.

BRONFENBRENNER, M., The dilemma of liberal economics, *Journal of Political Economy,* LIV (1946) 334–46.

DEMARIA, G., Sull'attendibilità di una tesi del Keynes a proposito di variazioni dei salari monetari e reali, *Giornale degli Economisti,* I, new series (1939) 681–91.

DUNLOP, J. T., Trends in the "rigidity" of English wage rates, *Review of Economic Studies,* VI (1939) 189–99.

FRIEDMAN, M., Lange on price flexibility and employment: A methodological criticism, *American Economic Review,* XXXVI (1946) 613–31.

HIGGINS, B., The optimum wage rate, *Review of Economic Statistics,* XXXI (1949) 130–39.

HUMPHREY, D. D., The nature and meaning of rigid prices 1890–1933, *Journal of Political Economy,* XLV (1937) 651–61.

MASCI, G., Variazioni dei salari e dei prezzi, *Economia Politica Contemporanea: Saggi di Economia e Finanzi in Onore del Prof. Camillo Supino,* Padova, Cedam, I (1930) 361–88.

MORGENSTERN, O., Free and fixed prices during the depression, *Harvard Business Review*, X (1931–32) 62–8.

*PATINKIN, D., Price flexibility and full employment, *American Economic Review*, XXXVIII (1948) 543–64.

STEIN, H., Price flexibility and full employment: Comment, *American Economic Review*, XXXIX (1949) 725–26.

PATINKIN, D., Price flexibility and full employment: Reply, *ibid.*, 726–28.

*PIGOU, A. C., Economic progress in a stable environment, *Economica*, XIV, new series (1947) 180–88.

REDER, M. W., Problems of a national wage-price policy, *Canadian Journal of Economics and Political Science*, XIV (1948) 46–61.

SCHELLING, T. C., The dynamics of price flexibility, *American Economic Review*, XXXIX (1949) 911–22.

SHISTER, J., A note on cyclical wage rigidity, *American Economic Review*, XXXIV (1944) 111–16.

SWAN, T. W., Price flexibility and employment, *Economic Record*, XXI (1945) 236–53.

WILLIAMS, B. R., Mr. Swan's theory of price flexibility, *Economic Record*, XXII (1946) 275–82.

SWAN, T. W., Rejoinder, *ibid.*, 282–84.

TIMLIN, M. F., Price flexibility and employment, *Canadian Journal of Economics and Political Science*, XII (1946) 204–13.

TSIANG, J. C., Professor Pigou on the relative movements of real wages and employment, *Economic Journal*, LIV (1944) 352–65.

I-F. Cycle Theory and the Determination of the Level of Employment

Includes monetary analysis of the cycle, but excludes purely nonmonetary analyses and models unaccompanied by discussion of monetary factors. For further references see the bibliography in *Readings in Business Cycle Theory*.

GORDON, R. A., A selected bibliography of literature on economic fluctuations, 1930–36, *Review of Economic Statistics*, XIX (1937) 37–68.

———, A selected bibliography of the literature on economic fluctuations, 1936–37, *Review of Economic Statistics*, XX (1938) 120–27.

SNIDER, J. L., Recent publications on business cycles, *Harvard Business Review*, XIV (1935–36) 241–47.

AMOROSO, L., La dinamica della circolazione, *Rivista Italiana di Statistica Economica e Finanza*, VI (1934) 823–36.

ARTHUR, H. B., Inventory profits in the business cycle, *American Economic Review*, XXVIII (1938) 27–40.

BENNING, B., Expansion und kontraktion der geldmenge, *Weltwirtschaftliches Archiv*, LVIII (1943) 205–45.

BENNION, E. G., Is unemployment chronic?, *Harvard Business Review*, XXIII (1944–45) 115–28.

BERGSON, A., Prices, wages, and income theory, *Econometrica*, X (1942) 275–89.

* Reprinted in the present volume.

BERHNARD, R. C., Myths and illogic in popular notions about business cycles, *Journal of Political Economy*, LI (1943) 53–60.

BERNSTEIN, E. M., War and the pattern of business cycles, *American Economic Review*, XXX (1940) 524–35.

BEVERIDGE, SIR W., The trade cycle in Britain before 1850, *Oxford Economic Papers*, No. III (1940) 74–109; No. IV (1940) 63–76.

BISSELL, R. M., JR., The rate of interest, *American Economic Review*, XXVIII (1938 supplement) 23–40.

BROCKIE, M. D., Theories of the 1937–38 crisis and depression, *Economic Journal*, LX (1950) 292–310.

BROWN, E. H. P., and SHACKLE, G. L. S., British economic fluctuations, 1924–38, *Oxford Economic Papers*, II (1939) 98–134.

BROWN, H. G., Two decades of decadence in economic theorying, *American Journal of Economics and Sociology*, VII (1947–48) 145–72.

BROWN, J. A., The nineteen thirty-seven recession in England, *Harvard Business Review*, XVIII (Winter 1940) 248–60.

BUCHANAN, N. S., Anticipations and industrial investment decisions, *American Economic Review*, XXXII (1942 supplement) 141–55.

CABBIATI, A., Grundzüge einer theorie der reflation, IX (1939) 54–85.

CANNAN, E., Growth and fluctuations of bankers' liabilities to customers, *The Manchester School*, VI (1935) 2–17.

CLARK, J. M., Convulsion in the price structure, *Yale Review*, XXII (1932–33) 496–510.

———, An appraisal of the workability of compensatory devices, *American Economic Review*, XXIX (1939 supplement) 194–209.

COURTIN, R., La production et le pouvoir d'achat dans la cycle économique, *Revue d'Economie Politique*, XLIX (1935) 45–94.

DAMPIER-WHETHAM, W., Money, prices and unemployment, *Lloyds Bank Limited Monthly Review*, II, No. 17, new series (July 1931) 255–73.

DEWING, A. S., Investment and the industrial cycle, *Harvard Business Review*, II (1923–24) 1–12.

DOBRETSBERGER, J., Die monetären konjunkturerklärungen und die erfahrungen der letzten krise, *Jahrbücher für Nationalökonomie und Statistik*, CXLI (1935) 385–403.

EDIE, L. D., The banks and the stock market crisis of 1929, *University of Chicago Journal of Business*, III (Jan. 1930) 16–21.

EZEKIEL, M., Productivity, wage rates, and employment, *American Economic Review*, XXX (1940) 507–23.

FANNO, M., Cicli di produzione, cicli di credito e fluttuazioni industriali, *Giornale degli Economisti*, XLVI (1931) 329–70.

FELLNER, W., Zum problem der universalen überproduktion, *Archiv für Sozialwissenschaft und Sozialpolitik*, LXVI (1931) 522–56.

———, Der Kriseneffekt bei verringerter zusätzlicher kraufkraftschöpfung, *Zeitschrift für Nationalökonomie*, VIII (1937) 91–102.

———, Employment theory and business cycles, *A Survey of Contemporary Economics*, Philadelphia, The Blakiston Company, 1948, 49–98.

FELS, R., The long-wave depression, 1873–97, *Review of Economic Statistics*, XXXI (1949) 69–73.

FELS, R., Warburton vs. Hansen and Keynes, *American Economic Review,* XXXIX (1949) 923–29.

FETTER, F. A., Lauderdale's oversaving theory, *American Economic Review,* XXXV (1945) 263–83.

PAGLIN, M., Fetter on Lauderdale, *American Economic Review,* XXXVI (1946) 391–93.

FISHER, W. E., Union wage and hour policies and employment, *American Economic Review,* XXX (1940) 290–99.

FLEMING, J. M., The determination of the rate of interest, *Economica,* V, new series (1938) 333–41.

FLOOD, M. M., Recursive methods in business-cycle analysis, *Econometrica,* VIII (1940) 333–53.

FOÀ, B., Recenti teorie monetarie del ciclo, *Giornale degli Economisti,* XLVI (1931) 847–73.

FORSTMANN, A., Zur theorie der beschäftigung, *Schmoller's Jahrbuch für Gesetzgebung, Verwaltung und Volkswirtschaft,* LXIX (1949) 421–72, 543–77.

FRISCH, R., On the notion of equilibrium and disequilibrium, *Review of Economic Studies,* III (1935–36) 100–5.

DE GRAAF, A., Price disparity and business cycles, *Kyklos,* I (1947) 358–69.

HAAVELMO, T., The inadequacy of testing dynamic theory by comparing theoretical solutions and observed cycles, *Econometrica,* VIII (1940) 312–21.

HANSEN, A. H., and TOUT, H. A., Annual survey of business cycle theory: Investment and saving, *Econometrica,* I (1933) 119–47.

HARDY, C. O., An appraisal of the factors ("natural" and "artificial") which stopped short the recovery development in the United States, *American Economic Review,* XXIX (1939 supplement) 170–82.

HARROD, R. F., An essay in dynamic theory, *Economic Journal,* XLIX (1939) 14–33.

HART, A. G., Uncertainty and inducements to invest, *Review of Economic Studies,* VIII (1940).

HAYEK, F. A., The paradox of saving, *Economica,* XI (1931) 125–69.

———, Investment that raises the demand for capital, *Review of Economic Statistics,* XIX (1937) 174–77.

———, The Ricardo effect, *Econometrica,* IX, new series (1942) 127–52.

———, Le plein emploi, *Economique Appliquée,* I (1948) 197–210.

HAYES, S. P., JR., The business cycle: Psychological approaches, *Political Science Quarterly,* LXIII (1948) 82–98.

HICKS, J. R., Mr. Harrod's dynamic theory, *Economica,* XVI, new series (1949) 106–21.

HIGGINS, B., Towards a dynamic economics, *Economic Record,* XXIV (1948) 173–90.

HINSHAW, R., Note on rising costs and business-cycle crisis, *American Economic Review,* XXVIII (1938) 707–10.

HOLDEN, G. R., Mr. Keynes' consumption function and the time-preference postulate, *Quarterly Journal of Economics,* LII (1937–38) 281–96.

KEYNES, J. M., Reply, *ibid.,* 708–9.

HOLDEN, G. R., Rejoinder, *ibid.*, 709–12.

KEYNES, J. M., Note, *Quarterly Journal of Economics,* LIII (1938–39) 160.

HUBBARD, J. C., A model of the forty-month or trade cycle, *Journal of Political Economy,* L (1943) 197–225.

ISLES, K. S., Employment and equilibrium: A theoretical discussion, *Economic Record,* XIX (1943) 212–24.

JAMES, R. W., and BELZ, M. H., The influence of distributed lags on Kalecki's theory of the trade cycle, *Econometrica,* VI (1938) 159–62.

JEVONS, H. S., Banking and the price level, *The Manchester School,* II (1931) 10–17.

———, The causes of fluctuations of industrial activity and the price level, *Journal of the Royal Statistical Society,* XCVI (1933) 545–88.

SNOW, E. C., and others, Discussion on Mr. Jevons' paper, *ibid.*, 588–605.

JONES, B., The relation of economic forces and a corresponding credit theory, *Economic Forum,* I (1932–33) 449–59.

KÄHLER, A., Scarcity and abundance of capital as cause of crises, *Social Research,* IV (1937) 74–90.

KALDOR, N., Speculation and economic stability, *Review of Economic Studies,* VII (1939) 1–27.

———, Review of *Employment and Equilibrium* by A. C. Pigou, *Economic Journal,* LI (1941) 458–73.

PIGOU, A. C., Models of short-period equilibrium, *Economic Journal,* LII (1942) 250–57.

———, Professor Hayek and the concertina-effect, *Economica,* IX, new series (1942) 359–82.

KLEIN, L. R., Theories of effective demand and employment, *Journal of Political Economy,* LV (1947) 108–31.

———, Notes on the theory of investment, *Kyklos,* II (1948) 97–117.

KOOPMANS, T., The degree of damping in business cycles, *Econometrica,* VIII (1940) 79–89.

———, Distributed lags in dynamic economics, *Econometrica,* IX (1941) 128–34.

———, The logic of economic business-cycle research, *Journal of Political Economy,* XLIX (1941) 157–81.

KUZNETS, S., Schumpeter's *Business Cycles, American Economic Review,* XXX (1940) 257–71.

LACEY, K., Commodity stocks and the trade cycle, *Economica,* XI (1944) 12–18.

LACHMANN, L. M., Commodity stocks and equilibrium, *Review of Economic Studies,* III (1935–36) 230–34.

———, Investment and costs of production, *American Economic Review,* XXVIII (1938) 469–81.

———, and SNAPPER, F., Commodity stocks in the trade cycle, *Economica,* V, new series (1938) 435–54.

LANDE, L., Kapital und kredit in konjunkturzyklus, *Archiv für Sozialwissenschaft und Sozialpolitik,* LXVIII (1933) 420–49.

LANGE, O., Say's law: A restatement and criticism, *Studies in Mathematical Economics and Econometrics,* Chicago, The University of Chicago Press, 1942. 49–68.

LESTER, R. A., The gold-parity depression in Norway and Denmark, 1925–28, *Journal of Political Economy*, XLV (1937) 433–65.

CHRISTENSON, C. L., A criticism, *ibid.*, 808–10.

LESTER, R. A., A rejoinder, *ibid.*, 810–13.

CHRISTENSON, C. L., A reply, *ibid.*, 813–15.

LITTLER, H. G., A pure theory of money, *Canadian Journal of Economics and Political Science*, X (1944) 422–47.

MAKOWER, H., The elasticity of demand and stabilization, *Review of Economic Studies*, VI (1939) 25–32.

MARRAMA, V., Short notes on a model of the trade cycle, *Review of Economic Studies*, XIV (1946–47) 34–40.

MARSCHAK, J., A cross section of business cycle discussion, *American Economic Review*, XXXV (1945) 368–81.

METZLER, L. A. The nature and stability of inventory cycles, *Review of Economic Statistics*, XXIII (1941) 113–29.

———, Business cycles and the modern theory of employment, *American Economic Review*, XXXVI (1946) 278–91.

MURAD, A., The Reichsbank in the financial crisis of 1931, *University of Chicago Journal of Business*, V (April 1932) 175–91.

NEISSER, H., The new economics of spending: A theoretical analysis, *Econometrica*, XII (1944) 237–55.

NÖLL VON DER NAHMER, R., Die Fehlinvestition und ihre volkswirtschaftlichen Probleme, *Zeitschrift für die Gesamten Staatswissenschaften*, XCVIII (1938) 436–55.

OHLIN, BERTIL, Alternative theories of the rate of interest, *Economic Journal*, XLVII (1937) 423–27.

PAISH, G., Credit, *Lloyds Bank Limited Monthly Review*, I, No. 10, new series (December 1930) 339–46.

PAPI, G. U., Studi sulla teoria monetaria dei cicli industriali: Rapporti fra interesse e sconto, *Giornale degli Economisti*, XLV (1930) 205–42.

PATINKIN, D., Involuntary unemployment and the Keynesian supply function, *Economic Journal*, LIX (1949) 360–83.

PIGOU, A. C., The classical stationary state, *Economic Journal*, LIII (1943) 343–51.

POLAK, J. J., Fluctuations in United States consumption, 1919–1932, *Review of Economic Statistics*, XXI (1939) 1–12, 88.

POLANYI, M., The "settling down" of capital and the trade cycle, *The Manchester School*, IX (1938) 153–69.

RADICE, E. A., A dynamic scheme for the British trade cycle, 1929–1937, *Econometrica*, VII (1939) 47–56.

ROBERTSON, D. H., The trade cycle—an academic view, *Lloyds Bank Limited Monthly Review*, VIII, No. 91, new series (September 1937) 502–11. Reprinted in *Essays in Monetary Theory*, London, King, 1940, 122–32.

ROBINSON, J., La théorie générale de l'emploi, *Economique Appliquée*, I (1948) 185–96.

———, Mr. Harrod's dynamics, *Economic Journal*, LIX (1949) 68–85.

Roos, C. F., and Von Szeliski, V. S., The demand for durable goods, *Econometrica,* XI (1943) 97–122.

Roose, K., The recession of 1937–38, *Journal of Political Economy,* LVI (1948) 239–48.

Salter, A., A year and a half of crisis, *Yale Review,* XXII (1932–33) 217–33.

Samuelson, P. A., The stability of equilibrium: Comparative statics and dynamics, *Econometrica,* IX (1941) 97–120.

———, Professor Pigou's employment and equilibrium, *American Economic Review,* XXXI (1941) 545–52.

———, The stability of equilibrium: Linear and non-linear systems, *Econometrica,* X (1942) 1–25.

Schumpeter, J. A., The explanation of the business cycle, *Economica,* VII (1927) 286–311.

———, Mitchell's *Business Cycles, Quarterly Journal of Economics,* XLV (1930–31) 150–72.

———, A theorist's comment on the current business cycle, *Journal of the American Statistical Association,* XXX (1935 supplement) 167–68.

Shackle, G. L. S., Expectations and employment, *Economic Journal,* XLIX (1939) 442–52.

———, The nature of the inducement to invest, *Review of Economic Studies,* VIII (1940) 44–8.

———, A means of promoting investment, *Economic Journal,* LI (1941) 249–60.

Simpson, P. B., Neoclassical economics and monetary problems, *American Economic Review,* XXXIX (1949) 861–82.

Singer, H. W., Price dispersion in periods of change, *Economic Journal,* XLVIII (1938) 658–73.

Slichter, S. H., The conditions of expansion, *American Economic Review,* XXXII (1942) 1–21.

Slutzky, E., The summation of random causes as the source of cyclic processes, *Econometrica,* V (1937) 105–46.

Smithies, A., Process analysis and equilibrium analysis, *Econometrica,* X (1942) 26–38.

———, The stability of competitive equilibrium, *Econometrica,* X (1942) 258–74.

Snider, J. L., Business cycle literature, *Harvard Business Review,* XVII (Spring 1939) 369–79.

Snow, E. C., and others, Is the trade cycle a myth? *Journal of the Royal Statistical Society,* CI (1938) 565–91.

Snyder, C., The influence of the rate of interest on the business cycle, *American Economic Review,* XV (1925) 684–99.

———, Overproduction and business cycles, *Academy of Political Science, Proceedings,* XIV (1930–32) 333–59.

Spengler, J. J., The physiocrats and Say's law of markets, *Journal of Political Economy,* LIII (1945) 193–211, 317–47.

Sprague, O. M. W., Bank management and the business cycle, *Harvard Business Review,* I (1922–23) 19–23.

Stafford, J., An aspect of the problem of unemployment, *The Manchester School,* V (1934) 54–69.

STAFFORD, J., A view of depression, *The Manchester School*, V (1934) 135–43.

——, The trade cycle, *The Manchester School*, VIII (1937) 69–84.

TANAKA, K., On Professor Hayek's theory of trade cycle, *Journal of the Kobe University of Commerce*, I (1939) No. 2, 1–30.

THORP, W. L., Postwar depressions, *American Economic Review*, XXXI (1941 supplement) 352–61.

TINBERGEN, J., Econometric business cycle research, *Review of Economic Studies*, VII (1940) 73–90.

——, Critical remarks on some business-cycle theories, *Econometrica*, X (1942) 129–46.

TINTNER, G., A "simple" theory of business fluctuations, *Econometrica*, X (1942) 317–20.

TIRANA, R., Behavior of bank deposits abroad, *American Economic Review*, XXX (1940 supplement) 92–105.

TUCKER, R. S., Estimates of savings of American families, *Review of Economic Statistics*, XXIV (1942) 9–21.

DE VEGH, I., Savings, investment, and consumption, *American Economic Review*, XXXI (1941 supplement) 237–47.

VITO, F., Il risparmio forzato e la teoria dei cicli economici, *Rivista Internazionale de Scienze Sociali*, XLII (1934) 3–46.

WAGNER, V., Die Zyklische Bewegung der Vorräte und die monetäre Wechsellagen-lehre, *Schmoller's Jahrbuch für Gesetzgebung, Verwaltung und Volkswirt-schaft*, LX (1936) 437–50.

WALKER, E. R., Structural changes and cyclical variations, *Economic Record*, XI (1935 supplement) 149–62.

*WARBURTON, C., The misplaced emphasis in contemporary business fluctuation theory, *Journal of Business of the University of Chicago*, XIX (1946) 199–220.

WILLIAMS, B. R., Types of competition and the theory of employment, *Oxford Economic Papers*, I, new series (1949) 121–44.

WILSON, T., A reconsideration of the theory of effective demand, *Economica*, XIV, new series (1947) 283–95.

WOLMAN, L., Wage rates, *American Economic Review*, XXVIII (1938 supplement) 126–31.

WRIGHT, D., Internal inconsistency in D. H. Robertson's "saving and hoarding" concepts, *Economic Journal*, LI (1941) 334–37.

ROBERTSON, D. H., Reply, *ibid.*, 337–38.

I-G. Multiplier and Acceleration Principles

Includes theoretical analyses but excludes the statistical determination of the consumption function.

ALEXANDER, S., The accelerator as a generator of steady growth, *Quarterly Journal of Economics*, LXIII (1949) 174–97.

* Reprinted in the present volume.

ANDERSON, C. J., The basic similarity of the monetary and investment theories of secondary employment, *American Journal of Economics and Sociology,* IV (1944–45) 203–11.

BARBER, C. L., The instantaneous theory of the multiplier, *Canadian Journal of Economics and Political Science,* XVI (1950) 78–82.

SOMERS, H. M., A comment, *ibid.,* 239–40.

BAUMOL, W. J., Notes on some dynamic models, *Economic Journal,* LVIII (1948) 506–21.

BENNSON, E. G., The multiplier, the acceleration principle, and fluctuating autonomous investment, *Review of Economic Statistics,* XXVII (1945) 85–92.

BODE, K., A note on the mathematical coincidence of the instantaneous and the serial multiplier, *Review of Economic Statistics,* XXVI (1944) 221–22.

BRESCIANI-TURRONI, C., The "multiplier" in practice: Some results of recent German experience, *Review of Economic Statistics,* XX (1938) 76–88.

————, Osservazioni sulla teoria del moltiplicatore, *Rivista Bancaria,* XX (1939) 693–714.

CHIPMAN, J. S., The generalized bi-system multiplier, *Canadian Journal of Economics and Political Science,* XV (1949) 176–89.

DYASON, J., A note on the multiplier in Australia, *Economic Record,* XV (1939) 114–18.

HORNER, F. B., The multiplier in Australia: A further comment, *ibid.,* 211–22.

GEHRELS, F., Inflationary effects of a balanced budget under full employment, *American Economic Review,* XXXIX (1949) 1276–78.

GIRARDEAU, E., Note sur la théorie du multiplicateur des effets d'investissement, *Revue d'Economique Politique,* LV (1945) 50–70.

GOODWIN, R. M., The multiplier as matrix, *Economic Journal,* LIX (1949) 537–55.

HAAVELMO, T., Multiplier effects of a balanced budget, *Econometrica,* XIII (1945) 311–18.

HABERLER, G., Multiplier effects of a balanced budget: Some monetary implications of Mr. Haavelmo's paper, *Econometrica,* XIV (1946) 148–49.

GOODWIN, R. M., The implications of a lag for Mr. Haavelmo's analysis, *ibid.,* 150–51.

HAGEN, E. E., Further analysis, *ibid.,* 152–55.

HAAVELMO, T., Reply, *ibid.,* 156–58.

LANGE, O., The theory of the multiplier, *Econometrica,* XI (1943) 227–45.

MANNE, A. S., Some notes on the acceleration principle, *Review of Economic Statistics,* XXVII (1945) 93–9.

MEADE, J. E., National income, national expenditure and the balance of payments, *Economic Journal,* LVIII (1948) 483–505; LIX (1949) 17–39.

MOSAK, J. L., Interrelations of production, price, and derived demand, *Journal of Political Economy,* XLVI (1938) 761–87.

NEISSER, H., The significance of foreign trade for domestic employment, *Social Research,* XIII (1946) 307–25.

SALANT, W. S., A note on the effects of a changing deficit, *Quarterly Journal of Economics,* LIII (1938–39) 298–304.

SAMUELSON, PAUL, Fiscal policy and income determination, *Quarterly Journal of Economics,* LVI (1941–42) 575–605.

SHACKLE, G. L. S., The deflative or inflative tendency of government receipts and disbursements, *Oxford Economic Papers*, No. VIII (November 1947) 46–64.

SMITHIES, A., The multiplier, *American Economic Review*, XXXVIII (1948 supplement) 299–305.

GARVY, G., and COHN, S. M., The multiplier: Discussion, *ibid.*, 306–10.

SOMERS, H. M., The impact of fiscal policy on national income, *Canadian Journal of Economics and Political Science*, VIII (1942) 364–85.

———, The multiplier in a tri-fiscal economy, *Quarterly Journal of Economics*, LXIII (1949) 258–72.

TEW, B., A note on the multiplier, *Economic Record*, XXIV (1948) 109–11.

ARNDT, H. W., Public finance and the national income, *ibid.*, 243–45.

TURVEY, R., The multiplier, *Economica*, XV, new series (1948) 259–69.

ULLMO, J., Une extension de la théorie du multiplicateur, *Economique Appliquée*, II (1949) 228–46.

WALLICH, H. C., Income-generating effects of a balanced budget, *Quarterly Journal of Economics*, LIX (1944–45) 78–91.

II. INTERNATIONAL MONETARY RELATIONSHIPS

The following articles form a supplement to the bibliography in *Readings in the Theory of International Trade*. Only articles appearing too late for inclusion in that bibliography are listed here.

ARMSTRONG, W. C., The Soviet approach to international trade, *Political Science Quarterly*, LXIII (1948) 368–82.

ARNDT, H. W., The International Monetary Fund and the treatment of cyclical balance of payments disequilibria, *Economic Record*, XXIII (1947) 186–97.

———, The concept of liquidity in international monetary theory, *Review of Economic Studies*, XV (1947–48) 20–6.

BALOGH, T., Exchange depreciation and economic readjustment, *Review of Economic Statistics*, XXX (1948) 276–85.

———, The concept of a dollar shortage, *The Manchester School*, XVII (1949) 186–201.

BEAN, R. W., European multilateral clearing, *Journal of Political Economy*, LVI (1948) 403–15.

BEHRMAN, J. N., A reappraisal of the United Kingdom's balance of payments problem under full employment, *Southern Economic Journal*, XIV (1947–48) 173–85.

BERLE, A. A., The Marshall plan in the European struggle, *Social Research*, XV (1948) 1–21.

BLOOMFIELD, A. I., Induced investment, overcomplete international adjustment, and chronic dollar shortage, *American Economic Review*, XXXIX (1949) 970–74.

KINDLEBERGER, C. P., Rejoinder, *ibid.*, 975.

BRESCIANI-TURRONI, C., Ancora i "cambi indiretti," *Rivista Bancaria*, IV, new series (1948) 307–15. (In English: *Review of the Economic Conditions of Italy* (1949) 385–94.)

————, Il problema dei "cambi indiretti" (cross rates), *Rivista bancaria,* IV, new series (1948) 190–97. (In English: *Review of the Economic Conditions of Italy* (1948) 147–59.)

CLARK, C., The value of the pound, *Economic Journal,* LIX (1949) 198–207.

CONAN, A. R., Changes in the dollar pool, *Canadian Journal of Economics and Political Science,* XVI (1950) 69–78.

DOMERATZKY, L., Outlook for international trade, *Yale Review,* XXXVII (1947–48) 668–85.

DUNCAN, A. J., South African capital imports, 1893–8, *Canadian Journal of Economics and Political Science,* XIV (1948) 20–45.

ELLIS, H. S., The dollar shortage in theory and fact, *Canadian Journal of Economics and Political Science,* XIV (1948) 358–72.

FEDERICI, L., Das problem des internationalen monetären gleichgewichts und die "Regel" von Cassel, *Kyklos,* I (1947) 230–41.

FIELD, H., A note on exchange stability, *Review of Economic Studies,* XV (1947–48) 46–9.

FREUND, R., Methods of financing the European Recovery Program, *Southern Economic Journal,* XV (1948–49) 267–78.

FRISCH, R., Outline of a system of multicompensatory trade, *Review of Economic Statistics,* XXX (1948) 265–71.

HINSHAW, R., Professor Frisch on discrimination and multilateral trade, *ibid.,* 271–75.

————, On the need for forecasting a multilateral balance of payments, *American Economic Review,* XXXVII (1947) 535–51.

POLAK, J. J., Balancing international trade—a comment on Professor Frisch's Paper, *American Economic Review,* XXXVIII (1948) 139–42.

MEIER, G. M., A further comment on Professor Frisch's Paper, *ibid.,* 624–26.

GINI, C., Scambi bilaterali e scambi plurilaterali, *Moneta e Credito-Rivista della Banca Nazionale del Lavoro* (1948) 454–63. (In English: *Banca Nazionale del Lavoro Quarterly Review* (1949) 3–11.)

GORDON, L., European Recovery Program in operation, *Harvard Business Review,* XXVII (1949) 129–50.

GOTTLIEB, M., The reparations problem again, *Canadian Journal of Economics and Political Science,* XVI (1950) 22–41.

GRAHAM, F. D., The cause and cure of "dollar shortage," *Essays in International Finance,* No. 10, Princeton, New Jersey, Princeton University Press, 1943.

GREGORY, T., The problems of the under-developed world, *Lloyds Bank Review,* X, new series (October 1948) 39–56.

GUTT, C., Exchange rates and the International Monetary Fund, *Review of Economic Statistics,* XXX (1948) 81–90.

HABERLER, G., The market for foreign exchange and the stability of the balance of payments: A theoretical analysis, *Kyklos,* III (1949) 193–218.

HARBERGER, A. C., Currency depreciation, income, and the balance of trade, *Journal of Political Economy,* LVIII (1950) 47–60.

HARRIS, S. E., Devaluation of the pound sterling, *Harvard Business Review,* XXVII (1949) 781–90.

HAWTREY, R. G., Multiplier analysis and the balance of payments, *Economic Journal*, LX (1950) 1–8.

HENDERSON, A., The restriction of foreign trade, *The Manchester School*, XVII (1949) 12–35.

HENDERSON, SIR H., The function of exchange rates, *Oxford Economic Series*, I, new series (1949) 1–17.

———, The moral of the British crisis, *Review of Economic Statistics*, XXXI (1949) 256–60.

HIRSCHMAN, A. O., Disinflation, discrimination, and the dollar shortage, *American Economic Review*, XXXVIII (1948) 886–92.

———, Devaluation and the trade balance: A note, *Review of Economic Statistics*, XXXI (1949) 50–3.

———, International aspects of a recession, *American Economic Review*, XXXIX (1949) 1245–53.

HOFFMAN, M. L., Capital movements and international payments in postwar Europe, *Review of Economic Statistics*, XXXI (1949) 261–65.

JOHNSON, H. G., The case for increasing the price of gold in terms of all currencies: A contrary view, *Canadian Journal of Economics and Political Science*, XVI (1950) 199–209.

KAHN, R. F., A possible intra-European payments scheme, *Economica*, XVI, new series (1949) 293–304.

KINDLEBERGER, C. P., The foreign-trade multiplier, the propensity to import and balance of payments equilibrium, *American Economic Review*, XXXIX (1949) 491–94.

KLEIN, L. R., A scheme of international compensation, *Econometrica*, XVII (1949) 145–49.

EKKER, M. H., A scheme of international compensation: Postscript, *ibid.*, 150–53.

KREPS, T. J., Toward a world economy, *Annals of the American Academy of Political and Social Science*, CCLVII (1948) 157–74.

KURIHARA, K. K., Toward a new theory of monetary sovereignty, *Journal of Political Economy*, LVII (1949) 162–70.

LENSCHOW, G., Long term economic significance of currency and trade restrictions, *Canadian Journal of Economics and Political Science*, XVI (1950) 63–9.

LEWIS, W. A., The prospect before us, *The Manchester School*, XVI (1948) 129–64.

LÖSCH, A., Theorie der Währung, *Weltwirtschaftliches Archiv*, LXII (1949) 35–88.

McCURRACH, D. F., Britain's U.S. dollar problems 1939–45, *Economic Journal*, LVIII (1948) 356–72.

MACDOUGALL, G. D. A., Britain's foreign trade problem, *Economic Journal*, LVII (1947) 69–113.

BALOGH, T., Britain's foreign trade problem: A comment, *Economic Journal*, LVIII (1948) 74–85.

MACDOUGALL, G. D. A., Britain's foreign trade problem: A reply, *ibid.*, 86–98.

MACHLUP, F., Three concepts of the balance of payments and the so-called dollar shortage, *Economic Journal*, LX (1950) 46–68.

MACKINTOSH, W. A., Canada and the world economy in the making, *Lloyds Bank Review*, XII, new series (April 1949) 12–29.

MEADE, J. E., Bretton Woods, Havana and the United Kingdom balance of payments, *Lloyds Bank Review*, VII, new series (January 1948) 1–18.

———, Planning without prices, *Economica*, XV, new series (1948) 28–35.

———, Financial policy and the balance of payments, *Economica*, XV, new series (1948) 101–15.

———, A geometrical representation of balance of payments policy, *Economica*, XVI, new series (1949) 305–20.

MENDERSHAUSEN, H., Future foreign financing, *Review of Economic Statistics*, XXXI (1949) 266–79.

METZLER, L. A.; TRIFFIN, R.; and HABERLER, G., International monetary policies, *Postwar Economic Studies*, No. 7, Washington, D.C., Board of Governors of the Federal Reserve System, 1947.

———, The theory of international trade, *A Survey of Contemporary Economics*, Philadelphia, The Blakiston Company, 1948, 210–54.

MIKESELL, R. F., Regional multilateral payments arrangements, *Quarterly Journal of Economics*, LXII (1947–48) 500–18.

———, International disequilibrium and the postwar world, *American Economic Review*, XXXIX (1949) 618–45.

———, The international monetary fund, *Journal of Political Economy*, LVII (1949) 395–412.

———, The role of the international monetary agreements in a world of planned economies, *Journal of Political Economy*, LV (1947) 497–512.

SALERA, V., Mikesell on international monetary agreements and planned economics, *Journal of Political Economy*, LVI (1948) 442–46.

MIKESELL, R. F., A reply, *ibid.*, 446–50.

MORGAN, D. J., The British Commonwealth and European economic cooperation, *Economic Journal*, LIX (1949) 307–25.

PÂQUET, R., The economic recovery of Belgium, *The Manchester School*, XVII (1949) 202–07.

PESMAZOGLU, J. S., Some international aspects of British cyclical fluctuations, 1870–1913, *Review of Economic Studies*, XVI (1949–50) 117–43.

POLK, J., and PATTERSON, G., The emerging pattern of bilateralism, *Quarterly Journal of Economics*, LXII (1947–48) 118–42.

RAPPARD, W. E., The economic position of Switzerland, *Lloyds Bank Review*, XI, new series (January 1949) 21–36.

REEVES, W. H., and DICKENS, P. D., Private foreign investments: A means of world economic development, *Political Science Quarterly*, LXIV (1949) 211–44.

RIPPY, J. F., Investments of citizens of the United States in Latin America, *Journal of Business of the University of Chicago*, XXII (1949) 17–29.

ROBBINS, L., Inquest on the crisis, *Lloyds Bank Review*, VI, new series (October 1947) 1–27.

ROBERTSON, D. H., Britain and European recovery, *Lloyds Bank Review*, XIII, new series (July 1949) 1–13.

SADIE, J. L., Further observations on foreign exchange rates, *South African Journal of Economics,* XVI (1948) 194–201.

WIJNHOLDS, H. W. J., Further observations on foreign exchange rates, *ibid.,* 309.

SAVOSNICK, K. M., National income, exchange rates and the balance of trade, *Economica,* XVII, new series (1950) 188–95.

SCHÜLLER, R., A free-trade area, *Social Research,* XVI (1949) 151–57.

SENSINI, G., Considerazioni intorno alla produzione dell'oro, *Rivista Bancaria,* V, new series (1949) 506–16.

SHANNON, H. A., The British payments and exchange control system, *Quarterly Journal of Economics,* LXIII (1949) 212–37.

SMITH, A. H., Evolution of the exchange control, *Economica,* XVI, new series (1949) 243–48.

SMITH, H. R., The future of the international economy, *Harvard Business Review,* XXVIII (1950) 110–20.

SMITHIES, A., Multilateral trade and employment, *American Economic Review,* XXXVII (1947 supplement) 560–68.

NURKSE, R., International monetary policy and the search for economic stability, *ibid.,* 569–80.

BLOOMFIELD, A. I.; ELLIS, H. S.; LERNER, A. P.; MIKESELL, R.; and WOOD, E., Domestic versus international economic equilibrium: Discussion, *ibid.,* 581–94.

————, European unification and the dollar problem, *Quarterly Journal of Economics,* LXIV (1950) 159–82.

HABERLER, G., A comment, *ibid.,* 306–10.

VON STACKELBERG, H., Die theorie des wechselkurses bei vollständiger konkurrenz, *Jahrbücher für Nationalökonomie und Statistik,* LXI (1949) 1–65.

STOLPER, W. F., Purchasing power parity and the pound sterling from 1919–1925, *Kyklos,* II (1948) 240–69.

————, American foreign economic policy, the dollar shortage, and Mr. Balogh, *Kyklos,* III (1949) 160–72.

————, Notes on the dollar shortage, *American Economic Review,* XL (1950) 285–300.

TEW, B., Sterling as an international currency, *Economic Record,* XXIV (1948) 42–55.

TINBERGEN, J., Observations sur le problème de la rareté de dollar, *Revue d' Economie Politique,* LVIII (1948) 36–56.

VINER, J., An American view of the British economic crisis, *Lloyds Bank Review,* VI, new series (Oct. 1947) 28–38.

VITO, F., Die wiederherstellung einer internationalen Währungsordnung, *Zeitschrift für Nationalökonomie,* XII (1949) 59–73.

WHITE, H. D., The International Monetary Fund: The first year, *Annals of the American Academy of Political and Social Science,* CCLII (1947) 21–9.

WILLIAMS, J. H., The world's monetary dilemma—internal versus external monetary stability, *Academy of Political Science, Proceedings,* XVI (1934) 62–8.

WOOD, E., Financial aspects of current international problems, *American Journal of Economics and Sociology,* IX (1950) 273–81.

III. Monetary and Fiscal Policy

III-A. Monetary-fiscal Policy in General

Includes the discussion of central banking, its relationship to fiscal operations, and articles on price level stabilization. For the concept of neutral money see also I-B.

ABBOTT, C. C., Administration of fiscal policy, *Harvard Business Review*, XXIII (Autumn 1944) 46–64.

ABBOTT, D. C., Prices and credit, *Academy of Political Science, Proceedings*, XXIII (1948) 82–94.

AMONN, A., Zur gegenwärtigen Krisenlage und inflationistischer Krisenbekämp-fungspolitik, *Zeitschrift für Nationalökonomie*, V (1934) 1–17.

ANDERSON, B. M., The fallacy of price stabilization, *Lloyds Bank Limited, Monthly Review*, I, No. 3, new series (May 1930) 67–78.

ANDERSON, B. M., JR., Currency stabilization—national and international, *Lloyds Bank Limited, Monthly Review*, VI, No. 63, new series (May 1935) 282–93.

ANDERSON, S. W., The federal reserve bank in its relation to inflation and deflation, *Harvard Business Review*, II (1923–24) 201–6.

BACH, G. L., The federal reserve and monetary policy formation, *American Economic Review*, XXXIX (1949) 1173–91.

———, Economic requisites for economic stability, *American Economic Review*, XL (1950 Supplement) 155–64.

BELL, J. W., Domestic and international monetary policies, *American Economic Review*, XXXVI (1946 supplement) 214–40.

BIDDULPH, G., The Bank of England's monetary policy, *Economic Forum*, II (1934–35) 313–26.

BOARD OF GOVERNORS, THE FEDERAL RESERVE SYSTEM, Proposals to maintain prices at fixed levels through monetary action, *Federal Reserve Bulletin*, XXV (1939) 255–59. See also *Federal Reserve Bulletin*, XXIII (1937) 827–28.

BOGGERI, M. L. and SUNDELSON, J. W., Italian theories of fiscal science, *Political Science Quarterly*, LIII (1938) 249–67.

BOPP, K. R., The government and the Bank of France, *Public Policy*, II (1941) 3–35.

———, Central banking at the crossroads, *American Economic Review*, XXXIV (1944 supplement) 260–77.

———, The Bank of England, *The Canadian Journal of Economics and Political Science*, XI (1945) 616–27.

BRAND, R. H., Stabilization, *Lloyds Bank Limited, Monthly Review*, VI, No. 70, new series (December 1935) 642–59.

BRATT, E. C., Business-cycle forecasting, *University of Chicago Journal of Business*, XXI (1948) 1–11.

———, Data needed to forecast the business cycle, *University of Chicago Journal of Business*, XXI (1948) 168–79.

BRONFENBRENNER, M., Sales taxation and the Mints plan, *Review of Economic Statistics*, XXIX (1947) 39–42.

BROWN, H. G., The danger in the mounting national debt, *American Journal of Economics and Sociology*, III (1943–44) 1–14.

BULLOCK, C. J.; SPRAGUE, O. M. W.; and DUNHAM, W. B., Federal Reserve Bank policy—the need of a definite statement, *Harvard Business Review*, I (1922–23) 132–38.

CARPENTER, C. C., The English specie resumption of 1821, *Southern Economic Journal*, V (1938–39) 45–54.

CARSON, W. J., Structure and powers of the Federal Reserve System in evolution, *Annals of the American Academy of Political and Social Science*, CLXXI (1934) 83–93.

COLM, G., On the road to economic stabilization, *Social Research*, XV (1948) 265–76.

COOMBS, H. C., General theory and Swedish economic practice, *Economic Record*, XV (1939 supplement) 135–51.

COPELAND, D. B., The commonwealth bank—cooperation or compulsion, *Economic Record*, XV (1939 supplement) 21–39.

CRICK, W. F., The role of statistics in monetary affairs, *The Manchester School*, IX (1938) 123–39.

CRUMP, N., The interrelation and distribution of prices and their incidence upon price stabilization, *Journal of the Royal Statistical Society*, LXXXVII (1924) 167–206.

EDGEWORTH, F. Y., and others, Discussion on Mr. Crump's paper, *ibid.*, 207–19.

DAY, J. P., The Reserve Bank of South Africa, *Canadian Journal of Economics and Political Science*, I (1935) 151–60.

DECHESNE, L., La stabilisation monetaire: Est-elle souhaitable? Est-elle possible?, *Revue d'Economie Politique*, LI (1937) 1–27.

DOUGHERTY, M. R., The currency-banking controversy, *Southern Economic Journal*, IX (1942–43) 140–55, 241–51.

EBERSOLE, J. F., Money management powers of the Treasury and Federal Reserve Banks, *Harvard Business Review*, XV (1936–37) 1–9.

EDIE, L. D., The Federal Reserve and the price level, *Annals of the American Academy of Political and Social Science*, CLXXI (1934) 104–6.

EGGLESTON, F. W., The political problems of a managed currency, *Economic Record*, XV (1939 supplement) 3–20.

FETTER, F. W., The Bullion Report reexamined, *Quarterly Journal of Economics*, LVI (1941–42) 655–65.

FISHER, I., Reflation and stabilization, *Annals of the American Academy of Political and Social Science*, CLXXI (1934) 127–31.

THOMAS, E., Money and its management, *ibid.*, 132–37.

WARBURG, J. P., Reply to Senator Elmer Thomas and Professor Irving Fisher, *ibid.*, 144–50.

FISHER, I., Discussion, *ibid.*, 150–51.

FOSTER, W. T., and CATCHINGS, W., Business conditions and currency control, *Harvard Business Review*, II (1923–24) 268–81.

*FRIEDMAN, M., A monetary and fiscal framework for economic stability, *American Economic Review*, XXXVIII (1948) 245–64.

NEFF, P., Professor Friedman's proposal: Comment, *American Economic Review*, XXXIX (1949) 946–49.

FRIEDMAN, M., Rejoinder, *ibid.*, 949–55.

NEFF, P., Final comment, *ibid.*, 955–56.

GIDEONSE, H. D., A planned currency system, *Report of the Commission of Inquiry into National Policy in International Economic Relations* (Robert M. Hutchins, Chairman), (1934) 196–209.

GOLDENWEISER, E. A., Significance of the lending function of the Federal Reserve Banks, *Journal of the American Statistical Association*, XXXI (1936) 95–102.

———, Federal Reserve objectives and policies: Retrospect and prospect, *American Economic Review*, XXXVII (1947) 320–38.

GORDON, R. A., Fiscal policy as a factor in stability, *Annals of the American Academy of Political and Social Science*, CCVI (1939) 106–13.

GRAGNANI, C., Sulla "moneta neutrale" di F. v. Hayek, *Rivista di Politica Economica*, XXIV (1934) 1131–43.

GRAHAM, F. D., Primary functions of money and their consummation in monetary policy, *American Economic Review*, XXX (1940 supplement) 1–16.

GREVEN, J., Die währungsausgleichsfonds im system der währungs- und kreditpolitik, *Finanzarchiv*, NF 6 (1938) 23–60.

HAMMOND, B., The Chestnut Street raid on Wall Street, 1839, *Quarterly Journal of Economics*, LXI (1946–47) 605–18.

HANCOCK, G. D., The present status of monetary and credit control, *Southern Economic Journal*, V (1938–39) 471–84.

HARDING, W. P. G., The Federal Reserve System in the light of changing banking conditions, *Harvard Business Review*, VIII (1929–30) 147–51.

HARDY, C. O., Liberalism in the modern state: The philosophy of Henry Simons, *Journal of Political Economy*, LVI (1948) 305–14.

*———, Fiscal operations as instruments of economic stabilization, *American Economic Review*, XXXVIII (1948) 395–403.

HENDERSON, H. D., The monetary problem, *Lloyds Bank Limited, Monthly Review*, VII, No. 82, new series (December 1936) 595–602.

———, The trade cycle and the budget outlook, *Lloyds Bank Limited, Monthly Review*, VIII, No. 88, new series (June 1937) 290–98.

HICKS, J. R., Mr. Hawtrey on bank rate and the long-term rate of interest, *The Manchester School*, X (1939) 21–37.

HAWTREY, R. G., Interest and bank rate, *ibid.*, 144–52.

HICKS, J. R., A reply, *ibid.*, 152–55.

HAWTREY, R. G., A rejoinder, *ibid.*, 155–56.

HORSEFIELD, J. K., The opinions of Horsley Palmer, Governor of the Bank of England, 1830–33, *Economica*, XVI, new series (1949) 143–58.

HUBBARD, J. B., Recent developments in Federal Reserve policy, *Harvard Business Review*, V (1926–27) 47–54.

HYTTEN, T. F., The limits of monetary policy, *Economic Record*, XV (1939 supplement) 76–93.

* Reprinted in the present volume.

JOHNSON, G. G., The significance of the government trust funds for monetary policy, *Public Policy*, I (1940) 212–46.

JONES, J. H., Exchange stability vs. internal price stability, *Journal of the Royal Statistical Society*, XCVII (1934) 277–99.

HAWTREY, R. G., and others, Discussion on Mr. Jones's paper, *ibid.*, 299–312.

EISLER, R., A note on Professor J. H. Jones's paper, *ibid.*, 478–83.

DE JONGH, T. W., Monetary and banking factors and the business cycle in the Union, *South African Journal of Economics*, IX (1941) 138–49.

KLEMME, E. H., Industrial loan operations of the Reconstruction Finance Corporation and the Federal Reserve Banks, *University of Chicago Journal of Business*, XII (October 1939) 365–85.

KOENIG, J., Nichtinflatorische Papiergeldausgabe? *Schmoller's Jahrbuch für Gesetzgebung, Verwaltung und Volkswirtschaft*, LIX (1935) 317–27.

KRIZ, M. A., Central banks and the state today, *American Economic Review*, XXXVIII (1948) 565–80.

KUNG, E., Staatswirtschaftliche konjunkturpolitik während des aufschwungs, *Weltwirtschaftliches Archiv*, LIV (1941) 80–119.

LEDERER, E., Das kreditproblem in der weltwirtschaftskrise, *Archiv für Sozialwissenschaft und Sozialpolitik*, LXVI (1931) 247–83.

LELAND, S. E., Our national debt, *Harvard Business Review*, XVI (Spring 1938) 257–72.

LUKAS, E., "Geldschleier" und zinspolitik, *Jahrbücher für Nationalökonomie und Statistik*, CLIII (1941) 415–30.

LUTZ, F. A., The interest rate and investment in a dynamic economy, *American Economic Review*, XXXV (1945) 811–30.

MCQUEEN, R., Central banking in the Dominions, *Canadian Journal of Economics and Political Science*, VI (1940) 599–610.

MAHR, A., Monetary stability, *Public Policy Pamphlet*, No. 9, 1933.

MAZZUCCHELLI, M., Economia "regolata" e controllo bancario, *Rivista Bancaria*, XII (1931) 862–70.

MIKESELL, R. F., Gold sales as an anti-inflationary device, *Review of Economic Statistics*, XXVIII (1946) 105–8.

MILLS, F. C., Price aspects of monetary problems, *Academy of Political Science, Proceedings*, XVI (1934–36) 3–10.

MINTS, L. W.; HANSEN, A. H.; ELLIS, H. S.; LERNER, A. P.; and KALECKI, M., A symposium on fiscal and monetary policy, *Review of Economic Statistics*, XXVIII (1946) 60–84

MÖLLER, H., Aktuelle grenzprobleme kreditärer mittelaufbringung in der staatswirtschaft, *Finanzarchiv*, NF 9 (1941–43) 95–116.

MORGENSTERN, O., Developments in the Federal Reserve System, *Harvard Business Review*, IX (1930–31) 1–7.

NIEBYL, K. H., and others, The changing character of money, *American Economic Review*, XXXVII (1947 supplement) 299–334.

NÖLL VON DER NAHMER, R., Möglichkeit und zweckmässigkeit nicht-inflatorische papiergeldausgabe, *Schmoller's Jahrbuch für Gesetzgebung, Verwaltung und Volkswirtschaft*, LX (1936) 59–73.

NORTON, J. E., The Bank of England and the money market, *Political Science Quarterly*, XXXVI (1921) 433–53.

NOYES, C. R., Free gold, *Harvard Business Review*, XI (1932–33) 35–44.

OHLIN, B., Knut Wichsell, father of the Swedish monetary experiment, *Economic Forum*, II (1934–35) 159–68.

LINDAHL, E., Sweden's monetary program: The experiment in operation, its results and lessons, *ibid.*, 169–81.

PAISH, F. W., Cheap money policy, *Economica*, XIV, new series (1947) 167–79.

PALYI, M., Economic significance of bank loans for stock-market transactions, *University of Chicago Journal of Business*, V (January 1932) 28–46.

———, A desirable monetary policy, *Report of the Commission of Inquiry into National Policy in International Economic Relations* (Robert M. Hutchins, Chairman), (1934) 236–45.

PERLOFF, H. S., Budgetary symbolism, *Public Policy*, II (1941) 36–62.

PREISER, E., Der begriff des preisniveaus und das problem der kaufkraftstabilisierung, *Jahrbücher für Nationalökonomie und Statistik*, CLVIII (1943) 186–206.

RIST, C., Stabilization, *Lloyds Bank Limited, Monthly Review*, VI, No. 65 (July 1935) 391–403.

ROBERTS, W. A., Elasticity in public finance, *Harvard Business Review*, XIV (1935–36) 235–40.

ROBERTSON, D. H., Theories of banking policy, *Economica*, VIII (1928) 131–46. Reprinted in *Essays in Monetary Theory*, London, King, 1940, 39–59.

ROBINSON, R. I., Central banks and the state: A comment, *American Economic Review*, XXXIX (1949) 494–96.

ROGERS, J. H., A supreme court of money: A bulwark against inflation, *Economic Forum*, III (1935–36) 149–54.

ROSENBERG, W., The evolution of central banking during the crisis, *Economic Record*, XIV (1938) 93–8.

ROSSI, L., "Gold standard" e moneta neutrale, *Rivista Italiana di Scienze Economiche*, VII (1935) 927–38.

SAYERS, R. S., Central banking in the light of recent British and American experience, *Quarterly Journal of Economics*, LXIII (1949) 198–211.

SCHNEIDER, E., Geldtheorie und geldpolitik: Zu dem gleichnamigen buch von Jörgen Pedersen, *Kyklos*, III (1949) 36–75.

SELTZER, L. H., The problem of our excessive banking reserves, *Journal of the American Statistical Association*, XXXV (1940) 24–36.

SHACKLE, G. L. S., Interest-rates and the pace of investment, *Economic Journal*, LVI (1946) 1–17.

SHAW, K. W., Credit control and central reserve banking, *Chinese Economic Journal and Bulletin*, XIX (1936) 515–18.

SIMKIN, C. G. F., The nationalization of the Bank of New Zealand, *Economic Record*, XXII (1946) 228–40.

SIMMONS, E. C., The role of selective credit control in monetary management, *American Economic Review*, XXXVII (1947) 633–41.

SIMONS, H. C., A positive program for laissez faire: Some proposals for a liberal economic policy, *Public Policy Pamphlet,* No. 15. Reprinted in *Economic Policy for a Free Society,* Chicago, The University of Chicago Press, 1948, 40–77.

*SIMONS, H. C., Rules vs. authorities in monetary policy, *Journal of Political Economy,* XLIV (1936) 1–30. Reprinted in *Economic Policy for a Free Society,* Chicago, The University of Chicago Press, 1948, 160–183.

SPROUL, A., Monetary management and credit control, *American Economic Review,* XXXVII (1947) 339–50.

STAFFORD, J., The relation of banking techniques to economic equilibria, *The Manchester School,* III (1932) 113–43.

————, The future of the rate of interest, *The Manchester School,* VIII (1937) 125–46.

STAMP, J., A stable price level, *Lloyds Bank Limited, Monthly Review,* I, No. 5, new series (July 1930) 143–48.

STUCKEN, R., Konjunkturbeeinflussung durch die notenbank, *Jahrbücher für Nationalökonomie und Statistik,* XL (1934) 35–52.

————, Kredit als finanzwirtschaftliches Deckungsmittel, *Finanzarchiv,* NF 5 (1937–38) 529–60.

STUDENSKI, P. (ed.), Government finance in the modern economy, *Annals of the American Academy of Political and Social Science,* CLXXXIII (1936).

TEW, B., The direct control of interest rates, *Economic Record,* XXIII (1947) 198–205.

TOCKER, A. H., The development of central banking, *Economic Record,* XV (New Zealand Centennial Supplement, October 1939) 45–57.

VANDERLIP, F. H., Stable money, *Economic Forum,* III (1935–36) 35–46.

WAGEMANN, E., and FEILEN, J., Die einkommenskomponente in der geldschöpfungslehre und geldschöpfungspolitik, *Jahrbücher für Nationalökonomie und Statistik,* CLIII (1941) 431–39.

WALKER, E. R., Sound finance, *Economic Record,* XV (1939 supplement) 61–75.

WALTERS, R. W., JR., The origins of the Second Bank of the United States, *Journal of Political Economy,* LIII (1945) 115–31.

WARBURG, P. M., The Federal Reserve Banks and the open market for acceptances, *Harvard Business Review,* I (1922–23) 257–68.

WARBURTON, C., Business stability and regulation of the cost of money, *American Journal of Economics and Sociology,* IV (1944–45) 175–84.

————, Monetary control under the Federal Reserve Act, *Political Science Quarterly,* LXI (1946) 505–34.

WELCKWER, J. W., The federal budget, a challenge to businessmen, *Harvard Business Review,* XXII (Summer 1944) 431–42.

WHALE, P. B., Central banks and the state, *The Manchester School,* X (1939) 38–49.

WHITTLESEY, C. R., A new instrument of central bank policy, *Quarterly Journal of Economics,* Vol. 54, (1939–40) 158–60.

————, Memorandum on the stability of demand deposits, *American Economic Review,* XXXIX (1949) 1192–1203.

* Reprinted in the present volume.

WILLIAMS, J. H., The world's monetary dilemma—internal versus external monetary stability, *Academy of Political Science, Proceedings,* XVI (1934–36) 62–8. Reprinted in *Postwar Monetary Plans and Other Essays,* New York, Knopf, 1944, 191–98.

————, The implications of fiscal policy for monetary policy and the banking system, *American Economic Review,* XXXII (1942 supplement) 234–49. Reprinted in *Postwar Monetary Plans and Other Essays,* New York, Knopf, 1944, 87–111.

WILLIS, H. P., The credit policies of the Federal Reserve System—a retrospect, *Annals of the American Academy of Political and Social Science,* CLXXI (1934) 94–103.

WILSON, J. S. G., Australia's Central Bank, *Journal of Political Economy,* LV (1947) 28–38.

YOUNG, J. P., Government management of currency and credit, *Annals of the American Academy of Political and Social Science,* CCVI (1939) 100–5.

III-B. The Problems of Recovery from Depression and of Maintaining Full Employment

Restricted to monetary-fiscal policies designed for such purposes. Wage and price policy articles, when related to expected monetary effects, are included in I-E.

ALDRICH, W., Credit control under a recovery program, *Academy of Political Science, Proceedings,* XVII (1936–38) 26–30.

ANDERSON, C. J., The development of the pump-priming theory, *Journal of Political Economy,* LII (1944) 144–59.

ANDERSON, R. V., Policy for full employment, *Canadian Journal of Economics and Political Science,* XII (1946) 192–203.

ANGELL, J. W., Gold, banks, and the new deal, *Political Science Quarterly,* XLIX (1934) 481–505.

APEL, H., Self-liquidating wages, *Social Research,* X (1943) 301–11.

ARNOLD, T. W., and STURGES, W. A., The progress of the new administration, *Yale Review,* XXII (1932–33) 656–77.

————, Must 1929 repeat itself?, *Harvard Business Review,* XXVI (1948) 32–45.

BACH, G. L., Monetary-fiscal policy reconsidered, *Journal of Political Economy,* LVII (1949) 383–94.

BALLANTINE, A. A., Employment and federal finance, *Academy of Political Science, Proceedings,* XVIII, No. 4 (January, 1940) 395–402.

BEATTIE, J. R., Some aspects of the problem of full employment, *Canadian Journal of Economics and Political Science,* X (1944) 328–42.

BECKHART, B. H., Domestic aspects of credit control and the recovery program, *Academy of Political Science, Proceedings,* XVII (1936–38) 31–5.

BENHAM, F., The muddle of the thirties, *Political Science Quarterly,* LIX (1944) 529–47.
   Also found in:
     BENHAM, F., The muddle of the thirties, *Economica,* XII, new series (1945) 1–9.

BERNSTEIN, E. M., Public expenditure, and the national income, *Southern Economic Journal*, II (1936) 34–46.

BERRIDGE, W. A., Observations on Beveridge's *Full Employment in a Free Society* and related matters, *Political Science Quarterly*, LX (1945) 176–87.

BEVERIDGE, W., The government's employment policy, *Economic Journal*, LIV (1944) 161–76.

——, Life, liberty and the pursuit of happiness (1950 model), *Review of Economic Statistics*, XXVIII (1946) 53–9.

BLACK, E. R., Financial policies for recovery, *Academy of Political Science, Proceedings*, XVI (1934–36) 110–16.

BOER, W., Equality and prosperity, *Social Research*, X (1943) 118–22.

BOOKER, H. S., Have we a full employment policy, *Economica*, XIV, new series (1947) 37–47.

BRAGDEN, J. B., The credit theory of full employment, *Economic Record*, XV (1939) 236–37.

BRATTER, H. M., The silver episode, *Journal of Political Economy*, XLVI (1938) 609–52, 802–37.

BROWN, H. G., Policies for full post-war employment, *American Journal of Economics and Sociology*, III (1943–44) 141–54.

BROWN, H. I., The coming reflation deadlock, *Economic Forum*, II (1934–35) 338–50.

CABOT, P., The crusade for national recovery, *Yale Review*, XXIII (1933–34) 1–19.

COOPER, W. W., Some implications of a program for full employment and economic stability, *Political Science Quarterly*, LXIII (1948) 230–56.

COPELAND, M. A., How achieve full and stable employment, *American Economic Review*, XXXIV (1944 supplement) 134–47.

COPPOLA D'ANNA, F., E' possibile una politica di "full employment" in Italia? *Previdenza Sociale*, II (1946) 132–35.

COVER, J. H., Our synthetic prosperity, *University of Chicago Journal of Business*, III (July 1930) 317–31.

COYLE, D. C., The dilemma of prosperity, *Yale Review*, XXXVI (1946–47) 193–209.

CROOME, H., Liberty, equality, and full empoyment, *Lloyds Bank Review*, No. 13, new series (July 1949) 14–32.

DONHAM, W. B., The attack on depression, *Harvard Business Review*, XI (1932–33) 45–56.

EBERSOLE, J. F., Banks can make more postwar jobs, *Harvard Business Review*, XXII (Autumn 1943) 1–9.

——, Government can help banks make more jobs, *Harvard Business Review*, XXII (Winter 1944) 167–77.

EDRE, L., Monetary inflation and price raising, *Yale Review*, XXIII (1933–34) 260–73.

EINAUDI, L., Il mio piano non è quello di Keynes, *Riforma Sociale*, XL (1933) 129–42.

——, Fondo disponibile di risparmio e lavori pubblici, *Riforma Sociale*, XL (1933) 340–52.

————, Risparmio disponibile, crisi e lavori pubblici, *Riforma Sociale*, XL (1933) 542–53.

EISLER, R., Un remède monétaire à la crise mondiale du chômage, *Revue d'Economie Politique*, XLV (1931) 333–57.

————, Reduce long-term interest rates, *Economic Forum*, II (1934–35) 458–68.

ELLIS, H. S., Postwar economic policies, *Review of Economic Statistics*, XXVIII (1946) 34–9.

FAIRCHILD, F. R., Government saves us from depression, *Yale Review*, XXI (1931–32) 661–83.

FELLNER, W., Hansen on full-employment policies, *Journal of Political Economy*, LV (1947) 254–56.

FISHER, A. G. B., Less stabilization: more stability, *Kyklos*, I (1947) 1–18.

FLEMING, J. M., Secular unemployment, *Quarterly Journal of Economics*, LIV (1939–40) 103–30.

FOSTER, W. T., Is fiat money any worse than fiat poverty?, *Economic Forum*, I (1932–33) 55–70.

FREDRIKSEN, D. M., Two financial roads leading out of depression, *Harvard Business Review*, X (1931–32) 137–48.

FURNESS, E. S., Reflections on the new dollar, *Yale Review*, XXIII (1933–34) 448–65.

GILBERT, J. C., Professor Polanyi's *Full Employment and Free Trade*, *The Manchester School*, XIV (1946) 85–97.

GOLDENWEISER, E. A., How can credit be controlled, *Academy of Political Science, Proceedings*, XVII (1936–38) 3–9.

GRAGY, C. I., and TEELE, S. F., The proposed full employment act, *Harvard Business Review*, XXIII (1944–45) 323–37.

GRAHAM, F. D., The creation of employment, *Economic Forum*, I (1932–33) 144–54.

GREGORY, T. E., The American experiment, *The Manchester School*, V (1934) 1–18.

GRIFFITH, E. C., Deficit financing and the future of capitalism, *Southern Economic Journal*, XII (1945–46) 130–40.

HAHN, A. L., Compensating reactions to compensatory spending, *American Economic Review*, XXXV (1945) 28–39.

HAIG, R. M., The state of the federal finances, *Yale Review*, XXII (1932–33) 234–51.

————, Facing the deficit, *Yale Review*, XXV (1935–36) 685–701.

HALEY, B. F., Federal budget: Economic consequences of deficit spending, *American Economic Review*, XXXI (1941 supplement) 67–87.

HANSEN, A. H., Capital goods and the restoration of purchasing power, *Academy of Political Science, Proceedings*, XVI (1934–36) 11–19.

————, A new goal of national policy: Full employment, *Review of Economic Statistics*, XXVII (1945) 102–3.

HARRIS, S. E.; HABERLER, G.; SLICHTER, S.; and McNAIR, M. P., Comments on the Murray bill, *ibid.*, 104–16.

————, The first reports under the Employment Act of 1946, *Review of Economic Statistics*, XXIX (1947) 69–74.

VINER, J., The Employment Act of 1946 in operation, *ibid.*, 74–9.

HARDY, C. O., Devaluation of the dollar, *Public Policy Pamphlet*, No. 8.

HARRIS, S. E., Monetary policy and recovery, *Economic Forum*, I (1932–33) 411–24.

HARROD, R. F., Full employment and security of livelihood, *Economic Journal*, LIII (1943) 321–42.

HART, A. G., Facts, issues, and policies, *American Economic Review*, XXXVI (1946 supplement) 280–90.

SWEEZY, A. R., Fiscal and monetary policy, *ibid.*, 291–303.

SLICHTER, S. H., Wage-price policy and employment, *ibid.*, 304–18.

PIERSON, J. H. G.; FELLNER, W. J.; WARBURTON, C.; and LERNER, A. P., The problem of full employment: Discussion, *ibid.*, 319–35.

HAVENS, R. M., Reactions of the federal government to the 1837–43 depression, *Southern Economic Journal*, VIII (1941–42) 380–90.

HAWTREY, R. G., Livelihood and full employment, *Economic Journal*, LIV (1944) 417–22.

HERRICK, L., Employment and post-war prosperity, *Yale Review*, XXXIV (1944–45) 270–81.

HIGGINS, B., Reder on wage-price policy, *Canadian Journal of Economics and Political Science*, XV (1949) 203–6.

REDER, M. W., A further comment on wage-price policy, *ibid.*, 206–10.

HIRSCH, J., Facts and fantasies concerning full employment, *American Economic Review*, XXXIV (1944 supplement) 118–27.

HOOVER, C. B., Economic planning and the problem of full employment, *American Economic Review*, XXX (1940 supplement) 263–71.

HOPKINS, J. L., Beware the spending panacea, *American Journal of Economics and Sociology*, VI (1946–47) 55–69.

HUBBARD, J. B., Easy money: Doctrine and results, *Harvard Business Review*, XIX (Autumn 1940) 52–65.

HUMPHREY, D. D., The relation of surpluses to income and employment during depression, *American Economic Review*, XXVIII (1938) 223–34.

HUTTON, D. G., Recovery and the rate of interest, *Lloyds Bank Limited, Monthly Review*, VI, No. 60, new series (February, 1935) 71–82.

JENNY, F., The American experiment and its consequences, *Lloyds Bank Limited, Monthly Review*, IV, No. 46, new series (December 1933) 498–519.

———, Some reflections upon the economic crisis and the way out, *Lloyds Bank Limited, Monthly Review*, V, No. 58, new series (December 1934) 522–39.

JENKES, J., Second thoughts on the white paper on employment policy, *The Manchester School*, XIV (1946) 65–89.

JOHNSON, A., Debt and the devil, *Yale Review*, XXII (1932–33) 450–64.

JORDAN, V., Stabilizing national prosperity, *Yale Review*, XVII (1927–28) 1–21.

KALECKI, M., Full employment by stimulating private investment, *Oxford Economic Papers*, No. 7 (March 1945) 83–92.

KAZEKEVICH, V. D., The dilemma of American banking, *Science and Society*, III (1939) 461–81.

LEAVENS, D. H., Silver and the business depression, *Harvard Business Review*, IX (1930–31) 330–38.

LESTER, R. A., Currency issues to overcome depressions in Pennsylvania, 1723 and 1729, *Journal of Political Economy*, XLVI (1938) 324–75.

———, Currency issues to overcome depressions in Delaware, New Jersey, New York, and Maryland, 1715–37, *Journal of Political Economy*, XLVII (1939) 182–217.

LUCAS, A. F., The bankers' industrial development company, *Harvard Business Review*, XI (1932–33) 270–79.

McDOUGALL, A., The white paper on employment policy, *Review of Social Economy*, III (1945) 18–33.

MACGIBBON, D. A., Inflation and inflationism, *Canadian Journal of Economics and Political Science*, I (1935) 325–36.

McLEOD, A. N., The financing of employment-maintaining expenditures, *American Economic Review*, XXXV (1945) 640–45.

McNAIR, M. P., The full employment problem, *Harvard Business Review*, XXIV (1945–46) 1–21.

MARRAMA, V., Some aspects of Italian economy and the theory of full employment, *Banca Nazionale del Lavoro Quarterly Review* (1948) 220–27.

MERRY, D. H., and BRUNS, G. R., Full employment, the British, Canadian and Australian white papers, *Economic Record*, XXI (1945) 223–35.

MEYER, A. L., Some implications of full-employment policy, *Journal of Political Economy*, LIV (1946) 258–65.

MILLS, O. L., Financial policies for recovery, *Academy of Political Science, Proceedings*, XVI (1934–36) 100–9.

MOULTON, H. G., The relation of credit and prices to business recovery, *Academy of Political Science, Proceedings*, XVI (1934–36) 20–6.

MUSGRAVE, R. A.; DOMAR, E. D.; ROBINSON, R. L.; WALLICH, H. C.; MITCHELL, G. W.; LITTERER, O. F.; HANSEN, A. H.; HARDY, C. O.; and LELAND, S. E., Public finance and full employment, *Postwar Economic Studies*, No. 3, Washington, D. C., Board of Governors of the Federal Reserve System, 1945.

NICHOLS, J. P., Silver diplomacy, *Political Science Quarterly*, XLVIII (1933) 565–88.

PAGNI, C., Fondo disponibile di risparmio e lavori pubblici, *Riforma Sociale*, XL (1933) 331–39.

PIERSON, J. H. G., The underwriting of aggregate consumer spending as a pillar of full-employment policy, *American Economic Review*, Vol. 34 (1944) 21–55.

———, The underwriting approach to full employment: A further explanation, *Review of Economic Statistics*, XXXI (1949) 182–92.

RIST, C.; MLYNARSKI, F.; ELVU, JENNY, F.; LAYTON, W. T.; ROGERS, J. H.; KOCK, K.; and MARTIN, P. G., Questions monétaires de l'heure présente, *Revue d'Economie Politique*, XLVI, 1932, 254–405.

ROBBINS, L., How to mitigate the next slump, *Lloyds Bank Limited, Monthly Review*, VIII, No. 87, new series (May 1937) 234–44.

ROBERTS, G. B., The silver purchase program and its consequences, *Academy of Political Science, Proceedings*, XVII (1936–38) 18–25.

ROBEY, R., Fiscal policy and credit control, *Academy of Political Science, Proceedings*, XVII (1936–38) 10–17.

ROGERS, J. H., Sound inflation, *Economic Forum*, I (1932–33) 119–28.

ROOSE, K. D., Federal Reserve policy and the recession of 1937–38, *Review of Economic Statistics*, XXXII (1950) 177–83.

RORTY, M. C., How may business revival be forced, *Harvard Business Review*, X (1931–32) 385–98.

ROSA, R. V., Small business and depression, *Harvard Business Review*, XXVI (1948) 58–62.

ROSTOW, W. W., The United Nations report on full employment, *Economic Journal*, LX (1950) 323–50.

SALANT, W. S., Foreign trade policy in the business cycle, *Public Policy*, II (1941) 208–31.

SALTER, A., The silver problem, *Political Science Quarterly*, XLVI (1931) 321–34.

——, Recovery: The present stage, *Yale Review*, XXIV (1934–35) 217–36.

SCHUMANN, C. G. W., Aspects of the problem of full employment in South Africa, *South African Journal of Economics*, XVI (1948) 115–32.

SELTZER, L. H., Deficit financing: Direct versus fiscal and institutional factors, *American Economic Review*, XXXI (1941 supplement) 99–107.

SIMONS, H. C., Hansen on fiscal policy, *Journal of Political Economy*, L (1942) 161–96. Reprinted in *Economic Policy for a Free Society*, Chicago, University of Chicago Press, 1948, 184–219.

——, The Beveridge program: An unsympathetic interpretation, *Journal of Political Economy*, LIII (1945) 212–33. Reprinted in *Economic Policy for a Free Society*, Chicago, University of Chicago Press, 1948, 277–312.

SIPHERD, L. W., The capital market and recovery in Canada, *Harvard Business Review*, XIV (1935–36) 494–501.

SLICHTER, S. H., How to stimulate postwar employment, *Annals of the American Academy of Political and Social Science*, CCXXXVIII (1945) 158–66.

SMITH, D. T., Economic consequences of deficit financing: A review, *American Economic Review*, XXXI (1941 supplement) 88–98.

SMITH, G. A., JR., Silver—its status and outlook, *Harvard Business Review*, XIII (1934–35) 44–53.

SMITHIES, A., Full employment in a free society, *American Economic Review*, XXXV (1945) 355–67.

SPRAGUE, O. M. W., Major and minor trade fluctuations, *Journal of the Royal Statistical Society*, XCIV (1931) 540–49.

HAWTREY, R. G., and others, Discussion on Dr. Sprague's paper, *ibid.*, 549–63.

STRAKOSCH, H., The road to recovery, *Economic Forum*, II (1934–35) Supplement.

EDIE, L. D., Stabilization: An American opinion, *Economic Forum*, III (1935–36) 10–22.

STRAUS, E. M., Prices, income flow, and employment, *Quarterly Journal of Economics*, LX (1945–46) 600–11.

TAUSSIG, F. W., Wanted, consumers, *Yale Review*, XXIII (1933–34) 433–47.

TIMLIN, M., General equilibrium analysis and public policy, *Canadian Journal of Economics and Political Science*, XII (1946) 483–95.

TYNDALL, D. G., A note, *Canadian Journal of Economics and Political Science*, XIII (1947) 118–20.

TIMLIN, M., A rejoinder, *ibid.*, 285–87.

TUCKER, R. S., Relief for debtors without inflation, *Economic Forum*, I (1932–33) 179–85.

UNIVERSITY OF CHICAGO ROUND TABLE, Balancing the budget: Federal fiscal policy during depression, *Public Policy Pamphlet*, No. 1.

URQUHART, M. C., Public investment in Canada, *Canadian Journal of Economics and Political Science*, XI (1945) 535–53.

VALLANCE, A., The problem of unemployment, *Lloyds Bank Limited, Monthly Review*, IV, No. 37, new series (March 1933) 86–98.

VAN SICKLE, J. J., Regional aspects of the problem of full employment at fair wages, *Southern Economic Journal*, XIII (1946–47) 36–45.

VEIT, O., Geldüberfluss und Wirtschaftslenkung, *Weltwirtschaftliches Archiv*, LVII (1943) 278–311.

WARBURTON, C., The monetary theory of deficit spending, *Review of Economic Statistics*, XXVII (1945) 74–84.

ARNDT, H. W., The monetary theory of deficit spending: A comment on Dr. Clark Warburton's article, *Review of Economic Statistics*, XXVIII (1946) 90–2.

WARBURTON, C., A reply, *ibid.*, 92–4.

———, Hansen and Fellner on full employment policies, *American Economic Review*, XXXVIII (1948) 128–34.

WASSON, R. G., Beveridge's *Full Employment in a Free Society*, *Harvard Business Review*, XXIII (1944–45) 507–18.

WILLIS, H. P., The future in banking, *Yale Review*, XXIII (1933–34) 233–47.

WIRTENBERGER, H. J., Public policy and postwar employment in the United States, *Review of Social Economy*, III (1945) 45–52.

MOGILNITZKY, T. A., Discussion, *ibid.*, 53–4.

WOLFF, A., The royal road to inflation, *Economic Forum*, III (1935–36) 61–70.

WOLMAN, L., Policies of post-war employment, *Political Science Quarterly*, LVIII (1943) 595–606.

WOOD, G. L., Some lessons of the American experiment, *Economic Record*, XV (1939 supplement) 119–34.

WRIGHT, D. M., Hopes and fears—the shape of things to come, *Econometrica*, XXVI (1944) 206–15.

YNTEMA, T. O., "Full" employment in a private enterprise system, *American Economic Review*, XXXIV (1944 supplement) 107–17.

III-C. Postwar Monetary-Fiscal Policy

Includes articles on the postwar inflation, liquid asset holdings, the changed problem of monetary policy, and debt management.

ABBOTT, C. C., Management of the federal debt, *Harvard Business Review*, XXIV (Autumn 1945) 96–108.

———, The commercial banks and the public debt, *American Economic Review*, XXXVII (1947 supplement) 265–76.

PRESTON, H. H., The commercial banks and the public debt: Discussion, *ibid.*, 289–92.

ALLEN, R. G. D., Post-war economic policy in the U. S., *Economic Journal,* LV (1945) 28–46.

BAFFI, P., Il problema monetario italiano sullo scorcio del 1944, *Giornale degli Economisti,* VI, new series (1948) 30–62.

BOPP, K. R.; ROSA, R. V.; PARRY, C. E.; THOMAS, W.; and YOUNG, R. A., Federal Reserve policy, *Postwar Economic Studies,* No. 8, Washington, D. C., Board of Governors of the Federal Reserve System, 1947.

BORGATTA, G., Interest rate policy and reconstruction requirements, *Banca Nazionale del Lavoro Quarterly Review* (1948) 407–15.

BRONFENBRENNER, M., Postwar political economy: The President's reports, *Journal of Political Economy,* LVI (1948) 373–91.

CARR, H. C., The problem of bank-held government debt, *American Economic Review,* XXXVI (1946) 833–42.

VILLARD, H. H., Comment, *American Economic Review,* XXXVII (1947) 936–37.

*CHANDLER, L. V., Federal Reserve policy and the federal debt, *American Economic Review,* XXXIX (1949) 405–29.

BERNSTEIN, P. L., A comment, *ibid.,* 1278–81.

DAGEY, W. M., The cheap money technique, *Lloyds Bank Review,* No. 3, new series (January 1947) 49–63.

———, Inflation under controls, *Lloyds Bank Review,* No. 4, new series (April, 1947 supplement).

DOWSETT, Delayed action inflation, *Economic Record,* XIX (1943) 64–70.

ECCLES, M., Economic conditions and public policy, *Federal Reserve Bulletin,* XXXII (1946) 1230–35.

FELLNER, W. J., Postscript on war inflation: A lesson from World War II, *American Economic Review,* XXXVII (1947) 76–91.

FETTER, F. W., The economic reports of the President and the problem of inflation, *Quarterly Journal of Economics,* LXIII (1949) 273–81.

GOLDENWEISER, E. A., Postwar problems and policies, *Federal Reserve Bulletin,* XXXI (1945) 112–21.

———; HAGEN, E. E.; and GARFIELD, F. R., Jobs, production and living standards, *Postwar Economic Studies,* No. 1, Washington, D. C., Board of Governors of the Federal Reserve System, 1945.

HANSEN, A. H., Inflation, *Yale Review,* XXXV (1945–46) 692–711.

HARDY, C. O., Federal Reserve System Report for 1945, *Harvard Business Review,* XXV (Winter 1947) 207–12.

———; WILLIAMS, K. B.; and ELLIS, H. S., Prices, wages, and employment, *Postwar Economic Studies,* No. 4, Washington, D. C., Board of Governors of the Federal Reserve System, 1946.

HARRIS, S. E.; SLICHTER, S. H.; and DUNLOP, J. T., Symposium: Wage policy, *Review of Economic Statistics,* XXIX (1947) 137–60.

———, and others, Ten economists on the inflation, *Review of Economic Statistics,* XXX (1948) 1–29.

———, and others, How to manage the national debt, *Review of Economic Statistics,* XXXI (1949) 15–32.

* Reprinted in the present volume.

HART, A. G., Postwar effects to be expected from wartime liquid accumulation, *American Economic Review,* XXXV (1945 supplement) 341–51.

HAWTREY, R. G., Monetary aspects of the economic situation, *American Economic Review,* XXXVIII (1948) 42–55.

HERMENS, F. A., Domestic postwar problems, *Review of Social Economy,* I (1942) 23–30.

HICKS, J. R., World Recovery after war—a theoretical analysis, *Economic Journal,* LVII (1947) 151–64.

————, The empty economy, *Lloyds Bank Review,* No. 5, new series (July 1947) 1–13.

HITCH, C., and others, The American economy in transition, *Review of Economic Statistics,* XXIX (1947) 16–38.

HUTT, W. H., Full employment and the future of industry, *South African Journal of Economics,* XIII (1945) 185–202.

HYSON, C. D., Notes on savings in relation to potential markets, *American Economic Review,* XXXVI (1946) 891–901.

JEWKES, J. H., and DEVONS, E., The economic surevy for 1947, *Lloyds Bank Review,* No. 4, new series (April 1947) 1–10.

JOHNSON, N. O., Problems of checking over-expansion of bank credit, *Academy of Political Science, Proceedings,* XXIII (1948) 11–18.

KÄHLER, A., The public debt in the financial structure, *Social Research,* XI (1944) 11–26.

LANSTON, A. G., Crucial problem of the federal debt, *Harvard Business Review,* XXIV (Winter 1946) 133–50.

LEFFINGWELL, R. C., Managing our economy, *Yale Review,* XXXIV (1944–45) 603–17.

LERNER, A. P., The inflationary process: 1. Some theoretical aspects, *Review of Economic Statistics,* XXXI (1949) 193–200.

HARRIS, S. E., The inflationary process: 2. In theory and recent history, *ibid.,* 200–10.

MACHLUP, F.; SOMERS, H. M.; and VILLARD, H. H., Comments, *ibid.,* 210–16.

LUTZ, F. A., Credit and finance policies, *Academy of Political Science, Proceedings,* XXIII (1948) 19–28.

LUTZ, H. L., The high cost of living, *Yale Review,* XXXVI (1946–47) 577–89.

MOSAK, J. L., National budgets and national policy, *American Economic Review* XXXVI (1946) 20–43.

NEISSER, H., Employment in 1947, *Social Research,* XIV (1947) 95–103.

REINHARDT, H., The great debt redemption 1946–1947, *Social Research,* XV (1948) 170–93.

RÖPKE, W., Repressed inflation, *Kyklos,* I (1947) 242–53.

ROTWEIN, E., Post-World War I price movements and price policy, *Journal of Political Economy,* LIII (1945) 234–57.

SAMUELSON, P. A., The effect of interest rate increases on the banking system, *American Economic Review,* XXXV, 16–27.

COLEMAN, G. W., The effect of interest rate increases on the banking system, *ibid.,* 671–73.

HARRIS, S. E., A one per cent war, *ibid.*, 667–71.

SAMUELSON, P. A., The turn of the screw, *ibid.*, 674–76.

SAULNIER, R. J., Institutional changes affecting the exercise of monetary controls, *Review of Social Economy*, V (1947) 19–34.

SELIGMAN, H. L., The problem of excessive commercial bank earnings, *Quarterly Journal of Economics*, LX (1945–46) 365–89.

SELTZER, L. H., Is a rise in interest rates desirable or inevitable?, *American Economic Review*, XXXV (1945) 831–50.

————, The changed environment of monetary-banking policy, *American Economic Review*, XXXVI (1946 supplement) 65–79.

WOODWARD, D. B., and YOUNG, R. A., The changed environment of monetary-banking policy: Discussion, *ibid.*, 87–92.

SIMMONS, E. C., The position of the Treasury Bill in the public debt, *Journal of Political Economy*, LV (1947) 333–45.

————, The monetary mechanism since the war, *Journal of Political Economy*, LVIII (1950) 124–41.

SIMONS, H. C., On debt policy, *Journal of Political Economy*, LII (1944) 356–61. Reprinted in *Economic Policy for a Free Society*, Chicago, University of Chicago Press, 1948, 220–30.

————, Debt policy and banking policy, *Review of Economic Statistics*, XXVIII (1946) 85–9. Reprinted in *Economic Policy for a Free Society*, Chicago, The University of Chicago Press, 1948, 231–39.

SLICHTER, S. H., Postwar boom or collapse?, *Harvard Business Review*, XXI (Autumn 1942) 5–42.

————, Present savings and postwar markets, *Harvard Business Review*, XXII (Autumn 1943) Part 2.

SPENGLER, J. J., The future of prices, *Southern Economic Journal*, XIII (1946–47) 1–35.

SPERO, H., and LEAVITT, J. A., Inflation as a post-war problem, *Journal of Political Economy*, LI (1943) 356–60.

THOMAS, W., The heritage of war finance, *American Economic Review*, XXXVII (1947 supplement) 205–15.

WILLIS, J. B., The case against the maintenance of the wartime pattern of yields on government securities, *ibid.*, 216–27.

BACH, G. L., Monetary-fiscal policy, debt policy, and the price level, *ibid.*, 228–42.

UNTERBERGER, S. H., and HENIG, G., Theory of wage control in the transition period, *Southern Economic Journal*, XII (1945–46) 283–89.

VINER, J., Can we check inflation?, *Yale Review*, XXXVII (1947–48) 193–211.

WALLICH, H. C., Debt management as an instrument of economic policy, *American Economic Review*, XXXVI (1946) 292–310.

————, The changing significance of the interest rate, *American Economic Review*, XXXVI (1946) 761–87.

WEINTRAUB, S., Compulsory savings in Great Britain, *Harvard Business Review*, XX (Autumn 1941) 53–64.

WHITTLESEY, C. R., Problems of our domestic money and banking system, *American Economic Review*, XXXIV (1944 supplement) 245–59.

————, Federal reserve policy in transition, *Quarterly Journal of Economics,* LX (1945–46) 340–50.

WIGGINS, A. L. M., Fiscal policy and debt management, *Academy of Political Science, Proceedings,* XXIII (1948) 69–80.

WILLIAMS, E., Two truisms and "price" inflation, *American Journal of Economics and Sociology,* VIII (1948–49) 17–9.

III-D. *Monetary and Banking Reform*

Includes articles on 100 per cent money, commodity money, social credit, nationalization of banking, and functional finance.

ALTMAN, I. B., A proposal for complete government ownership of currency and credit, *Annals of the American Academy of Political and Social Science,* CLXXXIII (1936) 157–62.

ANGELL, J. W., The 100 per cent reserve plan, *Quarterly Journal of Economics,* L (1935–36) 1–35.

ANONYMOUS, Nationalization of banks; an early phase of state socialism, *The Index,* XXVI (1946) No. 1, 13–24.

BAKER, J. G., The universal discount as a means of economic stabilization, *Econometrica,* XVI (1948) 155–84.

BASTER, A. S. J., The lessons of foreign experience, *Annals of the American Academy of Political and Social Science,* CLXXI (1934) 5–16.

BEALE, W. T. M.; KENNEDY, M. T.; and WINN, W. J., Commodity reserve currency: A critique, *Journal of Political Economy,* L (1942) 579–94.

GRAHAM, B., The critique of commodity-reserve currency: A point-by-point reply, *Quarterly Journal of Economics,* LI (1943) 66–9.

GRAHAM, F. D., Commodity-reserve currency: A criticism of the critique, *ibid.,* 70–5.

BEALE, W. T. M., Commodity-reserve currency: A rejoinder, *Journal of Political Economy,* LI, 175–77.

BRATTER, H. M., Should we turn to silver? *Public Policy Pamphlet,* No. 6.

BROWN, H. G., Objections to the 100 per cent reserve plan, *American Economic Review,* XXX (1940) 309–14.

BRUGGEN, B. N. E., An ABC of economics: An introduction to Soddy, *Economic Forum,* II (1934–35) 100–12.

BURKHEAD, J. V., Full employment and interest-free borrowing, *Southern Economic Journal,* XIV (1947–48) 1–13.

BURRELL, O. K., Essential elements in banking reconstruction, *Harvard Business Review,* XII (1933–34) 12–22.

CALSOYAS, C. D., Commodity currency and commodity storage, *American Economic Review,* XXXVIII (1948) 341–52.

CARTINHOW, G. T., Branch banks vs. unit banks, *Annals of the American Academy of Political and Social Science,* CLXXI (1934) 35–46.

DOUGLAS, C. H., The premises of social credit, *Economic Forum,* I (1932–33) 167–71.

FISHER, I., 100 per cent money and the public debt, *Economic Forum,* III (1935–36) 406–20.

FISHER, I., Note suggested by review of *100 per cent money, Journal of the Royal Statistical Society,* C (1937) 296–98.

FROMMER, J. C., A price formula for multiple-commodity monetary reserve, *Econometrica,* XIII (1945) 152–60.

GIDEONSE, H. D., The commodity dollar, *Association of Reserve City Bankers,* 1936. Also *Public Policy Pamphlet,* No. 26.

GRAHAM, B., Stabilized reflation, *Economic Forum,* I (1932–33) 186–93.

GRAHAM, F. D., Reserve money and the 100 per cent proposal, *American Economic Review,* XXVI (1936) 428–40.

——, Keynes vs. Hayek on a commodity reserve currency, *Economic Journal,* LIV (1944) 422–29.

KEYNES, J. M., Note by Lord Keynes, *ibid.,* 429–30.

*HART, A. G., The "Chicago plan" of banking reform, *Review of Economic Studies,* II (1935) 104–16.

HARVIE, C. H., A note on deferred export credits, *Economic Journal,* LVIII (1948) 425–28.

BOOKER, H. S., A note on deferred export credits, *Economic Journal,* LIX (1949) 253–58.

HAYEK, F. A., A commodity reserve currency, *Economic Journal,* LIII (1943) 176–84.

HEILPERIN, M. A., Economics of banking reform, *Political Science Quarterly,* L (1935) 359–76.

HIGGINS, B., Comments on 100 per cent money, *American Economic Review,* XXXI (1941) 91–6.

IRVING, J. A., The evolution of the social credit movement, *Canadian Journal of Economics and Political Science,* XIV (1948) 321–41.

LERNER, A. P., Functional finance and the federal debt, *Social Research,* X (1943) 38–51.

MALLERY, J. R., Disallowance and the national interest: The Alberta social credit legislation of 1937, *Canadian Journal of Economics and Political Science,* XIV (1948) 342–57.

MICHELL, H., Monetary reconstruction, *Canadian Journal of Economics and Political Science,* VIII (1942) 339–50.

MYERS, M. G., The nationalization of banks in France, *Political Science Quarterly,* LXIV (1949) 189–210.

NEUMAN, A. M., 100 per cent money, *The Manchester School,* VIII (1937) 56–62.

PEDERSEN, J., An evaluation of post-war monetary reforms, *Weltwirtschaftliches Archiv,* LXII (1949) 198–213.

PLIMSOLL, J., An Australian anticipation of Mr. Keynes, *Economic Record,* XV (1939) 108–10.

POINDEXTER, J. C., Fallacies of interest-free deficit financing, *Quarterly Journal of Economics,* LVIII (1943–44) 438–59.

WRIGHT, D. McC., A reply, *ibid.,* 637–46.

POINDEXTER, J. C., Rejoinder, *Quarterly Journal of Economics,* LX (1945–46) 154–65.

* Reprinted in the present volume.

————, A critique of functional finance through quasi-free bank credit, *American Economic Review,* XXXVI (1946) 311–23.

BENOIT-SMULLYAN, E., Interest-free deficit financing and full employment, *American Economic Review,* XXXVII (1947) 397–99.

PRITCHARD, L. J., The nature of bank credit: A comment, *ibid.,* 399–402.

POINDEXTER, J. C., Bank-financed functional deposits: Reply to Professors Pritchard and Benoit-Smullyan, *American Economic Review,* XXXVIII (1948) 391–94.

REED, H. L., *The commodity dollar.* New York, Farrar & Rinehart, 1934.

————, Principles of banking reform, *American Economic Review,* XXXVII (1947 supplement) 277–88.

WHITE, W. R., and WESTERFIELD, R. B., Principles of banking reform: Discussion, *ibid.,* 292–98.

ROBINSON, G. B., One hundred per cent bank reserves, *Harvard Business Review,* XV (1936–37) 438–47.

RÖPKE, W., Offene und zurückgestaute inflation, *Kyklos,* I (1947) 57–71.

RORTY, M. C., The commodity dollar, *Harvard Business Review,* XIV (1935–36) 133–45.

ROSENSON, A., International commodity reserve standard reconsidered, *Review of Economic Statistics,* XXX (1948) 135–40.

SALIN, E., Währungsexperimente und wahrungsreformen, *Kyklos,* III (1949) 97–115.

SODDY, F., Wealth, capital and money, a resume of my theories, *Economic Forum,* I (1932–33) 291–301.

THOMAS, R. G., 100 per cent money—the present status of the 100 per cent plan, *American Economic Review,* XXX (1943) 315–23.

VANDERLIP, F. H., A program for banking legislation, *Economic Forum,* II (1934–35) 1–12.

COPELAND, D. B., Commentary on the proposal for a federal monetary authority, *ibid.,* 13–14.

HARR, L. A., The need for a central bank, *ibid.,* 15–22.

WESTERFIELD, R. B., National vs. state banks, *Annals of the American Academy of Political and Social Science,* CLXXI (1934) 17–34.

WILSON, J. S. G., The future of banking in Australia, *Economic Journal,* LIX (1949) 208–18.

INDEX OF NAMES